Handbook of Research on Connecting Philosophy, Media, and Development in Developing Countries

Desmond Onyemechi Okocha
Bingham University, Nigeria

Melchizedec J. Onobe
Bingham University, Nigeria

Mirian Ngozi Alike
Nnamdi Azikiwe University, Nigeria

IGI Global
PUBLISHER of TIMELY KNOWLEDGE

A volume in the Advances in Media, Entertainment, and the Arts (AMEA) Book Series

Published in the United States of America by
IGI Global
Information Science Reference (an imprint of IGI Global)
701 E. Chocolate Avenue
Hershey PA, USA 17033
Tel: 717-533-8845
Fax: 717-533-8661
E-mail: cust@igi-global.com
Web site: http://www.igi-global.com

Library of Congress Cataloging-in-Publication Data

Names: Okocha, Desmond Onyemechi, 1983- editor. | Onobe, Melchizedec J., 1969- editor. | Alike, Mirian Ngozi, 1979- editor.
Title: Handbook of research on connecting philosophy, media, and development in developing countries / Desmond Onyemechi Okocha, Melchizedec J. Onobe, and Mirian Ngozi Alike, editors.
Description: Hershey, PA : Information Science Reference, [2022] | Includes bibliographical references and index. | Summary: "This book is for those who want to improve their understanding of the strategic role of philosophy, communication and media play in a country's history, identity formation, and progress, especially allowing developing countries of Africa and Asia the opportunity to explore their respective nation's unique experiences as they navigate on the journey towards survival, growth and international relevance"-- Provided by publisher.
Identifiers: LCCN 2021052898 (print) | LCCN 2021052899 (ebook) | ISBN 9781668441077 (hardcover) | ISBN 9781668441091 (ebook)
Subjects: LCSH: Developing countries--Africa. | Developing countries--Asia. | National characteristics, African. | National characteristics, Asian.
Classification: LCC BF753 .H36 2022 (print) | LCC BF753 (ebook) | DDC 155.8/9--dc23/eng/20211108
LC record available at https://lccn.loc.gov/2021052898
LC ebook record available at https://lccn.loc.gov/2021052899

This book is published in the IGI Global book series Advances in Media, Entertainment, and the Arts (AMEA) (ISSN: 2475-6814; eISSN: 2475-6830)

British Cataloguing in Publication Data
A Cataloguing in Publication record for this book is available from the British Library.

For electronic access to this publication, please contact: eresources@igi-global.com.

Advances in Media, Entertainment, and the Arts (AMEA) Book Series

Giuseppe Amoruso
Politecnico di Milano, Italy

ISSN:2475-6814
EISSN:2475-6830

Mission

Throughout time, technical and artistic cultures have integrated creative expression and innovation into industrial and craft processes. Art, entertainment and the media have provided means for societal self-expression and for economic and technical growth through creative processes.

The **Advances in Media, Entertainment, and the Arts (AMEA)** book series aims to explore current academic research in the field of artistic and design methodologies, applied arts, music, film, television, and news industries, as well as popular culture. Encompassing titles which focus on the latest research surrounding different design areas, services and strategies for communication and social innovation, cultural heritage, digital and print media, journalism, data visualization, gaming, design representation, television and film, as well as both the fine applied and performing arts, the AMEA book series is ideally suited for researchers, students, cultural theorists, and media professionals.

Coverage

- Color Studies
- Fine Arts
- Computer aided design and 3D Modelling
- Visual Computing
- Music & Performing Arts
- Sports & Entertainment
- Gaming
- Arts & Design
- Digital Heritage
- Environmental Design

IGI Global is currently accepting manuscripts for publication within this series. To submit a proposal for a volume in this series, please contact our Acquisition Editors at Acquisitions@igi-global.com or visit: http://www.igi-global.com/publish/.

The Advances in Media, Entertainment, and the Arts (AMEA) Book Series (ISSN 2475-6814) is published by IGI Global, 701 E. Chocolate Avenue, Hershey, PA 17033-1240, USA, www.igi-global.com. This series is composed of titles available for purchase individually; each title is edited to be contextually exclusive from any other title within the series. For pricing and ordering information please visit http://www.igi-global.com/book-series/advances-media-entertainment-arts/102257. Postmaster: Send all address changes to above address.

Titles in this Series

For a list of additional titles in this series, please visit: www.igi-global.com/book-series/advances-media-entertainment-arts/102257

Redefining Journalism in an Age of Technological Advancements, Changing Demographics, and Social Issues
Phylis Johnson (San Jose State University, USA) and Ian Punnett (Kansas State University, USA)
Information Science Reference • © 2022 • 284pp • H/C (ISBN: 9781799838449) • US $195.00

Handbook of Research on Global Media's Preternatural Influence on Global Technological Singularity, Culture, and Government
Stephen Brock Schafer (Independent Researcher, USA) and Alex Bennet (Mountain Quest Institute, USA)
Information Science Reference • © 2022 • 522pp • H/C (ISBN: 9781799888840) • US $265.00

Handbook of Research on Cyberchondria, Health Literacy, and the Role of Media in Society's Perception of Medical Information
Hacer Aker (Selcuk University, Turkey) and Mary Aiken (University of East London, UK)
Information Science Reference • © 2022 • 436pp • H/C (ISBN: 9781799886303) • US $275.00

Emerging Approaches in Design and New Connections With Nature
Esen Gökçe Özdamar (Tekirdağ Namık Kemal University, Turkey) and Okşan Tandoğan (Tekirdağ Namık Kemal University, Turkey)
Information Science Reference • © 2022 • 348pp • H/C (ISBN: 9781799867258) • US $195.00

Scientific Perspectives and Emerging Developments in Dance and the Performing Arts
Bárbara Pessali-Marques (Bastidores – Dance, Research, and Training, Brazil)
Information Science Reference • © 2021 • 361pp • H/C (ISBN: 9781799842613) • US $195.00

Handbook of Research on Contemporary Approaches to Orientalism in Media and Beyond
Işıl Tombul (Independent Researcher, Turkey) and Gülşah Sarı (Bolu Abant İzzet Baysal University, Turkey)
Information Science Reference • © 2021 • 990pp • H/C (ISBN: 9781799871804) • US $465.00

Handbook of Research on Narrative Interactions
Recep Yilmaz (Ondokuz Mayıs University, Turkey)
Information Science Reference • © 2021 • 401pp • H/C (ISBN: 9781799849032) • US $265.00

Engaging Communities Through Civic Engagement in Art Museum Education
Bryna Bobick (University of Memphis, USA) and Carissa DiCindio (University of Arizona, USA)
Information Science Reference • © 2021 • 350pp • H/C (ISBN: 9781799874263) • US $195.00

IGI Global
PUBLISHER of TIMELY KNOWLEDGE

701 East Chocolate Avenue, Hershey, PA 17033, USA
Tel: 717-533-8845 x100 • Fax: 717-533-8661
E-Mail: cust@igi-global.com • www.igi-global.com

Dedicated to our beloved family members and all in the struggle for a better world.

List of Reviewers

Damilare Agbele, *Bingham University, Nigeria*
Philomena Attah, *Bingham University, Nigeria*
John Nwanegbo Ben, *Federal University of Technology, Owerri, Nigeria*
Ampu Harikrishnan, *Bir Tikendrajit University, India*
Christiana Calice Ngozi Idika, *Catholic University of Applied Science, Germany*
Ejikemeuwa Ndubisi, *Tansian University Umunya, Nigeria*
Isaiah A. Negedu, *Federal University Lafia, Nigeria*
Tran Thi Hong Ngoc, *An Giang University, Vietnam*
Obinna Obi, *Benin Medical Care, Nigeria*
Ugochukwu Chinonso Okolie, *Alex Ekwueme Federal University, Nigeria*
Tobias Orji, *University of Nigeria, Nigeria*
Arvind Kumar Pal, *Sharda University, India*
Benazir Rahman, *Northern University, Bangladesh*
Suleiman Usani, *Ahmadu Bello University, Nigeria*
Vinit Kumar Jha Utpal, *Sharda University, India*
Samina Firoz Waglawala, *Parul University, Vadodara, India*

List of Contributors

Table of Contents

Detailed Table of Contents

awareness about philosophy cum philosophers, the public would change their perception, attitude, wrong thoughts, and shared falsehoods about the discipline, and also start seeing philosophers in good light.

Language is used in various ways and for various purposes, including for creating and solving various human problems. This chapter rises to demonstrate that language, as a medium of communication needed and used in all human endeavours, is what could be used to adequately bridge the gap between philosophy, media, and development in society. Using expository and analytic methods and qualitative approach, the chapter proves in its analysis that when language is used rightly and efficiently, the gap between philosophy, media, and development would be bridged adequately and the surrounding issues addressed significantly. It argues that the gap, which had been created and sustained by inefficient and wrong use of language in philosophical, media, and developmental matters, could be bridged through efficient and right use of language by professionals of these trio fields and other individuals in the society in general. The study submits that language is the panacea for the matters arising from the gap between philosophy, media, and development.

The term "cultural diplomacy" denotes a deliberate effort on the part of a government through its agencies to promote its national interest by projecting its culture to the world. This conception poses a great threat to other cultures, especially in this era of globalization. Through cultural diplomacy, cultures of presupposed lesser countries are swallowed by that of super-rich countries. What is seen as the emerging global culture is actually the culture of the few elitists countries projected on others through cultural diplomacy. This is another dimension of geopolitics, the promotion of cultural hegemony by the people of the Global North. Using philosophical methods of analysis and hermeneutics, the chapter contends that the people of the Global South, especially Africa, should also explore the avenue of cultural diplomacy to retain their identities in this era of globalization.

The chapter looks at the media and development in an era of digitalized economy and how this impacts on the growth of developing countries. It considers the growth in technology and how this has brought the world together as visualized by Herbert Marshall McLuhan in his academic coinage of the expressions 'the global village' and 'the medium is the message'. The chapter posits that embedded in McLuhan's concepts are recurring issues relating to the nature of modern media, media concentration or congregation, media efficiency or power, media control in relation to who keeps the media gate. The unfolding consequences of media concentration, media power patterns, rising power of digital media platforms with challenging implications for world economy in the face of growing 'paperlessness' of money raises concerns over digital money. The chapter posits that money is theoretically returning back to its 'barter era' due to the concentration and growing 'media power' as money mutates from paper to paperless digital reality.

Communication is fundamentally a toolbox of symbols used to create meaning in society. Its existence is a necessity spawned by circumstantial and society's contingencies at every turn. It is the reason languages, cues, imageries, and symbols—the building blocks of communication—continue to evolve with the times. The ritual of this dynamism is precipitated by a number of factors like socio-cultural identity crisis, economic and political variables, etc. This transitional socialisation continues to surge in the digital space of multi-platforms and the internet. Thus, this chapter attempts to evaluate the tenders of communication in the digital space, its influence on cultural identity, and the place of Africa in the narrative. The study submits that although the global nature of communication is believed to have overbearing influence on the continent's outlook, Africa being a culturally strong entity can outsource to the rest of the world and into the digital space its numerous rich cues, symbols, and signs to give the cultural identifiers indelibility and relevance on the global map.

In India, the purpose of television broadcasting is to clearly depict an ideology that reflects social development. In the chapter, the analysis of various case studies shows that the main objective of television broadcasting in India focuses on the social development of the youth and the society at large. From the initial days, television is mainly used to disseminate information. Along with this, it performs several other roles that are related to social development such as propagation of education, support in the development of knowledge society and in the progress of cultural promotion, creation of health awareness, etc. In contrast to the essential roles of television, the chapter also highlights the media contents that signify cultural imperialism and the growth of Indianisation in the media content. The chapter overall signifies how television is playing a significant role in the social development of the nation.

In contemporary media-saturated societies, media exercise a considerable influence on every aspect of our lives. The issues that reach public consciousness become significant and consequently exhibit more potential to influence the public policymaking process. Advocacy journalism carries a great potential to advocate human development issues to policymakers. This chapter reviews the role of advocacy journalism in human development journalism practices in a developing country such as Pakistan. It is not a comprehensive survey of the factors associated with media coverage of human development issues; instead, it offers empirical insight into the role of media in human development.

Foreword

One of the buzzwords in contemporary times is sustainable development. As nations of the world race against time to realise the goal of reaching development that impacts and/or transcends future generations, I can only get thrilled about this co-edited book by Drs Desmond Onyemechi Okocha, Melchizedec J. Onobe and Mirian Ngozi Alike that gives attention to the development needs of emerging economies. It is even more exciting as the chapters in the book critically look at unique contexts, informed by cultural norms and indigenous knowledge for development solutions, rather than looking for solutions cultivated elsewhere.

Unquestionably, one of the cornerstones of lasting development in any economy is research and innovation. Over the decades, developing countries have pumped lots of monies into research and innovation. Sadly, many in such countries are yet to profit from the yields of research as they continue to wallow in poverty and underdevelopment. It is little wonder that many believe the research conducted in these economies are only decorative pieces for the shelves of libraries and archival collections. Another view, which I tend to lean towards, is that, perhaps, the lenses for examining the issues that confront developing countries tend to be unfit-for-purpose, thus causing proffered research-based solutions to fall through.

The media also has a crucial place in any development agenda. This is because the media serve as a watchdog over the various arms of government by exposing the abuse of power, corruption and ensuring political accountability and transparency. The media also empower the public with information to make decisions on a personal level as well as to make democratic decisions. It is considering these that I am particularly excited about this book that seeks to connect philosophy, media and development. It is surely a welcome addition to the body of knowledge, more so when it speaks to issues confronting developing nations through the lenses of their unique socio-cultural contexts.

The book starts on a good philosophical note with an exploration of the fields of philosophy of language, film and literature with the aim of establishing the inherent connection between them on one hand, and to establish their existential relevance to humanity and society on the other. This phenomenal work leads us to a good discovery of the self in a time when there are various forces of influence which is leading to pollution of culture and identity. Yet again, the need to take the gown of philosophy to town is explored in the subsequent chapter with the idea that the media and philosophers can collaborate to make philosophy accessible to society in order to advance society rather than it being miles away from it.

There is a lot to learn from philosophy for the advancement of society. I also believe philosophies emanating from developing countries need more recognition than they currently do. I add my voice to the call in the hope that philosophies proposed by scholars in developing nations will be given the credence and acceptability they deserve and not relegated to the background. I dare say every knowledge is ethnic. Therefore, knowledge coming from emerging economies are as valuable as those coming from elsewhere; their validity and reliability must just be tested within the right contexts.

Developing nations need to reach development that is felt across every fibre of society. It needs to be noted that the notion and conceptualisations of development do not reside with certain people. Development must be indigenously driven. Thus, a people's unique cultural and socio-economic contexts must dictate their development agenda. The book covers important developmental issues in contexts like Nigeria, Pakistan and India, providing us with unique perspectives to handle issues of development.

Questions related to the role of participatory media in development, development aid for media and use of digital technologies, social media activism and digital governance have converging implications on human and societal development and their exploration in this book provides critical insights. I am also happy environmental issues are explored in the book. The environment is the nucleus of life, and by extension society. One cannot talk about development without including discussions on the environment. Without a safe environment, no human being can survive, let alone a development initiative.

This co-edited handbook rounds off discussions with a call to Africa to not simply swallow, hook-line-and-sinker, exogenous development initiatives suggested to Africa. Africa's challenges may not be unique but solutions to these challenges must be context driven to inspire long-lasting successes. Rightly so, the author encourages the nations of Africa to look within to tackle development challenges, bearing in mind its unique socio-cultural and economic circumstances. This is surely a good call on a good note!

I conclude by saying this book accomplishes something that is increasingly becoming critical in the scholarship of developing nations: decolonization of knowledge. Aside it being one of the blueprints of a decolonized scholarship, it serves as a motivation that it is possible to look within for real and lasting solutions for the challenges of emerging economies. It is my hope that this handbook serves the purpose for which all the authors stived for. It is an honour to have been asked to write the foreword to this tremendously important book.

Theodora Dame Adjin-Tettey
University of Ghana, Ghana & Rhodes University, South Africa

Preface

In the developing nations of Asia and Africa philosophy is a strong plank of sociological corporality. Much of it, however, is embedded in the traditions and cultures of the people and rarely do intelligentsias show its curious confluence with the rhythm of cosmic ideology and meta-manifestations in quarters of media and sustainable development. The veins on the body of knowledge are not worked out to show the fitness and muscularity of the African philosophical narratives in education today. The narrative is that Africa and other developing economies are disproportionately obese or terribly rattled by kwashi-orkor, idea and initiative-wise. This may be hereditary of the general malaise of colonialism, the beaten epistemological path and long tutelage of these nations by their colonial masters.

Beyond the surface mention and effects on the economic wellness of the nations, the gullies created by floods of Western incursion of the continent of Africa, for example, has swigged the crust of the socio-psychological outlook and political philosophy of the people. The crevice and the gully on the bloc of scholarship content and context in Africa are deep (Lodewyckx, 2020; Kasanda, 2015).

Media and development were twin forks that were valued as external implements in their operation-alization in the sphere. Both, in literature, have been systemically indigenized to Western development models and paced as mutually complimentary even as theorists of Diffusion of innovation suggests. That diffusion (media) and innovation (development so called) variant have asphyxiated organic evolution and adaptation.

What is remembered for the longest is that Africa as a continent is a consuming economy. The tale is strewn from concept to product and the potentials for indigenous ideation, the framework and production capacity all continue to be undermined, thanks to the leaders that went a borrowing. Their choice has derailed development and self-sustenance in the context of the socio-political organism leading to the absorption of the identity of the lands and people.

Even then some people see the binary for constructing development in Africa, Asia and Latin America within the corridors of technological paraphernalia and think of it as possessing singularly the propen-sity of ending poverty within the assumptive neoliberal economic principles in a blink. This is in utter disregard of "alternative development" thinking and practices. Clearly, the problem is rarely studied in a holistic manner. In Africa, much of the concern as scholars have noted is that development within the framework of expectations of modernity has engendered technicized, disembodied, depoliticized and sanitized approaches to "development" as a linear process of routinized, standardized, calculable and predictable practices (Ferguson 1990). Overall, the question is how sustainable is the hackneyed practice of undue emphasis on teleology and analogy than on the systematic study of ongoing processes of creative negotiation by Africans of the multiple encounters, influences, and perspectives evident throughout their continent?

The indices of measurement are strangely quantitative, when evaluating dividends; the euphoria of political correctness blinds from seeing the temporality of the gains. The often rehearsed and remix rhythm of millennia development goals is only a short stanza in the sum musical notation of poverty eradication and other millennial development objectives orchestrated by development watchers. Although these are World Bank benchmarks the calculus are graphed into limited prisms of evaluation and scientific rationality in measuring realities in the material turf of existential realities of developing nations. So are the right things being measured seriously? It seems that human development is parenthesized in the midst of other advances. The inadequacy is becoming apparent.

The saggy nature, for example, of both media structure, operations in developing economies of Africa, Asia and Latin America have stimulated a quest of innovative indigenization of media and development along the streams of philosophies that wear the nativity of the professors and the land of their cultivation. It is this situation that has inseminated a movement whose focal pursuit is shaped more-or-less by critical approaches to development, its mechanisms and articulations. From that extraction several African scholars involved in the process, regardless of their domain of investigation, are now bending over; cultivating vigorously topics and turfs that essentially reflect the grail such as "African knowledge and development (Wiredu 2000, Eboussi-Boulaga 2000, Karp and Masolo 2000), African culture and human rights (Njoku 2004), African economic growth and global economy (Moyo 2009), globalization, international cooperation and governance policy (Lauer 2007), African Journalism (Hallin and Mancini, 2004; Nyamnjoh, 2005) African Philosophy (Kasanda, 2015). Clearly this paradigm shift that is like a budding flower is seeking to unbalance the imbalance. That ignominious path has been the worn track popularized by leaders in most developing nations.

Experience reveals that the road to recovery is always niched in critical knowledge and illumination of a people. This treatise is part of a serial of many-sided intellectual renaissance that seeks to ignite cerebral fireworks to light up grown path that are pertinent and pathological to the evolution of development in nations of Africa and Asia. Creatively, the scholars in the different chapters of this work took dives into different segment of the deep from the realities of the sociological ambiance to the more serene turfs of philosophy and psychology, right through technology.

The first chapter, "The Nexus Between Philosophy of Language, Film, and Literature: A Hermeneutic Approach," deepens the discuss by exploring the nodes between literature and the filmic narratives of culture.

The second chapter, "Philosophers and the Press in the Collaborative Task of Demystifying Philosophy Through Increasing Public Awareness," advocates for a collaboration between philosophers and the press (the convenient media of communication) in the task of increasing public awareness regarding philosophy – the study of socio-psychological outlook of existence that has been so misunderstood and mystified.

Chapter 3, "Language as a Medium for Bridging the Gap Between Philosophy, Media, and Development" calls for a redefinition of language as the expressive linkage between philosophy, media, and development.

Chapter 4, "Cultural Diplomacy as a Dimension of Geopolitics," is a philosophical call to re-oxygenate suavely the values of unique culture in a society overcharged by abstracted ideology of smelting cultures into a bleep called globalization.

Chapter 5, "The Media and Development in an Era of Digitalized Economy," peels off an intriguing back revealing more than a nexus between media and development. It shows that the digital clock that spawned the media into a digital institution have given them the gene of second-generation parenthood to digital economy and money.

Chapter 6, "Symbolism in Digital Space and Transitional Society: New Forms of Communicative Meanings in Africa," is an epiphany of the tenders of communication in the digital space, its influence on cultural identity and the place of Africa in the divide.

Chapter 7, "Indian Television and the Ideologies of Social Development in India," is a testament of how cultural imperialism that subverts the core objective of television - social development – can be circumvented with a typical case of India's Indianization in media content in the plate.

Chapter 8, "Human Development and Advocacy Journalism in the Spotlight: Evidence From a Developing Country," cups journalism as a socio-cultural science that could use the dynamics of peoples' realism as a buffer for needs attention, agenda and measurement indices of performance or otherwise in human development.

Chapter 9, "Public Sphere, Development, and the Challenge of Media Censorship in a Dictatorial Democracy: The African Dilemma," unveils the beatitude of public sphere as the rudiment of public communication and the foundation of any enduring governance in society.

Chapter 10, "How Generous Are Foreign Aid Donors in Media Development? A Descriptive Analysis," looks at the political economy of media aid particularly from established democracies.

Chapter 11, "Participatory Communication and Digital Media in Africa: A New Paradigm," premises digital media within the ridges of participatory communication. It advocates that the technology could be the fuse that lights the way for self-determinism for Africa and the rest of the developing nations.

Chapter 12, "Post-Truth Politics as a Threat to Democracy," examines the concept of post-truth and the politics of post-truth – and the taste that leaves in the mouth is whether the variegation of truth in the economy of world politics is a 'matterization' of truth.

Chapter 13, "National Security, Media and Cybersecurity Threats: A Strategic Framework for Secure Cyberspace Governance in Developing Countries," meets the challenge of globalization and its fallout in a nifty and an organic triangulation of policy makers with keys to improve effectiveness of national security, counter crimes and advance public governance.

Chapter 14, "Digital Governance in Post-Modern Africa: Evolving Realities of a New Communication Paradigm," critically analysis governance in the context of new reality of Netizens and the theoretical aspiration of post-modernist clamor for more purposeful and community-centric leadership style.

Chapter 15, "Social Media Activism, Championing, and Reconstructing Causes and Values: Mapping the Social Media Ecology of 'EndSARS' Protest of 2020 in Nigeria," evaluates activism and protest within the borders of existentialism, interrogating the epistemology and the ontological underpinnings of #ENDSARS press ecology traced to populace social media interactivity and feedback systems.

Chapter 16, "Global Partnership in Technical and Vocational Education and Training: A Pathway to Sustainable Development," makes a unique proposition that vocational education should be seeded within the fertile grounds of the core cultural values of a milieu in order to reap sustainable development dividends.

Chapter 17, "Artificial Intelligence as Catalyst for Socio-Economic Development: Challenges and Prospects," combs the future of socio-economic development and stretch its brightest furs on AI, but objectively points to the pitfalls for a poorly prepared economy to take on with a solid grid on its national identity.

Chapter 18, "Adopting of Artificial Intelligence and Development in Developing Countries: Perspective of Economic Transformation," is a philosophical investigation into the wisdom of man using technology to replace himself. If Africa must proceed along that path, it provides salient philosophical considerations that should not be ignored

Chapter 19, "Africa in the Face of AI Wave and Fourth Industrial Revolution: Leapfrog Opportunities, Development Backlogs, and Impediments," assesses the opportunity of Africa diving into the current of Artificial Intelligence in the Fourth economic revolution that has dawned.

Chapter 20, "African Multi-Wives Culture: Human Fatality and the Media in Nigeria," is a philosophical heel turner on the imposed monogamy preachment of Judeo-Western tradition with a renaissance call on media to make that an agenda that could be a panacea for the rising fatality rate from bouts in marriages.

Chapter 21, "A Critical Evaluation of Social Media and Human Development in Nigeria," evaluates the flabby influence of social media with its consequence of misinformation, fake news and seeming vista for scam and submits a compelling call for media literacy across board for all content consumers.

Chapter 22, "The Environment and the Challenge of Technological Development: Perspectives, Problems, and Prescription," looks at pushbacks of nature against technology's many violations of the environment. It pumps up the metaphysical dimension of nature's consciousness to self-defend and submits a safe capsule of operation called law of mutual complementary exchange.

Chapter 23, "Environmental Degradation and Its Implication for Environmental Sustainability in Niger Delta," squares in on a typical example in the Niger Delta and reveals that man and nature share a simultaneous healing space in the of ecosystem development.

Chapter 24, "Nigerian Media's Poor Representation and Negligence of Minorities as Breach of Ethical Journalism," gauges the derailment of local media from values of objective humanist empathy influenced by Western doctrine of impassionate representation and values of capitalist (economic/personality cult) prominence.

Chapter 25, "Radio Programmes for Youth Empowerment and National Development," stretches the sublimity of radio as a mobilizing force of youth empowerment by particularizing on areas that have not been explored in conscription campaigns.

Chapter 26, "Queen Bee and Her Female Subordinate in Ifeoma Okoye's "Between Women": An Intra-Gendered Discourse," is an antithetical searchlight against the popular media agenda of patriarchal violence calling on a multi approach spectacle to the socio-psychological dysfunctionality. Violence could be intra gender not only inter gender.

Chapter 27, "The Fate of Nigerian Women in Armed Conflict Situation: An Appraisal of Adichie and Agbasimalo's Novels," investigates conflict as a fallout of patriarchal society dominance, revealing that the collateral impact of conflict is harder on women and can be better told by them.

Chapter 28, "Rethinking the Idea of Sustainable Development in Africa," x-rays philosophically the numerous programs saddled to cure Africa's malaise. The crux of the chapter deflates the casuistry of many flavors of recycled programs as cure and re-gears development adventurers to endogenous page flip as a lease of fresh breath.

Desmond Onyemechi Okocha
Bingham University, Nigeria

Melchizedec J. Onobe
Bingham University, Nigeria

Mirian Ngozi Alike
Nnamdi Azikiwe University, Nigeria

REFERENCES

Eboussi-Boulaga, F. (2000). The Topic of Change. In African Philosophy as Cultural Inquiry. Indiana University Press.

Hallin, D. C., & Mancini, P. (2004). Comparing media systems: Three models of media and politics. *Cambridge University Press Journalism, 2*(2), 123–147. doi:10.1017/CBO9780511790867

Karp, I., & Masolo, D. A. (Eds.). (2000). African philosophy as cultural Inquiry. Indiana University Press.

Kasanda, A. (2015). *Analyzing African social and political philosophy: Trends and challenges*. International Association for East-West Studies. https://www.iaesonline.org/

Lauer, H. (2007). Depreciating African political culture. *Journal of Black Studies*, *2*(2), 288–307. doi:10.1177/0021934706286905

Lodewyckx, H. (2020). *Africa and philosophy at the rendezvous*. http://www.antwerpfvg.org

Moyo, D. (2009). *Dead aid: why aid is not working and how there is another way for Africa?* Farrar, Strauss and Giroux.

Njoku, F. O. (2004). *Development and African philosophy. a theoretical reconstruction of African socio-political economy*. Universe.

Nyamnjoh, F. B. (2005, November). Journalism in Africa: Modernity. *Africanity Rhodes Journalism Review*, (25), 3–6.

Wiredu, K. (2000). Our problem of knowledge: brief reflections on knowledge and development. In I. Karp & D. A. Masolo (Eds.), *African Philosophy as Cultural Inquiry*. Indiana University Press.

Acknowledgment

We could not have accomplished this on our own. Therefore, as editors, we would like to acknowledge the help and support of those who have made this journey possible for us. We owe a great debt of gratitude to our dear academics from different countries and diverse academic disciplines who wrote chapters for this book.

As depicted by the title, this book will shed light on researchers, policymakers, students and academics interested in the field of media, philosophy, communication, development and their allied areas in developing countries, thanks to the contributions of valuable authors. We would also like to express our gratitude to the academics of the editorial advisory board who provided full support in the constitution of the book.

Finally, we would like to thank the IGI Global publishing house for giving us the chance to publish our edited book.

Chapter 1
The Nexus Between Philosophy of Language, Film, and Literature:
A Hermeneutic Approach

Osemwegie Taiwo Wesley
University of Benin, Nigeria

ABSTRACT

The work explores the fields of philosophy of language, film, and literature with the aim of establishing the intrinsic nexus between them on one hand, and to establish their existential relevance to humanity and society. Man as an existential, social, and cultural being, and no doubt finds this expression in his use of language and artistic creations. The imperative question is, how is it possible to use language to communicate what is not real and what is real? The work argues that though language somewhat sets the limit or demarcate the boundary between what is real/meaningful and what is not/meaningless according to the view expressed by Wittgenstein and the logical positivists, is that enough to abandon or jettison human artistic works as constituting nothing but mere entertainment? The work submits that consideration of film and literature as ersatz and which sole purpose is amusement is mistaken. Rather, the work advanced the argument that film and literature and every other human artistic works represent existential reflections of man's true self in the "life-world."

INTRODUCTION

The corporeal nature of the human person sets him/her as part of the natural order. The human person, from a naturalistic outlook, could be seen or viewed as a material or physical substance. Certain traits displayed by man, not only sets him as superior specie among the hierarchy of beings but also far above other species of creation. Humans are believed to exhibit a superior communication ability which distinguished them from other animals. His language ability which is seen in speech construction and cognitive capacity to learn, decode and use language attests to man's organizational skill and this confers on

DOI: 10.4018/978-1-6684-4107-7.ch001

him a social nature, "hence by giving man the gift of speech nature intends him to live in a community" (Omoregbe, 1991, p. 159). By and large, language makes it compulsory for humans to necessarily exist in a society. This peculiar characteristic coupled with a very developed rational mental faculty bestows control and mastery on man which has not only aided him to relate with his kind but also made him to assert his subjugation or dominance of his environment and the universe in general. This follow from the level of civilization humans have evolved over time. It may not be surprising given the remarkable manner humans have organized their society and set order in the global sphere, inevitably may have elevated humans to the level of intelligent and rational beings.

Humans, in comparison to other animals, though arguable, have a highly developed mental faculty. This display of intelligence and mental cognition is demonstrated in his inventiveness and creativity. Human being is believed to be the only specie who is able to entertain himself and other humans through artistic creations such as film and literature. Whether in written or unwritten form, the intention or message is usually conveyed through language. Hence, language is vital to film and literature if their usefulness or pragmatic relevant is to be felt by their intended audience. Film as well as literature is not a creation for itself. It is not an end in itself but a means to an end. For the end to be completely grasped and understood; the language must be clearly devoid of any form of ambiguity or esoteric coloration. Not only are syntax and semantics important in language, meaning and clarification are also fundamental in the matrix of communication. This informed why philosophy of language *ab-initio*, from the ancient time to modern and contemporary epochs has continuously apt on the distinction between language that is meaningful/useful/sensible and language that is meaningless/useless/nonsensical. Consequently, if the idea/message of film and literature are largely conveyed using language, then these ideas/messages must be subjected to the scrutiny/interrogation and interpretation of philosophy of language.

One of the focuses of this paper is centered on the question how well are ideas in the mind of the novelists/playwrights and filmmakers exactly replicated using language/words in their works such that the imagery and the motive of the playwrights/filmmakers are conveyed without ambiguity to the audience? For scholars of philosophy of language, the relationship between ideas and reality is a fundamental question that must be approached if the knowledge of film and literature are to serve the aesthetic purpose of humanity. The approach to this work begins with conceptual clarification of main terms, the nexus or connection between philosophy of language, the analysis of film and literature and their relevance to man and societal development, followed by the role of language in distinguishing what is real and what is not and the argument(s) to refute the idea that film & literature are for mere amusement/entertainment.

CONCEPTUAL CLARIFICATION OF TERMS

The concepts or terms to be clarified here are philosophy of language, film and literature. We shall begin with philosophy of language. Philosophy of language as the name implies is philosophy examining language. It is "concerned with four central problems: the nature of meaning, language use, language cognition, and the relationship between language and reality" (Philosophy of language, 2019). Generally, it is an inquiry or investigation into the origin, nature and the use of language. Basically, with reference to "Philosophy of Language" (2019), scholars of language, especially in the domain of philosophy, would like to understand what speakers and listeners do with language in communication, and how it is used socially. Secondly, would like to know how language relates to the minds of both the speaker and the interpreter and finally, they investigate how language and meaning relate to truth and the world.

At the domain of language is linguistics— the scientific study of human language (Halliday & Jonathan, 2006). In this regard, "linguists have developed at least two general methods of understanding the relationship between the parts of a linguistic string and how it is put together: syntactic and semantic trees. Syntactic trees draw upon the words of a sentence with the *grammar* of the sentence in mind. Semantic trees, on the other hand, focus upon the role of the *meaning* of the words and how those meanings combine in order to provide insight onto the genesis of semantic facts" (Philosophy of language, 2019). While language is the vehicle for conveying meanings, it must be conveyed explicitly to the audience or hearer/listener. In Achebe's words, language may be described as the "palm-oil with which words are eating" (Achebe, 1958).

By and large, philosophy of language "is the general attempt to understand the components of a working language, the relationship, the understanding speaker *or writer* has to its elements, and the relationship they bear to the world. The subject therefore embraces the traditional division of semiotics into syntax, semantics, and pragmatics. The philosophy of language thus mingles with the philosophy of mind, since it needs an account of what it is in our understanding that enables us to use language. It also mingles with the metaphysics of truth and the relationship between sign and object" (Blackburn, 2005).

The earliest interest in language perhaps during the ancient Greek era was as a result of the need or role of language. It was mainly used for philosophical argumentation. As knowledge evolves, this instrumental use of language gave way to the analysis of language. It was at this stage that language becomes an object of philosophical inquiry.

Accordingly, philosophers at least from time of Plato conducted inquiries proper to philosophy of language. They investigated the following; 1. how words acquire their semantic values; 2. how proper names and other singular terms refer, 3. How words combine to form larger semantic units; 4. The compositional principles necessary for language understanding; 5. How sentences, statements, or propositions come to be truth-evaluable; and among later figures of the classical period, 6. How propositions, as abstract, mind-and language-independent entities, are to be (a) characterized in terms of their constituents, (b) related to minds and the natural languages used to express them, and (c) related to the language-independent world (Craig, 1998).

Film is the representation of life on stage. It could be movie, fiction and nonfiction. Film has become a global industry with very large participants comprising filmmakers, actors/actresses, the audience and all what not. All over the globe, film has become a hug business for lots of persons. Beside this business, some films are designed to instill morals and shape human character or behavior. As said earlier, a film is a reproduction of true life story or situation on stage, cinema, media and any other electronic media. Film transmits knowledge. Sometimes, it does not only capture past events but also future events. It has the capacity to reveal what has been suppressed or hidden. It is also informative and educative by breaching the gap between people's or societal historical past, culture, tradition or a way of reverberating a societal historical cum cultural past. Film is used to communicate and remodel wrong, mistake for the purpose of avoiding or repeating same error. Film also can be used to promote culture, unity, among a dissenting group/people. It could also be used as a satire, that is, to criticize a popular misleading idea, policy, ideology or traditional belief such as killing of twins, slave trade, child labor/abuse, bad governance and other social maladies.

Film is very germane as it relates to people's emotions, psychology and thought formative process. It has a way of connecting people to themselves, especially watching a film or movie that steers or creates empathy. One is able to connect and relate one's self evoking emotions and creating feelings as if the actors were oneself. It becomes a mirror to examine or x-ray oneself and character. Without necessarily having to read about one's past, film or movie could become the mirror one examines himself/herself. It re-enacts the Socratic dictum that an unexamined life is not worth living. Film becomes the means to examine oneself morally.

Literature is a literal performance. Most times, if not all times, literature could mean a person's (written or dramatists) attempt to reproduce certain view of the world or reproduce his intentions. Majorly, literature is in written form and it is received from the following contexts: cultural, economic, political and religious. It is basically refers to written works, particularly those with superior artistic or intellectual merit. As a subject, it mainly refers to the study of written work. However, there is also oral literature (Hasa, 2018). Literature may manifest in the following perspectives; form, politics, ideology, consciousness etc. In the view of Kennedy & Gioia (1995), literature may be an artifact, a product of social consciousness, a world vision and also an industry. It is germane to state that not all forms of literature could be expressed /written or done using language. The point here is that though language is not in written or spoken form; it could be non-verbal or "visual poetry" as Neff (1998) described it. Typical example is the type of drama in *The Water Station*, "first created and performed in 1981 by Japanese playwright/director Ota Shogo (1939-2006) and the Theatre of Transformation (Tenkei Gekijo) (Zarrilli, 2009)."

Furthermore, Sapir (1991) defines 'literature' as an 'expression' of 'unusual significance,' but 'does not exactly know how to measure this. Similarly, he opines that 'literature' has two distinct kinds or levels of art: 'a generalized, non-linguistic art; and 'a specifically linguistic art'. The medium intertwines the latent content of language-our intuition record of experience-with the particular confirmation of a given language-the specific "how" of our record of experience. This definition of literature brings to the fore the nexus between language, literature and human experience. Language here is the vehicle for communicating human experiences whether in the area of film or literature. That such a connection exists and that language is at the centre of human experience presupposes a meticulous analysis of language.

THE NEXUS BETWEEN PHILOSOPHY OF LANGUAGE, FILM AND LITERATURE

Before x-raying the nexus between philosophy of language, film and literature, it is germane to first establish the nexus between film and literature in order to appreciate the context upon which both terms intertwine in the ongoing discourse. As a point of departure, one of the ways to look at the relationship/connection between film and literature is through the work of Edward Huddlin. According to Huddlin (1979[a]), "one way of regarding film as analogous to literature is based on a comparison between the structure of verbal language and the function of visual imagery in the cinema." Elucidating further, Huddlin (1979[b]) stressed that "films are thought to be "read" like novels, meaning that (1) the filmic image is considered logomorphic, and (2) editing is thought to constitute a syntax. Thus words are compared with shots, sentences with sequences, paragraphs with scenes, cuts and fades with punctuation, etc."

Furthermore, "Pudovkin's view of cinema, then, is that the semantic and syntactic structure of film parallels that of literature. Images are analogous to words, editing is analogous to syntax, and the processes of artistic creation and appreciation are the same in each case" (Huddlin, 1979). In the same way philosophy of language cross-checks ideas with reality; so did Pudovkin to film and literature when examining their relationship thus "… the process of making a film is one in which the scenario writer begins with some set of preconceived ideas, set out in a rough script, and then "writes" directly on the film, substituting an image for each word, until the written word is translated onto the screen and appears in plastic, visual form" (Pudovkin, 1950). So far, we have seen that film is analogous to literature in some ways. Another way to compare their similarity is that both come under the umbrella of aesthetics discourse. Having explicated their similarity, let's proceed to establish their connection with philosophy of language.

Film is a narrative or experience transmitted to the audience using language. Whether the idea or thought transmitted is a moral lesson or not, mere fantasies, fiction or non-fiction, requires language. Though film could create in the individual comic relief or hilarious feeling, the language must be well thought out. Philosophy of language is not only just clarification of our ideas or thoughts but also the intention behind those who created the film. Language is crucial to meaning. To understand the intended meaning conveyed by any film or work of literature, the tool use in conveying the idea; which is language has to be thoroughly scrutinized. Most film's languages are served to mislead the intended audience or language users. This is where clarification of thought or idea comes in. The intention must be clearly pointed out. Every film or movie is designed to serve a given or specific purpose. It is not the case that film or movie is intended to depict what has no bearing in reality. Fictional movie of whatever kind may be intended to steer morals, evoke emotions and pleasure, it must be narrated using language that really depicts such scenario or situation.

One of the goals of philosophers of language is that language must correspond to actual or true state of affairs. For example, when I assert that Wesley is the current President of America, such language must correspond to real or actual state of affairs. Otherwise, it will be regarded as false, thus making the statement meaningless and fallacious. In this regard, language becomes the means for demarcating "what is" from "what is not." The language philosophers, especially the linguistic analysts of British origin call for the usefulness of language. Though the American counterparts did not really focus on the relevance or meaning convey by language, their focus or emphasis was on the pragmatic use or purpose of language. Care must be taken here, because the usefulness or pragmatic use of language got less attention or favor from philosophers who were critical about metaphysical or transcendental realities.

Some films/movies or novels have metaphysical contents/outlook. In fact, fictional and non-concrete movies such as matrix, space-x, etc composed of some metaphysical stuff. Whether these films convey morals or knowledge, for those opposed to metaphysical language would regard it as meaningless and nonsensical. X-raying movies/novels from this perspective call to question the essence and purpose attach to such aesthetic works of art. Aesthetic creation is not only the goal of film or movie and work of literature. The question of actual or real importance of such an art comes into limelight. For this reason, films/literature must be categorized according to the bearing they have on the concrete or existential terrain of man. Film/literature therefore cannot attempt to establish or set its own standard as to what (constitute) "essence," "truth," "beauty", "relevance" etc. in its work. Rather, it is philosophy of language that does this assigning and clarification.

In literature, reference must be made to the connection between what is depicted and what is portrayed, so also is the language. Though here emphasis is not on the distinction between depiction and portrayal, in order to change what is portrayed, the words which make up the work itself would also have to be changed (Hudlin, 1979). It must be stressed that it is words that convey both the entities that is depicted and what is portrayed. The language or words must be intrinsically connected or hold similarity to what is depicted and what is portrayed. This is synonymous with or related to "the "substitution" theory of metaphor associated with Aristotle, since he seems to insist on (1) the reduction of visual metaphor to verbal metaphor and (2) the reduction of these two to literal meaning" (Hudlin, 1979).

One way to clearly say that the nexus between philosophy of language and film/literature has been achieved or established is when filmmakers/novelists/playwrights reflect on or are critical of the language adopted in their works couple with whether it clearly captures or convey the intentions/motives in their minds to the end audience. Otherwise, when this is not the case, the dichotomy or disconnect between philosophy of language and film/literature becomes inevitable. Filmmakers and playwrights/poets must take the role/place of the language philosopher. They must bring into their works the critical mindset and thinking skill required of the philosopher of language. In fact, they must become philosophers of language in their works. They must constantly ask the question of how language connects ideas in the mind to reality. They must concern themselves with the use of language and the language game, and how language can set the limit to what we know or not. In as much as film and literature cannot do without the use of language to be meaningful, they all play essential role in the development of man and the society.

RELEVANCE OF PHILOSOPHY OF LANGUAGE, FILM AND LITERATURE TO SOCIETAL AND HUMAN DEVELOPMENT

Language, film and literature do not only serve as bridge between philosophy, media and development, especially in developing countries, they have somewhat become the indices for rating the social advancement of a country. The fundamental question is how do language, film and literature represent the reflection of man's true self in the life-world? Philosophy as the search for wisdom and ultimate reality that underlay all things raises pertinent questions concerning the existence of the universe, man and society. One of the goals is to discover the purpose and the meaning of existence. Philosophers have rightly posed the question, why existence instead of non-existence? Why being instead of non-being? Why do humans exist instead of the opposite? What is the purpose of the universe? What is the reason for the existence of the society? These and many more are critical to man's understanding of his self, his environment and his place in the world.

The media has played a critical role in the development or advancement of man's world. Man's constant interrogation of things around himself and his environment has not only stimulated development but also in the organization of his society. Man has set order in the society and his environment thanks to his critical thinking nature. In so far man is a question seeking being, he must also fashion solutions emanating from the problems lurking in the questions. One of the ways to unlock the problem of development that confronts man's world is the introduction and invention of the media. The introduction of the media has revealed many hegemony and social maladies that plague the development of the society. It may be right to assert that the long absence of the media may have been responsible in the slow pace of development in third world countries. Many injustices perpetrated by colonialism and neo-colonialism thrive smoothly for decades due to the absent of social media and where there was one, it either lacks objective coverage or it was manipulated to shield the evils of the imperialists and their collaborators.

Since philosophy of language is the use of language to state facts or things the way they are and reasserting the real meaning of things and their correspondence to nature, it becomes easy for philosophy of language to align with human artistic creations such as film and literature. The media, through film and literature, has been critical of man's activities in the globe. The media has become the watch-dog of man's actions towards others and his environment. The media has been able to regulate and check the excessiveness of man. Be it in the political, social, religious and cultural spheres. Many crimes (war crimes) committed in the past have been exposed to a wider audience through the instrument of film and literature. The various systems and forms of government are not left behind. The media has exposed the advantages and disadvantages of the following systems of government, feudalism, monarchy, autocracy, totalitarianism, democracy etc.

The media, via film and literature has also served as a vital proliferations and wide criticisms/ condemnations of oppressive regimes in Africa and developing countries. The literary writings of the apartheid regime in South Africa, worse human-slavery in history, European domination/subjugation of Africa, economic exploitations, child abuse, rape, sexual violence, racism etc cannot be overemphasized. Even in the contemporary developing countries, film and literature are means that continuously canvass against human trafficking, drug abuse, terrorism, religious extremism, intolerance, bad governance, corruption, etc and stand for social rights; such as child rights, women's rights, gender equality, social justice, good governance, etc.

There is hardly any area in human spheres that have not found place in film and literature and by extension, the media. The activities of media have made it easy to transmit happenings in developing countries to the outside world. This has made it possible for the intervention of the developed economy of the world to send aids through the various agencies such as UN, World Bank, World Health Organization and World Trade Centre to developing countries. Over the years many developing countries have received aids and still continue to receive supports in the area of health such as the Covid 19th vaccines, polio vaccines, and others such as loans to developing countries, infrastructural supports, environmental climate support, funding in the areas of research, education, provisions of technical support to mention a few.

In all, the prevalence of philosophy and the media has had more beneficial impacts on developing countries. The world is not what it used to be, thanks to the advancement in technology and human artistic creations. Film and literature have revolutionized the way people live and think. It has entered into and become the part and parcel of many cultures in the world. Literary criticisms and humor are acceptable ways of seeing the world. The shaping and reshaping of the world through the means of film and literature will continue to be appreciated by many. No wonder, the subjects have gained relevance in both conservative and nonconservative institutions of learning.

In another vein, language though it has been argued by some linguists is a natural or innate feature of humans, others scholars believed is something learnt from experience, especially behaviourists school of thought, as an instrument or mode of communication that drives both film and literature. Language may not be a human creation but film and literature are. The meeting point is that film and literature depend on the use of language in order for their meanings to be understood by society and man. The relevance of film and literature to man is embedded in meaning. Language is also tied to meaning. Meaning therefore is at the centre of language and film as well as literature. The message to be conveyed by film and literature are intended, they are deliberate and willful by the individual from which is emanating. The intentions of the artists are revealed in a clear use of language without compromising meaning. Film and literature will not be able to convey any meaning other than through language. The place/role of philosophers in the use of language is proper clarification of meaning.

It does not in any way suggest that philosophy of language is superior to literature. They both serve the same purpose in driving or making meaning explicit to man. More so, literature has much practical knowledge to offer an individual. As an art of words, it can help a person to become more sensitive to language, both your own and other people's. It can make you aware of the difference between the word that is exactly right and the word that is merely good enough (Kennedy & Gioia, 1995).

In addition, film and literature have fostered the development of human societies, especially developing societies. The scene production in film/movies has impacted in the crucial reordering and reorganizing of many societies in Third World countries. It has a way of producing a comparative knowledge and status between the developed and the developing countries. Sometimes, this may not be the intention of the playwright or scriptwriter. The scene and setting have a way of producing some psychological effects in the mind of the audience. It may not only be psychological, it could be epistemic as well. Transmitting knowledge from one culture to another has been done or achieved either consciously or unconsciously through films and literature. Movies and prose/novels sometimes have ways of connecting people to each other such that the existential circumstances/situation of one person is felt by another. Film (drama-acting) humanizes. Besides impacting knowledge, it makes us to become others. It places one in the other's shoes. To feel what they are feeling/thinking etc.

Clearly, some of the benefits of films and literature to the human societies may be summarized thus, (i) the ability or capacity to influence and impact the minds of the younger generation or population. It creates avenue for knowledge acquisition and learning of important values. Dissenting groups or social hegemony and varying social maladies/conflicts have been addressed and resolved through the platform and instrument of film. For example, the resentment and discrimination against the *Osu caste system*— an alleged outcast group or tribe of the people of Imo state, eastern Nigeria, has been almost completely deescalated through sensitization and the education of the people on the value of human dignity through film and movies. (ii) Film has been discovered to have the capacity to stimulate critical thinking and independent decision making on the individual. Science-fiction movies in this regard have stimulated deep critical thinking on the mind of the audience and this has in turn sharpened the society. (iii) Films as well as literature have influenced not just behaviour but also speaking. Public speaking is very important as it creates or builds confidence in the individual. Most good public speakers learn the art/skill of public speaking by watching movies/films or reading novels. The audience's vocabulary is further broadened and they are exposed or introduced to new words. (iv) In movies and novels, many characters are seen as role-models. People imitate their action and behaviour. Consequently, people are able to differentiate between behaviour that is morally good and behaviour that is morally bad. Cinema or film helps the audience connect with the moment more closely; whether past or told tales (Cruz, 2014) and Cinema or film is also thought of to be philosophically provocative and insightful and it is considered as mode of reflective thought (Robert, 2019).

THE ROLE OF LANGUAGE IN DISTINGUISHING WHAT IS REAL AND WHAT IS NOT

Wittgenstein in the *Tractatus Logico-Philosophicus* develops the picture theory of meaning. He stated that a sentence must share a pictorial form with whatever state of affairs it reports. Wittgenstein was impressed by the way a model, for instance of a traffic accident, could be used to illustrate the actual events, and the picture theory takes the relationship of model to situation as the fundamental semantic relationship. It requires that elements of the model correspond to elements of the situation, and that the structure of the model is shared with that of the situation (Blackburn, 2005).

In the domain of language, certain discourse and aspect of literature such as fiction is merely a written piece that is invented or imaginative, devoid of real facts. In contrast the written piece containing facts or real life phenomena is called non-fiction. The distinctive characteristic of a fiction is that its content cannot be verified or subjected to empirical verification because it is made up or invented by the author. This dichotomy between invented or imaginary creation and the attendant use of language to describe them and the real facts that exist in the world, separated pseudo expressions/statements from authentic expressions/statements. Philosophy of language therefore becomes the standard and yardstick for demarcating genuine statements from false or fake statements. This controversy about the use of language to separate 'what is' from 'what is not' became the instrument enacted by the logical positivists in establishing statements that are meaningful/significant and statements that are meaningless and insignificant.

"Literary works also pose issues concerning truth and the philosophy of language. For example, in educated opinion, at least, it is commonly reputed as true that Sherlock Holmes lived in London" (David, 1978) whereas this statement is false. Furthermore, the relationship between philosophy of language, truth and our understanding of film and literature's language are illustrated thus:

It is also considered true that Samuel Pepys lived in London. Yet Sherlock Holmes never lived anywhere at all; he is a fictional character. Samuel Pepys, contrarily, is judged to have been a real person. Contemporary interest in Holmes and in Pepys share strong similarities; the only reason why anyone knows either of their names is because of an abiding interest in reading about their alleged deeds and words. These two statements would appear to belong to two different orders of truth. Further problems arise concerning the truth value of statements about fictional worlds and characters that can be implied but are nowhere explicitly stated by the sources for our knowledge about them, such as Sherlock Holmes had only one head or Sherlock Holmes never travelled to the moon (Philosophy and Literature, n. p.).

ARGUMENT(S) TO REFUTE THE IDEA THAT FILM AND LITERATURE ARE FOR MERE AMUSEMENT/ENTERTAINMENT

What are the ways to test the validity or otherwise of the ideas convey by film and literature? Clearly, one way to test the validity of a film or movie is through its language. The same applies to literature. By validity, the paper means the coherence of thoughts exhibited by characters with reality as well as how the audience or readers are able to comprehend or decipher the motive of the film producer or playwright. To begin with, film is an expression, mainly of an idea, communicated to others, often the end recipient called audience. Truth is important in establishing validity. The imperative question therefore is what truth does film or movies communicate? By virtue of some films being fictional (invented stories) for example, can it be said that such films communicate truth to its audience? To answer the question, let us first try to establish what truth is. Truth is whatever is real, whatever is, truth is one. Truth is what is immutable, unchanging and certain. In philosophy, especially epistemology which is the science or study of knowledge, truth may be seen as that which corresponds to reality or an actual state of affairs. In another vein, truth among the coherentists is that which coheres with an acceptable standard or norm. For the pragmatists, truth is whatever works, whatever is useful and of value, especially cash value.

Therefore, to evaluate the validity of the term film, giving all the above conceptions of truth, one could say that a film though a representation of life on stage or cinema has some cash value. This pragmatic conception is seen in the way film has been revolutionized. It has become a big industry that actors thrive to make themselves relevance and attain fame and wealth. There are many examples of movies' industry such as Bollywood America and Europe have grown to become multi-billion dollars industries. The usefulness of this industry is tied to the films or movies that they constantly dish out. Whether the idea communicated makes sense or not, whether the film is fictional or not, the unprecedented popularity and the entertainment created by the industries to the vast population of the world makes film to be useful and having practical relevance to human society.

There are also films or movies that idea corresponds to historical past such that the past is reenacted or re-evented to educate the present generation of historical wrong. For example, the genocide of Rwanda, the Biafra civil war that took place in Nigeria, the great genocide committed by Adolf Hitler of Germany against the Jewish population, the apartheid in South Africa, etc have been acted and communicated through movies/films to those who were not given birth when the event happened. Watching such movies come with a great moral lesson, to remind one of the consequences of war. The language used to communicate the ideals of the film though not exactly how it was used in the real event, in as much as the language clearly captures the ideas, it is commendable. Main while, the language employed in some films and novels are either literal or figurative. While "literal language uses words exactly according to their conventionally accepted meanings or denotation, figurative (or non-literal) language uses words in a way that deviates from their conventionally accepted definitions in order to convey a more complicated meaning or heightened effect" (Hasa, 2018). This has some serious implications. Presentation of words or associating words with unrelated meanings could obstruct the audience or readers' understanding of the objective of the film or novel. More so, the moment a language is rendered obscure, meaning is almost totally lost and the purpose of such venture is defeated.

Films are also used to showcase or predict future events, particularly relating to certain segment of the society and international relation between countries. As affirmed by Lewis (2007), "Shakespeare intended to entertain the masses, inform them and reflect on past and present events." The use of biological or chemical weapon, uncontrolled research which may lead to virus and human genetic mutations, highly developed and technological control of man etc. though these films or movies have not really happened in real life, it is a prediction of the future happenings, would the language used be described or interpreted as false and therefore meaningless? To communicate in futuristic term using language is an acceptable norm. According to scholars in the field of language, using language in futuristic manner only conveys probability and has nothing to do with truth. It merely expresses the possibility that an event would happen. In logic for example, modality and possibility have been analyzed to communicate ideas that lack certainty. In the words of William James (1907) cited in the *New World Encycliopedia,* "truth is found by attending to the practical consequences of ideas." The inevitable question is how does language relates to truth and the world? If this is the case, in what sense would film or movies be interpreted?

It is true that some artistic works are only intended for the purpose of monetary value or gain. Majority of the film or movie producers are interested in the amount of money that a movie would generate or produced. They may not be interested as such on the ideals and other associated positive values. While it is also true that some film or movie producers aim at evoking emotions in their audience irrespective of whether the content of the film or movie mirrors actual state of affairs, which is the concern of the philosophers of language, the utter disregard and dichotomy between film and philosophy of language must be reconciled.

Plato in the *Republic* is notable for his critique of literature. He expressed grave reservation/negative attitude towards literature and therefore calls for its censorship by the state. The main reason advanced is that literature more or less expresses fictional character and these characters are imitation of the real. Already Plato is appalled by the fact that the physical world is an imitation of the real and ideal world. In his transcendental philosophy, he made a distinction between the world of forms and ideas and the physical world. The world of forms which is transcendental is the perfect world. The physical world is the imitation of this perfect ideal world of forms. Anything that is a copy of the physical world for Plato is an imitation, therefore not real. The physical imperfect world is the world of sense experience and as such no knowledge can be attained from it. It is constantly changing. No indubitable truth can be ascribed to the physical except the world of forms and ideas which is unchanging, static and real.

It may be the case that the meanings of words are conventionally fixed, based on context. As a result, filmmakers or novelists ought to use language in their works that reflects the convention and context of certain culture and people. To this end, the goal of filmmaking and literature should not only be for its own sake or pecuniary value, but also for the development, understanding and transformational value of their target audience. For example, a movie produced in Great Britain, with hundred per cent British culture and sophisticated British language, may be hard to comprehend in other socio-cultural climate like Africa with an entirely varied language background. Though the intention or motive of the filmmaker or novelist may have been well thought out, the intention/motive may be misconstrued if not acted/written with language that aligns explicitly with the culture and worldview of a people. Against this backdrop, it may be correct to affirm that there is no such thing as a universal language but relative. The peculiarities of each cultural background and worldview must be taking into consideration in the process of filmmaking and novel/prose writing. Each society— conservative, mainstream, modern etc. may act as social/cultural conditioning in the determination of the language of Film and literature.

CONCLUSION

So far, the paper has explored the intrinsic link between philosophy of language and film/literature. The main connection that has been pointed out in this discourse is language. Language is used to express the existential realities of a society and it is through society that language finds meaning. The paper has pointed out that film and literature states and reinstates the historical past to the present. It is said to portray the missing link between the present and the past, and the culture of a people is revealed through language. A society values or norms can be unfolded by the characters and language in a play or novel. Literature and film are aesthetic works that have fostered the development of man and his world. The constant creation and recreation of man's environment have been enhanced through filmmaking and literature. They address man and society as well as the existential relation of man as a being with others. As man relates with other members of the society, the need of language and the clarification of our thoughts/ideas is considered sacrosanct. The paper has demonstrated that language, literature and film cannot only act as moral educators but also modes of reflective thoughts.

Essentially, the work presumed that most filmmakers do not carry within their works the goal or requirement of the language philosopher. The work therefore becomes useful to filmmakers/ scholars of literature to often set in their mind the role of language philosopher not only in the visual or imagery aspect of their production but also the language employed in their work. The take home in this essay is that creative artists, especially in the arena of film and literature should not only focus on the content of their works but also the language. Whether the content is fictional or not, meticulous attention has to be paid to the language used. It is in this regard philosophers of language are canvassing for and calling for the strict adherence to language of communication that stands for all ethical and social engineering in speaking and writing.

REFERENCES

Achebe, C. (1958). *Things Fall Apart*. Heinemann Educational Books.

Blackburn, S. (2005), The Oxford Dictionary of Philosophy (2nd ed.). Oxford University Press.

Craig, E. (n.d.). *Routledge Encyclopedia of Philosophy*. Routledge.

Halliday, M. A. K., & Webster, J. (2006). *On Language and Linguistics*. Continuum International Publishing Group.

Hasa. (2018). *Difference between Philosophy and Literature*. Retrieved from www.differencebetween.com/difference-between-philosophy-and-literature/

Huddlin, W. E. (1979). Film Language. *The Journal of Aesthetics Education*, *13*(2). doi:10.2307/3331928

James, W. (1907). *A New Nature for Some Old Ways of Thinking*. Longman Green & Co.

Kennedy, X. J. & Gioia, D. (1995), *Literature: An Introduction to Fiction, Poetry, & Drama*. Harper Collins College Publishers.

Lewis, D. (1978, January). Truth in Fiction. *American Philosophical Quarterly*, *15*(1).

Neff, D. (1998, Nov. 16). The Water Station. The Capital Times.

Omoregbe, J. I. (1991). *A Simplified History of Western Philosophy: Ancient and Medieval Philosophy* (Vol. 1). Joja Educational Research and Publishers Limited.

Philosophy and Literature. (n.d.). Retrieved from https://en.wikipedia.org/wiki/Philosophy_and_literature

Philosophy of Language. (2019, March 25). *New World Encyclopedia*. Retrieved 19:35, January 15, 2022 from https://www.newworldencyclopedia.org/p/index.php?title=Philosophy_of_language&oldid=1019212

Pudovkin, V. I. (n.d.). *Film Technique and Film Acting*. New York: Dutton.

Robert, B. P. (2019). *Filmed Thought: Cinema as Reflective Form*. University of Chicago Press.

Sapir. (1991). *Linguistic Theory: The Discourse of Fundamental Works*. Longman.

Torres, C. D. (2014). *Literature and Film in Postmodern Metanarratives*. Palgrave Macmillan. doi:10.1057/9781137439734_3

Zarrilli, B. P. (2009). *Psychological Acting: An Intercultural Approach after Stanislavski*. Routledge Taylor & Francis Group.

Chapter 2
Philosophers and the Press in the Collaborative Task of Demystifying Philosophy Through Increasing Public Awareness

Christiana Danjuma
Federal University of Lafia, Nigeria

ABSTRACT

The low level of public awareness about philosophy makes the public hold and share wrong notions about it. This study makes a case for significant collaboration between philosophers and the press in the task of increasing public awareness about philosophy, towards demystifying philosophy, righting the wrong thoughts about philosophy and philosophers, and rousing the deserving interest of the public to philosophy. Drawing from focus group discussion, observation and intuition, and secondary data, the study reveals that public awareness about philosophy is currently very low. Philosophers and the press ought to collaborate meaningfully and change the widespread wrong notions about philosophy cum philosophers. The study concludes that once philosophers and the press collaborate significantly in creating public awareness about philosophy cum philosophers, the public would change their perception, attitude, wrong thoughts, and shared falsehoods about the discipline, and also start seeing philosophers in good light.

INTRODUCTION

Over the years, public awareness about philosophy and philosophers has remained low or poor. To state in brief here, this study argues that public awareness about philosophy and philosophers is currently very low. Consequently, most members of the public know little or nothing about philosophy and philosophers. They only keep assuming this and that about philosophy and philosophers. In fact, the way most

DOI: 10.4018/978-1-6684-4107-7.ch002

of them conceive philosophy, as a discipline, is the way they conceive philosophers, its professionals. Being ignorant of what philosophy really entails and what philosophers do and who they really are, such members of the public hold and share negative thoughts and falsehoods about philosophy, as a field of study/human endeavor, and philosophers, as professionals. This thought is echoed by Besong and Robert (2018) too. In fact, most members of the public remain ignorant of the realities and misconceptions about the field and its professionals. The reasons for this backdrop are not farfetched. These include the evil of ignorance; the evil of mind concealment; misconceptions and wrong perception; the popularized and shared wrong notions, tales, myths and falsehoods about philosophy and philosophers; and the low public awareness about this field as well as its professionals; among others.

Given the foregoing, it is imperative to make a change in that direction. To do so, a significant collaboration between the philosophers and the press is imperative. The aim is to increase public awareness about philosophy and philosophers and get rid of all what not that are held and shared about philosophy and philosophers in error. That is the advocacy advanced by this study, with a view to calling for meaningful scholastic works, socialization and pedagogic and media contents that would breach the current gap between philosophy and the media, on one hand, and philosophy and the public, on the other. The study seeks to show how philosophers and the press can collaborate in the task of creating high level of awareness among the public in order to change their commonly held and shared wrong perception, views, thoughts, tales and myths about philosophy as well as philosophers. Considering the implications of these wrongs, this paper will call for a harmonious collaboration between philosophers and the press. It hopes that the collaboration would bring about a new world order in the fields of philosophy and media and communication as well as the society at large. In the course of the analysis, the study will prove the degree of public awareness about philosophy/philosophers in Africa– especially Nigeria, where most members of the public largely misconceive philosophy as well as philosophers as being mystical, immoral, blasphemous, too radical and confusing, and what have you.

Finally, the study will also demonstrate the extent to which the collaboration between philosophers and the press could increase the level of public awareness among non-philosopher members of the public, who continuously misconceive philosophy/philosophers and consequently dread philosophy, hate and label philosophers variously and poison the minds of others around them against philosophy and philosophers. Thus, in the long run, the study will show that the ageing failure of philosophers and the press to collaborate and take up the thankless task of duly creating high level of public awareness about philosophy and philosophers has been the bane of the widespread misconceptions, tales, myths and falsehoods about philosophy and philosophers across the ages. Thus, to change these, professionals of these two fields must unceasingly create and sustain avenues for a meaningful collaboration between the two fields as well as them, the professionals of the fields. They have to rightly key into the existential inevitable interdependence between them, which constitutes the avenue for harmonizing their existential opposites, which are their missing links (Asouzu, 2007; Ijiomah, 2014).

CONCEPTUALIZING PHILOSOPHER

Etymologically, the concept of philosopher describes 'a lover of wisdom'. Pythagoras was the person who coined and used the word 'philosophy', when he called himself a lover of wisdom (Abakare & Okeke, 2016, p. 4). The philosopher is one who loves wisdom; who seeks to know this and that about the Supreme Being, the universe, substance, knowledge, humans, nonhumans and all existential phenomena.

Within the ordinary sense, the philosopher is one who does what any philosopher does or could do; one who rationalizes and asks questions about things, persons and the Supreme Being –God; one who goes critical about everything in order to prove or disprove what exists materially and/or idealistically. The philosopher is also one who thinks critically, creatively and logically and adopts various systematic and valid means of finding answers and solutions to ultimate questions and problems of life and all that exists on Earth and beyond. Omoregbe (1985, p. 1) agrees that the philosopher continuously finds answers to the ultimate questions about life and existence.

The foregoing descriptions are what this study makes of the ordinary conceptual description of the philosopher. Going by the foregoing, the philosopher is not necessarily or only the formally trained philosopher. It is in line with the foregoing thought that no nation (culture) can be objectively or rightly adjudged as not having had philosophers from time being. In what lends credence to the foregoing, Abakare and Okeke (2016, p. 5) maintains that 'the fact that one is a rational being is enough for one to be called a philosopher. We can say without mincing words that philosophy is a prerogative of human beings.' Thus, Abakare and Okeke agree that one must not have a formal training in philosophy to be a philosopher or to philosophize. They also agree in the same publication that just as philosophy is conceived from the ordinary or general sense and professional or technical sense so also there are some philosophers with formal training, while others have no formal training in philosophy (Abakare& Okeke, 2016, p. 5-6).

Professionally, the philosopher is one who has (had) formal training in philosophy. It is in this context that learners (students) and teachers (trainers) of, and other experts in philosophy discipline are called philosophers. Beyond the professional description of the concept of philosophers, there are also philosophers who have had little or no professional training in philosophy. These are persons who rationalize, think critically, creatively and logically and adopt/use systematic philosophical processes, approaches, methods and principles in most of what they do, especially in rationalizing. Based on this consideration, it is clear that not all philosophers have had and/or are undergoing training in philosophy. Based on this line of thought, it could be understood that there are core professional philosophers and other philosophers. Therefore, philosophers are those who rationalize either as core philosophers, or as other philosophers that have no core professional training in the field of philosophy.

For some philosophers, anyone without a formal training in philosophy is not qualified to be called a philosopher. This work argues otherwise that formal training is not the basis of critical thinking, rationality, rationalizing or philosophizing. Without any sentiments, there are a good number of persons without formal training in philosophy, who do rationalize and engage deeper or better in philosophical themes. Thus, in that context, one cannot merely argue against the philosopher status of such non-core philosophers, merely because they have had no formal training in philosophy. In what lends credence to the foregoing notion of who is or not a philosopher, Nelson (1998, p. 741) dismisses the claim that because Aldo Leopold had no formal training in philosophy, he does not qualify for the philosopher status, title or nomenclature. Meanwhile, Aldo Leopold had made a ground contribution to environmental philosophy cum environmental ethics. While some philosophers (e.g. Robin Attfield) reject the idea that Leopold is a philosopher, some others (e.g. Michael Nelson) continuously argue that by virtue of Leopold's enormous philosophical contributions to philosophy, environmental ethics and several other sub-disciplines of philosophy, even when philosophers were still quiet about some issues, Leopold is a great philosopher.

As a way of refuting the philosopher status of Leopold, Robin Attfield claims thus: 'Leopold the philosopher is something of a disaster, and I dread the thought of the student whose concept of philosophy is modeled principally on these extracts' (Attfield, 1984, 294). Reacting to these words as well as such others expressed by Attfield, like his fellows, Nelson remarks, '...However, I contend that Leopold, who never held a degree or position in philosophy, made many contributions to the discipline of philosophy...' (Nelson, 1998, p. 741). Nelson reiterates the fact that Leopold is one of those who laid the foundation for today environmental philosophy as well as environmental ethics. Despite not being a philosopher by formal training, Leopold made significant contributions to philosophy, particularly in the field of environmental ethics (Nelson, 1998, pp. 741-4). He (Leopold) is affirmed to have greatly influenced environmental ethics right from inception (RolstonII, 1988; Callicott, 1989; Nelson, 1993; RolstonII, 1994; Callicott, 1999).

To prove Leopold's unique place in philosophy, Nelson (1998, p. 741) mentions that 'the most fully formulated and defended environmental ethical theory to date, *the Land Ethic*, is an extension of Leopold's ethical thought, presented in his now legendary 50-year-old treatise: A Sand County Almanac' (1949).' In a brief reflection on Leopold's views in the context of this paper, it could be understood from Leopold that ecological science has the potential of altering the worldviews and ethical behavior of those outside philosophy world about and towards philosophy and philosophers. Nelson (1998, p. 744) thinks this way too, as he observes that Leopold's idea has the capacity of changing people's rudimentary thoughts or mindset and worldview about and consciousness towards the land. In the same vein, his thoughts and those of others without formal training in philosophy are capable of changing the thoughts, worldviews and consciousness of many who currently misconceive and blaspheme against philosophy and philosophers. Given the foregoing, it is quite clear that philosophers are not necessarily or only those who have (had) formal training in philosophy. It is also understood that both core and non-core philosophers think beyond asking questions about God and the universe, unlike what many people assume in error and ignorance.

CONCEPTUALIZING THE PRESS

'The press' is a technical term used in the plural form, though it is linguistically or grammatically singular, to refer to mass media professionals. That is, these are professionals, who have formal professional training in the field of media and journalism. 'The press', like 'the media', is an encompassing technical term for broadcasters, journalists, public relations officers and teachers, learners, and trainees of the media profession (Robert & Besong, 2016). Here, those who are not professionally trained in the field of mass communication (media and journalism) are not considered as 'the Press' or 'the media.' However, they are affirmed to be media professionals. These include media scholars, experts, researchers, and several other sets of non- or less formally trained persons who practice media and journalism or take up the roles of the Press.

It is imperative to note the 'the press' or 'the media' are of two broad categories. These are the modern media/press and the traditional media/press. Those with traditional and informal training in media activities are the traditional press/media. On the other hand, those with modern and formal training are the modern press/media. Here, both traditional and modern Press ought to be well informed, educated, trained and socialized on what they ought to transmit and create attraction to the masses. The task lies with philosophers. Setting agenda and making the image of philosophy and philosophers by the media (press) come only after philosophers had/have fed the media (press) with what they need to know and share as the truth and the lies about philosophy and philosophers to the public. Thus, these two sets of professionals must rely on each other in carrying out the thankless task of letting the public know what they do not really know about philosophy and philosophers. The reliance calls for significant collaboration. In the parlance of this study, collaborating task refers to the thankless task of doing what has to be done, as responsibilities that need to be undertaken to rightly inform the masses about philosophy and philosophers and change their held and shared negative thoughts and exhibited attitude towards the duo.

Essentially, the press would have to go beyond socialization, education, sensitization, entertainment, information dissemination and their other traditional roles of the mass media to the mobilization of the public through agenda-setting and image-making by involving sustained publicity. Publicity, Belch and Belch (2001, p. 22) note, refers to non-personal communications regarding an organization, product, service or idea not directly paid for or run under identified sponsorship. Within the context of media publicity, 'it usually comes in the form of a news story, editorial or announcement about an organization and/or its products and services' (Belch and Belch, 2001, p. 22). Since the mass media are the widest heterogeneous sources of publicity, information, knowledge, entertainment, marketing, advertisement, etc., they are the uppermost actors in the task of creating the right awareness about philosophy and philosophers among members of the public. The kind of role they play in creating the awareness would largely determine what the public subsequently hold and share about the field and its professionals. Once they play positive role in this regard, which depends largely on philosophers for quality media contents, the press would undoubtedly cause the change envisaged by this paper.

The media are affirmed to play significant role in causing social change, new world order, and development in various phases, and in addressing issues public concern (Ajala, 1999, p. 117; Adomeh, 2008, p. 28; Chiakaan & Ahmad, 2011, pp. 54-5, 59; Chiakaan, 2013, p. 128; Dibie & Robert, 2015, p. 14). Chiakaan and Ahmad (2011, p. 54) reiterate the fact that the press inform the entire society about everything that occurs in it, whether good or bad, so that it can help it to grow and develop. Similarly, Moemeka (1991) has observed that the press (media) help unify society and increase social cohesion by holding and teaching a broad base of common social norms, values and collective experience. The mass media also help transmit culture from generation to generation through their organized and designed media contents, activities, programs and what have you. In the same vein, philosophy is known to play a crucial role in fostering development, social change and new world order, and addressing critical issues, among others (Ekei, 2017; Asouzu, 2017).

PHILOSOPHY, ONE FIELD OF MANY FIELDS

Philosophy is one broad field of study found in every field of study, because of its nature, scope and multidisciplinary approaches (Besong & Robert, 2018). Despite its complex nature and vast scope, philosophy is essentially a rational enterprise. According to Abakare and Okeke (2016, p. 5), 'what characterizes the nature of philosophy is rationality, and so every human person that possesses or exhibits rationality is a philosopher.' Following its nature and scope, philosophy has limitless career opportunities for its graduates. But because most people either dread the course or simply hate it for flimsy reasons, they see it as having nothing to offer its graduates. Such reasons include shared wrong notions and falsehoods about philosophy and philosophers; the misconception of philosophy as an esoteric field; regarding philosophy as a field in which its professionals (philosophers) are all atheists and heresies; all that philosophers do is arguments; the wrong thinking that the career prospects of philosophy are only in teaching; negative internalized socialization had about philosophy and philosophers; the assumption that being in Arts and Humanities, philosophy is not a science (Dibie & Robert, 2016, p. 45; Besong & Robert, 2018, p. 3); and what have you.

There is the dire need for philosophers to collaborate with the press and rightly educate the public on the realities and misconceptions about philosophy cum philosophers, and to dismiss such fallacious reasons as what one should erroneously conceive about philosophy and philosophers. For example, by doing so, the public would be duly sensitized that 'no course is science; what makes a course scientific is the methods and principles employed by such course before arriving at a conclusion' (Nwala, 2008, p. 18). By this orientation, those who hold on to science as a parameter for judging philosophy or a reason for not wanting to delve into philosophy would become better informed about what makes a course a science or not. Convinced or influenced by this orientation, many members of the public are bound to become aware of what make a course a science and upon realizing that philosophy has those things (attributes) that make a course a science, they could wholeheartedly delve into it. Upon getting into philosophy, they would come in contact with philosophy of science and some of the scientific methods that make a course a science. Such persons will realize, as they progress with time in the field of philosophy, that philosophy makes use of scientific methods and thus it is a science too.

As Dibie and Robert (2014), Dibie and Robert (2016), Besong and Robert (2018) and Robert (2018) argue, although Philosophy and Linguistics are science courses, their founders had deliberately situated them in Arts and Humanities that existed then. That is, Arts and Humanities had emerged long before faculties of sciences came into being. Dibie and Robert (2014) stress that even when pure sciences became well-established independently, earliest linguists (called philologists then) and philosophers took interest in having them in Arts and Humanities and thus never bothered about moving them to faculties of sciences or the group of formal endeavors known today as pure sciences. According to Robert (2018), if the Classics had put these two fields in the same group with any science(s) one could think of, the contemporaneous would today not argue about the scientific or not scientific nature of these fields. That is, if for examples, the earliest scholars and elites had situated Biology, Physics and Mathematics in Arts/Humanities, Social Science, Management Science or thereabouts, there would not have been any current reference to them as fields in pure, natural and applied sciences. The same would have been the case with Philosophy and Linguistics, the two most diverse fields that are found in all other fields (Agbedo, 2000; Nwala, 2008; Dibie & Robert, 2014; Dibie & Robert, 2016; Besong & Robert, 2018; Robert, 2018).

WHY MANY HATE PHILOSOPHY AND PHILOSOPHERS

In developing nations in particular, as evidenced in Nigeria and many other religious nations, philosophy and philosophers are hated, basically because of the philosophical, empirical and skeptical arguments and engagements of philosophers. It should also be note that even among developed nations, most of the religious and most of those in the realm of power have never had it easy with philosophers. The harsh experiences of many past Western philosophers in their societies, which led to exile, punishment, assassination, rejection of their works and what have you, prove the postulation that philosophers as well as philosophy are hated overtime among many members of different nations of the world. Among many examples are the experiences of Socrates, Plato, Thomas Hobbes, Karl Marx, Friedrich Nietzsche, Peter Singer, Walter Rodney, Frantz Fanon, Odera Oruka, etc., who had it tough with society because of their philosophical ideas. These days, religiosity is defunct in developed nations, especially Western nations. However, it trends in developing nations till date. So, the ideological and phenomenological clashes between philosophy and religion constitute the bane of the hatred for philosophy and philosophers in contemporary developing nations. To cause a significant change, philosophers and the press have to meaningfully collaborate and reorient the masses of developing nations that are largely ignorant of what philosophy really is and who the philosopher really is. Doing so should be a sustained task for them, because if it is not sustained, the hatred will continue afterwards, once they stop keeping the masses abreast of the realities about philosophy and the philosopher.

Most members of the public so hate philosophy and philosophers that they see nothing good about them and would not want to hear anything about the field and its professionals. When introduced to elementary philosophy course at tertiary level, most students belonging to such group of the public often complain a lot about the course and see nothing good about the courses. The phobia makes most of them not to read the courses and thus keep carrying-over the courses. Then, in further expression of their hatred for the philosopher teacher, they simply say 'The wicked philosophy lecturer gave/gives me carryover.' It should be noted that this statement does not exonerate some of the philosophy lecturers who deliberately fail some students for their varied personal, sentimental and subjective reasons. Such reasons may be for want of sex and/or money from certain students, not buying their made-compulsory textbooks, having personal conflict with a student or some students, clash of interests and/or personality, and what have you (Dibe & Robert, 2017; Robert, 2017; Aper and Iorhemen, 2015). Also, metaphysics and historical aspects of philosophy are the most hated by students and most other members of the public. The haters of philosophy and philosophers usually spread the hatred to even those who would have ordinarily loved it as well as its professionals – philosophers.

The nature and the scope of philosophy add to the above identified sources of hatred against philosophy and philosophers. Philosophy is too elusive and thus makes its professionals multidisciplinary. They seem to be jack of all trades, master of none. More so, the ideas of philosophers are another set of factors that culminate to the hatred philosophy and philosophers receive from the public. Radical and critical ideas of philosophers do not go down well with most members of the public. Such ideas are more associated with Western philosophers, most of whose ontological views counter the existence of God, negate or fault religious doctrines and dogmas, condemn the conventional and ordinary views of the non-philosophers in society, and so on. They had laid the foundation of such ideas. Thus, having their pictures in mind, the public views all philosophers as such – as same. As such, extensive public awareness is imperatively needed to let the public know that all philosophers are not the same. Their individual differences do not simply disappear into the thin air because of their profession– philosophy. Again, what philosophers suffer from the public are manifestations of work or career hazards. Most members of the public fail to realize that philosophy influences each philosopher differently and not all philosophers practice what they argue out and institutionalize. Some of their views are only theoretical and not practicable. As such, they do not practice some of their expressed ideas.

Thus, most members of the public often conceive the duo from narrow or esoteric perspective. Consequently, they fail to look beyond the periphery. Viewing philosophy from the esoteric perspective makes many persons outside the field to see nothing good about philosophy, except that it is a 'mystic thing'. On this line of thought, its professionals are thus conceived as mystics who serve as priests and priestesses of philosophy. The esoteric approach to or conception of philosophy sees philosophy with its professionals as being purely mystical and thus the exclusive preserved field of mystics trained in the field. In other words, based on the esoteric conception of philosophy, the public holds different wrong and misleading thoughts, notions and falsehoods about philosophy as well as philosophers. These ill-thoughts, often shared among members of the public, are the bane of the hatred philosophy along with its professionals (philosophers) suffers from most members of the public. Therefore, the need to change the mentality of such members of the public about philosophy as well as philosophers is why this study rose. Given the foregoing, it suffices to say that the hatred arises from the various misconceptions of what philosophy is, even when those views are not what philosophy really is.

The advocacy of this paper is scholarly depicted by Abakare and Okeke (2016), who point out what philosophy is not, so as to clarify the public of some come misconceptions about what some people think philosophy is. First, they point out that philosophy is not an abstract discipline of the past, as many members of the contemporary public claim. It is not what had served its purpose in the past and ceased to be relevant in contemporary time. Philosophy does not connote or imply 'the dexterity of telling lies', as some persons think. It is also not the art or science of telling lies. So, the philosopher is not a liar, as many think (Abakare & Okeke, 2016, pp. 4-5). Also, despite being an art, philosophy is not sophistry, as some people think. Sophistry is the use of powerful and sometimes fallacious arguments to distort the bane of issues (Ugwuanyi, 2006, p. 1; Popkin & Stroll, 1993, p. xiii). That some Greek philosophers made use of sophistry does not mean philosophy is sophistry.

In addition, philosophy is misconceived as the anti-worldly activity of certain individual philosophers, whose views attack others' and stand opposed to those of others in and outside the field of philosophy (Ugwuanyi, 2006, p. 1; Popkin & Stroll, 1993, p. xiii). For some other persons, philosophy is merely one's or a people's distinct way of life and of handling situations. Although individuals and groups have their distinct philosophies respectively, philosophy means and entails much more than just that. When looked at from in this context, philosophy is often disregarded, though not necessarily dreaded. It is disregarded as a common or general thing that need not be studied formally. Again, creating public awareness is imperative to change such mentality.

TOWARDS TRUE KNOWLEDGE OF PHILOSOPHY AND PHILOSOPHERS: PUBLIC AWARENESS IMPERATIVE

The low level of public awareness about philosophy makes the public hold and share wrong notions about it. Also, the ageing gap between philosophers and the press largely accounts for the failure of the philosophers to feed the press with the basics, and realities about philosophy and philosophers. This study argues that philosophers currently fail to do the needful in keeping the media as well as the public abreast of the real information they need to have/know about philosophy and philosophers. They merely concentrate on teaching philosophy to students in the department and those electing courses from Philosophy. To make the matter worse, most of them mystify the philosophy discipline by the ways they teach and practice philosophy. As Besong and Robert (2018) note, it is imperative to create deserving attraction to the public about philosophy and philosophers; for by so doing, the interest of the public would be roused to both the field and the professionals, and the negative perception about them would be dropped for good. Once these are attained, the negative attitude and the widespread wrong notions about the field as well as its professionals would get changed, reduced and dropped.

Against the foregoing backdrop, this study makes a case for significant collaboration between philosophers and the press in the task of increasing public awareness about philosophy, towards demystifying philosophy, and righting the wrong thoughts about philosophy and philosophers. Obviously, doing so would rouse the deserving interest of the public to philosophy. To increase public awareness about philosophy and philosophers in true, real and/or good light, the right knowledge has to be indiscriminately imparted in members of the public so that those who are ignorant of the realities and truths about the field and its professionals would become well informed and knowledgeable to that end. Meanwhile, the other non-philosopher and non-press members of the public, who are already conversant with what philosophy really is and who philosophers really are, would increase their knowledge of and interest in, and better their attitude towards philosophy and philosophers.

The held and shared wrong notions that philosophy is a mystic field engaged in arguing against the existence of God alone and against the thoughts of other non-philosopher individuals are bound to cease or at least reduce drastically, when there is a significant rise in public awareness about philosophy and philosophers. The ignorance about the numerous career opportunities of this field would also be got rid of, as the public realizes that the philosopher can work anywhere, just like the linguist (Nwala, 2008, pp. 32-3). The philosopher can work anywhere because philosophy runs into and operates in all disciplines/human endeavors. Besong and Robert (2018) note that philosophy and linguistics have vast scope, branches and career opportunities; adding that no other fields can ever do without linguistics and philosophy. They go on to note that despite this reality, these fields do not exist in isolation but depend on others too, just as others depend on them.

Knowing the real thing that has to be known about philosophy and philosophers requires having the real information about them, rather than the otherwise wrong notions held and shared as a result of misinformation and ignorance. Information, as the press often says, is life. One who is not informed is deformed. Also, an individual may feel that s/he knows a thing or a person without truly knowing them. When Socrates realized this fact, he voiced out: 'All I know, I know nothing.' Given the foregoing, it is through the collaborative teaching and sensitization offered by philosophers and the press alongside various other agents of socialization and participants/actors in teaching-learning processes that most members of the public would get to know what they really ought to know about philosophy and philosophers, other than what they feel they know about philosophy and philosophers. Apart from intuitive knowledge, the individual knows or acquires knowledge externally from other sources through different processes. The sources as well as the processes include socialization, education (teaching-learning), training, instruction, indoctrination, traditional knowledge sources, learned authorities and experts, experience and research, among others (Ocheje, 2020).

By taking up the thankless task of rightly informing, educating and socializing the masses about philosophy and philosophers, philosophers and the press engage in liberating ignorant masses from ignorance and mind concealment, and salvage them from the problems these phenomena cause them. Once these two sets of professionals disseminate the right information to the public and sustain the gesture, the misconceptions, wrong notions, tales, myths and falsehoods held and shared about philosophy and philosophers would drop drastically and get changed or replaced with the right ones –the opposites. The rightness or otherwise of the media contents about philosophy and its professionals depends on philosophers; for it is what philosophers offer the media (press) that they (the latter) would transmit and make prominent to the public (audience).

The press is capable of carrying out the task by projecting the image of philosophy/philosophers in good light through the agenda setting role. What this means is that the media would set agenda for changing all what ought not to about philosophy and philosophers. Doing so involves verbal and non-verbal sensitization, sustained publicity, evolving and articulating needful and impactful media contents on and public awareness programs and campaigns about philosophy and philosophers. It is an indisputable fact that by doing so and thereby changing what ought to be changed through increased public awareness about philosophy and philosophers, members of the public would change their perception and attitude towards philosophy and philosophers. In the course of the envisaged collaborative task of causing a new world order by philosophers and the press, the public would undoubtedly hold on to the factual information given about philosophy and philosophers by the press. For the press to be able to give the public factual and ideal information, they ought to be kept abreast of the needed background information by the philosophers.

In both cases, effective use of language is needed (Besong & Robert, 2018; Dibie & Robert, 2016; Dibie & Robert, 2014). It is with that aim of creating public awareness and changing the perception and the attitude of members of the public that this study advocates a significant collaboration between philosophers and the press in the shared task of telling the public about what they need to know and do not know about philosophy and philosophers in society. Again, philosophers have to first of all teach and train the press to be well informed, educated, trained and socialized on the basics of philosophy and the core and real, rather than the wrongly assumed, attributes of philosophers. Once the press get well-armed (enough) by philosophers, the task of clearing the looming misconceptions, tales, myths, wrong notions and so on about philosophy and philosophers would become easy for the press (media). The media have to be guided by philosophers. Then in turn, the media guide the masses on how to relate with philosophers without sentiments that are shrouded in misconceptions, worldviews, ignorance, and so on. They also go on to educate the masses on the nitty-gritty of philosophy and what philosophers do as it its professionals. Early career guidance and counseling is one way of getting to change the widespread negative attitude towards philosophy as well as philosophers (Besong & Robert, 2018).

Beyond publicity, early career guidance and counseling would equip many members of the public with proper and adequate (re)orientation, information and education on the real truths about philosophy and philosophers. In the context of the concern of this study, the task of early career guidance and counseling basically lies on family, particularly parents/guardians, and school, particularly philosopher-teachers who are well grounded in philosophy. These two sets of socialization agents are well grounded because they have the ordinary and the professional or technical knowledge, information and the nitty-gritty of philosophy. Philosophers and the press in general context are those this study sees to as playing the role of socialization, education, training, authoritative teaching-learning, information resources and dissemination and so on. There are philosophers and the press at home, in the school setting and the public arena. So, once they are up and doing and live up to expectation in collaboratively sensitizing the public on what are true and those that are false about philosophy and philosophers, the task of demystifying philosophy would be easily carried out sustainably and the objectives realized.

Although Besong and Robert (2018) do not state categorically that the press and the philosophers have to increase public awareness about philosophy and linguistics, they insinuate that the gap 'allows [for] misinformation, misconception and poor orientation about these fields to continuously thrive' (Besong & Robert, 2018, p.1). For them, poor interest in and negative attitude towards, misconception, wrong notions, tales, myths and falsehoods about philosophy and linguistics arise from the near-absence of early career guidance and counseling, and misinformation, misconception and poor orientation. Again, in attempting to change what currently prevail against philosophy and its professionals, it is imperative for language to be used efficiently, technically, rightly and persuasively (Besong and Robert, 2018; Dibie & Robert, 2014). According to Dibie and Robert (2014), the extent to which science and/or any other fields can go depends largely on language; for without language, nothing about a field would be expressed, revealed or known.

CONCLUSION

As so far demonstrated, there currently exists a gap between philosophers and the press, which is why little or nothing is done by the media to create deserving public awareness about philosophy and philosophers. This study concludes that given the current gap between philosophers and the media and the public, for which realities about philosophy and philosophers are known to philosophers themselves alone and a few other members of the public, philosophers and the press ought to collaborate significantly in creating public awareness about philosophy and philosophers. Such 'knowing few members' of the public are those who go the extra mile of knowing what they need to know about philosophy and philosophers. Engaging in creating significant public awareness about philosophy and philosophers to the public would change their perception, attitude, wrong thoughts and shared falsehoods about the discipline, and make them to start seeing both philosophy and philosophers in good light.

First and foremost, the media have to be well educated and informed about what philosophy truly entails, its nature and scope; and who philosophers truly are pragmatically, what they do and do not, and so on. Philosophers owe the press this responsibility, just as the media owe the public (masses) the responsibility too. The responsibility is that of making all needed to be made known about philosophy and philosophers to the press and the masses respectively. The media can only teach what they know. They can set agenda and make positive image of philosophy and philosophers, once they get all they need to know about philosophy from philosophers. It is after getting all they need to know about philosophy from philosophers that they could appropriately disseminate the core knowledge of philosophy to the masses and clarify the masses of different lingering misconceptions about philosophy and philosophers. So, the whole processes of correcting the wrongs bedeviling philosophy and philosophers in society begin with philosophers themselves. They have to rise to the challenges before them and take the bull by the horns. They have to set the right tone and set standards and good examples. However, in the sustained efforts to correct the wrongs beclouding all their good sides and meaningful contributions, and the prospects of philosophy, philosophers have to be objective. By being objective, the philosophers must reveal the good, the bad and the ugly about themselves and their profession to the media and the masses, while advancing for changes that would make up for their bad sides. They have to take responsibility for their own wrongs and havoc to their profession.

In other words, philosophers have to avoid the act of telling the media and the masses only everything good about themselves and their career, and hiding or rejecting their bad sides and those of their profession. This study argues here that contemporary philosophers have the task of righting the wrongs of their past fellow philosophers. They have to change the habit of arguing for the fond of arguing against the ideas of others and against well established realities, merely bifurcating realities. It is no crime accepting other people's views and then adding one's own. Contemporary philosophers must make efforts to demystify philosophy, just as Ludwig Wittgenstein attempted in his works on language and by calling for the demystification of philosophy from flamboyant and impressionistic use of language to cause confusion in philosophy, especially to scare away those outside philosophy world. Wittgenstein lashed the medieval philosophers for such use of language, which create problem for philosophy. One of the problems is that of mystifying philosophy.

REFERENCES

Abakare, C. O., & Okeke, V. C. (2016, July). Philosophy in contemporary time: Relevance vs. public perception. *Mgbakoigba. Journal of African Studies, 6*(1).

Adomed, I. O. C. (2008). Sociology theories of education. In R. O. A. Aluede & E. O. Omoregie (Eds.), *Sociology of education*. Alltime Publishing Company.

Agbedo, C. U. (2000). *General linguistics: An introductory reader*. ACE Resources Konsult.

Ajala, J. (1991). *Public relations: In search of professional excellence*. African Link Book Ltd.

Aper, I.C., & Iorhemen, I.P. (2015). Dissecting academic and church corruption in Nigeria: The way forward. *Fidei Journal of Management and Business Studies, 1*(1).

Asouzu, I.I. (2007). *Ibuanyidanda: New complementary ontology beyond world-immanetism, ethnocentric reduction and impositions*. LitverlagGmBh & Co. KGWien.

Asouzu, I. I. (2017). *Changes, adaptation and complementary noetic transformation*. A Keynote Address delivered at the 2nd African Philosophy World Conference (UNICAL 2017): Jointly Hosted by the University of Calabar, Nnamdi Azikiwe University, Awka, and the University of the Witwatersrand in Collaboration with the Conversational School of Philosophy (CPS), University of Calabar.

Attfield, R. (1984). Value in the wilderness. *Metaphilosophy*, 15.

Belch, G. E., & Belch, M. A. (2001). *Advertising and promotion: An integrated marketing communication approach*. McGraw Hill.

Besong, E. N., & Robert, O. S. (2018). *Rousing parents' and students' interest to Arts/Humanities through early career guidance and counselling*. Paper presented at the International Conference on 'The arts/ humanities: Past, present and future', University of Calabar.

Callicott, B. J. (1989). *In defense of the land ethic*. State University of New York Press.

Callicott, B. J. (1999). *Beyond the land ethic: More essays in environmental philosophy*. State University of New York Press.

Chiakaan, G. J. (2013). *Broadcasting and the broadcast media in Nigeria*. Eagle Prints.

Chiakaan, G. J., & Ahmad, J. I. (2011). *Mass communication for beginners*. Azaben Publishers.

Dibie, G. A., & Robert, O. S. (2014). Appraising the significance of arts and languages in polytechnic education. *5th National Conference of the Nasarawa state: Polytechnic ASUP chapter.*

Dibie, G. A., & Robert, O. S. (2015). *A thankless task for Nasarawa parents, schools and mass media in marketing library resources. International Journal and Publications.*

Dibie, G.A., & Robert, O.S. (2016). Significance of arts and languages in polytechnic education. *International Journal of Education Research.*

Dibie, G. A., & Robert, O. S. (2017). Highlevel of corruption in Nigerian tertiary institutions. *National Annual Conference of ASUP.*

Ekei, J. (2017). *Philosophy, human development and national question* (Special edition). UJAH. http://dx.doi./org/10.4314/ujah.v18i2.1

Ijiomah, C. (2014). *'Harmonious monism' a philosophical logic of explanation for ontological issues in supematuralism in African thought*. Jochrisam Publishers.

Moemeka, A. (1994). *Communicating for development: A new pan-disciplinary perspective*. State University of New York Press.

Nelson, M. P. (1993). A defense of environmental ethics: A reply to Janna Thompson. *Environmental Ethics, 15*(3), 147–160. doi:10.5840/enviroethics199315318

Nelson, M. P. (1998). Aldo Leopold, environmental ethics, and the land ethic. *Wildlife Society Bulletin, 26*(4), 741–744. www.jstor.org/stable/3783545

Nwala, M. A. (2008). *Introduction to linguistics: A first course* (rev. ed.). Osi and Alozie Ltd.

Ocheje, D. O. (2020). *Philosophy of education* (2nd ed.). Yinkus and Sons Ent.

Omoregbe, J. (1985). African philosophy, yesterday and today. In P. Bodurin (Ed.), *Philosophy in Africa: trends and perspectives*. University of Ife Press.

Popkin, R. H., & Stroll, A. (1993). *Philosophy made simple*. W.H. Allen.

Robert, O. S. (2017). *Contemporary trends plaguing Public schools in Nigeria*. Kindle Direct Publishing.

Robert, O. S. (2018). Formation, types and processes of questions in Bekwarra language of Northern Cross River. *International Journal of Language, Literature and Culture, 5*(3), 27–34.

Robert, O. S., & Besong, E. N. (2016). Nigerian media and indigenous cultures transformation: The journey so far. *J Mass Communicat Journalism, 6*, 317.

Rolston, H. I. II. (1988). *Environmental ethics: Duties to and values in the natural world*. Temple University Press.

Rolston, H. I. II. (1994). *Conserving natural value*. Columbia University Press.

Ugwuanyi, L. (2006). Disabusing the mind of the prejudices against the world of philosophy. In Philosophy and Africa. UNIZIK UNESCO World Philosophy Day Celebrations, Lumos Nig Ltd.

Chapter 3
Language as a Medium for Bridging the Gap Between Philosophy, Media, and Development

Odey Simon Robert
FCT College of Education, Zuba, Nigeria

ABSTRACT

Language is used in various ways and for various purposes, including for creating and solving various human problems. This chapter rises to demonstrate that language, as a medium of communication needed and used in all human endeavours, is what could be used to adequately bridge the gap between philosophy, media, and development in society. Using expository and analytic methods and qualitative approach, the chapter proves in its analysis that when language is used rightly and efficiently, the gap between philosophy, media, and development would be bridged adequately and the surrounding issues addressed significantly. It argues that the gap, which had been created and sustained by inefficient and wrong use of language in philosophical, media, and developmental matters, could be bridged through efficient and right use of language by professionals of these trio fields and other individuals in the society in general. The study submits that language is the panacea for the matters arising from the gap between philosophy, media, and development.

INTRODUCTION

All human activities depend on language for survival, sustenance and continuity (Uche, 1994; Emeka-Nwobia, 2007; Dibie & Robert, 2014; Emeka-Nwobia, 2015). That is, no human activities can either be known or carried out without language use. So, beyond the communication purpose, language serves various other purposes. To that end, this study seeks to show that language aptly serves the purpose of bridging the gap between philosophy, media and development in society. It seeks to prove its assertion that language is the number one existential link between philosophy and media, philosophy and develop-

DOI: 10.4018/978-1-6684-4107-7.ch003

ment, media and philosophy and media and development respectively. Given the link, this study argues that language has been a veritable medium for bridging the gap between/among these endeavors from time immemorial. The problem has been the failure to use language appropriately for what it has to be used for and how to use it well. Meanwhile, legion studies affirm the place of language in the progress, development, survival and entirety of human activities, and the imperative of duly evolving, using and sustaining language-based techniques for development, growth, security, peace, integration, unity, ethnocentrism, new ways of life, new world order, science and technology, innovations and discoveries, (Uche, 1994; Emeka-Nwobia, 2007; Dibie & Robert, 2014; Dibie & Robert, 2014; Emeka-Nwobia, 2015; Osuagwu & Chimakonam, 2018; Oyedeji, 2018).

For this study, the above noted failure is a result of the sustained negligence of the place of language in bridging the age-long gap between one field as well as one phenomenal endeavor and another. The negligence is extended to the place of language in solving human problems in general, as many tend to continuously neglect the potentials of language in solving human problems. In the same vein, most people either undermine or refute the fact that the misuse of language is the bane of human problems in society across ages, while its right use leads to tapping from and realizing the neglected potentials of language in solving human problems. The dire need to rouse the deserving attention of the public to the imperative of using language rightly and effectively is what informed this study. In the course of its analysis, the study shall make an empirical exposition of how language could be used to affect and attain development in every society. In addition, it shall explain how language can be used to get rid of what cause the gap between philosophy, media and development, and how to bridge the gap so as to attain harmony between philosophy and media. Then, with the attained harmony, philosophy and media would engender as well as do more in societal development.

PHILOSOPHY AND DEVELOPMENT

The commonly noted definition of philosophy is that of its etymology, which has it that philosophy simply means the 'love of wisdom' or the 'quest to know'. This study reiterates and sustains that definition here. It is needless engaging in the various attempted definitions of philosophy, since every definition presupposes a conception not likely to be shared by other philosophers. Rather each definition is subjected to criticisms by other philosophers. Talking about the concern of philosophy, Uduma (2000, p. 7) notes that the most outstanding goal of philosophy is to deal with 'ultimate things', which are ultimate reality, ultimate truth and ultimate matters affecting human fate and conduct. He also states that in the course of its concern with human existence, philosophy indisputably deals with the deepest problems and issues of man and his existence (Uduma, 2000, p. 22). Here, this study considers the problem of the gap between philosophy, media and development as one of such problems of 'man and his existence'. The gap is not just a problem, but also a challenging factor in the growth and development of philosophy and the media in societies, such as those in developing nations, where the gap is still vast, and development remains a mirage.

As Inya-Egwu (2018, 499) notes, to philosophize is a natural imprint of wonder on the human intellect, and reason is its tool. Reason is an essential tool used for philosophizing and transmitting philosophized ideas, thoughts, knowledge, arguments, speculations, etc. in both written and oral forms, though more in written forms these days. Myths, folklores, poems, proverbs, legendaries, various other cultural objects, individuals' prose write-ups, etc. are affirmed to be ingredients of the philosophies of various peoples, including Western and African philosophies (Inya-Egwu, 2018, 499; Udofia, 2014, pp. 14-5; Uduigwomen, 2014, pp. 2-6; Lawhead, 2002, p. 6). Etieyibo and Chimakonam (2018, p. 73) argue that 'reason is responsible for the development of cultures and growth of civilizations.' This point concisely tells of the place of philosophy in development. Being that reason is the corpus of philosophy, it is quite clear that through reason, philosophers become charged and bent on contributing to the development and growth of cultures. Armed with and influenced by reason, philosophers also apply reason to media and matters concerning/affecting media. It should be noted that culture and civilization are synonyms and so this work makes use of one to stand for both of them used by Etieyibo and Chimakonam (2018, p. 73).

Given the above brief on philosophy, the study now turns to development. Development is variously defined. This study leaves out the legion definitions of development. Only several definitions are taken to suffice for the legion definitions in the literature. Accordingly, in the words of Besong (2017, p. 59), development 'simply implies significant all-round improvement, change, innovation, growth, increase, advancement and capacity that were hitherto lacking in a place and among a people.' Drawing insight from Nyerere's development philosophy and deeds, for which he accorded importance to people's active participation and control of their own development, Besong (2016, p. 29) observes that when development is otherwise, as in the case of Nigeria since independence, it is underdevelopment. Similarly, Dibie and Robert (2018, p. 160) explain that:

Development is the situation of a better standard of living, all-round change, improvement, growth, increase, innovations, betterment, transformation and at least fair availability of basic human needs, infrastructure and good governance impact. It involves the advancement of human; natural (phenomena) and the society at large in all capacities so as to attain (reach) certain appreciable standards, level and ways of life and operation. Human development entails the state of advancing (bettering) the standards and ways of life of a people, both individually and collectively.

It can be deduced from the above that development means improvement in the standard of living of a people, which involves all-round growth and change in welfare and ways of living; adequately or fairly meeting basic needs for both present and future uses; and using available resources for the realization of human personality through wealth, finance, resources, employment and equality. So, an area could be considered developed when there is at least an appreciable improvement in the standard of living for the people; increase in infrastructure and social amenities that are made available to the citizenry by its government; and the eradication or reasonable reduction of common socio-economic problems, such as poverty and lack, illiteracy, hunger and starvation, unemployment, health issues and epidemics, and inequality; and the rise to advanced ways of doing things like civility and the exposure to and the extent of the use of new resources (e.g. modern technologies).

For Ekei (2017, p. 10), development includes both economic growth and human development, whereby economic growth and other indices of overall development are got from human development. These indices include health, nutrition, education, clean environment, economic and infrastructural development, etc., which are all made possible by humans who are agents of human and non-human development (Ekei, 2017, p. 10). Having said the foregoing, it is important to note here that philosophy develops humans, who in turn develop infrastructure and other phenomena. It lays foundation for and contributes to societal development –non-human development– by acting upon human reason, developing humans and rousing in them the consciousness towards, the critical thinking and the burning quest to do what have to bring about development. Indices of human development are noted to include provision of health, leading to long life, political freedom, building people's capacities, and education, especially the nurturing of human mind, etc. (Ekei, 2017, p. 10). Influenced by reason, critical thinking and the quest to know, philosophers ask questions about development and find logical and substantial answers to the questions that the non-philosophers would be unable to answer. With historic references to ancient philosophers, Ekei (2017, pp. 10-14) demonstrates that philosophy reserves a great pride of place in development, as a field engaged in mind-training.

Given that human mind, also regarded by the ancients as soul, is the bedrock of all human activities, its place in efforts and deeds that lead to or bring to place development in society cannot be emphasized. Indeed, mind-training is imperative because the mind houses, begins and ends everything human beings do in life. In fact life itself humanly rests on the mind, when considered as soul. That is why when the soul ceases to function or live in a human's body, that particular body becomes empty, motionless and lifeless. The act of training the mind philosophically is what Asouzu (2007, p. 233) calls 'noetic propaedeutic'. In his words, 'noetic propaedeutic is the pedagogical and psychotherapeutic dimension of ibuanyidanda philosophy' (Asouzu, 2011, p. 46). Noetic propaedeutic is a pedagogy of philosophical pre-education and re-education of mind and human reason with a view to overcoming the broken unity in human consciousness caused by the challenges of tension-laden human ambivalent existential situations and *ihe mkpuchi anya,* meaning literally as 'phenomenon of concealment' (Asouzu, 2004, p. 61-69; Asouzu, 2007, pp. 57, 235, 358; Asouzu, 2011, p. 49). Noetic propaedeutic teaches that the mind has to be well-trained to be aware of the existential complementarity between and among humans and non-humans, phenomena and groups of all spheres. Like Aristotle (1947), Asouzu believes that to get rid of concealment, the mind has to be trained to see reality in relational modes. He holds that all modes of complementary relationship demand what is needed to mediate meaningfully the tension that mistakes contraries for contradictories, generated in the mind (Asouzu, 2017, p. 3).

Asouzu's noetic propaedeutic is an integral part of his Ibuanyidanda philosophy. Asouzu's Ibuanyidanda philosophy is that of complementary ontology, which emphasizes the need for mutual complementarity between and among persons, people, groups and phenomena for the realisation of the greatest possible thriving and gaining the collective good. Asouzu (2011, p. 104) notes that Ibuanyidanda philosophy is that which aims at harmonizing and complementing reality rather than seeking or exhibiting, dividing, polarizing and bifurcating of reality. For Asouzu, any relationship that is the like of ibuanyidanda or that is anchored on ibuanyidanda usually seeks to proffer solutions to 'the fracture in the mind that makes harmony of differences difficult, if not impossible' (Asouzu, 2004, p. 277). Essentially, the simple message being passed here in view of mind training is that philosophy has the resourcefulness of (re)training, pre-educating and (re)educating the mind in such ways that development could be attained.

Rather than polarizing the reality of the gap emphasized by this study, a relationship anchored on ibuanyidanda should be built between philosophy and the media so as to attain meaningful development and let it (development) strive. Building such a relationship rather than allowing for, creating or emphasizing a gap between philosophy and the media as well as other fields would eliminate mind concealment, differences that are missing links, and proffer solutions to 'the fracture in the mind' (Asouzu, 2004, p. 277). Thus, bridging the gap would be of immense benefits to media, other fields and the society at large, and engender development, as developmental problems get resolved. Also, with the teaching of noetic propaedeutic, mind training is imperative to bridge the gap between philosophy, media, development and other fields and phenomena in society through expelling the phenomenon of mind concealment that polarizes realities and creates problems between/among the fields under study, other fields/endeavors, phenomena, things and humans.

MEDIA AND THEIR CORE ROLES

Media is a polysemous word with more than one contextual meaning. It is a register in linguistics, media profession/mass communication, anatomy and history. It has variances in meaning within the context of each of these fields. This paper considers its usage in the contexts of linguistics and mass communication. Media is used to refer to journalists and other professionals of the field of mass communication– media organization (NOUN, 2008; Chiakaan and Ahmad, 2011; Robert & Besong, 2016). The concept also refers to the plural of 'medium' – a channel. It also refers to 'means' and 'institutions' for publishing and broadcasting information. It is imperative to note that the concept of 'media' refers to the channels of communication in the process of communication. Sometimes, it is used as a short form of 'mass media' (Robert & Besong, 2016). Some persons use 'media' and 'mass media' interchangeably as synonyms. Media is also used as an adjective to qualify nouns that concern mass communication (e.g. media organization, media professional, media content, etc.). In addition, media is used to refer to the mass media. By this reference, the term is used to describe channels of communication by professionals of mass communication, who communicate to a heterogeneous audience.

Channels of public (mass) communication are termed mass media. The mass media are channels of communication to a heterogeneous audience, which include television, radio, computers, microfilms, newspaper, magazine, internet, social media, etc. The term 'mass' suggests 'many', where the communication exercise is undertaken by a few selected persons or a person and passed on, or disseminated to many persons who make up the public– the masses. Communication of all kinds involves the use of language. When the communication involves two or more individuals, it is regarded as interpersonal communication. On the other hand, when it is between a person or a few persons and a large audience of many people, it is mass communication. Mass communication has two sets of communication media, means or channels. Technological mass media are the audio and audio-visual means of mass communication, such as television (TV), radio, computers, telephones, cinema, video recording, etc. They are called electronic (mass) media. In other words, the new mass media, which are technology-based, involve a two side communication in which both parties are producers and consumers of the media contents– information respectively. Examples include GSM and telephone conversations and short message services (SMS), emails, social media posts, blog posts, and various other internet data/information sources (Crosbie, 2002). There are other channels of mass communication that are visual and manual. These other channels are called print media. Examples of print media include newspapers, magazines, books, journals, etc. Basically, some channels (media) of communication are visual, audio and audio-visual respectively.

What the foregoing suggests is that there are mass media are two main sets of mass media. These are print and electronic media, through which information or message is transmitted or disseminated to a heterogeneous audience (Chiakaan and Ahmad, 2011; Dibie & Robert, 2015; Robert & Besong, 2016). The importance of the media in society cannot be over-emphasized. The media play significant roles in the affairs of society. The primary roles or functions include information, entertainment, instruction, awareness, surveillance, education and socialization (Chiakaan and Ahmad, 2011; Dibie & Robert, 2015; Robert & Besong, 2016). Through their primary roles, the media usually take up various secondary functions of immense benefits to society. They teach and uphold norms, values, customs, tradition, literature, and other aspects of culture of the society where they operate. They also play crucial contributory role in development, growth, welfare, sustenance and continuity of society. Besides, they play a significant contributory role in governance, polity, leadership and democratization in society. As Chiakaan and Ahmad (2011, p. 55) rightly note, in the course of carrying out the aforementioned roles, educational media surfaces to educate, inform, instruct and develop individuals socially, psychologically, academically and otherwise. By this reality, it is understood that mass media are used for educational or instructional purposes.

In spite of their enormous contribution to society in almost all spheres, the (mass) media also exert negative impact or influence on society. This assertion is echoed by Chiakaan and Ahmad (2011), Chiakaan (2013) and Robert and Besong (2016), among others, as they praise the media for their good deeds and blame them for their bad deeds and negative influence on the masses of all societies. This means that the media exert both positive and negative impacts on their audience– the masses. Mass media are said to 'help manipulate public mind' (Puiu et al., 2015, p. 131). This simply tells how influential the media are to the public. The manipulation is realised through their agenda and image-making tactics, which also constitute some of their other secondary roles. The implication of the foregoing is that the mass media could either make or mar the development, wellbeing, success and various activities of individuals, groups and nations respectively. The kinds of roles they play determine their significant or insignificant contributions to the society. The postulation of this paper that the media has the capacity of bridging the current gap between them, philosophy and development through effective language use is sustained by Moemeka's (1991) affirmation of the socialization role of the mass media. According to Moemeka (1991), the mass media help unify society and increase social cohesion by upholding and teaching a broad base of common social norms, values and collective experience. By implication, once the media begin to do the needful on what has to be done to bridge the current gap between media, philosophy and development, the postulation of this study would be obviously made manifest and sustained.

By getting immensely concerned with and involved in development matters and deeds, the media would bridge the gap between the mass media and development. Secondly, while being and remaining committed to and acting actively in development, the media, as professionals of mass communication making use of both language and mass media, would have a meaningful entangle with philosophers– development philosophers. Apart from entangling with philosophers therein, the media would get some philosophers involved in development concerns and activities. This is possible because the media are known to exert reasonable influence on members of the public, manipulate their mind, rouse their interest and attention to what they erstwhile paid no attention to and had no interest in, socialize them on the imperative of doing this and/or that, and so on (Moemeka, 1991; Chiakaan and Ahmad, 2011; Dibie & Robert, 2015; Puiu et al., 2015; Robert & Besong, 2016). Besides, the media would also succeed in influencing the philosophers preoccupied with developmental concerns and activities in several regards. The influence would yield several positive results, which would together help bridge the current extant gap. Once the media become and remain up and doing, unifying philosophy and the mass media fields of human endeavor would be attained in no distant time.

The unification would undoubtedly guarantee significant development in society. That is because both philosophers and the press will connect and collaborate more to search for, evolve, do and sustain what would bring development to place as well as advance the extant development in their societies respectively. Publicity is one means through which media could play the role of bridging the gap between media, philosophy and development (Belch and Belch (2001, p. 22). The impacts of the media on society in general and their role in developing the society in particular have been affirmed by different scholars (e.g. Chiakaan, 2013, p. 128; Adomeh, 2008, p. 28). Through socialization and educational media, the media help transmit culture from one generation to another (Moemeka, 1991; Chiakaan and Ahmad, 2011; Dibie & Robert, 2015; Robert & Besong, 2016). They are affirmed to be viable mechanisms for national development (Ajala, 1999, p. 117; Chiakaan and Ahmad, 2011, p. 59). The mass media are also seen as playing the role of motivating and mobilizing people to attain their political, socio-economic and educational goals (Ajala, 1999, p. 117; Chiakaan and Ahmad, 2011, p. 59).

PHILOSOPHY, MEDIA AND DEVELOPMENT

Cassirer (1985) is said to be the one who made significant advances and introduced a strong movement towards understanding the relationship between philosophy and a deeper and widely understood concept of the medium (Alić, 2010, p. 206). That follows his reaction to, and analysis of Kant's inversion as a possibility that the priority of the function over the subject from the field of cognition spreads onto myth, religion and art (Alić, 2010, p. 206). Alić (2010) holds media high in terms of what they are and could do. According to Alić (2010, p. 207), all the symbols of the world are media for shaping it wherever the symbols apply. Stressing the use of the symbols, Alić (2010, p. 207) posits, 'Everything that exists, we form creatively; we shape and produce and mediate with our symbols. We are only through mediation; we are only through the mediation of the media.' One implication of these quoted assertions in the context of this study is that philosophy, media and development exist because we (humans) have created them. Secondly, human beings can neither live nor function without mediation and the existential symbols of language and mediation.

Apart from assets of nature, human beings create all that exists by nurture rather than nature through symbols and media, which are both of language. Mediation is realized with the use of language through symbols and media. Self-liberating thoughts do take cognizance of the significance of mediation and each medium of mediation (Alić, 2010, 207). Self-liberating thoughts involve self-consciousness, which holds within itself, just as 'the inner language form' enables 'the outer or surface language form' to manifest, operate and function. In the same vein, individual symbols of myth, religion or art contain their own whole within themselves. Linguistically, 'the inner language form' is the generative phase of language at the deep structure (in the mental faculty of the individual, where the linguistic repertoire exists). The inner language is behind mediation, upon which expressed thoughts at the surface structure– the outer or surface language form acts and presents itself, using both internal and external media. The internal media are the speech organs of the body (lungs, trachea, gullet, alveolar ridge, tongue, nose, lips, etc.), while the external media are those man-made communication media (e.g. radio, television, books, etc.), which are non-human organs.

In understanding the world, art has been giving itself to philosophy as a partner (Alić, 2010; Cassirer, 1985). The scopes of art have been implanted into philosophical systems, where forms of dialogue or stories were used, yet art has always been left at the sidelines and was actually thought of as a lower form of cognition (Alić, 2010; Cassirer, 1985; Hegel, 1955). Like philosophy and media, myth and religion make use of symbols. However, myth and religion use symbols that philosophy could not implement into its grammatical and logical edifice. Only the discovery of the constant production of the existing world revealed the meaning of each symbol for shaping the truth as a whole, namely the importance of each medium (Alić, 2010; Cassirer, 1985; Hegel, 1955). Producing media contents and reportages, inclusive of covering news and anchoring studio programs, are ways of un/consciously creating realities (Alić, 2010, p. 205; Thompson, 1988, p. 48), using language and media/mediums of mass communication. Interestingly, both philosophy and the media engage in producing the realities created and promoted by the media, using language and various communication media. Arts, such as dance, performance, drama, poetry, folklores, myths, pictures, sculptures, writing, carving, etc. have been the mediums or media of philosophy of media from time immemorial.

It is averred that myth, religion and art along with cognition make up the world in which we live (Alić, 2010; Cassirer, 1985). The world is not merely a world of pure impressions but rather a product of language, science, myths, religion and art (Alić, 2010; Cassirer, 1985). It is on the basis of religion that the world is conceived as a world of 'spiritual expression' (Alic, 2010, p. 207; Hegel, 1955, pp. 46, 65). It could be recalled that philosophy has a trace to poetry. This tells of how philosophy came to being poetically, whereby poetry was one of its foundational instruments of communication. Poetry, myth (mythology), folktale, and legendary, which philosophers across all periods agreed to be the mother of philosophy (Udofia, 2014, pp. 14-9; Uduigwomen, 2014, pp. 2-6, 8-12; Lawhead, 2002, p. 6; James, 1988; Olela, 1984; among others), are the elements, aspects or thrust of oral literature. And, literature is an art. These days in contemporary times, science and technology have put forward new media. The new media cannot do away with the old communication media. The old media only silenced by the new media and have become less in vogue.

Alić (2010, p. 203) is of the view that sciences, religion and arts took over and impoverish the philosophy of media for ages until recently when changes began to surface. The philosophy of (the) media covers theoretical, practical and poetical aspects of mass media as well as mass communication. Rather than striving to be determined by image, grammar, concept, context, performance, performance psychology or technology, philosophy of media strives to preserve and overcome all these things within it (Alić, 2010, p. 201). Alić (2010, p. 202) avers that all efforts of contemporary philosophical approaches are collected and realized within philosophy of media, which basically questions the issues of mediation of media, opinions, knowledge and philosophy per se. Although this position is arguable on the ground that some persons are bound to consider it an overstatement, it is not but a reality. It is realistic in that by giving it a critical consideration, one realizes that philosophizing and all activities of philosophy involve communication of ideas, thoughts, arguments, propositions, knowledge, information, innovation, findings, discoveries, inventions, and so on through language. In doing so through language, various communication media or mediums are used.

In addition, Alić (2010, p. 203) maintains that various philosophical questions, such as questions on language, image, cognition, epistemology, history of philosophy, and the ontological level of question, basically deal with media mediation. According to Alić (2010, p. 203), it is only at the level of philosophy of media that it is possible to answer all these questions all at the same time, because it is a contemporary, appearing, self-critical and self-conscious philosophy. This philosophy 'returns to its beginnings, reinterprets history, and releases elements of the highest quality from tradition and delivers them to the future' (Alić, 2010, p. 203). The core questions of philosophy of media bother on the possibilities of receiving a system of symbols; what makes the differential experience of the phonetic highway better or worse; and which language media (mediums) are/could be more efficient for the transmission of thoughts, experience, knowledge, etc. from encoder(s) or transmitter to the decoder(s) or audience making up the network of human reception Alić (2010, p. 205). According to Alić (2010, p. 206), the motive of philosophy of media is to reveal what is seductive in fictional texts as well as philosophical discourses, offer purposeful orientation that aid attaining its own goals and those of the media as well as other phenomena.

WHY THE GAP BETWEEN PHILOSOPHY, MEDIA AND DEVELOPMENT?

The seeming negligence to the influences of technology and the media on philosophy is one factor behind the gap between philosophy and the media (Alić, 2010). The gap has grave development implications for both fields. This is simply because the interdisciplinary contributions of these two fields to the development of each other are not duly made. For instance, borne not for the extant gap, the media would have done much more than what obtains currently in contributing to the development of philosophy and vice versa. It is a clear manifestation of the maxim 'United, we stand; divided, we fall.' Put the other way round, it becomes 'Divided, we fall; united, we stand.' The gap between philosophy and the media is a product of undeserving division on professional lanes and subjective sentiments about each other.

Alić (2010, p. 204) argues that 'until philosophy of media formally and legally finds its place at the universities,' the gap between philosophy and media remained unfilled. The gap has been there for many years and it will also take many years to bridge it (Alić, 2010, p. 204). The age-long gap is why philosophy of media is yet to find its right place in academic circles and activities. In the same vein, Hegel (1952, p. 13) has lamented the gap between philosophy and media, as he notes 'A systematically developed media philosophy has until now remained a desideratum for research.' This view points to the unfilled gap in research on media philosophy (philosophy of media). Meanwhile, as Hegel (1952, p. 13) notes, media psychology, media sociology, media education, media law and media economics had long ago found their right places in professional research and teaching at both micro- and macro-levels (i.e., at both discipline-specific and interdisciplinary phases and engagements). Thus, given the above, it is important to bridge the gap between philosophy, media and development as well as other fields.

More so, variances in cultural and social settings also account for the gap. Bridging the gap is imperative to allow for having good and right knowledge of who the other party truly is rather than the otherwise. It is also imperative to allow for group tolerance, integration and smooth intergroup and interpersonal relations and communication. Language misuse about and against each other has been responsible for the age-long gap between philosophy and media. This manifests, as professionals of the two fields preach and hold on to separation rather than interdisciplinary unity and integration. Integration and interdisciplinary imperatives are affirmed and emphasized by the Integrationist Approach theory, noted to be problem-oriented and to insist that no single discipline or approach can satisfactorily and independently address a particular problem (van Leeuwen, 2005, p. 8; Ahmed, 2017, p. 94).

Rather, since disciplines and approaches are existentially interdependent, they could work well and address problems better when they are integrated (van Leeuwen, 2005). In her own contribution as well as affirmation of the necessity to interdisciplinary co-operation and integration, Malek (2018) observes that 'when applying arguments and conclusions to actual practice, it is necessary to see problems through a wide-angle lens that doesn't leave concerns about the larger context in our peripheral vision.' Wide-angle lens suggests considering, adopting and using multiple approaches and means to get the best results or solutions. Besides, she hints that philosophers in bioethics, as in philosophy of media under study, face the challenge of maintaining clarity and rigor while expanding the scope of their work to include real world complexities (Malek, 2018, p. 7).

Another reason for the gap is the extreme or exclusive focus on conceptual distinctions, semantic differences and/or nuanced details, whereby how these considerations matter in practice is being neglected (Malek, 2018, p. 3). Malek (2018, p. 3) emphasizes that describing principled resolutions without considering the realities of their implementation 'can generate skepticism about the value a philosophical approach has to offer.' Malek (2018, p. 3) also notes that while hypothetical scenarios can help illustrate key points, 'when those scenarios become too far removed from actual possible cases or events, they may lose their intuitive force or educational value.' Philosophy is fond of describing principled resolutions without taking into consideration the realities of implementation. This practice does not go down well with the media in practice or some practical cases or events. Thus, the media rather tend to maintain a gap between itself and philosophy. Secondly, philosophy, through philosophers, too often takes hypothetical scenarios too far to the point of removing the actual possible cases or events. This makes philosophy to lose its intuitive force or educational value, as hypothetical scenarios lose their intuitive force or educational value as a result of taking them too far and removing them from the actual possible cases or events.

BRIDGING GAP BETWEEN PHILOSOPHY, MEDIA AND DEVELOPMENT: LANGUAGE IMPERATIVE

Bridging the gap would allow for philosophy to make manifest its resourcefulness of solving human problems and those associated with nature. In the words of Asouzu (2017, p. 1), 'philosophy has much to do with the resourcefulness with which we handle the changes [and challenges] we encounter in life.' This implies that the gap between them has been hampering or shattering the resourcefulness of philosophy to make changes that culminate to indices of development. The challenges encountered in life as a result of underdevelopment and poor communication could be handled by philosophy borne not for the gap. Also, the media would have been tapping more significantly from philosophy borne not for the extant gap. Thus, it is imperative to bridge the gap using language as a viable medium for mediation and communication. The imperative of effective use of language to philosophically solve human and existential problems is echoed by Ekpenyong and Ikegbu (2018), who admonish that 'languages, linguistics and communications must be added to the list of the allied challenges of humanity, where there is a high increase in knowledge upon which philosophical thought is increasingly needed to deal with them.'

Concisely, language is a natural phenomenon that serves as a means of communication between and among individuals and groups, humans and animals alike (Dibie & Robert, 2014; Monday & Eze, 2012; Nwala, 2008). This phenomenon is both general and specific. It is specific to a group or a people, when regarding to the language or speech form inherent to a given people or group. It is general when talking about the phenomenon in general context, from which the specific forms derive or rest on. The foregoing brief explanation is captured by Hockett (1958), as he noted that every language displays the core functions of language. Clearly, he talks about a language [every language] and language. Language is both written and oral, vocal or auditory, creative, symbolic, innate, versatile, unique, rule-governed, dynamic, systematic, learnable, dualistic, arbitrary, productive, discrete, semantic, interchangeable, displaceable, conventional, culture transmission and universal, etc. (Hockett, 1958; Agbedo, 2000; Nwala, 2008; Monday & Eze, 2012; Dibie & Robert, 2014). Language performs communicative, expressive, informative, performative, directive, ideational, unification and humanization functions. It is used to communicate knowledge, etc; give information, directives, orders, and instructions; perform various activities; and share interactions and exchange of pleasantries, as in greetings, wishes, love and business transactions (Nwala, 2008; Anagbogu et al., 2001; Monday and Eze, 2012; Dibie & Robert, 2014).

Language imperative in the task of bridging the gap between philosophy, media and development is given credence by Alić (2010, p. 207), who observes that philosophy has always relied on language as well as language medium [or media]; found validity in the grammar structure of sentences it suggested to be used as laws of thought– objective laws of everything that exists; and acknowledged the language medium, while at the same time negating the completeness of that medium. The loose, insufficient and inappropriate communication between philosophy and media accounts for the extant gap between them, which transcend to the gap between them and development. The misuse of language for communication leads to underdevelopment. For instance, the indictment of African with its embodiments variously by the West continues to work against its development. Consider a contemporary Westerner, who intends to relocate to Africa, invest, establish a multinational business and settle down in Africa for the rest of his/her life. Then, in the course of discussing his/her thoughts with a fellow Westerner, who is a racist or holds/exhibits ethnic hate against Africa, the prospective alien developer of Africa is bound to be discouraged by this racist. Such a person could also get discouraged by certain Western mass media that engage in penchant broadcast, news and media programs, which transmit nothing good but all bad about Africa.

Such Western media, which sustain Western falsehoods of olden days about/against Africa and promote them in contemporary time, would also thwart the prospective development of Africa, no matter how small the proposed business may be and contribute to development in Africa. Since that Westerner has not visited Africa before, whatever convincing or influential stories framed up for him/her that individual Westerner could be taken as true stories. If the media also worsen the situation with such framed stories, that foreigner would believe the stories because of media influence, which is additional to that of the individual Westerner. Consequently, he or she gets discouraged. For example, insecurity arising from religious fundamentalism and hostage kidnapping could be a scary issue put forward to such a person for conviction. Meanwhile, there are many other foreigners (inclusive of Westerners) doing businesses prosperously in Africa amidst the claimed insecurity. It should be noted that it is language is that is used persuasively to convince the person to believe the stories and subsequently succumb to the discouragement. In using language for mass communication, some media are used to pass across the message to micro or macro audience of interpersonal and/or mass communication. It is important to note that development is not dependent on foreign investment alone. However, investments by foreigners undoubtedly bring to place even development. That is, foreign investments contribute to development. Of course, that is how urbanization begins and how urban development is attained (Dibie & Robert, 2018).

With reason (rationality), such a person would apply critical thinking to arrive at a logical conclusion that in as much there are other persons doing businesses well therein, s/he could also move to Africa and successfully invest in and do businesses and settle down on the continent. Borne not for the gap, the media would have also been the solace of the person intending to move to Africa to settle down and invest therein. Thus, bridging the gap between philosophy, media and development is indeed very imperative. Language, which is used to create the gap through the various communication media, remains the same medium for bridging the gap between philosophy and media, which paves way for even development. As such, the bridged gap becomes a meeting point for philosophy, media and development. Similarly, philosophy and media ought to bridge the current gap so as to ensure that the gap in communication between them is got rid of. With that, the philosophically informed media of one nation or continent would be able to adequately and factually transmit the right information about another nation/continent, including the right information about its philosophy. In view of the foregoing, this study argues that the misinformation packaged and spread by some Westerners then and now about Africa and its philosophy is what grounds the negative sentiments many Westerners have, exhibit and express about and against Africa, and its peoples, cultures and all that belongs to it. It is to that end that African philosophy is often debated and relegated by Western philosophers.

The foregoing explanation could be further illustrated with the social situation in which certain persons are hated by some other individuals because of the false information they have had from those persons' covert adversaries/haters about them. Having been 'nailed to the cross' by their adversaries, some of those close to those adversaries are bound to hold same negative thoughts and sentiments about/against these innocent individuals. Some persons have suffered man-tailored plagues on them, because of either the (mis)deeds of their close persons, ethnic groups, religions or thereabouts, or the prejudiced information spread about them or their close persons or groups. Bridging the gap between philosophy, media and development requires (re)building the broken link between them. In fact, by (re)building the broken link between philosophy and media, the link between these duo and development would automatically get (re)built. The imperative of (re)building the link between philosophy and other fields and phenomena is somewhat echoed by Innis (1964, p. 10), who observes viz: 'Alexandria broke the link between science and philosophy. The library was an imperial instrument to offset the influence of Egyptian priesthood.' Clearly, the broken link between philosophy and science is what Innis (1964, p. 10) decries, which means that the link ought not to have been broken. Thus, there is the dire need for philosophy to continuously have strong unbroken link with media, development and other fields and phenomena in society across ages. McLuhan (1964, p. 52) has voiced out the power of electronic media, when he observed that the student of media and communication could have the key to the power in all media to reshape any lives they touch, if they 'meditate on the power of this medium of electric light to transform every structure of time and space and work and society that it penetrates or contacts.'

To the above, this study avers that language is what is behind the voiced out power of the (electronic) media. Without language, the medium of communication with which media contents are aired out and written, the power of the media would ever remain void and unknown. The power of the media is showcased through the use of language. For example, with the use of language, McLuhan (1964, p. 52) tells the media student of the power of the media, with which they could transform societal structures alongside the society and the lives the media touch. Also, as Plato had prophesied, media literate people are more capable of forgetting than the media illiterate ones (Alić, 2010, 209). The philosopher, not being in the media proper, is a media illiterate person, whose literacy is in ideology, which rides again and again. Fortunately, the philosopher is not capable of not forgetting and thus has the capability of dealing with the forgetfulness of the media, if there is no separation gap between them. Philosophers are also quite fortunate to have the training that enables them break down claims into their core components, and identify premises and assumptions that can be analyzed for their individual veracity and collective soundness (Malek, 2018). This training remains valuable for analyzing complex issues such as personal identity, societal well-being, and moral responsibility (Parfit, 1984). Such components can then be used as building blocks for discussions and negotiations among members of society with differing worldviews (Engelhardt, 1996; Malek, 2018).

As (Alić, 2010, 209) notes, 'nowadays, we try to make Man media literate by teaching him techniques of inclusion into the production of spectacular media lie.' So, it is by bridging the gap that the Press would duly teach the philosopher and make him a media literate man. Then, with the bridged gap, for which collaboration becomes inevitable and sustainable, the philosopher teaches the Press philosophical knowledge and exposes them to reason, critical thinking and the questions concerning media that the philosophy of media answers. Bridging the gap between philosophy and media for a strong sustainable link would afford for philosophy the avenues for self-question and wide dissemination of information about itself to wide heterogeneous audiences across the globe. Essentially, bridging the gap for a strong sustainable link would allow for meaningful intermediation between philosophy and the media in both specific and non-specific professional areas and activities. On the other hand, the intermediation between them would stretch to working together in several regards to achieve the development goals of the society, where they are domicile in. The intermediation would also rouse self-consciousness in philosophers and the Press, the professionals and human representatives of philosophy and media. The roused self-consciousness would lead to self-development, which extends to interpersonal and intergroup development. Both philosophy and media are viable instruments of development. The meaningful contributions and/or otherwise to societal development are communicated through various media of communication. It is an indisputable fact that language is the medium of communication with which everything about philosophy and media is communicated, revealed, taught, expressed, documented, transmitted across generation, and what have you. In fact, the activities of both philosophy and media, like those of all other fields, are dependent on language. Without one form of language or the other, no activities can be carried out.

Leaning on Halliday's notion of language on holidays (Halliday, 1985), this study posits that the gap between philosophy, media and development has linguistic traces and so bridging the gap requires linguistic solution. By having linguistic traces, it is quite reasonable that the solution to the problem at stake has to be linguistically sorted and offered. This requires language-based techniques, approaches, measures and sustained efforts. That is, the gap could be bridged through efficient and right use of language by professionals of these trio fields and other individuals in the society in general. The study argues that this is because the gap had been created and sustained by inefficient and wrong use of language to address issues in the fields of philosophy, media and development. The implication of the foregoing is that once the professionals of these fields make language to cease from being on holidays on matters concerning them as well as their fields of endeavor, the gap between them will be sustainably bridged. Language does not have to go on holidays because its moments of holidays portend and bring forth untold dangers and harm to various endeavors.

CONCLUSION

This study has so far demonstrated that there exists an existential link between philosophy and media, which rightly situates both of them in development. That is, they have development potentials and do contribute immensely to the development of society. Nevertheless, the extent of their respective and combined contributions to development as well as their own development is hampered by the age-long gap between them. The study considers the professionals of these fields as those responsible for the gap. It demands that they have to bridge the gap using language efficiently and rightly. Language, as a medium of communication, has various media which constitute the channels of mass communication used by the media (professionals). In all, this study submits that since language is the panacea for the matters arising from the gap between philosophy, media and development, it remains the viable medium for bridging the gap between philosophy, media and development. Language is an instrument for developing both philosophy and media and for expressing all that concerns them. The task of bridging the gap requires efficient and right use of language by professionals of philosophy, media and development.

REFERENCES

Agbedo, C. U. (2000). *General linguistics: An introductory reader.* ACE Resources Konsult.

Ahmed, Y. (2017). *Language, rhetoric, and politics in a global context: A decolonial critical discourse perspective on Nigeria's 2015 presidential campaign* (Dissertation). Michigan Technological University. doi:10.37099/mtu.dc.etdr/400

Ajala, J. (1999). *Public relations: In search of professional excellence.* African Link Book Ltd.

Alić, S. (2010). Philosophy of media – Is the message. *Synthesis Philosophica, 50*(2), 201–210.

Anagbogu, P. N. (2001). *Introduction to linguistics.* J.F.C. Ltd.

Aristotle. (1947). Metaphysics. In R. McKeon (Ed.), The basic works of Aristotle. Clarendon.

Asouzu, I. I. (2004). *The method and principles of complementary.* Calabar University Press.

Asouzu, I. I. (2007). Ibuanyidanda: New complementary ontology, beyond world-immanentism, ethnocentric reduction and imposition. *Trans-Action.*

Asouzu, I. I. (2011). Ibuanyidanda and the philosophy of essence. *Filosofia Theoretica: African Journal of Invention and Ideas, 1*(1), 79–118.

Asouzu, I. I. (2012). Ibuanyidanda and the philosophy of essence (philosophy, the science of missing links of reality). 50th Inaugural Lecture, University Calabar, Calabar, Nigeria.

Asouzu, I. I. (2017). *Changes, adaptation and complementary noetic transformation.* A Keynote Address delivered at the 2nd African Philosophy World Conference (UNICAL 2017): Jointly Hosted by the University of Calabar, Nnamdi Azikiwe University, Awka, and the University of the Witwatersrand in Collaboration with the Conversational School of Philosophy (CPS), University of Calabar.

Besong, E. N. (2016). *Lingering aspects of human bondage in Nigeria: A reflection on Nyerere's true freedom.* Paper presented at the Nigeria Philosopher Association Annual Conference, University of Uyo.

Besong, E. N. (2017). The imperative of indiscriminate and rural-centred educational broadcasting in Nigeria. In O. S. Robert & E. N. Besong (Eds.), *Unresolved degenerating nat'l issues: Nigerian govt & media's failure* (pp. 49–64). LAP Lambert Academic Publishing.

Cassirer, E. (1985). *Filozofija simboličkih oblika* [Philosophy of symbolic forms]. Dnevnik-Književna zajednica Novog Sada.

Chiakaan, G. J. (2013). *Broadcasting and the broadcast media in Nigeria.* Eagle Prints.

Chiakaan, G. J., & Ahmad, J. I. (2011). *Mass communication for beginners.* Azaben Publishers.

Crosbie, V. (2002). *What is new media? Digital deliverance.* www.digitaldeliverance.com

Dibie, G. A., & Robert, O. S. (2014). Appraising the significance of arts and languages in polytechnic education. *5th National Conference of the Nasarawa state: Polytechnic ASUP chapter.*

Dibie, G. A., & Robert, O. S. (2015). *A thankless task for Nasarawa parents, schools and mass media in marketing library resources. International Journal and Publications.*

Dibie, G. A., & Robert, O. S. (2018, January). Towards transforming sub-Sahara Africa through collective rural development. *International Journal of Engineering and Information Systems*, *2*(1), 159–167.

Ekei, J. (2017). *Philosophy, human development and national question* (Special edition). UJAH. http://dx.doi./org/10.4314/ujah.v18i2.1

Ekpenyong, B., & Ikegbu, E. A. (2018). The language of philosophy and the philosophy of language: A symbiotic paradigm. Budapest International Research and Critics Institute- Journal, 1(3), 296-305.

Emeka-Nwobia, N. (2007). *Sociolinguistics: An introductory reader*. Larry Caleb- Copy Craft International Ltd.

Emeka-Nwobia, N. U. (2015). The place of indigenous Nigerian languages in national development. *Research on Humanities and Social Sciences*, *5*(12). www.iiste.org

Engelhardt, H. T. Jr. (1996). *The foundations of bioethics* (2nd ed.). Oxford University Press.

Etieyibo, E. E., & Chimakonam, J. O. (2018). The state of African philosophy in Africa. In E. E. Etieyibo (Ed.), *Method, substance, and the future of African philosophy*. doi:10.1007/978-3-319-70226-1_5

Halliday, M. A. K. (1985). *An introduction to functional grammar*. Edward Arnold.

Hegel, G.W.F. (1955). *Fenomenologija duha* [The phenomenology of spirit]. Grafički zavod Hrvatske.

Hockett, C. F. (1958). *A course in modern linguistics*. Macmillan. doi:10.1111/j.1467-1770.1958.tb00870.x

Innis, H. A. (1964). *The bias of communications, with a new introduction by Marshall McLuhan*. University of Toronto Press.

Inya-Egwu, A. (2018). Philosophy in diverse modes: An appraisal of the musicsophical contents in the music of Fela Anikulapokuti and Prince Nico Mbarga. In P.B. Bisong & O.J. Alexander (Eds.), Essays on feminism in honour of Prince Nico Mbarga (pp. 498-515). e20Media Limited.

James, G. (1988). *The stolen legacy*. Julian Richard.

Lawhead, W. F. (2002). The voyage of discovery: A historical introduction to philosophy (2nd ed.). Wadsworth/Thomson Learning.

Malek, J. (2018). Bridging the gap between theory and practice: Philosophy through a wide- angle lens. *The Journal of Medicine and Philosophy*, *43*(1), 1–7. doi:10.1093/jmp/jhx031

McLuhan, M. (1964). *Understanding media*. Routledge & Kegan Paul.

Moemeka, A. (1991). *Communicating for development: A new pan-disciplinary perspective*. State University of New York Press.

Monday, H. G., & Eze, C. C. (2012). *Basic studies in English and communication skill for tertiary institutions*. Shola Publishers.

NOUN. (2008). *MAC 111 Introduction to mass communication: Course guide*. National Open University of Nigeria.

Nwala, M. A. (2008). *Introduction to linguistics: A first course* (rev. ed.). Osi and Alozie Ltd.

Olela, H. (1984). The African foundations of Greek philosophy. In R. Wright (Ed.), *African philosophy: An introduction*. University Press of America.

Osuagwu, N., & Chimakonam, J.O. (2018). African Studies through language-based techniques. *Filosofia Theoretica: Journal of African Philosophy, Culture and Religions, 7*(1), 101-124. . doi:10.4314/ft.v7i1.5

Oyedeji, V. A. (2018). *Indigenous Language Education and the Challenges of Insecurity in Nigeria. Zaria Journal of Educational Studies* (special edition, Vol. 19). ZAJES.

Parfit, D. (1984). *Reasons and persons*. Oxford University Press.

Puiu, Y. V., Puiu, D. A., Sablin, I. V., Georgieva, E. S., Vladimirovich, I., & Bykov, A. Y. (2015). Conceptual framework of mass media manipulative models forming. *International Review of Management and Marketing*, *5*(special issue). http: www.econjournals.com

Robert, O. S., & Besong, E. N. (2016). *Nigerian media and indigenous cultures transformation: The journey so far* (Vol. 6). J Mass Communicat Journalism.

Thompson, A. (1988). The news media and international relations: Experience and the media reality. *Canadian Journal of Communication, 13*(1). doi:10.22230/cjc.1987v13n1a440

Uche, B. G. (1994). The interaction between science and language. *The Nigeria Teacher Today: A Journal of Teacher Education*, *3*(1), 101.

Udigwomen, A. F. (2014). The Greek cultural context: The transition from poetry to philosophy. In A. F. Udigwomen & C. A. Udofia (Eds.), *A critical history of philosophy: Ancient and medieval* (pp. 1–13). Ultimate Index Book Publishers.

Udofia, C. A. (2014). Early pioneers: The myth and reality about their authorship and origination of Western philosophy. In A. F. Udigwomen & C. A. Udofia (Eds.), *A critical history of philosophy: Ancient and medieval* (pp. 14–20). Ultimate Index Book Publishers.

Uduma, O. U. (2000). *The fundamentals of philosophy*. WAP Coy.

van Leeuwen, T. (2005). Three models of interdisciplinarity. In R. Wodak & P. Chilton (Eds.), A new agenda in (Critical) discourse analysis: Theory, methodology and interdisciplinarity (pp. 3-18). John Benjamins. doi:10.1075/dapsac.13.04lee

Chapter 4
Cultural Diplomacy as a Dimension of Geopolitics

Uchenna Azubuike Ezeogu
https://orcid.org/0000-0001-6167-666X
Nigeria Maritime University Okerenkoko, Nigeria

ABSTRACT

The term "cultural diplomacy" denotes a deliberate effort on the part of a government through its agencies to promote its national interest by projecting its culture to the world. This conception poses a great threat to other cultures, especially in this era of globalization. Through cultural diplomacy, cultures of presupposed lesser countries are swallowed by that of super-rich countries. What is seen as the emerging global culture is actually the culture of the few elitists countries projected on others through cultural diplomacy. This is another dimension of geopolitics, the promotion of cultural hegemony by the people of the Global North. Using philosophical methods of analysis and hermeneutics, the chapter contends that the people of the Global South, especially Africa, should also explore the avenue of cultural diplomacy to retain their identities in this era of globalization.

INTRODUCTION

The focus of this chapter is to establish that cultural diplomacy is actually another dimension of geopolitics. This chapter tries to argue that beyond what is explicitly presented as the focus or goal of cultural diplomacy, that there exist implicit motives which are covert and may not be in the interest of all parties. Cultural diplomacy is an instrument of competitive struggle by elitists' countries to assert their interest on the rest of the world. It is a geo-political movement. One of the popular definitions of politics was given by Harold Lasswell. For him, politics is all about, who gets what, when and how. Cultural Diplomacy is a subtle way through which countries from the Global North, continues to dominate and dictate for those in the Global South especially Africa. In geopolitics, there is this continuous battle for who gets what, when and how. Countries of the world struggle for better positioning to achieve this. Each has specific and personal interest to protect or gains to make. This chapter argues that what is today known and seen as cultural diplomacy is actually another dimension of geopolitics. It involves a

DOI: 10.4018/978-1-6684-4107-7.ch004

situation where countries, especially those from the Global North project and sell their interest to the rest of the world through culture. To a large extent one may refer to it as the act of enforcing cultural hegemony or cultural imperialism.

In this chapter, the paper will mainly focus on the impact of cultural diplomacy on Africa, with particular reference to Nigeria. The concept or idea of cultural diplomacy is multi-disciplinary in nature, but this chapter will approach it from a philosophical perspective. It is obvious that the politics involved in cultural diplomacy is actually dividing Africa as a war spoil. The Asians are already getting it right while Africa continues to play the ostrich. It is interesting to note that Asians have started taking advantage of cultural diplomacy in selling their image to the world. The question is; how is Africa going to turn the tide that is already against her? In recent time, the Euro-American world has succeeded in what this paper will refer to as image propaganda; presenting itself as the modern ideal for almost everything, while African culture is projected to represent the opposite. The challenge for Africa is that the West through cultural diplomacy has impressed their culture so much in the psychic of the average African mind that, Africans are on their own rejecting everything indigenous to them and at the same time, have become agents of promotion to Western values and culture. This has permeated all facets of life ranging from religion, dress code, language, movies, food, marriage, consumption, system of learning and so on. To buttress this point further; on the issue of religion, in most African society especially in Nigeria, African Traditional Religion worshippers are seen as being fetish and magical while followers of Western religion are held in high esteem. This was pointed out by Chimamanda Adichie (2021) in her speech at the Humboldt Forum, where she posed the question; "what could be more magical than the story of a man who dies and magically rises again?" She was trying to make a comparison between Euro-Christian Religion and Traditional African Religion. Her point is, if we can fault African Traditional Religion on the ground that there are certain illogical or magical elements associated with it, the same illogical or magical elements also exist in Euro-Christian Religion. For Adichie, so long as a belief system fills the spiritual need of a people, it is valid. On the aspect of marriage, in some African societies, one is not considered fully married until he or she performs the white wedding, even after performing all Africa traditional rites. In the area of consumption, the average African mind prefers to patronize Euro-American products to local (made in Africa) products. The list is unending, but all these were achieved through cultural diplomacy. This probably might be part of what has inspired the decolonization movement.

In the view of Iver B. Neumann (2018), diplomacy is about communicating with the other and the essence of this communication is to change people's minds. This boils down to impression management which is a face work. There is this constant cultural propaganda in the form of cultural diplomacy by the people of the Global North to place their values and culture as the paradigm others should follow. The West started with colonization, and currently through the instrumentality of cultural diplomacy they have continued to plunder Africa to their advantage. They currently represent the standard for everything. The idea of International Poverty line, how does it reflect the actual state of an African woman in an African village who may not need to go to the market to buy her food since she has all her needed food in her farm. She goes to her farm every morning to gather enough food to take care of her family. By Western standard, she might be classified as being poor, because she has no earnings, or when the earnings are translated to Dollar does not meet certain specified range. Yet, her daily needs are met through the farm.

This chapter will consider the meaning and nature of cultural diplomacy. Effort will be made to explore the concept *vis a vis* philosophical hermeneutics. This will open up the geopolitics inherent in the concept, the soft power politics and the negative implications of ignoring it. The paper will further argue on how Africa can also explore this avenue of cultural diplomacy to retain her cultural identity.

This will raise anew the already existing skepticism towards globalization and economic openness as it tends to benefit the rich countries of the Global North and further impoverish the poor countries of the Global South.

THE CONCEPT OF CULTURAL DIPLOMACY

What is cultural diplomacy? There is no univocal definition of this concept. The concept is multi-disciplinary in nature and has a very long history. For Piros S. and Koops J. (2020), cultural diplomacy is difficult to define given the ambiguous and often all-encompassing nature and meaning of culture. On the nature and meaning of 'diplomacy' it has also been in flux with recent debates centering on the dichotomy between 'orthodox' or 'classical' state-centric diplomacy versus the latest iteration of modern or decentralized 'new diplomacy' driven by globalization (Kelley, 2010). For a proper understanding of the concept of cultural diplomacy, one has to explore the meaning of 'public diplomacy', 'international relation', 'soft power' and the like. For Martina Topic and Cassandra Sciortino (2012), the term cultural diplomacy is often used interchangeably with the term public diplomacy, though they posit that current scholarship generally views cultural diplomacy as conceptually and practically a subset of public diplomacy. By implication, cultural diplomacy may be seen as an aspect of public diplomacy. The idea of cultural diplomacy is of a recent origin while public diplomacy is as old as statecraft (Topic & Sciortino 2012). For a better understanding of the concept of cultural diplomacy, one has to explore the concept of public diplomacy. The effort of this chapter is not just to explore the meaning of the concept as it is, but rather to employ hermeneutics in such explanation. Through hermeneutics both the overt and covert meanings are made clear.

On the idea of public diplomacy, by way of analysis the concept is divided into two; 'public' and 'diplomacy'. Diplomacy is conventionally understood to mean government-to-government (diplomat -to- diplomat) exchange. The idea of 'public' makes reference to the people generally. The idea of 'public diplomacy' hermeneutically could be said to connote contradiction going by conventional meaning of the term 'diplomacy'. Ideally, diplomacy implies government to government relationship. Public diplomacy implies a relationship between government and the people. Government of a particular country instead of relating to the government of another country steps down to relate to the people of that country. This generates a philosophical question; why would a government bypass a fellow government to relate directly with the citizens of that country, if the intentions are pure? The unequal nature of such relationship subjects it to various forms of suspicion and philosophical scrutiny. For Signitzer (2008), "Public diplomacy is a government's process of communicating with foreign publics in an attempt to bring about understanding for its nation's ideas and ideals, its institutions and cultures, as well as its national goals and current policies". This brings to question the idea of 'diplomacy', if the relationship is no longer between government and government, can such relationship still be classified as diplomatic? On the goal of public diplomacy, Signitzer went further to assert that "the goal of public diplomacy is to influence the behavior of a foreign government by influencing the attitudes of its citizens". This also raises concern on the genuineness of the goal of public diplomacy. Philosophically speaking, this goal of public diplomacy has some elements of coercion embedded in it. The main focus of this chapter is not on public diplomacy per se but on cultural diplomacy. Our exploration of the idea of public diplomacy is for a better and more holistic understanding of cultural diplomacy since the former precedes the later historically. Having looked at the idea of public diplomacy, let us consider the idea of cultural diplomacy.

Martina Topic and Cassandra Sciortino argue that it is long-term relationship building that distinguishes between cultural diplomacy and public diplomacy. In citing Leonard M. (1997) three-tiered conceptualization of public diplomacy; short-term, medium-term and long-term they refer to cultural diplomacy as the third tier (long-term). The short-term takes hours or days, the medium-term is executed within months and the long-term relationship building takes years. This long-term relationship building is what they referred to as cultural diplomacy. According to Signitzer, just as in public diplomacy, "the goal of cultural diplomacy is to produce positive attitudes towards one's own country with the hope that this may be beneficial to over-all diplomatic goal achievement". Cultural diplomacy and public diplomacy are seen as examples of soft power (Topic, M. & Sciortino, C. 2012, 16). Soft power is a term coined by Joseph Nye (2008) "it is the ability to affect others to obtain the outcome one wants through attraction rather than coercion or payment". For Nye, a country's soft power rests on its resources of culture, values and policies. Hermeneutically we can deduce and agree with Topic and Sciortino that both public diplomacy and cultural diplomacy are instruments or examples of 'soft power' politics.

Cultural diplomacy, public diplomacy and soft power are closely related terms. Patricia M. Goff (2013) in analyzing various views on cultural diplomacy concludes that cultural diplomacy is first and foremost about bridging differences and facilitating mutual understanding. This position is based on her two premises; first, that good relations can take root in the fertile ground of understanding and respect. Second, that cultural diplomacy rests on the assumption that art, language, and education are among the most significant entry points into culture. The term cultural diplomacy is inexhaustible as it continues to take various forms and meanings. Our focus is to consider it from a philosophical perspective. In as much as this paper agrees with Goff on what may appear as the essence of cultural diplomacy; 'bridging differences and facilitating mutual understanding', it questions the usage of the term diplomacy. Silviu Piros and Joachim Koops (2020) argue that cultural diplomacy and education diplomacy are intimately intertwined in historical, conceptual and policy practice terms, and that we cannot understand the full extent of cultural diplomacy without also understanding and exploring the education diplomacy dimension. The perspectives are unending, but the chapter will like to establish, going by hermeneutical implication of the term, that the concept has both overt and covert meaning. The idea of cultural diplomacy tilting towards mutual understanding between countries is overt. But the unequal coming together for this mutual understanding creates an unequal relationship, this dimension is covert. The unequal nature of this coming together creates unequal outcome in the mutual understanding. One country stands the possibility of being accused of trying to dominate the other with its culture and values. This is explainable when one empirically observes the relationship between The Global South and The Global North with particular reference to Africa. A situation where citizens of Africa countries are trying to adopt Euro-American culture as ideal culture to the detriment of their indigenous culture. This opens us to the geopolitical dimension of cultural diplomacy.

THE GEOPOLITICS OF CULTURAL DIPLOMACY

The idea or concept of cultural diplomacy is multi-facets. While some scholars may have argued on the political neutrality of the concept stating the promotion of 'mutual understanding' as the main aim of cultural diplomacy, some have also seen it from the perspective of promoting imperialism. Carta, C. and Higgott, R. (2020), writing on the EU cultural diplomacy posit that the main challenge or allegation against EU's cultural diplomacy is that it aims more at the promotion of Europe than the promotion of cultural relations. They argue that a deliberate choice to change this narrative will help prevent allegations of arrogance and cultural imperialism. This points to the fact that there are wide range of suspicion or allegation on the intention of European cultural diplomacy. In the view of Taylor, P. M. (2007) cultural diplomacy ought to be a government undertaking which communicates to other nations via the media and in a supposedly non-political manner. But for him, in reality it is a political activity which serves the national interest under the cover of culture.

Cultural diplomacy for Ryniejska-Kieldanowics (2009) is a conduit in implementing a government policy abroad with the aim of popularizing its culture as being more valuable than the culture of other countries. What takes place is an unequal exchange of culture or a domination of a given culture by another. If we consider the idea of 'mutual understanding' associated with cultural diplomacy as we have stated earlier and argued by some scholars, it implies 'give and take'. Each country has what they are dishing out and at the same time what they are receiving from each other as a mark of mutual understanding. One may see it as a dialectical intercultural dialogue. Dialectical in the sense that, there is a process of mutual cultural transformation on the both sides. But a situation where a country mainly focuses on dishing out its culture to foreign audience with the sole aim of promoting it, this questions the suitability of adopting the idea of 'mutual understanding'. This paper will like to argue that, cultural diplomacy which does not involve mutual exchange of cultures, operates by mathematical law of substitution or what the paper will like to refer to as cultural substitution; a country trying to substitute the culture of another with its culture. This brings us to the geopolitical question; the question of who dominates the political arena.

We have earlier explored the meanings of the following terms: public diplomacy, cultural diplomacy and soft power. Cultural diplomacy is seen as a long term public diplomacy. That is to say, a public diplomacy with a long term focus. Both public and cultural diplomacy are seen as important tools in the arsenal of smart power. Nye argues that in international politics, the resources that produce soft power arise in large part from the values an organization or country expresses in its culture. At this point, there is need to connect all the dots in relation to our argument, and address all the linguistic fluidity associated with the terms. First to be addressed is public diplomacy; diplomacy entails government to government relationship. It is the coming together of two or more independent equals. But when diplomatic relationship moves from government of a country to the people of another country it becomes an unequal relationship which to a large extent may be worrisome. One may argue that the idea of 'diplomacy' implying government to government relation is orthodox or classical and that there is a modern or decentralized understanding of the term which is driven by globalization and technological advances where non-state actors are empowered. The goal or aim of the both remains the same, whether we look at it from the classical or the modern understanding. The idea is to sell a particular country's culture to a foreign audience with the aim of influencing the government through its people. When this becomes a long term plan, it is seen as cultural diplomacy. For Nye, one can affect others' behavior in three main ways: threat of coercion (sticks), inducements and payments (carrots) and attraction that makes others want what you want. Cultural diplomacy which is an instrument of soft power falls in the third category. For John Lamola (2021), under the prevailing ideology of globalization modern technologies that are produced for global consumption comes from a particular political and geo-cultural place. In his view, Euro-American epistemic tradition and intellectual heritage have ascended into a position of hegemony on scientific research and technological innovation. This paper will like to add that the entire epistemic or cultural dominance started with cultural diplomacy. Through cultural diplomacy Euro-American world have come to dominate all spheres of human endeavor, substituting other peoples' culture with theirs.

Paulin Hountondji (1990) pointed out the area of scientific dependence in Africa, though he did not link it as a by-product of cultural diplomacy, rather he argued on the negative implications of such dependency system. For Hountondji, the system of education in Africa is structured in such a way and manner that African scholars of whatever field of study believes that everything that matters for them in their field is taking place elsewhere outside Africa. “Elsewhere, outside Africa, are located the most fully equipped laboratories, the best universities, the most powerful research centers, the editorial teams and offices of the most prestigious scientific journals, the most complete reference libraries and publishing houses, and last but not the least, the world’s major concentration of practicing scientists”. On the question concerning how African scholars react to this situation, for Hountonji, they hardly question it. They tend to take it for granted. It is on this note that this paper tends to make clear the implicit effect of cultural diplomacy. Through cultural diplomacy, the Euro-American world have projected their culture to serve as paradigm in all spheres of life in Africa. This is a clear case of geopolitics, and identity struggle. For Africa to retain its identity at the global stage without serving the copycat role for Euro-American world, there is need for Africa to also employ this method of cultural diplomacy in projecting its culture to the rest of the world.

The structure created by geopolitics of cultural diplomacy is of a very long origin, only that it has been viewed from different interpretative perspectives. Just as Grosfoguel in Lamola M. J. (2021) captures it;

We (people of the ‘Global South’) went from the sixteenth century characterization of ‘people without writing’ to eighteenth and nineteenth-century characterization of ‘people without history’, to the twentieth-century characterization of ‘people without development’ and more recently, to the early twenty-first century of ‘people without democracy’.

The geo-political structure of the globe has always been in favor of Euro-American hegemony. This they have achieved through cultural diplomacy. They favorably project their narrative to the rest of the world and negatively interpret African narrative. This to a large extent has continued to influence the fate of Africa in the global space.

CONCLUSION

At this juncture, with the advent of globalization it suffices to argue that, countries of the Global North through cultural diplomacy are making desperate efforts at the global stage to project their culture as the global culture thereby eliminating other cultures. It is a truism that nature avoids vacuum, in projecting their culture as the ideal global culture they are indirectly eliminating other cultures. Hence, this paper from a philosophical perspective posits cultural diplomacy as cultural substitution based on its one-sided approach to cultural relation. Ezeogu and Ezugwu (2021), in arguing on the domination of Eurocentric concepts and categories in African philosophy have argued that, cultural encounter between the West and Africa degenerated to relationship of domination and subordination. A situation where Western philosophical concepts and categories tend to shape or influence discourse on African philosophy. Today some African scholars are crying against epistemic marginalization (Chimakonam, 2017), while the West through cultural diplomacy are busy expanding their frontiers. It is the position of this chapter that cultural diplomacy in this age of globalization is currently giving the world a new identity. This new identity, represents the culture of few elitists’ countries of the world. The only way Africa and the rest of the Global South can be part of this changing new identity is to also play the game of cultural diplomacy. China and some Asian countries have come to understand this new dynamics and they are already playing along. It will be to the detriment of African continent if the continent continues to play the ostrich.

REFERENCES

Adichie, C. N. (2021). *Speech at the Humboldt Forum*. YouTube.

Carta, C., & Higgott, R. (2020). Conclusion: On the Strategic Deployment of Culture in Europe and Beyond. In Cultural Diplomacy in Europe. The European Union in International Affairs.

Chimakonam, J. O. (2017). African Philosophy and Global Epistemic Injustice. *Journal of Global Ethics*, *13*(2), 120–137.

Ezeogu, U. A., & Ezugwu, U. J. (2021). African Philosophy beyond Eurocentric Concepts and Categories. *Nnamdi Azikiwe Journal of Philosophy*, *12*(2), 1–10.

Goff, P. M. (2013). Cultural Diplomacy. In The Oxford Handbook of Modern Diplomacy. Oxford University Press. doi:10.1093/oxfordhb/9780199588862.013.0024

Hountondji, P. (1990). Scientific Dependence in Africa Today. *Research in African Literatures*, *21*(3), 5–15.

Kelley, J. R. (2010). The New Diplomacy: Evolution of a Revolution. *Diplomacy and Statecraft*, *21*(2), 286–305. doi:10.1080/09592296.2010.482474

Lamola, J. M. (2021). *Africa in the Fourth Industrial Revolution: A Status Questionis, from the Cultural to the Phenomenological. In African Values, Ethics and Technology*. Palgrave Macmillan.

Lasswell, H. D. (1951). The Political Writings of Harold D. Lasswell. The Free Press.

Neumann, I. B. (2018). Diplomacy, the Arts, and Popular Culture. In G. Martel (Ed.), *The Encyclopedia of Diplomacy*. John Wiley & Sons, Ltd. doi:10.1002/9781118885154.dipl0080

Nye, J. S. Jr. (2008, March). Public Diplomacy and Soft Power. *The Annals of the American Academy of Political and Social Science*, *616*(1), 94–109. doi:10.1177/0002716207311699

Ryniejska-Kieldanowics, M. (2009). *Cultural Diplomacy as a Form of International Communication*. Institute for Public Relation BledCom Special Prize for the best New Research on the Cultural Variables in Public Relations Practice.

Signitzer, B. (2008). Public Relations and Public Diplomacy: Some Conceptual Explorations. In A. Zerfab, A. A. Van Ruler, B. Van Ruler, & K. Sriramesh (Eds.), *Public Relations Research: European and International Perspectives and Innovations*. VS Verlag fur Sozialwissenschaften. doi:10.1007/978-3-531-90918-9_13

Taylor, P. M. (2007). *Global Communications, International Affairs and the Media since 1945*. Routledge.

Topic, M., & Sciortino, C. (2012). Cultural Diplomacy and Cultural Hegemony: A Framework for the Analysis. In Cultural Diplomacy and Cultural Imperialism: European Perspective(s). Peterlang.

Chapter 5
The Media and Development in an Era of Digitalized Economy

Bassey Okon
NAF School of Public Relations and Information, Nigeria

ABSTRACT

The chapter looks at the media and development in an era of digitalized economy and how this impacts on the growth of developing countries. It considers the growth in technology and how this has brought the world together as visualized by Herbert Marshall McLuhan in his academic coinage of the expressions 'the global village' and 'the medium is the message'. The chapter posits that embedded in McLuhan's concepts are recurring issues relating to the nature of modern media, media concentration or congregation, media efficiency or power, media control in relation to who keeps the media gate. The unfolding consequences of media concentration, media power patterns, rising power of digital media platforms with challenging implications for world economy in the face of growing 'paperlessness' of money raises concerns over digital money. The chapter posits that money is theoretically returning back to its 'barter era' due to the concentration and growing 'media power' as money mutates from paper to paperless digital reality.

INTRODUCTION

The rapid growth in the media has redefined society in perplexing ways. The perplexity itself is a function of the impact of evolving information channels on the social, economic, cultural, religious, political and psychological spheres of human interaction. The security, health, sports and education domains are not excluded from the growing transformation of human interaction as a result of the media. The differentiation in access to media domains raises the same issues previously addressed by the controversial World Information Order or news flow between the north and south poles. It is expedient to begin any inquiry into the interrelationship between the media and development by looking at the development within the media itself. It is interesting to note that communication is described today in different ways reflecting how information ebbs and flows from senders to receivers. Scholars define communication in terms of old, modern, interactive and hybrid media depending on their angle of analysis. However,

DOI: 10.4018/978-1-6684-4107-7.ch005

Figure 1. The mediating influence of media on the rational spheres

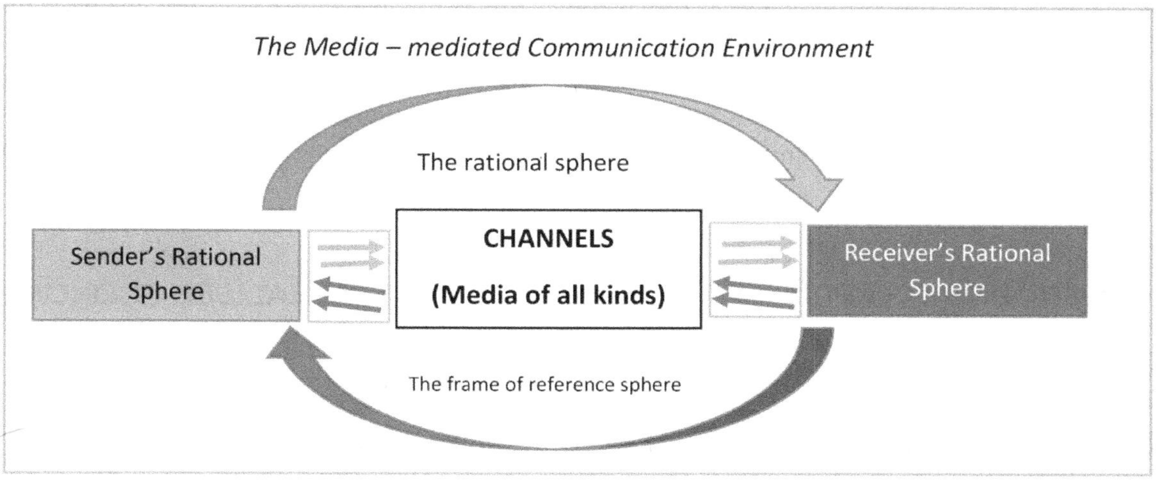

communication itself is not the media, but relates to how information gets to its end destination. In this instance, the media are mere channels through which communication radiates.

Communication is therefore considered here in its traditional broader perspective to encompass the rational sphere of the sender, the media and the rational sphere of the receiver as reflected in Figure 1. The sender, in the presence of divergent media and a wide range of conduits, now has an unimaginable spectrum of engagement options with the receiver, who equally has numerous outlets to send his feedback to the originating source of the communication chain. The media therefore are a multiplicity of communication options made readily available by positive developments in technology. The media, incorporating the internet, print and broadcast media function, through a nexus of mediating variables (Klapper, 1960). These variables, according to Klapper, affect how the media impacts on the audience. Consequently, if the media influence is mediated as postulated, it raises concerns on the extent to which these mediating variables influence the effect of the media on development. This, on its own, raises a lot of perplexing complexities prominent among which is the question: Does the media indeed influence development? If the media do, how does that happen at the global sphere of human society where the system is differentiated by first, second and third world countries? In responding to this contradictory concern, it would be necessary to separate effects as a function of the message and effects as a function of easy access and extreme reach by modern media. The ease of access is indeed the underlying basis for stating that the media indeed influences development. It is the media as the medium but not the message that creates this differentiation within the context of this book chapter.

This position does not necessarily contradict the postulations of McLuhan who stated that the "medium is the message" (McLuhan, 1967). It rather re-enforces it in that it agrees with Logan who concurred that McLuhan, in making that statement, "proposes that the media, not the content that they carry, should be the focus of study" (Logan, 2021). The influence of the media, rather than the content, forms the basis of the deduction that development is functionally influenced by the media in an era of digitalized economy. The economy, politics, culture and social relations within each sub-system are helplessly dependent on the nature of communication and media power within each social system. This is critical in understanding how the 'advent and massive expansion of the Internet and planetary scale digital platforms' impact on data-driven trends in the market space and political sphere of global businesses. Development itself is tied to economic operations within each social system. However, what constitutes development within different substructures and what is visualized as a digitalized economy in today's media varies from society to society. It is only when development is analysed from a universal media perspective covering the different rational spheres that a realistic conclusion can be meaningfully deducted in a digitalized world. Accordingly, it is important to provide a conceptual background to media and development in a digitalised economy.

BACKGROUND TO MEDIA AND DEVELOPMENT IN A DIGITALISED ECONOMY

The media are mere channels. They do not generate the message. They transmit it. The way a message is transmitted plays a critical role in its acceptance, believability and credibility. For instance, a message that people should stay indoors, if aired by a credible medium would tend to generate more positive response than a medium that is known for carrying phony news. However, conceptualizing the media to reflect only channels would be limiting in this context. Hence the media, as used here goes beyond the conduits to incorporate the content that is transmitted through the medium. In this instance, the media and the contents they carry are considered synonymous to each other making the medium the same thing as the message and vice versa. As noted by McLuhan, the form of the medium in this instance embeds itself in the message thereby creating a symbiotic relationship between the medium and the message (McLuhan, 1967). Similarly, development connotes different things to different people. What constitutes development in one location may be considered retrogression in another location. It is therefore expedient to define what is considered as development within the context of this chapter. Furthermore, human interaction with machines have moved from analogue to the digital era. Technologies and equipment that could not keep pace with the rapid transformation have already been relegated to the abyss of history. Money has also moved on to "paperlessness" as the digitalised world evolves. Consequently, it is imperative to take a closer look at the nature of today's media, what constitutes development within different substructures, and the era of digitalised economy.

The Nature of Today's Media

The arrival of new communication technology keeps reshaping the nature of media existing at any time. The creation of the font or movable type in 1455 by Johan Guttenberg (Robert S. Fortner, 2021) transformed information dissemination by making the newspapers possible. Subsequent developments in signal message transmission and receiving sets moved communication to the radio era and then television with the arrival of visualization. Today, the media has moved to the digital era with devices of different sizes bringing information from divergent, sometimes inexperienced, purveyors of news to an indeterminate audience. It is an era of participatory journalism also tagged citizen journalism or "we journalism" (Shayne Bowman and Chris Willis, 2003). Kovach and Rosenstiel posit that there would be a shift in modern media trends with the combination of new technology, globalization and the conglomeration of media. Trends however show that while emerging media may displace existing forms in terms of preference, these do not replace or eliminate them completely. Radio could not replace the print just as television could not replace the radio. Emerging media simply complement or re-enforce existing media systems. The growing digitalization of the media space may only increase the continuous

Figure 2. Illustration of the nature of today's media

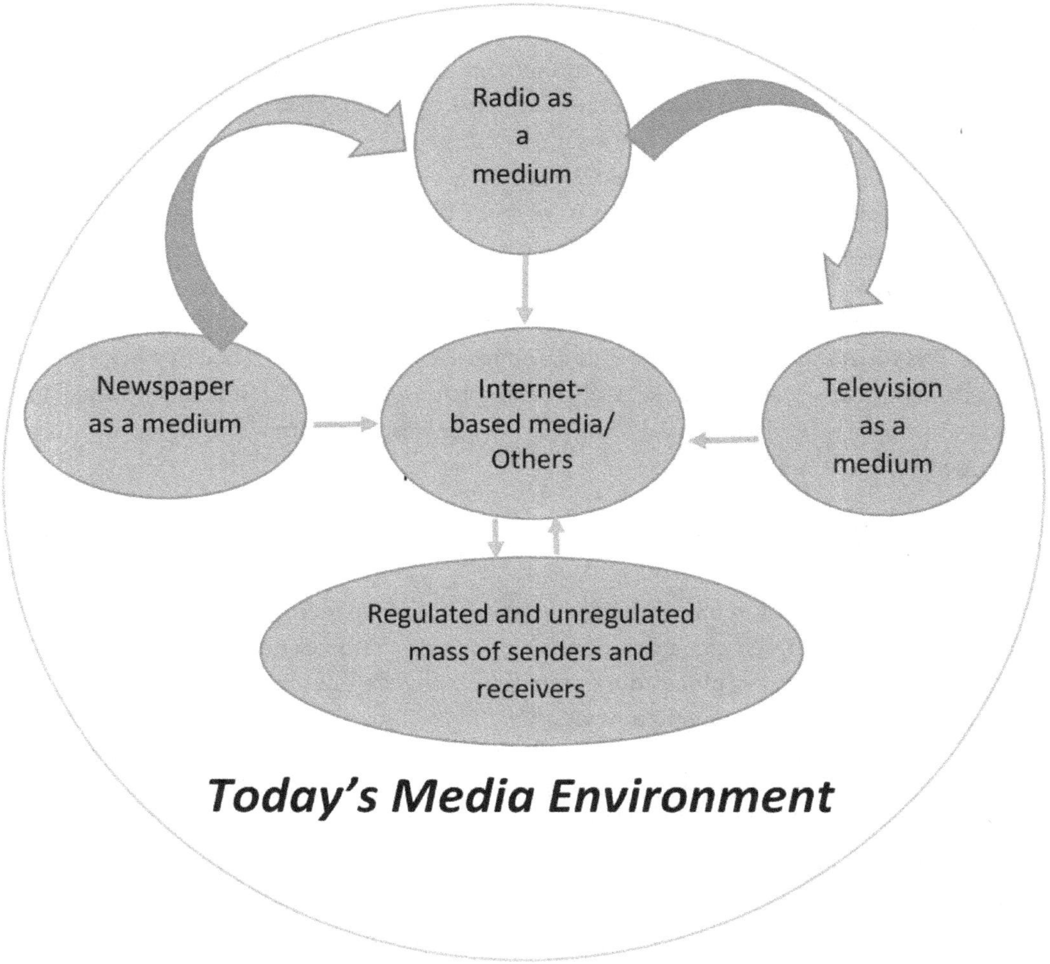

information implosion compelling the media consumers to selectively expose themselves to the media based on individual preferences. News is simply a click away with the multiplicity of communication channels. Audience do not necessarily have to wait for scheduled programming to expose themselves to media content. Consequently, today's media environment is simply a nexus of different media platforms as illustrated in Figure 2.

The media space, as illustrated in Figure 2, appears very simplistic. The figure provides a web that is encompassing. Newspapers, radio and television houses now have websites where their contents could be viewed 24 hours of the day. The gradual concentration of media channels through the internet and web systems into a collective whole has somewhat eliminated, to some extent, the previous inability of the distant audience to review and "listen again" to a news item that has been aired by either the radio or television. Today, a curious listener can go to the website of a media house, two or more days after the newscast, to replay a news story thereby defeating the hitherto "passing nature" of electronic news where news broadcast by the radio and television decades ago cannot be repeated to ascertain the content aired.

However, when this is considered within a global perspective, there are various levels of differentiation in modern media outreach that make this illustration self-defeating. There are several communities that are cut off from the media web either due to economic backwardness, technological deficiency, lack of electricity, internet access and a combination of other factors. Ironically, a bulk of those cut off from the media web are from the traditional less developed or third world countries. This, in itself, raises concern on how these less developed societies can take advantage of the media to develop communities that are cut off from the news channels. As noted, by Ithiel Pool, "the less developed countries of the world require large injections of information in the form of technology transfer if they are to have economic growth and development" (Pool, 1979, p. 150). Regrettably, the "means of acquiring it are largely beyond their reach" (Pool, 1979, p. 150). The inequality among nations in the area of information diffusion led to the agitation for a new world information order which again echoes the importance of the media to development. The media is therefore conceptualized here to mean all the processes involved in the production and distribution of content at all levels to one or more persons in time and space. This concept of the media aligns with Denis McQuail who saw it as means of communicating openly to many over space and time (McQuail, 1983).

The Concept of Development

Developments in communication have brought humanity together such that people are able to visualize what is happening globally. Disasters, wars, conflicts, progress, famines and other human developmental incidents can be aired across the globe to a diversified audience due to the nature of today's media. It is therefore not difficult to conceptualize what constitutes globally acceptable development standards across different substructures in the world. These development indices which vary from region to region, have been synchronized by the United Nations. The world has been classified based on their perceived or assessed development index into first, second and third world countries alternatively referred to as developed, developing and underdeveloped countries respectively. Developing countries have been grouped into 6 regions namely: Arab States comprising 20 countries and territories, East Asia and the Pacific with 26 countries, Europe and Central Asia with 17 countries, Latin America and the Caribbean with 33 countries, South Asia with 9 countries, and Sub-Sahara with 46 countries.

It is difficult to provide a universally acceptable definition of development without generating some sort of argument. Development has been defined in different ways to depict political, economic and social growth within given societies. Thomas argues that development has been given theoretical and political connotations that have made the concept inherently complex and ambiguous. He equates its understanding to "the limited meaning of the practice of development agencies, especially in aiming at reducing poverty and the Millennium Development Goals" (Thomas, 2004, pp. 1,2). The contradiction of using poverty or economic indices in defining development lies in the contrast between "development as immanent and unintentional process and development as an intentional activity" (Cowen and Shenton, 1998, p. 50). However, by using economic indices, it is easier to define if a country is growing progressively or retrogressively. Opinion is divided on whether development should depend on values or alternative conceptions of the quality of life. The disagreement lies in who defines a good life and positive values. Kanbur (2006) states that "there is no uniform or unique answer" to what constitutes development. Thomas (2000, p. 1) argues that, "development is contested, complex and ambiguous' while Gore (2000, p. 794-5) posits that it could, depending on the era, be construed as a "vision of the liberation of people and peoples' dominated, based on structural transformation".

Figure 3. Illustration of development as conceptualized in this chapter

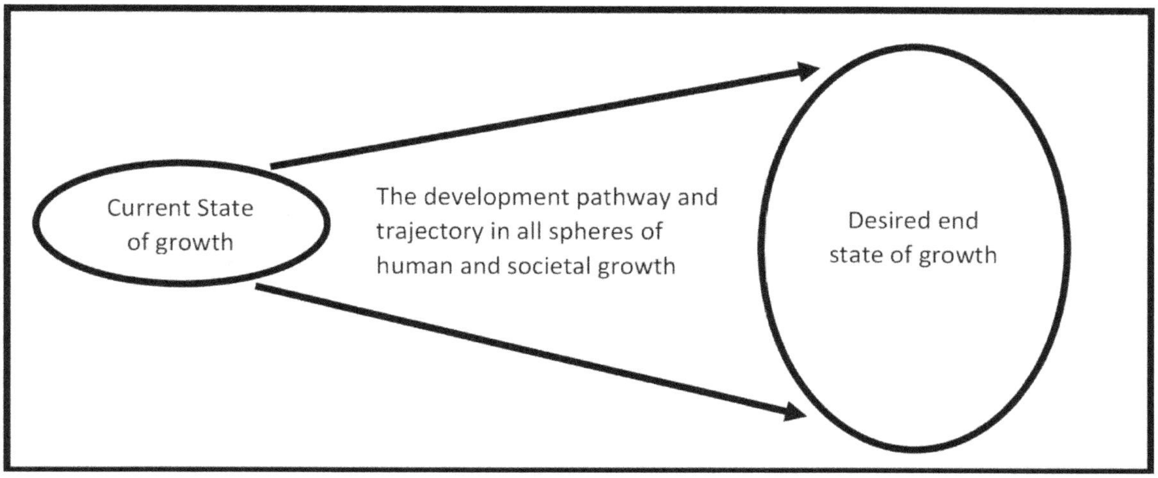

Development can therefore be construed as a progressive trajectory from comparatively low positions in different societal fields to positively higher dimensions over time. It is the attainment of set targets, from the Millennium Development Goals' perspective, to attainment of better standards of living as defined by western modernity. This view of development aligns with the structural societal transformation perspective where Thomas (2000) sees development as 'a process of historical change'. Embedded in this perspective is the concept of prescriptive and non-prescriptive values of progress towards acceptable modernity. This view of development can be visualized as two fulcrums at each end of a trajectory where one point is occupied by the inferior undeveloped societies and the second position occupied by the superior societies. This view raises the North and South debate where the North is considered as the developed or superior position that must be attained while the south is seen as the unacceptable inferior position. The inferior-superior paradigm as argued by post-modernists invariably follows the differentiation pathway where nations are categorized as First, Second and Third World countries. The Third World countries must grow within the defined indices of progress to attain the acceptable standard of modernity. It is the movement from the inferior state to the superior state that is then considered as development. This view does not consider such inherent attributes like the cultural identity of individual societies. Consequently, another way to look at the description of development as presented in Figure 3 is to consider one side of the trajectory as the current state of a society and the other end as the desired end state of the society as it moves along the development pathway.

Development thinkers like Marx, Hagel, Condorcet and Kant, construe it philosophically as "progress in a distinct manner from that resulting from the idea of conscience" (Soares and Quintella, 2008). To them, development is "the potentially infinite concept of progress" (Soares and Quintella, 2008). Their line of thought is in "a certain proximity with Augustinian thinking, of conceiving history as a totality, a firm march of civilization, a continual, albeit inconstant and non-linear process, in the direction of a common well-being" (Soares and Quintella, 2008). Rist considers this view of development as "a constant evolution, based on the belief of human perfectibility and motivated by the incessant search for well-being" (Rist, 2001, p. 70). This conceptualization of development agrees with Rostow's seminal work which reclaims Social Darwinism "to explain development as a process of evolutional succession in stages, where human societies leave a rudimentary model until they arrive at a western industrialized civilization consumption model, which is considered unique and universal' (Rostow, 1971).

Digitalised Economy

A digitalised economy refers to the widespread use of information communication technology to address and manage different spheres of human engagement ranging from the economic to the social within a society including its out borders. It relates to the digital production of goods and services. It now extends to transactions as money continues to transform to intangible 'paperlessness' or digital dots. Rumana and Richard (2019) consider digital economy as "that part of economic output derived solely or primarily from digital technologies with a business model based on digital goods or services." Digitalisation is a critical pathway towards the attainment of modernized development. The United Nations Development Programme (UNDP) presents an integrated development solution to be driven by country priorities which follows a synchronized pathway consisting of digitalisation, strategic innovation and development financing. The global supporting countries are expected to build inclusive, ethical and sustainable digital societies. The digitalisation is expected to impact on such indices as poverty and inequality, governance, resilience, environment, energy and gender equality (UNDP, 2021). The positive technological improvements in communication, especially in the area of connectivity or internet of things, new devices, digital models and associated robotic technologies, have combined to make digital technology readily available across borders (OECD, 2015).

Tapscott (1996) defines a digital economy as the "Age of Networked Intelligence" by looking at how humans take advantage of emerging technology to manage the economy. Lane (1999) focused on electronic commerce and wider issues of innovation, privacy, standards and digital divide. He sees it as "the convergence of computing and communication technologies in the Internet and the resulting flow of information and technology that is stimulating all of electronic commerce and vast organisational changes" (Lane, 1999). Kling and Lamb (2000) went further to break digital economy into 4 categories namely highly digital goods and services, mixed digital goods and services, IT- intensive services of goods production and the IT industry itself. The first referred to online information services while the second was associated with online sales and marketing like booking hotels online and ordering items electronically. The third part was about computer engineering services while the fourth was about the communication equipment that support the other three categories. Mesenbourg (2001) presented digitalised economy as "having three primary components" namely the E-business infrastructure, which relates to the economic infrastructure used to support business processes and electronic commerce; E-business which considers how businesses are conducted over computer-mediated networks; and the E-commerce which relates to the value of goods and services sold over computer-mediated networks.

It was Rouse (2016) who provided a more succinct definition of a digital economy when he wrote that "digital economy is the worldwide network of economic activities enabled by information and communication technologies (ICT)". He went on to simplify it further by adding that it is "an economy based on digital technologies" (Rouse, 2016). A digitalised economy, drawing from Rouse (2016) submission and considering Brennen and Kreiss (2014) definition, can be said to cover "all economic activity based on digital technologies" (Brennen and Kreiss, 2014). It involves the "application of digitisation to organisational and social processes." (Brennen and Kreiss, 2014). It must be noted that while digitisation refers to the conversion of data from analogue to digital form, digitalisation incorporates a wide range of digital activities and relates to "the way in which many domains of social life are restructured around digital communication and media infrastructures" (Brennen and Kreiss, 2014). Digitalised economy therefore covers all forms of information communication technology consumption and application. This is illustrated below.

Figure 4. Illustration of digitalised economy as conceptualized in this chapter

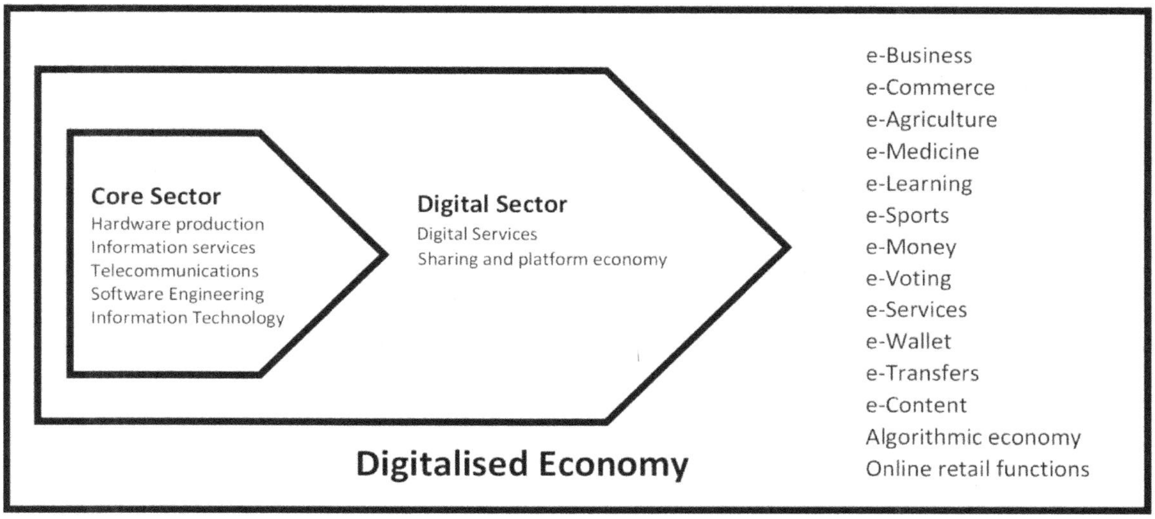

MEDIA AND DEVELOPMENT IN A DIGITALISED ECONOMY

The media support development in various spheres of human engagement in this era of digitalised economy. These spheres are the social, economic, cultural, religious, political, security, psychological, health, education, recreation and sports domains. Growth in technological development has led to media concentration in such a way that information now circulates in cyclic dimensions across the broad spectrum of multi-dimensional conduits. This has resulted in the mediastratification of information such that issues relating to any aspect of human life can be readily obtained through the internet. Mediastratification, as a concept, relates to the trend where traditional or mainstream media, namely television, radio and print now compete for space and audience in the social media environment. There is a coming together of multiple media, creating digital information concentration as various media strive to put out as much information as their media space can contain. Furthermore, there are opportunities now for anybody to create a blog and become a purveyor of news overnight without requisite training. The consequence of this media 'gatelessness,' which is a product of the digital era, has resulted in all kinds of information dysfunctions, including fake news. These negative aspects of mediastratification equally have an impact on the positive developmental capabilities of the media. Fraud, crime and all kinds of negative societal developments associated with the traditional south pole countries have also arisen as the media undergoes the digital transformation.

Gatelessness itself is the gradual erosion of the primary functions of editors and other media gatekeepers as the traditional media structure continue to collapse in the face of citizen journalism. Citizen or participatory journalism is in itself a healthy trend within the developing and underdeveloped countries as it creates opportunity for democratic media engagement. The brand of journalism, where everyone who has access to an online device and can send and receive media news, could make practitioners manifestly uncomfortable thereby "raising new questions of trust and veracity" which may require the collective development of acceptable standards of trust (Bowman and Willis, 2003, p. vi). The easy access to media channels by all could help hitherto excluded communities to establish contact with people of like minds and interest. It could also lead to societal unrest. It was this ease of access to the new media that gave rise to the Endsars protest and subsequent burning of the Ikoyi tollgate in Lagos, Nigeria (Sotunde, 2021). Participatory journalism therefore brings people who are passionate about specific issues together quickly. This could have positive or negative developmental implications. Those who participate in online platforms usually create content to inform and entertain others. Citizen journalism helps different people to create content and this, as noted by Bowman and Willis (2003), builds self-esteem as people derive satisfaction from the act of creation.

The controversy, as to who now controls the gate, has resurfaced in the public domain as opinion is divided on the effective access to evolving media platforms by the global south. The contention that there is actually no gatelessness arises from the proposition that there are indeed multiplicity of gates with various gatekeepers who delete unwanted content and allow only materials peculiar to that media outlet as information passes from one channel to another. This proposition is however faulty as anybody that has access to the social media could write, video, or take images of events and transmit same within minutes to a diversified audience. The fact remains that controllers of social media outlets like facebook, snapchat, twitter and others could attempt to delete or bring down controversial content. Those actions taken to prevent such content from further spread cannot be considered as gatekeeping as the gate has already been breached. Such breaches often lead to negative consequences which challenge the developmental capability of the media. As rightly noted by Pałka-Suchojad (2021) "the turbulent and dynamic conditions of the digital environment require a new look at the phenomenon of gatekeeping". The two dimensions to the gatekeeping debate as stated by Pałka-Suchojad (2021) are "the concept of social gatekeeping, which places the focus on users acting as guards, and the influence of algorithms on this process, as an inherent element of social media architecture". Traditional gatekeeping, as presented by Schoemaker, is "the process by which billions of information available around the world are selected and transformed into hundreds of information that reaches a given person on any given day" (Barzilai-Nahon, 2008, p. 1495). The concern over the media gates comes from the understanding that whoever keeps the gate, controls the media power. The North-South information dichotomy or imbalance would continue to resonate if gatekeeping is considered within the threshold of the influence of algorithms on the gatekeeping role. The owners of the social media platforms do, to a significant level, control what can go through their social media channels and by implication what can be brought to the public domain. This gatekeeping role is systematically carried out within the social media through channeling, censorship, internationalization, security, cost-effect mechanism, adaptability, infrastructure, level of interactivity, content editing; and regulation metamechanism (Pałka-Suchojad, 2021).

The media may be credited with the power to transform society and facilitate development. This power of the media to transform is manifestly latent. In an attempt to give meaning to the concept of media power, Freedman (2014) came up with the consensus, chaos, control and contradiction paradigms. The approach did not address the issues of media impact on the economy, politics, attitudes and beliefs effectively but answered the questions which he posed. The questions relate to the ability of media to provide state or corporate actors with a valuable tool to assert their own dominance and the locus of power as well as the ability of the media to constitute the space where power is decided (Freedman,

2014). The powers of the media to effect change and promote development may indeed have been exaggerated. This does not suggest that the media do not have enormous powers. It however depends on the dimension or function the media are performing at any given time. The power of the media to inform, especially when it relates to the immediacy of the news, and when the recipients are uninformed, has been unparalleled. Similarly, the power of the media to educate has been impactful. Nevertheless, when it comes to the ability of the media to persuade, a lot of intervening variables may make the effect of little consequence. This, however depends on the content of the communication, its production and intended consequence. In this instance, strategic communication, which is disseminated through well selected conduits and directed to specific audience, would yield a much better effect than a routine communication. It is equally noteworthy to state that a seemingly harmless communication not targeted to any particular audience could result in unintended consequences. The strength of the assumption that media indeed influences development is based on the ability of the media to reach and target specific fields of human engagement.

It may be necessary to consider the differentiations in the presentations of media power. For Foucault, "power, as well as the resistance it generates, are diffused and not localized in some points." Simply put, power is everywhere which implies that each medium also carries its own power relations (Daldal, 2014). The media, by setting the agenda of public discussion, could unconsciously, empower a set of people who are prominent within the agenda. Knowledge, from the Foucauldian approach, is power and the media provide knowledge (Gramsci, 1975). McNair (2018) seems to be between a Foucauldian approach, which itself considers power as productive and the economic versions of the pluralist projections where Cater presents media power as a form of 'mobile and transitory' power in highly segmented decision-making situations. Brian McNair, while examining the role of the media in the political process, considered the influence of communication on "the referendum vote for the UK's withdrawal from the European Union, the rise of nationalist populism in Europe, and the victory of Donald Trump in the 2016 US presidential election". He also considered the negative side of media power by looking at the use of communication as a weapon by Putin's Russia and the Islamic State as well as other insurgent organisations (McNair, 2018). McNair (2018) argues that "an expanding globalised public sphere and digital media network have transformed political communication, allowing political actors, from politicians and pressure groups to trade unions and terrorist organisations, to bypass traditional, established media in communicating their messages". Cater presents media power as a form of 'mobile and transitory' power in highly segmented decision-making situations (Cater, 1965, p. 4). These differentiations by media scholars, even if uncertain, merely demonstrate ongoing insights into an old media held postulation that the 'pen is mightier than the sword.' This age-long media perception ascribe imaginary power to the outcomes of media effects which seemed to be hypodermic (Media, 2021) in nature, even if false. Lippman and others, in trying to rejig the effects paradigm through the introduction of intervening variables in media effects outcome (Lippmann, 2004); uses and gratification pathway (Ruggiero, 2000); impart of frames of reference to differential responses to same media messages (Chandler and Munday, 2011); gradually opened the floodgate to the theoretical might of media power in the face of technology-induced concentration. The media power has helped developed, developing and underdeveloped nations in the different human domains covering the social, economic, cultural, religious, political, psychological, health and educational domains.

The Social Sphere

The media has helped to develop social relations within and among nations. The social development relates to the relationships and cohesion of people within defined territories. It refers to the linear progress, positively or negatively, that a group of people make in their interactions and how they move from outdated to modern methods or lifestyles. The media has played key roles in the eradication of open defecation in different countries. The availability of multiple channels has redefined social engagements. Regrettably, while the developed North continue to use these channels to maintain payment systems, provision of social amenities, a significant number of countries from the global south now see these new technologies as a pathway to crime, insurgency and banditry. The sahel region has been overtaken by insurgency using the same media channels that would have been deployed for more functional social interactions.

The social media now makes it quite easy to connect and maintain contact with friends and groups with common interest. It is easier to establish business contacts and transfer vital documents within the comfort of people's homes. Simply put, the digitalised communication space opens a new way of social interaction among peers, business associates and family members who may be living several kilometres away. The media environment is now an open social and market space. One can state explicitly that "No one owns it. Everyone can use it. Anyone can improve it" (Barzilai-Nahon, 2008). In Nigeria, the advent of the social media reduced traditional letter writing as mails and messages could be sent in seconds through the internet. The two-way journalism that the modern participatory news reporting has brought enables closer interface between news purveyors and news analysts. The sender and receiver are technically brought closer unlike the regimented and hierarchical system operated by the traditional media. Anybody can become a commentator or reporter without any training. The citizen could talk online about his field of endeavour and offer expert guidance directly to those who need such services via the internet. The journalist could double as a 'forum leader,' mediator, teacher or counsellor. "The audience becomes not consumers, but 'pro-sumers,' a hybrid of consumer and producer (Kovach and Rosenstiel, 2001, p. 24).

The Economic Sphere

In the economic sphere, the advent of modern media has reduced the difficulties previously encountered in doing business. Economic transactions now occur within minutes and goods are ordered and paid for over the internet from different parts of the world. There are several new opportunities created by the massive availability of information. Today, there are options in e-commerce and the wellbeing of the people has been significantly improved. The wealth, finances and business transactions of nations have been impacted positively. However, there are negative aspects of the economic perspective. These negative effects include identity theft, massive financial fraud, fraudulent domestic and foreign transfers, money laundering and massive corruption as a result of availability of different payment options. Money has also moved away from its traditional paper state to paperless digital dots. Electronic currencies like bitcoin, cryto-currencies and others have appeared on the scene. Money, today, is considered theoretical as returning to its 'barter era' in what can be classified as the full transformation of money. This presumes that money, as it mutates from paper to paperless digital reality, would, theoretically return interactions to contact between 'demand and supply' with the media now filling the intermediary role. The media, in this instance, is not acting from the promotional or advertorial constructs, but from the standpoint of a strategic key player in economic decisions between buyers and sellers.

In the barter system, goods and services are exchanged through bartering. This is in contrast to the currency system where a form of acceptable intermediary in the form of paper or coin is used in the exchange of goods and services. The currency system enables buyers and sellers to exchange goods based on a need-and-value system eliminating the burden of mismatch present in the barter process. The history of bartering, as noted by Hall (2021), goes back to 6000 BC. It took place mostly in local community settings where tangible and intangible goods and services are exchanged on the basis of need. Progress in the areas of technology and transportation facilitated barter on a global scale with acceptable intermediaries that acted as currency. The same growth in Information Communication Technology and the evolving media environment is beginning to return money to its barter era with unexamined possibilities. The outcome of this silent but growing phenomenon could threaten world trade possibilities which may affect the global exchange system and distort the currency imbalance between the developed north and developing south poles. The exchange rate of different currencies, which is dependent on the dollar, and now threatened by the yen, could lead countries to resort to trade-by-need with unpredictable consequences on world power relations. Nigeria attempted a direct currency transaction with China which bypassed the dollar by replacing it with an agreed transaction rate between the naira and yen. There is no globally accepted currency in bartering and purchasing goods and services is dependent on need and not value-rated deposit process calculated to the value of gold. In the current dollar-dependent system, the value of a country's currency is dependent on its import and export ratio. Figure 5 is an illustration of a possible barter return with the changing media environment in the face of a digitalised economy.

Modern technology is expanding contact between buyers and sellers and the media, as a collective term representing all forms of communication, may begin to play the international intermediaries in the exchange system. This could challenge the value of different currencies in the global market as the current indices used to determine the market value of each currency may collapse. The acceptability of the demand-supply paradigm in assessing the exchange rate of currencies, based on dollar and gold reserves, may be challenged. This scenario opens fresh opportunities for the global south to look at the areas they have comparative cost advantage in their international trade transactions. The rise of the internet of things, artificial intelligence and other communication technologies have "revived the barter system, allowing participants to trade goods and services" (Hall, 2021). Countries like Thailand, the world's largest exporter of rice and Iran, with abundance of oil, agreed to trade their goods under the barter system (Hall, 2021).

Cultural Perspective

In the view of futurist and author Watts Wacker, the question is not about greater personalization but about greater perspectives. According to Wacker, the world is moving faster than people can keep up with it. As a result, there are fewer common cultural references that can be agreed upon. Ideas, styles, products and mores accelerate their way from the fringe to the mainstream with increasing speed. To combat the confusion, consumers are seeking more perspectives. They research an automobile for purchase by spending time online and reading both professional and amateur reviews alike. (Wacker, 2002)

The media environment has a culture which ensures that standards are met. However, Rosenberg states that "it should be obvious that weblogs aren't competing with the work of the professional journalism establishment, but rather complementing it. If the pros are criticized as being cautious, impersonal,

Figure 5. Illustration of the gradual return to the barter era in international trade

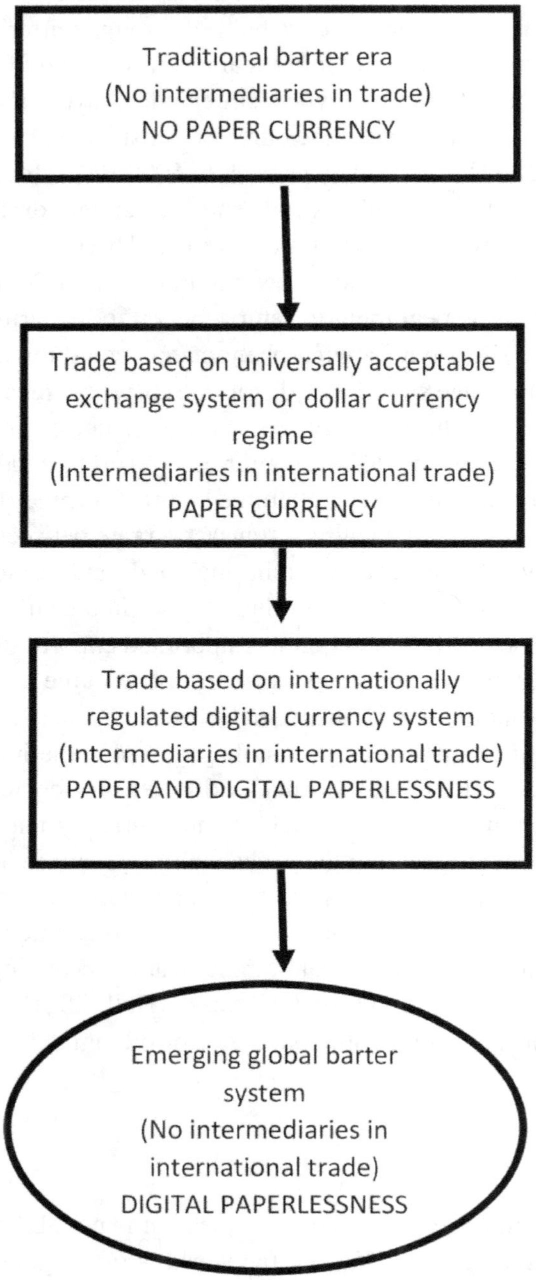

corporate and herdlike, the bloggers are the opposite in, well, almost every respect: They're reckless, confessional, funky — and herdlike (Rosenberg, 2002). The media culture is therefore gradually giving way to an unpredictable media culture where standards are difficult to regulate across boundaries. It's not just the Internet that threatens the culture and status quo of the news business. Kovach and Rosenstiel make a compelling argument that the news business is undergoing "a momentous transition" (Kovach and Rosenstiel, 2001). This transformation tends to favour the traditional south pole countries as access to the media, though not absolute, is nevertheless better in the evolving media culture. Mainstream media are created with commercial bias. They are structured culturally to compete in the broadcast and advertising space and earn income which is used to sustain the media business. Traditional media men therefore value rigorous editorial work, profitability and integrity. On the other side, the culture of participatory journalism is "created by networked communities that value conversation, collaboration and egalitarianism over profitability (Shayne Bowman and Chris Willis, 2003, p. 12).

Religious Perspective

The global south, especially some Asian and African countries, is largely religious in nature. Religion play key roles in the mobilisation of people towards development programmes. The advent of participatory journalism has provided a greater opportunity for self-acclaimed religious leaders and preachers to broadcast information to a diversified audience. The media are now exploited positively and in some unfortunate instances, negatively. The ability of citizens to play active roles in information gathering, processing, analyzing, reporting and dissemination has increased religious growth within the developing societies with its attendant fanaticism. Participation in the media world could have provided "independent, reliable, accurate, wide-ranging and relevant information that a democracy requires (Bowman and Willis, 2003) but issues of religious intolerance have negated the positive potentials for development. A significant number of religious groups have gone digital, reaching members and conducting religious services online. It has been argued that the increased participation of religious bodies in the media, especially after the arrival of the COVID-19 pandemic with its attendant restrictions, helped to redirect the efforts of youths towards positive developmental engagements. This assertion is yet to be proven with verifiable data. The religious sphere has therefore been impacted by the bottom-up nature of participatory journalism where "little or no editorial oversight or formal journalistic workflow is needed in dictating the decisions of a staff but rather the result of many simultaneous, distributed conversations that either blossom or quickly atrophy in each religious group's social network (Bowman and Willis, 2003).

Political Dimension

The political sphere has also been affected by the nature of today's media. Citizen journalism has resulted in significant positive developments in political systems, nature of media freedom, security and freedom of association enjoyed by the people as they progress along the development pathway. The centrality of electronic media has been effective in compelling the people to participate in politics. In Nigeria, the modern media galvanised the people to form over 90 new political parties which were later reduced to about 27. Youth activism in the political domain increased and the government was kept on its toes. Political activism again led to the banning of a social media platform, Twitter, over political disagreements.

It was easier for the government to manipulate the mainstream media before the arrival of digitalisation. However, with the multiplicity of channels, such stifling of the press by politicians and political interest became difficult. Increased movement from autocratic regimes and sit-tight rulers towards democratic reforms occurred in most underdeveloped and developing societies. The expansion of the media space could therefore be considered as a necessary aspect of basic human rights and fundamental to determinations of what is just and unjust. Scholars in political communication posit that "political expression on social media can foster deeper engagement in democratic life" (Boulianne, 2015). The opportunities given to social media influencers and other citizens to hold and air political opinion have developed the political space with people knowing their rights and demanding more responsibility from their leaders. "There is increasing acknowledgement that social media may play a more dynamic role in shaping how individuals come to see themselves as political actors. Social media are not simply vehicles for political news, campaign advertisements, or collective action, but are also important social environments in which people engage in the messy process of sorting out how they "fit" into the world of politics (Thorson, 2014).

Educational and Health Dimension

The digitalization of media channels has opened up online training of professionals, online educational conferencing and academic meetings, workshops and seminars. The use of the broadcast media for educational purposes has been amplified. Today, several universities offer online postgraduate training for several fields of human endeavor. There are open universities, distance learning centres and other educational programmes that have been assisted by the digital age. The advent of COVID-19 pandemic has shown that massive digitalization in education is possible. It opened up a lot of possibilities for online education.

The manpower needs of second and third world countries have been addressed through the internet. However, the slow pace of making internet facilities available to a significant number of people within these regions and the educational backwardness act as impediments. The environment has also benefited from the growing online education of the people about the state of the environment and to guide the people on how to care for the environment. Issues relating to logging, afforestation, pollution and associated environmental abuses have been addressed through educational programmes that were brought to the people through the modern media. The environmental dimension is not limited to the quality of the air, water and soil. It also includes how education through modern media has impacted on environmental security, recreation, sports, health and psychological state of the people. Classrooms have moved from face-to-face or physical interaction to online spaces. Sports education has moved from outdoor instructor-led physical exercises to online indoor physical do-it-yourself exercises.

Today, people can access their hospitals and preferred medical experts through tele-health medicine. This positive development is a result of modern medicine. It is however necessary to add that the attainment of the UN development goals can only be achieved if successfully education strategies empower learners of all ages with the knowledge, skills, values, and attitudes to transform themselves, their communities, and societies. Online educational institutions could contribute in achieving a lot if the various governments in the global south can facilitate and support the massive online access by supporting relevant communication agencies within their domains. Training and educational institutions must be transformed digitally to fulfill their roles in the educational development of the people. It is important to note that it is only when the learners and their teachers have the requisite competencies that digitalization can make a valuable contribution to empower people. Teachers must have the capacity to produce digital content and there must be energy to power digital devices.

CHARTING THE WAY FORWARD

The arrival of modern media has given great opportunity to people of the global south to develop their societies. Media channels now open up opportunities for development in several areas of human interaction. However, for developing nations to gain meaningfully from the evolving digital age, there is need for them to prevent the negative use of these emergent technologies to scuttle the growth of their economies.

The manifest dangers to be tackled include religious fanaticism, illiteracy and the dangers of exclusion from opportunities. Such exclusion come from low levels of digital skill and technology penetration both within and between countries (Dahlman et al, 2016). There are also dangers of adverse incorporation into the digital economy due to liminality (lack of resources, capabilities, institutions, relations) (Murphy and Carmody, 2015). It is equally important to look at the specific volatility of digital enterprises in developing countries (Foster and Heeks, 2010). There is also the problem of marginalisation of developing country workers within any strengthening of digital labour driven from and for the global North (Martin, 2016). There are certain dangers of digital economy within developing countries, like growth in vulnerabilities around digital security and privacy (Manyika et al, 2013). There is yet the issue that between global North and South, there are risks that digital technologies will contribute to the "re-shoring of production" and thus augment "premature deindustrialisation" across the developing world (Dahlman et al, 2016). The sudden transformation of uninformed citizens to overnight reporters without requisite training has resulted in all kinds of information dysfunctions, including fake news. There is need to regulate the media field to guide against libel, slander and defamation. Finally, the global south countries must mitigate the negative aspects of mediastratification which affects the positive developmental capabilities of the media. Fraud, crime and all kinds of negative societal developments must be curtailed for developing countries to benefit from the power of the media to develop different spheres of the society.

CONCLUSION

The growth in the information communication field has bridged the information gap between the rich and poor in the global south as a significant portion of the population in those countries now gain access to communication equipment and media spaces. There were several individuals who could not afford a telephone or other communication equipment in the traditional south pole. It was not until 1992, following the deregulation of the media and approval for private communication companies to operate in Nigeria that a vast majority of Nigerians gained access to telephone services on a commercial scale. The government owned Nigerian Telecommunications Limited (NITEL) only supplied lines to privileged politicians and government officials. The arrival of other communication companies expanded the media space and opened up internet access to the hitherto excluded mass of rural inhabitants. Today, the Nigerian internet space has created jobs, improved the economy and provided additional source of income to several private business entrepreneurs. The media therefore impacts on different spheres of human activity covering the social, economic, political and other domains.

It is anticipated, with the continuous improvement in communication and increasing media concentration, the economic sphere may witness a drastic return to the barter era with great implications for trade across the global north and south. However, there is need for the global south to look at the challenges of media power and abuse of the internet by criminal elements from these countries if the citizens must develop and benefit positively from the opportunities created by the modern media.

REFERENCES

Barzilai-Nahon, K. (2008). Toward a theory of Networking Gatekeeping: A Framework for Exploring Information Control. *Journal of the American Society for Information Science and Technology, 59*(9), 1493–1512.

Boulianne, S. (2015). Social media use and participation: a meta-analysis of current research. *Information, Communication & Society, 18.* doi:.1008542 doi:10.1080/1369118X.2015

Bukht & Heeks. (2019, February 17). *Defining, Conceptualising and Measuring the Digital Economy.* Retrieved from Centre for Development Informatics, University of Manchester, UK: https://www.gdi.manchester.ac.uk/research/publications/working-papers/di/

Cater, D. (1965). *Power in Washington: A critical look at today's struggle to govern in the U.S.A.* Collins.

Chandler, D., & Munday, R. (2011). *A Dictionary of Media and Communication.* Oxford University Press. doi:10.1093/acref/9780199568758.001.0001

Cowen, M., & Shenton, R. (1998). *Doctrines of Development.* Routledge.

Dahlman, C. M. (2016). *Harnessing the Digital Economy for Developing Countries.* Retrieved from OECD, Paris: https://www.oecd-ilibrary.org/docserver/download/4adffb24-en.pdf

Daldal, A. (2014). Power and Ideology in Michel Foucault and Antonio Gramsci: A Comparative Analysis. *Review of History and Political Science, 2*(2), 149–167.

Fortner. (2021, March 31). *The Origins of Media Theory: An Alternative View.* Retrieved from Researchgate: https://www.researchgate.net/publication/278316913

Foster, C. (2010). *Researching ICT micro-enterprise in developing countries.* Retrieved from The Electronic Journal of Information Systems in Developing Countries: https://www.ejisdc.org/ojs2/index.php/ejisdc/article/view/695

Freedman, D. (2014, June 16). *Paradigms of Media Power.* Goldsmiths.

Gore, C. (2000). The rise and fall of the Washington consensus as a paradigm for developing countries. *World Development, 28*(5), 789–804. doi:10.1016/S0305-750X(99)00160-6

Gramsci, A. (1975). History, Philosophy and Culture. In The Young Gramsci ed. (pp. 352-353). New York: Telos Press.

Hall, M. (2021, July 21). *Barter System vs. Currency System.* Retrieved from Economics and Macroeconomics: https://www.investopedia.com/ask/answers/061615/what-difference-between-barter-and-currency-systems.asp

Kanbur, R. (2006). *What's Social Policy got to do with Economic Growth?* Retrieved from https://www.arts.cornell.edu/poverty/kanbur/

Klapper, J. T. (1960). *The Effects of Mass Communication.* Free Press.

Kling, R., & Lamb, R. (2000). IT and organizational change in digital economies. In Understanding the Digital Economy. Cambridge, MA: MIT Press.

Kovach & Rosenstiel. (2001). *The Elements of Journalism: What Newspeople Should Know and the Public Should Expect*. Three Rivers Press.

Lane, N. (1999). Advancing the digital economy into the 21st century. *Information Systems Frontiers*, *1*(13), 317–320. doi:10.1023/A:1010010630396

Lippmann, W. (2004). *Public Opinion*. Dover Publications.

Logan, R. (2021, December 24). *Understanding Man: The Extensions of Digital Media.* Retrieved from https://www.researchgate.net/publication/313601251 doi:10.13140/RG.2.2.32821.47847

Maitland, D. (1994). Forging New Links for Telecom Development. *Transnational Data and Communications Report*, (March/April), 17–20.

Manyika, J. e. (2013). *Lions Go Digital: The Internet's Transformative Potential in Africa*. Retrieved from McKinsey Global Institute. https://www.mckinsey.com/industries/high-tech/our-insights/lions-go-digital-the-internets-transformative-potential-in-af

Manyika, J. e. (2016). *Digital Globalization: The New Era of Global Flows*. https://www.mckinsey.de/sites/mck_files/files/mgi_digital_globalization.pdf

Martin, D. (2016, June 20-21). *Socio-digital practices of collective action in online labour platforms.* Paper presented at Connected Life Conference.

McLuhan, M. (1967). *The Medium is the Massage. New York*. Bantam Books.

McNair, B. (2018). *An Introduction to Political Communication*. Routledge.

McQuail, D. (1983). *Mass Communication Theory: An Introduction*. Sage.

Media. (2021, December 23). Hypodermic Needle Theory. *Media - The study of what we hear, watch and read*. http://www.mediaknite.org/hypodermic-needle-theory/

Mesenbourg, T. (2001). *Measuring the Digital Economy*. Retrieved from US Bureau of the Census, Suitland, MD.: https://www.census.gov/content/dam/Census/library/working-papers/2001/econ/umdigital.pdf

Murphy, J. A. (2015). *Africa's Information Revolution*. John Wiley.

Negroponte, N. (1996). *Being Digital*. Vintage Books.

OECD. (2015). *OECD Digital Economy Outlook*. Retrieved from OECD: https://www.oecd.org/sti/oecddigital-economy-outlook-2015-9789264232440-en.htm

Pałka-Suchojad, K. (2021). *Who Keeps the Gate? Digital Gatekeeping in New Media*. Retrieved from Zeszyty PRASOZNAWCZE: https://www.ejournals.eu/Zeszyty-Prasoznawcze/ doi:10.4467/22996362PZ.21.012.13477

Pool, I. d. (1979). The Influence of International Communication on Development. *Media Asia 6*(3), 149-156.

Rist, G. (2001). *Le developement: une histoire de croyance ocidentale*. Presses de Science Po.

Rosenberg, S. (2002, May 10). *Much Ado About Blogging*. Retrieved from Salon.com: https://www.salon.com/tech/col/rose/2002/05/10/blogs/

Rostow, W. (1971). *Etapas do desenvolvimento econômico*. Zahar Editores.

Rouse, M. P. (2016). *Digital Economy*. Retrieved from Techtarget, Newton, MA.: https://searchcio.techtarget.com/definition/digital-economy

Ruggiero, T. (2000). Uses and Gratifications Theory in the 21st Century. *Mass Communication & Society*, *3*(1), 3–37. doi:10.1207/S15327825MCS0301_02

Scott Brennen and Daniel Kreiss. (2014, September 8). *Digitalization and digitization*. Retrieved from Culture Digitally: https://culturedigitally.org/2014/09/digitalization-and-digitization/

Shayne Bowman and Chris Willis. (2003). *We Media: How audiences are shaping the future of news and information*. Retrieved from Academia: www.hypergene.net/wemedia/

Soares & Quintella. (2008, April 28). *Development: An Analysis of Concepts, Measurement and Indicators*. Retrieved from Brazilian Administrative Review: http://www.anpad.org.br/bar

Sotunde, A. (2021, October 2). *#ENDSARS movement: From Twitter to Nigerian streets - The "soro soke" generation won't give up*. Retrieved from Amnesty International: https://www.amnesty.org/en/latest/campaigns/2021/02/nigeria-end-impunity-for-police-violence-by-sars-endsars/

Tapscott, D. (1996). *The Digital Economy: Promise and Peril in the Age of Networked Intelligence*. McGraw-Hill.

Thomas, A. (2000). Development as practice in a liberal capitalist world. *Journal of International Development*, *12*(6), 773–787. doi:10.1002/1099-1328(200008)12:6<773::AID-JID716>3.0.CO;2-7

Thomas, A. (2004). *The Study of Development*. Paper prepared for DSA Annual Conference.

Thorson, K. (2014). Sampling from the civic buffet: Youth, new media, and do-it-yourself citizenship. In New technologies & civic engagement: New agendas in communication series (pp. 3 - 22). New York, NY: Routledge.

UNDP. (2021). *United Nations Development Programme strategic plan 2022 - 2025*. UNDP.

Vaccari, C., Valeriani, A., Barberá, P., Bonneau, R., Jost, J. T., Nagler, J., & Tucker, J. A. (2015). Political expression and action on social media: Exploring the relationship between lower- and higher-threshold political activities among Twitter users in Italy. *Journal of Computer-Mediated Communication*, *20*(2), 221–239. doi:10.1111/jcc4.12108

Wacker, W. (2002). *The Deviant's Advantage*. Crown Publishing.

Chapter 6
Symbolism in Digital Space and Transitional Society:
New Forms of Communicative Meanings in Africa

Melchizedec J. Onobe
Bingham University, Karu, Nigeria

ABSTRACT

Communication is fundamentally a toolbox of symbols used to create meaning in society. Its existence is a necessity spawned by circumstantial and society's contingencies at every turn. It is the reason languages, cues, imageries, and symbols—the building blocks of communication—continue to evolve with the times. The ritual of this dynamism is precipitated by a number of factors like socio-cultural identity crisis, economic and political variables, etc. This transitional socialisation continues to surge in the digital space of multi-platforms and the internet. Thus, this chapter attempts to evaluate the tenders of communication in the digital space, its influence on cultural identity, and the place of Africa in the narrative. The study submits that although the global nature of communication is believed to have overbearing influence on the continent's outlook, Africa being a culturally strong entity can outsource to the rest of the world and into the digital space its numerous rich cues, symbols, and signs to give the cultural identifiers indelibility and relevance on the global map.

INTRODUCTION

Communicative symbols have always been like a flouting vessel in human existence and society. They have always had a condescending characteristic that is amendable to any user under any circumstance. Using Africa's picturesque analogy, they are like the servile donkey that waits to be burdened, shown where to go, told where to stop and squat, with innate unique intrinsic indifference to the rider of the thoughts who animates meaning as he/she pleases. Such portals and carts are what the communicative

DOI: 10.4018/978-1-6684-4107-7.ch006

symbols and their traditions afford the living with here-and-there tinges of ethnicity, cultural mappings, attribution or prohibitions, coloration and biases; but they nevertheless carry the weights thrust at them.

Perhaps, symbolisms can be rigid and also dynamic at the same time. The meanings that are auctioned by them are reflective of society's political, social and economic mappings and acculturation (Parker, 2012). It is through them that power and dominance are decided and conceded. In clusters of any course, when linguistically arranged to denote power equation, they portend conquest or describe subordinates. This interestingly fluid nature of ciphers is the hub of power in ancient and modern society. Like the planetary system, they have a revolving circumference around human socio-psychological space and evolutionary interactivity. They serve as entrance as well as exit portal for some epochal developments of society (Cohn, Engelen and Schileroord, 2019) such as heralding new civilization and socialization, starting an era and ending another in an organic, discreetly overlapping style.

From symbols grow constant interactions, social relationships and meaning sharing. Berger and Luckmann (1971, p.114) observe that even in them the universe can be micro scoped, analyzed, understood and consequently animated.

The symbolic universe is conceived of as the matrix of all socially objectivized and subjectively real meanings; the entire historic society and the entire biography of the individual are seen as events taking place within this universe.

Thus, symbols are generally and always metaphorical in communicative context, giving them expressive three-dimensionality; a buffer for richer context of viewing issues. This "multi-faceted nature of symbols" as Luuk (2018, p.258) describes it is a flexibility that engages meta-communication/socialization. More often than not they have been used as the ladder of communicative evolution, overlapping cultures negotiated by either confab or happenstance (O'Reilly, 2017) on a wide range of splitter issues. In every civilization and culture, in Africa and elsewhere, they abound in arrays of rhetoric, text art and cultural science.

A little over a decade ago, Steen (2008) proposed a three-way model of language, thought and communication all sandwiched in deliberate metaphor theory (DMT). The DMT suggests that *deliberate* metaphors are linguistic metaphors that "explicitly invite the addressee to conceptualize one thing as another thing, often for rhetorical or persuasive purposes" (Steen, 2008, p. 213). A metaphorical interpretation thrives usually when there is reason to interrogate a literal interpretation because some element of falsity has been established in a narrative (Searle, 1993) resulting in withering stereotypes foist on unsuspecting masses that consume, misappropriate the icons. The incomplete information and inaccurate knowledge, if left, breeds and ventilates indiscriminate misinterpretation from a pond of falsity. And in a market place of ideas truth and falsehood are wares that inadvertently and contentiously intersect and symbols act like a wolverine magnetic codes to denominate the two.

Nevertheless, literature makes a distinction between symbols. Generally, they try to draw a line between ornamental symbols depicted by personalized representation and linguistic denotation acknowledging though that the point of difference may be minor. In communal usage and quarters, for example, various degrees of iconicity are tacitly accepted into existence and symbols (e.g. the Christian cross, or onomatopoetic words like *knock, bump, crash)* such as they represent exhibit iconicity as well (Luuk, 2013). Not taking anything away from the concepts of many linguists, this chapter submits that the blustery nature of symbols or representational icons permits a duality, a mobility, and somewhat a vista for ornamental symbols to transit also freely to formal usage in media register depending on the clot of prominence that they command from dominant adoption or personality (celebrity) endorsement (Morris, 2010).

What is to be found outside language that might determine the role that words can play as Morris (2010) quizzed? Well it may be naïve to insist, for example, that language and the form of expressing them are formalities that defy the tide of change sweeping through (Sirbu, 2015). As it is apparent, cold signs and algorithmic expressions called emojis have rudely violated the exclusivity held by traditional linguistic language expressed in text. Their roots go to Japanese manga where 'emoji'—picture (e) character (moji)— became integrated into digital keyboards (Moschini, 2016). The popularity of this unconventional communication mode eclipsed emoticons that were in vogue before its advent (Pavalanathan and Eisenstein, 2016).

Emojis are symbols that rarely had universalized meaning until they were socially negotiated by use, misuse and pervasiveness. Cohn, Engelen and Schileroord (2019) observe that emoji vocabulary is now integrated into operating systems as a relatively fixed list controlled by the Unicode Consortium, a conglomerate of technology companies that decide how computers encode typed information. Thus, this governing body largely decides variants to emoji and creation of new emoji.

Brilliant as the idea appears, what is the cultural composition of the Unicode Consortium? What are the parameters of accepting and canonizing an emoji? How heterogeneously constituted is the consortium to reflect the diversity of cultures and people that are likely to interact and do corresponding exchange with emojis that are created, used, applied and indifferently segregated out of reservation about there appeal? These are questions that gnaw away at the heart, begging for answers. The problem may just be one of one habit replacing another – one freedom becoming a new fiat, a prison yard; one free style becoming statute-closed, I mean a convention that shuts the door for further appreciation.

Many studies so far conducted (Kelly and Watts, 2015; Lu et al, 2016; Berengueres and Castro, 2017; Markman and Oshima, 2017) show that many emojis are, in a way, subordinated to text. Other works (Danesi, 2016; Cohn, Engelen and Schileroord (2019) are conversely inclined, showing that in some independent ways emoji can be used as rebuses or calquing, substituting directly for words like names of the images depicted. It is hardly predictable how far they may go and what form they will assume in years to come. The point is expressional communication mode, whether linguistic or ornamental, interweave and go through dynamics of change. Conventions of interpretations, spectacles and structures of evaluation ought to go with the motion and dynamics of the time.

Like Chen (2018) corresponds, "for a language to remain vital and relevant it needs to evolve as its practitioners evolve. As new awareness awakens so do new viewpoints emerge—all of which affect the ways that we observe and record our world." This is the challenge facing expressive innovation of any kind. I think concepts should not be cast in concrete. Pedagogues could air the space of reasoning a bit. To forestall censorship in evolution of language, pedagogues should focus on the social utility, aesthetics and dynamism of language evolution and less on its calcification.

SYMBOLISM AND ITS LINGO IN COMMUNICATIVE VALUE

As noted earlier, some symbols double as linguistics characters in certain climes. Whether as linguistic characters or ornamental representations, symbols conjure psychological images as O'Connell and O'Connell (2008) aver with more resilient indelibility far many times more than people care to consider. "Ours is a world shaped by symbols and images. We are bound to select from and simplify the infinite complexity of what we perceive. Somehow we must choose and act, must decide what to value and strive for" (961).

Poon (2017) submits that investigations carried out by adepts, in varied disciplines, like structuralists, anthropologists, sociologists, semioticians, linguists and artists recognize the heterogeneity, universality and commonality of ideas and concepts behind symbols essentially in their service as "metaphorical texts of social transformation, cultural change [and of various] scenarios and possibilities" (Hall, 1996, p. 286).

Let's face it, the arability of symbols, their meta-mobility and meaning-making schemas in social narratives allow strategists and many brand promoters and scribes to manipulate, position and reposition them for target-precision impact. The chess nature of the game is reason to institute a planned active play and stamina development of the image that is wheeled around for endorsement.

Like cards that are beveled in arrangement when laid, symbols even when reordered, rejigged and reconstituted don't exactly depart from their roots as Poon (2017) and others (Luuk) alarm, except they are phenomenal in dimension like matters of cultural identity correction. Ordinarily, they just reveal their pedigreed pattern and progressive wheel of relevance. What that implies is that symbols must evolve with the time to represent unitary, individual or group's communicative relevance in society.

A perverse consequence of an attempt to draw a line between the sphere of identity from which "interests" are said to emerge, and the sphere of rationality or instrumentality where actors try to maximize their interests, is that this may make it impossible to understand the social construction of identity. Rather than being separate, strategy and choice are in fact fundamental to, and inextricably bound up in the processes of the social construction of identity. Hariman and Luciates (2007, p.289) observe that: "icons, always, are equally articulate images available for communicating civic virtue or dissent, national resolve, or the horror of war, achievement or hubris, continuity or change. The icon emerges from the welter of images because it evokes the vital center of mainstream public culture. Iconic images capture both the central contradiction and the deepest commonality defining a polity".

Symbolic identity operates like a strategic axle motorized by progressive plans immersed in the brightest selling hues of culture. It is what curators of national image do. The flag of every nation on earth, as simplistic as it is, is a mix of some color, shape, icon or emblem. No national flag is a bland pennon. The colors that are depicted in each alongside the other components are communally emblematized, once curated with a certain linguistic connotation.

Thus, a nationalistic identity relatable to the value-philosophy of its infused pride stands out. In many cases, these emblematic collages retain notoriety after their creation by social negotiation, although it appears the values they represent soon become ephemeral in some cases as they go through ideological vicissitude. Typical is the recent BBC and other news agencies report that France had changed its flag without anyone noticing.

The change was not diametrically off. It was just in the shades of the color interpreted to represent the French President's, Emmanuel Macron, political leaning (see CNews and Europe1 https://news.sky.com/story/emmanuel-macron-changed-colour-of-french-flag-to-revive-a-symbol-of-the-revolution- and https://www.europe1.fr/politique/info-e1-le-drapeau-francais-a-change-de-couleur- respectively). The color change is a return to a darker navy shade that was used before 1976, when then-president Valéry Giscard d'Estaing decided to make the colors lighter to better match the European Union's flag. The new shade is also a hat tip to the French Revolution and a "very political" attempt to reconnect with the past, French site Europe1 reported.

Point is often, symbolic interaction attempts to manipulate the attention of, or shares attention with, another individual… This attempt, quite often, involves both (a) reference; or inviting the other to share attention to some outside entity (broadly construed), and (b) predication, or directing the other's attention to some currently *unshared* features or aspects of that entity (in the hopes of sharing attention to the new aspect as well). Comprehension of an act of symbolic communication thus consists in understanding for example that 'She is attempting to direct my attention to X' or 'She is attempting to direct my attention to Y with respect to X's (Tomasello 2010, p.95) ace conceptual drift.

In marketing communication when an icon is left on auto drive the locomotion is comparatively slow like a slot. The currency in most enlightenment these days is to balloon and propel it to a fast lane so it can cruise ambitiously. Anything but lethargic whims will sell in shoring up the stateliness of the personality, identity and product being advertised. Communicative symbols have 360 chances to engage, influence socio-political dispositions and commodification of global narratives. At infancy, symbols may just denote feebly derivative meanings, which make them humanistic and sometimes irritable. However, when they are padded and modified with cues, codes and signals, they appear assertive and significantly iconic, almost larger than life. They become flawless immortals, the gaze-objects with elastically stretching influence that hypnotizes admirers. In other words symbols are positioned to denote, they are politicized to connote period.

IMAGES OF AFRICA IN INTERNATIONAL NARRATIVE

Reality is an abstraction outside human experience. Many times they are reconstructed and hatched by imageries, symbols and signifiers that play roles of doors to let the uninitiated in. It is an intercourse of two different orientations, worlds of ideology. In the end one capitulates to the other that eventually becomes the active intelligence of that alliance. Thus, Berger and Luckmann (1971, p.115) state that, "The symbolic universe provides order for the subjective apprehension of biographical experience. Experiences belonging to different spheres of reality are integrated by incorporation in the same, overarching universe of meaning."

Thus, the abstracted world may be described by symbols employed by creators of worldviews intended to predominate others (Bruner, 1991; Herman, 2011; Polletta, 2009) with hypnotic force to alter weaker narratives (McAdams, Josselson, and Lieblich, 2006; Herman, 2011; Stephens and McCallum, 2013; Marchant, 2018). Globalization as a concept is an abstracted world of economic, social and political convergence with stronger symbols in art, designs, architecture, currencies, icons of trade, movies etc. than text and speeches; that has invaded the literal world. For example some cultural symbols (actually American in reflective origin) like Hollywood, McDonald's, Kentucky Fried Chicken, Coca-Cola, Nike, Levis, Disneyland and, more recently, Yahoo!, Microsoft, Google, and Motorola are eradicating regional and local eccentricities (Daghrir, 2013 p.19).

There are growing concerns that local cultural and national identities are dissolving into a cross-cultural American consumerism. The American culture is iconized in artifacts, trademark symbols, logos and figurines of deified personalities like Elvis Presley, Rockefeller, and Michael Jackson, Michael Jordan, Nike etc. Africa is worst heat, although other parts of the world are just as agitated. The rat race for dominance is conveyed in the thoughts of a French producer Martin Karmitz. Karmitz, cited in Blakley (2001, p.13) states, "sound and pictures have always been used for propaganda, and the real battle at the moment is over who is going to be allowed to control the world's images, and so sell a certain lifestyle, a certain culture, certain products, certain ideas".

The strategy used is often the contrastive approach that borrows steam from the manipulative tactics. Such tactics "was driven by the search for cultural forms that would be able to transcend separate national and ethnic traditions and would constitute a "universal" code of communication. In this search, linguistic communication had obvious limits. Images and music, on the other hand, had obvious advantages" (Fluck, 2011, p.243).

Nature forbids vacuum. There's no picture of reckon except there is one to be replaced by another especially when there is a fixation to be achieved by unctuous subterfuge. Contrastive appeals are stronger and appear quite notorious to deal with once fixed. So how was the subtle negotiation like on and about Africa in the international arena?

The land (America) that holds the largest African immigrant population prides itself and is signified by imageries of Disney land with the catch bait, "the American dream: land of opportunities". In contrast, the imageries of Africa as a continent, over time, has been one hell of a "mass grave" dug by ravaging self-inflicted poor living condition (Fluck, 2011). It is adjudged a disease stricken belt, a hold of 'thugs', a baleful valley of collateral misfortune in even basic civility with shambled economy; the continent where the sun that shines is the scourge from corruption and wars of attrition and a place where one is constantly confronted by horrifyingly surreptitious variants of psychological wreckage. The contrast is day and darkness by imageries that suggest such and so the carrot is a pass to migrate to the land of bright prospects.

Black lives are labeled craftily as less valuable. Stereotypes of black men are generally a depiction of hood-wearing harmful lot (Downing, 2001) even in movie roles. The film *Birth of a Nation*, made in 1915, shows Black men as savages trying to attack White women (Smiley and Fakunle, 2017). Their brutality is met with propaganda depicting the Ku Klux Klan as heroic and honorable. The result was Blackness as a pigmentation becoming closely associated with criminalization (Davis, 1998; Alexander, 2010; Muhammad, 2010). If it is devilish it is black, if it is godly it is white.

Smiley and Fakunle, (2017, p.4) remind that, during the institution of slavery, the image of Black people, specifically Black males, was a docile character. Lavished images of buffoonery, blissful ignorance, and juvenile angst were seen as the primary traits of enslaved Blacks. That quickly gained acceptability resonating with stoic stereotypes among the white audience about the underdog race in several portrayals of Black males of the time. The use of Blackface – a type of performance that generally used White actors wearing black make-up to portray Black people in stereotypes – became banal as well in the 19th century. White actors popularized minstrel shows, depicting stereotypes of Black life as foolish, messy, and overall comedic at the expense of Black culture (Lhamon Jr., 2000; Strausbaugh, 2006). In addition, other popular literature and media characterized antebellum enslaved Blacks as contents with their place in society. In literature, the character of Uncle Tom in *Uncle Tom's Cabin* is portrayed as an older Black slave who is faithful and dutiful to his White master. The film *Gone with the Wind* depicts content slaves, specifically the role of Mammy who even fends off freedmen. The Disney film, *Song of the South* depicts Uncle Remus as an elderly Black freedman who was satisfied with his place in society, singing the famous happy song, "Zip-a-Dee-Doo-Dah."

Thus, the imageries and hues that Africa and Africans are represented perpetuate negative forms of micro-insults and micro-invalidations. The stereotypes convulse with images of demonization, bleakness, confusion, incredulity and pain even when they are exported to the land of opportunities. The stereotyping that pervades the African outside Africa is because the symbols of the spectacle in which Africa was viewed persist years after linguistic repudiation and repatriation were made. If the Blacks' lives matter, the stereotypes need to change radically.

Socio-linguistic enlightenment popularized by the mystics of Western ideology like David Hume, Immanuel Kant, and Thomas Jefferson may have amplified the decibel in literature and theory behind biological racial differences. In his essays, *Notes on the State of Virginia* William Jefferson, a founding father of the United States, third U.S. President, and slave owner, wrote about the differences between the races such as skin color and hair texture as the basis for scientific distinction. He states, "The difference is fixed in nature, and is as real as if its seat and causer were better known to us". Jefferson uses observable data – presumably his own slaves – to come to his conclusions, stating:

"Besides those of color, figure, and hair, there are other physical distinctions proving a difference of race. They have less hair on the face and body. They secrete less by the kidneys, and more by the glands of the skin...They seem to require less sleep...They are at least as brave, and more adventuresome...They are more ardent after their female; but love seems with them to be more an eager desire, than a tender delicate mixture of sentiment and sensation (Jefferson, 1997, p. 98).

Many of the harbingers of misrepresentation are shy descriptors of experiences they never witnessed or shared in, only perhaps as emissaries of figments of crude imaginations. Such was Sir Edgar Burroughs, the creator of *Tarzan of the Apes*. He created a theatrical for puerile fantasies and imagination called the Tarzan series that became the authoritative introduction to savage Africa for Euro-American children. To his skewed credit, however, that series may have negatively influenced the imaginations of millions, adults and children alike, about Africa and earned him a reputation from Ray Bradbury as 'the most influential writer in the entire history of the world' (cited in Kerridge 2016). Buroughs fame gained notoriety for his derogatory and fantastic imaging of Africa. Explorer narratives were not objective records of events as they unfolded in Africa, but biased attempts to confirm some pre-existing mythologies especially because of creations like the Tarzan series (Dokotum, 2020). Their electrifying influence may have invalidated caution that the account was illusory, after all.

In the same light, the racial dynamics and superiority doctrine has not been obliterated years after the statutory abolition of the obnoxious trade. The economic imperative and the humongous leviathan that America and Europe wants to be in order to maintain a grip of world trade demanded a surreptitious cheap labor minefield. So Africa had to continue its role as the largest supplier of workforce for a modern American production farmhouse surreptitiously packaged as Green Card to the land of "opportunity", to work. As it seems, editorially and linguistically the obscenity of racial discrimination may have been spruced and blurred, the symbols of the stereotype are nevertheless visible (Eze, 1997; Fields, 1990; Memmi, 2000).

SHAPING SYMBOLS OF AFRICAN NARRATIVE

Steve Jobs, the Silicon Valley genius is quoted to have said the "most powerful person in the world is the storyteller," the reason according to him is that the storyteller sets "the vision, values and agenda of an entire generation" (Yarow, 2013). Well that position may be partly correct except that it is deficient when viewed intrinsically. Ideas and traditions sometimes outrun the harbinger of the message. Under many circumstances, a better conclusion will be that narratives and their cast are formidable Machos, the real competition, in the game of influence because they far outlive their curators.

Many Americans who have visited Africa as tourists, relief workers, government officials and students on exchange programs and even journalists, as Machira (2002) relays, all get "shocked" about what the reality concerning Africa is when compared with how the symbols of the continent in Western media led by the American pack of reporters makes the world believe. A member of a group of journalists who recently visited Africa was "pleased" to "discover" that the continent is not a land of unrelenting disaster as portrayed by the American media. He said: "Americans only see and read about war, famine, HIV/AIDS, depleted economies, and all sorts of awful things, as if the continent is on fire. Where is the fire?"

Well, the fire may be in the inflammatory images, symbols, context of meaning and syntax variously assembled around issues and stoked with misplaced emotional sparks. The local narrators of the African development are just as guilty as their foreign counterparts in all mediatized communications. The furnace of different informal 'art schools' and cosmetic face makers on the streets of Africa are not homogenous and creatively diverse enough in laying the forms and colors, the fillers and strokes that can brightly out-dust, showcase and wreath the profile of the continent's space in the narrative belt. Ama Biney notes that, "Misinformation about Africa has become a growth industry in the West." Shouldn't re-structuring be Africa's new game turf and pass time?

What influence do the pictorial imageries foretell or advance in the construction of Africa, even though it is tactically being under-valued for supposed lack of credibility? Ngu~g̃ı wa Thiong'o reminds that "culture does not just reflect the world in images but actually, through those very images, conditions a child to see that world in a certain way. The colonial child was made to see the world and where he stands in it as seen and defined by or reflected in the culture of the language of imposition."

Sources like the American film industry are so influential and widespread; they have been injected into the home of every American leaving little reflection regarding the accuracy of what is produced (Lemarchand 2009). A lot of adventurers planning trips to Africa, as Bork (2011) observes, are often cautioned by comments like "have you seen *Hotel Rwanda*?" despite the fact that the movie has sparked much controversy over inaccuracies and misrepresentation of basic facts about a genocide that happened over two decades ago. McCormick (2006, p.42) notes that films of that ilk do "hold up a stark and unflattering mirror to the colonial and neo-colonial footprint these adventurers have left upon the continent and its people"

Already the image hemisphere of international politics and narrative of representation is crowded by contents, symbols, icons and compositions that are untoward signifiers, corralling and disfavoring the profile of Africa. James (1999, p.152) avows that some icons as droll of subtle campaigns are objects of uncritical devotion. However the testament of their position in this information age can be tested for their potency. They may hold out conversely as withering symbols perhaps because of certain insipidity that may have crept up consequently displaying vista for alternate options, with less clout and popularity, to replace them. A communication's channel devotional and instrumental functions can be artfully maximized for remedial and reparatory purposes by the teeming community of creativity that feel it behooves decency for records to be put straight for the continent to regain its virtuosity in the glow of dignity. Doing that will be paying tribute to Edmond Burke's thesis: "the only thing necessary for the triumph of evil, is for good men to do nothing."

DIGITALIZATION OF AFRICAN SYMBOLS

How ardent is the task of wielding the flag of the new narrative of Africa and other symbolic 'universes' step-motherly treated? A lot that went down may have been cultured by generational paranoia because of pervasive ignorance - aided and abated – and a lean information alternative of previous generations. Back in the day there was usually a star icon and a monopolistic symbol of representation of society, nations and continents; now a constellation full of them can simultaneously exist with true heterogeneous characteristics, thanks to many communicative windows.

The mobility of communicative platforms (from stationary to movable and virtual), it is argued, demystifies the sacredness in constituting symbols to communicate or plough them into one icon to represent all; more like a bandwagon effect, good or bad. There are many franchises in the symbolic gallery that, though have not been formally conventionalized by patency, trade their creations with considerable patronage in the market. This is a new vista, as (Onobe and Beida, 2016) submit, with limitless opportunity to package the African flavors.

The flurry of platforms makes the single story phenomenon, unitary and linear spectacle beholden to Africa; a dusty path disinteresting to ply or be taken through. Challenging actively stereotypes, examining and redesigning the media frameworks that currently allow these negative characterizations to remain unquestioned is a more dignifying way to represent Africa and Africans. This demystification characterizes what Ndlovu-Gatshen and Ndlovu (2021, p.37) calls the many "inaudible refutation of Western definitions of Africa, denunciation of what the West has done and continue to do to Africa, and disqualification of the West's claims to monopoly of what it means to be human".

In the old technology with its jaundiced tendencies, the African rarely goes pass the gatekeepers even when he/she has articulated African cultural identities in creative works. Their voices are muffed and abridged before they are appropriated in the West (Wright 2002). This follows a pattern even in the natural science as Hlabangane (2021, p.185) relates, "Western science fashions itself as universal, objective, logo-centric, apolitical and impartial; effectively casting itself as having a god-eye view of the world, outside and above world power dynamics and other wordily concerns, except to add to knowledge in aid of human civilization and progress. By implication, other knowledge systems are thought of as local, intuitive, subject and partial and fraught with human frailties such as emotions, politics and attendant short-sightedness." It is a bit different now with new technologies. Personalized media allow statements to be made by curators themselves not by proxy.

There are many technologically midwifed means of communication in this era. Cheng (2018) points to Motif as a new symbolic notation language and stresses variant utility that can be gleaned. However, for all its utility, Motif Notation is currently hampered in its adoption and evolution by a number of challenges. Even those who are familiar with Motif Notation (including certified Laban Movement Analysts) often do not prioritize it in their personal or professional practices. This conversational mode loosely exists uncoordinatedly. Cheng (2018) identifies the informality of their existence as a problem, either registering or evolving the Motif symbol base, which makes adoption of new symbols haphazard and arrhythmic. More salient is the fact that the tools for creating graphical Motifs are few in number, largely unsupported or stalled in development, and often difficult to use, as Cheng (ibid) stresses plus an observable absence of a standard, interoperable digital format for storing Motifs or transferring them between applications, as is routinely done with documents in other domains. As a result, Motifs are difficult to preserve and share.

When one learns a movement quality and also learns to associate that experience with a symbol, the symbol is "charged up" with a visceral body memory. One need only see the symbol to recall the lived experience of that movement quality. The esoteric nature of symbols helps root the concepts in the unconscious as it holds a kind of power - its ability to bridge between the abstract conceptual framework of LMA and the sub-/un-conscious world of body experience. All the same, some things may be getting in the way of it being used everywhere and feeling vital in the 21st century.

Cheng (2018) for example, notes that there are swaths of concepts for which we don't yet have symbols, such as the meta-themes of Exertion/Recuperation, Stability/Mobility (as meta-themes rather than Effort States), Inner/ Outer, and Subtle/Simple/Complex. Currently, we lack effective tools for doing so. Very small groups with limited resources can use software programs ostensibly designed for Labanotation that can be used as well to create Motifs. Updates are irregular.

"Designs are not closed units," as Dyer and Petersen (2021, p.4501) point, "which for a long time has been the modernist designer's ideal illusion. Instead they are open and multi-stage, and may exist beyond the designer's intent. Consequently, when they undermine the apotheosis of artifacts confined to exist within designer-given determinate possibilities, they are in the same motion also emphasizing the indeterminate kinetic pluralism of designed artifacts. They give an example of Projected Realities".

As a living language, Motif require continual evaluation of its on-going usefulness within current context, addressing questions like, does it serve our movement observation needs? Can everything be represented that we want to express? Is anything left out? Can the existing system be made more intuitive? Easier to read and write? At the same time, any evolution of the language needs to carry forward its core values, its fundamental principles, otherwise referred to by some as "first principles." It should ideally address issues of principles by recording the following as concerns:

1. How to make symbols simple and fast to write, with a minimum number of pen/brush strokes.
2. How to make symbols have legibility irrespective of size or constraints of time, or demand for urgency.
3. How to make symbols writable, duplicable, with a preferably monolithic characteristic (single color).
4. Making symbols not to be tied to a particular human language or alphabet.
5. How to make complex symbols be built from basic symbols, where possible.
6. Ensuring that most general forms of symbols are simplest to express.
7. How to make symbols either stretchable or non-stretchable.
8. Not stretched, symbols should have a bounding box of consistent height.
9. Ensure inclusion of both sides of a polarity within the same symbol (such as Rising and Sinking written together) means that either or both polarities are present.
10. Motif Notation itself is not a static system but can evolve over time.

There are attempts to ensure that evolution of Motif Notation tend to maintain compatibility with past versions. No doubt, tools are needed at all levels of application, from creating simple Motif graphics for embedding in social media posts to doing complete page layouts with control over all aspects of printing. With the aid of digitalization, devices that allow for maneuvering and interphase between crude means and digital mix may be more advantageous.

Outside the motif turf there is now computer-mediated communication with emoticons. An Emoticon, a word that is formed by a neologism that is made up of terms such as icon and emotion, is a text-based smiley face, frowning faces and other inventive compositions created with symbols available on your keyboard. They have been used for years on the Internet via messaging and emails. They made their first appearance in an issue of a magazine back in the year 1881. It was just about 100 years later, in 1982 that Emoticons were first incorporated into computer language.

Emoticons have become a part of almost all forms of computer-mediated communication (CMC) and represent an adequate replacement for facial expressions in their role in nonverbal communication (Jibril

Figure 1.

& Abdullah, 2013). Reeves and Nass (1996) found that individuals interact with computers, television and new media in a fundamentally social and natural way that is equal to interactions in real life. Emoticons can push receivers into a specific direction of interpretation. When used in that capacity, emoticons and emojis operate as clarifiers of intent—powerful enough to convey meaning that could be perceived as opposite of the language used (Bliss-Carroll, 2016). This way of interaction is not conscious or intuitive it is automatic. It is important to consider the analogy that media equals real life in order to reconsider issues like cross-cultural nonverbal display of emotions in CMC (Gerritsen, Gagnon, Stefanucci & Drews, 2012; Reeves & Nass, 1996).

Another digitally graphical symbols that have particularly impressive showing, as an innovation of the digital evolution, are the emoji. Yassin (2021) avers that, "Modern communication technology may have created Emojis, which has tremendously appreciated to a status of a brand new symbolic language that is more an active interpersonal means of communication taking over mainstream communication.

As common phenomenon in most platforms, emojis are appropriated in disciplines like marketing, law, healthcare, food-related and addictive context (Ai et al., 2017; Danesi, 2016; Tran et al., 2018), (Ge and Gretzel, 2018; Vidal et al., 2016; Goldman, 2018; Willoughby and Liu, 2018). Yassin (2021, p.109) relays that if a brand is interested in expanding into a new state or country, using Emojis as part of the initial marketing strategy could be a great way to gain the attention of the targeted customers. It may not be because the emojis address the people in their native language, quite the opposite. A lot of people now hold multiple citizenships, the perennial and the associative citizenship. The later is a virtual citizenship with borderless constitution. Many people refer to themselves now as Netizens, especially youth. It is this universe that has normalized and adopted emojis as a communicative lingo.

Emojis offer larger scope for creativity and innovation. There are around 3000 Emojis in use today, and brands can even create their own Emojis to convey their unique message to the consumers. A number of techniques like intrusion, illusion, metaphors, exaggerations; association transformation and installation (Tellis, 2007; Sherin, 2013; Stoklossa, 2007; Velarde, 2017; Eskilson, 2019) are variously used with impressive success stories.

As part of a text and drive campaign, Volkswagen using transformation technique featured a pretty bruised and battered Emoji with bandaged heads, knocked out teeth, smashed up sunglasses and bloodied face, showing the dangers of distracted driving Without having to use very many words at all, just Emojis (Yassin, 2021, p.111). The possibilities of ingeniously creating newer emojis are endless in marketing.

Beyond that, they have crossed the threshold seizing advertising messages especially targeted at a computer and digital-savvy generation that is mobile-devices-focused and their primary way of communicating is through mobile devices that has thousands of Emojis. Typical was when Pepsi used more than 70 global and locally uniquely designed Emojis printed on cans, bottles and cups all over the world. They called it the PepsiMoji language, sparking unexpected conversations and action around the world in a unique advertising campaign titled “Say it with Pepsi”. There are now Emoji translators; EMOJIPEDIA is the most well known website to look for Emojis meanings.

Social media hold a large degree of credit in helping to popularize Emojis. They provided advertisers with a welcome opportunity to interact and connect with a new generation of consumers that expect more meaningful and creative engagement. The opportunity to infuse the value-laden prosaic culture of Africa, spruced with prized corrective lens impression, on the stand is incontrovertibly now. The concern is beyond the talk, it should be upped to the touch. The creative squad is the youth that should match up with others their age, using their skills and know-how to digitally launder the image and identity of Africa before the world.

The technology is firmly in their grip, well so it may seem. Now the talk is that there are new tech creators savvy with all digital technology. What is the cultural mix of the gatekeepers of digital ivory tower - the Silicon Valley? How many emojis reflect cultural diversity, since that is the dominant digital currency of communication? How many emojis, emoticons capture the complex, traditions of Africa? If cultures and languages are being digitized, Africa’s is endangered. The computer mediated communication era seems to be an equalizer as it gives anyone able to use it the vista to create emotionally representative messages and propagate it. Nevertheless, much of the messages symbolized by digital shortcuts called emoticons or emojis are linearly constructed to dominantly reflect relationships that tend toward connubiality or other kinds of casual relationships that are so far from the existing templates. Even then how much of Africa’s symbolism of love gestures, kind gestures, African hospitality, selflessness, life styles and social expressions are reflected in the existing digital lingo – emojis, emoticons and Motif Notation? Practically none. In the language frame symbols are the strongest sockets that are likely to hold when word fittings fall of or into disuse. The concern is palpable considering that whatever is digital is eclipsing what is not. Already the language and framework for digital communication has been cast with nothing of Africa earning a spot in it. Language is a modern algorithm of reassembling and culture resettlement (Sibanda, 2021).

It seems the economic and social direction of communication has eclipsed and blunts the edge of other agitations of identity, political imbalance, ideological enslavement etc. The template and the creators of what have become popular in the digital language lexicon are blind to the inordinate issues gripping society, especially cultural and identity questions. The ideas that dominate digital messaging dummy cat now might become the biggest and easiest colonizing threads of all time unless the tapestry is woven with variegated threads of multi-uniformity and more issues of counterpart input, not democratized control system. Africa cannot ask for an affirmative action to get a space. It needs to actively engage and create its space in the digital track and run along. People perceive the world in cultural models and behave accordingly in cultural ways in a social context. It follows that cultural and social context are necessities for communication because actions and communication are the subject’s adaption to context (Mantovani, 1996).

CONCLUSION

The context of this discussion has revolved around the significance of cultural communication in a digital era. The thoughts roamed around how pristine symbols, imageries, have created stereotypes of Africa and Africans; viewed and related to in most contexts of social, political and economic narratives. Biased impressionable images and motifs can only be replaced by another use of stronger impressionable cues. The computer mediated communication era seems to be an equalizer as it gives anyone able to use it the vista to create emotionally representative messages and propagate it. Nevertheless, much of the messages symbolized by digital shortcuts called emoticons or emojis are linearly constructed to dominantly reflect relationships that tend toward connubiality or other kinds of casual relationships. They are limited and inadequate in representing other deeper issues of socio-political imbalance in society. Cultural identity issues are not reflected. The digitally communicative symbols appear to be homogenized agents of globalization and the penetrable force and influence of African youth is terribly austere. They need to be mentored by older patriots on the politics of narrative manipulation for them to significantly be imbued to raise a high identity flag.

REFERENCES

Ai, W., Lu, X., Liu, X., Wang, N., Huang, G., & Mei, Q. (2017). Untangling Emoji popularity through semantic embeddings. *Proceedings of the International AAAI Conference on Web and Social Media*, 11.

Alexander, M. (2010). *The new Jim Crow: Mass incarceration in the age of colorblindness*. The New Press.

Berger, L. P., & Luckmann, T. (1971). *The social construction of reality: a treatise in the Sociology of knowledge*. Hamondswoth Penguin.

Blakley, J. (2001). *Entertainment goes global: mass culture in a transforming world*. The Norman Lear Center Publications.

Berengueres, J., & Castro, D. (2017). *Differences in emoji sentiment perception between readers and writers*. A Paper presented at the 2017 IEEE International Conference on Big Data. https://arxiv.org/pdf/1710.0888

Bliss-Carroll, L. N. (2016). *The nature, function, and value of Emojis as contemporary tools of digital interpersonal communication*. https://digitalcommons.gardner-webb.edu/english_etd

Bork, P. (2011). *Misunderstanding Africa: The West's misrepresentation of Africa, an insufficient notion of evil seen through the lens of the Rwanda genocide and child slavery in Ghana*. https://keep.lib.asu.edu/items/150395

Bruner, J. (1991). The narrative construction of reality. *Critical Inquiry*, *18*(1), 1–21. doi:10.1086/448619

Cheng, B. (2018). *21st Century Motif: relevance and (r)evolution*. Paper presented at the LABAN 2018 International Conference Celebrating the 40th Anniversary of the Laban/Bartenieff Institute of Movement Studies. https://labaninstitute.org/wp-content/uploads/2018/07/21st-Century-Motif-Relevance-and-REvolution-Brenton-Cheng.pdf

Cohn, N., Engelen, J., & Schileroord, J. (2019). The grammar of emoji? Constraints on communicative pictorial sequencing. In *cognitive research: Principles and implications*. doi:10.1186/s41235-019-0177-0

Daghrir, W. (2013). Globalization as Americanization? Beyond the Conspiracy Theory. *IOSR Journal of Applied Physics, 5*(2), 19-24.

Danesi, M. (2016). *The semiotics of Emoji: the rise of visual language in the age of the Internet*. Bloomsbury.

Davis, Y. A. (1998). Race and criminalization: Black Americans and the punishment industry. In J. Jones (Ed.), *The Angela Y Davis Reader* (pp. 61–73). Blackwell Publishing.

Dokotum, O.O. (2020). *Hollywood and Africa recycling the 'Dark Continent' myth, 1908–2020*. NISC African Humanities Program.

Downing, D. H. J. (2001). *Radical Media Rebellious Communication and Social Movements*. Sage Publications, Inc.

Dyer & Petersen. (2021). Design culture of thinking: the theory, history and critics. *Cumulus Conference Proceedings*.

Eskilson, J. S. (2019). *Graphic Design: a New History* (3rd ed.). Yale University Press.

Eze, E. (1997). *Race and the Enlightenment: A Reader*. Wiley-Blackwell.

Fields, B. J. (1990). Slavery, race and ideology in the United States of America. *New Left Review*, *181*, 95–118.

Fluck, W. (2011). The Americanization of modern culture: A cultural history of the popular media. In *Romance with America? Essays on culture, literature, and American Studies*. https://www.jfki.fu-berlin.de/en/v/publications_fluck/2000/Romance_with_America/Fluck__Winfried_-_The_Americanization_of_Modern_Culture.pdf

Ge, J., & Gretzel, U. (2018). Emoji rhetoric: A social media influencer perspective. *Journal of Marketing Management*, *34*(15-16), 1272–1295. doi:10.1080/0267257X.2018.1483960

Gerritsen, D., Gagnon, K., Stefanucci, J., & Drews, F. (2012). I'd Like to Introduce you to my desktop: toward a theory of social, human-computer interaction. In *Proceedings of the Human Factors and Ergonomics Society Annual Meeting* (Vol. 56, No. 1, pp. 2098-2102). SAGE Publications. 10.1177/1071181312561445

Goldman, E. (2018). Emojis and the law. *Washington Law Review (Seattle, Wash.)*, *93*, 1227.

Hall, S. (1996). *Critical Dialogues In Cultural Studies*. Routledge.

Hariman, R., & Luciates, L. J. (2007). *No Caption Needed: Iconic Photographs, Public Culture, and Liberal Democracy*. University of Chicago Press.

Hlabangane, N. (2021). The underside of modern knowledge: an epistemic break from Western science. In M. Steyn & W. Mpofu (Eds.), *Decolonizing the human: reflections from Africa on difference and oppressions*. Wits University Press. doi:10.18772/22021036512.12

James, J. (1999). Black revolutionary icons and 'neoslave' narratives. *Social Identities*, *5*(2), 135–159. doi:10.1080/13504639951536

Jefferson, T. (1787). Notes on the state of Virginia. In Race and the enlightenment: A reader. Wiley-Blackwell.

Jibril, A. T., & Abdullah, H. M. (2012). Relevance of emoticons in computer-mediated communication context: A review. *Asian Social Science*, *9*(4), 201–207. doi:10.5539/ass.v9n4p201

Kelly, R., and Watts, L (2015). Characterizing the inventive appropriation of Emoji as relationally meaningful in mediated close personal relationships. In *Experiences of technology appropriation: Unanticipated users, usage, circumstances, and design*. Academic Press.

Lemarchand, R. (2009). The dynamics of violence in Central Africa. University of Pennsylvania Press. doi:10.9783/9780812202595

Lhamon, W. T. Jr. (2000). *Raising Cain: Blackface performance from Jim Crow To hip hop*. Harvard University Press.

Lu, X., Ai, W., Liu, X., Li, Q., Wang, N., Huang, G., & Mei, Q. (2016). Learning from the ubiquitous language: an empirical analysis of emoji usage of smartphone users. *Proceedings of the 2016 ACM International Joint Conference on Pervasive and Ubiquitous Computing*.

Luuk, E. (2013). The structure and evolution of symbol. *New Ideas in Psychology*, *31*(2), 87–97. doi:10.1016/j.newideapsych.2012.06.001

Luuk, E. (2018). *Symbol and its evolution*. doi:10.12775/3991-1.064

Marchant, R. E. (2018). Anyone anywhere: narrating African innovation in a global community of practice. *Publicly Accessible Penn Dissertations*. 2746. https://repository.upenn.edu/edissertations/2746

Markman, K., & Oshima, S. (2017). *Pragmatic play? Some possible functions of English emoticons and Japanese Kaomoji In computer-mediated discourse*. Paper presented at the Association of Internet Researchers Annual Conference 8.0: Let's play! Vancouver. 10.31235/osf.io/qa764

McAdams, P. D., Josselson, R., & Lieblich, A. (2006). *Identity and story: creating self in narrative*. American Psychological Association. Retrieved from http://psycnet.apa.org/psycinfo/2006-01746-000/

McCormick, P. (2006). Our hearts of darkness. *U.S. Catholic*, (May), 42–43.

Memmi, A. (1999). *Racism*. University of Minnesota Press.

Mantovani, G. (1996). Social context in HCI: A new framework for mental models, cooperation and communication. *Cognitive Science*, *20*(2), 237–296. doi:10.120715516709cog2002_3

Morris, M. (2010). The idea of words as signs. In *Philosophy of language and linguistics* (Vol. II). The Philosophical Turn. Ontos Verlag.

Moschini, I. (2016). The 'face with tears of joy' emoji. A Socio-Semiotic and multimodal insight into a Japan-America Mash-Up. *HERMES-Journal of Language and Communication in Business*, *55*, 11–25.

Muhammad, K. (2010). *The condemnation of blackness: race, crime, and the making of modern urban America*. Harvard University Press. doi:10.2307/j.ctvjsf4fx

Ndlovu-Gatshen, S. J., & Ndlovu, P. P. (2021). The invention of blackness on a world scale. In Decolonizing the human: reflections from Africa on difference and oppressions. Wits University Press. doi:10.18772/22021036512

O'Connell, J., & O'Connell, K. (2008). Rabrindranath Tagore as cultural icon. *University of Toronto Quarterly, 77*(4), 961-970.

Onobe, J. M., & Beida, O. J. (2016). Commoditization of cultural communication: buying back Nollywood from the trans-Atlantic and neo-classic market of alien values. *Journal of Communication and Media Research, 8*(1).

O'Reilly, M. D. (2017). *An investigation into metaphoric competence in the L2: A linguistic approach.* https://etheses.whiterose.ac.uk/19853/2/An%20investigation%20into%20metaphoric%20competence%20in%20the%20L2%2C%20a%20linguistic%20approach_O%27Reilly%2C%20D_PhD%20thesis%202017.pdf

Pavalanathan, U., & Eisenstein, J. (2016). More emojis, less: The competition for paralinguistic function in micro blog writing. *First Monday, 21*(11). Advance online publication. doi:10.5210/fm.v21i11.6879

Polletta, F. (2009). *It was like a fever: Storytelling in protest and politics.* University of Chicago Press. https://proxy.library.upenn.edu:2265/books/about/It_Was_Like_a_Fever.html?id=hBY2OUKingUC

Reeves, B., & Nass, C. (1996). *How people treat computers, television, and new media like real people and places.* CSLI Publications and Cambridge University Press.

Sherin, A. (2013). *Design elements, using images to create graphic impact.* Rockport Publishers.

Sirbu, A. (2015). The significance of language as a tool of communication. 'Mircea cel Batran'. *Naval Academy Scientific Bulletin, 18*(2), 405–406.

Sibanda, B. (2021). 'Language as Being' in the politics of Ngugi wa Thiongo. In M. Steyn & W. Mpofu (Eds.), *Decolonizing the human: reflections from Africa on difference and oppressions.* Wits University Press. doi:10.18772/22021036512.11

Smiley, C., & Fakunke, D. (2017). From "brute" to "thug:" The demonization and criminalization of unarmed black male victims in America. *Human Behavior Society Environ., 26*(3-4), 350–366. doi:10.1080/10911359.2015.1129256 PMID:27594778

Steen, G. (2008). The paradox of metaphor: Why we need a three-dimensional model of metaphor. *Metaphor and Symbol, 23*(4), 213–241. doi:10.1080/10926480802426753

Stephens, J., & McCallum, R. (2013). *Retelling stories, framing culture: traditional story and metanarratives in children's literature.* Routledge. doi:10.4324/9780203357750

Stoklossa, U. (2007). *Advertising: New techniques for visual seduction.* Thames and Hudson.

Strausbaugh, J. (2006). *Black like you: Blackface, whiteface, insult and imitation in American popular culture.* Tarcher.

Tellis, J. G. (2007). *The sage handbook of Advertising* (1st ed.). SAGE Publications Ltd. doi:10.4135/9781848607897Tran, T., Nguyen, D., Nguyen, A., & Golenz, E. (2018). Sentiment analysis of emoji-based reactions on marijuana-related topical posts on Facebook. *IEEE International Conference on Communications (ICC).*

Tomasello, M. (2010). On the different origins of symbols and grammar. In Language evolution. doi:10.1093/acprof:oso/9780199244843.001.0001

Velarde, O. (2017). *Commonly used Advertising techniques in visual marketing*. https://visme.co/blog/visual-advertising-techniques/#XAcjK-wo0ApoBc8Gf.99

Vidal, L., Ares, G., & Jaeger, R. S. (2016). Use of emoticon and emoji In Tweets for food-related emotional expression. *Food Quality and Preference*, *49*, 119–128. doi:10.1016/j.foodqual.2015.12.002

Willoughby, F. J., & Liu, S. (2018). Do pictures help tell the story? An experimental test of narrative and emojis in a health text message intervention. *Computers in Human Behavior*, *79*, 75–82. doi:10.1016/j.chb.2017.10.031

Wright, H. K. (2002). Editorial: Notes on the (Im) Possibility of articulating continental African identity. *Critical Arts: a Journal of Media Studies.*, *16*(2), 1–18. doi:10.1080/02560240285310111

Yarow, J. (2013). *Here's an awesome story about Steve Jobs telling an employee he's going to become the world's best story teller in 1994*. https://www.businessinsider.com/steve-jobs-story-teller-2013-7

Yassin, A. K. (2021). Emojis as a new visual language in Advertising creativity. *Journal of Design Sciences and Applied Arts*. doi:10.21608/jdsaa.2021.29904.1037

Chapter 7
Indian Television and the Ideologies of Social Development in India

Subir Sinha
https://orcid.org/0000-0001-7578-9809
Dum Dum Motijheel College, India

ABSTRACT

In India, the purpose of television broadcasting is to clearly depict an ideology that reflects social development. In the chapter, the analysis of various case studies shows that the main objective of television broadcasting in India focuses on the social development of the youth and the society at large. From the initial days, television is mainly used to disseminate information. Along with this, it performs several other roles that are related to social development such as propagation of education, support in the development of knowledge society and in the progress of cultural promotion, creation of health awareness, etc. In contrast to the essential roles of television, the chapter also highlights the media contents that signify cultural imperialism and the growth of Indianisation in the media content. The chapter overall signifies how television is playing a significant role in the social development of the nation.

INTRODUCTION

The term 'ideology' is a complex word used to describe a particular set of principles, beliefs, ideas, concepts or doctrines. It was used by various scholars, groups and organisations in different ways to describe numerous set of principle, concepts, basic beliefs or guiding principles of a person or a group. Michael Freeden in the opening chapter of his book -*'IDEOLOGY: A Very Short Introduction'*- define the term ideology as *"Ideology is a word that evokes strong emotion"*- (Freeden. M, 2003). In *Merriam-Webster*, it's defined as *"a manner or the content of thinking characteristic of an individual, group, or culture" "the integrated assertions, theories and aims that constitute a socio-political program"*. In contrast, Stanley J. Baran and Dennis K. Devis in their book -*'Mass Communication Theory: Foundations, Ferment and Future'*- define the term 'Ideology' while discussing the Marxist theory as *"In*

DOI: 10.4018/978-1-6684-4107-7.ch007

Marxist theory, idea present in a culture that mislead average people and encourage them to act against their own interest" (Baran and Davis, 2010). The term varies and signifies different meanings in distinct contexts. However, in the context of television broadcasting the term ideology tries to explain or depict a set of principles, ideas or doctrines which a television broadcasting system uses or follows. Television is a gift of technology which is serving mankind from the very beginning of its arrival and helping to bring a new era of modernity. Television from its early days is acting as a vital tool that helps to disseminate information related to various news, education, health awareness, cultural promotion, rural developments along with entertainment.

In India, television arrived in the middle of the twentieth century with a clear objective of social development. The broadcasting system of India depicts that Indian television is not only associated with entertainment, rather it has shown a wider purpose in the field of social development. The ideology that reflects from the content of Indian television broadcasting is nothing but an ideology of social development of the youth and the development of the entire society at large. The sentiments of Indian television broadcasting are highly nationalistic and developmental in nature. The propagation of the positive ideological content that is related to social development through various programmes is at high priority from the initial days of Indian television. Prasar Bharati, the autonomous body that controlled television broadcast in India gave high priority to social development and especially to the development of the children and youth. Prasar Bharati appealed to Doordarshan the autonomous public service broadcaster of India and to the several other private satellite channels of India to broadcast programmes on information, education, health awareness, rural development and cultural promotion which are highly valued and socially relevant. While focusing on the appeal of Prasar Bharati and the recommendation of various committees, Doordarshan and various satellite channels of India focus on the programme based on information, education, knowledge development, health awareness creation and cultural promotions. The programmes are highly necessary for the development of the younger generation and the society at large. The programmes motivate society and the younger generation to move on the right path. They reflect that the ideology of Indian television broadcasting is mainly based on the social development and the development of the youth.

THE ARRIVAL OF TELEVISION AND SATELLITE TELEVISION IN INDIA

In India, television has shown a significant contribution in the field of social development and the development of the youth since its arrival in 1959. During the early days, Philips (India) demonstrates the use of television and transmitter in an exhibition in New Delhi and made an offer to the Government of India to provide transmitter and television at a low cost. In the meantime, UNESCO provides a grant of $20,000 for the purchase of community receiver sets and the United States offer some equipment all these offers boost the rise of a television system in India. On 15 September 1959, Delhi Television Centre came into existence. The range of the transmitter was forty kilometres around Delhi, and it was beamed twice a week, each of twenty minutes duration. In Delhi, in 1961, school educational programmes were introduced through television for the development of the youth. In 1965, the duration of the television programme was increased and informational, cultural, developmental, and entertainment based programmes were introduced. In 1967, a renowned developmental programme based on agricultural "Krishi Darshan" started to be broadcasted. The programme was developed with the help of the Department of Atomic Energy, the Indian Agricultural Research Institute, the Delhi Administration, the State

Government of Uttar Pradesh and the State Government of Haryana. The programme Krishi Darshan was introduced to eighty villages, and the range of the transmitter for broadcasting the programme was extended to sixty kilometres. – (Kumar, K, J, 2007).

After the opening of the Delhi Television Centre, Bombay Centre for television broadcast came into existence in 1972, and it was followed by Srinagar of Kashmir and Jalandhar the city of Punjab in 1973. Kolkata, Chennai and Lucknow got their own television broadcasting centre in 1975. The broadcasting centre in Hyderabad and Jaipur opened in 1977 whereas the centre in Bhubaneswar opened in 1987, and gradually with time Doordarshan set up various other centres at various places within the nation for the welfare of the society and to the nation at large. A significant event occurred in 1976 when Doordarshan separated from All India Radio and formed a separate unit under the Ministry of Information and Broadcasting.

In India, the marks of globalisation on media were started by the arrival of satellite television during the early days of the nineties. They entered with a great motive of serving the Indian audience by providing a wide range of information, entertainment and global culture. It begins with Ted Turner's Cable News Network (CNN); the American satellite channel which telecasts the entire First Gulf War during 1991 in India on the other side the bombing of Kuwait by Saddam Hussein in the First Gulf War raises the demand for satellite dishes. The demand of the satellite dishes and the phenomenon of information sharing through audio visual mode put the light on Indian media business and encourage various groups to enter into the new form of business (media business).

Rupert Murdoch within a short time launches his STAR Group with only four channels, and during October 1991 the group launched its fifth satellite channel BBC. STAR is followed by the Indian private satellite network group called 'ZEE' which was launched by Subhash Chandra in 1992 and within a couple of years SONY arrives in India on the early days of 1995. It was being noted that not only the American and Indian networks attempt to enter into the Indian media world but also various European satellite channels also try to enter. However, the early days of 1992 show the record of around 4500 household satellite user through cable networks and during 1993 it was seen the number of households increased to around 3.3 million and by the end of 1994, it reached around 11.8 million according to a survey report. - (IndiaNetzone, 2013).

These networks bring a wide range of information along with entertainment and foreign culture to India. The presentations of these networks are different and attractive which started to attract a greater number of Indian audiences from various sectors and within a short time the networks started to gain huge popularity. Indian society and the younger generation started to use these networks not only for information but also they become a medium to decode modernity and entertainment. The networks started to telecast various programmes for various ages, even in few cases it was seen that networks launch separate channels for a specific target audience such as CNN IBN, NDTV PROFIT, and ZEE Business. They are for the audience who are deeply attached with the share markets. Disney Channel, Cartoon Network, Pogo are for the children, Star Plus, Star Jalsha are now specifically for the women and housewife, similarly MTV, Channel V, and B4U are for youth and teenagers. This network tries to refresh the youth and teenagers by various musical and informational programmes where as men and women are opened to various movies and soap operas. These programmes bring in front of the Indian audience several new customs, food habits and a new style of living. The programmes are ideologically different from the Indian one, but the Indian audience especially the children and the youth started to adopt the content of the satellite television in an openhearted way. In January 1992, Indian Institute of Mass Communication (IIMC) conducted a survey in New Delhi which shows that around 84 percent of the respondent suggests MTV having a socio-cultural effect on the younger generation of India. – (Kumar. K. J, 2007)

TELEVISION AND THE INFORMATION DISSEMINATION RELATED TO SOCIAL DEVELOPMENT

In India, television is one of the most vital forms of mass media used to disseminate information. Television is the medium which is mainly used by various governments and private agencies to disseminate various messages and information for promoting various programmes related to social development. The government of India focuses on its abilities of information dissemination from the very beginning of its arrival. Doordarshan the autonomous public service broadcaster of India has started to disseminate news from the very beginning, but Prasar Bharati and Union Cabinet have approved a separate 24-hour news channel 'DD News' on 03 October 2003. The channel runs under the supervision of Doordarshan and disseminates only news and information. DD News broadcast over 16 hours of live news bulletin daily in Hindi, English, Sanskrit and Urdu. One of the main reasons for its huge popularity is the ideology of fair and balanced presentation. A sister channel of Doordarshan, 'DD India' also become popular for the presentation of current affairs and news in the English version (DD NEWS). Along with Doordarshan various private satellite channels also provide their own news bulletin. Private satellite news channels including NDTV, TIMES NOW, Headline Today, ABP ANANDA, 24 GHANTA presenting the news round the clock. They collect and present various news stories according to the necessity and popularity of the story. The news room of these channels is always in hurry in the production of news stories which makes society and the younger generation always well informed. These news channels are maintaining their duties and social responsibilities by disseminating facts and unbiased news stories among the society for social development.

The government and other agencies are using the television not only for news broadcast and but also for the propagation of various essential messages. During the pandemic period of COVID-19, television performs a great function of information dissemination and helping the society from various dimensions. The Indian government declared lockdown on 24th March 2020 with the outbreak of COVID-19 – (Hebbar, 2000). Nearly 1.3 billion Indians locked themselves within their residents and for them television has become one of the vital sources of information. Through television, they received various data and information related to the situation of various places, medical facilities, government activities and various announcements. Television provided continuously significant national and international news about Corona virus and COVID-19 on a regular basis which makes the youth and the society well informed. The value of television in the field of information dissemination is enormous.

Information disseminated by the Indian television plays a significant role in the social development of the society and especially the children and the young adults. Information provided by the television satisfies their cognitive mind by providing enormous data which they use according their own necessity. They used data and information in several ways for their own self development. The data provided by the television make them well informed and helps to develop curious and cognitive behaviours. It makes them aware about the news, latest events, and activities happening around them. The data and information provided by the television channels also helps the children and young adult in quick decision making process. Along with this, television also provides various advices related to children and young adults which ultimately focus on the social development of the younger generation. It plays a significant role in the dissemination of information which is ideologically relevant for the social development of the children and the young adults.

TELEVISION AND THE PROPAGATION OF EDUCATION

In India, television used to disseminate a wide range of formal and informal educational programmes for the benefit of society and especially for the benefit of the children and young adults. It shows a positive experience by developing intellect within children and young adults. Through television children and young adults decodes a wide variety of education which makes them well educated and technically skilled. The objective is to promote social development through the progress of quality education and the promotion of Right to Education within the nation. Due to the frequent use of television mainly by the children and young adults they are widely used as a medium of teaching and learning.

Television acts as a powerful tool of education. It opened a new medium for imparting teaching and learning as it shows the capacity of wide dissemination of data and information. The government of India has taken it from the early days of its arrival as a medium for imparting education and reflects a developmental and progressive ideology. In 1961, on an experimental basis, India's first school television service began in Delhi. It was projected as 'Educational Television' with an aim of imparting education through television. Later, television was used to broadcast for the propagation of educational programme from several Indian states in different languages covering both formal and informal education. The main intention was to improve the basic concept of science and develop a new teaching tool.

In 1975, Satellite Instructional Television Experiment (SITE) displayed how television can be used as a medium of education. In this experiment, the Department of Atomic Energy agreed with the National Aeronautics and Space Administration (NASA) of the United States for a satellite which will be used for an experiment on social development starting from August 1975. The experiment covered around two thousand four hundred villages of six states of India –Orissa (presently Odisha), Madhya Pradesh, Bihar, Rajasthan, Andhra Pradesh and Karnataka. Within these states, an experimental telecasting was conducted on Education along with Agriculture, Health and Family Planning programmes. The programmes were planned and produced by All India Radio (AIR) at the production centre set up in Delhi, Hyderabad and Cuttack with the help of representatives from Central and State Government and from various universities – (Kumar. K. J, 2007). The main objectives of the educational programme of this experiment are:

- To reduce the drop rate in school
- To make the school more attractive in front of students
- To impart a proper centralised education
- To improve the concept of the student
- To make students well informed and well educated
- To create awareness
- Motivate to adopt a scientific and healthy lifestyle

The experiment has changed the concept of teaching techniques and highlighted how television can be used to propagate education to a wide range of audiences. This experiment proved that television can be used as an agent of social development.

Later in 1984, the University Grand Commission's (UGC) higher education project known as "Country Wide Class Room" was launched to broadcast educational programmes through television. The main aim of this programme was to disseminate higher education across the nation. Television took a significant role in this educational programme and proved its success as a medium for imparting meaningful education. In this programme around one thousand seven hundred colleges were provided free colour television and few colleges bought their own television set for the propagation of higher education programme. According to ADMAR (1993) study report, the UGC's programme Country Wide Classroom had a viewership of over 19 million of which 12 million watches at least once a week and around 7 million are regular viewers – (Kumar. K. J, 2007). This case study has reflects the importance of television in the propagation of education and how the Indian government used television for social development as well as for the development of the children and the youth.

TELEVISION AND THE DEVELOPMENT OF KNOWLEDGE SOCIETY

The term 'Knowledge Society' has gained importance in the recent days. The concept of knowledge society gain pace with the development of communication and information technology. The term signifies essentiality and value of knowledge within human society. Knowledge is the central figure of the concept. In the initial part of the book 'Public Service Broadcasting: A Best Practices Source Book' Indrajit Banerjee and Kalinga Seneviratne discussed about the concept of knowledge society as follow:

The concept of knowledge societies, which UNESCO is advocating, offers a holistic and comprehensive vision (cutting across all UNESCO's domains) with a clear development oriented perspective that captures the complexity and dynamism of current global trends and prospects. Knowledge societies require an empowering social vision which encompasses plurality, inclusion, solidarity, and participation. Based on the principles of freedom of expression, universal access to information and knowledge, promotion of cultural diversity and equal access to quality education, the concept of knowledge societies is progressively recognized as essential for attaining major development goals. (Banerjee and Seneviratne, 2005).

In a developing nation like India, knowledge and information both are playing a vital role in the development of the nation. Globalisation and mass media are changing the entire world into a knowledge hub. Mass media, especially television is playing a major role in this change. Indian public service television broadcasting channel Doordarshan continuously propagates various programmes based on education and knowledge. In addition to Doordarshan various private satellite television channels are also disseminating regularly a wide range of knowledge among the audience. The broadcasting of these educational and knowledge programmes is desperately trying to change the nation into a 'Knowledge Society'.

Knowledge is no longer remaining within a single cluster of people, television disseminating them among the masses. It tells the audience about various fields. Knowledge through television plays a special role in the career of children and young adult. The knowledge propagated by the television shows essentiality in their life. Television provides wide variety of knowledge which helps the children and young adults to develop their mind and conceptions. It took them beyond their class room and academic lessons. The several contents of the television reflect moral values of life which socialise the children and the young adults.

Along with Doordarshan various private satellite channels reflects panoramic view of various knowledge. Television channels like 'HISTORY CHANNEL', 'DISCOVERY CHANNEL', 'NATIONAL GEOGRAPHY', 'DISCOVERY SCIENCE', 'ANIMAL PLANETS' are spontaneously broadcasting various programmes related to science, geography, history, art and culture. Geographical and financial barriers are no longer creating problems, as satellite television bringing these programmes directly among the audience. Television is also widely propagating knowledge about various professional fields in a wonderful manner among society. Youth who are attracted from these channels are getting benefited by gaining knowledge of various fields.

TELEVISION AND THE CREATION OF HEALTH AWARENESS

Television has taken a significant role in the creation of health awareness. Television is an effective electronic mass media playing a vital role in the propagation of information related to health awareness. While dealing with the health awareness campaign through television, Indian television channels have shown a dominant nationalistic ideology of public service. Indian television channels desperately try to give public service for the benefit of not only the youth but also for the entire society. In 1975, the case study of India's Satellite Instructional Television Experiment (SITE) has shown programme broadcasted on Health and Family Planning along with Educational and Agricultural Programme. The health programme of the SITE Experiment mainly focuses on medical aid for the delivery of babies, improvement in health and nutrition, creation of awareness about health issues, health knowledge, where as the main aim of the family planning programme was how to reduce the birth rate, the adaption of vasectomy and to propagate the knowledge about the benefit of a small family.

Television was also used by various private satellite channels to create health awareness among the viewers. The case study of Sony Picture Network along with Viacom 18 youth channel MTV shows how satellite channel starts a campaign against HIV/AIDS on World AIDS day – (Best Media Info, 2016). They provide moral support for the patients who are affected by the deadly virus and create awareness about the deadly diseases. The campaign of Pulse polio in India is another case study showing the role of television in health awareness. Pulse Polio campaign was initiated by the Government of India to eradicate Poliomyelitis from India. The programme was supported by World Health Organisation and UNICEF – (Wikipedia. Pulse Polio, 2021). The Indian veteran actor Amitabh Bachchan became associated with the programme and played a role in the public service television advertisement of the Pulse Polio. In 2008, The Tobacco Control Cell along with The Ministry of Health and Family Welfare presented a public service advertisement on television "The Child Stop Smoking" which tries to create awareness among the cigarette smoker about the harmful and negative effects of smoking. In 2010, the Ministry of Health and Family Welfare presented an anti-tobacco campaign through a testimonial public service television advertisement, revolving around a twenty-four year old young man, called "Mukesh" who became the victim of cancer due to the consumption of tobacco. The advertisement tries to create awareness about the harmful effect of tobacco and instruct the youth and the society not to use any tobacco products for the maintenance of good health- (Ghosh, 2012).

Television also proved beneficial for the children and young adults. Most of the children and young adults spend a big time in watching television. They directly learn from various programmes several healthy style of living. Television suggests them several tips for healthy and joyful life. Several children and young adults are now over weight due to consumption of unhealthy food and without physical activities and yoga. Several Indian television channels are now broadcasting various programmes on fitness and yoga for the benefit of children and young adults. Television also shows impact on food habits. A research study shows children who watched a child oriented cooking show featuring healthy food found 2.7 times more likely to make a healthy food choice than those who watch a different episode of the same show featuring unhealthy food (Ochsner Health, 2020). Television is also being used by governments and various private organisations especially for the health awareness of children and young adults.

During the days of COVID-19 pandemic, Indian television actively propagate various news stories related to COVID-19, the corona virus and the safety precautions from COVID-19. Their impact on the public was in the highest form. Governmental and several non-governmental organisations used television to propagate information for public awareness about COVID-19 and corona virus. In the initial days of the outbreak of COVID-19, television started to inform how COVID-19 is spreading among the public, source of transmission, Symptom of COVID-19 and various precautions and preventive measures such as staying home staying safe, using mask and gloves, frequently washing hands with soap, using high alcohol based sanitizer for hand sanitising. All this information propagated by television tried to create health awareness among the society.

TELEVISION AND THE PROGRESS OF CULTURAL PROMOTION

India is a democratic secular nation which consists of various religion and diverse culture. Each Indian state has its own culture which is different from the culture of the other states in numerous ways. Along with the culture, every religion that exists in India also shows its own tradition and customs. The fusion of these cultures, traditions and customs became the strength of India. Cultures and traditions are the heritage of the society and the cultural programmes are the programme that reflects in front of the society about the heritage of culture and traditions. These cultural programmes refresh the youth and society mainly with the traditional classical forms of art, dance and music. Television on the other hand became a vital medium that promotes and presents these cultural elements and traditions through various programmes. Television highlights the Indian culture and displays it in front of the entire world. The cultural programme that is broadcasted through television encourages the youth to get involved with the cultural programme to continue the tradition.

Television promotes culture among the children and young adults. It reflects in front of the children and young adults the culture maintained for thousands of years through an audio visual panoramic view. Several histories based cultural programmes focus on the art and the flawless architecture of various ancient statues, monuments, temples, monasteries, and ancient universities. The programmes reflect excellent flawless architectural works of ancient India. On the other cultural classical programmes mainly focus on traditional dance and music which signifies the interest of India in classical art. The projection of these programmes in front of the children and young adults help them to understand the age old culture and tradition of India and pursue them to continue it.

Prasar Bharati and Doordarshan show interest in the cultural promotion. In various channels of Doordarshan, cultural programmes are broadcasted. They exhibit various cultural dances, folk songs, musical programmes, Indian novels and dramas that highlight Indian culture, tradition and customs. Doordarshan also shows concern with various Indian films that depict Indian culture. In satellite channels like STAR PLUS and STAR JALSA, several serial and programmes are putting the focus on the culture of Indian families, and various other Indian social norms and issues. Star groups create serial like 'Kyunki Saas

Bhi Kabhi Bahu Thi', 'Kahaani Ghar Ghar Kii', 'Siya Ke Ram' that display Indian culture, mythology and customs. Television turns into a vital medium of cultural promotion not only within the nation but also across the globe.

TELEVISION, CULTURAL IMPERIALISM AND THE INDIANISATION OF THE MEDIA CONTENT

The contents of the Indian television also give wide exposure to the Western culture. The Western cultures are propagated through Indian television channels, deriving Indians far from their own tradition and forcing them to adopt a new tradition and customs. The younger generation of twenty first century started to adopt the Western likes and dislikes, even in several cases, it was seen that teenagers prefer to speak in some foreign language among their groups rather than their own mother language which highlights that the Indian youth shifts from their own tradition and culture. The content of the satellite television channel playing a vital role in this change, from news programmes to various musical programmes all are dominated by the Western style. Most news channels prefer that anchors should perform in front of the camera in a Western gentleman outfit. The anchors of various musical programmes always try to imitate the Hip Hop culture of Western nations. These Western influences act as a 'Cultural Dopes' for the youth and the Indian society. It tries to change the native tradition and produce a hybrid culture which Ronald Robertson defines as 'Glocalization' – (Robertson,), which means the merge of global culture with local tradition.

The impacts of the Western culture are developing several new trends among the youth. The dress code and behaviour of teenagers are changing; they start to prefer Western outfits such as jeans, t-shirt, sneakers to traditional Indian outfits. Moreover in verbal communication they also use words like "Hi", "Hello" in the phatic phase of communication and depart with words like "Bye", "See You". The impact does not restrict within the trends. It also has effect on food habits. The younger generation highly prefers entering Pizza Hut, KFC, McDonald's and in various restaurants for foreign and intercontinental foods.

After the invasion of the Western culture through mass media, Indian audience started to realise the impact of cultural imperialism. The audience and the government immediately try to obstruct all the negative aspects of the Western influence after absorbing the positive ones. In 1991, the Vardhan Committee suggested only ten percent of the total time of the programmes should be foreign in nature and the remaining should be nationalise in character – (Kumar. K. J, 2007). Later in 1995, Ram Vilas Paswan Committee also highlighted about foreign programmes and their influence. It was clearly noted that based on the recommendation of various committees, private satellite channels started to telecast programmes with national sentiments. In satellite channels including STAR PLUS, several programmes put focus on the culture of Indian families, and various other Indian social norms and issues. Even the hip hop Hindi remix songs also started to convert into a nationalise one. It was a mark of 'Indianisation'. Songs like "Made in India" by Alisha Chinai put a mark of nationality on Indian remix song later A.R.Rahamann remixed and composed the famous patriotic song "Vandaa Ma Taramm" which also reflects the nationality and patriotism. The Indian producer on those days also produces Indian super hero like 'SHAKTIMAN' which was telecasted through a serial programme with a same name in Doordarshan. Cartoon channels also started to present Indian cartoon characters like 'Chota Bheem' 'Krishna', 'Tanali Raman' instead of foreign characters like Mickey Mouse or Donald Duck.

CONCLUSION

The ideology reflected through the broadcasting of Indian television system is highly social and developmental in nature. The apolitical television broadcasting mainly focuses on the development of the youth and the development of the society. The ultimate objective is the overall social development of the nation. Television broadcasting has been widely used to bring social changes throughout the nation. In this article, the wide discussion of the role of television in information dissemination, education propagation, development of the knowledge society, creation of health awareness and the progress of cultural promotion signify that television plays a significant role in various fields of social development. The ideology of social development benefits the public of all classes of the Indian society who decode information from television. Along with the entire society, the ideology of social development proves highly beneficial especially for the growth of the children and the young adults. They are openly receiving various data, information, knowledge and culture learning directly from the television which helping them to develop in various ways. The ideology of social development in the field of television broadcasting plays a vital role in the overall progress of the nation which transforming India into a new modern society.

REFERENCES

Banerjee, I., & Seneviratne, K. (2005). *Public Service Broadcasting: A Best Practices Source Book*. UNESCO.

Baran, S. J., & Davis, D. K. (2010). *Mass Communication Theory: Foundations, Ferment and Future*. Wadsworth Cengage Learning.

Best Media Info. (2016). *TV Channels create awareness about AIDS*. Retrieved from https://bestmediainfo.com/2016/12/tv-channels-create-awareness-about-aids/

David, R. (2020). *India Confirm its first corona virus case*. CNBC. https://www.cnbc.com/2020/01/30/india-confirms-first-case-of-the-coronavirus.html

DD News. (n.d.). *About us*. Retrieved from http://ddnews.gov.in/about/about-us

Freeden, M. (2003). *Ideology: A Very Short Introduction*. Oxford University Press. doi:10.1093/actrade/9780192802811.001.0001

Ghosh. (2012). *Dead son face of anti – cancer fight, family lives in penury*. Retrieved from http://archive.indianexpress.com/news/dead-son-face-of-anticancer-fight-family-lives-in-penury/1049922/1

Hebbar, N. (2020). P.M. Modi announces 21- day lockdown as COVID-19 toll touches 12. *The Hindu*. https://www.thehindu.com/news/national/pm-announces-21-day-lockdown-as-covid-19-toll-touches-10/article31156691.ece

IMDB. (n.d.). *All Shows of Star Plus*. Retrieved from https://m.imdb.com/list/ls021951507

IndiaNetzone. (2013). *History of Private Television in India*. Retrieved from https://www.indianetzone.com/42/history_private_television_india.htm

Kumar, K. J. (2007). *Mass Communication in India*. Jaico Publication House.

Mehta, N. (2008). *India on Television: How Satellite News Channel have Changed the Way We Think and Act?* Harper Collins.

News, D. D. (2020). *Actor Amitabh Bachchan shares precautionary measures on Coronavirus*. Retrieved from http://ddnews.gov.in/videos/health/actor-amitabh-bachchan-shares-precautionary-measures-corona-virus

Ochsner Health. (2020). *How TV can Help Kids Eat Healthy Foods*. Retrieved from https://blog.ochsner.org/articles/how-tv-can-help-kids-eat-healthy-foods

Robertson, R. (n.d.). *Glocalization: Time-Space and Homogeneity-Hetrogeneity*. https://warwick.ac.uk/fac/arts/history/students/modules/hi31v/syllabus/week18/robertson-1995.pdf

Wikipedia. (2021a). *DD News*. Retrieved from https://en.m.wikipedia.org/wiki/DD_ News

Wikipedia. (2021b). *Pulse Polio*. Retrieved from https://en.wikipedia.org/wiki/Pulse_Polio

Chapter 8
Human Development and Advocacy Journalism in the Spotlight:
Evidence From a Developing Country

Muhammad Yousaf
University of Gujrat, Gujrat, Pakistan

Syed Hassan Raza
https://orcid.org/0000-0002-1318-7818
Bahauddin Zakariya University, Multan, Pakistan

Shafiq Ahmad Kamboh
University of the Punjab, Lahore, Pakistan

ABSTRACT

In contemporary media-saturated societies, media exercise a considerable influence on every aspect of our lives. The issues that reach public consciousness become significant and consequently exhibit more potential to influence the public policymaking process. Advocacy journalism carries a great potential to advocate human development issues to policymakers. This chapter reviews the role of advocacy journalism in human development journalism practices in a developing country such as Pakistan. It is not a comprehensive survey of the factors associated with media coverage of human development issues; instead, it offers empirical insight into the role of media in human development.

INTRODUCTION

The Millennium Development Goals (hereafter MDGs) identified certain human development spheres, including human capital, infrastructure and human rights, that is necessary to raise the quality of life (Bedriñana, Martín, & Añaños, 2021; Das, 2018). Scholars affirmed a critical role of media in achieving

DOI: 10.4018/978-1-6684-4107-7.ch008

the MDG's through adopting advocacy journalism practices (Kamboh & Yousaf, 2020). The advocacy journalism paradigm suggests media coverage to immerse stories to aid human development goals through fostering societal changes (ElAlfy, Darwish, & Weber, 2020). However, mainstream media coverage remains limited in reporting facts instead of implementing advocacy journalism while covering human development issues (Alvares, Cardoso, Crespo, & Pinto-Martinho, 2021; Charles, 2019). To embark upon human development goals, a transformation of mainstream media journalistic practices has been observed in the form of advocacy journalism (Williams Fayne, 2021). This paradigm has shifted the locus of journalism from captivating sides to tap what creates news stories (Laursen & Trapp, 2021). To this point, advocacy journalism revolutionizes the journalistic practices and necessities participation of the audience. Compared to the traditional media practices that are limited to reporting the mere facts, this genre of journalism guides how to find and act-oriented engagement of the audience. In this way, advocacy journalism serves as an alternative model of journalistic practices to enhance people's engagement in human development issues (Pearson, 2021). This emerging advocacy model gradually counters mainstream media news values and influences journalistic practices. As such, the reliance of the advocacy journalists moves into profoundly transformed journalistic practices focusing on human development issues instead of objectivity (Charles, 2013). Previous understandings of the news values in reporting human development issues are now in question. For example, do delineation facts in a news story regarding human development can accomplish the objective of people engagement? Scholars (e.g., Charles, 2013; Pearson 2021) affirmed that advocacy journalistic arguably had shifted away from mainstream media objectivity and new values into more ethical and action-oriented practices (Peuchaud, 2021).

In this standard, media plays an imperative role in the change and development of society by engaging people with stories. Advocacy journalism encourages public participation, so it can be applied to improve a country's human development landscape. In this regard, Roger noted, "a participatory process of social change in a society, intended to bring about both social and martial advancement (including greater equality, freedom, and other valued qualities) for the majority of the people through their gaining greater control over their environment" (Roger, 1978, p. 68). Several studies have acknowledged a strong correlation between media and human development in societies (Lerner, 1958; Lerner & Schramm, 1967; Schramm, 1964). Some of these studies treat media as an independent variable that plays a crucial role in development. The amount of communication correlates with the level of development in society (Lerner & Schramm, 1967; Schramm, 1964).

In contrast, other studies outline that media were necessary to change the traditional values customs of the traditional Middle Eastern societies. It was found that the traditional values and habits of these societies were inconsistent with the Western-centered values; therefore, communication was an essential factor to transform the values and bring them in conformity with the western values to make the development process smoothly take place in these societies (Lerner, 1958). However, this Western-oriented modernization paradigm failed to bring any significant change and bridge the gap in poverty in developing countries. Another reason was that development was not only based on amount and knowledge but also ethos, values and religion. Therefore, new inclusive and participatory approaches such as Human Development from 1990, the Millennium Development Goals (MDGs) in 2000 and the Sustainable Development Goals (SDGs) in 2015 were introduced and propagated (UNESCO, 2015). Although these studies have pointed out different reasons for the failure of the modern paradigm, however, these all studies shared a common conclusion that the western paradigm of modernizing the underdeveloped countries did not meet the desired targets and is dead (McAnany, 1978; Moemeka, 1994; Parker, 1978;

Porat, 1978; Rogers, 1978). The modern paradigm failed because it was one way from, i.e., center to the periphery, had inherent epistemological bias and intellectual ethnocentrism. Moreover,

ADVOCACY JOURNALISM

Advocacy journalism refers to the media practitioners' active role in interpreting and participating in the voices of marginalized groups and speaking on behalf of them (Charles, 2019; Laws & Chojnicka, 2020). In this sort of journalism, the journalist becomes the voice of those less representative people in the mainstream media (Alvares et al., 2021). Hence, some media practitioners represent their issues and intervene to protect their developmental interests for the reparation of power disparities in society and media (Williams Fayne, 2021). This paradigm is derived from the "campaigner instinct" to endorse standpoints that are characteristically below or untouched in the media coverage. For instance, people with disabilities are less represented in the media. In comparison, advocacy journalists shed light on their sufferings and issues (Fisher, 2018).

Similarly, media stereotyping towards several groups is an instance of media representation (Raza, Zaman, & Iftikhar, 2021). Thereby, scholars have noted that the advocacy journalistic paradigm is contradictory to the gatekeeping paradigm, wherein the concept of journalistic practices is directed by the principles of objectivity (e.g., facts) (Alvares et al., 2021; Fisher, 2016; Peuchaud, 2021). In typology, advocacy journalists work with the communities rather than only relying on the facts. Thus, advocacy journalism encounter media routines through interpreting and representing the marginalized or less representative groups.

Historically, advocacy journalism seems in an extent of research and is applied in a wide-ranging setting (Charles, 2013). Primarily, specific attributes are devoted to advocacy journalism, namely; (1) specific media reporting style, (2) subjective reporting of the story and (3) engagement of the audience (Alvares et al., 2021; Charles, 2019). These attributes make advocacy journalism a form of journalism devoted to promoting specific political, societal and community causes. Henceforth, advocacy journalism has been deliberated as an opposing viewpoint of the objective media coverage model (Fisher, 2016; Laws & Chojnicka, 2020). The traditional prevailing media journalistic routines are curious to find the facts to remain objective. However, that legacy has been entirely shifted towards adopting new journalistic practices whereby media coverage somehow becomes subjective by incorporating viewpoints of the less representative groups (Laursen & Trapp, 2021). In this way, the detachment of the journalists with the event has been rectified to foster social change.

The literature underlined that the dominant practices of journalism involved a dependence model practiced by the news organizations (Fisher, 2016; Pearson, 2021). This dominant media content and routines model is highly reliant **on** external factors such as governments or business organizations. Therefore, such media practices have also been criticized owing to the anti-professionalism viewpoint that somehow supports and watches the benefits of the government or business at the expense of critical societal issues (Pearson, 2021). However, the neo-communication environment has facilitated advocacy journalism due to its distinct base on several factors; (1) multiple information sources, (2) availability of multiple free platforms such as digital media, and (3) emergence of the mindful audience (Charles, 2019; Laursen & Trapp, 2021). The aforementioned factors altogether promote advocacy journalism beyond prejudice and merely enchanting sides. To illustrate, the audience has become more resourceful in terms of cross-checking the facts and increasingly, social media usage is making them more aware of communal issues (Iftikhar & Yousaf, 2021). In this situation where the audience is more mindful, advocacy journalism has emerged as a new phenomenon by becoming the people's voice. Therefore, the obstructive viewpoints about advocacy journalism to support the objectivity news media model are also seemingly turn out to be a false dichotomy (Alvares et al., 2021).

Furthermore, Fisher (2016) also outlined aspects that can impact advocacy journalism's outcome (e.g., story). She noted that the advocacy stories are under certain conations that can be influenced and become "understated" or "evident" because of organizational or individual situations. Therefore, these conditions can contrarily shape journalistic advocacy practices in different regions of the world. For example, in the global south, the dominant idea of advocacy journalism is resistance towards the government. In contrast, a widespread practice in an authoritarian state is taking the side of the ideas related to autonomy and human rights. Certain advocacy practices have been delineated in more detail in the next section.

PRACTICES OF ADVOCACY JOURNALISM

Advocacy journalism is the most recent perspective among more inclusive and multidimensional approaches. It is "a broad church of subjective forms of reporting that promote social issues and causes" (Firmstone, 2019, p. 714). In other words, it adopts a non-objective viewpoint to promote social issues with a targeted purpose in mind. Media advocacy intends to increase coverage of social issues such as tobacco and is a source of providing a platform to ordinary public voices (Stillman, Cronin, Evans, & Ulasevich, 2001). Waisbord (2009) categorized the advocacy journalism model into "advocate-journalist" and "civic model of advocacy journalism" (p. 371). In the advocate journalist model, journalists speak on behalf of voiceless and powerless segments of the society as a spokesperson to address inequality injustice for the underrepresented segments of the society (Janowitz, 1975, p. 619). According to Janowitz, this model is different from the gatekeeping concept guided by the spirit of objective criterion to choose news for publication. In the latter, organized groups use the news media to get sufficient space and voice for the issues vis-à-vis mobilization to get government attention to address the issues. However, the advocate journalist model is not meeting its normative role in the developing countries owning to many reasons. In Waisbord's conception, "as long as [Global Southern] governments and politicians continue to wield substantial power on press economies, news organizations are likely to act as vehicles for promoting their political interests" instead of following the notion of "journalists as social mobilizers" (Waisbord, 2009, p. 374). Thus, owing to these pressures and compulsions, media in developing countries fails to provide sufficient time and space to the issues of the voiceless ordinary public.

There exist different forms of advocacy journalism, including newspaper editorials. While establishing a link between advocacy and editorial journalism, Firmstone (2019, p.8) reported:

Although editorial journalism can be considered as a specific form of advocacy journalism, it is rarely theorized or empirically researched as such. Historically, editorial and advocacy journalism share an ethos for journalism that endeavors to effect social or political change.

ADVOCACY JOURNALISM PRACTICES IN PAKISTAN

According to the year 2019 Human Development Report, Pakistan's HDI value for 2018 is 0.560 (in the medium human development category), placing it at 152 out of 189 countries and territories and that ranks it lower than all other South Asian countries ("Human Development Index", 2019). This alarming situation is constantly persisting, which is evident from the data in Table 1.4 that reveals that growth in HDI value for the country has almost stagnated over the last five years.

However, despite this deplorable state of human development index, Pakistani print media keeps providing precious space to political, showbiz and other such issues instead of becoming a voice for the voiceless and marginalized segments of the society (Kamboh & Yousaf, 2020). Most of the media content focuses on conflicts in society, conflicts among politicians, showbiz and other such issues and neglect the human development issues at large such as education, health, environment, poverty (Hussain, 2000; Umber, 1999). A most comprehensive study conducted to explore the editorial coverage of human development and other issues concluded that print in Pakistan provides low to moderate coverage to human development issues compared to other tissues (Kamboh & Yousaf, 2020). More precisely, human development received (17.2%), (37.7%) on political issues, (30.4%), international relations (30.4%)), security issues ((10.9% and miscellaneous issues received (3.9%) editorials (pp. 653-654). In a more recent study, Kamboh, Ittefaq, and Yousaf (in press) concluded that media either failed to link environmental issues to the pandemic or ignored the environmental issues. These studies indicate that despite appalling statistics of human development issues, media gives negligible coverage to these issues. Most media coverage goes to internal and external political conflicts regarding conflict with India, Afghanistan, security issues, showbiz, sensational news, and sports. Writing about the plausible reason for this deplorable coverage of human development issues, Kamboh (2019) argued that universities syllabi are not practical oriented to orient the graduates with the significance of coverage of human development issues. He suggested a D-J-M model wherein he proposed that universities syllabi should be prepared by a team that is a blend of academicians, media professionals and development experts to instill the training to fresh graduates vis-à-vis these revised syllabi sensitize them to develop spirit for the coverage of human development issues. The literature mentioned above shows that media gives less coverage to human development issues than other issues. Therefore, based on the preceding review, we proposed three research questions:

Research Questions

RQ1: Was there a difference between editorial coverage of human development issues and other issues among Pakistani newspapers during the first time period (T1)?

RQ2: Was there a difference in the number of editorials coverage of human development issues and other issues among Pakistani newspapers during the second period (T2)?

RESEARCH DESIGN

This study used a longitudinal research design to track the change in the proportion of editorials published in two different periods. A quantitative content analysis method was used to accomplish the analysis. For data collection, we selected the editorial contents of two mainstream newspapers, one from each

Figure 1. Models of advocacy journalism described by Waisbord (2009)

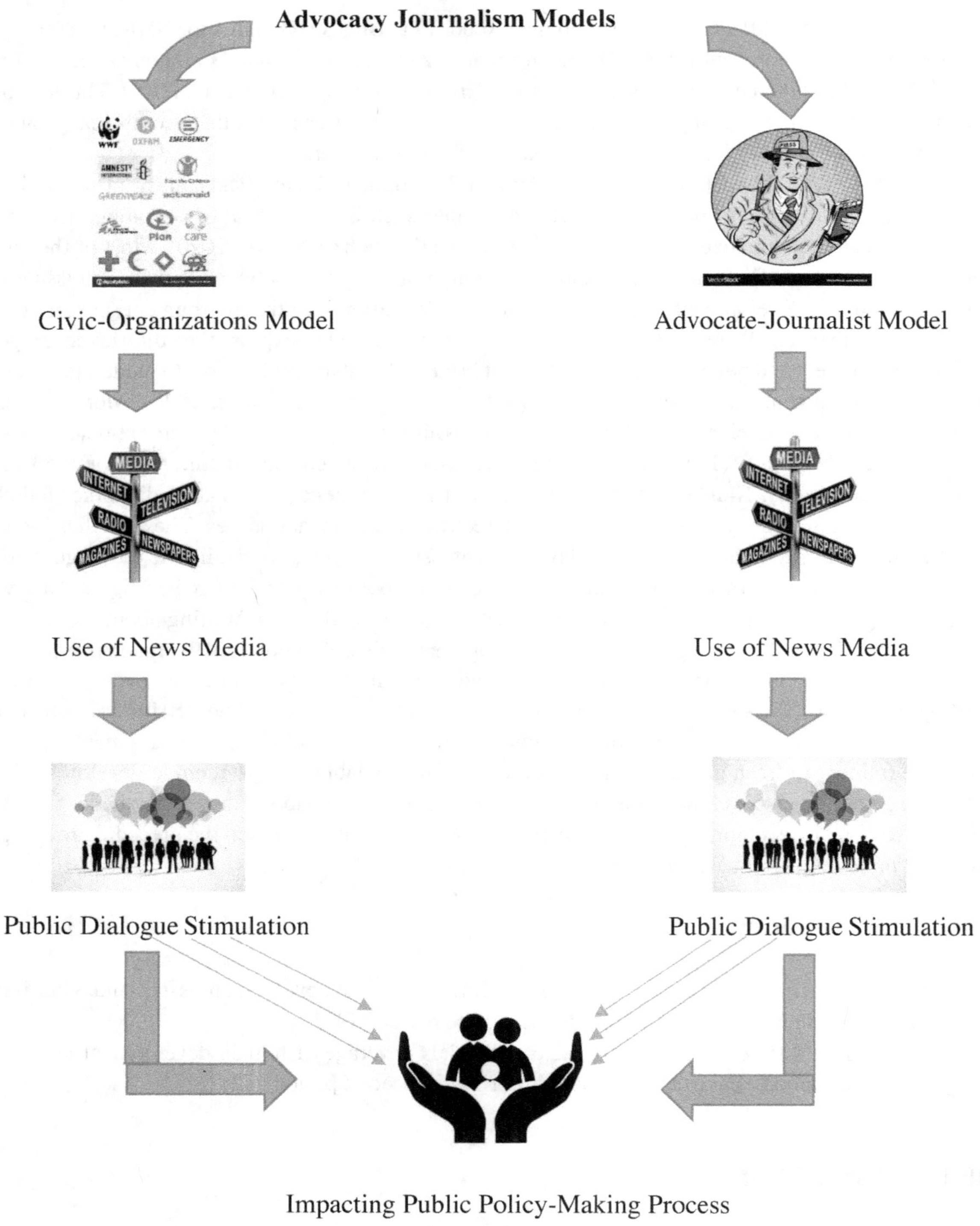

Table 1. Yearly human development trends (Pakistan)

Year	HDI Value	Ranking	Category
2014	0.546	148 out of 188 countries	Low
2015	0.550	147 out of 188 countries	Medium
2016	0.556	149 out of 189 countries	Medium
2017	0.558	150 out of 189 countries	Medium
2018	0.560	152 out of 189 countries	Medium
2019	0.557	154 out of 189 countries	Medium

Note. Human Development Data (1990-2018), Retrieved from https://hdr.undp.org/en/data

Urdu and English press. These newspapers are considered representative of Urdu and English medium newspapers in the country. We selected Daily Dunya among Urdu newspapers and daily Dawn among English newspapers.

Though Firmstone (2019, p.8) has underlined a few differences between editorial and advocacy journalism as well, this study considers the 'editorialists' as 'advocate-journalists' because the term advocacy journalism is not as clearly defined in the scholarship as concepts such as gatekeeping or agenda-setting. Moreover, Pakistani editorialists have historically been known for taking the role of 'advocate-journalists' right from the period of the Indian Independence movement (Jensen, 2008).

We adopted the categories scheme developed by Kamboh and Yousaf (2020). The content was categorized into five operationalized categories. The complete editorial was considered as a unit of analysis. The analysis is divided into two time periods. The first period was between July 2015-30 June 2016, and the second time period selected was August 2018-18 August 2019. There was a rationale for selecting these two time periods for the analysis. For instance, during the time period, Sustainable Development Goals (SDGs) were introduced by UNESCO. The second time is significant because a pro-human development government came into power in Pakistan. Therefore, it is vital to investigate the newspaper's editorialists' attitude towards human development issues vis-a-vis other issues advocated in the editorials published in the selected newspapers.

We used Scott's pi to measure intercoder reliability for the time period (T1) and time period (T2). For the T1, a coding of 100 editorials produced Scott's pi of between .77 and .90, with the following ranges: human development issues (between .78 and .87); international relations and issues (between .77 and .84); Security operations issues (between .78 and .81), State and political parties' policy issues (between .80 and .89), and miscellaneous (between .80 and .83). Similarly, for the T2, coding of the same amount of editorials produced Scott's pi of between .77 and .91, with the following ranges: human development issues (between .85 and .89); international relations and issues (between .79 and .82); Security operations issues (between .78 and .84), State and political parties' policy issues (between .81 and .90), and miscellaneous (between .78 and .86).

RESULTS

We analyzed 3,745 editorials to answer selected research questions. In the first place, this study through RQ1 aimed primarily to compare five major content categories to explore the difference in editorial

Table 2. Five categories and their definitions

Categories	Definitions
A: Human development	This category includes the issues such as public health, environment, religious intolerance, drinking water, food safety, malnutrition-related issues, poverty, unemployment, increasing inflation rate, energy, population planning, gender, and social injustice, etc.
B: International Relations and Issues	It contains editorials relating to Pakistan's foreign policy issues, including conflicts and agreements with other countries. It also includes editorials that referred to such issues in other countries having either no direct relevance to or suggesting an indirect lesson for Pakistan.
Security operations issues	It contains editorials advocating Pakistan military-led counter security operations/measures being carried out as per The National Action Plan of 2015 (NAP) to eradicate terrorism, militancy and insurgency from various parts of the country.
State & political parties policy	This major category includes editorials published on the policy issues of state institutions and political parties advocating institutional reforms, good governance issues, constitutional, civil and democratic supremacy to keep the state/government/democracy/parties moving smoothly.
Miscellaneous	These editorials include those that deal with showbiz sports-related news.

Source: Kamboh & Yousaf (2020)

coverage between human development issues and other issues. The ultimate findings indicate that the human development category (A) issues were among those which received the least attention by the editorial boards of mainstream Pakistani newspapers. The highest number of editorials were published on state and political parties' policy issues (category D); followed by international relations and issues (category B).

Although the editorial writers started publishing more content on human development issues during the second time period, the overall coverage of human development issues (the mean of both time periods) still seems inadequate, particularly when it comes to comparing with the category B and D issues coverage against the backdrop of carrying bad human development indicators for the last many years.

A comparison of Urdu and English newspapers in terms of giving editorial coverage to various content categories shows that both language newspapers almost equally ignored to address human development issues, with the exception of daily *Dawn that* gave a slightly higher significance to such issues than their Urdu counterpart. Contrarily, both selected newspapers gave equal and fair coverage to security operations issues, particularly during the first time period. Interestingly, the selected English newspaper (daily Dawn) dedicated more editorial space to the country's internal issues (i.e., on category A, category C and category D issues) than the Urdu language newspaper Daily Dunya, which conversely gave more significance to the external world issues (i.e., category B issues). It looks as despite carrying the persistently bad HDI value (which is evident from the data in Table 1) and being a major recipient of the negative repercussions of global climate change (Eckstein et al., 2019), Pakistani advocate-journalists (editorial writers) still consider terrorism and associated issues a much bigger threat to the existence of the country.

Secondly, this study aimed to find the change in editorial agenda with the change in policy agenda. Eventually, the data reveal that both language newspapers have increased editorial content on human development issues with the arrival of influential agenda-builders in power. Additionally, the data further shows that the decrease in the editorial content on category C issues (owing to the end of military operations) and category B issues (owing to relatively smoother relations with the neighbors) during the second time period also contributed to improving coverage on human development category (A) issues.

Table 3. Comparison between the newspapers and issues of five content categories in T1

Newspaper	Human development T1	International Relations T1	Security operations issues T1	State and political parties policy issues T1	Other T1	Total
Dawn	206	264	124	468	15	1077
Dunya	142	203	111	255	8	719
Total	348	467	235	723	23	1,796

Table 3 shows the number of editorials published on the five given categories in the first period. Overall, *Dawn*, the English newspaper, published more editorials on the given five categories than *Dunya*, the Urdu newspaper. It indicates that the number of editorials published on human development issues is less than published on international relations and state political parties policy issues. Of 1.796 editorials published during the first time period, only 348 (19.4%) were written on human development issues, and the remaining (80.6%) were published on the other issues.

In contrast, the number of editorials published on human development during the send time period improved compared to the first time period. Of 1,949 editorials published during the second period, 661 (33.9%) were written on human development issues. Put it differently; there was a 14.5% increase in the proportion of editorials during this period.

Table 4. Comparison between the newspapers and issues of five content categories in T2

Newspaper	Human development T2	International Relations T2	Security operations issues T2	State and political parties policy issues T2	Other T2	Total
Dawn	335	227 (21.2%)	64	433	12	1071
Dunya	326	117 ()	23	406	6	878
Total	661	344	87	839	18	1,949

It indicates that the government agenda influenced the media agenda during the second period. Moreover, Urdu and English newspapers differed in terms of their editorials on human development issues.

DISCUSSION

The present study's findings reveal contemporary Pakistani advocacy journalism trends (i.e., in terms of not adequately covering human development issues unless such issues come on the policy agenda and with their inter-media agenda differences between Urdu and English newspapers) seem under the influence of several factors. Let us discuss those factors in light of the hierarchy of influence model.

Individual-Level Influences

At the most micro level, the individual level assumes that news content is affected by the individual workers' personal characteristics and traits, including their educational and professional background, their motivation level, the news values they adhere to, their personal attitudes, values and beliefs towards mass media discourse, and their demographic features (Shoemaker & Reese, 1996:59–99). While quoting a working journalist's views, Jamil (2020, p.281) reported a similar observation in her study:

Journalists' knowledge about issues of development is very important. Higher Education Commission of Pakistan (HEC) and major public-sector universities (like Karachi, Punjab and Peshawar Universities) do not pay attention to revising their curriculum regularly. Consequently, the courses on Development Communication that are taught to journalism students in these universities are not enough to train them for understandably reporting on complex issues for their readers or audience.

Several existing studies also reveal that the media content production process has to face many challenges from journalists' individual-level background, demographics, traits, and characteristics in the Pakistani context. In this regard, Jamil and Appiah-Adjei (2020: 98-99) highlighted an important aspect of gender difference as:

gender plays a crucial role in deciding challenges related to the journalistic practice in Pakistan, and specifically to combat the problem of reporting reliable information to the public amid pandemics. There is a huge dominance of male journalists in the Pakistani news media, which deprives female journalists of coming forward to communicate pandemic-related information and preventive measures to women and keep them away from false cures and unreliable information. When talking about how journalists' gender influences their ability to deal with disinfodemic, a female journalist highlights: In Pakistan, there is a significant problem of women's and girls' access to accurate information, which is often restricted in the country's rural and tribal areas.

While revealing the role of journalists' educational background, Jamil and Appiah-Adjei (2020: 99) stated that:

In addition to gender, this study finds that a lack of journalists' education in science journalism and their training to filter reliable information deprives Pakistani people of access to verified information about COVID-19 disease. "We do not have science journalists in Pakistan. Journalists are not trained to handle infodemic and disinfodemic in the country. Unintentionally, they may share inaccurate facts", states a news producer from a private television news channel.

In this perspective, Ejaz et al. (2021, p. 10) further added the lack of science-oriented knowledge background of Pakistani journalists in negatively impacting the journalistic content on environmental issues in Pakistan as:

At an individual level, this study finds that except for a few respondents (5), most journalists lack the domain-specific knowledge required to cover the complex issue of climate change. It could be because all participants in this study have qualifications related to journalism, whereas none has educational background concerning climate and environment sciences. Hence, this lack of relevant expertise significantly influences the news content on environmental issues in Pakistan.

Ejaz et al. (2021, p. 11) found the role of individual journalist's heightened motivation level in media content production as a critical factor, despite having limited domain-specific knowledge and lack of training to report some development-related issues:

Regarding personal motivation, 20 respondents have expressed that they began covering climate issues owing to their interest, whereas one was assigned to report on environmental stories. Thus, their affective affiliation to the issue has often influenced their content in various ways, including their choice of medium, news format, and time they are willing to spend on each story. One veteran journalist narrated his reason as I belong to the Thar desert (a rural and economically less developed area in Sindh province) and bear witness to the actual consequences of climate change because it has made my family migrate three times in the last few years. This personal experience has shaped my identity as a climate journalist, which reflects in my coverage.

In this connection, Ittefaq et al. (2021, p. 9) added a few other journalists concerns, for instance:

the lack of resources for training to integrate media convergence into the industry in Pakistan. Journalists explained that a lack of training has made their jobs difficult because of the extra pressure of self-learning they feel is required to be able to produce content for different and distinct media platforms. However, despite voicing all of these concerns, the journalists recognized they continue to work under such conditions because the alternative to compliance is the scary thought of unemployment.

Routine-Level Influences

Journalistic routines are defined as "patterned, routinized, repeated practices, and forms that media workers use to do their jobs" (Shoemaker and Reese, 1995:105) and include, for example, *news sourcing practices*, *news values*, *priority given to news*, *gatekeeping*, *selection patterns of more profit-oriented content*, *audience appeal* and many others (Shoemaker & Reese, 1996, p. 100–132; Tandoc and Duffy, 2019).

Findings of the previous studies undertaken in the Pakistani context also reveal those news routines substantially impact local news content. While quoting an example of selecting more profit-oriented content, commonly practiced news routines in Pakistan that eventually affect the work of local environmental journalists, Ejaz et al. (2021, p. 11) revealed that:

climate reporting is a very resource and time-intensive beat. Therefore, the restriction of both does not allow them to pursue stories in-depth and in non-urban areas, e.g., in the remote Hindu Kush Mountain range where climate change is rapidly changing the landscape (Mayewski et al. 2020) or the rural areas of Punjab that once had abundant water but now is experiencing frequent droughts (Ali et al. 2020).

In this connection, Kamboh et al. (2021, para 8) presented a case from local health settings, where journalists routinely prefer to pick and translate stories from Western media houses due to Pakistani media owners' ineptitude to produce any local content:

This analysis of weaker local science journalism culture looks quite relevant because instead of generating local content on various ongoing clinical trials of Chinese COVID-19 vaccines and current national rollout in Pakistan concerning their safety, efficacy and side effects; or including insight of local vaccine experts on incidents of adverse effects abroad, Urdu language newspapers are merely preferring to pick, translate and report such content from foreign sources.

In this perspective, Nguyen and Tran (2019:979) further added that:

Research in Asia and Africa has found over the years that science-related topics are allocated comparatively little space and often used as space/time fillers, rarely as leading news items, and occasionally left out to give the space for last-minute paid advertisements (Dutt and Garg, 2012; Ekanem, 2003; Michael and Binta, 2013; Schanne et al., 2009). Not surprisingly, in that climate, dedicated science teams and sections are a 'luxury' in newsrooms. In Pakistan, Bangladesh, Nepal and Central America, the media see regular ups and downs, with continuous launches and closures of science sections and shows due to the lack of a professional will and/or financial support (Ahmed, 2005; Massarani, 2014; Patairiya, 2007).

Ejaz et al.'s (2021, p. 11), while interviewing local journalists, further added that due to the absence of new ideas and climate experts in Pakistan, working journalists have been left with no options but to deliberately follow the Western news sources and style of climate journalism:

While working on a story often feel that there is a dearth of Pakistani experts on an issue, or we have the same climate experts whom all the journalists are also quoting. Consequently, we have to seek opinions from international experts or read their work which often gives new ideas. This indicates that the climate journalism process in Pakistan relies on elite (experts and international) sources, Western-style journalism, and prescribed limitations regarding reporter's routine influence its coverage while reducing climate change to a very few areas and experts and limiting the public understanding of this very expansive issue.

Organizational Influences

The *organizational* level of influences is referred to the policies and economic imperatives of a media organization (Reese, 2019, p. 2) and include such factors, for instance, *the prime importance of financial goals, organizational policies* and *the owners' political and personal interests* (Shoemaker & Reese, 1996, p. 133–165).

Pakistani journalist fraternity has many concerns regarding media convergence policies of local cross-media owners. In this connection, Ittefaq et al. (2021, p. 9) has aptly summarised the hazards of Pakistan's current media convergence model.

By specifying the augmented expectation to submit a publish-ready news story simultaneously for different mediums, our interviewees noted that it has caused severe pressures and even forced many to quit the profession. A reporter from The News stated: 'management has used convergence as a cost-cutting tool rather than bringing innovation and quality to journalism'. Such perceptions mirror the findings of Hanitzsch et al. (2010), who argued that organizational policies are implemented to balance commercial and professional concerns and satisfy ownership and financial goals accordingly.

REFERENCES

Alvares, C., Cardoso, G., Crespo, M., & Pinto-Martinho, A. (2021). Seeking the Legitimation of Mainstream Journalism: A Portuguese Case-Study. *Journalism Practice*, 1–16. doi:10.1080/17512786.2021.2008808

Bedriñana, K. G. A., Martín, J. A. R., & Añaños, F. T. (2021). Human Rights in the Least Developed Countries of Asia: An Index for Quantifying Sustainable Development Goal 3 (Good Health and Wellbeing). *International Journal of Environmental Research and Public Health*, *18*(9), 4747. doi:10.3390/ijerph18094747 PMID:33946837

Charles, M. (2013). News, Documentary and Advocacy Journalism. In K. Fowler-Watt & S. Allan (Eds.), *Journalism: New Challenges* (pp. 384–392). Centre for Journalism and Communication Research: Bournemouth University.

Charles, M. (2019). Advocacy Journalism. In T. P. Vos & F. Hanusch (Eds.), *the International Encyclopedia of Journalism Studies* (pp. 1–5). John Wiley & Sons.

Das, S. (2018). Maternal health, human rights, and the politics of state accountability: Lessons from the Millennium Development Goals and implications for the Sustainable Development Goals. *Journal of Human Rights*, *17*(5), 550–567. doi:10.1080/14754835.2018.1496012

Eckstein, D., Künzel, V., Schäfer, L., & Winges, M. (2019). Global climate risk index 2020. *Germanwatch*. Available at https://germanwatch.org/en/17307

Ejaz, W., Ittefaq, M., & Arif, M. (2021). Understanding Influences, Misinformation, and Fact-Checking Concerning Climate-Change Journalism in Pakistan. *Journalism Practice*, 1–21. doi:10.1080/17512786.2021.1972029

ElAlfy, A., Darwish, K. M., & Weber, O. (2020). Corporations and sustainable development goals communication on social media: Corporate social responsibility or just another buzzword? *Sustainable Development, 28*(5), 1418-1430. doi:10.1002/sd.2095

Firmstone, J. (2019). Editorial journalism and newspapers' editorial opinions. In J. Nussbaum (Ed.), *Oxford Research Encyclopedia of Communication*. Oxford University Press. doi:10.1093/acrefore/9780190228613.013.803

Fisher, C. (2016). The advocacy continuum: Towards a theory of advocacy in journalism. *Journalism*, *17*(6), 711–726. doi:10.1177/1464884915582311

Fisher, C. (2018). News Sources and Journalist/Source Interaction. In J. F. Nussbaum (Ed.), *Oxford Research Encyclopedia of Communication* (pp. 1–18). Oxford Oxford University Press. doi:10.1093/acrefore/9780190228613.013.849

Human Development Index 2019: Pakistan ranks lower than all South Asian countries. (2019, December 13). *The News*. Retrieved from https://www.thenews.com.pk/print/582826

Iftikhar, M., & Yousaf, M. (2021). The Impact of Climate Change Coverage on Public Adherence towards Health Threat: An Empirical Validation of the Health Belief Model. *Sir Syed Journal of Education & Social Research*, *4*(2), 402–413. doi:10.36902jesr-vol4-iss2-2021(402-413)

Ittefaq, M., Ejaz, W., Fahmy, S. S., & Sheikh, A. M. (2021). Converged journalism: Practices and influences in Pakistan. *Media International Australia*, *181*(1), 167–182. doi:10.1177/1329878X211017329

Jamil, S., & Appiah-Adjei, G. (2020). Battling with infodemic and disinfodemic: The quandary of journalists to report on COVID-19 pandemic in Pakistan. *Media Asia*, *47*(3-4), 88–109. doi:10.1080/01296612.2020.1853393

Janowitz, M. (1975). Professional models in journalism: The gatekeeper and the advocate. *The Journalism Quarterly*, *52*(4), 618–626. doi:10.1177/107769907505200402

Jensen, R. (2008). *Advocacy journalism*. The International Encyclopaedia of Communication., doi:10.1002/9781405186407.wbieca029

Ji, D., Hu, Z., & Muhammad, Y. (2016). Neighboring competitor? Indian image in Chinese media. *Global Media and China*, *1*(3), 234–250. doi:10.1177/2059436416668186

Kamboh, S. A. (2019). Missing links in practical journalism in developing Pakistan. In B. Dernbach & B. Illg (Eds.), *Journalism and journalism education in developing countries* (pp. 157–168). Manipal University Press.

Kamboh, S. A., Ittefaq, M., & Sahi, A. A. (2021). Journalistic routines as factors promoting COVID-19 vaccine hesitancy in Pakistan. *Third World Quarterly*. Advance online publication. doi:10.1080/01436597.2021.1995713

Kamboh, S. A., Ittefaq, M., & Yousaf, M. (in press). COVID-19: A window of opportunity to influence environmental policies through media advocacy in global south. *International Journal of Communication*.

Kamboh, S. A., & Yousaf, M. (2020). Human development and advocacy journalism: Analysis of low editorial coverage in Pakistan. *Development Policy Review*, *38*(5), 646–663. doi:10.1111/dpr.12443

Laursen, B., & Trapp, N. L. (2021). Experts or advocates: Shifting roles of central sources used by journalists in news stories? *Journalism Practice*, *15*(1), 1–18. doi:10.1080/17512786.2019.1695537

Laws, N., & Chojnicka, J. (2020). "A Future to Believe in": Introducing Varieties of Advocacy Journalism. The Examples Sustainability and the Sanders Campaign. *Journalism Studies*, *21*(9), 1261–1283. doi:10.1080/1461670X.2020.1742773

Lerner, D. (1958). *The passing of traditional society: Modernizing the Middle East*. Free Press.

Lerner, D., & Schramm, W. L. (1967). *Communication and change in the developing countries*. East-West Center P. doi:10.1515/9780824885663

McAnany, E. G. (1978). Does Information Really Work? *Journal of Communication*, *28*(1), 84–90. doi:10.1111/j.1460-2466.1978.tb01568.x

Moemeka, A. A. (1994). Development communication: A historical and conceptual overview. In A. A. Moemeka (Ed.), *Communicating for development: A new pan-disciplinary perspective* (pp. 3–22). State University of New York Press.

Parker, E. B. (1978). An Information-Based Hypothesis. *Journal of Communication*, *28*(1), 81–83. doi:10.1111/j.1460-2466.1978.tb01567.x

Pearson, M. (2021). Global Justice, Factual Reporting and Advocacy Journalism. In S. J. A. Ward (Ed.), *Handbook of Global Media Ethics*. Springer. doi:10.1007/978-3-319-32103-5_30

Peuchaud, S. R. (2021). Objectivity, advocacy, and critical pedagogy in the race, gender, and media classroom: Individual, interpersonal, and structural tensions and recommendations. *Journalism*, *22*(2), 519–536. doi:10.1177/1464884918779943

Pitts, L. (2001, December 17). Objectivity might be impossible, so we strive for fairness. *Austin American Statesman*, p. A13.

Porat, M. U. (1978). Global Implications of the Information Society. *Journal of Communication*, *28*(1), 70–80. doi:10.1111/j.1460-2466.1978.tb01565.x

Raza, S. H., Zaman, U., & Iftikhar, M. (2021). Examining the Effects of Media-Generated Stereotypes on Receivers' Trust and Attitude in Pakistan. Moderating Influence of Ethnicity and Gender. *Information (Basel)*, *12*(1), 35. doi:10.3390/info12010035

Rogers, E. M. (1978). The Rise and Fall of the Dominant Paradigm. *Journal of Communication*, *28*(1), 64–69. doi:10.1111/j.1460-2466.1978.tb01564.x

Schramm, W. L. (1964). *Mass media and national development: The role of information in the developing countries*. University Press Stanford.

Shoemaker, P. J., & Reese, S. D. (1996). *Mediating the message: Theories of influences on mass media content* (2nd ed.). Longman.

Stillman, F. A., Cronin, K. A., Evans, W. D., & Ulasevich, A. (2001). Can media advocacy influence newspaper coverage of tobacco: Measuring the effectiveness of the American stop smoking intervention study's (ASSIST) media advocacy strategies. *Tobacco Control*, *10*(2), 137–144. doi:10.1136/tc.10.2.137 PMID:11387534

Tandoc, E. C. Jr, & Duffy, A. (2019). *Routines in Journalism*. Oxford Research Encyclopedia of Communication., doi:10.1093/acrefore/9780190228613.013.870

Waisbord, S. (2009). Advocacy journalism in a global context. In K. Wahl-Jorgensen & T. Hanitzsch (Eds.), *The handbook of journalism studies* (pp. 371–385). Routledge.

Williams Fayne, M. (2021). Advocacy journalism in the 21st century: Rethinking entertainment in digital Black press outlets. *Journalism*. doi:10.1177/14648849211023166

Yousaf, M., Rahman, B. H., & Yousaf, Z. (2020). Constructing reality: Framing of the Kashmir conflict in dictatorial and democratic regimes in the Pakistani English Press. *Media Watch*, *11*(3), 401–415. doi:10.15655/mw/2020/v11i3/203045

Chapter 9
Public Sphere, Development, and the Challenge of Media Censorship in a Dictatorial Democracy:
The African Dilemma

Thaddeus A. Oparah
Madonna University, Nigeria

Ejike Akpa
Madonna University, Nigeria

ABSTRACT

The post-independence mantra of most African states signaled a continent with varied ability to advance her developmental frontiers. However, this has remained elusive owing to many factors among which is the disillusionment with the 'public sphere' by the ruling class because the public sphere presupposes and guarantees the consent of the governed in policy formulation, better governmental process, and the possibility of sustainable and true development. This makes the idea of public sphere very important and a normative concept, as it is an ideal for good/accountable governance. On the contrary, the absence of the public sphere, à la media censorship, has resulted in a leadership failure in its entirety, which in turn has truncated and subverted development. Through critical textual and qualitative analysis, the authors advance the argument that there exists a nexus between public sphere, good governance, and development. And the connection has almost been rendered a nullity through the actions/inactions of the political class whose hatred for the public sphere necessitates its negation.

INTRODUCTION

The context of this work is the many years of postcolonial rule in Africa, when most African countries

DOI: 10.4018/978-1-6684-4107-7.ch009

and their leaders claimed to have achieved 'independence' and hence self-rule. The outcome of such claim ought to be an embrace of civil democratic rule which is considered the best governmental system. Best system, because, it ideally comes with perks and inherent tenets (such as self-reliance, free speech, right to govern and to be governed, etc), that make it unique from other systems, (Gilley, 2009, p.114). However, more than six decades after political independence and despite her numerous endowments, most of these goals have remained unrealized because of some intractable problems. Among these problems is the disillusionment with the 'public sphere' by the ruling elites because the public sphere presupposes and guarantees the consent of the governed in policy formulation, better governmental process and the possibility of sustainable and true development (Ake, 1996).[1] Without functional and democratic public sphere, government officials cannot be held accountable for their actions and citizens will not be able to influence political decisions. This makes the idea of public sphere very important and a normative concept, as it is an ideal of good and accountable governance. Still, its normativity specifies the "ideal characteristics of public communication, as well as conditions conducive to their realization, and help to evaluate critically existing communication". Public sphere hinges on the following essential features: free flow of information, free expression, and free debate. It is a buffer against power abuse as it is truly participatory. In actualizing these objectives, therefore, the role and function of the media cannot be overemphasized.

The media is the purveyor of the contents (opinion) of the public sphere better called the public opinion. Its bound is marked by the transcendence of the private sphere in its involvement in the revealing and/or uncovering of the contents of the private sphere. This runs on the assumption that though there is a distinction between the public and private realms, one cannot be tightly secluded from the other in the contemporary social discourse since what is public has an implication for the private order and vice versa. In the engagement with the media, the destination is generally the entire society but specifically the government as it (media) acts like the Socratic gadfly that wakes everyone to his/her respective responsibilities. This work, therefore, raises socio-philosophical issues that bother on unity of purpose by participants in a polity, the relation between part and whole, the connection between individual and state, and the nature of reason. It investigates the governmental agentive role and reason in narrowing the public sphere through media censorship; and so, acts as a clarion call to every member of the society to the antics of the ruling class in stifling their 'voice'.

THE CONCEPT OF A PUBLIC SPHERE

The concept of the public sphere, developed by Jürgen Habermas, is at the core of (participatory) democracy. Public sphere, originally a German term, *'Öffentlichkeit',* connotes a public arena where citizens gather to exchange views regarding public concerns, carry out discussions with the aim of forging public opinion.[2] In the words of Habermas (1997), it is "a domain of our social life where such a thing as public opinion can be formed [to enable] citizens act as a public when they deal with matters of general interest without being subject to coercion; with the guarantee that they may assemble and unite freely, [to] express and publicize their opinion freely" (p.105). It essentially includes all channels of communications through which citizens can send and receive information and where if the two-way-flow of communication is absent, it implies that a public sphere does not exist.

The public sphere can be a physical arena as community square, town hall, etc., but does not necessarily need to be so, as it can be any forum or infrastructure (virtual), other than physical, for communication and information exchange among citizens. The philosophical presuppositions of the public sphere is captured by the gregarious nature of humanity which demonstrates the impossibility of humans acting in isolation but always in common (Fuchs, 2014, p. 61), which Hannah Arendt (1958) describes as "the common world [that] gathers us together and yet prevents our falling over each other" (p. 52), and the Aristotelian distinction between the *polis* and *oikos*, a reference to formal body politic and the household, respectively. The *polis*, according to Aristotle, is the realm of freedom, while the *oikos* was that of necessity. As such, public sphere does not necessarily exist in any identifiable space. So, it is, according to Hartley (1992), a metaphorical concept (a better illustration of which in the contemporary times are the internet, social media, radio and TV talk shows/phone-in programs), used to describe the virtual space where people can interact, find out and participate in what is happening in their immediate communities, especially socio-politico-cultural matters. The virtuality of the public sphere is not to discredit the fact that the public sphere is seen as a physical arena symbolized by community square, or town hall, rather, it tries to underscore the fact that its virtual nature makes the congregation of an entire social conglomeration of a society possible, since it is open to all citizens. In this sense and context, it is practically impossible to bring together the entire Nigerian populace into a physical space of a town hall or community square where they could all discuss issues that affect them. It is on this basis that Habermas (1997) underscores the necessity of 'means' of reaching a wider public (p. 105).

Historically and prior to the emergence of the modern conception of public sphere, cultures and societies, especially Western societies, were modeled as feudal systems that were strictly hierarchical. In this arrangement, the monarch was decked with absolute power that was only a direct derivative from God; he was simply God's vicegerent. Accordingly, the Qur'an says: "It is He Who has appointed you vicegerents in the earth, and has raised some of you in ranks above others ..." (Qur'an 6: 165). This puts his/her subjects squarely under his control in all ramifications as he is God's dignified trustee on earth.[3] The distinction between the concepts of public and private revolves around the power that the monarch wields over the subjects. While the monarch was the *de facto* 'public' that epitomizes the state, every one of his subjects makes up the 'private'. Goode (2005), aptly observes that the "'Publicness' was still the preserve of the feudal powers and it remained primarily oral, theatrical and immediate" (p. 4). Under feudalism, public realm existed for mere representation rather than as a realm of interaction and debate. However, from the seventeenth century, when new set of radical ideas began to emerge, this trend took completely new dimension. The ideas were centred on the assumptions of social justice and inclusiveness, which make equal treatment of every person in a society a *sine qua non*. This thereby launched the Western societies into a new historical epoch christened "modernity". Modernity is an epoch that is assumed to have achieved profound socio-structural and intellectual transformations, characterized with, among other things, order, certainty, harmony, humanity, etc (Sarup, 1996, p. 50).

Habermas (1998) goes further to describe modernity as an expression of epochal consciousness of antiquity with bounds between the old and new (p. 3). To this extent, modernity, in what sounds like social revolution, sets the tone for public sphere. Some of the preceding social norms it sets as a prelude to the claims of public sphere include: equality, justice, freedom and comfort. It is to this that Alan McKee (2005) attests that modernity connotes different manner of visualizing the world as guarantor of peoples' freedom, justice, equality and comfort (p. 7).

Why the stress on modernity? Habermas in theorizing on the modernity project evinces tremendous optimism in view of the rationalization of everyday life. In his view, the eighteenth century project of modernity articulated by the philosophers of Enlightenment, consisted in their efforts to develop objectivity from its inner logic with the aim of releasing its cognitive potentials from their esoteric forms.

This, for the Enlightenment philosophers, would guarantee the enrichment of the rational organization of everyday social life (Habermas, 1998, p. 9), as part of the Enlightenment project, was an attempt to purge Europe of the censorship that found political despotism allied with religious traditionalism.

Thus, of all the norms listed above, equality commands tremendous impact in the public sphere project. The idea of equality aligns with the Enlightenment project giving to citizens the appropriate power to partake in the decision making process of their society. In this way, modernity upstages the feudal and hierarchical structure of societies which hitherto, according to Habermas (1989 [1962], p. 26), offered no opportunity to citizens to partake in political decision making. Consequently, citizens found ways of exchanging information and ideas, reaching consensus about what they wanted done, and sharing or communicating that information to members of their society. Sharing and communicating decisions require the formation of public channels and publications to make effective communication possible. Thus emerged public sphere as a vital part of modernity, and its Enlightenment commitment to equality (McKee, 2005, p. 8), which in the words of Habermas (1997), constitutes "the publicness that once had to win out against the secret politics of monarchs and that since then has permitted democratic control of state activity" (p. 105).

The publicness or better still, the representative publicness (or the principle of control) that was the exclusive preserve of the monarch ("the feudal powers, the Church, the prince, and the nobility") was lost (Habermas, 1989 [1962], p. 11; Goode 2005, p. 5) and publicness rather became the property of the Habermasian *bourgeois public sphere*. The bourgeois public sphere is the assemblage of private persons; it is a "precursor to a more directly political public sphere" (Goode, 2005, p. 7). This is isolating the concept of the 'public' from a representative vested with authority and reverting such "competence-regulated activity of an apparatus furnished with a monopoly on the legitimate use of force" (Habermas, 1997, p. 107). The trademark of bourgeois public sphere is its egalitarianism in dialogue. Thus, apart from the concern for 'truth', the bourgeois public engages in a critical dialogue that aims at dismantling dogmatism. This is achieved by allowing wider discursive latitude to new participants who approach the dialogue with valid claims in every open discourse (Goode 2005, p. 9; Habermas, 1962, p. 37).

THE AIM AND USEFULNESS OF PUBLIC SPHERE

The public sphere has short, medium and long term goals. Its short term goals include transforming the individual/private members of a society in their opinion with the aim of molding public opinion and to specifically influence individual opinions. It is to this end that Bankler (2006) suggests that all citizens are duly allowed to identify with public sphere as guarantee of transiting from consumers and public spectators to creators and primary subjects. (p. 272). This makes the public sphere akin to a "free marketplace of ideas," a libertarian ideal where everyone is able to propose ideas, and where the best idea is given consideration. Far beyond Bankler's observation, McKee (2005) highlights the essential function of the metaphor that is public sphere in relation to molding the ordinary members of a society to the realization and awareness of their ability to contribute to the functioning of their society (p. 10). He compares this metaphor with alternative media metaphors that predominate in totalitarian societies and which aim to perpetuate the aspirations and powers of privileged powerful group who use their power and privilege to suppress less powerful (p. 10).

Essentially, the medium term aim of public sphere is to "legitimate authority in any functioning democracy" (Rutherford, 2000, p. 18). This is considering its insistence that "an ideal democratic polity be defined by features beyond those that formally enable political participation" (Schudson, 1992, p. 147), which among other things, include "a broader sense of political practice as the constitution of ways of living together" (Calhoun, 1996, p. 451), as against mere happenings in the parliament. This is why Schudson (1992) alleges that for Habermas, no plebiscitary democracy would qualify as having a functioning public sphere because, not only does participation need to be widespread, it must also be rational (pp. 146-7). To this end therefore, public opinion forms the basis of political power and legitimacy, such that any government can measure its level of security from the willing consents of the ruled to obey (Odugbemi, 2008, p. 17). This underscores the crucial nature of public opinion in politics, given credence by David Hume's claim that "it is therefore, on opinion only that government is founded" (Hume, 1994, p. 16).

Public sphere has a long term desire to build good governance. As a concept, public sphere is a pointer to the understanding of how societies are organized, especially in cultures that are structured by Enlightenment values of equality, freedom, justice and comfort, rather than cultures with feudal values of strong hierarchical ladder, tradition and respect for authority. In such manner, it gives impetus to the understanding of how 'liberal' societies function, in contrast to the workings of totalitarian ones. Liberal forms of social organization bear the hallmark of a commitment to the individual 'private' realm of existence, over which individuals are allowed some reasonable control of their affairs. This form of social organization is of concern to Plato who believes "every man has license to do as he likes" and "would arrange a plan for leading his own life in the way that pleases him." This contrasts with the totalitarian societies in which every element of the individual's life, like in the Platonian ideal society, is regimented and squarely managed for the individual by the state personified in the aristocrats (the carefully trained guardians) (IV, 445D). The public sphere is not a government/governmental project; it is not formed by the government and not managed by government. It maintains absolute independence from the government which, according to Fraser (1990), makes possible a balance between society and the state where the state is accountable to the society (p. 58). Socrates in the *Republic* and the *Apology* was recorded to have recognized that cities with bad regimes do not permit their misconduct to be questioned and corrected. Splichal (1999) situates this by advancing a view that equates what public sphere is to the state to what market is to the economy. In this instance, in the public sphere goods and currencies are not exchanged as in economics, rather what is traded and exchanged is public opinion and ideas.

Though the three aims conflate, the third is of utmost importance since good governance is pivotal to development. The claim by the bourgeoisie to stand as the locus of reason and justice, served as a check on the state secrecy.

Historically, the polemical claim of this kind of rationality was developed, in conjunction with the critical public debate among private people, against the reliance of princely authority on secrets of state. Just as secrecy was supposed to serve the maintenance of sovereignty based on voluntas, so publicity was supposed to serve the promotion of legislation based on ratio (Habermas, 1962, p. 53).

PUBLIC SPHERE AND DEMOCRACY

In the ancient period, Aristotle feared that democracy, as a system of government, leads to mob rule, although he favored stable and just rule by the many in what he called a polity (*polis*). His loathsome mindset against democracy, underscores his deepest derision of a form of governance that empowers most, if not all members of the society. Similarly, many of his contemporaries paraded like mindset. For example, Plato deeply distrusted democracy on the ground that it tended to numerous excesses.[4] This attitude was inherited by scholars of the Middle Ages who opposed democratic rule on the grounds of it being antithetical to the divine institution of leadership as vested in the monarch. This is a position which was later contested by the modern scholarship, especially the Enlightenment, when democracy assumes the toga of what seems a popular revolt against the monarchs and rich oligarchs. According to Plato, in this democratic trend, "the people are granted an equal share in citizenship and political office" (VIII, 556E-557B), and individual liberty and equality remain unequal as well as unrivaled virtues. Iris Marion Young (2000) situates this in her conception of deliberative democracy. For her, deliberative democracy has the attributes of inclusion, equality, reasonableness and publicity (Schiff, 2015, p.86), where norm of inclusion requires that "a democratic decision is normatively legitimate only if all those affected by it are included in the process of discussion and decision making" (Young, 2000, p. 23). Inclusion connotes political equality, that is, imposing on all affected parties "an equal right and effective opportunity to express their interests and concerns" (Young, 2000, p. 23). While equality, on the other hand, entails reasonableness, which involves the willingness to hear an opposing side (Young, 2000, p. 24). So, deliberative principle is both "individualist and democratic. . . ." The willingness to listen to others confers legitimacy on deliberations, as according to Manin (1987), "the source of legitimacy is not the predetermined will of individuals, but rather the process of its formation, that is, deliberation itself. ... A legitimate decision does not represent the will of all, but is one that results from the deliberation of all" (pp. 351ff) It is in this light that Jean Cohen (1989) defines the concept of deliberative democracy in its rootedness in public argument, free public deliberation and reasoning among equal citizens who aim at resolving issues (problems) of collective choice (pp. 12-24).

The emphasis here is on the conduciveness of specific processes of the democratic formation of opinion and will, presumed to have the potential for generating rational outcomes, of actually leading to such results (Habermas, 1992, p. 446). This led Immanuel Kant to theorize on the principle of publicity as a legal maxim and as a fundamental principle of democracy. Kant in his anti-utilitarian disposition, unequivocally holds all actions that affect other people to be wrong if they are not accessible or open to public scrutiny, to which end, he designates the public sphere to be the space for "public use of reason" or communicative rationality. The public use of reason is hinged on the ethics of communication, which renders imperative the respect for opposing speakers and viewpoints, the ability to compromise, and other principles of fair public debate. In any ideal rational public sphere, Habermas (1989) conceives knowledge and argument to be dominant, rather than "violent conflict" (p. 132) or the use of "power" (Habermas, 1992, p. 451) or other non-communicative forms such as "hypnosis . . . deception, or perhaps by appealing to authority" (Outhwaite, 1996, pp. 11–12). In this circumstance, the legitimacy of an action or a statement, in principle, lies in equal participation of individuals as justificatory ground for free debate (Baert, 1998, p. 142). This bestows on rationality an attribute or quality that does not belong to individuals, but is grounded in human group interactions where, communication with others disavows emotional forms of information gathering or communications are disallowed in preference for only logical forms of argument (Outhwaite, 1996; Poole, 1989). Essentially, therefore, emotional forms of information gathering or communication fail to meet the condition of being a rational project, and consequently cease to be public because they do not really involve an attempt to communicate.

(DEMOCRACY) PUBLIC SPHERE, PUBLICITY AND CENSORSHIP

Iris Young linked deliberative democracy to the press/media. This she did on the assumption that there necessarily had to be a mode of expression thereby effectively underscoring the need for publicity, which normally found effect in the press. The press is "a site of engagement in which deliberators can be held accountable" (Schiff, 2015, p. 85). Thus, publicity is the unveiling and making public where, according to Young (2000), a public is an aggregation of individuals in dialogical confrontation with one another with the aim of addressing collective problems using a common procedure (p. 25). But in confronting issues and persons in a dialogue, the quintessential constraint in any communicative encounter is for participants to take responsibility for their arguments to ensure publicly acceptable reasons (Schiff, 2015, p. 86). This is given impetus by the Habermasian theory of communicative action which is conceived as a "rationalization of the life-word". The theory of communicative action is rooted in the ideal of transparency, undistorted and rational communication, where all parties strive to reach a consensus. This thereby creates room for a developing relationship between the media and politics. To this end, the failures of communication have very wide implication. It leads to pathological distortions in communication which constitutes "significant barriers for communication" (Schiff, 2015, p. 64). Communication is pathological where inclusivity in deliberations is absent; where participants are not on equal terms; where there is absence of willingness to listen to others; and where public accountability is lacking. Pathological distortions parade an obvious implication of frustrating transparent, rational communication in the public sphere. The concern against pathological distortion is to forestall uncertainty and fear, which could result to the colonization of the life-world. Colonization of a life-world translates to, "the manipulation of things by the individual subject or knower [through] the application of technological approaches and instrumental rationality to the realm of human communication" (Dusek, 2006, p. 61). This attitude, essentially, renders some traditional forms of rationality unacceptable to Habermas because they possess certain repressive and destructive tendencies. Take the case of 'strategic rationality', for example, which is a means-end way of seeing the world, becomes a way of sacrificing individuals to a mechanistic notion of doing what is best for society.

In "The Media and the Public Sphere", Nicholas Garnham (1992) advances a position that has it as axiomatic, the assumption that "some version of communicative action lies at the heart of both the theory and practice of democracy" (p. 364), where the rights and duties of a citizen are largely characterized in terms of freedom of assembly and freedom to impart and receive information. He posits that where such freedoms are absent, the citizens risk being denied access to the views of others necessary to come to an agreement amongst themselves, be such agreement consensual or majoritarian. The absence also hampers the possession of knowledge of the actions of those to whom executive responsibilities are delegated in order to hold them accountable. As well as equipping the citizens with the necessary knowledge of the external environment required to arrive at appropriate judgment of both personal and societal interests. Garnham further notes that the debate on the relationship between public communication and democracy is considerably dominated by the free press model. The free press model being an idealist transposition of face-to-face communication to mediated communication where encumbrances associated with mediated communication are removed (p. 361).

Public sphere approached ideal state through the removal of ethnic, gender, and class exclusions but, at the same time, had to be hampered by the advance of social welfare, the growth of culture industries, and the evolution of large private interests. This is why Habermas (1962) alleges that (talking of the proprietorship of large newspapers devoted to profit), it provided avenue for the invasion of the public sphere by privileged private interests (p. 185). For him, the misuse of publicity undermines the public sphere. This is evident in "manipulative publicity" which, at a time, became very common. Accordingly, he avers: "even arguments are translated into symbols to which again one cannot respond by *arguing* but only by *identifying* with them" (p. 206). Such propaganda manages views, fosters political theatre, and conveys "authorized opinions" (p. 245). Visual display – "showy pomp" (p. 185) and "staged display" (p. 206) – are used by those in authority to assert dominance or entitlement. The result is the scenario painted by Herbert Marcuse, who in his *One Dimensional Man,* alleges in his analysis of the new "voice of command" used by managers, educators, experts, and politicians, that could only create the "one-dimensional" citizens, who will be incapable of protest or refusal. Similarly, Frank Webster (1975) argues public sphere is deeply wounded by the intrusion of PR, which, to Habermas, violates the claim to truthfulness, and marks the abandonment of criteria of rationality which formerly shaped public debate. In entering public debate, public relation is alleged to disguise the interests it represents by making them bear welfarist outlook and representing national interest (p. 103). Thus, in his analysis of the development of internal sites for political debate in the eighteenth century Europe such as the salons, coffee houses, clubs and newspapers, Habermas gave impetus to such informal venues to provide avenue away from the institutionalized political system for citizens to ventilate their views and inform themselves, and to form political opinions that could then be transmitted through various democratic access points to the political system. So the question here is if, actually, society is denied reliable information, how can true democracy possibly be realized?

The role of the media (traditional mass media and social media inclusive), cannot be overemphasized in any public sphere project. It is so vital to the extent that its consideration in the public sphere is seen as motor to the public opinion phenomenon. However, it is a role highly loathed by African despotic leaders who masquerade as democrats and whose fear is popular revolt and/or revolution. The inclusivity in deciding policy direction remains abhorred as it is reminiscent of the Athenian leaders in their disgust to the influence of Socrates on the Athenian youths and for which he paid the supreme price. Thus, the only effective way to check the 'menacing' influence of public sphere on African leaders and their leadership style is to gag the media in the name of censorship. This comes on the assumption that once the media is censored, it becomes selective of what it disseminates (tells the people) and thus becomes very redundant and narrowly focused in projecting governmental inactivity, ineffectiveness and excessiveness. There are, therefore, issues concerning repressive nature of the rules of balance and objectivity within which public service broadcasting is forced to operate.

Far from thinking or advancing the view that media regulation is not necessary, we advance a candid opinion that Media regulation should provide institutional framework and enablement for the media to fulfill its democratic roles without political or economic pressures and/or strangulations as "it should be evident that a people entrusted with the power of self-government must be able to exercise a disciplined judgment: not everything goes". For example, it is said that much of what is said in the *Republic* and elsewhere reflects the belief that the vital opinions of the community could be shaped by law and that men could be penalized for saying things that offended public sensibilities, undermined common morality, or subverted the institutions of the community (Anastaplo, 2021). So, media rule of engagement cannot equal media censorship as every public expression shall be made within the law uninfluenced by personal whims and caprices.

The Nigerian clime is suffused with such common refrain as "hate speech". Yes, censorship can be an instrument to curtail hate speech and other societal anomalies, but the problem arises when censorship is used to target a particular group or when the censor is not called to account for its own infractions.

Take for instance, though there is the desire to curtail hate speech by the government of Nigeria, but when utterances considered hateful oozes from the law giver/enforcer, who enforces the law on him/her? It smirks of deceit. A typical case in point is President Buhari's alleged comment considered to be hate speech and which became the cause of action by Twitter, a microblogging and social media network, that acted to remove the comment. So, the refrain "hate speech" by the government, may be viewed as a subtle ploy to dictating, and restricting the media on what to or not to say. It allows a dominant group (government) to create a specific narrative in society to be regarded as truth (whatever the president says is law). It is usually targeted primarily to the public to frustrate opposing expressions against the government. In this instance, censorship creates a psychological impact in the people, through its ability to swerve their mind and attitude toward the view to be advocated by the media, by increasing the desire to receive or detest that information.

In a clime where censorship festers, alternative voices which hitherto were expressed through public sphere/opinion are claimed to be only legitimately expressible through the 'elected' parliamentarians, even when it is certain that the parliaments have fallen short of raising people's voices, hopes, aspirations and opinions honestly and dispassionately. The reason is that the members of the African parliaments are products of a doctored form of, or adulterated democratic practice seen in most African states which only represents political base that bears elitist and bourgeois trappings and clout.[5] It is contra public sphere as "public power in Africa continues to serve the interests of those in power more than it serves African citizens, and the latter continue to suffer the consequences" (Ganahl, 2013, p.4). Still on other hand, censorship makes people redundant to using their initiative to create opportunities for themselves. A situation where everything receives censorship, then it would be a place where nothing could get done without specific permission from someone in charge. That means every business, each idea, and even the foods that one eats each night would require an official stamp of approval. This, indeed, is part of the shenanigans of 'African democracy' where enormous power is bestowed on the ruler who dishes same out based not on rule of law but at the discretion of the ruler.

PUBLIC SPHERE AND DEVELOPMENT: THE AFRICAN CHALLENGE

The interest here is to probe the intersection of public sphere and development and how this interchange has been effectively hampered by what we have decided to describe here as dictatorial democracy. Dictatorial democracy here implies antithesis (counterfeit) of ideal democracy because it is devoid of the appurtenances of democracy. Thus, despite the claim of most African states to have democratized, a critical overview of most of them would reveal that the goal of democracy has been most difficult to realize and this can be traced to, among other things, the erosion of the public sphere as effective feedback mechanism for good (public) governance. Such democracy is antithetical to development because of its zeal to gag, through censorship, the media, perceived to be the means of popular expression of desires, frustration and disgust. Since it is the responsibility of the media, to circulate unhindered, the outcome of public sphere to both citizens and government, this underscores the responsibilities of the media as essential instrument for the success of the public sphere and societal reinforcement.

The African form of democracy[6] is suspect here. The African democratic enterprise does not permit alternative view points away from that of the leader and ruling party. It is characterized by obvious breakdown of social consensus to a form of dissensus with considerable societal anomie. Little wonder Ake (1996) blames African political conditions as the greatest impediment to development. Accordingly,

African leaders in struggling to advance their interests, pay little or no consideration about conformity to norms of legality or legitimacy. Nigerian politics was, invariably, reduced to "the crude mechanics of opposing forces driven by the calculus of power", where for everyone in such political configuration, "security lay only in the accumulation of power that is self-serving. [And] the result was an unprecedented drive for power; power was made the top priority in all circumstances and sought by all means" (Ake, 1996, p. 3). This singular attitude greatly endangers democracy as parties engage in serious electoral gerrymandering to enable them grab power. Such democracy is akin to what Young identifies as neglected forms or aspects of communication by democratic theorists in their distinction between concepts of "appropriate" and "inappropriate" modes of communication. This distinction, for her, is too "constricted" (Young, 2000, as cited in Schiff, 2015, p. 86), in that the norm of appropriateness threatens to exclude from deliberative processes those people who, for a variety of reasons, cannot engage in styles of communication that are deemed appropriate by those who set the terms of deliberation. This is a situation when one can talk of censorship.

Censorship in this manner is understood as the "supervision and control of the information and ideas that are circulated among the people within a society." The *raison d'etre* of censorship can be located in the assumption that it is necessary for the protection of basic social institutions, especially the state. There are added reasons why proponents of censorship feel it is necessary; it is, among other things, claimed to debase the public taste, corrupt all sense of decency and civility, and even undermine civilization (Konvitz, 2007). This description foregrounds a statist intervention in a people's freedom and liberty. So, despite the avowed protection granted the media in some countries' constitutions in Africa (e.g., the Nigeria's 1999 Constitution), governments still find basis to still muzzle the media.[7] This makes some to define censorship *via negativa* as "the oppressive exercise of centralized power by defined 'others' ... who decide on the inclusion or exclusion of certain texts" (Smejkalovd-Strickland, 1994, p. 195). However, part of its positive tendencies may include limiting access to contents that might be disruptive to society. Without this understanding, certain classified information bothering on state security could be divulged publicly with a simple request. Proprietary ingredients would vanish because of the need for disclosure. It is so believed that by limiting certain types of information from the primary flow of society, there is less of a potential for harm to that community. This brings to mind the question of how well the Freedom of Information (FOI) law has worked in granting people access to vital government documents in Nigeria. Though the (FOI) law grants that every citizen of Nigeria can request and be given access to certain official documents within the shortest possible time, that is, it aims to mandate a disclosure of public documents, but the reality of its implementation remains a mirage (see Oluwasemilore, 2018). It is this scenario that Habermas claims to be the fault line for the failure of public sphere. It is made possible "by the rise of the complex bureaucracies and highly organized state apparatuses" (Pensky, 2014, p. 23). He announced the alleged demise of the public sphere, as "it sunk from the level of critical discourse in the 19th century to merely affirmative publicity in the 20th century" (Wessler & Freudenthaler, 2018).

The form of 'democracy' prevalent in Africa is one, which by intent, does not promote, but, indeed, abhors, development in the truest sense of it. This is done through tactical isolation of the media, an ideal source of public opinion exchange. When this happens, the leader tactically subverts democracy and development. According to Ake (1996), "African elites have placed great obstacles in the way of development by their antipathy to democracy" (p. 119). In such circumstance, development becomes unrealizable project because its logic is antithetical to social will that characterizes endogenous developmental agenda of a people.

Our claim, here, is predicated on the notion of development as "a process of self-empowerment, [characterized by] a long process of struggle for liberation from structures of domination and control, including mental constructs and the use of language" (Tendon, 2015, p. 146).[8] Placing development in some historical perspective, Hettne and other development optimists, give development thinking a 'modern' context. In this sense, development thinking becomes a product of enlightenment that aims at improving the society from the point of view of rationalist principles. This group of development optimists argues that despite its ups and downs, it is however laded with possibilities, since development dovetails to choices people make to improve themselves. This conception of development is in consonance with the Habermasian conception of the goal of democratic societies to be the erection of a "democratic dam against the colonizing encroachment of system of imperatives on areas of the life-world" (Habermas, 1992), which Claude Ake firmly establishes its nexus in his book *Democracy and Development in Africa.* Ake (1996), advocated for endogenous developmental strategy to be harmonized peoples' social needs. By so conceived, the social will of a people becomes the 'germ' as it remains the driving force that propels the wheel of development where the people play the role of both means and end of development (p. 119).

Generally, good governance bears serious correlation with development. And usually, the two are related and indeed, overlap when developmental issues are tossed up. Invariably, the correlation between the public sphere and good governance is a *sine qua non* for development. Good governance embraces common participation, social inclusiveness, responsiveness, consensus, transparency and equality. These are components found in broader public sphere. The effective public sphere guarantees consent in policy formulation and the possibility of sustainable and true development. Good governance is about how citizens, leaders and public institutions communicate with each other to make developmental goals realizable. This is why Ganahl (2013), following Daniel Kaufmann and others, posits that "good governance not only matters for economic development, but could even be regarded as a central determinant of a nation's economic performance" (p. 2). This is possible through free flow of information, free expression, and free debate which are requisites of public sphere. Governance also implies a manner in which power is exercised to guarantee welfare and development anchored in efficiency, accountability, responsiveness, and participation. Therefore, the phenomenon of the public sphere centers on the idea of participatory democracy, and how public opinion becomes political action. The outcome of the public sphere or public opinion generated through the public sphere is very critical for societal transformation. It is the pedestal upon which good governance is rested. In good governance, leaders and public institutions interface for the purpose of effecting societal change and enhancement. The legitimacy of the public sphere issues from the fact of it being open to all and sundry, rendering it a mini-referendum.

CONCLUSION

The concept of the public sphere is at the core of (participatory) democracy. Public sphere connotes an arena where citizens gather to exchange views regarding public concerns, carry out discussions with the aim of forging public opinion. The aims of public sphere include transformation of the individual/private members of a society in their opinion with the aim of molding public opinion and specifically influence individual opinions; legitimatization of authority in a functional democracy; and to guarantee good governance. Good governance is pivotal to development and can be achieved when there is openness, and rational approach to policy formulation. Implied in this is the possibility of 'all' in the society to make imputes into the decision organs of the society. The role of the media cannot be overemphasized in any public sphere project. It is so vital to the extent that its consideration in the public sphere is seen as vehicle to the public opinion phenomenon. However, it is a role highly loathed by African despotic leaders who masquerade as democrats and whose fear is popular revolt and/or revolution. The inclusivity in deciding policy direction remains abhorred leaving the African leader with censorship as the only option of forcefully checkmating the 'menacing' influence of public sphere on their authority and leadership style. This comes on the assumption that a guided (censored) media reduces, if not totally removes, its influence on the masses who it would educate to quest for good governance. In addition, the media, when censored, becomes redundant and narrow minded in projecting governmental inactivity, ineffectiveness and excessiveness. Censorship, in the African context, is simply self-serving. In such situation, development as a conscious movement of a people towards better society and self-reliance becomes a mirage. The feasibility of self-reliance can only be possible within the ambit of a thorough democratic society, where members are seen not just as means, but the very end of development. Thus, the phenomenon of development becomes synonymous with the pursuit and realization of objectives set by the people (society) themselves in their own interest and benefit through openly, freely and rationally expression of their desires. Where such is not possible, the consequence becomes a severe developmental lapse; an eclipse of a sort.

REFERENCES

Ake, C. (1996). *Democracy and development in Africa*. The Brookings Institution.

Anastaplo, G. (2021). *Censorship. Encyclopædia Britannica*. Ultimate Reference Suite. Encyclopædia Britannica Inc.

Arendt, H. (1958). *The human condition* (2nd ed.). The University of Chicago Press.

Bankler, Y. (2006). *The wealth of networks*. Yale University Press.

Calhoun, C. (1996). Social theory and the public sphere. In B. S. Turner (Ed.), *The Blackwell companion to social theory*. Blackwell Publishing.

Cohen, J. (1989). Deliberation and democratic legitimacy. In A. Hamlin & P. Pettit (Eds.), *The good polity* (pp. 12–24).

Dusek, V. (2006). *Philosophy of technology: An introduction*. Blackwell.

Fraser, N. (1990). Rethinking the public sphere: A contribution to the critique of actually existing democracy. *Social Text*, (25/26), 56–80. doi:10.2307/466240

Fuchs, C. (2014). Social media and the public sphere. *TripleC*, *12*(1), 57–101. doi:10.31269/triplec.v12i1.552

Ganahl, J. P. (2013). *Corruption, good governance, and the African state: A critical analysis of the political-economic foundations of corruption in sub-Saharan Africa*. Postdam University Press.

Garnham, N. The media and the public sphere. In C. Calhoun (Ed.), *Habermas and the public sphere* (pp. 359–376). The MIT Press.

Gilley, B. (2009). Is democracy possible? *Journal of Democracy, 20*(1), 113–127. doi:10.1353/jod.0.0052

Goode, L. (2005). *Jurgen Habermas: Democracy and the public sphere*. Pluto Press.

Habermas, J. (1962). *The structural transformation of the public sphere: An inquiry into a category of bourgeois society.* The MIT Press.

Habermas, J. (1984). *The theory of communicative action*. Beacon Press.

Habermas, J. (1992). Further reflections on the public sphere. In C. Calhoun (Ed.), *Habermas and the public sphere* (pp. 421–461). The MIT Press.

Habermas, J. (1997). The public sphere. In R. E. Goodin & P. Pettit (Eds.), *Contemporary political philosophy: An Anthology* (pp. 143–146). Blackwell Publishers.

Habermas, J. (1998). Modernity – An incomplete project. In H. Foster (Ed.), *The anti-aesthetic: Essays on postmodern culture* (pp. 3–15). The New Press.

Hartley, J. (1992). *The politics of pictures: The creation of the public in the age of popular media.* Routledge.

Hartmut, W., & Freudenthaler, R. (2018). Public sphere. In P. Moy (Ed.), *Oxford bibliographies in communication*. Oxford University Press., doi:10.1093/obo/9780199756841-0030

Hettne, B. (2002). Current trends and future options in development studies. In V. Desai & R. B. Potter (Eds.), *The companion to development studies*. Arnold.

Hume, D. (1994). *Political essays* (K. Haakonssen, Ed.). Cambridge University Press. doi:10.1017/CBO9781139170765

Kant, I. (1983). To perpetual peace. In *Immanuel Kant: Perpetual peace and other essays on politics, history, and morals* (pp. 107–144). Hackett. (Original work published 1795)

Konvitz, M. R. (2006). Censorship. *Microsoft Encarta 2007* [DVD]. Microsoft Corporation.

Manin, B. (1987). On legitimacy and political deliberation. *Political Theory, 15*(3). DOI: doi:10.2307/191208

McKee, A. (2005). *The public sphere: An introduction*. Cambridge University Press.

Odugbemi, A. (2008). Public opinion, the public sphere, and quality of governance: An exploration. In A. Odugbemi & T. Jacobson (Eds.), *Governance reform under real-world conditions: Citizens, stakeholders, and voice* (pp. 15–37). The World Bank. doi:10.1596/978-0-8213-7456-6

Oluwasemilore, I. (2018). A critical analysis of Nigeria's freedom of information act. *The Gravitas Review of Business and Property Law, 9*(2).

Outhwaite, W. (1996). General introduction. In W. Outhwaite (Ed.), *The Habermas Reader* (pp. 1–22). Polity Press.

Pensky, M. (2014). Historical and intellectual contexts. In B. Fultner (Ed.), *Jurgen Habermas: Key concepts* (pp. 13–32). Routledge.

Poole, R. (1989). Public spheres. In H. Wilson (Ed.), *Australian Communications and the Public Sphere: essays in memory of Bill Bonney* (pp. 6–26). The Macmillan Company of Australia. doi:10.1007/978-1-349-11077-3_2

Rutherford, P. (2000). *Endless propaganda: The advertising of public goals*. University of Toronto Press. doi:10.3138/9781442674455

Sarup, M. (1996). *Identity, culture and the postmodern world* (T. Raja, Ed.). Edinburgh University Press.

Schiff, J. L. (2015). Repressive democracy: Pathological and ontological distortion in Habermas' theory of communicative action. In B. Fischer & M. Mergenthaler (Eds.), *Cultural transformations of the public sphere: Contemporary and historical perspectives* (pp. 65–92). Peter Lang.

Schudson, M. (1992). Was there ever a public sphere? If so, when? Reflections on the American case. In C. Calhoun (Ed.), *Habermas and the public sphere* (pp. 143–164). The MIT Press.

Sidaway, D. J. (2002). Post-development. In V. Desai & R. B. Potter (Eds.), *The companion to development studies*. Arnold.

Smejkalovd-Strickland, J. (1994). Censoring canons: Transitions and prospects of literary institutions in Czechoslovakia. In R. Burtn (Ed.), *The Administration of aesthetics: Censorship, political criticism, and the public sphere* (pp. 195–215). University of Minnesota Press.

Splichal, S. (1999). *Public opinion, developments and controversies in the twentieth century*. Rowman & Littlefield.

Tandon, Y. (2015). Development is resistance. *Africa Development. Afrique et Developpement*, *XL*(3), 139–159.

Thornton, S. H., & Thornton, W. H. (2008). *Development without freedom: The politics of Asian globalization*. Ashgate Publishing Limited.

Webster, F. (1975). *Theories of the information society*. Routledge.

Wessler, H., & Freudenthaler, R. (2018). Public sphere. In P. Moy (Ed.), *Oxford bibliographies in communication*. Oxford University Press., doi:10.1093/obo/9780199756841-0030

Wiredu, K. (1999). Society and democracy in Africa. *New Political Science*, *21*(1), 33–44. doi:10.1080/07393149908429850

Young, I. M. (2000). *Inclusion and democracy*. Oxford University Press.

ENDNOTES

1 Claude Ake believes that political conditions are the greatest obstacle to development in Africa because many factors among which "social pluralism and its centrifugal tendencies", converged to make developmental failure possible. Consequently, there was discontent and disillusionment among citizens leading to the enforcement of political conformity through coercion, constraint of

the political expression of the masses and the imposition of 'political unity' in the midst of considerable social pluralism that had become very divisive for being politicized. Claude Ake, *Democracy and Development in Africa* (Washington, D.C: The Brookings Institution, 1996), p. 6.

2 Public sphere is akin to the *agora* in ancient Greece. *Agora* in the ancient Greek cities is an open space that served as a meeting ground for various activities of the citizens. The name, first traceable to the works of Homer, has a connotation of both the assembly of the people as well as the physical setting; it was applied by the classical Greeks of the 5th century BC to what they regarded as a typical feature of their life: their daily religious, political, judicial, social, and commercial activity.

3 Habermas asserts "public discussions that are institutionally protected and that take, with critical intent, the exercise of political authority as their theme have not existed since time immemorial - they developed only in a specific phase of bourgeois society, and only by virtue of a specific constellation of interests could they be incorporated into the order of the bourgeois constitutional state". See Habermas, "The public sphere", in *Contemporary Political Philosophy*, p. 106.

4 Despite his disapproval of democracy as the best and possibly, desirable system of government, he nevertheless professes the democratic leader as a "manifold man stuffed with most excellent differences,… containing within himself the greatest number of patterns of constitutions and qualities". (VIII, 561E)

5 Kwasi Wiredu in "Society and Democracy in Africa", argues that "the majoritarian form of democracy seen in the multiparty systems in Britain and the USA is drastically antithetic to ... the complexities of our contemporary situation". "Society and democracy in Africa", *New Political Science*, vol. 21:1 (1999), p. 36.

6 The form of democracy practiced in Africa has the imprint of her foreign colonial 'other' whose aims have been seen to be selfish and insincere. Such democracy came with very wide implications as articulated in Joseph Patrick Ganahl, *Corruption, Good Governance, and the African State: A Critical Analysis of the Political-Economic Foundations of Corruption in Sub-Saharan Africa* (Postdam: Postdam University Press, 2013).

7 Section 22 of the 1999 Constitution of the Federal Republic of Nigeria states that the press, radio, television and other agencies or the mass media shall at all times be free to uphold the fundamental objectives contained in this chapter and uphold the responsibility and accountability of the government to the people.

8 Yash Tandon, "Development is resistance", *Africa Development,* XL (2015), p. 146; cf. Songok Han Thornton and William H. Thornton, *Development Without Freedom: The Politics of Asian Globalization* (Hampshire: Ashgate Publishing Limited, 2008), especially the introduction which bothers on Amartya Sen's book *Development as Freedom*, where Sen makes strong and unequivocal claim that "development requires the removal of tyranny and social deprivation as well as poverty per se".

Chapter 10
How Generous Are Foreign Aid Donors in Media Development?
A Descriptive Analysis

Sevinc Ozturk
Bitlis Eren University, Turkey

ABSTRACT

Media assistance has arisen as a significant tool of media development and democracy initiatives, particularly in the last 20 years. While the research in foreign aid and democracy aid is rich, studies on media assistance are quite limited in number due to its novelty. Moreover, existing research on media assistance usually focuses on the role and/or impact of media assistance on recipient nations' media capacity or media independence. Differing from this existing research, this study focuses on the donors of media assistance and asks how generous foreign aid donors are in media development and what type of donors provide media assistance. Using data from the OECD, Freedom House, Reporters Without Borders, and Comparative Political dataset, this study finds that democratic countries, countries with higher independence in their media, and governments with center ideology are more likely to provide a higher amount of media assistance compared to others.

INTRODUCTION

Since the Cold War, foreign assistance has become an important foreign policy instrument for donor countries. Donor countries aim to support economic development and promote democracy, including media freedom, through foreign assistance in developing countries. With these aims, the members of the Development Assistance Committee (DAC) have provided 161.2 billion $ foreign assistance to the developing countries in 2020 (OECD, 2021). Some of this assistance has been shared for media support by the donor countries. According to the Center for International Media Assistance (CIMA), only 0.3 percent of the total amount of aid has been allocated for media support, and bilateral donors (excluding China) have provided an average of 454 million $ per year for media development between the years of 2010 and 2015 (Myers et al., 2018). Aid for media aims for many targets such as training journalists,

DOI: 10.4018/978-1-6684-4107-7.ch010

supporting the development of the media organizations, promoting freedom of expression, and supporting media independence.

Despite the million dollars spent on media development, the function and the impact of media assistance are still debated. Although media assistance is supposed to boost media freedom, and African, Asian, and Eastern European countries are the main target regions of media assistance, these regions still suffer from censorship, violence, and abuse in the media sector. The index of Reporters Without Borders indicates that many African and Asian countries witness intense abuses and violence against their media actors (Reporters Without Borders, 2021). The censorship, abuses, and violence against the media workers have significantly increased in the last decade with the rise of populist and personalist regimes (Repucci, 2019).

The potential benefits of foreign aid on media development have been analyzed by scholars of political science and media; however, these studies have inconclusive findings. Some of these studies find that foreign development or media aid has a positive impact on media development (e.g., Brownee, 2019; Lugo-Ocando, 2018), while some of them find conditional impact or no impact (e.g., Dutta & Williamson, 2016). The problem regarding the impact and effectiveness of media assistance is critical to address because policymakers and aid organizations still spend a high amount of funding, time, and effort on an issue, although its impact is not clearly known. This does not only cause wasting the resources but also could harm democracy or inhibit democratization. Addressing the problem can inform policymakers and organizations to implement more efficient media assistance policies or take specific measures.

Current studies mainly evaluate if the received aid increases the media development or media freedom in the recipient nation (e.g., Dutta & Williamson, 2016; Galus, 2020). However, the research on foreign aid and media development overlooks the impact of donor's regime type, level of media freedom, and government ideology when examining the relationship between aid and media development. On the other hand, research on foreign aid's impact on recipient nations specifically notes that donors' intentions and motivations directly determine the aid effectiveness (Bearce and Tirone, 2010). The studies on donor motivation and intention; therefore, consider the factors such as donor ideology and regime type to understand why aid is given (e.g., Lumsdaine, 1987; De Mesquita and Smith, 2007, 2009).

This study aims to apply this argument on the relationship between donors' domestic politics and foreign aid policies to media assistance policies. Therefore, it examines the relationship between the type of donor and media assistance. More specifically, this study is interested in analyzing what type of donors provide more assistance for media by focusing on the regime type, level of media freedom, and government ideology of the donor countries. Therefore, this study asks, 'to what extent do donors provide foreign assistance for media development to developing countries, how much of their total foreign assistance is spent on the media and what type of donors provide more media assistance to developing countries?'.

This study will contribute to the literature on aid and media development in two ways: First, as discussed above, existing studies predominantly examine the impact of foreign aid on media development or freedom of press in the recipient countries based on the type of recipient (e.g., Dutta and Williamson, 2016). Instead of the recipient countries, this study will focus on the type of donor countries. Second, current literature is primarily interested in the specific country cases such that they examine individual donor country's media aid to only one or two recipient country cases (e.g., Brownlee, 2017; Harris, 2018; Galus, 2020). Because it is difficult to make general inferences from specific country cases, this paper attempts to analyze all donors' efforts to provide an overall descriptive picture of donors of media assistance.

This study employs descriptive analysis to explain the media assistance given by different types of donors of media assistance. To demonstrate the media assistance of each donor, this study uses the OECD's Official Development Assistance (ODA) data from the Creditor Reporting System (CRS). In this database, OECD presents data on donor countries' foreign assistance in US dollars for various sectors, including the media sector as "Media and Flow of Information" (Creditor Reporting System, 2021). However, this data does not provide us with information on how much of the total aid of each donor is spent for media. To calculate the share of the media assistance, this study will benefit from OECD total Official Development Assistance (ODA) data and divide the amount of media assistance into the total amount of ODA.

To compare democratic donors' media assistance with autocratic donors, this study benefits from the democracy scores from the Freedom House (2021). The OECD's data consists of aid information of thirty-five donor countries between 2002 and 2020 (Creditor Reporting System, 2021). Twenty-nine of these countries are DAC countries, many of them being democratic. On the other hand, there are six non-DAC donors, including autocratic countries. Additionally, this study uses data from the Media Freedom Index of Reporters Without Borders (Reporters Without Borders, 2021) to analyze if the donors' level of media freedom correlates with their generosity in media assistance. Finally, the data for government ideology will be used from the Comparative Political data (Armingeon et al., 2021) to identify the governments' ideology of media assistance donors.

This chapter has four main sections. Following the introduction, the first section reviews the literature on the relationship between foreign assistance and media development by providing conceptual definitions. The second section focuses on the donors and discusses the donors' motivation in providing media assistance to the recipient countries from the theoretical background. In the third section, this study will describe the top donors of media assistance and explain how generous the donor countries are when it comes to the media; in other words, how much of the donors' GNI and total foreign assistance is spent for media by each donor country will be explained. In the last section, the relationship between the regime types, levels of media freedom, and government ideology of donors and media assistance will be evaluated before the conclusion.

AIDING FOR MEDIA DEVELOPMENT

The relationship between foreign assistance and media development has become a rising research area in media and political science studies, particularly in the last decade. In previous studies on foreign aid, the aid's impact on the recipient nation is usually studied on the recipient nations' economic development and growth (e.g., Easterly, 2003; Raghuram and Arvind, 2008; Kim, 2011), recipient nations' democratization and good governance (e. g., McMahon, 2002; Knack, 2004; Yuichi Kono & Montinola, 2009) and recipient nations' conflict level (e.g., Uvin, 1997; Savun and Tirone, 2011). Many of these studies are clustered on the effectiveness of foreign assistance; however, they found inconclusive results regarding the positive impact of aid.

In previous years, media assistance has not been allocated separately. Donor countries have been providing development assistance or democracy assistance to support the economic development or democratization in the recipient nations. It has been considered that media development could be achieved when economic development and democratization could increase in the recipient nation as a result of foreign aid rather than allocating resources specifically for media. However, in the last 20 years, foreign assistance began to be given directly for media development under the flow of media assistance. Therefore, it can be considered that foreign aid could influence the media in the recipient nations in three main ways: Economic development, democratization and good governance, and media development.

The Role of the Link Between the Foreign Assistance and Economic Development in Media Development

The relationship between economic development and the media sector is two-way: While media development can influence economic development, economic development can also create media development. Media development can influence economic development by advertising, creating market structures, influencing consumer behavior, and enabling communication between politicians, consumers, and producers. On the other hand, economic development can create media development when the communication infrastructures, information and communication technology tools, and media independence are ensured as a result of economic development.

Foreign aid is among this relationship. When economic development could be achieved as a result of foreign aid, media development can be enabled as a result of this economic development. Also, as modernization theorists explain (Lipset, 1959), economic development can cause democratization. If foreign aid could contribute to economic development, and in turn, democratization, media development could be achieved along with this democratization. To be more concrete, economic development brings modernization with industrialization, high income, low inflation rates, urbanization high education level in the society. Modernization will contribute to the democratic culture, and the higher standard of living under modernization will provide legitimacy for the regime to survive. When foreign aid contributes to economic development, it can also foster the modernization process and causes democratization. Therefore, foreign aid could also increase media development via economic development when recipient nations' spending for ICT tools and structures increases as a result of the economic development. Foreign aid for economic development could also enhance media development via democratization. If the economic development in the recipient nation causes democratization, media development can be ensured within this democratization process.

On the other hand, research on the relationship between foreign aid and economic development provides mixed results. While the main aim of the development assistance is to increase the economic development of the recipient nation by providing extra funding resources, some scholars find the result of foreign assistance is not meeting this aim such that foreign aid does not contribute to the economic development nor the economic growth (e.g., Easterly, 2003; Raghuram and Arvind, 2008). However, other scholars find that foreign aid could contribute to economic growth or development, even if it has a conditional impact (e.g., Fayissa and El-Kaissy, 1999; Burnside and Dollar, 2000; Karras, 2006; Yiew and Lau, 2018).

The Role of the Link Between the Foreign Assistance and Democratization in Media Development

Democracy promotion and economic development have been the main aims for the donor countries such as the US and the EU. With these aims, foreign aid has become the primary tool of donors in Latin America, the Middle East, and Africa. Donor countries have been providing democracy assistance to technically assist the process of electoral support, to strengthen legislatures and judiciaries, and to assist the election. While foreign assistance, foreign aid, or official development assistance refers to the total amount of assistance, democracy assistance only refers to the assistance that is given for reform and improvement of political parties, elections, the rule of law and judiciary, human rights, and civil society organizations in the recipient countries. By providing democracy assistance, donor nations aim to increase democratization in the recipient country. However, there have also been many critics about the effectiveness of foreign aid on democratization.

According to theoretical analysis of foreign aid policies and democratization, foreign assistance may contribute to democratization in three ways: 1) Donor countries can technically assist for the electoral process of recipient countries by strengthening the legislatures and judiciaries and assisting the elections. 2) Foreign assistance can contribute to democratization by increasing the level of income and economic development, decreasing the inequality in the recipient countries. It can also lead to democratization by improving the education level and, more generally, enabling modernization. Foreign assistance can be given to the recipient country conditionally to develop democratic policies. In this way, to gain assistance, the recipient country's government prioritizes fulfilling the conditions that could lead to democratization (Knack, 2004, p. 251).

However, research on democracy and foreign aid finds mixed results as research on foreign aid and economic development does. While some studies find no relationship between foreign aid and democratization, some find a positive relationship. For example, in a comprehensive quantitative study, Knack (2004 p. 257-258) finds no evidence that foreign assistance positively impacts democratization. To uncover the reasons behind the ineffectiveness of foreign aid on democracy, Brown (2005) examines two recipient countries, Botswana and Mauritius, and finds that lack of commitment and understanding of the donors, as well as impediments to democratization or conditionality, are the main reasons for this ineffectiveness. In another study, Yuichi Kono and Montinola (2009, p. 2) analyze if foreign aid has an impact on leaders' survival and conclude that there is only a little evidence to argue for foreign assistance's contribution to democracy. Moreover, they even find that the recipient country's regime type and time horizon are critical for the leader's survival in those regimes such that the sustained aid transfer can help autocrats' survival in the autocratic regimes in the long run compared to democrats (Yuichi Kono & Montinola, 2009, p. 2). On the other hand, McMahon (2002) argues that foreign assistance has led to a relatively positive democratic transition process in recipient countries, and some elements of the assistance are quite helpful in democratization. He (McMahon, 2002) argues that causal relationships can be inferred in civil society; in other words, foreign assistance is positively effective in improving the civil society in Benin.

Media independence, including the elements of free media, freedom of the press, freedom of expression, is a significant dimension of democracy and a fundamental human right. By contributing to the democracy or causing democratization in the recipient nation, foreign aid or democracy aid can develop the media in the recipient nation. Therefore, media development has arisen as a more specific area for democratization.

Foreign Aid as Direct Tool for Media Development

Media Development

As previously stated, media development is a novel concept. Center for International Media Assistance (CIMA), one of the leading institutions that work on media development, defines media development as "the term that refers to evolution and change in the news media and communications" (CIMA, n.d.). These changes not only include the reforms in the rule of law and freedom of media but also involve educational adjustments for media staff and even business opportunities in media. CIMA also notes that this development can be supported by the donors and private investments while it could be achieved by media owners, managers, journalists, media industry associations, and other collective efforts (CIMA, n.d.).

UNESCO develops a framework, Media Development Indicators, which consists of the ways in which media can contribute to and be influenced by good governance and democratization. These indicators are combined under five categories below (UNESCO, 2008):

- "A system of regulation conducive to freedom of expression, pluralism, and diversity of the media
- Plurality and diversity of media, a level economic playing field, and transparency of ownership
- Media as a platform for democratic discourse
- Professional capacity building and supporting institutions that underpins freedom of expression, pluralism, and diversity
- Infrastructural capacity is sufficient to support independent and pluralistic media."

Media Assistance

The origins of media development can be found in the Cold War era, but it has taken particular attention since the end of the Cold War. To achieve media development and enable democratization and good governance, international aid donors and aid workers have been providing and managing aid transfer since the 1980s and 1990s. Especially in the last twenty years, the donors have been contributing to media development by providing development assistance or democracy assistance and specifically sharing and transferring resources for media development to developing countries under the name of "media assistance."

Media assistance is defined as "everything from using the media to encourage people to vote, to a national program to train investigative journalists, or support to a website that exposes corruption" (Myers et al., 2017, p. 4). Media assistance, therefore, consists of support to information and communications technology or infrastructures, support to any media sector for production, and benefiting from the media for establishing the relationship between recipient countries' public and donor country.

On the other hand, Terzis (2015, p.1) defines media assistance as "an attempt to influence the media governance of a country or region in order to support the development of the proper functioning of liberal democracies in conditions of peace and respect of human rights." According to Terzis (2015), there are several instruments and actors in the media assistance process. The actors include the donors and donor implementers, intermediaries, agencies, and contractors, as well as local partners such as media outlets, media organizations, NGOs, professional media associations, journalism schools, universities, policymakers, and government institutions.

Media assistance includes the provision of media content, hardware and tools, and institutional core funding that could be used for training and education. CIMA explains that media assistance has seven categories which include training, organization development and management, policies and institutions, financial support for news production, research on media systems, mixed approaches, and media development (unspecified).

Media Assistance could influence media development in two main ways: support for media freedom and support for media capacity. First, theoretically, media assistance could increase the independence of media by creating incentives for the recipient government to diminish the institutional barriers and regulations for the media sector and by increasing the role of the government for media freedom (Dutta and Williamson, 2018, p. 604). While this argument sounds logical and achievable theoretically, Dutta and Williamson (2016) find that foreign aid does not lead to press freedom in autocracies, and it contributes to press freedom only if the recipient country is already democratic.

Second, foreign assistance and, more particularly, media assistance can boost media capacity in the recipient nation by increasing the capacity of ICT technology, training the journalists, providing financial support for news production, and increasing the capacity of media institutions in the recipient countries. Poland, for example, provides media assistance to Ukraine, focusing on media capacity development, though it is highly under-financed (Galus, 2020; p. 390).

DOMESTIC POLITICS OF DONORS AND MEDIA ASSISTANCE

Literature on the effectiveness of foreign aid also focuses on the donor's motivation to understand why aid can be ineffective. A significant study by Alesina and Dollar (2000) indicates that donors' motivation to give aid originates from their interests, such as in trade or support in the United Nations Security Council (UNSC). For that reason, if the aid is given solely for the strategic interests of donors and targeted only to meet these interests, it might not meet the recipients' needs.

To uncover donors' motivation in providing foreign assistance, a branch of studies examines the regime type and ideology of the donor countries and governments (e.g., Lumsdaine, 1987; Lancaster, 2006; De Mesquita and Smith, 2007; 2009). In one of the leading studies, Lancaster (2006) explains the impact of domestic politics of donors on foreign aid policies and argues that ideas, institutions, organizations, and interest groups determine the foreign aid policies of donor countries. Also, De Mesquita and Smith (2007, 2009) apply the Selectorate Theory of foreign policy on foreign aid motivations of donor countries and examine the impact of regime type on the foreign aid motivations of the leaders. Accordingly, democratic countries give assistance to receive some policy concessions from the recipient countries, which could help to provide public goods to their citizens. Conversely, the leaders in autocratic countries aid to provide private goods to their supporters in their small size winning coalition. Their explanation (De Mesquita and Smith, 2007; 2009) clarifies that not only the recipient countries' regime type but also the donors' regime type matter on the aid motivation. In another study, Annen and Strickland (2017) also take the donor's regime type into account and argue that governments can use this assistance to justify to the public in the media what they spend for due to the visible nature of humanitarian assistance. As a result, donors spend more on humanitarian assistance if the election date is close. Some studies also consider the government ideology as a motivation for aid giving. Lumsdaine (1987) explains that leftist parties in donor countries can be influential in the provision of foreign assistance due to their emphasis on equality and freedom. Tingley (2010) also argues that liberal governments are more likely to provide a higher amount of foreign assistance compared to conservative ones.

On the other hand, donor motivation based on their regime type and ideology in providing particularly for media assistance has yet to be examined in the literature. If the regime type and ideology of donors have an impact on the amount of foreign assistance they give, then they should influence the media assistance provided. Relying on that, different types of regimes of donors might provide different amounts of media assistance. More specifically, democracies might provide media assistance in a higher amount compared to autocracies, given their interests in freedom of expression, freedom of media, human rights, and media. Autocracies, on the other hand, are also usually considered to provide aid to transfer their regime and ideology to the recipient nation. Therefore, they might provide foreign aid directly to governments, not specifically for media. Moreover, the donors with higher media independence might provide a higher amount of media assistance than the donors with lower media independence because if the donors care about media independence in their countries, they might be more interested in increasing media independence in the recipient nation as well.

In addition to regime type and level of media independence in donor countries, the ideology of the donor government might influence the amount of media assistance provided. As Lumsdaine (1987) notes, governments heavily formed of leftist parties could provide a higher amount of media assistance to further emphasize the importance of freedom in the recipient nation compared to the governments primarily formed of the parties from the right ideology.

WHICH DONOR COUNTRIES PROVIDE MORE MEDIA ASSISTANCE?

The scholarly attention on media assistance is limited with a few case studies, while the Center for International Media Assistance has been paying particular focus to the area. The existing studies usually focus on whether the media assistance or foreign aid, in general, has any impact on the media development (whether it is media independence or media capacity) (e.g., Dutta and Williamson, Brownlee, 2017; Harris, 2018; Galus, 2020). In other words, in most of these studies, media assistance or foreign aid is used as an independent variable.

The current literature on media assistance lacks studies that consider media assistance as a dependent variable and that examine what leads donor countries to provide media assistance or why do specific donor countries provide a higher amount of media assistance compared to others. While CIMA describes the top donors of media assistance as well as their recipients in its reports (Myers et al., 2017; 2018), these reports lack sufficient explanation regarding the specific characteristics of the donor countries. To fill this gap in the literature, this study describes the top donors of media assistance and identifies the regime type, level of press freedom, and government ideology of more generous donors of media aid.

There are two primary datasets that the researchers benefit from in foreign assistance studies. One of them is AidData (Tierney et al., 2011) which offers project-level foreign assistance data. In CIMA's reports, this dataset has been used to identify the aid projects that are in different categories of media (Myers et al., 2018). The more commonly used dataset is OECD's Official Development Assistance data in Creditor Reporting System. The OECD classifies the official development assistance within 270 sectors in this database. One of these sectors is presented as Media and Free Flow of Information (Creditor Reporting System, 2021). This study benefits from OECD's data to describe the characteristics of media assistance providers.

In this database, there is media assistance data for both DAC and non-DAC donors, which provide media assistance. The OECD provides media assistance data for between the years 2002 and 2020. Unfortunately, there is no information regarding the media assistance of some countries such as China in this database. Also, some countries' media assistance data is missing for some years in this dataset. There is no information on whether these countries did not provide any media assistance in those years or whether the OECD does not simply have this information. Nevertheless, since the OECD is one of the prominent institutions that systematically records foreign assistance data, this study uses the OECD's database.

In OECD's database, it is seen that 35 donor countries in total have provided media assistance between the years 2002 and 2020. Therefore, on a yearly basis, there are 665 country-year level observations. The donor countries on this dataset are listed in Appendix 1. According to the data of the OECD, 29 of these countries are DAC members, while 6 of them are non-DAC media assistance providers. Table 1 below shows the top ten providers of media assistance in the last 19 years, while Table 2 presents the donors which provide the least amount of media assistance among the donors.

As shown in Table 1, Germany has provided the highest amount of media assistance in the last 19 years with 2453,284 million dollars. The United States follows Germany with total media assistance of 1038,359 million US dollars and the United Kingdom with a total of 644,2171 million US dollars in 19 years. While Germany, the US, and the UK have been the top three providers of media assistance in the

Table 1. Top donor countries of media assistance between the years of 2002 and 2020

Donor Country	Media Assistance Between 2002-2020 (US Million $)
Germany	2453,284
United States	1038,359
United Kingdom	644,2171
Sweden	434,549
Norway	167,5946
France	127,9767
Netherlands	127,7071
Denmark	78,94743
Poland	65,89352
Switzerland	55,44086

Source: OECD, Creditor Reporting System (2021)

Table 2. Donors that provide the least amount of media assistance between 2002 and 2020

Donor Country	Total Media Assistance between 2002-2020 (US Million $)
Lithuania	0,9036
Turkey	0,647972
United Arab Emirates	0,613249
Romania	0,239009
Greece	0,216417
Latvia	0,192914
Iceland	0,13053
Slovak Republic	0,128739
Hungary	0,069909
Slovenia	0,03852

Source: OECD, Creditor Reporting System (2021)

last 19 years, Sweden, Norway, France, Netherlands, Denmark, Poland, and Switzerland also provide a significant amount of assistance for media and information flow.

Besides, Table 2 demonstrates that among 35 media assistance providers, Slovenia, Hungary, and the Slovak Republic have provided the least amount of media assistance in the last 19 years. They are followed by Iceland, Latvia, Greece, Romania, United Arab Emirates, Turkey, and Lithuania.

On the other hand, the higher amount of media assistance does not always indicate that the top providers indeed care about media development the most. Wealthier donors might provide higher amounts not just because they care the most but because they have more resources than the others. Therefore, the higher amount of media assistance does not reflect the generosity of the donor country on behalf of the media development. Besides identifying the top donors, this chapter also examines how generous the donor countries are when it comes to media development.

The generosity of donors can be examined in two ways. First, the countries' media assistance relative to its national income can be a useful indicator to understand to what extent the donor country is interested in the media development in recipient countries. Another way can be estimating the generosity relative to donor countries' total official foreign assistance. In this way, this study shows to what extent the donor country cares about media development relative to the other sectors in the provision of foreign aid.

To understand the generosity of donors, this study follows both ways, therefore, collects data for gross national income of the media assistance donor countries from the World Bank database (the World Bank, 2021) and total official development assistance data of these donors from OECD's Official Development Assistance data (OECD Creditor Reporting System, 2021). To calculate the generosity of donors in media assistance, this study calculates the share of the media assistance relative to the donor countries' gross national income by multiplying the yearly media assistance by 100 and dividing the result into the gross national income of the donor country. Moreover, to examine the share of the media assistance among the total yearly official development assistance, the amount of media assistance is multiplied by 100 and then divided into the amount of total yearly official development assistance of donors. Table 3 shows the most generous donors of media assistance relative to their GNI, while Table

Table 3. The most generous donors of media assistance between the years of 2002 and 2020 (relative to their GNI)

Donor Country	Years	Share of Media Assistance Relative to the GNI (US Million $)
Germany	2015	0,648960823
Germany	2019	0,63514738
Germany	2016	0,606484795
Germany	2014	0,603172463
Germany	2013	0,592730254
Germany	2018	0,588701983
Germany	2017	0,587413421
United Kingdom	2019	0,508205131
United Kingdom	2017	0,50457
United Kingdom	2018	0,462037579

Source: OECD, Creditor Reporting System (2021)

Table 4. The most generous donors of media assistance between the years of 2002 and 2020 (relative to their Total ODA)

Donor Country	Years	Share of Media Assistance Relative to the total ODA (US Million $)
Poland	2014	7,906046158
Poland	2015	7,543617705
Poland	2013	5,848761029
Poland	2019	5,002415718
Poland	2016	4,843966497
Poland	2018	4,072917211
Poland	2017	3,825466566
Germany	2013	2,052812393
Latvia	2020	1,946154952
Estonia	2018	1,916559385

Source: OECD, Creditor Reporting System (2021)

4 demonstrates the donors that provide the highest amount of media assistance relative to their total official development assistance.

Table 3 shows the top ten generous donors of the media assistance in a given year between 2002 and 2020. As is seen in Table 3, Germany has been the most generous donor of media assistance for multiple years in the last 19 years. It has provided the highest share of its national income for media development in other countries in many years, such as 2013, 2014, 2015, 2016, 2017, 2018, 2019. Germany is followed by the United Kingdom. The United Kingdom has also shared a high amount of media assistance from their national income, particularly in 2017, 2018, and 2019.

Table 3 demonstrates which donor countries provide the highest share of their total official development assistance for the media. According to Table 4, Poland has been the leading donor, which shares the highest amount of media assistance from its yearly official development assistance in multiple years. It has provided the highest share of its official development assistance for media in 2013, 2014, 2015, 2016, 2017, 2018, and 2019 among the last 19 years. In addition to Poland, Germany in the year 2013, Latvia in the year 2020, and Estonia in the year 2018 are the countries that have provided the largest share of their ODA for media compared to other countries between 2002 and 2020.

Table 4 shows that the most generous donors of media assistance are also among the top donors of media assistance. However, although the United States is among the top donors, it is seen that the US has not been sharing its GNI for media assistance as much as Germany or the United Kingdom does. On the other hand, Table 4 verifies that the donors which provide the highest amount of media assistance are not always the ones that attach the highest importance to media development. Interestingly, none of the top media assistance donor countries except Germany spends the highest share of their official development assistance for media development. Poland appears to be sharing a larger part of its ODA for media compared to other donors in multiple years. Moreover, while Latvia and Estonia are also not among the top media assistance donors, they appear as the countries which are most interested in the media sector compared to the other donors' interests.

WHAT TYPE OF DONORS PROVIDE MORE MEDIA ASSISTANCE?

In the previous section of this chapter, the generosity of the media assistance donors has been evaluated. While it explains which donors are more generous, it still does not indicate any characteristic features of the top or generous donors. This section focuses on uncovering some of the significant characteristics of the top media assistance donors. To analyze what type of donors provide a higher amount of media assistance, this study uses the variables regarding the domestic politics of donors, such as donors' level of democracy, donors' level of media independence, and donor governments' ideology.

As discussed above, media development is seen as an essential part of democracy. A critical motivation of donor countries is influencing the domestic politics of recipient countries. This influence could be achieved by foreign assistance, whether given conditionally or unconditionally. Because democratic donor countries might aim to influence the recipient countries by transferring their democratic values, it can be expected that they focus on media development as a part of their aim in spreading democracy. Therefore, it is expected that democratic donor countries are more likely to provide a higher amount of media assistance. To demonstrate if the democratic donors provide a higher amount of media assistance, this study uses the democracy score data of Freedom House (2021). Figure 1 shows that democratic donor countries (free) of media assistance spend a much higher amount of assistance with about 17 million US dollars for media development compared to non-democratic and hybrid regimes (not free and partly free). Figure 2 also shows that media assistance donors with higher democracy scores provide a higher amount of media assistance compared to the donors with lower democracy scores.

Figure 1. Mean of media assistance based on regime type of media assistance donors
Source: Freedom House, (2021) and OECD, Creditor Reporting System (2021)

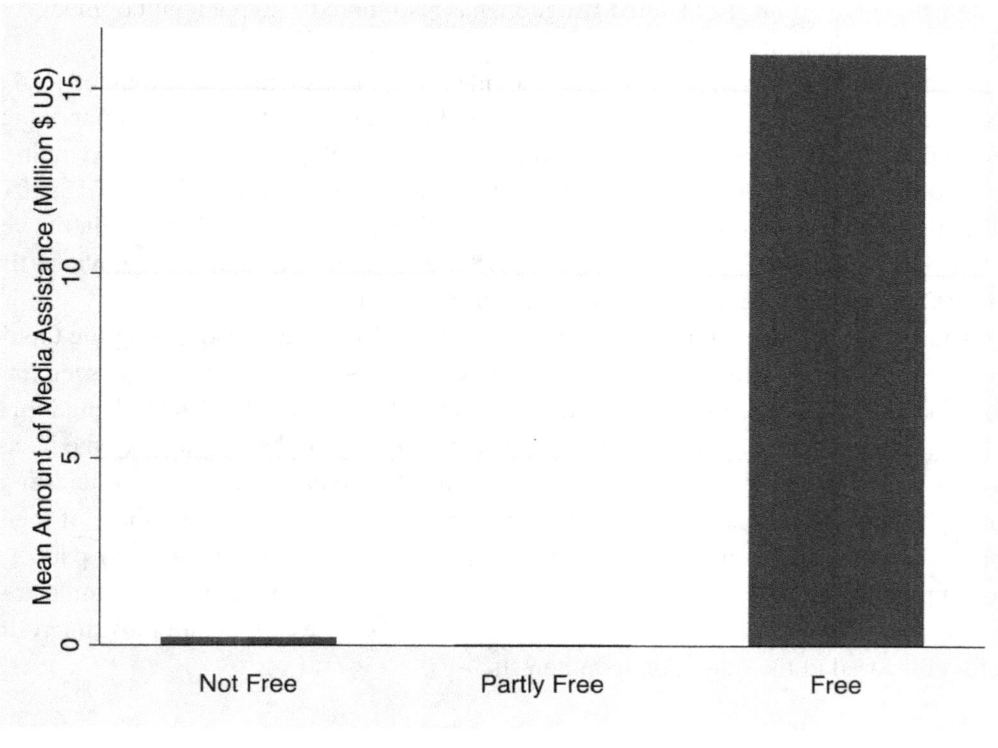

Figure 2. Amount of media assistance based on the donors' level of democracy
Source: Freedom House, (2021) and OECD, Creditor Reporting System (2021)

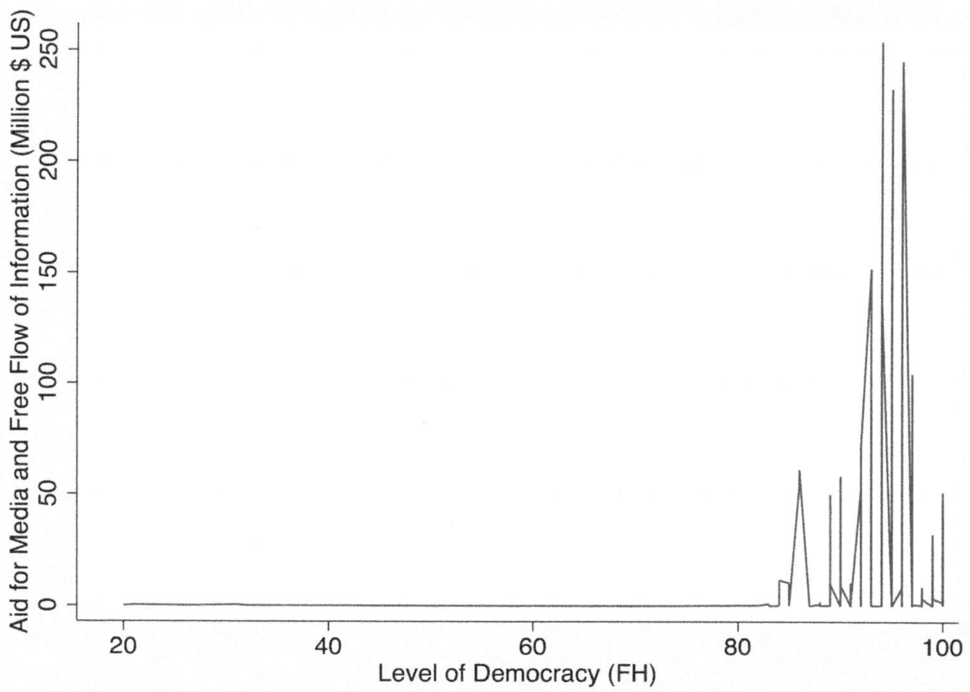

While the regime type of the donor countries might determine the amount of media assistance given, it could also affect the generosity of the donor country. In other words, democratic donors might be more interested in providing media assistance relative to their GNI and their total foreign aid. Therefore, this study also examines if the regime type of the donor country determines the generosity of donors in the transfer of media aid. Figure 3 indicates that media assistance donors with a higher level of democracy are more generous in providing media assistance relative to their GNI, while Figure 4 also shows media assistance donors with a higher level of democracy provide a higher share of their ODA for media assistance compared to donors with a lower level of democracy.

Media assistance is given for media development which involves media capacity and media independence. It could be expected that the countries with a higher level of media independence might be more interested in media independence in other countries as well. Therefore, this study also examines if the donor's level of media independence determines the amount of media assistance given and the donor's generosity in media assistance provision. To analyze this, level of press independence variable has been used from the Reporters Without Borders index (Reporters Without Borders, 2021). This index has two different variables; one measures the ranking of the country in a given year, while the other one measures the level of press independence. For the aim of this study, the level of press independence data is used. The data in this variable ranges between 0 and 100, with 0 being the highest level of freedom of the press and 100 being the least level of freedom of the press. Figure 5 demonstrates that the donors with a higher level of press freedom are more likely to provide a higher amount of media assistance. Figure 6 and Figure 7 show that the donors with a higher level of press independence are more likely to share

Figure 3. Spending of donors' media assistance relative to their GNI and based on their level of democracy
Source: Freedom House, (2021) and OECD, Creditor Reporting System (2021)

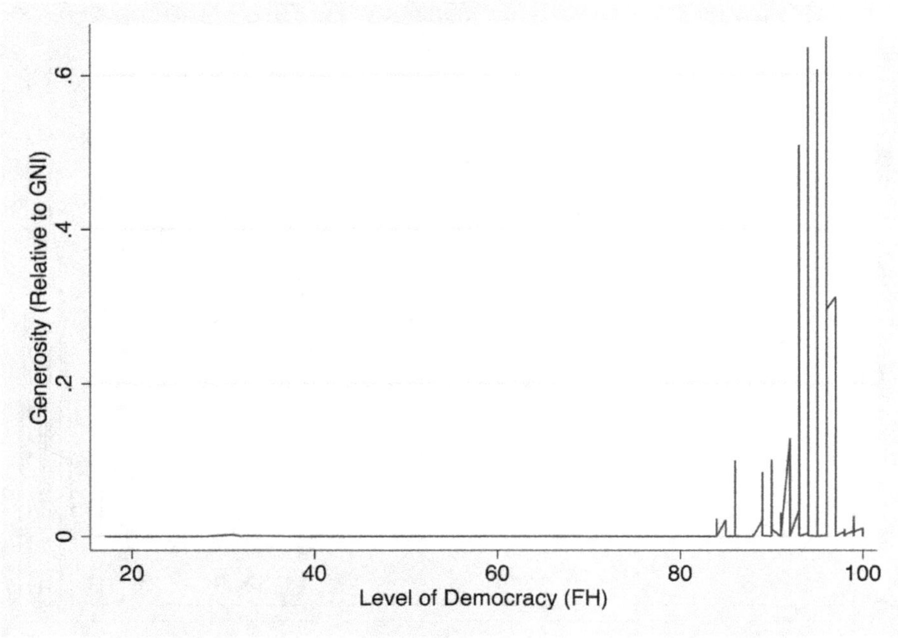

Figure 4. Spending of donors' media assistance relative to their total ODA and based on their level of democracy
Source: Freedom House, (2021) and OECD, Creditor Reporting System (2021)

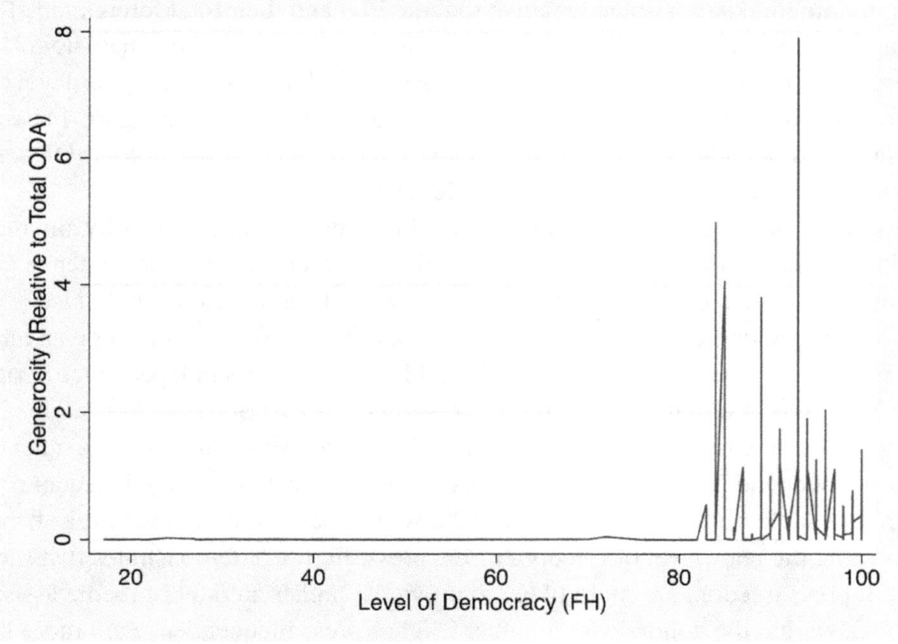

Figure 5. The relationship between the level of press freedom in donors of media assistance and their media assistance
Source: Reporters Without Borders (2021) and OECD, Creditor Reporting System (2021)

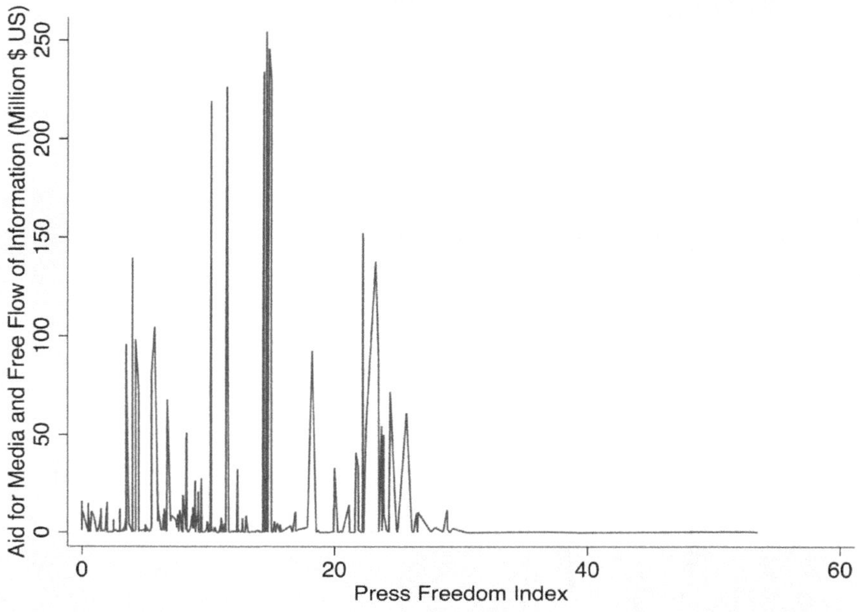

Figure 6. Spending of donors' media assistance relative to their GNI and based on their level of press freedom
Source: Reporters Without Borders (2021) and OECD, Creditor Reporting System (2021)

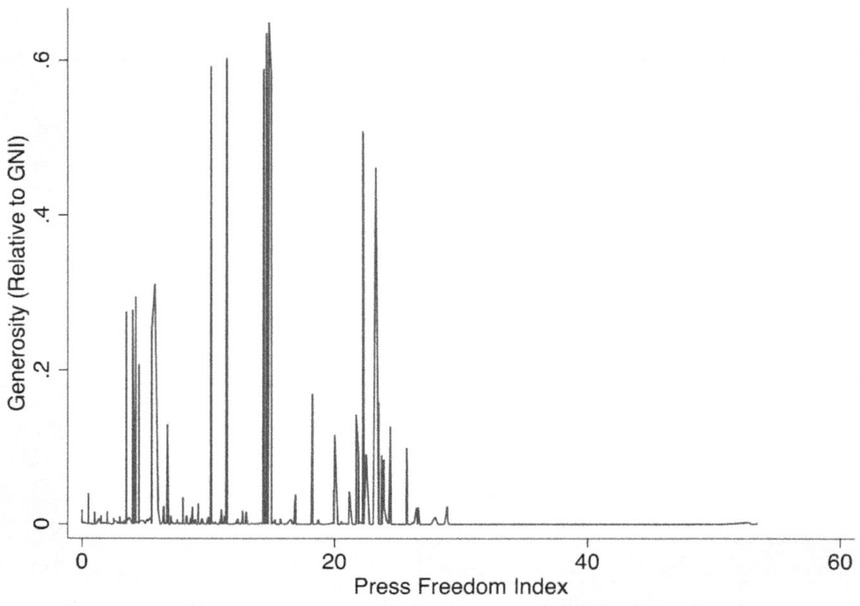

Figure 7. Spending of donors' media assistance relative to their total ODA and based on their level of press freedom
Source: Reporters Without Borders (2021) and OECD, Creditor Reporting System (2021)

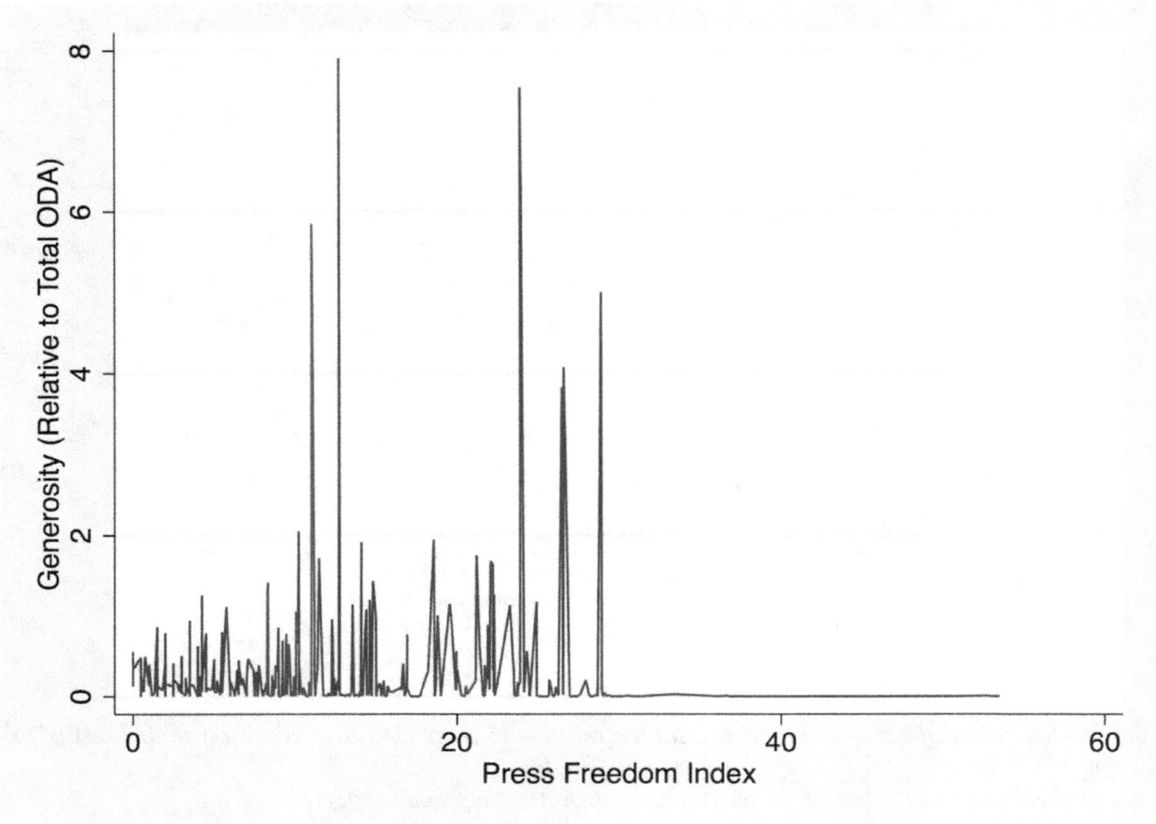

the higher amount of their GNI for media assistance, and these countries are also more likely to share a higher amount of their total ODA for media development.

Moreover, media assistance provision might be motivated by the ideology of the donor government. This study also analyzes if the government's right, left, and center ideology influences the amount of media assistance and their generosity in media assistance. To do so, this study uses the government left ideology, government right ideology, and government center ideology data from the Comparative Political Dataset (Armingeon et al., 2021). Comparative Political Dataset has three variables regarding the government's ideology in a country in a given year. These variables are called gov_right2, gov_cent2, and gov_left2, and each of these measures "the relative power position of right/center/left parties in government based on their seat share in parliament, measured in percentage of the total parliamentary seat share of all governing parties" (Armingeon et al., 2021). To be able to compare the amount of media assistance by different donors with different ideologies, this study creates a new variable based on the most common ideology in the government. In this new variable, if the highest percentage of seat share is right, then the country is coded as right for that year. If the highest percentage of seat share is left, then the country is coded as left for that year, and if the seat share is center, then the country is coded as center. Moreover, some countries have an equal percentage in the share of seats for a given year. In

Figure 8. Mean amount of media assistance based on the donor governments` ideology
Source: Comparative Political Dataset (Armingeon et al., 2021) and OECD, Creditor Reporting System (2021)

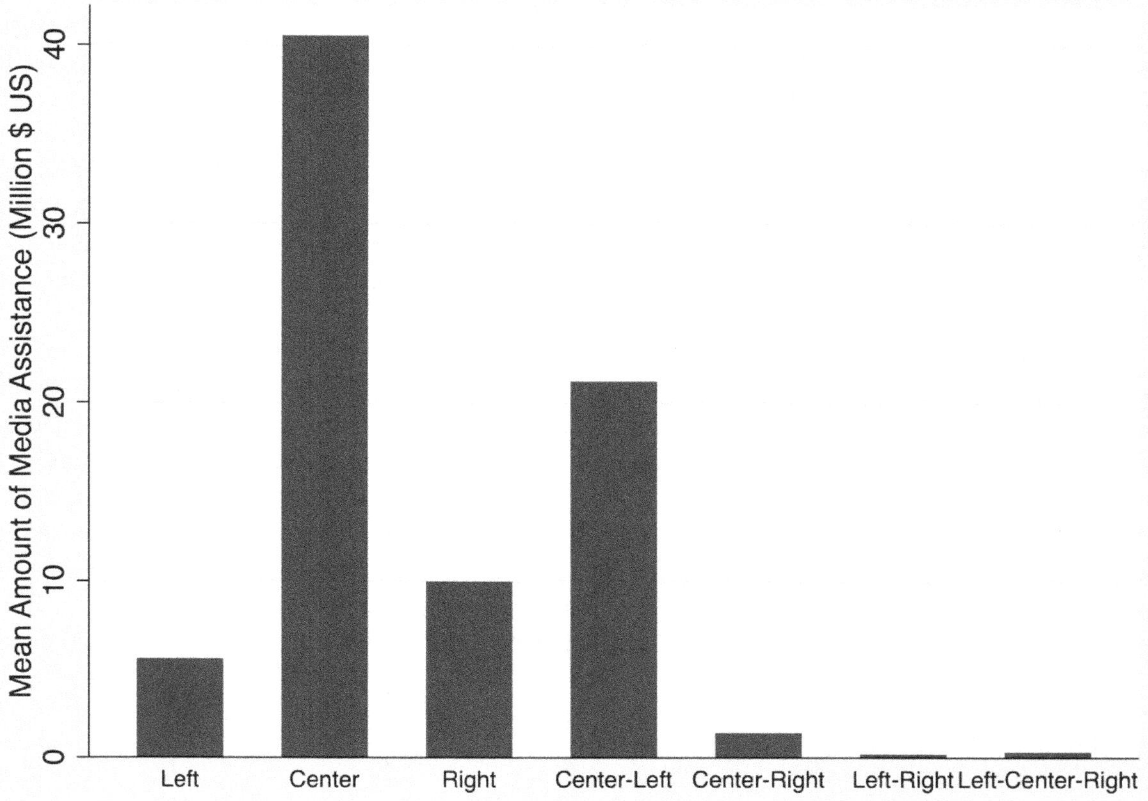

those cases, all ideologies have been coded, such as left-center, right-center, left-right, left-center-right. Interestingly, as Figure 8 shows, donor governments of media assistance with center ideology appear to be giving the highest amount of media assistance compared to the right and left governments. These center governments are followed by donor governments with center-left ideology.

CONCLUSION

Donors of foreign assistance have been paying specific attention to media development in recent years. These donors share some of their development assistance to the media sector to increase media capacity and media independence in the recipient countries. However, the literature in media assistance is highly limited in numbers and overlooks the donors' domestic political factors to understand donors' motivation in the provision of media assistance. This chapter focuses on the donors' regime type, level of press freedom, and government ideology to uncover which and what type of donors have been providing the highest amount of media assistance.

With this aim, this chapter first identifies the top donors and most generous countries of media assistance by benefiting from the OECD's data on media and information flow. Then, using data from the Freedom House, Reporters Without Borders, and Comparative Political datasets, this chapter examines what type of donor countries provide the highest amount of media assistance based on their regime type, level of press independence, and government ideology. As a result, this study finds that Germany, the US, and the UK are the top donors of media assistance while Germany and the UK are also the most generous countries in media assistance based on their GNI between the years of 2002 and 2020. On the other hand, in those years, Poland, Germany, Latvia, and Estonia have provided the highest share of its ODA for media assistance. Moreover, this study finds that democratic donor countries, donors with a higher level of press independence, and donor governments with center ideology provide a higher amount of media assistance compared to autocratic donors, donors with a lower level of press independence, and donor governments with other ideologies.

This study offers a detailed and useful description to understand the donors' motivation in giving media assistance. However, it also has limitations. First of all, this study does not employ any inferential test to analyze the domestic political motivations of donors. Future studies that employ inferential tests to analyze the domestic motivations of donors in media assistance can be quite useful to understand if the findings of this study are statistically significant. Second, the countries which do not provide any amount of media assistance between 2002 and 2020 are not included in the analysis of this paper. A future study that can compare the countries which provide media assistance with the countries that do not provide media assistance might be beneficial to understand why some countries prefer to be donors of media assistance in the first place while the others do not pay particular attention to the media development.

ACKNOWLEDGMENT

This research received no specific grant from any funding agency in the public, commercial, or not-for-profit sectors.

REFERENCES

Alesina, A., & Dollar, D. (2000). Who Gives Foreign Aid to Whom and Why? *Journal of Economic Growth*, *5*(1), 33–63. doi:10.1023/A:1009874203400

Armingeon, K., Engler, S., & Leemann, L. (2021). *Supplement to the Comparative Political Data Set – Government Composition 1960-2019*. Institute of Political Science, University of Zurich.

Bearce, D. H., & Tirone, D. C. (2010). Foreign aid effectiveness and the strategic goals of donor governments. *The Journal of Politics*, *72*(3), 837–851. doi:10.1017/S0022381610000204

Berry, W. D., Ringquist, E. J., Fording, R. C., & Hanson, R. L. (1998). Measuring citizen and government ideology in the American states, 1960-93. *American Journal of Political Science*, *42*(1), 327–348. doi:10.2307/2991759

Brownlee, B. J. (2017). Media development in Syria: The Janus-faced nature of foreign aid assistance. *Third World Quarterly*, *38*(10), 2276–2294. doi:10.1080/01436597.2017.1333420

Burnside, C., & Dollar, D. (2000). Aid, policies, and growth. *The American Economic Review*, *90*(4), 847–868. doi:10.1257/aer.90.4.847

Center for International Media Assistance. (n.d.). *What is media development?* Center for International Media Assistance. Retrieved December 02, 2021, from https://www.cima.ned.org/what-is-media-development/

De Mesquita, B., & Smith, A. (2009). A Political Economy of Aid. *International Organization*, *63*(2), 309–340. doi:10.1017/S0020818309090109

De Mesquita, B. B., & Smith, A. (2007). Foreign Aid and Policy Concessions. *Journal of Conflict Resolution, 51*(2), 251–284. . doi:10.1177/0022002706297696

Dutta, N., & Williamson, C. (2016). Can foreign aid free the press? *Journal of Institutional Economics*, *12*(3), 603–621. doi:10.1017/S1744137415000557

Easterly, W. (2003). Can foreign aid buy growth? *The Journal of Economic Perspectives*, *17*(3), 23–48. doi:10.1257/089533003769204344

Fayissa, B., & El-Kaissy, M. I. (1999). Foreign aid and the economic growth of developing countries (LDCs): Further evidence. *Studies in Comparative International Development*, *34*(3), 37–50. doi:10.1007/BF02687626

Galus, A. (2020). What is Media Assistance and (Why) Does It Matter? The Case of Polish Foreign Aid to the Media in Belarus and Ukraine. *Central European Journal of Communication*, *13*(27), 390–408.

Harris, S. T. G. (2018). Questioning the Role of Foreign Aid in Media System Research. In B. Mutsvairo (Ed.), *The Palgrave Handbook of Media and Communication Research in Africa*. Palgrave Macmillan., doi:10.1007/978-3-319-70443-2_22

Karras, G. (2006). Foreign aid and long-run economic growth: Empirical evidence for a panel of developing countries. *Journal of International Development: The Journal of the Development Studies Association*, *18*(1), 15–28. doi:10.1002/jid.1187

Kim, J. (2011). Foreign aid and economic development: The success story of South Korea. *Pacific Focus*, *26*(2), 260–286. doi:10.1111/j.1976-5118.2011.01065.x

Lugo-Ocando, J. (2018). A Mouthpiece for Truth: Foreign Aid for Media Development and the Making for Journalism in the Global South. *Brazilian Journalism Research*, *14*(2), 412–431. doi:10.25200/BJR.v14n2.2018.1101

Myers, M., Harford, N., & Bartholomew, K. (2017). *Media Assistance: Review of the Recent Literature and Other Donors' Approaches*. Imedia Associates.

Myers, M., Juma, L. A., & O'Maley, D. (2018). *Defending independent media: A Comprehensive analysis of aid flows*. Center for International Media Assistance. https://stats.oecd.org/Index.aspx?DataSetCode=crs1

OECD. (2021, April 13). *COVID-19 spending helped to lift foreign aid to an all-time high in 2020*. OECD Detailed Note. Retrieved December 02, 2021, from https://www.oecd.org/dac/financing-sustainable-development/development-finance-data/ODA-2020-detailed-summary.pdf

Rajan, R. G., & Subramanian, A. (2008). Aid and growth: What does the cross-country evidence really show? *The Review of Economics and Statistics*, *90*(4), 643–665. doi:10.1162/rest.90.4.643

Reporters Without Borders. (n.d.a). *2021 World Press Freedom Index: Journalism, the vaccine against disinformation, blocked more than 130 countries*. Reporters Without Borders. Retrieved November 2, 2021, from https://rsf.org/en/2021-world-press-freedom-index-journalism-vaccine-against-disinformation-blocked-more-130-countries

Reporters Without Borders. (n.d.b). *World Press Freedom Index 2021*. Retrieved October 10, 2021, from https://rsf.org/en/ranking_table

Repucci, S. (2019). *Freedom and Media 2019: Media Freedom: A Downward Spiral*. Freedom House. https://freedomhouse.org/report/freedom-and-media/2019/media-freedom-downward-spiral

Savun, B., & Tirone, D. C. (2011). Foreign Aid, Democratization, and Civil Conflict: How Does Democracy Aid Affect Civil Conflict? *American Journal of Political Science*, *55*(2), 233–246. doi:10.1111/j.1540-5907.2010.00501.x

Terzis, G. (2015). *INFOCORE Definitions: "Media Assistance"*. Brussels: Global Governance Institute. Retrieved November 30, 2021, from https://www.infocore.eu/results/definitions/

The World Bank, World Development Indicators. (2021). *GNI*. Retrieved November 10,2021, from https://data.worldbank.org/indicator/NY.GNP.PCAP.CD

Tierney, M. J., Nielson, D. L., Hawkins, D. G., Roberts, J. T., Findley, M. G., Powers, R. M., Parks, B., Wilson, S. E., & Hicks, R. L. (2011). More dollars than sense: Refining our knowledge of development finance using AidData. *World Development*, *39*(11), 1891–1906. doi:10.1016/j.worlddev.2011.07.029

UNESCO. (2008, March 26-28). *Media Development Indicators: A Framework for assessing media development.* Intergovernmental Council of the International Programme for the Development of Communication (IPDC). Retrieved December 02, 2021, from https://unesdoc.unesco.org/ark:/48223/pf0000163102

Uvin, P. (1998). *Aiding Violence: The Development Enterprise in Rwanda*. Kumarian Press.

Yiew, T. H., & Lau, E. (2018). Does foreign aid contribute to or impeded economic growth? *Journal of International Students*, *11*(3), 21–30. doi:10.14254/2071-8330.2018/11-3/2

APPENDIX

Table 5. List of media assistance donors

Donors	Years
Australia	2002-2020
Austria	2002-2020
Belgium	2002-2020
Canada	2002-2020
Czech Republic	2002-2020
Denmark	2002-2020
Finland	2002-2020
France	2002-2020
Germany	2002-2020
Greece	2002-2020
Hungary	2002-2020
Iceland	2002-2020
Ireland	2002-2020
Italy	2002-2020
Japan	2002-2020
Korea	2002-2020
Luxembourg	2002-2020
Netherlands	2002-2020
New Zealand	2002-2020
Norway	2002-2020
Poland	2002-2020
Portugal	2002-2020
Slovak Republic	2002-2020
Slovenia	2002-2020
Spain	2002-2020
Sweden	2002-2020
Switzerland	2002-2020
United Kingdom	2002-2020
United States	2002-2020
Estonia	2002-2020
Latvia	2002-2020
Lithuania	2002-2020
Romania	2002-2020
Turkey	2002-2020
United Arab Emirates	2002-2020

Chapter 11
Participatory Communication and Digital Media in Africa:
A New Paradigm

Desmond Onyemechi Okocha
https://orcid.org/0000-0001-5070-280X
Bingham University, Nigeria

Roxie Ojoma Ola-Akuma
Bingham University, Nigeria

ABSTRACT

Digital media has had an unquestionable impact on participatory communication. The use of digital media has become a part of the community development framework for inclusive participation. Premised on the foregoing, this chapter sought to examine how digital media, an emerging development in Africa, has changed the status of participatory communication across the continent. Furthermore, it reviewed how this new phenomenon has paved the way for empowerment journalism and digital participation, thereby making participatory communication a community development tool in the 21st century that heightens collaborations. The study was anchored on theories of new media and development communication. The methodology employed a desk review. Findings showed that aside from vitalizing participatory communication for rural development, community journalists needed to be conscious that they create a new twist that clashes with what the mainstream media professionals do from a community's viewpoint, which can impede participation.

INTRODUCTION

Community Participation in Primary Health Care, Community Participation in Tourism Planning and Development, infrastructure development, education and agriculture have been sustainable development strategies between development agencies and the government intended for the government and the community especially in low-income countries. There is, however, evidence about the nature of some

DOI: 10.4018/978-1-6684-4107-7.ch011

partnerships that lacks the perspective of community members. Through participatory communication, communities experience development because community member who are involved in problem-solving and decision-making not only improve the community but also gain new skills, change behaviour, and adopt change.

What Africa has been long subjected to have been the rise of a small number of persons tagged as key stakeholders deciding for the entire local government area, state, regions, province, or nation. For example, the Nigerian Constitution enacted in 1999 starts with a phrase

We the people of the Federal Republic of Nigeria Having firmly and solemnly resolve, to live in unity and harmony as one indivisible and indissoluble sovereign nation under God, dedicated to the promotion of inter-African solidarity, world peace, international co-operation and understanding And to provide for a Constitution for the purpose of promoting the good government and welfare of all persons in our country, on the principles of freedom, equality and justice, and for the purpose of consolidating the unity of our people Do hereby make, enact and give to ourselves the following Constitution- (Constitution of the Federal Republic of Nigeria, 1999).

Indeed, the question an individual will be asking will be "when was I even consulted for this? How? Even after being enacted, except in some formal education settings where the Nigerian constitution is taught as part of a topic in subjects such as – civic education, government, and history or then in the university for Political Science, Mass Communication and International Relations Students, the researcher is not aware of any other system that has been deliberately employed to breakdown or dissect the sections in the constitution to the citizens. What we have proliferating the internet are fragments and misinterpretations of the constitution on social media which has significantly turned sour in the mouths of Nigerians for example.

According to a World Bank and African Development Bank (AFDB) estimate from 2013, Africa had 650 million mobile users, far more than the United States or Europe. Africa had 507.9 million Internet users in 2021, accounting for 10.9 percent of web users globally at the time of this study. West Africa is one of the three leading regions with the highest Internet penetration rate, at 42 percent. In terms of social media, Africa accounts for 6.6 percent of the world's active users, or over 277 million across 200 miles on the continent. Digital media have had an unquestionable impact on participatory communication: from the community town hall meetings to community radio, participatory documentary, and social media platforms. The use of digital media has become a part of the community development framework for inclusive participation. A small group meeting that could only host 50 community members with a projector slammed on a wall has translated to use of transferrable message platforms where a whole community can be connected with live from a remote location via the internet.

Premised on the foregoing, this paper reviewed how this new phenomenon has paved the way for digital participation thereby making digital media a community development tool in the 21st century that is not only increasing participation but also promoting mass literacy and awareness.

OBJECTIVE OF THE STUDY

1. To examine how digital media has changed the status for participatory communication in Africa.
2. To highlight the use of digital media in participatory communication in selected African Countries.

3. To identify factors affecting participatory communication in Africa

THEORETICAL FRAMEWORK

New Media Theory

New media theory, broadly speaking, conceptualizes the implications of digital technologies: from the novel sociopolitical configurations fostered by computer-mediated communication to the aesthetic and cultural significance of digital culture. New media are enabling development agents to accomplish their goals in peculiar ways never before seen. Videoconferencing, teleconferencing, e-mail chat areas, and podcasting allow people like to provide teams with the opportunity to share and react to great amounts of information simultaneously. Development agencies can now decide what information is necessary to aid their responsibilities or seek extra information that will be needed in the future thanks to the availability of digital media. The introduction of new technology into organizations is clearly changing conventional organizational structures and activities (West & Turner, 2010).

In addition to the aforementioned, new media theories, like any theories, have their detractors. In research on Critical Theory and Social Media published in 2018, Philippe E. Becker Marcano presented the alternatives and new sensibility that new media consumers require. He claims that social media platforms like Facebook, Twitter, LinkedIn, and others are technical communication tools that have taken over our social lives. New media theory has been chastised for its dominance and for giving users little control over these platforms and their impact on human behavior.

Development Communication Theory

Leading scholars such as Daniel Lerner, Wilbur Schramm, and Everett Rogers championed what is called the development communication theory. Rogers is regarded as one of the founding fathers of development communication due to his pioneering effect. By gauging the needs and views of local communities that should be improved and seeking to build a consensus about development project plans that are to be carried out, participatory development seeks to ensure that attention is paid to enhancing the benefits to local people and lessening negative consequences. Information transmission and education, behavior change, social marketing, and social mobilization are all examples of development communication approaches. Other components of development communication theory incorporate media advocacy to create a homogenous entry for implementation with key stakeholders - including communication for social change, and community support.

However, critiques have contended that development communication hypothesis limits the media to be subordinated to only political, financial, social, and social needs subsequently constraining their scope. Scholars argue that too often, development communication implements westernization more than modernization because it draws in a culture of authority in its execution.

For the purpose of this study, the researcher will be focusing on communities, agencies, and government's use of the media for participatory communication to stabilize and homogenise views within a community around socio-economic and other developmental issues.

Conceptual Framework

Mefalopulos (2007) describes participatory communication as a relevant theory and practice that involves individuals in the growth process and decision-making. Participatory communication, which is distinctive from other forms of communication allows for a horizontal flow of communication based mostly on dialogue and is becoming a more important part of development efforts around the world. Participatory communication necessitates a shift in emphasis from communication as a dissemination or campaigning tool used to inform and persuade individuals to change their behavior or attitude to communication as a tool for empowerment (Haider, Mcloughlin, & Scott, 2011).

Traditional media is defined as media that existed before the rise of the internet. That includes newspapers, magazines, billboards, radio, and broadcast TV and direct mail. Digital media is any digitized content (Including digitalisation of traditional medium) that can be transmitted over the internet or computer networks. This can include text, audio, video, and graphics (Sikarwar, 2016). This means that news from a television network, newspaper, magazine, or other source that is available online via a website or blog is considered digital media. There are a wide range of digital media applications that allow for accessing digital images, digital photography, digital video, digital audio, computer games. Another form of digital media is what can be described as multimedia productions, animations, digital video film making, e-books, web pages, data, and databases. Digital media practically mean everything you can view digitally. It can also be transmitted such as online advertising, search engines, social media, video streaming services, and websites.

LITERATURE REVIEW

The Emergence of Participatory Communication in Africa

Participatory communication is a dialogue-based technique that provides an avenue for various stakeholders to share information, perceptions, and opinions, thereby facilitating their empowerment. This includes Communication for Development also known as C4D which refers to the exchange of information, ideas, knowledge, and concepts in order to improve a people's well-being particularly the rural poor. Communication for Development is built around four axes as shown in the diagram below:

1. Com4Prom: Communication for Promotion is a strategy for promoting development aid in donor countries by demonstrating how and why funds are utilized. This can be accomplished through some form of social marketing, in which the agency can use communication materials such as activity and project reports to highlight its cause or idea, as well as how the support received has aided or will aide a key program or project. Careful study needs to be carried out on the models adopted by other development or humanitarian agencies to have a clear understanding of what differentiates them and continue to persuade the donor of what is the unique proposition in terms of benefit to the beneficiary or what they could stand to lose otherwise.
2. Com4Imple: By explaining development programs to local populations, Communication for Implementation enhances the implementation of development aid in developing countries (Drouet, 2014). This can be accomplished also with the help of social media marketing where commercial marketing tactics are used in social marketing to promote public health, agriculture, educational and

Figure 1.
Source: Researchers' construct, 2021

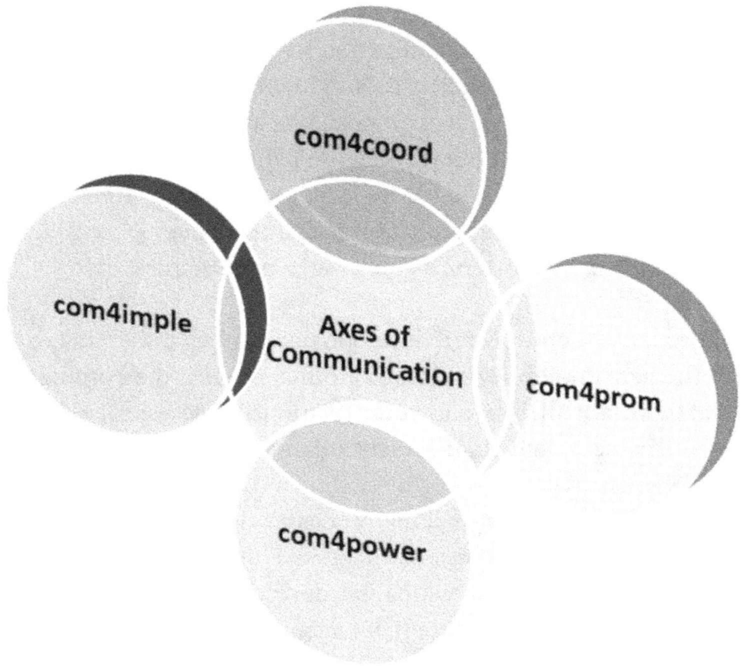

social campaigns. On a population level, social marketing is effective, and farmers, for example, can be sensitised on peculiar issues. In the book 'Marketing Social Change', Andreasen defines social marketing as "the application of proven concepts and techniques drawn from the commercial sector to promote changes in diverse socially important behaviours such as drug use, smoking, sexual behaviour, nutrition and even child labour. This marketing approach has an immense potential to affect major social problems if harnessed (Evans, 2006).

3. Com4Power: This refers to a situation where the local populations are given the ability, platform, or opportunity to speak or report on the implementation of development aid received from donor countries. Without factoring Communication for Empowerment various problems in project execution, such as inadequate communication between agencies and community people, might have a negative impact on project outcomes. Hence specific communication characteristics such as transparency, fairness, and understanding can be used by Com4Power to ensure that community buy-in is increased so that the intermediate and ultimate outcomes are achieved. Furthermore, by emphasizing empowerment, development communication professionals must visit the communities where interventions are supposedly taking place. and where they are not to allow community members the chance to evaluate the projects by institutions and agencies such as education, governance, healthcare. In this dimension, community reported outcome measures the indicators, then takes centre-stage in implementing strategies to increase their empowerment. With a consideration of community members' empowerment this can serve as a directly measurable community reported outcome for targeted issues to be addressed. An example is the case of patient empowerment in healthcare that provides them with an opportunity and tool to evaluate the kind of care they are

receiving this in turn will allow for healthcare providers to quickly attend to these issues when adopting the patient empowerment paradigm (McAllister, Dunn, Payne, Davies, & Todd, 2012).

4. Com4Coord: Communication for Coordination allows donor entities to coordinate their activities on a global scale through a series of coordination tools and rules. In case of implementing partners, to ensure proper coordination means promotional and communication material such as the websites, social media platforms, and also proposals and annual reports can play role in promotion of the cause. Experts point out that non-profits are using new innovative approaches to promote social causes, such as Facebook, Talking Books, blogs, and many others; social media campaigns raise awareness, which in turn reaches a larger global audience, increasing the agency's chances of generating more funds or supporters, as the case may be (Arora 2016)

C4D takes several forms like Top-down (a development catalyst disseminates information from development agencies to the general public). In top-bottom approach, the communication is usually one way with one source that thinks for all. This shows the relationship between communication, government accountability and responsiveness, and state-society relations in developing countries (Scott, Haider, & Mcloughlin, 2011). A variety of case studies have shown that when a development programme tries to exclude the beneficiaries from decision-making processes, it leads to nonparticipation, and exposes itself to risks that lower the project's chances of success. This becomes a Top-down approach. Parks (2021), duly notes that bottom-up approach which is a development catalyst means that information is disseminated from the general public to development agencies

The evolution of communication for development (C4D) has mirrored broader shifts in theories and models of economic and social development. From the ground up (the people are the agents of development and development agencies only prime the people up). What C4D does is to employ a participatory approach for transmission of attitudes, practices, and technologies. When this type of participation is encouraged among community members, it also supports in promoting local stakeholders' sense of ownership, which improves sustainability of an initiative. Correspondingly, communication for development initiatives adopt a diffusion approach, which uses communication tools to carry out a transfer of information such as large-scale media campaigns, social marketing, and dissemination of printed materials, 'education-entertainment' and other forms of one-way transmission of information from the sender to the receiver (Scott, Haider, & Mcloughlin, 2011).

Participatory methods employed by media and development agencies enables better identification of WHO is affected in WHICH ways and proffers WHAT can be done. In particular they enable the voices of the very poor, women, children, and vulnerable groups to be heard (Mayoux, 2018).

Types of Participation

There are different types of participation and reasons for them. Millington (2012) notes that every type of community can be classified by the purpose that brings them together along five areas: interest, action, place, practice, and circumstance. To ensure inclusive participation, community members must be segmented into the following categories and addressed accordingly.

However, through the ladder of participation as illustrated by (Cousins & Friedman, 1993) one can see the eight steps in the citizen contribution ladder, each demonstrating a different level of involvement. The ladder explains the level of public participation and how much real power the citizens have over the process and outcomes from bottom to top.

Figure 2.
The Ladder of Participation. Source: Cousins & Friedman (1993)

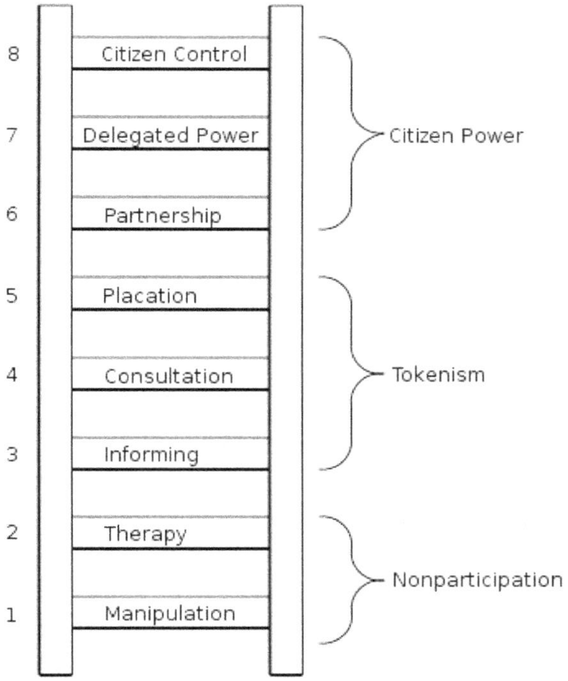

The ladder is a valuable tool for figuring out what 'participation' means in programmes and regulations. For the citizens to have power, they need to be treated according to their heterogeneous needs, and that each grouping contains people with varying degrees of authority.

Powerful actors use forms of non-participation at the bottom of the hierarchy to enforce their objectives.

The ladder above illustrates how powerful actors use forms of non-participation at the bottom of the hierarchy to enforce their objectives. When community members can discuss an intervention and decide to share their views, this is referred to as 'input' by power holders. Community members not voicing out, on the other hand, will have no impact on the project; consequently, that lack of involvement will not result in transformation.

METHODOLOGY

This is a descriptive study that took a look at a variety of community participations and cases of interactive participation with spontaneous mobilisation in Africa which includes: Sudan, Ghana, Ethiopia, Uganda, Burkina Faso, Kenya. Through the mass media and digital media tools, development agencies are effectively finding ways to include community members voices or their stories in a project. This section takes a look at some of the case studies across the African continent.

On-Air Dialogues Making Participatory Communication Audible Through Community Radio

When decisions come from community members, the goal of a project has a higher chance of being achieved. In Sudan, the IFAD Project did employ a participatory communication methodology Radio can inform people, and it is also a two-way medium that brings people into the conversation who would not otherwise be heard, like women in areas where they are prevented from speaking publicly. She further notes that confidence is built for community members as on radio, identities are protected as such they can speak openly. When people are listened to, they have hope, they have agency. When it comes to issues of climate change for example, Helene Papper, IFAD's Director of Global Communications and External Advocacy explains the need to hear the voices of people in remote rural areas, especially women and youth and this is because they are at the first to be displaced by the changing climate yet have not been equipped to weather the impacts (Raja, 2021).

Purchase for Progress (P4P) was a World Food Programme (WFP) pilot project in Ghana that aimed to connect small-scale farmers to formal markets. The project attempted to guarantee that rural residents in the Ejura-Sekyeredumase district received timely and appropriate information about optimum agricultural methods. The research was able to uncover 16 farmers' organizations because farmers are frequently organized in small groups or cooperatives. Farmers were compelled to use information to enhance agronomic techniques as a result of the market opportunity, which resulted in much higher yields and higher quality crops. The process for delivering market and business information radio program, which projects the voices of farmers through the community radio program, was spelled out in an interactive session. Educating community people about the information collected by a project can be done through films, community theaters, and news programs. Of course, these community members may have heard other radio programs previously, but they have never handled a responsibility like providing frequent market reports to other farmers, as seen in the Ghana case study. To continue to expand, they will want technical assistance to keep them informed about the best ways to conduct business.

Community radio has also aided in the provision of services and amenities for numerous parts of society's development, such as education, health, water and sanitation, disaster relief, addressing social concerns at the community level, and connecting rural populations with the government (Khan, Khan, Hassan, Ahmed, & Haque, 2017). This is due to the fact that community radio stations can be managed, owned, and influenced by the people who live within. It operates through a non-profit organization that aims to create a platform for individuals, groups, and communities to tell their own stories and share their experiences in a media-rich world. Community radios have been used by community members in various Ghanaian communities who have become creators and contributors within the media space. For example, in a study that explored the contribution of Simli Radio to the livelihood improvement of the people in the Tolon-Kumbungu and Savelugu-Nanton Districts of the Northern Region of Ghana, Al-hassan, et.al. (2011) describes that the activities of the radio have promoted the decentralisation of government improving accountability and transparency. This is made possible through an interactive session provided by the station for local authorities to explain government policies and programmes and then the people get the opportunity to question certain actions and commissions of the authorities through the "listeners' comments" sessions. So not only are the authorities speaking but community members are offered a chance to also participate.

Gender sensitivity in participatory communication is key as it allows for community members to be aware of how gender plays a role in their lives through their treatment of other members of the community especially the generally marginalised groups. In the course of ensuring participation by community members, care must be taken to also include the voices of the minority groups of women and youths. Gender sensitivity trainings should also be included to educate especially community leaders, gatekeepers, and major actors so they become more aware of and sensitive to gender as it plays out in their communities.

Participatory Communication also involves the use of the media as an initiative to increase the involvement of vulnerable groups such as women in the media. This is refereed to as Gender Sensitive Participatory Communication which projects the activities women are involved in, showcasing their strengths, and promoting them as reliable assets. Allowing for vulnerable groups such as women to contribute to the media content can change the perception the community has about them (Pavarala, Malik, and Cheeli, 2006). Through some of such participatory communication through the media, women and girls have been encouraged to venture into technical areas taking key decisions including determining the direction for others to try. A similar synthetic world appears to exist on community radios according to the facts of cultivation theory. Whatever is shared on community radios informs an opinion and might end up with a judgement.

Community Health Promoters in Uganda

Recognising the value of community members in addressing health issues and preventing ill health at the grassroot level, living Goods a nongovernmental organisation whose mission is to decrease maternal child mortality from preventable diseases in low-income countries initiated a Community Health Promoters platform in Uganda. These CHPs serve as the first point of access to the health care system. These CHPs were recruited based on referral from community members, religious leaders and subsequently existing CHPs who then go through a 13-day training programme that will equip them to continue to serve their communities. The project recognised that the advantages of a community participation approach in primary health care (PHC) are a cost-effective way to extend a health care system to the geographical and social periphery of a country. And when communities are well sensitised to begin to understand their health status, they may be moved to take a series of preventive measures (MacCormack, 1983)

Water Solutions in Ethiopia

Individuals, groups, and institutions who are stakeholders are participating in identifying and addressing local concerns that influence water supply functions in Ethiopia through community-based watershed management approach. The watershed management project was developed to reduce harsh water constraints affecting local stakeholders by introducing ways to direct any surface area from which rainfall runs off then it is collected and drained through a common convergence point.

In executing the PWSD in Ethiopia, the Ministry of Agriculture principally did seek to ensure that the watershed communities were involved in all stages of planning, implementation, and management of watershed development activities. Through a user guideline, it also factored the process was a continuous type and not a one-time exercise. Different participatory techniques were used based on existing and innovative experience with a gender consideration because women were the most affected by environmental hardships, for example, they need to walk long distances to fetch water which is gradually becoming more and more scarce by the day. Their involvement in watershed development planning, implementation and management were also key to ensuring that they equally benefit from the various measures that were put in place (Ali, 2013).

Subsequently, the community members were also involved in what is referred to as Participatory Monitoring and Evaluation (PM&E) which is different from the conventional monitoring and evaluation because this style involves participation. An effective PM&E makes use of a participatory planning approach so the community can achieve sound resource management in any watershed development or natural resources management.

According to the report by the Ethiopia Ministry for Agriculture, various African countries, including Kenya, Niger, Burkina Faso, and Mali, have successfully implemented, and expanded participatory conservation and watershed-based approaches. Such programs have been realized within the context of combating desertification and poverty reduction efforts (Debebe, 2017).

Although referring to infrastructure development, Wattam (1998), opines that not only would community participation in project maintenance be more cost effective, but it would also have significant developmental implications. These findings on community engagement obtained over three years from research in Uganda, Tanzania, and Kenya included enhanced cash and income options, skill development, and a higher sense of ownership (Wattam, 1998). This, according to the researcher, is applicable and can be gained in any region where community members participate.

Burkina Faso Youth Participating in Improving Reproductive Health

Through participatory communication in Burkina Faso, the locals were encouraged to initiate action, set the agenda, and work towards a commonly defined goal. This is because involving communities in development is good practice, as the community members know their own needs and understand issues that influence their health. Youth from Burkina Faso offer a practical definition of community participation (Hause, 2002) in an example of collective action these youth were mobilised to work with organizations in their communities to improve adolescent reproductive and sexual health. It is one of the principles of primary healthcare, a way in which members of a community are organised, sensitised, and mobilised towards participating in health programmes affecting their health and existence. It is a very important component of the health and development of every community

Participatory Communication for Community Budgeting

Since 2012, Fahamu Networks for Social Justice, has been working with communities in Kenya to engage in participatory budgeting processes to help guide and direct public spending. Working with local government representatives, community activists, and existing social movements, citizens collectively identify priorities and make decisions about public monies. The projects are working in Kajiado, Kwale, Makueni, Kakamega, and Kisumu counties (The Communication Initiative Network, 2015). In a 30 minutes documentary, Fahamu describes the process so far and how Kenyans have been allowed to set the agenda as a way of democratising democracy. In a district like Kwale, the documentary revealed that they lacked basic amenities including education and clean water. The video also served a s a tool to educate the people about their constitutional rights and provisions for their participation. Through 5 stages, community members get the chance to list out their priorities and vote with one voice.

The Constitution of Kenya (2010) calls for citizens to participate in the governance management and decision-making socially, economically, and politically. One of the demands arising from citizens during the Fahamu-led Change Initiative forums was for citizens to be involved in this governance and to be part of determining their own development path. The Participatory Budgeting (PB) project was created in response to these demands, as a way of ensuring that agenda setting begins at the community level. The Participatory Budgeting process allows communities to work collectively at smaller community levels to decide how to allocate part of a municipal or public budget. Report shows that the practice did allow for the citizens to identify, discuss, and prioritize public spending on projects, and support them to make actual decisions on which projects to undertake as a matter of priority. Community wards delegate members who will be in charge of developing specific spending proposals which will later be presented to the community for validation. If the community then approves of the proposals, they are then forwarded to the county government to be considered for implementation.

According to Fahamu, participatory budgeting is a more in-depth and meaningful technique to include local citizens in decision-making than typical consultation processes. This entails including residents and community groups who represent a varied cross group of the population in developing expenditure proposals based on the needs of the community and collectively deciding on budgetary allocations. Furthermore, the method involves citizens in the inspection and monitoring of the process and the implementation which is intended to inform annual or periodic decision making. The initiative has created a manual, 'Facilitating Participatory Budgeting in Kenya', to aid communities and guide them through the process.

Social Dialogues as a Form of Participatory Communication

In Uganda, community social dialogue served as a participatory communication tool to address the issues of Child abuse when UNICEF partnered with Save the Children International (SCI) to fund their programme for training community members on knowing and protecting children's rights and creating Child Friendly Spaces (CFS) for children to enjoy their rights safely (Asobora, 2021).

To ensure success, organisations, and their partners, will need to engage in a series of community and social dialogues, beginning with a comprehensive assessment through meetings with influential leaders, chiefs, social groups, political leaders, community meetings, etc. This builds expands and deepens the dialogue process to include more groups and people for example with what happened in Ghana, it led to the signing of the "Kumasi Accord".

The programme also includes capacity-building elements and establishing institutions, structures and networks that help to respond to emerging issues.

CSDs are now avenues in which knowledge, norms, and traditions are examined, rather than places where cultural authority is asserted. During CSDs, gatekeepers and stakeholders collaborate in the making of meaning reviewing existing practices against social and economic implications. These community leaders have lived through a particular time, the process enables those involved in the dialogues to explore images of themselves, their histories, and communities. This shift within the participatory communication has resulted in the continuous implementation of community social dialogues among community members through Town hall meetings where issues in the community are sometimes presented in the form of dramas, songs, and diagrams. This shift within the community has resulted in participatory cultural communication. Through CDSs also, more people are motivated to participate in planned activities by participatory communication, which changes their behavior and attitudes and empowers them to focus on getting results

Community Engagement Solving Water Crises

Generally, the demand for a water project comes from one of two places - either the community themselves or by an external agency that uncovers an unmet need. Often times, people who are coping without access to clean, safe water actively go out and try to find someone who can help them. When a community chooses to organise their water project. This is known as community demand because the local village is the initiator. They have a desire to get clean, safe water and have organized enough to begin the process of finding it.

Sometimes though, those with the greatest need have not yet found their voice. It's necessary to go out and find these communities - by talking to local people, driving out into remote areas, or using government data. Then, our partners work with them to develop a plan together so that they too are engaged in a shared process from day one. Regardless of how we come to meet the communities we serve, and before anything else happens, a lot of talking needs to happen. We require our partners to open and maintain a dialogue with each community. We want to be sure everyone has answers to questions like: Who are you? What do you want? Why are you here? What is it like living here? What do you need? and then hopefully, how can we work together? When these kinds of questions are asked, by both sides, the community and the NGO build a strong foundation of cooperation and respect by seeing each other's points of view. It's an important step that takes time. In the long run it pays huge dividends.

Community Participation Bridging Financial Access and Transforming Communities

In one of the most remarkable stories so far, Village Savings and Loans Agents (VSLAs) in the Sanaag region donated $USD1,000 of their social fund to support the most vulnerable people in the drought-stricken region. The model is for interested participants (mostly women) to come together to form groups of 19 to 25 members, who pool in money by buying an agreed number of shares at an agreed time that creates a fund from which members could borrow with minimal and agreed interest rates. It usually runs for an agreed cycle of 9 – 12 months after. Throughout the cycle, shares are bought, loans are disbursed, and members pay back loans with agreed interest within a certain period. At the end of the cycle, members would have also earned a return on their savings which is shared to all according to the shares purchased all through the cycle. The result has been seen across communities in Ghana, Malawi, and Uganda where VSLAs have led to increased savings and access to finance, improved micro-enterprise performance, and increased community empowerment (IPA, 2011).

Participatory Rural Communication through Digital Media

Major projects worldwide employ the use of digital media because they can be created, viewed, distributed, modified, Listened, and preserved beyond the paper and the pen. Through the use of digital electronics devices, social media also such as blogs, podcasts and other content sharing devices are used to engage users via participatory communication. This marks a shift in how digital media is playing a publicly communicative role so that community members can continue to be custodians of their cultural content and share their concerns through the media. It also signifies a new possible direction for community learning through a wide range of initiatives that demonstrate how participatory communication through digital media can be integrated into community development practices. The use of digital media tools presents an ideal opportunity for community members to provide authentic cultural information, that will receive media attention.

Development projects are increasingly open to cultural diversity, local knowledge, and popular memory. Participatory Communication approach helps the projects to connect with the identities, and socio-cultural issues that exist within them. This approach has supported the deconstruction of grand narratives and have affirmed the role of audiences in social learning and development. Experts on the field can tap a form of community intelligence that will certainly create a path from top-down approach to community networking which demands an engagement with the people. This is also changing the ways that the media are responding to the challenges of providing authentic and authoritative information within the increasing participatory environment.

In 2016, Mzwandile Makhanya conducted a study around Using the participatory mode of documentary filmmaking for knowledge exchange and empowerment exploring the usefulness of a participatory video approach to facilitate knowledge exchange and community empowerment in the uMgungundlovu district of South. This shows how media tools can support participatory communication research project. Makhanya's goal was to enable positive communication between Willowfontein (a peri-urban1 community of South Africa) and numerous other stakeholders through the participatory video project. The documentary was used to examine and address issues around food security/insecurity in this community which served as an empowerment tool for the community which did not have usually have the opportunity to participate in a decision-making process and to communicate at a constructive level with persons such as governmental practitioners, and agricultural and academic experts. With the video captured, this can be extended to these key stakeholders who are usually recognised in decision-making processes. Why do community members participate in film projects such as this? According to Kolanisi (2013), People become interested in participating in such (film) initiatives because it provides them hope that someone will finally hear their tale.

In Ghana, Farm Radio International (FRI) collaborated with commercial radio stations Obouba and Akyeaa FM to improve the knowledge and skills of small-scale farmers in the sustainable production and post-harvest handling of high-quality staple foods. Research informed their design of a comprehensive programme to produce and broadcast participatory Farm Radio programmes, in collaboration with partners such as the Adventist Development and Relief Agency (ADRA) and Ghana's Ministry of Food and Agriculture. This programme is reported to have reached a total audience of one million farmers, including those directly supported by P4P. The project also provided selected farmers' organizations with a mobile phone including technical support to encourage participatory communication. Through the digital device, they are able to foster interactivity between the radio station and the rural populace who are often isolated, farmers. Additionally, these phones, is supporting them to receive weather forecasts and market information on a weekly basis.

Mzwandile (2016) states that In South Africa, there have been many interventions and projects from the government and other community out-reach organisations in an attempt to assist such communities with crop production. However, most of the projects are consistently unsuccessful. The government had been employing the top-bottom conventional strategies through community out-reach which does not facilitate collaboration that encourages the contribution of community members. As a result, the community development projects had all failed since they lack this most fundamental component of community development. Participatory video, though a process works in collaboration with the community, offers an appropriate approach to explore any community development cause, including food security/insecurity. The documentary film, Freedom from Hunger, Hunger for Freedom, produced with the community supported the examination, the factors that were contributing to failing crop gardens in this community which the government had struggled hard to solve because the root of any community development can only come from positive participation between different stakeholders, including the community. But then how does Mzwandile's project and others become digital? Through streaming platforms such as YouTube, Facebook, blogs, and digital news channels.

Another example can be seen in December 2007 the BBC launched its online streaming and download service, the iPlayer. By the end of 2009, over 729 million requests to view programs had been made via the service, which offers U.K. viewers a chance to watch programs screened on the BBC's television channels in the last seven days or listen to radio broadcast over any BBC radio station over the same period via their computer or a range of mobile media devices. The BBC Pidgin is a language service for digital platforms in English-based Pidgin for West and Central Africa which was launched in 2017 by the BBC World Service. This is an example of inclusive digital participation offering a platform that can serve a younger audience and women with social media playing a key role.

Citizen Journalists and New Media Participatory Communication

Citizen Journalism can be defined broadly as the dissemination of information through facilitated online communication, networking, and/or collaboration. Citizen journalists are employing social software, social networking and Web 2.0 as tools and platforms that enable user interaction. With this kind of facilitation which not new what makes the difference are the tools in their hands. While social media technologies such as Facebook were designed primarily as network communication tools to connect with friends and family, citizen journalists are currently employing the use of these social media applications—including blogs, podcasts, and vlogs to facilitate a participative cultural, community and communication experience by a number of people.

The information and communication technology (ICT) and digitalization innovation is providing more platforms and empower people opportunity to voice out and engage actions to issues that they felt worth advocating for and long been neglected by the mainstream media by utilizing mew media platforms including among rural communities and their sustainability. Citizen journalism is making an attempt to address this problem by enabling rural communities to obtain and report news, and, to facilitate coverage of their concerns and interest, by connecting those communities and a virtual news outlets prospect to ensure their voice is also heard to initiate actions and mobilization towards a more sustainable rural community.

What was ordinarily aired or broadcasted by mainstream media with limited timeslots, can now be streamed online with the convergence of multiple mainstream media now available. Digital media facilitates social interaction and empowers people. Through digital media community members have a voice which is increasing their civic participation and facilitating the creation of communities with a purpose. Among the benefits of digital media is the way it is changing how work can be done, boosting productivity, and enhancing flexibility for workers and employers. It has enabled unprecedented levels of communication, community building, and social interaction, breaking the barriers of location, time, and social context. The spread of digital media has made possible the rise of new methods of learning, providing underserved communities with better opportunities.

Digital technologies like social media have allowed us to communicate and share in real time around the globe and across traditional cultural boundaries. The digital divide, however, may in fact create an even greater separation between cultures that are connected from those that are not. The social media space has created a platform for a variety of participatory communication as a platform for social change, political action and e-governance including on the spot polls/surveys to gauge users' perceptions and opinions. The widespread availability of low-cost information and communication technology, such as cell phones and the internet, has expanded the media landscape and relocated it from the institutional to the modern communication arena. What we have seen is how civil society and the public sphere around the world today have taken advantage of platforms such as Facebook, Twitter, and Instagram to operate independently of political institutions. As seen in the ENDSARS protest of 2020 where Nigerian Youths took on to the street to speak against police brutality, social media is serving as a tool for organizing and mobilization, as well as a forum for discourse, interaction, and democratic decision. Quasi political actors are also relying on channels of communication and mass media networks such as Channels News Television, The Sun Newspaper and ThisDay newspaper who all have all converged online to influence public discussion, shape opinions, and promote social change.

One such instance in Nigeria is how influencers and activists such as Aisha Somtochukwu Yesufu who is Nigerian activist and businesswoman along with the former vice president of the World Bank Oby Ezekwesili together championed the #BringBackOurGirls movement, on Twitter which was used to draw the attention of the public and the world at large to the abduction of over 200 girls from a secondary school in Chibok, Borno State Nigeria. Through social media, they rallied students and other civil based organisation who marched to the National Assembly to seek for action from the government (Nwabufo, 2020). A report by Statista, an online global research website, did reveal the percentage change in internet usage in West Africa between 2000 and 2021. The chart below shows the access by country:

The chart above shows data on the internet usage in West Africa which rose rapidly between 2000 and 2021. Togo's growth rate was 912 percent, making it the fastest-growing country in the world. Internet usage increased by 882 percent in So Tomé and Principe. While Cabo Verde, Mali, and Nigeria, according to data on internet users in Africa, have the highest rates, with web density of over 60%. The internet is providing for participation in a new sort of public realm that is impossible for the state to govern which has been enabled by new media technologies as seen in the chart from the growth of the internet.

Mobile phones and other new media technologies are supporting displaced persons in Nigeria who are typically excluded from the social, economic, cultural, and public system of their new locations. Internally displaced people were utilizing their phones to earn money, obtain emotional and psychological support from family and friends, study online, and follow political news and participate in discussions, according to The Conversation a News Blog. They were also able to solicit financial assistance from the general public via social media. (Sikhakhane, 2021).

Empowerment Journalism

Community-based form of reporting that seeks to not just gather, sort, and tell stories but seeks out community member's perspectives to telling the story is referred to empowerment journalism. This includes the use of Media advocacy which is as the strategic use of mass media to advance public policy initiatives (Wallack, 1994). Heywood (2021) describes access to information as the route to empowerment. She points out that in a country like Mali, where there are 170 private radio stations, 121 of which are volunteer-run community stations, radio remains the primary source of information. Heywood discovered that Studio Tamani, as a radio studio, was normalizing dialogue on women's concerns by broadcasting women-related programs through a content analysis of a series of women-related radio programmes produced and broadcast by Fondation Hirondelle's Studio Tamani in 2018-2020. This is the first step toward

Figure 3.
Source - https://www.statista.com/statistics/1139345/internet-growth-in-west-african-countries/

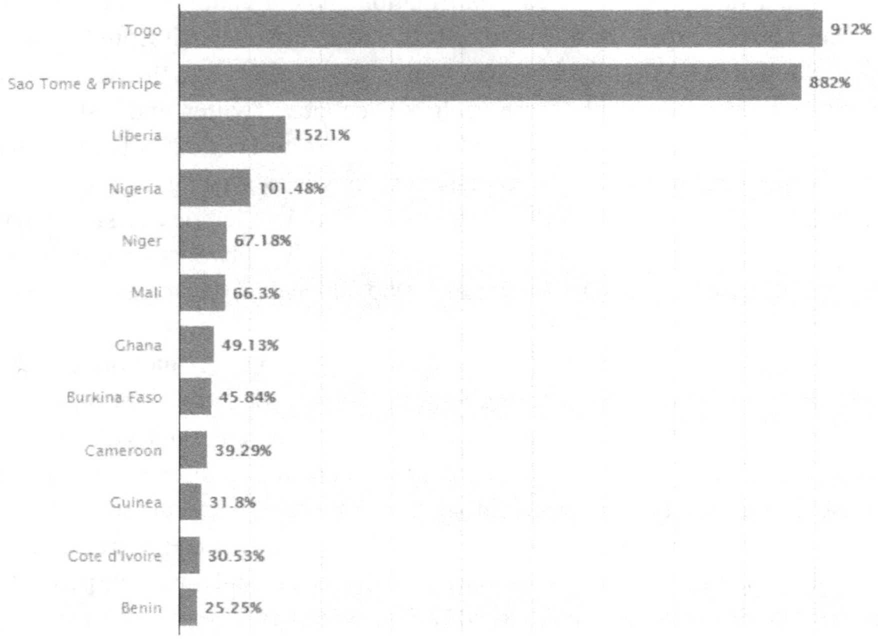

utilizing radio as a powerful tool for creating an empowered environment. However, women must not be removed from their web of associations in order for this to be effective for communal empowerment.

Empowerment journalism can be achieved through media advocacy actions. The purpose of media advocacy is to promote good public policy, which is fundamental in community empowerment. There are several ways in which it differs from standard mass media techniques. Wallack notes that the focus of media advocacy goes from discussing and promoting personal interests to that of the society in general. Hence empowerment journalism is not about the individual but the socio-political, socio-economic behaviors that should translate into development policies for the environment. Now while the traditional media attempts to bridge the "knowledge gap," media advocacy seeks to bridge the "power gap" (Wallack, 1994). It means that getting the community members to have more power over the environmental policy by speaking collectively about their issues, would serve more than merely trying to inform the people about their development issues.

In 2010, Futhi, et al., did try to ascertain to what extent the local governments in South Africa were following accepted participatory communication principles and practices to communicate with the community particularly in the Kungwini Local Municipality. The findings showed that although the participatory approach and the role of effective communication were well acknowledged and appreciated at the local government levels as being critical for facilitating, enhancing, and driving development yet the communities were not empowered to take full responsibility for driving the development process and the evaluation of the development. This leads to mistrust between the community and the municipality as the community is often not satisfied with the manner in which the identified projects are implemented.

Another tool is employing a documentary strategy such as the video produced in Zambia – done in the framework of aquatic agricultural systems program it aimed at diversifying diets and improving livelihoods through use of locally available seasonal foods. Although women organised themselves into cooking groups to showcase their recipes and knowledge around food processing the documentary approach allowed for better understanding of what the community was used to. In participatory communication, it is a continuous process to find out what the community wants to say. Through this initiative, the women in the community discovered that they had been getting it all wrong from the way they were processing their staple food which was majorly maize.

Working within the communities allows for the media to project the shortcomings, important lessons around health, agriculture, and general empowerment of members of the communities.

Gender Sensitivity in Participatory Communication

A 2021 report by world Bank, disclosed that women in Morocco have continued to face obstacles in social, economic, and political participation. The report notes that Women's economic participation in Morocco was at 26% which is among the lowest in the world and has not changed since 1990. But then through the Morocco WID Sector Strategy, poor rural and urban women were given the opportunity to articulate their needs and priorities through a participatory rural appraisal (PRA) process which provoked discussion among community members about development and gender issues and sought their views in formulating national policy objectives. By engaging the local populations in development projects, it provided the opportunity for even women to become a part in initiatives designed for their benefit which drives sustainability (Cornwall, 2002).

They have the potential to develop the capacities of women as sociopolitical actors. They also have the potential to promote a balanced and non-stereotyped portrayal of women in the media and to challenge the status quo. In Zambia, women who took part in a participatory video project presented themselves as active citizens who made significant contributions to their families and communities. These recorded images improved the status of women in the minds of government bureaucrats.

Gender sensitivity is the process by which people are made aware of how gender plays a role in life through their treatment of others. To ensure participatory communication is effective and complete, gender sensitivity trainings should be deliberate used to educate people, usually employees, to become more aware of and sensitive to gender in their lives or workplaces. This is also called inclusive participation. To be effective, development agencies and the media must be deliberate in identifying the marginalised groups, build relationships with them, conduct a needs assessment, and then conduct group action meetings. Through a gender-sensitive approach various agencies can employ tools for understanding and assessing the impacts, of their methodologies and practices to ensure that both men's and women's concerns, aspirations, opportunities, and capacities are considered.

Another case was in the Amhara Region of North Ethiopia where a project run by Search for common Ground intended to promote gender equality and increase the participation of women in decision-making on food security at the household and community levels. The communication strategy included the design of a series of interactive, multimedia communication tools such as radio spots, participatory theatre, image boxes, comic books and a video documentary to be screened using mobile cinemas. Also, through the provision of technical assistance to staff of their partners in Amhara the goal was to achieve an equitable participation and benefits for both women and men in addressing food security issues at the community level.

Similarly, the UN project in Lebanon which provided a platform between May 2019 and December 2020, where the Centre for Professional Mediation held trainings—including on active listening, building positive relations, mediations, and negotiations—for members of the network. under the project "Fostering Stabilization and Social Cohesion in Lebanon through Women's Engagement in Conflict Prevention and Management" some women participated in a training of trainers' programme where others are now part of the legal support unit that trains armed personnel in all 12 Palestinian camps on international human rights and humanitarian law. The final phase of the project involved bringing together women trained on conflict resolution to brainstorm ideas for peacebuilding, with the aim of developing a plan to prevent conflict within the community.

Participatory Research Communication

According to Ewa Hermanowicz, a Communications Specialist at EUFORGEN, who shares her thoughts and stories about the relevance of participatory communication describes it as a relevant research tool for reaching out to external audiences and feedback-it to the communities with which an agency has worked with. Hermanowicz (2016) adds that through a research project, community members can be the source of primary first-hand data validating the exercise. Though it is worth proper planning and budgeting in a project there are 3 reasons which makes it key – it serves to achieve impact, relevance, and outreach because it is constantly seeking to increase communication between different parties within the community.

Factors Affecting Participatory Communication

While the researcher was able to pull out various initiatives that have been able to strengthen accountability, human rights, and most of all citizen participation, it is worthy of note that there are also some factors mitigating participatory communication such as technological constraints and institutional constraints as discussed below.

Technological Constraints

The use of participatory communication in development remains limited because informational approaches such as the Top-Bottom are still favoured across Africa where a few determine the kind of technology to deploy without proper consideration for how many community members have access to or can afford it. The presence of new technologies which the community members may not yet be conversant with becomes a major hindrance for effective participation. Some beneficiaries or community members become still or mute in the face of a microphone, tape recorder or even a video camera.

Institutional Constraints

This is quite a major setback for development communication as development agencies tend to choose communication approaches based on a perceived expectation, rather than on their systematic value which should target the people. Hence there is a slow acceptance by the communities they work in. Communication is usually taken as a last option without prior consideration for the tasks. Ali & Sonderling (2017) notes that institutional decisions such as adopted by some development agencies like Organization for

Rehabilitation and Development in Amhara (ORDA) will mean that development projects are designed without the dynamic engagements of the local community. Where this approach is employed, then the local needs and concerns of the community members will be rarely prioritized. Some agencies have only one communication officer who is burdened with the responsibility to draft strategies, implement these strategies, and equally report on the outcomes. As opposed to other units which have teams that collaborate to make the field programmes a reality.

Others includes local resistance to monitoring, the need for constant resource investment, and the difficulty of ensuring sustained community engagement. These challenges centre on a concern that plagues participatory approaches as a whole – that is, why should people participate?

Liquid Democracy: A New Frontier for Participatory Communication

Aside all the dimensions and tenets of participatory communication, there is an additional concept that emerged elsewhere in Europe referred to as liquid democracy. The concept at the moment is still fluid and evolving. Liquid democracy is a type of delegative democracy in which a community member can participate directly in collective decision-making through dynamic representation and direct engagement with other members. This democratic system incorporates both direct and representative democracy aspects. This paradigm has created new potentials for social interaction and decision-making among diverse communities.

Through liquid democracy, communities are getting involved in meaningful and consistent participation across activities as they are free to delegate those, they are confident would work to support and improve their social wellbeing. Unlike conventional democracy where delegates run for a particular tenure, the representatives can be changed at will especially when the community members are no longer satisfied with the outcomes. Community involvement examples include mobilising youths, working with community volunteers to manage projects to ensure sustainability. This approach equips people with the knowledge and skills to be their own best advocate. In view of the World Economic Forum Report, Sub-Saharan Africa risks landscape, which shows that communities across Africa are faced with a variety of issues such as unemployment/underemployment, underinvestment in infrastructure, Fiscal crises, Political change, and Climate change. The researcher believes that in the near future the concept of liquid democracy will be adopted even in Africa this is because, where liquid democracy is present, a community has the ability to present even liquid feedbacks at any time. There are established standardized protocols that will allow community members to adjust even their delegated authority without compromising the main aim they seek to achieve through mutual agreements. This implies that the system is participatory and encourages open dialogue. As a result, when liquid democracy is applied, community-based socio-economic issues as noted by the WEC and others such as water, sanitation, maternal health, poor healthcare systems, weak educational systems, and access to market knowledge and financing can be appropriately addressed.

DISCUSSION AND SUMMARY OF FINDINGS

From the voices of people in Simli community radio in Ghana, to the Water Solutions in Ethiopia, Community Health Promoters in Uganda and the Community Budgeting in Kenya, this study was able to scrutinise the use of digital media, in participatory communication across the African continent. It is important to reiterate that participatory communication cannot be complete if it becomes a one-way communication approach because it is a dialogue-based technique that provides an avenue for various stakeholders to share information, that leads to empowerment. The implication as argued by the new media theory is fostering digital based communications where community meetings are not just notes but also voices recorded and transferred over the phone through participatory call-in community radio programmes. The four axes of Communication for Development shows that Communication for Empowerment can give power to local population when they are allowed to function as a part of the project and also report on the implementation of the development aid received from donor countries.

The game has changed as communication tools such as phones, cameras and recorders are no longer serving as mere dissemination or campaigning mechanisms that simply inform and persuade people to change their behavior or attitude but more of an empowering tool. People are empowered by digital media because it enhances wider social interactions which is not limited by time or space. In many cases, members of the community have a voice thanks to digital media, which is also expanding civic participation and supporting the formation of purpose-driven communities.

Another advantage of digital media is how it is changing the way people work, increasing productivity, through multimedia products, journalists and development agencies now have more freedom to produce engaging documentaries like what was done in Zambia where women organised themselves to share what they had learned around balanced diets. Here they can relay the needs and choices of the communities they serve. Citizen participation through digital media has permitted unparalleled amounts of communication, community development, and social involvement by removing geographical, temporal, and social context restrictions.

The growth of community participation means new platforms are enabling learning by the proliferation of digital media, offering improved chances for underserved areas such as can be seen with the BBC Pidgin News Service which has a segment that projects activities within various communities across west and central Africa which can be streamed and is uploaded online for viewers across the globe. Digital technologies like social media have allowed us to communicate and share in real time around the globe and across traditional cultural boundaries.

Findings also revealed that media cultivation is evident in the way communities, agencies and government make use of the media for participatory communication to stabilize and homogenise views within various communities around socio-economic and other developmental issues. This shows that that the use of digital media has become a necessary part of the community development framework for inclusive participation.

RECOMMENDATIONS

Apart from vitalizing participatory communication for rural development, there are major constraints around technology, institutions and finances that are factors hindering the actualisation of effective participatory communication. The following are some recommendations drawn from the study:

1. Media practitioners to be conscious in recognising that they are responsible for birthing a new twist around development communication from the community viewpoints, which can further improve cultivation of innovations.
2. Participatory communication should not be ignored when planning any programme.

3. Social media as a platform for participatory communication should be well harnessed to facilitate change for the larger society.
4. Community members should be introduced early enough to the project's goal for easy collaboration with all levels of stakeholders.
5. Development agencies must be intentional about projecting issues of community interests and fostering community participation through interactive, educative, and informative media platforms. The more community voices are heard, the quicker issues will be solved in a practicable and sustainable way.

CONCLUSION

What we have seen from communities in Africa is that participation could be voluntary or co-opted. In any way, community members serve as token representatives who eventually take part in making decisions or a collective action. The Project Evaluation and Monitoring process for example what was done in Ethiopia, enhances skills and confidence of local people on management of development projects. It is also evident that although social media technologies such as Facebook were designed primarily as network communication tools to connect with friends and family, but it is now shifted to being utilised by citizen journalists who are currently employing the use of these social media applications through blogging, podcasts, and vlogs to facilitate a participative cultural, community and communication experience by a number of people. The participatory communication platforms can be seen in the ways social media platforms are used to mobilise and facilitate social and political events such as was seen with the #EndSARS and the #BringBackOurGirls in Nigeria.

As development agencies strive to be more intentional about projecting issues of community interests and fostering community participation through interactive, educative, and informative media platforms, the more marginalised voices will be heard, and the quicker issues will be solved in a practicable and sustainable way.

REFERENCES

Ali, W. (2013). *Introduction: Watershed, Principles of Watershed Management.* National Centre of Excellence in Geology University of Peshawar. Retrieved 2021, from http://nceg.uop.edu.pk/workshops/workshop-geoscience/WorkshopMaterial/Lectures/Day4/lecture-1-wajidali.pdf

Copeland, B. J. (2020). The Modern History of Computing. *The Stanford Encyclopedia of Philosophy.* Retrieved from Stanford Encyclopedia of Philosophy: https://plato.stanford.edu/archives/win2020/entries/computing-history/

Debebe, A. D. (2017). Socio-Economic Contributions of Community Based Participatory Watershed Development on Rural Farm Households at Gammo Gofa Zone of Demba Gofa Woreda, Ethiopia. *Journal of Economics and Sustainable Development, 8*(13), 15–27. Retrieved 2021, from https://core.ac.uk/download/pdf/234647914.pdf

Evans, W. D. (2006). How social marketing works in health care. *BMJ, 332*(7551), 1207-1210. Retrieved 10 8, 2021, from https://bmj.com/content/332/7551/1207.2

Haider, H., Mcloughlin, C., & Scott, Z. (2011). *Topic Guide on Communication and Governance*. Academic Press.

IPA. (2011). *The Impact of Savings Groups on the*. Innovations For Poverty Action. Retrieved 2021, from https://www.poverty-action.org/study/evaluating-village-savings-and-loan-associations-ghana

Khan, M. A., Khan, M. M., Hassan, M., Ahmed, F., & Haque, S. M. (2017). *Role of Community Radio for Community Development in Bangladesh. The International Technology Management Review*. doi:10.2991/itmr.2017.6.3.3

MacCormack, C. (1983). Community Participation in Primary Health Care. *Tropical Doctor, 13*(2), 51-54. Retrieved 9 18, 2021, from https://ncbi.nlm.nih.gov/pubmed/6679395

Mayoux, L. (2018). *Participatory Methods*. Retrieved 2021, from Watsan Mission Assistant: https://www.google.com/url?sa=t&rct=j&q=&esrc=s&source=web&cd=&cad=rja&uact=8&ved=2ahUKEwiV-bXWjsnzAhUGlhQKHanlBJAQFnoECCAQAQ&url=https%3A%2F%2Fwatsanmissionassistant.org%2Fwp-content%2Fuploads%2F2018%2F08%2Fparticipatory-methods-_linda-mayoux.pdf&usg=AOv

McAllister, M., Dunn, G., Payne, K., Davies, L., & Todd, C. (2012). Patient empowerment: The need to consider it as a measurable patient-reported outcome for chronic conditions. *BMC Health Services Research, 12*(1), 157-157. Retrieved 10 8, 2021, from https://bmchealthservres.biomedcentral.com/articles/10.1186/1472-6963-12-157

Mefalopulos, P. (2007). Theory and Practice of Participatory Communication - The Case of the FAO Project "Communication for Development in Southern Africa. *Communication Initiative Network*. Retrieved 2021, from https://www.comminit.com/africa/content/theory-and-practice-participatory-communication

Millington, R. (2012). *Types Of Community And Activity Within The Community*. Retrieved July 2021, from https://www.feverbee.com/types-of-community-and-activity-within-the-community/

Msibi, F., & Penzhorn, C. (2010). Participatory communication for local government in South Africa: A study of the Kungwini Local Municipality. Information Development. *Information Development, 26*(3), 225–236. doi:10.1177/0266666910376216

Nabi, R. L., & Riddle, K. (2008). Personality Traits, Television Viewing, and the Cultivation Effect. *Journal of Broadcasting & Electronic Media, 52*(3), 327–348. doi:10.1080/08838150802205181

Nigeria. (1999). *Constitution of the Federal Republic of Nigeria 1999*. Federal Government of Nigeria. Retrieved 2021, from https://www.icnl.org/wp-content/uploads/Nigeria_constitution2.pdf

Raja, F. (2021). *Amplifying rural needs and voices: A conversation with Helene Papper*. Retrieved 2021, from IFAD: https://www.ifad.org/en/web/latest/-/amplifying-rural-needs-and-voices-helene-papper

Scott, Z., Haider, H., & Mcloughlin, C. (2011). *Topic guide on communication and governance*. Retrieved 10 8, 2021, from http://gsdrc.org/docs/open/commgap1.pdf

Sikarwar, R. (2016, december 29). *Definition of Digital Media.* Retrieved 2021, from Linkedin: https://www.linkedin.com/pulse/definition-digital-media-rahul-sikarwar-digital-marketing-expert

The Communication Initiative Network. (2015, June 9). Retrieved 9 23, 2021, from https://www.comminit.com/governance-africa/content/participatory-budgeting-project

Wallack, L. (1994). Media Advocacy: A Strategy for Empowering People and Communities. *Journal of Public Health Policy, 15*(4), 420-436. Retrieved 9 14, 2021, from https://ncbi.nlm.nih.gov/pubmed/7883943

West, R., & Turner, L. (2010). *Introducing Communication Theory. Analysis and Application. Fourth Edition* (4th ed.). McGraw-Hill. Retrieved 2021, from https://silo.pub/introducing-communication-theory-analysis-and-application-fourth-edition.html

Chapter 12
Post-Truth Politics as a Threat to Democracy

Kingsley Mbamara Sabastine
https://orcid.org/0000-0002-4046-7858
The John Paul II Catholic University of Lublin, Poland

ABSTRACT

Politics for long has been associated with mendacity, disinformation, manipulation, and at odds with the truth. In recent times, the term post-truth is used to further characterise politics, which implies a fresh phenomenon in the conflict between truth and politics. The chapter examines the concept of post-truth and post-truth politics. The chapter argues that the application of post-truth rhetoric in politics implies a novelty in politics and in the relationship between truth and politics which undermines democracy. It is arguable that post-truth condition negatively impacts individual ability to discriminate between what is true or false taking into consideration the volume of disinformation on the one hand and on the other hand the need to make informed decisions and choices without having to consult experts at the critical time that the stakes involved in such decisions and choices are urgent and crucial.

INTRODUCTION

The term post-truth does not mean or imply that the idea and concern for truth is a thing of the past. Instead, post-truth describes and denounces the trending manner of communication that reflects a disregard for truth and deflect from reliable means of knowing what is true. Arguably, people's readiness to discover and accept the truth correlates with their overall development: the ability to stand up for what is right, the capacity for social critique, and the capacity to stand up to power. The post-truth condition is counterproductive because misinformation and manipulation negatively affect people's decision-making process at a time when the stakes involved in these decisions and choices are becoming increasingly high (McIntyre 2018, Block 2019, and Kalpokas 2019).

DOI: 10.4018/978-1-6684-4107-7.ch012

In 2016 the term "post-truth" was declared the word of the year by the Oxford English Dictionary (OED) following a hick in its usage (cf. McIntyre 2018, 1). The declaration further popularised it, leading to "a rise in its use in a growing number of domains as its original meaning becomes stretched and mangled" (Block, 2019, 3). As a result, it has caught the interest of the Media and intellectuals. That is evident in the growing number of literature and media coverage on the phenomenon of post-truth, which has resulted in a more precise conceptualisation and description of its manifestations, consequences, origin and relations to various domains such as philosophy, religion, psychology, economy, science and technology, particularly the Internet, media and specifically the social media.

Earlier characterisation and conceptualisation of the idea of post-truth appeared in the year 2004 by Ralph Keyes in a book he titled *The Post-Truth Era: Dishonesty and Deception in Contemporary Life.* Keyes in this publication offers a broad critique of the lack of sincerity and the prevalence of deceit in contemporary society. A year later, Harry G. Frankfurt, in his essay *On bullshit* (2005), offers a similar critique of modern society. He says that "one of the most salient features of our culture is that there is so much bullshit. Everyone knows this. Each of us contributes his share" (2005, 1). However, the term "post-truth" has been used increasingly to describe the contemporary era (McIntyre 2018, Lockie 2017, Block 2019, and Kalpokas 2019). The close association of post-truth with populist politics and new communication technologies coupled with the understanding of it as manipulative and relying on misrepresentation gives post-truth the status of being both familiar and strange, old and new. However, this does not undermine the fact that "there are still differences between old-style lies and conspiracies, and post-truth manipulation" (Yilmaz 2019, 240).

The paper analyses the contemporary association of politics with post-truth and defends the thesis that this association not only denigrates politics but undermines the value and trust in democracy (cf. Suiter 2016, 17-25). The argument is developed in three steps. The first section explores the concept of post-truth and post-truth politics to argue that the phenomenon of post-truth politics poses a significant threat to democratic politics in particular. These threats are illustrated by explicating the consequences and implications of post-truth rhetoric in the recent political campaigns as manifestations of post-truth politics. The second section situates the challenges of post-truth and post-truth politics in the broader context of the crisis of truth to argue that post-truth politics poses a threat to democracy in general by undermining the value of truthfulness in democratic politics. The final section concludes with a proposal on countering the challenge of post-truth and post-truth politics.

THE CONCEPT OF POST-TRUTH

According to McIntyre (2019, 123 -125), post-truth has its remote origin within the academic discussions concerning the "standard of evidence, critical thinking, scepticism, cognitive bias, and so on" but in connection with postmodernists' approach that questioned everything. That ended up in perspectivism that denied the possibility of objective truth and indirectly attacked evidence-based reasoning. However, the term "post-truth" was meant to describe the kind of political rhetoric known today as post-truth politics. Hopkin and Rosamond (2017, 3) described the contemporary context in which post-truth emerged as word of the year as follows: "The rise of populist and anti-elite movements and the rejection of basic principles of reason and veracity characteristic of much of their political discourse." That was evident in the political discourse that characterised the Brexit campaign, the presidential campaign of Donald Trump in 2016. We may place the change campaign in Nigeria in 2015 in the same category. The political rhetoric that accompanied these political campaigns raised perennial concern about the relationship between truth and politics to new levels. The campaign rhetoric was primarily based not on evidence/facts, truth and viable policies (cf. Hopkin and Rosamond 2017, 5). Narratives were coloured by sentiments, fabricated facts, and misleading data used to create political rhetoric that had no direct bearing on the truth or the concrete situation of things. Hence, in the words of Rose (2017, 555-558), "[t]hese electoral outcomes not only represented serious challenges to the established political norms, but they also exposed serious fault lines between different groups of citizens." Within that context, the term "post-truth" emerged as an expression of that concern. It highlights a new form of politics and relationship between politics and truth that is the combination of all that was traditionally known as political lies, mendacity, political spin, bullshit with manipulation and exploitation of passions through the power of rhetoric to win arguments and consequently electoral votes and endorsement rather than the use of logic/reason and evidence. According to Suiter (2016, 17-25): "currently, what seems to matter most is not the truth of any given interpretation on this history but the ability of a nativist or populist leader to appeal to instincts and nostalgic emotions of his group." That is what post-truth is about. Taking Donald Trump as an example, Zerilli (2020, p. 4) states:

With Trumpism, however, we seem to be moving from the register of the deliberate lie into another register [...]. In this new register, the lie is not so much put forward and taken for truth. Rather, the very distinction between true and false cease to exist with consequences far more corrosive of democratic politics than anything cooked up by inveterate liars such as Nixon.

According to Hopkin and Rosamond (2017, 2) post-truth, "rhetorical utterances can be understood as typical of a particular mode of reasoning [...] or indeed as a form of politics that more or less manifests itself *in toto* as a distinctive mode of communication [...]" that appeals to emotions instead of facts or evidence. The current hype in the use of the term is a phenomenon peculiar to contemporary time. That point is sufficiently made in the 2016 OED definition of post-truth. The term was defined as "Relating to or denoting circumstances in which objective facts are less influential in shaping public opinion than appeals to emotion and personal belief" (OED 2016 as cited in McIntyre 2019, 1). Closely following that definition, McIntyre (2019, 3-9) asserts that post-truth means more than the prevalence of falsehood, lying, deceit, manipulation, misinterpretation and falsification of facts, self-deception and delusion. McIntyre concludes that:

Yet all seem sufficiently hostile to the truth to qualify as post-truth. [...] As presented in the current debate, the word post-truth is irreducibly normative. It is an expression of concern by those who care about the concept of truth and feel that it is under attack. [...] In its purest form, post-truth is when one thinks that the crowd's reaction does change the facts about a lie.

Similarly, Kalpokas (2019, 12-13) asserts that:

Any claims that post-truth consists of 'misrepresentations at best, and at worst, lies', even including a routinisation of blatant lies ... are somewhat simplistic, since the idea of a 'lie' is itself anachronistic in the post-truth environment. [...] Hence, the prefix 'post-' does not indicate that we have moved to 'beyond' or 'after' truth as such but that we have entered an era where the distinction between truth and lie is no longer important; hence, we had also moved beyond an era when a consensus about the content of truth was possible.

Furthermore, post-truth entails a conscious and deliberate manner of speaking and acting or relating with the truth that is in disagreement with the facts of the situation or disregard of evidence but not without an interior motive. In that sense, Kalpokas (2019, 2) states that "post-truth does not have to involve discarding truth and embracing lies; it refers, instead, to the blurring of the distinction between the two." In the typical political lie, the distinction between true and false still holds, but in post-truth, the difference between true and false is erased. In a sense, it is a cognitive manipulation; hence, post-truth actors like their populists' counterparts "cannot be accused of lying any longer since it has succeeded in abrogating the very idea of truth" (Jay, 2010, 149). Post-truth political actors exploit the resulting atmosphere of scepticism and confusion as Arendt (1973 in Bendall and Robertson 2018, 6) explained: "Left vulnerable by socio-economic upheavals, a muddled mass could be susceptible to Goebbelian big lies."

I agree with McIntyre (2019) and Kalpokas (2019) on their definitions of post-truth. However, there is still more about post-truth that these definitions do not capture and therefore do not translate seamlessly to our current predicament concerning the relationship between truth, politics, and the public that is genuinely new in our situation. The public seemingly accepts the lies and cooperates with the liars to further their interests. As long as the lies do not immediately negatively affect their well-being, nobody cares. The pursuit of truth for its sake does not matter and could be ignored if it does not bring any material benefit. Zerilli (2020, 3-4) aptly describes this new situation as a result of post-truth:

On this view of the problem of so-called post-truth democracies, people know they are being lied to, but they refuse to acknowledge it. They refuse to accord the lie any public significance because buying into the lie pays, so to speak. Accordingly, material interests outweigh fidelity to truth, but truth itself remains in principle knowable. It assumes that citizens are poised to recognise what is right before their eyes if only their material interests could be properly aligned with what is real. It is a view of mystification and deception familiar to anyone who has worked on the classic question of ideology, where how things appear is a distortion of what really is, but a distortion in which subjects are invested because it aligns with what they take their interests to be. Understood as ideological mystification, this account of post-truth suggests that reality is there to be seen by all those who have an interest in seeing it and are conscious of what that interest is.

The above condition explains what post-truth is all about. Truth does not matter as much as emotions/feelings and the existing situation in which one cannot objectively say what is true and what is untrue (cf. McIntyre 2018, 116). We are not hallowing or romanticising any period or exempting any side of the political divide, party and political actor as free of post-truth but exploring the idea of post-truth as a mode of expression, which has become a defining characteristic of recent times. "Whether we are liberals or conservatives, we are all prone to the sorts of cognitive biases that can lead to post-truth. One should not assume that post-truth arises only from others, or that its results are somebody else's problem" (McIntyre 2019, 172). Hence according to Keane (2018, 2), "post-truth is not simply the opposite of truth, however, that is defined; it is more complicated. It is better described as an omnibus term, a word for communication comprising a salmagundi or assemblage of different but interconnected phenomena [...]. Post-truth has recombinant qualities."

THE NATURE OF POST-TRUTH POLITICS

When applied to politics, the concept of post-truth has a deeper meaning beyond dishonesty and deceit and must be distinguished from a long tradition of political lies, propaganda, fake news, and mendacity. McIntyre (2019, 13) claims that post-truth politics

amounts to a form of ideological supremacy, whereby its practitioners are trying to compel someone to believe in something whether there is good evidence for it or not. And this is a recipe for political domination. [...] If one looks at the Oxford definition, and how all of this has played out in the recent public debate, one gets the sense that post-truth is not so much a claim that truth does not exist but that facts are subordinate to our political point of view.

In view of what has been dubbed post-truth and post-truth politics in the preceding, appeals to non-cognitive faculties such as feelings, emotions, and guts are dominant and form the basis for decisions and choices. Consequently, facts are ignored, objectivity in judgment is abandoned, and priority is given to appearances and subjective assessment that results in holding a different perspective so that "there is no such thing as objective truth. [...] any profession of truth is nothing more than a reflection of the political ideology of the person who is making it" (McIntyre, 2019, 126). This sort of situation as Suiter (2016, 25-27) notes in reference to Brexit produced arguably swathes of expressive voters moved by dangerous rhetoric, nativism, irritation and anger to vote in a certain direction without regard to facts or for evidence. But the crucial question that may be asked is how was that possible?

Advancement in science and technology have created new and effective forms of communication that have made it easy and in particular through social media, for post-truth political actors to tape in and create online communities that cut across borders and class distinctions with shared interests, desires, aspirations and a common sensitivity, cognitive bias and worldview. This is possible through mining and harvesting of personal data of individuals and communities on a larger scale delegated to algorithms, statistical and computing programs (Kalpokas 2019, 22-28). Once created these communities become crucial hubs for the dissemination of post-truth fiction. Davis (in Kalpokas 2019, 29) states that "It is by now clear that post-truth involves political actors openly tailoring a pitch to a selected segment of the population by entertaining its members with fantasies and myths that have a particular appeal to them."

Furthermore, Kalpokas (2019, 2) notes that post-truth should be "seen as deeply embedded in everyday practices and developments (most notably, mediatisation) and innermost human drives (primarily, the striving for pleasure as a means of persevering in existence). Hence, what matters is how we experience and emotionally connect with information." In this case, cognitive bias becomes a factor as people tend to follow only information consonant with their sentiments which are made readily available or preselected for them through algorism online. Thus, according to Yilmaz (2019, 237-238),

While considering post-truth and its application by politicians, one needs to consider the reception side, namely the public's perceptions and acceptance of post-truth statements. As stressed, public opinion is inclined towards arguments with misinformation, fake and/or falsified stories, untruths and half-truths, and assertions without factual basis if the arguments appeal emotionally and if they are closer to one's own belief system.

Kalpokas further argues that this scenario is not possible without the complacency and cooperation of the wider society with post-truth political actors. Hence post-truth politics is not merely a manipulation but a co-created fiction and in fact, a collusion between the post-truth political actors and the wider society (Kalpokas, 2019, 18). The reason being that;

Data is created by users themselves, which is a permanent process in the current era of ubiquitous connectivity: messaging records, social media posts, browsing and search history etc as well as data generated by various connected smart devices and appliances that gather and transmit data by default is collected, collated, and analysed, sparing data users the need to specifically collect what is necessary for them, ultimately allowing for complete quantification and datafication of the subject, from their walking patterns to meals ordered and friends met. The more convenience, user-specific tailoring, and proactivity there is in the services one uses, the more data is ultimately being collected (Kalpokas 2019, 29).

However, the fact that people's data online are collected and used without their knowledge and approval for such political manipulations and intent, make them unconscious or unwilling co-operators (Kalpokas 2019, 29-31) which rules out the possibility of meaningful consent and responsible political action. This threatens the heart of democracy, for democracy is not merely about a system of voting. Democracy is an expression of political freedom which is akin to human dignity. It is about a choice that has a moral value that a candidate or political party represents. Or it is a choice of a value that a party represents, and therefore it is a moral choice. It is a violation of conscience to persuade and manipulate peoples' emotions or sentiments to make the wrong choice or come to the wrong conclusion. The significance of that cannot be overemphasised in connection to democracy because it creates forms of participating politically that are separated from the satisfaction of desire or the endorsement and promotion of what is in vogue over that which is good.

The Cambridge Analytica scandal is illustrative here: while the harvesting of user data has allowed for campaign planning in the most rational-qua-efficiency-maximising sense, it may not have led to the most rational outcome as far as electoral choices of the affected societies are concerned (Kalpokas 2019, 30).

This raises many concerns. First, regarding the moral and legal permissibility of taping into the private lives of citizens and using such data or information for political purposes. Second, concerning the legitimacy of the advantage and the results due to such an advantage over an opponent. Third, it raises legitimate moral and legal concern over the use of such indirect means for political campaigns and the extent to which the public have been manipulated into giving their consent notwithstanding whether it is for their good or not. Fourth, the lack of shame and guilt on the part of post-truth political actors for manipulating the public further raises concern over the intent of gaining political power (Chen et al., 2019, 57-72). Political rhetoric as employed by post-truth politicians is primarily concerned not about truth but power and the sustenance of that power. To sustain that power, it is important, that the public is not only bewildered and confused by rhetoric that blurs the line between truth and falsity so that their capacity for veracity is lost, especially if they are at the same time offered narratives that they would like to believe as true (Pinter 2012, 10). Therefore, in the words of Zerilli (2020, 6),

[T]he real danger of what we call post-truth politics is not so much ideological fervour or political provocation but the erosion of a common world in which things can be judged to be true or false. ... This distinction is not eroded overnight of course but emerges through, among other things, continual lying: The result of a consistent and total substitution of lies for factual truth is not that the lies will now be accepted as truth, and the truth be defamed as lies, but that the sense by which we take our bearings in the real world—and the category of truth vs. falsehood is among the mental means to this end—is being destroyed. That was the condition that characterised 20th Century totalitarianism and that is the condition into which we seem to be moving today.

Therefore, post-truth politics is a well-calculated strategy in some advanced democracies to entrench neoliberalism with its emphasis on individual political action that places cognitive responsibility on citizens to shape and make sense of their political world but would restrict the extent of political actions and decisions that democratic and social institutions are allowed to pursue (cf. Hopkin and Rosamond 2017, 2).

Post-truth politics may represent a modern form of grasping power achieved through (the force of) datafication to claim to some form of democratic endorsement in elections. According to Kalpokas (2019, 30) "datafication is a key term here, referring to a process whereby any online action is turned into exploitable data, and that data, in turn, becomes the epicentre of business models, either as a tradable commodity or as a key input into business planning." Legitimate questions can therefore be raised about the use of datafication as a campaign strategy or mechanism for mass persuasion and profiling, particularly the extent to which online personal data are used to create political/campaign content that deliberately distracts the public from core political issues and into making bad decisions and choices. Political rhetoric produced through datafication is tailored and can be understood as a distinct type of reasoning and communication that is manipulative by intentionally anchoring political utterances on emotions/feelings instead of basing them on verifiable facts. This form of politics is consequential as it is employed to keep rhetoric at bay with the truth and can be illustrated in contemporary campaigns in which we have seen the apparent disconnection in the relationship between political rhetoric and truth. For instance, research by Blyth (as cited by Hopkin and Rosamond 2017, 2-3) shows that the austerity policies widely adopted by many countries as the result of the world economic meltdown were contrary to expert opinions of academicians and the austerity policies were sustained despite this opposition being borne out by the expected poor results. Hence, the popularity of ideas that prove to be unviable in the political sphere were evidence of their operation as bullshit but actually should be understood as post-truth politics because the decision was not based on existing true knowledge and evidence. According to Forough, Gabriel, and Fotaki (2019, 18), "Human progress is not assured, and the environment in which post-truth narratives have taken hold poses many threats." The continuous rise of post-truth politics despite these threats is rooted in the erosion of the culture of good democratic politics and campaign culture (cf. Hopkin and Rosamond (2017, 3).

POST-TRUTH AS ANTI-DEMOCRACY

Politics and truth have for long been considered to be at odds. Rose (2017, 555) asserts that "The belief among voters that politicians lie is near-ubiquitous in contemporary political systems, and politicians, in general, are routinely placed at or towards the bottom of indices of truth." It is arguable whether this has any significant effect during democratic elections involving such politicians. Likewise, post-truth rhetoric is known to be untruths or half-truths and manipulations. Nevertheless, it happens that such knowledge or discovery has little or no impact on the legitimacy of post-truth political actors where sentiments or emotions outweigh the judgement of reason. This situation, in the long run, could lead to indifference and denial of established truths and values. Kinna (in Yilmaz 2019, 240-241) stresses the fact that lies are

[N]o longer told with the pretence of upholding a public good, the lies that characterise post-truth are not designed to pass undetected, as Machiavellian lie was indented to do. A prince discovered to be dishonest and to tell untruths was hardly well equipped to rule a virtuous republic.' In other words, today's [...] politicians employing a post-truth strategy do not even pretend they are not misinforming the public, nor that the 'facts' they are creating or rewriting are for the public good. Interestingly, despite their detection, politicians employing post-truth strategies have so far not suffered major repercussions or delegitimization.

In political and democratic cultures where liars are not reprimanded or punished for mendacities, they are at liberty to invent non-existent realities that match their aspirations/ambitions (cf. Yilmaz, 2019, 241). This scenario is cementing the belief that politics is a dirty game, with no clear-cut moral norms for good political conduct. Living ethically and actively involved in politics does no longer resonate with what is acceptable in a political and democratic community. Notably according to Shapin (2019, 8),

English High Court judges, asked to consider a summons against Boris Johnson for demonstrable falsehoods in the referendum on EU membership, ruled against the petitioners, saying that everyone knew that lying was part of politics.

Similarly, we know about post-truth and the post-truth politics and its combination with new technologies, social media, fake news and populism to manipulate, polarise and "with the specific intention of shaping voter opinion and exciting emotions through inciting fear and hatred of the "other"" (Yilmaz 2019, 237-238). Yet, there seems to be a quiet resignation from the public notwithstanding that fact-checking tools are accessible, there seems not much willingness and need in that area. This is happening at a time when according to Yilmaz, (2019, 240) the multiplication of means of communication such as social media due to advancement in media technology has propelled post-truth politics to new heights and at the same has dwindled the impact and influence of traditional journalism and traditional media.

There is no doubt about the effectiveness of social media networks to easily spread unverified information, misinformation, as well as fake news to a large population across borders. Political actors can easily attract a large group of followers across borders, thereby making social media not only a platform to circulate fake news and post-truth utterances that misinform the public on purpose. Media technology has given politicians direct access to communicate with the public which again has the impact of decreasing the influence of mass rallies and party influence while empowering and popularising individual politicians and at the same time increasing individual voting autonomy. "In the end, 'the value or credibility of the media has somewhat faded in comparison to personal opinions. The facts themselves take second place, while "how" a story is told takes precedence over what. It is, therefore [. . .] about listening, seeing and reading the version of facts which more closely fits with each person's ideology" (Yilmaz 2019, 240). At a time when political lies and fake news are shaking the very foundations of democracy and the world as we know it, the increasing use of post-truth politics assisted by social media as a campaign strategy and weapon by political actors further exacerbates such concerns and creating new challenges.

Post-truth situation significantly undermines the ability of individuals and arguably the society at large to differentiate what is false or true and to know what is accurate or inaccurate in a society full of [mis]information vis-à-vis the challenge of making informed decisions and choices without the requisite expertise at the crucial times that the stakes involved in these decisions and choices are critical. Post-truth has left ordinary citizens without access to the truth by misusing the technological power of the internet and Media in particular and as a result, undermines human potential and orientation to truth. We thought that with access to the internet it could no longer be possible to isolate people from the truth and manipulate them. However, with the same internet we are doomed switching from one source of information to the other in search of objectivity and truth without any hope of reaching certainty.

Consequently, public trust in the credibility of experts and authorities is low in many areas or aspects of public interests, for instance; the media/press, economics/finance, policies, medicine and so on. This is fuelled by misinformation, truth denial and the dissemination of which constitute partly what is called fake news. For instance; the recent connection in some quarters of the spread of coronavirus pandemic and 5G telecommunication technology and the connection between coronavirus vaccine, the implants of chips and the biblical mark of the beats called 666 and so on. It is important to note in passing how this sort of misinformation or fake news touch on critical sensibilities of the public beginning from science, technology, religion and culture (cf. COSMOS). It is a crisis because the line separating truth and false, facts and mere opinions are blurred by all shades of emotions/sentiments and reasoning that fact-checking does immediately tell you where the truth lies. This is the era and situation of post-truth society where truth is not just relative but it is no longer a truth as *adequatio intellectus et rei*. It should be noted that because there is a concept of truth as consistency within a system, now we have post-truth, which says adequacy to emotions or consistency with feelings is a criterion of what is true and false. This means that to influence the choice I have to influence not reason with facts but emotions. In this critical circumstance, a lot is at stake and there is no reason for the ignorance that some of our natural virtues such as trust, reasonableness and sincerity are undermined or compromised. There arises immediately the need to re-examine or diagnose some aspects of our current culture which are in a critical state and isolate them and determine, what the solutions are. Firstly, our task is to break the wall of lies. It is a difficult challenge. We need to mobilise our technological and human potentials to win the battle for truth. Our emphasis is on the human potentials and orientation to truth. In which case, the individual through personation has a significant role to play. This is moral duty that we owe to each other.

Secondly, there is the problem with some contemporary philosophical accounts of truth, which do not only misunderstand but ignore the moral nature of truth. Hence, academic discussion of truth is far removed from real life, its metaphysical relation and, restricted to inference/logic and placeholder of reality. This is only a clue about how narrowly truth is understood or conceived; so that what is missed or not stated or understated is significant enough not to be ignored and can be against the very truth which is defended. This is the case with half-truths or when truth becomes a matter of personal convenience, that is, truth as it suits one's situation and needs. Hence, the objectivity and universality of truth are denied and rejected in favour of a subjective and individualistic approach to and affirmation of truth. Consequently, it is difficult if not impossible to see the current problem of truth as a crisis. The crisis might be missed or go unnoticed because the demand for truth and its usage is hardly made in daily living. The question of truth will normally arise in situations that entail a search, a questioning, and an inquiry about the state of an affair or what is/was the case. A proposition about the state of an affair may describe a situation or state the truth about a particular case, for instance, in a testimonial or attestation in a law court. The demand for truth is made in efforts to delineate it from falsehood and when it is considered that the integrity and trust have been tempered or compromised, for instance, when the owner of Facebook, Mark Zuckerberg was questioned about the privacy and safety of personal information of users and how they are used (cf. Quartiroli 2011, 7). Another example is the demand to know the truth about the safety and morality of Artificial Intelligence such as when robots perform some duties like driving and health diagnoses on human beings.

Discussion about truth is heard and the truth is sought at critical and crucial circumstances. Truth matters when public officials, experts, and commissions/committees make statements or declarations of intent and purpose. However, truth matters not less but more in intellectual pursuit and is akin to such disciplines as philosophy, religion, and science. What is truth or what is the nature of truth and what is the truth of the case, feature more in the abovementioned disciplines but especially in philosophy where different and competing theories of truth have been propounded and debated without a clear winner. This is an indication that we commonly know that there exists such a thing as truth. We recognise that truth is important but as to what it is and how it should be construed or understood, philosophers do not agree.

Such disagreements do not exist when it comes to the recognition of truth or absence of truth and the important need to disentangle truth from falsehood. Failure in this respect gives the problem of truth a moral charge. We are strictly careful besides human error and ignorance that truth is not made to look like a lie and a lie is not made to look like truth by any form of rhetoric and description. A lie is not just the opposite of truth but a statement that has no match in the actual world and neither realisable in any world or circumstance; for instance, when religious persons or scientists make so-called 'future predictions'; or when politicians make promises that cannot be fulfilled, or when scientists in valedictory speech say there are out in search of the reality. Further instances can be made from other areas such as the economy, finance, national security, social security, and general public safety concerning consumer goods and services. The least consideration we can make of any such statement or claim is that it is nonsense. But it is fraudulent and constitutes mendacity, that is, intentional deception of people. It is depressing that such fears, concerns and questions are raised in virtually every aspect of life. Shapin (2019, 10) notes that

credibility and legitimacy problems attending a number of cultural institutions aren't new. We've never needed critical analysis to support the belief that governments lie. Machiavelli recommended deceit as sound policy, and, in a famous 17th-century formulation, the English diplomat Henry Wotton defined an ambassador as "an honest gentleman sent to lie abroad for the good of his country.

Therefore, it is evident we are dealing with a crisis which is merely the lack or absence of truth but it is more of the situation in which people appeal and respond more to emotions than to truth or facts. This is typical of post-truth politics. Hence, the supposition or the claim that we are living in a Post-Truth Culture. The consequences are both psychological and material as the result of the widespread culture of lying, covering up the truth, and fraud. It weakens trust, spread suspicion and increases the burden and scope of verification and vigilance. We want other persons to trust and believe what we say and do, in the same manner, and for the same reasons that we want to trust and believe what they say and do. Thus, where there are persons, authority or experts, we take for granted their responsibilities and our expectations of mutual reliability, integrity, and trust. Public awareness and involvement in the detailed technicalities and intricacies of government, politics, economy, health policies and issues, finances, investments manufacturing, security, and so on is limited for lack of knowledge or ignorance. To take advantage of this ignorance to lie and deceive ask questions about the essence of representative democracy.

Besides, to know that some institutions and their representatives lack credibility and still leave them as normal without challenging the status quo as unacceptable is partly the expression of the Post-Truth Culture. The practice of feeding the electorates with lies and false campaign promises in the name of politics is the abnormal culture or practice that has become normal. Stamping out bad politics and entrenching a healthy political and democratic culture necessarily means a zero-tolerance to lies and liars. Morality is absent where truth is lacking and both morality and truth are needed for the rise of any social group and the advancement of human well-being more than the appeal to emotions.

THE RESPONSE TO POST-TRUTH IN POLITICS

This way of understanding and interpreting the post-truth phenomenon demonstrates that countering post-truth demands more than fact-checking skills, truth-telling or standing up for a notion of truth or even the idea of allowing the facts to speak for themselves. These may not be sufficient to counter post-truth narratives. We may quickly recall that Kalpokas (2019) describes post-truth as collusion between politicians and the public. Besides that, Zerilli (2020) has exposed post-truth as an interest-based phenomenon both from the end of politicians and the general public. McIntyre (2019) and likewise Kalpokas (2019) link post-truth with manipulation and exploitation but in connection to our cognitive biases, affectivity, and science through new technologies such as social media to effectively shape public opinion and perception of reality. These accounts of post-truth suggest that it is a deliberate act that has a premeditated outcome. Thus, the post-truth problem is not due to ignorance or as a result of error; nor is it a problem of understanding. Post-truth politics knowingly reject truth/facts for political ends. Thus, it is not a cognitive issue. That means post-truth politicians know the facts and fact-checking does little to change the narrative or sway public opinion, particularly where and when the facts in question are not commonly accepted and upheld as objective truths (cf. Zerilli, 2020, 6). There is often more than one perspective about reality supported by different sets of facts. From this perspective fact-checking is not enough. Zerilli asserts (2020, 5);

what if the obsessive fact-checking that has become second-nature to those who would contest the delusional reality show (Dietz) of Trumpism actually worked against the public acceptance of the facts that are checked? What if fact-checking undermines the truth of opinion […] crucial to caring about factual truths at all? If the problem of post-truth is the loss of our allegiance to a fact-based reality, we need to understand wherein that allegiance consists, that is, the worldly atmosphere in which facts, once checked, can be received as true in a politically significant way.

Similarly, McIntyre basing his arguments on research work and experimental results in psychology has noted the limitations of fact-checking as a strategy in dealing with post-truth. He acknowledges that the repetition of facts does in the long run have an effect (McIntyre, 2019, 158). But he further argues that merely exposing people to facts or truths is often not enough to make them change their beliefs. This is because McIntyre (2019, 34) notes, "the selective use of facts that prop up one's position, and the complete rejection of facts that do not, seem part and parcel of creating the new post-truth reality."

Furthermore, fact-checking offers very little in countering post-truth amidst growing "media fragmentation, information bias, the decline of objectivity, the threat of not just to knowing the truth but to the idea of truth itself" (McIntyre 2019, 153). Hence, McIntyre's proposal in dealing with post-truth is to stand up for a notion of truth and fight back. He states that "in the era of post-truth we must challenge each and every attempt to obfuscate a factual matter and challenge falsehoods before they are allowed to fester" (McIntyre 2019, 157). It is a moral duty not to accord any form of tolerance to lies and structures or organisations that support them. Consequently, McIntyre (2019, 157 - 158) has challenged and rejected the idea of a media balancing act, which means telling both sides of the story. The rule of media balancing act accords the same time to opposing views at the split-screen debates hosted by television media houses. The practice accords a lie the status of a competing opinion while being in actual fact a falsehood that should have been outrightly rejected. In effect, all facts become mere opinions in the subjective sense of it. Zerilli (2020, 9) notes that "this transformation of fact into mere opinion destroys the common world about which to exchange opinions and form judgment." For that reason, Zerilli's solution to post-truth is centred on her idea of the truth-teller as a fact-checker. It is in substance the same with McIntyre's proposal, particularly where she argues that "whatever resilience factual truths have ultimately depended on the continual testimony of human beings. In our ordinary speech and action, it is we who affirm a world held in common, reality as shared" (Zerilli, 2020, 8).

There is no doubt to the merits of McIntyre's, and Zerilli's solutions and others of like minds to the problem of post-truth. However, their positions and solutions suffer the same weakness for which fact-checking is judged to be insufficient in countering post-truth. Those solutions are reactionary responses to the problem. In other words, the solutions arose only at those instances that truth is known or on suspicion to have been violated and necessitate a response, otherwise, there would be none. However, post-truth like a political lie and manipulation are all designed not to be dictated by their victims which is often the case. Thus, Williams (2002, 207) argues that "if it is a good thing, other things being equal, for the people to be truthful, it is a good thing for people in government to be truthful." Where and when post-truth (political lie or bullshit) succeeds, it takes advantage of public trust as one of the primary virtue and condition of democracy in liberal societies, which is the basis of the consent to govern. That trust is not and should not be dependent on the ability of citizens to be able to know when those saddled with the responsibility to govern are dishonest. Where and when that ability is lacking "the search for truth as the telos of inquiry and action" (Jay, 2010, 23) would hardly arise. It is on this basis that it is argued here that fact-checking, truth-telling and standing up for a notion of truth come short of solving the problem of post-truth. These solutions confine the responsibility and pursuit of truth and truthfulness to only those who know. Meanwhile, a great number of citizens are ignorant not only in many matters of politics but of life in general and are not less concerned about truth. Due to human weakness, our knowledge is limited in many areas of interest/need, in which others are experts. This necessitates our mutual dependence, trust and truthfulness. Liberal democratic societies are made of interdependent relationships based on mutual trust and truthfulness that democratic leadership cannot be dispensed from, for the continued sustenance and maintenance of the consent to govern and consequently, for the growth and survival of democracy and society (cf. MacIntyre, 2014, 1-13).

Walzer (1997, 9) asserts that "coexistence requires a politically stable and morally legitimate arrangement and this too is an object of value." From the foregoing, the fight against post-truth should be a commitment to living, acting and speaking truthfully/frankly that take cognisance of our human interdependence and mutual relationship as agents. "Truthfulness implies a respect for the truth" (Jay, 2010, 11). And truthfulness is akin to the virtue of accuracy, sincerity, honesty, and commitment to acquire true beliefs and knowledge, so that what one says and does reveal what he/she knows and believes. Authority should be rooted first in truthfulness before competence so that it is careful not to lie and ruin trust. What must be emphasised, however, is that the basic cultivation of truthfulness in relation to everyday truth is only the beginning, not the whole story" (Jay, 2010, 12). This recognition makes truth an independent value acceptable as a natural virtue not measured exclusively in terms of its effects. Williams (2002, 210) makes the same argument in a slightly different manner.

Liberal societies are democracies, and it may look as though it is the democratic element in the liberal complex that has a particular connection with a demand for government truthfulness. The people are the source of the government's authority (under various substantial restrictions) even of its policies. Government is in some sense a trust; there is a special relationship between government and people, and it is a violation of this conception for secrecy or falsehood to come between trustee and people. It is a feature of democracy, obviously that the citizens are supposed to be able to trust the government. ... One relationship that by its nature excludes deceit is agency, in the sense of an agent's doing things on behalf of the or in place of a principal, things that the principal is poorly placed, for instance, or too occupied to do for himself.

Agency is an existential human condition that engenders trusting others on the things and areas of life that we do not know or have the capacity to understand. In this sense, trust and sincerity are natural virtues and the exercise of which are duties we owe each other without exceptions. "The general rule is, that truth should never be violated, because it is of utmost importance to the comfort of life, that we should have a full security by mutual faith..." (McIntyre 2006, 102). From this perspective, the bridge of trust or compromise of sincerity has moral and legal implications. If everyone lies or conceals the truth to everyone in our common and personal search for meaning and truth, common actions/goals will be impossible and our long-time survival and progress will be frustrated. Human beings are by nature social and political animals that embody those relationships of giving and receiving through which our individual and common goods can be achieved (MacIntyre 2014, 129). Thus, we have roles and responsibilities arising from belonging to the political community. This sort of shared human survival depends largely on the collective recognition of the virtues of truth, trust and sincerity as the foundation of the liberal democratic society. According to MacIntyre (2006, 114) "What is needed is the identification of some mode of institutionalised social practice within which generally established norms and reflective habits of judgment and action could sustain a coherent and rationally justifiable allegiance to a rule concerning truth and lying in a way and to a degree very different from the present dominant culture."

Politics is a genuine human activity that engenders responsibility which often comes in conflict with morals or truth. In such a situation of conflict, truth is a virtue and a value when removed or neglected or even concealed is a deliberate choice with implications. It is a failure not to live up to the moral truth and even to recognise certain higher standards or values. More accurately, it is a failure not to recognise that truth does not merely regulate a practice or activity; truth defines the kind of practice or activity called politics and at the same time legitimises it. We give away or concede too much to politics if politics is allowed to determine truth. Truth should determine politics.

ACKNOWLEDGMENT

Disclosure Statement: No potential conflict of interest was reported by the author.

REFERENCES

Arendt, H. (1973). *Origin of Totalitarianism*. A Harvest Books.

Bendall, M. J., & Robertson, C. (2018). Crisis of democratic culture. *International Journal of Media and Cultural Politics*, *14*(3), 383–391. doi:10.1386/macp.14.3.383_7

Block, D. (2019). *Post-Truth and Political Discourse*. Springer Nature Publishers. doi:10.1007/978-3-030-00497-2

Cerovac, I. (2016). 'The Role of Experts in a Democratic Society'. *Journal of Education Culture and Society*, *2*(2), 75–88. doi:10.15503/jecs20162.75.88

Chen, M. (2019). Modelling Public Mood and Emotion: Blog and News Sentiment and Politico-economic Phenomena. In A. Visvizi & M. D. Lytras Effat (Eds.), *Politics And Technology In The Post-Truth Era* (pp. 57–72). Emerald Publishing Limited. doi:10.1108/978-1-78756-983-620191005

Collaboratarium for Social Media and Online Behavioural Studies (COSMOS). (2020). https://www.cosmos.ualr.edu/misinformation

Elkins, J. (2012). Concerning Practices of Truth. In J. Elkins & A. Norris (Eds.), *Truth and Democracy*. University of Pennsylvania Press. doi:10.9783/9780812206227.19

Ellington, J. W. (Ed.). (1994). *Immanuel Kant Ethical Philosophy*. Hackett Publishing Company.

Forough, H., Gabriel, Y., & Fotaki, M. (2019). Leadership in a Post-Truth Era: A new Narrative Disorder? Sage. doi:10.1177/1742715019835369

Frankfurt, H. (2005). *On Bullshit*. Princeton University Press. doi:10.1515/9781400826537

Gaita, R. (2016). *When Politicians Lie: Reflections On Truth, Politics And Patriotism*. https://griffithreview.com/contributors/raimond-gaita/

Greenberg, D. (2015). *Truth in Politics Now*. https://prospect.org/article/truthpolitics-now

Hopkin, J., & Rosamond, B. (2017). Post-truth Politics, Bullshit and Bad Ideas: 'Deficit Fetishism' in the UK. *New Political Economy*. Advance online publication. doi:10.1080/13563467.2017.1373757

Human Rights Watch. (2019). *Nigeria: Widespread Violence Ushers in President's New Term*. Human Rights Watch. https://www.hrw.org/news/2019/06/10/nigeria-widespread-violence-ushers-presidents-new-term

Jay, M. (2010). *The Virtues of Mendacity*. University of Virginia Press.

Kalpokas, I. (2019). *A Political Theory of Post-Truth*. Springer Nature Publishers. doi:10.1007/978-3-319-97713-3

Keane, J. (2018). *Post-Truth Politics and why the Antidote isn't simply 'Fact-Checking' and Truth*. https://theconversation.com/post-truth-politics-and-why-the-antidoteisnt-simply-fact-checking-and-truth-87364

Keyes, R. (2004). *The Post-Truth Era*. St Martin's Press.

Lee, M. Y. H. (2015). Donald Trump's False Comments connecting Mexican immigrant and Crime. *The Washington Post*. https://www.washingtonpost.com/news/fact-checker/wp/2015/07/08/donald-trumps-false-comments-connecting-mexican-immigrants-and-crime/

Lockie, S. (2017). Post-truth Politics and the Social Sciences. *Environmental Sociology*, *3*(1), 1–5. doi:10.1080/23251042.2016.1273444

Mair, P. (2013). *Ruling the Void. The Hollowing of Western Democracy*. Verso.

Marty, E. M., & Moore, J. (2000). *Politics Religion and the Common Good*. Jesse-Bass Publisher.

Maryniarczyk, A. (2016). *Rationality and Finality of the World of Persons and Things*. Polskie Towarzyztwo Tomasza z Akwinu.

McInery, R. (Ed.). (1998). *Aquinas, T. Selected Writings*. Penguin Books.

McIntyre, A. (2006). *Ethics and Politics: Selected Essays* (Vol. 2). Cambridge University Press. doi:10.1017/CBO9780511606670

McIntyre, A. (2007). *After Virtue* (3rd ed.). University of Notre Dame Press.

McIntyre, L. (2019). *Post-Truth*. The MIT Press.

Mearsheimer, J. J. (2011). *Why Leaders Lie: The Truth About Lying in International Politics*. Oxford Press.

Pashkova, V. (2016). *Arendt's political thought: the relationship between truth and politics*. http://hdl.handle.net/1959.7/uws:37675

Pinter, H. (2012). Art, Truth and Politics. In J. Elkins & A. Norris (Eds.), *Truth and Democracy*. University of Pennsylvania Press. doi:10.9783/9780812206227.9

Quartiroli, I. (2011). *The Digitally Divided Self: Relinquishing Our Awareness to the Internet*. Silens Publishers.

Rose, J. (2017). Brexit, Trump, and Post-Truth Politics. *Public Integrity*, *19*(6), 555–558. doi:10.1080/10999922.2017.1285540

Shapin, S. (2019). Is there a Crisis of Truth. *Los Angeles Review of Books*. https://lareviewofbooks.org/article/is-there-a-crisis-of-truth/

Suiter, J. (2016). Post-Truth Politics. Political Insight, 7(3), 25-27. doi:10.1177/2041905816680417

Vogler, C. (2016). Anscombe on Two Jesuits and Lying. In L. Gormally, D. A. Jones, & R. Teichmann (Eds.), *The Moral Philosophy of Elizabeth Anscombe*. Imprint Academic.

Williams, B. (2002). *Truth and Truthfulness: An Essay in Genealogy*. Princeton University Press.

Yilmaz, G. (2019). Post-truth politics in the 2017 Euro-Turkish crisis. *Journal of Contemporary European Studies*, *27*(2), 237–246. doi:10.1080/14782804.2019.1587390

Zerilli, L. M. G. (2020). Fact-Checking and Truth-Telling in an Age of Alternative Facts. *Le foucaldien, 6*(1), 1–22. doi:10.16995/lefou.68

Chapter 13
National Security, Media, and Cybersecurity Threats:
A Strategic Framework for Secure Cyberspace Governance in Developing Countries

Kursim Leonard Fwa
National Institute for Policy and Strategic Studies, Nigeria

ABSTRACT

This chapter discusses the nexus between national security, media, and cybercrime in cyberspace governance. To achieve good governance within nations cyberspace, it becomes essential for the policymakers to exercise political, economic, and judicial procedures in a manner that ensures that the people are given their freedom to fulfil their duties and resolve their disputes in accordance with rule of law. The chapter provides policymakers with insights on how to improve the effectiveness of national security, counter cybercrimes within cyber governance institutions, and processes in the face of the changing nature of the use of media and its platforms. The chapter discuss the problematic, the concept cyberspace, cyberspace, and the changing dynamics and cybersecurity crime: trends, method, risks, and vulnerabilities. The chapter provides a strategic framework for a secure cyberspace in developing countries, taking cognisance of the realities and constraints within a developing milieu of the developing countries.

In battle, there are not more than two methods of attack—the direct and the indirect; yet these two in combination give rise to an endless series of manoeuvres.

—Sun Tzu, The Art of War

DOI: 10.4018/978-1-6684-4107-7.ch013

INTRODUCTION

The mass espousal of the Internet in the 1990s brought about an era of hope and optimism. Here was a platform that enabled instant communication and the sharing of and access to information. Early proponents asserted that access to the Internet would democratise societies in the long run. However, as The Economist points out, 'these days it is the Internet's defects, from monopoly power to corporate snooping and online radicalisation, that dominate the headlines.'(The Economist, 2019). Indeed, disregard for personal data by media by extension the social media networks, the notoriety of fake news and deep fake content, as well as the growth of cybercrime have dampened the early enthusiasm for connected societies. There is also an increase in cyber fatigue, as Internet users are constantly bombarded with privacy and safety warnings.

At the outset of the digital age, it was hoped that technology would inevitably bring about more openness, freedom and democracy. Unfortunately, since then authoritarian states have learnt how to manipulate technologies to silence dissidents and use the Internet as a propaganda outlet. These states furthermore cite security concerns, claiming protection of their citizens when they limit their rights to access social media platforms and messaging apps. The rise of fake news in a post-truth world has indeed been exploited by certain states, non-states actors, individuals and politicians, who create their own narratives as part of information warfare against local and foreign dissenters and critics. Anyone who has an opposing point of view is typically labelled as a 'foreign agent'. This is often followed by attacks on the person's integrity and character on social media and may be coupled with physical harassment or intimidation in the real world.

However, now that humanity is no longer viewing technology through rose-tinted glasses, it may be more mature about the regulations required. The road ahead is not paved or even well lit. Legislation and regulation are necessary to both enable the rights of citizens on the Internet and protect them from cybercrime and the unauthorised use of personal data (Turianskyi,2020:p 3). Governments need to perform a balancing act in these matters to ensure that there are appropriate regulations in place that allow them to deal with cybercrime without infringing on online freedoms or providing opportunities for security services to spy on their citizens. Maintaining a balance between protecting citizens from cybercrime and maintaining their Internet freedoms is indisputably difficult and is further complicated by the fact that technology tends to be years ahead of policy. Therefore, policymakers need to work with technology experts to stay up to date with the latest developments, as well as to ensure that regulation does not stifle innovation

The continuous development of the internet in the last few decades together with the resulting growth, innovation and capital investment in related technologies, compel developing nations to establish and mature its cybersecurity environment in order to mitigate the threats that accompany the vast capabilities that these innovations provide. The growing access of developing countries to cyberspace, requires that all such countries should have a proper plan to help secure their cyberspace. Although some documents for this purpose do exist, they are usually long and complex and do not provide simple and clear-cut guidance on where to start securing cyberspace. Developing countries, because of financial and expertise constraints, cannot do everything at the same time – so a more basic document is needed with clear steps on how to start

The structure of the Internet itself, which comes down to interconnected networks using standardised routing protocols and websites that may reside anywhere in the world, even on privately owned infrastructure, exacerbates the regulatory problems resulting in jurisdictional issues. The Internet is decentralised and so is its governance, yet the rate at which people are connecting is also increasing dramatically and cybercrime repression requires international coordination. Domestic laws are insufficient – technology is borderless. Furthermore, global solutions tend to be challenging to implement, given the multitude of perspectives, ideologies and technical requirements. Significant differences remain between countries on how the Internet should be governed and it is unlikely that consensus will be reached any time soon. In addition, there are ideological divisions on the standardisation of data protection and Internet usage. The extreme sides of this debate propagate either no data privacy regulations whatsoever or extremely strict ones, which would make conducting business untenable. These divisions are similar to between those countries that make no effort to control or regulate Internet usage and those which strictly control it.

Debates on cybersecurity, media and cyberspace governance start with its very definition, which are reflected in various perspectives, approaches and policy interests. Computer specialists focus on standards and applications, human rights activists are concerned with freedom of expression and privacy, while policymakers view it through the prism of cybersecurity. (Kurbalija J,2019). Two camps can be identified: those advocating for multi-stakeholder governance of the Internet and cyberspace, on the one hand, and those in favour of state control, on the other. Multi-stakeholder governance of the Internet is indeed an interesting idea. Currently, many global initiatives exist to address development challenges, entrench democratic practices and strengthen regulatory frameworks through multi-stakeholder partnerships between governments, civil society and the private sector. (Gruzd S et al., 2018). What is therefore needed is a strategic framework for developing countries to secure cyberspace, to provide a starting point for developing countries when implementing its cybersecurity strategy. Such a framework can then be utilised as best practice or a blueprint by developing countries as a starting point in designing their own framework and strategy. Therefore, this paper present a framework in order to establish a guidance based on relevant factors and to encourage developing countries to address the securing of cyberspace in a comprehensively approach, instead of just focussing on a narrow scope of activities.

THE PROBLEMATIC

Cyberspace touches practically everything and everyone. It provides a platform for innovation and prosperity and the means to improve general welfare around the globe. But with the broad reach of a loose and lightly regulated digital infrastructure, great risks threaten nations, private enterprises, and individual rights. Governments have responsibility to address these strategic vulnerabilities to ensure that, together with the larger community of nations, can realize the full potential of the information technology revolution. The cyberspace activities has changed the world in ways hitherto unknown. The international financial system, air, land and maritime transport systems are all digitally linked. Similarly, most militaries are fully or partially networked. This has not only sped up the decision-making processes at all levels, but it has also rendered these systems vulnerable to cyber-attacks. Cyberspace-warfare is now recognized as the most potent form of non-kinetic war fighting. In order to prevent large scale network-attacks, cyber-powers are simultaneously spending a lot of time, money and effort to erect redundant cyber-defences and enhancing their offensive cyber capabilities. Difficulties in creating a stable environment in information-space stem from differing national, regional and global perceptions regarding the freedom of the Internet, application of international law and problems associated with attribution.

At the beginning of this century, a new type of crisis surfaced which is the control of cyberspace. Cyberspace is a new environment where no country is immune to the threats that its use occasions. With the rapid growth came possibilities in development and new ways to empower people: however, this is accompanied by new vulnerabilities, risks and challenges. It is therefore crucial to research how to build cyberspace-capacities in developing countries and simultaneously how to secure these. The main dilemma being faced in cyberspace is lack of universal understanding of definitions, norms, values, rules, regulations and laws on the use of internet in general and the prosecution of criminals in particular. Developed countries have started exploiting the threats and vulnerabilities of the cyberspace to gain hegemony and influence over their rivals. To be able to use the cyberspace, the developing countries rely on the products and capabilities made and presented by the western world and what is more important is that they use the technology developed by the same countries to protect their information.

Nation's critical infrastructures are composed of public and private institutions in the sectors of agriculture, food, water, public health, emergency services, government, defence industrial base, information and telecommunications, energy, transportation, banking and finance, chemicals and hazardous materials, and postal and shipping to say the least. Cyberspace is their nervous system—the control system of countries worldwide. Cyberspace is composed of hundreds of thousands of interconnected computers, servers, routers, switches, and fibre optic cables that allow our critical infrastructures to work. Thus, the healthy functioning of cyberspace is essential to nation`s economy and national securities. Needless to say, that the Cyberspace is today the defining feature of modern life. The governance and security of the cyberspace is currently the major concern confronting the international community, thus, without doubt, a vital environment for global insecurity.

Therefore, governance of the cyberspace is and must fundamentally be tied to the good-governance of cyberspace domain. So, the relationship between cyberspace governance and cybersecurity is of vital importance for putting in place a Strategic framework, adopting efficient strategies and policies regarding the cyberspace. Governments, individuals and communities worldwide connect, socialize, and organize themselves in and through cyberspace. From 2000 to 2021 and beyond, global Internet usage has continue to increase from over 360 million to over 6 billion people. As Internet usage continues to expand, cyberspace will become increasingly woven into the fabric of everyday life across the globe. Therefore, the objective is to research paper is to interrogate the relationship between national security, media, cybersecurity-threats and cyberspace governance, in order to confirm or deny the existence of interdependence between the levels of nations security, media influence, cybersecurity-crime and the quality of cyberspace governance particularly from the developing countries perspectives.

Furthermore, can the nation security challenges, media, cybersecurity-crime dilemmas be resolve peacefully through good governance. Can good governance contribute to the prevention and the peaceful resolution of the cybersecurity-threats and cyberspace predicaments. Therefore, depending on the consistency of this assumption, the first challenge is to cross-examine the nexus or interdependence between the state's security, media and the quality of cyberspace governance. The secondary is to identify the main reasons for which we might consider the cyberspace a strategic domain alongside land, air, sea and space. Thus, backing the assumption that the security and governance of cyberspace as vital interest for the developing countries. The dynamics of recent international events such as "The Arab Spring" or "The Twitter Revolution" shows that the proper understanding of the phenomena which take place on the "cyber arena" is particularly important for the study of contemporary international relations and security.

The continuous development of the internet should compel the developing countries to establish and mature its cybersecurity environment in order to mitigate the threats and vulnerabilities that accompany the vast capabilities that these innovations provides. The growing access of developing countries to cyberspace, requires that all such countries should have a proper strategic framework and or plan to help secure their cyberspace. Such a framework can then be utilised as best practice or a blueprint by developing countries as a starting point in designing their own framework and strategy. It a truism that there is an increasing awareness among scholars, policymakers in the developing countries that stronger efforts are needed to better protect states interests in cyberspace against a wide array of dangerous threats. It is useful to think about addressing security challenges in cyberspace as a matter of managing risk. Here "risk" is expressed as being a composite of three things: threat, vulnerability, and consequences. Threat is a product of both intention and capability. In cyberspace, some of the greatest indications of intention and capability are the wide variety of ongoing malicious activities, many of which are difficult to attribute to specific attackers and sources. Vulnerability depends on the characteristics of the target and the probability that an attempted attack will be successful. Lastly, consequences are the political, social, or economic damages or costs inflicted by a successful attack. One of the useful aspects of a risk management approach to security challenges in the cyber realm is that it illuminates the fact that efforts to increase cybersecurity could be focused on any combination of the following: reducing threats, reducing vulnerability, or reducing the consequences of a successful attack.

WHAT CYBERSPACE?

It worthy to state from the onset that the cyberspace is not immune to insecurity, crime and competition. Cases of cybercrimes, cyberwarfare, cyberespionage, propaganda, data losses, compromised networks and cyber-doom scenarios fill the headlines on a daily basis. States, international organizations, private companies and human rights activists are struggling to regulate a wide range of activities that take place in cyberspace and at the same time balance between critical infrastructure protection, civil liberties, technical standards and cost. Cyberspace poses a great challenge to the traditional idea of global governance that is mainly state-centric. Due to its asymmetrical, anonymous and dual-use features, cyberspace challenges traditional understanding of key concepts such as security, borders, human rights, privacy and sovereignty (Emerson 2016; Slack 2016). The reason is that the socio-political and technological characteristics of this new domain are constantly being redefined (Choucri 2012: 4).

The rapid pace of technological developments and changes and the way societies respond in the digital realm is affecting the interests of state and non-state actors in cyberspace. Advances in the field of information technology, like the Internet of Things (Weber 2013), Big Data (Cukier and Mayer-Schoenberger 2013) and the Dark Web (Chertoff and Simon 2015), have surpassed the ability of states and international organizations to offer efficient governance. States lack the necessary human capital and technical resources to provide cyber security to its citizens. The public-private sector relationship in cyberspace resembles a paradox. On the one hand, governments cannot act as a security provider and protect the private sector from all cyber threats. On the other hand, the private sector is asked to assist the government in cyber security matters, by conducting censorship and surveillance.

Today the cyberspace has become pervasive within contemporary societies. "At its essence, cyberspace is the realm of computer networks (and the users behind them) in which information is stored, shared, and communicated online." It is an information environment handling digitized data in different ways (copying, moving, storing, …), at the same time it is the computers and networking technologies on which this happens. So, cyberspace is both something virtual, but not exclusively, it has its physical aspects. In essence, cyberspace is a manmade domain (in opposition to the other four domains of warfare) and people behind their computers and in charge of managing the infrastructure are also an important part of cyberspace. As most expert put it: "cyberspace is explained as much by the cognitive realm as by the physical or digital." (Singer and Friedman, 2014). In principle the cyberspace is constantly evolving. First, cyberspace is evolving in its size and scale over the past decennia and has evolved from a computer network fully controlled by states to the present-day situation, where people around the world connect and disconnect their devices with it constantly. Secondly, the technologies that form cyberspace evolve, for example, until recently it was mostly wired connections, whilst today wireless connections of e.g., smartphones are also omnipresent and lastly, the politics of cyberspace is evolving in multiplicities and dimensions.

The vulnerability of this cyberspace domain networked resource to criminality has become an important issue of international policy for governments. States, individuals, corporations and non-states actors are harnessing cyberspace to create new industries, a vibrant social space, and a new economic sphere that are intertwined with our everyday lives. At the same time, these same individuals, subnational groups, and governments are using cyberspace to advance interests through malicious activity. Terrorist's recruit, train, and target through the Internet, hackers steal data, and intelligence services conduct espionage. Still, the vast majority of cyber domain is civilian space used by individuals, businesses, and governments for legitimate purposes. These challenges have provoked scholars, policy analysts, information technology executives and security and intelligence experts to interrogate existing and future threats to cyberspace governance. How to find ways, approaches to advance and defend national, subregional and regional interests and recommend new ways and means to prevent, defend interests in cyberspace with a view to develop offensive capabilities to compete there.

Over the past two decades, states, non-state actors, non-governmental organizations and transnational organized criminals have also expanded in size, scope, and menace, destabilizing globalized political, social, cultural, economies and the likes, creating insecurities in communities around the world and in particular the developing countries. As criminal entrepreneurs, non-states actors, international and transnational illicit networks hijacked these advances in developments (technological, financial, health and communications etc,) for unlawful gains, they continue to present new harms to the cyberspace domain and security of all nations. Thus, the cyberspace security has become a governance concern since 2007 when for example, Estonia and Georgia and host of others suffered large-scale cyber-attacks. These attacks were proof to many governments and corporations that the cyberspace-security domain requires governance. The proliferation of these networks and the convergence of their criminal activities threaten not only the global, regional but national interdependence and transactional systems that facilitate governance, and also the movement of people, jeopardizing cyberspace structures, economic development, security, and supply chain integrity.

To emphasis the crisis in the cyberspace domain, it is important to state that proxies have existed around the world for centuries. Thucydides writes about proxies, including mercenaries and privateers used in the Peloponnesian war. Geraint Hughes's book on proxy warfare carries the title 'My Enemy's Enemy', a phrase taken out of the Arthashastra, a treatise on statecraft from India dating back to the fourth century BC (Walt, 1985). Machiavelli wrote 'Mercenaries and auxiliaries are at once useless and dangerous, and he who holds his State by means of mercenary troops can never be solidly or securely seated.'(Machiavelli,2010). In Chinese history, the 36 stratagems include one recommending 'Kill with a borrowed sword'. According to an article published by the Shanghai Daily in 2013, 'the true meaning of this stratagem is to attack your enemy by using the forces or strength of a third party, or to entice your ally into attacking your enemy instead of doing it yourself.'

The cyberspace threatened environment is characterized by the convergence-the merging and blending of an ever-expanding array of illicit actors and networks. The interconnected pipelines linking these threat actors and networks cut across borders, infiltrated and corrupted licit business, penetrated fragile governments, and undercut the interests and security of our partners across the international community. The direct links among specific states actors, cybercriminals, illicit actors and the use of media institutions in particular social media for propaganda, psychological warfare have worsened the security dilemma, through the activities of the growing illegal economies that supports and enables corrupt officials, criminals, terrorists, and insurgents. The Cyberspace-security has, thus become a major contemporary governance challenge. As the public and private sectors continue to deliver goods through digital means, the cyber domain will only continue to expand and become more relevant to the field of security governance. This new domain poses threats to governance in the form of cyber-crime, cyber-warfare, cyber-terrorism, and cyber-espionage, and creates new vulnerabilities to the Critical Infrastructures and Big data. As the cyber domain cuts across national borders and is not congruent with national boundaries, how the developing countries would governed their cyberspace-security domain is the thrust of this paper. The motivation for this is the urge that policymakers and strategists from developing countries would find this piece an invaluable resource in their efforts to ensure the safeguard of their national security and answer concerns about future secure cyberspace governance.

THE CYBERSPACE AND THE CHANGING DYNAMICS

Human beings are social animals. They communicate with each other in complex ways, using a variety of spoken and written languages. Homo sapiens have the distinct reputation of inventing the sign language and the braille for those amongst them without the natural ability to see or hear. There are thousands of languages and dialects in the world. Over the millennia some of these have died out, a few have been revived and newer ones have emerged including computer languages. An elaborate system of encryption ranging from simple codes and cyphers to exotic algorithms has been developed to keep the content of the messages secret. The Oxford dictionary defines communication as "imparting or exchanging of information or news." Means of communication collectively form the integrated management backbone for all kinds of human undertakings extending from family matters to corporate and government dealings, as well as interstate relationships. Different kinds of agents, instruments and methods are used to pass information. These range from primitive means such as the word of mouth, drumbeats, smoke signals, bugles, messengers, carrier pigeons, and semaphore to the more sophisticated ones like modern computer networks. The area, where information resides, is the information-space. In the Internet lexicon terms like cyberspace and information-space are used interchangeably. For most people cyberspace signifies the world of computer networks. The Bing Dictionary describes cyberspace as the "imagined place where electronic data goes," or the "the notional realm in which electronic information exists or is exchanged." Others have defined cyberspace in similar terms e.g. The environment formed by physical and non-physical components, characterized by the use of computers and electro-magnetic spectrum, to store, modify, and exchange data using computer networks. A domain characterized by the use of electronics and the electromagnetic spectrum to store, modify, and exchange data via networked systems and associated physical infrastructures.

The nature of the digital systems we are creating today represents a significant evolution away from the technology of the past – where we could design systems with a clear scope and function. Our future will see a cyberspace underpinned by technologies that together form a platform for innovation whose New technology brings significant opportunity. Business and government have understood the potential of technology for many years and are engaged in ongoing programmes of digital transformation. This will now feel like a continuous journey – no longer a project with a clear end point, but rather a move towards embracing a constant level of technology change within the core of our organizations. It has been clear for some time that technology will critically underpin solutions to key global challenges.

Furthermore, Cyberspace is growing rapidly, as new connected devices, networks, services and data emerge. This brings changes in the scale not only of networks, but also of data volumes, storage capacity, processing systems and the knowledge space that we collectively create. The scale of cyberspace is already difficult for most to conceptualize. Communications and data-processing can be carried out at an ever-accelerating pace, and this enables a speeding up of business transactions and processes, relationship creation, publishing and sharing of content and ideas, and generation of value. The change in speed and or pace is so substantial that it may mean current forms of management for our relationships, content, image and processes are too slow and no longer fit for purpose. There is an increasing level of interconnectivity of systems and interdependence of actors across cyberspace, throughout organizations and supply chains. Together these changes result in a fundamental shift in the dynamism with which we experience cyberspace. Many feel that that is so complex, with increasingly sophisticated characteristics, that our role will change so that we become observers of a system increasingly outside our control. significant progress to be made in the areas of health, carbon footprint reduction, delivering new economic opportunities to the poorest nations, farming in order to feed the world's population, and making our public and critical infrastructures safer and more efficient. These characteristics, represents the dynamism and transformation in technologies that is contributing to the changing dynamics of cyberspace. We do not claim that this is the complete set of technology innovations that will define our futures, nor that they illustrate all the risks we face. However, they are sufficiently representative to illuminate the range of risk we are likely to face in the next 10–20 years. The structure, components, relationships and processes are constantly changing to support emerging ideas, services, security and business needs. As a result, the underlying dynamics of cyberspace are changing.

As Gibson's notional 'cyberspace' (1984) has materialised as the 'network of networks' that constitutes the internet and the communication and content services made available over it, so there has been an inevitable growth in the criminality associated with this environment. Cyberspace spawn's cybercrime and 'since crime tends to follow opportunity and the internet provides many new opportunities, then new crimes will certainly emerge (Wall, 2003: p xv). Cybercriminals are driven by a range of motivations, from intellectual joy riding to political protest (Jordan & Taylor,1998: pp. 757 – 780). Post-September 11, cybercrime has inevitably become one element of the developed nation's fascination with terrorism. Attention has focused on the possibilities for 'cyber-terrorism', cybercrime with a premeditated political motivation, (Denning, 2000, pp. 29-37) as well as for 'cyberwar', State-based activity, with the image of a future 'electronic pearl harbour' haunting policy-makers. The healthy functioning of cyberspace is essential to nations economy and national security. However, as with other areas of internet-based activities, addressing cybercrime raises complex issues in international relations, challenging traditional conceptions of sovereignty, jurisdiction and territoriality, though not inevitably or necessarily to their detriment (Perritt, 1998: pp pp. 475 – 491).

Such complexities are recast as three core questions: regulate what, regulate when and regulate how. In terms of the 'regulate what', there is a need to identify those activities that threaten the security of cyberspace without over-criminalising enforcement activities to safeguard the rights of others, whether sovereign rights or privacy rights. In terms of 'when' to regulate, the problem has been succinctly stated in the following terms: That in a networked world, where all points are equidistant from all others and all are accessible from anywhere, the principles of the international legal system cannot impose obligations on everyone to comply with all law. If this is considered a self-evident truth, what criteria render a nation's criminal law and procedure applicable? Is it one of mere accessibility from the territory or actual effect or harm on those in the territory? The 'how' of regulation involves issues of legal treatment and law enforcement. To minimise regulatory arbitrage, the exploitation of differential laws by cybercriminals, Governments have both extended the application of national law as well as promoted harmonisation between legal systems.

According to Jason Andress and Steve Winterfeld, (2014: pp 3-5) cyberspace is a "notional environment" or "global domain" that consists of independent networks of information technology infrastructure including telecom networks, computers, internet, controllers and embedded processors to collect, analyse, modify, transmit, store and secure the information (pp3-4). It was originally designed to enhance communication and connectivity. However, the ever-increasing human dependency on cyberspace and destructive technological innovations have transformed the cyberspace into an arena where information technology and data are being used as the tools as well as the target of warfare for causing instability, destruction of critical infrastructure and espionage. For most developing countries, cyberspace has become a criminalised and militarised zone, posing threats to its national security. (Ghernaouti, 2013). Most developing countries are exposed to extensive cyber threats ranging from computer malware, identity theft, financial data theft, cyber frauds, surveillance on critical infrastructure and critical infrastructure information. They cannot ensure comprehensive national security without effectively coping with these threats.

A successful response to transnational cybercrime thus requires a degree of cooperation between states—cooperation that may not be automatically forthcoming. The governance of cyberspace is no less a pluralistic endeavour than is the governance of physical territory. Current literature on the regulation of cyberspace is no longer focused on whether cyberspace can be regulated. Instead, conversation focuses on how cyberspace is regulated and who are the regulators. It is generally conceded that the state cannot adequately control cyberspace via laws and regulations. Even when laws and regulations are kept up to date with developments in technology, the functions and effectiveness of laws and regulations will be limited; the transnational dimensions of much cyber illegality and the architectures of digital technology all but guarantee this (Grabosky et al. 2001; Katyal 2003). Other regulatory methods such as code and system design, self-regulation by the private sector and co-regulation via public and private cooperation have been proposed as alternatives with which to govern cyberspace.

CYBERSECURITY CRIME: TRENDS, METHOD, RISKS AND VULNERABILITIES

Cybercrime appears to be partially supplanting traditional forms of crime. Cybercrime is crime that is enabled by, or that targets computers. It is argued that there is no agreed-upon definition for "cybercrime" because "cyberspace" is just a new specific instrument used to help commit crimes that are not new at all. Cybercrime can involve theft of intellectual property, a violation of patent, trade secret, or copyright laws. It could also include attacks against computers to deliberately disrupt processing or an espionage to make unauthorized copies of classified data or harms that result from opportunities created by networked technologies. According to FBI data, bank robberies have been decreasing since 2008 while cybercrime has been increasing during the same period of time. This should not be surprising as cybercrime is considerably safer than bank robbery and the perpetrator has a far greater chance of avoiding arrest and prosecution. Cybercrime falls into a variety of categories including several types of fraud, sale in contraband and counterfeit items, and scams.

Cybercrime is attractive, in part, because it is often hard to investigate and prosecute. Cybercriminals exploit jurisdictional boundaries - a cybercriminal may be based in one country, use a server in another country, and defraud victims in yet another country, meaning that the suspect, the evidence, and the victim, may all fall under different national jurisdictions, legal systems, and enforcement and investigative agencies. This makes for tremendous challenges in coordinating a multi-national law enforcement response and dealing with very different legal frameworks and restrictions. Effective cybercriminals also enjoy a high degree of anonymity, manipulating the Internet and other computer networks to hide their identity and location thus making it difficult to identify and convict criminals.

The motives that drive these cybercriminal groups now may differ from those of their paying customers, who may possess little or no technical skills. New technologies continue to outpace policy for law enforcement. Problems of coordination among agencies of different countries, along with conflicting national policies about crime in cyberspace, work to the advantage of cybercriminals who can choose to operate from geographic locations where penalties for some forms of cybercrime may not yet exist. Sophisticated tools for cyberattack can now be found for sale or for rent on the Internet, where highly-organized underground cybercrime businesses host websites that advertise a variety of disruptive software products and malicious technical services. High-end cybercrime groups use standard software business development techniques to keep their products updated with the latest ant security features and seek to recruit new and talented software engineering students into their organizations.

Where illicit profits are potentially very large, some high-end criminal groups have reportedly adopted standard IT business practices to systematically develop more efficient and effective computer code for cybercrime. Studies also show that organized crime groups now actively recruit college engineering graduates and technical expert members of computer societies and sponsor them to attend more information technology (IT) courses to further their technical expertise. However, in some cases, targeted students may not realize that a criminal organization is behind the recruitment offer (McAfee Virtual Criminology Report: Organized Crime and the Internet, December 2006). Cyber-crime has become a major problem for the 21st century, in relation to both prevention and detection of the growing number of associated activities. In fact, cybercrime is the fastest-growing area of crime. As more countries around the world are becoming increasingly dependent on digital networks and the opportunities for committing cybercrime are increasing, as "the computer" increasingly becomes a central component of commerce, entertainment, and government. This now means the opportunities for committing cybercrime are growing exponentially as more and more people utilise handheld devices capable of exploitation and the accessing of personal and professional data. Crimes such as committing fraud, hacking, trafficking in child pornography and intellectual property, stealing identities, or violating privacy are becoming everyday activities for those involved in committing cyber-crime. Cyber-crime has not created new crimes, simply provided an alternative method through which to commit crimes such as theft, extortion, illegal protest, and terrorism.

Cybercrime vulnerabilities can be distinguished into three broad categories of activity. First, computer-related cybercrime, such as fraud and theft, where computers are simply the tools for the crime, manipulating data to commit traditional criminal activities. Second, content-based cybercrimes, such as criminal copyright infringement and child pornography, where computer and communications technologies facilitate the distribution of illegal data. The third category of cybercrime are those activities where the intention is to compromise the integrity, availability and confidentiality of the computers and systems connected to the internet and the data being processed on them, such as hacking and the distribution of viruses. To address the threat of cybercrime and to enhance the security of cyberspace, governments from developing countries must be keen to establish an appropriate legal framework that deters such attacks. Such a framework must not only appropriately criminalise the different forms of cybercrime, but also enable law enforcement agencies to adequately investigate and prosecute such activities.

The transnational nature of cybercrime activities, as well as concerns to avoid the proliferation of jurisdictional havens, has driven harmonisation initiatives within a number of international fora, such as the G8 and the Council of Europe. However, most developing countries are left out, with the acceleration, magnification, diffusion, entropy and empowerment within the developing countries environment and the international system evolving at a hypervelocity. A consensus is emerging among policymakers, scholars, and practitioners that recent sweeping developments in information technology, communication, transportation, demographics, and conflict are making cyberspace governance more challenging. Some argue these developments have transformed the international system, making it more vulnerable than ever to the predations of terrorists and criminals. Others argue that despite this significant evolution, organized crime, transnational terrorism, and non-state networks been endemic and an unpleasant features of human society throughout history, that they represent nothing new, and that our traditional means of countering them—primarily conventional law enforcement—are adequate.

Even among those who perceive substantial differences in the contemporary manifestations of these persistent maladies, they are viewed as major nuisances not adding up to a significant national or international security threat, much less an existential threat. Why because reliable statistics about the scale of cybercrime are notoriously difficult to come by. A lack of consensus about what constitutes cybercrime is clearly one obstacle to the collection of data. However, a range of factors contribute to this absence of data. First, there is a lack of reporting by victims as commercial organisations avoid adverse publicity to protect their reputation and share price. Second, a lack of experience and resources among law enforcement and prosecuting authorities has often meant that investigations and prosecutions are not considered a priority area, particularly when competing for attention with other public concerns, such as violent crime. This second factor obviously contributes to the first, underreporting, since where victims perceive that they will receive a poor response from law enforcement agencies, they will be less likely to make the effort to report.

A third factor is the recording of relevant statistics. Law enforcement agencies often fail to specifically collate data in relation to cybercrime. This may be due to a lack of resources but is more likely due to the complexities of recording such events, since a fraud committed over the internet can be recorded as both fraud and cybercrime, which may artificially inflate the crime statistics through double counting. A fourth factor is the transnational nature of cybercrime and the associated jurisdictional problems that contribute to the complexity of investigating and prosecuting offenders. All law enforcement agencies are under pressure to perform and are short of resources. Tackling transnational crime is resource intensive, yet has low clear-up rates, in terms of successful prosecutions. Finally, computers, particularly when networked, create significant forensic challenges to law enforcement agencies when obtaining evidence and subsequently presenting it before the courts.

NATIONAL SECURITY

National security, from the perspective of this paper, is seen as a multidisciplinary subject which ranges from the core values of our society, national enterprise such as defence, internal security, economic security, food security, security interest of the people and technological security. Concept of national security has become an extremely challenging task where restrictions have been introduced to State issues. Unfortunately, the term "national security" has long been used as a symbolic concept of a policy which has a wide and ambiguous meanings. Some definitions equate the concept of national security to the "State and Centre" all related policies revolving around nation. However, there has been a change in the school of thought of strategists wherein the concept of national security has changed merely from the security of the "State to the security of the citizens". In the view of Water Lippmann (1943), a nation is secure to the extent to which it is not in danger of having to sacrifice societal core values. The need to safeguard the political system, society and its people have become important to the overall national security. Consequently, national security, as a concept in the contemporary structure of a nation, is highly entwined with the ease of governance of national and international space and states constitution provides the key to its national security policy.

In a similar way, national security questions has seen its profile (and focus) increase due to the parallel approach to which attacks can take place. No longer are physical attacks the only approach to undermining or overcoming a nation's security. Todays' modern interconnected digital networks provide an almost parallel approach that is, in certain circumstances less costly, more discreet and more damaging than the once sole approach to physical attack. Seemingly, the link between or nexus between cyber-crime and national security in global cyberspace governance has become increasingly prevalent, as technology has advanced, the criminal capacity to cause harm and annoyance to individuals, and a nation's critical infrastructure by undermining its vital instrumentalities are increasing in greater proportion. What this has therefore created is a new approach to the emerging ways in which old problems like protecting national security can be addressed, utilising in some instances, changes in a nation's law. As decision-makers continue to tackle the myriad of security challenges posed by today's interconnected digital world—which is inherently international, a change in practices has co-developed across law enforcement and the intelligence and security agencies. This coordinated approach to confront the merger between cybersecurity-crime and national security threat has led to the adoption of national strategies, particularly for the cyberspace governance.

MEDIA FRAMING

In the last two decades, electronic media emerged as one of the key power brokers and played a substantial role in the social construction of security threats. The media brought to light the psychological, economic, social, cultural and political setting in which cyber securitisations are introduced. Furthermore, the media is today a platform through which the spectators, listeners, and the general audience react to these security concerns. With respect to the cybersecurity dynamics in the developing countries, the media has become part of the audience when one uses the phrase "effects in media." However, "effects of media" makes it a crucial functional actor with the ability either to play down or amplify the cyber security dilemma moves. This is a point wherein lies the challenge. Instead of highlighting the growing existential cyber threats and vulnerabilities, the media could compel the audience to focus more on human rights violations and excessive investigative powers instead of positive protective measures. Cyberspace is relatively a new realm of security about which the audience has limited knowledge. A securitising actor or governments of developing countries can use media framing to create a desired and suitable context by activating the positive aspects of cyberspace security initiatives. By sending credible voices, they should utilise this platform to achieve the support of the political opposition, neutral actors and human rights organisations.

The prime focus of the media should be on issues that benefit the general public. The media has a responsibility to uphold fairness, justice, national unity and international cooperation. The traditional role of the media in any society is to inform, educate, entertain, publicize and most importantly correct the excesses in any society. The media is a means of communication that reaches or influences people widely. It has a significant place in the statecraft machinery especially in the age of information revolution. It is the source of information for a society regarding any issue, be it local, regional or global. People rely on and even trust what is presented to them by the media. The media as the fourth estate and watchdog of the society plays crucial role in national development. The media shapes the perceptions of government, and influences public opinion, promote democracy, good governance as well as influence peoples' behaviour and support people- oriented policies.

The media as a strong instrument for nation sovereignty is also referred to as the vanguard for political, economic and social development. As stated earlier, the dynamics of media impact on national security varies from country to country and cannot be underestimated. In develop countries and to some extent in the developing countries, the attention and support people give to issues is in direct proportion to the amount media coverage. Today governments have invaded and fought several wars against each other, for example, the media was embedded in the war reporting. This enabled a constant flow of braking news report to both local and international audiences through television cable channels and their internet web sites. The integration of the media in the prosecution of the war greatly influenced the opinion of the global populations. It is on record that the media coverage swayed options in favour of the certain government.

As stated earlier, cyber-crimes and cyber-security has become a matter of national, international, economic, and societal importance that affects multiple nations (Walker, 2012). Since the 1990s users and or cyber-criminals have exploited vulnerabilities to gain access to networks for malicious purposes. In recent years, the number of attacks on States networks has continued to grow at an exponential rate. This includes malicious embedded code, exploitation of backdoors, and more. These attacks can be initiated from anywhere in the world from behind a computer with a masked Internet Protocol (IP) address. This type of warfare, cyber warfare, has changed the landscape of war itself (Beidleman, 2009). This type of warfare removes the need to have a physically capable military and requires the demand for a force that has a strong technical capacity e.g., computer science skills. The developed countries and other have come to understand that this is an issue and have started developing policies framework to handle this in an effort to mitigate the threats and vulnerabilities within and outside the cyberspace.

With the rise of the contemporary state, formal institutions of social control have evolved to provide rules of behaviour, forums for the resolution of disputes between citizens and institutions for preventing, deterring, policing, prosecution, adjudication and punishment of the most serious transgressions. However, it is now generally accepted that governmental agencies of social control are neither omnipresent nor omnipotent, thus creating a demand for supplementary countering, reducing or policing the security threats particularly of the cyberspace and or domain that knows no borders. These state institutions are complemented by a variety of non-state bodies that 'coproduce' security. Such entities vary widely in size and role, from large private security agencies and the manufacturers and distributors of technologies such as closed-circuit television (CCTV), to the good friend who keeps an eye on her neighbour's house at vacation time.

CYBERSPACE SECURITY GOVERNANCE CHALLENGES

Since the year 2000, the number of Internet users has increased almost ten-fold from 394 million users to 2.9 billion users in 2014 (Statista.com, Internet users). Though we had 4.88 billion devices connected to the Internet of Things in current times, it is predicted that 25 billion devices will be connected by the year 2020 (Gartner, 2011) and even double that by the end of the twenty first century. The Internet of Things is the broader Internet network consisting of computers, routers, modems, and all users' devices that it communicates with it. When speaking of connectivity, it refers to the high amount of devices that are connected to the Internet of Things. Society now makes extensive use of connected systems ranging from our communications to the services and products we consume. As connectivity proliferates, it provides industry and governments more ways to make use of the cyber domain. This trend will push for more of our services and goods to continue being digitized.

The cyberspace ecosystem is built upon the physical infrastructure of the Internet and is basically composed of users, points of online interaction (websites, for instance) and the volume of activity that occurs online. The online ecosystem gets larger as the number of users, points of interaction and volume of activity increases. This section lays out a three-part framework for understanding the scope, size, width and breadth of cyberspace. Cyberspace is essentially an amalgamation of the number of users (people and devices, etc.), the number of points of interaction (websites and domains, etc.) and the activity linking these broad categories (data flows and commerce, etc.). The basic point is that the ecosystem of cyberspace is big and getting a lot bigger at a fairly rapid pace. This growth is akin to the growth of a population in a city or country, in the sense that a fixed amount of crime and a growing population will result in a lower crime rate or a better chance that one will not be subject to a crime.

The number of Internet users is a good measure of the size of cyberspace because it shows the actual number of people that are a part of the "network of networks." In this sense, it is akin to the number of people in a city or country. It is also a good proxy for the number of devices online, although this number surpassed that of humans on the network around 2008 (Evans 2011). Data on the number of Internet users from 2008 to the end of 2014 was taken from the website Internet Live Stats, which provides real-time statistics on various indicators of the size of the Internet (Internet Live Stats 2015a). Email is one of the most basic uses of the Internet. The number of email users online is a good measure of the size of the active population base of the online ecosystem because it captures not just the number of people who have web access (as done via Internet users' statistics), but also the number of people who actually use the Internet as a part of their daily lives. Email users, therefore, are an active subset of all Internet users. In 2014, for example, there were 421,249,355 more Internet users than email users for that year. Data on email users from 2008 to 2012 was taken from a data aggregation blog called Royal Pingdom, which is operated by the website monitoring company Pingdom (Royal Pingdom 2009; 2010; 2011; 2012; 2013). Data for email users for 2013 and 2014 were taken from a Radicati Group (2013) study of the email market.

Increasingly, people access the Internet via a mobile platform rather than a traditional desktop computer. In January 2014, mobile usage surpassed desktop usage in the United States for the first time

(O'Toole, 2014). The trend is even more pronounced in the developing world, where Internet access has expanded primarily by skipping the fixed access/desktop stage and moving directly into the mobile/wireless broadband stage. The Internet is also, as it is colloquially known, an "information superhighway." Another measure of the activity that occurs on the Internet, therefore, is the number of search engine queries per year. Data on the annual number of Google searches was used as a measure for Internet search queries (Statistics Brain 2015). Globally, Google Chrome is also the largest web browser in every region of the world (Stats Counter 2015). These trends suggest that Google searches are a good proxy for the occurrence of Internet-based searches more generally. The Internet is becoming increasingly integrated into every aspect of society. One of the most meaningful (or at least most measurable) effects of this growing integration and importance is the Internet's share of global GDP. Currently, no comprehensive time series data exists for this measure.

The security of cyberspace can be conceptualized best from a user's perspective, broadly defined. A secure cyberspace is one in which a user can make use of the Internet without an unreasonable fear of suffering a high cost, with cost being defined in some combination of reputational, monetary and rights violations terms. An insecure cyberspace environment is the opposite, or basically one in which using the Internet is likely to impose a large cost upon the user. The occurrence of online cyber-attacks and the costs of successful attacks, together, these three categories give a sense of how insecure cyberspace is for an individual user. Many aspects of the security of cyberspace are worsening over time, but many others are actually remaining fairly static year over year. In the odd case, a given indicator is actually improving. These measures of the insecurity of cyberspace are akin to the crime rate in a city or country. If they are increasingly slower than the population, staying the same size as the population grows, or improving as the population increases, the common result is an improved crime rate.

The sheer volume of users and increasing volume of person to person, person to business, business to business, government to person and business transactions that take place must be testament to the fact that the Internet is currently working. If a good quality security product is installed and Internet browsers are used wisely then users will reduce levels of risk. Despite this, there remains the underlying public concern, propagated by media reportage and adverse commentary, that the Internet is not only criminogenic, but downright dangerous in that hackers can still make planes fall from the sky and interfere disastrously with aspects of the critical infrastructure. Yet, longstanding critical incident management plans mean that very few aspects (if any) of critical infrastructure are still connected directly to the Internet – if they are, then this is extremely problematic, if not negligent, and needs to be remedied. The main concerns about infrastructure are not so much the environment itself, but the management of the large amounts of critical information within it, especially when it is concentrated within one source such as a database.

This issue became highlighted in November 2007, when CD-ROM disks containing the personal information of 25 million child benefit claimants were lost in postal (not electronic) transit from one public agency to another. The resulting panic not only brought to light other losses, but it has also illustrated how potentially vulnerable such concentrations of data are and how important security policies are to the politics of personal security. Although no evidence has yet been presented to suggest that any of the missing data has caused loss through fraud. In addition to outlining potential vulnerabilities, the data losses also emphasise the importance of maintaining existing security policies when critical functions are increasingly being outsourced, especially the security of public data when it is shared across the public and private sectors. Yet, these possibilities should also be part of information management plans. What these incidents do highlight most of all is that all activities within cyberspace will carry risks, as they do in the normal world, and such risks have to be identified and remedied, however, as the events have illustrated, the risk lies more in human failings than in the virtual environment.

These virtual forums play an important role in shaping contemporary discourses and perceptions of crime and penal system. Valier (2004) argues that the Internet has become a site for different kinds of 'technological populism' by urging participation in online polls, surveys, and debates about crime and punishment. Examples include 'name and shame' sections of sex offenders, 'soft judges', and so on. Cyberspace provides retributivist tendencies among the public a new forum, which assumes significance when we juxtapose it with the fact that, to a considerable extent, it is not constrained by the limitations enforced upon print and television by legal and professional journalistic ethics. 'It permits anyone to act as report or publisher of images and information, to transmit material on any topic to a potentially global audience, as well as allowing people to participate in real-time conversations with distant others' (Valier, 2004:97).

The argument is that the Internet is not an instrument of anomie and individualism, or an epithet of libertarian ideas; rather it has provided space for the emergence of online groups and solidarity with respect to issues of race, gender, religion, and crime and punishment. What is to be noted here is that the extraterritorial nature of the Internet changes the dynamics of penal discourse and identity, which has conventionally been associated with bounded local and national societies. The Internet is therefore also a platform for constructing images and notions of 'the other'. For instance, the portrayal of Iran as an alleged 'axis of evil' is solidified in 'real' terms mainly through different forms of virtually mediated reality such as videos, recordings posted on, say, YouTube. Afzal Guru's hanging made it to the headlines of not just Indian leading dailies but also The Guardian and The Washington Post. An image of India being 'tough' was created thereof.

Cyberspace is a part of the 'mediascapes' and 'technoscapes' (Appadurai, 1996) and are becoming increasingly salient for constituting identities. Online technologies therefore need to be analyzed within the wider framework of how they are etched into everyday life, including political mobilization, crime prevention and control. For instance, the Megan's Law website provides information about registered sex offenders in a particular neighbourhood. In this regard, the virtually mediated dangers can seem more 'real' than individuals' actual, real-world experiences, thus producing a realm of 'hyper-real' threat in the neighbourhood. The Megan's Law mapping system can be seen as yet another example of the emerging 'surveillance society' (Lyon, 2001). Nevertheless, it also provides a key understanding of how notions of community, safety, and risk have transformed.

Online mapping of 'real world' dangers is on the rise. Geographic Information Systems (GIS) have now become a standard item in the police armoury. Introducing the language of 'crime hotspots' and 'criminogenic areas', these systems provide and create images of low and high-risk communities to the law enforcement agencies (Gundhus, 2006). In the US, partner agencies can obtain information not only about 'criminal' matters, but also of the racial configuration of a community, demographic trends, as well as income and educational levels of the people. Crime mapping thus transforms the community from a concrete, local entity into an abstract simulation (Aas, 2007). The interactivity provided by cyberspace is a further step in actively involving citizens in the governance of crime.

Cyber-communities can have a substantial influence on local group by mobilizing ideas, opinions, capital, and linkages, as is illustrated by penal populism, football supporters etc. The online and offline realms are therefore not mutually exclusive. 'People who choose to enter online social spaces do not leave their offline world behind when they do so, but rather begin a process of weaving online communications and activities into their existing offline lives' (Kendall, 2002: 16). To quote Arjun Appadurai: 'These virtual neighbourhoods seem on the face of it to represent just that absence of face-to face links, spatial contiguity, and multiplex social interaction that the idea of a neighbourhood seems centrally to imply. Yet we must not be too quick to oppose highly spatialized neighbourhoods to these virtual neighbourhoods of international electronic communication. The relationship between these two forms of neighbourhood is considerably more complex '(Appadurai, 1996: 195).

CYBERSECURITY THREATS AND NATIONAL SECURITY IN CYBERSPACE

The concept of national security has altered significantly in recent years (Grabosky, 2014). Gone are the days when a country's main security threats were territorial in nature and purely military in solution. No longer does a country require a physical or military invasion to take place for there to be a threat to domestic security issues such as public health, national economy, or social cohesion (Grabosky, 2014). Distance and isolation that once afforded countries the relatively low possibility of attack are now all but irrelevant (Burton, 2013b). One particular type of crime that exemplifies this new attack capability better than any other is that of cyber-crime. Cyber activities are increasing with significant velocity, allowing connection speeds to be almost instantaneous. Sophistication has reached levels never witnessed before representing a serious threat to society. The perception of how long things take to happen has reduced significantly owing to the speed in which cyber technology is advancing. Criminal gangs are also responding to the pressure placed upon such activities by law enforcement by reorganising their operations and attracting a new generation of coders and cyber experts. The concept that the world is a smaller place has influenced how countries now view security. In a globalised and cyber dependant world, countries and individuals can be attacked at any time, from anywhere, in a whole manner of different ways at an incredible speed. These factors and the relatively low operating costs of cyber-crime exemplify why it is likely to pose a direct threat to national security.

Today we should note that government, infrastructure, intellectual property, and personal information are all potentially threatened. These types of threats are of national security significance due to the potential for significant disruption or harm to the functioning of society. This is of particular concern when one considers that these threats are not only posed by other states who have significant resources at their disposal but by rogue individuals who need only the know-how and access to a computer to be considered a potential threat. One of the key issues surrounding the debate as to whether cyber-crime should be considered a threat to national security is that of classification. Cyber-crime, similar to transnational crime encompasses an array of crimes not all of which are considered a potential threat to national security. While cyber-crime generally encompasses crimes such as child exploitation, fraud, money laundering, "hacktivism", espionage, terrorism and so on, in most countries especially the developing countries.

Our lives are mediated by an increasing number of technologies. The Internet can be seen as an exemplar of global connectivity, which is a hallmark of the globalized era we live in. Increasingly, our professional and recreational activities are moulded by this connectivity. The challenges to global governance are probably best illustrated by the extra-territorial, seemingly unregulated nature of cyberspace. Cyberspace illustrates a highly complex interaction between global and local forces which make it difficult to regulate by individual nation-states. We live in a world where "local transformation is as much a part of globalization as the lateral extension of social connections across time and space… what happens in a local neighbourhood is likely to be influenced by factors – such as world money and commodity markets – operating at an indefinite distance away from that neighbourhood itself" (Giddens

1990, p. 64). Morley (2002, p. 2) expresses the role of media and ICTs (information and communication technologies) in this regard in a most succinct manner: 'the sitting room is a place where, in a variety of mediate forms, the global meets the local'. Technology has always been seen as a key instrument of social change. From the invention of railways and atom bomb to cell phones and computers, technological change has had a powerful impact on social behaviour. In recent decades, information and communication technologies have come to increasingly mould our lives, the societal and state institutions that are in place, and knowledge production. Castells argues that the Internet can be seen as the backbone of these transformations and its impact is difficult to discount (Castells, 1996, 2001).

Today, the Internet is like in 1990s a revolutionary force which has brought the 'death of distance', and the emergence of the virtual society, the changing nature of warfare, and so on. Castells sees it as the best example of the 'space of flows', as the truly global technology which characterizes the essence of the 'network society'. The Internet in essence has become 'the technological basis for the organizational form of the Information Age to which the core economic, social, political, and cultural activities throughout the planet are being structured. In fact, exclusion from these networks is one of the most damaging forms of exclusion in our economy and in our culture'. (Castells, 2001:3, quoted in Aas 2007, p. 175). On the other hand, critical scholars, who have tried to temper this celebration of the Net as an emancipatory agent, have pointed out that technology may have far less vivid and less foreseeable consequences. The so-called 'social shaping of technology' approach contends that technological change has to be understood within the larger framework of social and economic change (Aas, 2007:154). The Internet is not only a global, 'unrestricted' medium, but is also used in local spaces and conditioned by local contexts. How it is used is determined by a number of social, economic, and cultural factors. Rather than being a universal medium, the Internet reflects a deeply stratified and divided global condition. Internet access is unequally distributed, creating a digital divide along class, racial and ethnic lines within countries, as well as between the global North and the global South (Castells, 2001). Cyber-connectivity should therefore be perceived as a symbol of privilege at the global level.

Cyberspace is not only a space of freedom from physical constrictions and state intervention but has increasingly emerged as a necessary medium through which contemporary social, economic, and political mobilizations occur. Online communication has become 'an important site for the contestation of group values. Indeed, it is through this very contestation that new forms of collectivity are imagined and performed' (Valier, 2004:93). The issues related to cyberspace, cybercrime and the governance of it provide insights to some of the most fundamental changes of the globalizing era such as the questions of disembedding of social relations, risk, social construction of crime, deterritorialization of crime, issues of surveillance, and plural policing. To quote Aas (2007: 169), "life on the screen may not be so different and far removed from the 'real' world as its proponents and critics sometimes seem to suggest."

The 'global' spread of cybercrimes is constituted by specific, 'local' acts of deviance and crime. A good example, apart from the ones mentioned throughout the paper, would be that of piracy. We know Torrent is 'illegal' in most, if not all, countries. The act of downloading a movie illegally is a highly 'local' act and can be considered a crime or offense in one country or region and may not be in another. However, this 'local' act is part of a wider 'global' network of Torrent users (who mainly consist of those who upload the videos called 'seeders', those who download it, and those who provide the platform for it). This 'global-local' or 'glocal' nexus is mediated by the Internet. Although governing cyberspace crimes has been quite difficult because of its nebulous nature, inter alia, national governments have been relatively successful in their attempts to mitigate, if not eliminate, this phenomenon. And this has been possible precisely because this 'offense' involves a 'local' dimension too.

The 'local' part of it is best illustrated by an individual user's IP address which can be tracked by the authorities when they wish to penalize him/her. While remaining part of the 'global' network, each user still retains this local element in him/her. Therefore, the 'global' should not be seen as some kind of overarching phenomenon which is above and beyond our lives. To quote Ericson et al. (2000), "The global only exists to the extent that it is being created through ongoing social life." What cyber governance requires is a 'global' effort towards tackling it, an effective coordination among all countries, especially the developing countries, be it with respect to intelligence sharing or technology transfer. Although Interpol has made great advances in this regard in its collaborative ventures with national law enforcement agencies, much more needs to be done. This is easier said than done. Different countries have different legal stances on particular acts and this becomes complicated when we seek to analyze them in the context of cybercrime which is a relatively new phenomenon. Nevertheless, there's no denying the importance of the issue and the action it calls for. An important limitation of this paper is that it does not problematize concepts like 'cybercrime', which is a loaded and often contested term. Crime as a category of study is itself far from being straightforward. However, we have to take certain categories and definitions for granted, owing to time and space constraints. The expectation is that this does not inhibit the insights that can be generated on the interplay of global and local forces in the arena of cyberspace governance.

DEALINGS WITH CYBERSECURITY THREATS

Information security constitutes a driving force for the economic development of states and regions and must be carried out simultaneously with ICT infrastructure. Benefits from information technology services deployment are dependent upon an accompanying development of ICT infrastructure, sufficient security measures and a legal and regulatory framework. Cybersecurity in a broad sense, including the legal framework, is critical to attract economic actors for developing a favourable business environment. The global information society and knowledge economy are constrained by the development and overall acceptance of an international cybersecurity framework. The validity of such a framework or model requires a challenging multidimensional cybersecurity approach for everyone – from individuals to organizations and states. Each actor dealing with an information and communication device, tool or service, for professional or private issues, needs information security.

It is true for governmental institutions as for big or small organisations and individuals. The security answer should satisfy particular protection and defence levels requirements, in regards of the actor's need. The end user's perspective and the reason for security should never be forgotten as well as the particular needs for privacy and fundamental human rights protection. Developing security models and solutions is not enough to protect informational resources. If technical security measures have to be developed and implemented, concomitant legal measures have to exist as well to prevent and deter criminal behaviour that uses pervasive networks as a target of crime (new technology – new crimes) or uses pervasive network as a means to realize a crime (old crime with new technology). The legal dimension of ICT security should be considered as a global business enabler that will contribute to minimizing criminal opportunities.

For developing countries, attempts to reduce the digital divide through investment in infrastructure only, without taking into account the need for security and control of ICT risks (unsolicited incident, malevolent acts, ...), would result in the creation of a security divide as prejudicial for developing countries as the digital divide. It has become imperative that developing countries not only introduce measures to fight against cyber- crime, but also control the security of their infrastructure and information technologies departments. The use of an ICT technological and legal approach would help not to further widen the digital divide by adding a second "security divide", and to quickly create a reliable infrastructure which meets needs at the international level.

Cybersecurity tools and legal framework constitute an additional challenge for developing countries. It is the responsibility of developed countries to help developing countries find their own good practices by transferring knowledge and skills. It is everyone's responsibility to promote a safe and reliable cyberspace environment in the context of an emerging information society. A minimum level of security for information and communication technologies must be provided at an affordable cost. Security must not become an exclusion factor for anyone who would like to conduct private or business activities over the Internet.

In the context of information security some basic recommendations could be proposed: Educate the end-user; Increase public awareness to enhance security user's behaviour; Give to the end-user tools and means to be responsible; Design an end-user centric security model within a given technical and legal framework; Information technology and content providers should improve the security of their products and services. Products or services must integrate, in native, simple and flexible security measures and mechanisms. Products should be well-documented and comprehensible and security mechanisms should be readily understood and configured easily by untrained users. Security must be integrated at the beginning of information technologies' infrastructure development life cycles.

It is fundamental that the international community, including developing countries: Understand cybercrime from a global perspective; Define a national cybersecurity strategy; Develop public awareness of cybercrime and cyber security challenges (economic and management issues, political issues, social issues, technical issues, legal and law enforcement issues); Promote a cyber security culture (information on stakes and risks, dissemination of simple recommendations, such as: use secure systems, reduce vulnerability by avoiding dangerous situations or behaviour, etc.); Train and inform on information and communication technologies and on security issues, and relevant legal provisions; Develop cyber security education; Propose a unified cybersecurity framework which includes, in a complementary fashion, the human, regulatory, organizational, economic, technical and operational dimensions of cyber security; Put in place organizational structures to support a national cybersecurity strategy; Create regional alert points for the provision of technical information and assistance regarding security risks and cybercrime; Create effective cybercrime laws that are enforceable at national and international levels (global and harmonized legal framework taking into account the right to privacy (Protection of public safety, with protection of privacy and civil liberties)); Redefine law enforcement and legal framework in order to bring cybercrime perpetrators to justice; Manage jurisdictional issues; Fight cybercrime (deterrence, detection, investigation, prosecution of cybercriminal activities, crime reporting, crime analysis, practices and experiences on search and seizure of digital evidence, organizing capacities to combat cybercrime, information sharing, promotion of effective public and private sector cooperation); Develop acceptable practices for ICT protection and reaction; Establish effective cooperation and promote cooperation and coordination at national and international levels.

STRATEGIC FRAMEWORK FOR SECURE CYBERSPACE GOVERNANCE

A Global Approach

The word global should be understood as a systemic security framework including the political, social, economic and technical dimensions of cybersecurity. The systemic approach concerns all actors of the information society: from all kinds of end users (including children), technologies, services or contents providers and professionals, to policy makers, passing by organization's owners, shareholders, managers, justice and police professionals as judge, prosecutors, law enforcement people for example. In a cybersecurity context, global also imply the necessity to think security in terms of collaboration, cooperation and know how sharing. From public awareness to policy makers, a global and schedulable cybersecurity approach should be available to answers all kind of security issues and challenges. Each actor at his level has a role to play in the security chain. In another hand, security is strongly linked to local culture, ethic, politic, law, as to say to specific national environments, which means that in an interconnected global information society, cybersecurity should answer the challenge to be locally significant and efficient for a particular national context and interoperable and compatible at the international level. Only an international open approach and cooperation, including international standardization process could contribute to achieve these goals. Strategic and operational answers should bring to all kind of actors belonging to political, legal, organisational, technical and social dimension of cybersecurity because cybersecurity is not just a cultural problem that has a technology or legal dimension.

POLITICAL DIMENSION

Since Cybersecurity and cybercrime issues are governmental issues, and national security issues, government people should understand the links between social and economic development with crime and security issues in a connected society with interrelated infrastructures. ICT related threats and risks for states, organizations and citizens including privacy and economic crime issues needs protection at national, regional and international levels. The role of all relevant stakeholders and relationships between private and public sectors should define general measures to be taken to obtain a satisfying level of ICT security and protection assets (including privacy issues

LEGAL DIMENSION

A cyberspace regulatory framework could help to transform the Internet into a safer place to conduct activities. An adapted legal framework and laws that are applicable to the digital world must be operational at the national level and internationally compatible. Security solutions can protect a given environment in a particular context but cannot prevent criminal behaviour altogether. Legal institutions and the law exist to dissuade criminal behaviour and to bring to justice people who carry out illegal acts. At the same time qualified justice system and police authorities skilled in new technologies and cybercrime should enforce the legal aspects of information technologies and cooperate with their partners at the international level. Taking into account the legal dimension and specific needs for justice and police professionals,

Global understanding of legal issues related to Internet and misuses should be apprehended. That means the understanding of the legal requirements at national and international levels; Computer investigation and forensic methodologies and tools; how to interpret and implement existing international regulation as Cybercrime doctrine that could be considered as an international reference model to develop legal frameworks and international cooperation. This requires a common understanding of computer related crime and of international collaboration in order to fight against cybercrime and deals with global cyberthreats. They should be able to define a legal framework, appropriate cyberlaws enforceable at national level and compatible at the international level and develop measures to fight against cybercrime and to be able to collaborate at an international level.

TECHNOLOGICAL DIMENSION

Concerning the technology dimension of cybersecurity, professionals should understand technical vulnerabilities and misuse. Understand Internet related risks, cyberthreats and cyberattacks. Understand societal and organizational issues and values. In order to be able to decrease the number of vulnerabilities of digital environments, define, design, produce, and implement efficient security tools and measures of protection and reaction to support availability, integrity and confidentiality of Internet infrastructures and develop confidence into e-services. Security technologies should be cost effective, user friendly, transparent, auditable and third party controllable.

Social Dimension

All citizens should understand threats for the end-user (virus, spam, identity usurpation, fraud, swindle, privacy offence, etc…) and their impacts. Understand how to build a national, regional and global cybersecurity culture based on well recognized international standards and recommendations involving several kinds of stakeholders. In order to raise awareness among all interested parties to empower human resource in a global perspective. This concern as well developed country or developing countries. Education is the key factor to become an actor of the information society and it is the cornerstone of a knowledge-based society. Therefore, to enhance confidence and security in the use of ICT and cybersecurity education should not be considered as an option.

Develop a Cybersecurity Culture

Protecting the information is a crucial issue to take into consideration in developing the information society. At the crossroads of technological, legal, sociological, economic, and political fields, cybersecurity is an interdisciplinary domain by nature. Depending on the country, a national cybersecurity approach must reflect the vision, the culture and the civilization of a nation as well as meeting the specific security needs of the local context in which it is introduced.

Awareness as a Cybersecurity Pillar

Using computers and information resources via the Internet implies increasing dependency, ICT access and vulnerability. This introduces a new kind of risk that must be taken into account when developing e-services. Master technological and informational risks have to be done in allowing an efficient use of information and communication technology, and also allowing privacy in respect of fundamental human rights. It is not enough to promote development of connecting points to the Internet for accessibility; the information infrastructure must be reliable. This means that ad hoc performances, continued services, quality of service and quality of data must be guaranteed. At the same time, national legal frameworks should be developed in conformity with international regulations

Capacity Building to Sustain Cybersecurity Culture

Capacity building contributes to the creation of an enabling environment with appropriate policy and legal frameworks, institutional development, including community participation, human resources development and strengthening of managerial systems. Capacity building includes human resource development, organizational development and institutional and legal framework development. Human resource development, the process of equipping individuals with the understanding, skills and access to information, knowledge and training that enables them to perform effectively. Appropriate cybersecurity education programs should exist at several levels (schools, university, and continuing education) in all cybersecurity fields (political sciences, business and economics, engineering, social and legal fields, ...). Because education is a key factor to strengthen competitiveness, employment and social cohesion, education is the key factor in becoming an actor in the information society and it constitutes the cornerstone of a knowledge-based society. Education contributes to developing a layer of defence in deep security approach and is the cornerstone of the information society. Education constitutes a real human capacity challenge that governments of developing countries have to face. Education contributes to building a safe and inclusive information society. Considering cybersecurity education is a long-term approach that is efficient for a sustainable information society.

CONCLUSION

Cyberspace has become severely contested. The challenge is not only the traditional power politics game between states, but also the loss of power within states. States compete with each other in their attempt to create norms and institutions that will shape the future of governance, but at the same time, they have to fill in the sovereignty gap and compete with the private sector. As a result, cyberspace governance is still under construction. Establishing a social contract for cyberspace, that would involve governments, companies and civil society actors, seems unrealistic for the near future. The available institutions and the existing body of international law provide adequate tools to regulate a wide range of state activities in cyberspace. Cyberspace lacks a single forum or international organization that is responsible for regulating its activities. Thus, governance is spread throughout technical standard setting fora, private sector organizations, civil society groups, states and international organizations. Governance ranges from developing norms and codes of conduct, to signing regional treaties and imposing regulations. The future of cyberspace governance lies in balancing between great power competition and power asymmetries both between and within states especially the developing countries

REFERENCES

Aas, K. F. (2007). Beyond "the desert of the real": Crime control in a virtualised reality. In Y. Jewkes (Ed.), *Crime Online*. Willan.

Addis, A. (2004). The Thin State in Thick Globalisation Sovereignty in the Information Age. *Vanderbilt Journal of Transnational Law*, (January), 3–107.

Andress & Winterfeld. (2014). What is Cyber Warfare. In *Cyber Warfare: Techniques, Tactics and Tools for Security Practitioners*. Elsevier.

Appadurai, A. (1996). *Modernity at large: Cultural dimensions of globalization*. University of Minneapolis Press.

Baudrillard, J. (1998). The Consumer Society: Myths and Structures. *Sage (Atlanta, Ga.)*.

Bauman, Z. (2000). *Liquid modernity*. Polity Press.

Brenner, S. W. (2007). Cybercrime: Rethinking crime control strategies. In Y. Jewkes (Ed.), *Crime Online*. Willan.

Castells, M. (2001). *The internet galaxy*. Oxford University Press. doi:10.1007/978-3-322-89613-1

Choucri, N. (2012). *Cyber-politics in international relations*. The MIT Press. doi:10.7551/mitpress/7736.001.0001

Cohen, S. (2002). *Folk devils and moral panics: The creation of the mods and rockers* (3rd ed.). Routledge.

Denning, D. (2000). Cyber-terrorism: The Logic Bomb versus the Truck Bomb. *Global Dialogue*.

Emerson, R. G. (2016). Limits to a cyber-threat. *Contemporary Politics*, *22*(2), 178–196. doi:10.1080/13569775.2016.1153284

Ericson, R., & Stehr, N. (2000). The ungovernability of modern societies: states, democracies, markets, participation, and citizens. In R. Ericson & N. Stehr (Eds.), *Governing Modern Societies*. University of Toronto Press. doi:10.3138/9781442675452

Garland, D. (2001). *The Culture of Control*. Oxford University Press.

Gartner. (2011). *Gartner Says 4.9 Billion Connected*. Retrieved January 12, 2022, from https://www.gartner.com/newsroom/id/2905717

Ghernaouti, S. (2013). Cyber Conflicts, Cyberwars and Cyber Power. In *Cyber Power: Crime, Conflict and Security in Cyberspace*. EPFL Press.

Giddens, A. (1990). *The consequences of modernity*. Polity Press.

Grabosky, P. N. (2001). Virtual criminality: Old wine in new bottles?'. *Social & Legal Studies*, *10*(2), 243–249. doi:10.1177/a017405

Gruzd, S. (2018). *Multi-Stakeholder Initiatives: Lessons Learned*. SAIIA Research Paper.

Innes, M. (2004). Reinventing Tradition? Reassurance, Neighbourhood Security and Policing. *Criminal Justice*, *4*(2), 151–171. doi:10.1177/1466802504044914

Innes, M. (2005). Why Disorder Matters? Antisocial Behaviour and Incivility as Signals of Risk. Paper given to the *Social Contexts and Responses to Risk (SCARR) Conference*, Kent, UK.

Jewkes, Y. (Ed.). (2003). Dot. In Cons: Crime, deviance, and identity on the internet. Cullompton.

Jewkes, Y., & Andrews, C. (2007). Internet child pornography: international responses. In Y. Jewkes (Ed.), *Crime Online*. Willan.

Jewkes, Y., & Sharp, K. (2003). Crime, deviance and the disembodied self: Transcending the dangers of corporeality. In Y. Jewkes (Ed.), *Dot. Cons: Crime, Deviance, and Identity on the Internet*. Willan.

Kendall, L. (2002). *Hanging out in the virtual pub: Masculinities and relationships Online*. University of California Press. doi:10.1525/california/9780520230361.001.0001

Kurbalija, J. (2019). An Introduction to Internet Governance (6th ed.). Princeton University Press.

Lyon, D. (2001). *Surveillance society: Monitoring everyday life*. Open University Press.

Lyon, D. (2003a). *Surveillance after September 11*. Polity Press.

Lyon, D. (2003b). Surveillance as social sorting: Computer codes and mobile bodies. In D. Lyon (Ed.), *Surveillance as Social Sorting: Privacy, Risk, and Digital Discrimination*. Routledge.

Machiavelli, N. (1992). Of Auxiliary, Mixed, and One's Own Soldiers. In *The Prince*. University of Chicago Press. (Originally published 1532)

Mathiesen, T. (1997). The viewer society: Michel Foucualt's "Panopticon" revisited. *Theoretical Criminology*, *1*(2), 215–234. doi:10.1177/1362480697001002003

Morley, D. (2000). *Home territories: Media, mobility, and identity*. Routledge.

Orwell, G. (1990). *1984 Nineteen Eighty-Four*. Penguin Books.

Perritt, H. H. (1998). The internet as a threat to sovereignty? Thoughts on the internet's role in strengthening national and global governance. *Global Legal Stud.*, *2*, 475–491.

Rasmussen, T. (2000). *Social theory and communication technology*. Ashgate.

Report, S. I. S. T. (2016). *Trends for January–June 07* (Vol. XII). Symantec.https://www.symantec.com/content/dam/symantec/docs/reports/cyber-security-trends-report-africa-interactive-en.pdf

Sheptycki, J. (2002a). Accountability across the policing field: Towards a general cartography of accountability for post-modern policing. *Policing and Society*, *12*(4), 323–338. doi:10.1080/10439460220000055

Shields, R. (2003). *The virtual*. Routledge.

Simon, J. (2007). *Governing through Crime: How the War on Crime Transformed American Democracy and Created a Culture of Fear*. Oxford University Press.

Singer, P. W., & Friedman, A. (2014). *Cybersecurity and Cyberwar: What Everyone Needs to Know*. Oxford University Press. doi:10.1093/wentk/9780199918096.001.0001

Smith, G. (n.d.). An Electronic Pearl Harbor? Not likely. *Issues on Science and Technology*.

Statista. (2015). *Internet users' number 2005-2015*. Author.

Symantec. (2015). *Internet Security Threat Report* (April ed., Vol. 20). Symantec.

Toffler. (1970). *Future Shock*. Bantam Books.

Turianskyi, Y. (2020). *Policy Insights 77, Africa And Europe: Cyber Governance Lessons African perspectives Global insights. The South African Institute of International Affairs*. SAIIA.

Valier, C. (2004). *Crime and punishment in contemporary culture*. Routledge.

Walt, S. (1985). 'Alliance Formation and the Balance of Power' 9. *International Security*, *9*(4), 3. doi:10.2307/2538540

Yar, M. (2006). *Cybercrime and society*. Sage. doi:10.4135/9781446212196

Chapter 14
Digital Governance in Post-Modern Africa:
Evolving Realities of a New Communication Paradigm

Melchizedec J. Onobe
Bingham University, Nigeria

Desmond Onyemechi Okocha
https://orcid.org/0000-0001-5070-280X
Bingham University, Nigeria

Michael Agbo John
Bingham University, Nigeria

ABSTRACT

A strong reason democracy continues to be favored in the 21st century is because it is presented as more fluid and amendable to political evolution in digitization. While digitization of governance is an advantage worth exploring, in Africa, Western democracy remains a challenge especially for young and experimental governments and particularly that the system lacks indigenous organism in origin. A fundamental thrust of this chapter therefore is to interrogate how nations of Africa are grappling with the many variables of democracy as a Sphinx, how good governance, postmodernist demands jump in the fray of theories and practices to shape the form of governance evolving in Africa. The chapter is a positional outlook on the development as they unfold. It suggests that though there is a speed deficit of Africa catching up with the hypothetical perfect Western system's demand, the dawn of e-governance in the continent should be uniquely organismic to sync with Africa's heterogeneous cultural diversity in order to achieve desired results of speed and all-around development.

DOI: 10.4018/978-1-6684-4107-7.ch014

INTRODUCTION

Every society's strength, guaranteed post-humus applause, may be in the investment and commitment it makes to the class it has groomed to further its gene. There is growing concern that many African societies are not investing in the development of their human capital. Nowhere perhaps is this truer than in the realm of politics and leadership in managing resources. Africa is believed to have a "notoriety" of leadership complex that believes it is messianic and should continue to be dominant else things will fall apart irredeemably. The erstwhile President of Nigeria, General Ibrahim Badamasi Babangida once granted African Independent Television (AIT) an interview in early 2000, responding to a question "why Nigeria keeps recycling ex-rulers". He said Nigeria would continue on the path of recycling leaders for another 50 years because those that are recycled into leadership are mature; they have been tested and should be trusted. His response encapsulates a threadbare mental stereotype, and this may be reflective of Africa.

The leaders are over-protective of the political experiment that trusting a younger generation may seem like running against general norms. This sit tight syndrome is characteristic and Sesay (2014, p.4) describes it as, "One of the defining features of African governance systems … the phenomenon of 'sit tight' leaders and 'presidents for life' in many countries". That aberrant behavior, wrong as it is without justifying the unjustifiable, begs a nifty question. Is it exclusively African or a dis-contextualization to demonize African nations? Are the rules the same in measuring all, or there is a pedagogic manipulation in conceptualization that has initiated a rite of reasoning and a color of perception? What about the Queen of England, other Presidents in the European countries that have ruled well over a decade?

However that mental frame of "birth-right-ship" to rule perhaps heavily contradicts common aphorism in most African communities that, "youth are leaders of tomorrow" in political leadership and sectors of managerial responsibilities. It may be a carry over of a normative that children and youth do not lead. They are too inexperience and full of exuberance to steer, since in many African cultural settings particularly with mixed demographics, it is the elders that hold leadership responsibilities in society. We can admit that a stereotype that lives in denial of present day reality is stunted and trapped in the past, which is the case with many African states; but it may, after all, not necessarily be a seminally African trait.

Africa has youth age groups that are led by youth with no umbilical attachment or waiting on elders to cheer their courses (Sesay, 2014). The history of African modern political structure can be annotated by taking a cue from the structure of the capital to which it's system of rule is annexed. If we defer to the leadership of the colonial masters of many parts of Africa like the British Monarchy, it may reveal a revisit pattern. A parenthetical age class that cannot be described as youth holds the Queen's stool and much of the leadership in Europe. Middle age and old in society dominated the leadership of many European countries, until quite recently. The same pattern is true of North America, until recently as well. Their demographic characteristics, arguably, reflect the index of those societies as investigation reveals.

Eurostat (2021, para 8, 18) shows, "the share of the population aged 65 years and over is increasing in every EU Member State. Another aspect of population ageing is the progressive ageing of the older population itself, as the relative significance of the very old is growing at a faster pace than any other age segment of the EU's population. The share of those aged 80 years or above in the EU's population is projected to have a two and a half fold increase between 2020 and 2100, from 5.9% to 14.6%" The leadership from this class will dominate, as it has, for more than half the EU countries. However, when the same scenario plays out in Africa with a diametrically opposite wealth of youth and work force latched in a bracket of youthful generation whose population is projected according to Hamdok (2015) to "represent over 40 per cent of the world's young people, in less than three generations", the aberration is dangerously rigged with potentials to plummet the polity into unimaginable abyss.

The ability of countries to harness the demographic dividend depends critically on their investments in human capital, particularly young people poised to enter the labor force, whose productivity, entrepreneurship and innovation will drive future economic growth (African Union, 2020). If human capital investment falls short and the labor market is unable to absorb new workers, the opportunity of this demographic dividend may be squandered. The future of the collective dream of the founding fathers of many African states and the aspiration of many youth will drown in the fears of short-circuitry leadership and mentorship.

GOVERNANCE IN POST-MODERN AFRICA

Governance as a concept is that mechanisms of coordination of human productivity in political, economic, social and psychological sphere for the purpose of harmonious productivity and sustainability in any milieu by public authorities or private organizations.

Governance in Africa is a malnourished concept because of its complex bowel and situational given regarding reality at every circumstance. From the get go a chunk of the system of governance practiced in Africa today is contrived, and has been since a long time ago. Indigenous system in places were collectively weighed in a balance and found wanting by the conquistadors.

Policies on international relations involving power states and blocs of economic control were made to align with political arrangements across the globe. Democracy was the currency and on that shaft Western policies regarding African nations were made to answer particularly after the collapse of the Berlin Wall in October 1989, the year that closed the Cold War (Sesay, 2014).

The corollary of that on Africa was the pressure point towards ratification of democracy in the continent championed by civil society forces and some political actors that were apparently the underdogs in the power tussle with either military rulers or rival political groups. The ignition for political reform enjoyed the support by self-styled Africa's development partners that institutionalized conditions for friendship and aids. Acceptance of those codified prerequisites became keys to foreign aids, grants and technical supports. More pertinent were the agitations that became the fallout of much disquiet over a scripted political system that was not organic with manifest difficulties and signs of adaptation. Many protestations on the choreographed system were framed not as evidence of organic repudiation of a system but as symptoms of secondary concerns like economic problems, social and other political sutures.

The spectacle of yardstick used de-standardizes the African craft and by fiat foist a systems on Africa (Rahman, 2001). Somehow the continent had to stay in line. The line was drawn by Western nations with capitalist democracy as the rule. When the yardstick was "modernity", Africa was "primitive", now that the gauge is post-modernism Africa is intermediately modern. The continent seems to have the problem of size, not because there is no existing size for it but because people have always looked for its size in the wrong shops. Kataoka (n.d, p.6) states:

During the era of colonial rule, European powers tried to "civilize" Africa but they lacked an understanding of the values of traditional African society. Such misperceptions and these powers' imposition of their structures and concepts on African countries gave rise to incomprehension in many aspects. Thus, although African leaders inherited states from their former colonial rulers at independence, these political and governmental structures were artificial constructs of the suzerain states rather than structures derived from traditional African society.

A contumelious irony is that Africans have denounced Africa's system in many wide and loud proclamations. Many elites of African descent hypnotically praise democracy as the best system of governance for Africa although there have been innumerable cases of its crass failures. Lots of African countries, for example, have become consistent example of a failed state on the balance of that modeled system of government. Kataoka (nd, p.7) observes "When African countries achieved freedom from colonial rule by Western powers, their newly-created states were modeled after those of Western countries; African leaders attempted to introduce mechanisms of government from these models". It is easy to find the blame in Africa as a problem state than in the system since the benchmark system democracy is almost venerated as a perfect system.

The interesting thing is that the anatomical superstructure of the African's body seems to have unique features that make it easy to tell the skeleton of an African from a European, as studies have variously suggested (Kaur, Miller, Freitas, Bemben and Bemben, 2019; Looker, 2002). Wouldn't it therefore indicate that the architecture of governance for every race is a manual organically shaped by nature in a way for a people to follow? Is it civilization to be traditional in the way we dress? Is it primitive to not look and dress like a man from a different tradition? Would it be absurd to organize a society based on a system a people are comfortable in? Who labels and whose standardizes?

While it may not be too apparent, some lights are beginning to reveal that even the inerrant system of democracy may need some overhaul and re-evaluation by those that hold the ace on its pertinence. There are many greasepaints on the recorded successes that appear to eclipse internal combustions in the countries that hold the right to the system. Sabel (2001, p.121) avers:

The exhaustion of the party politics of Left and Right, together with assaults on central governments and spasmodic efforts to reform them, encouraged these developments. National governments of nearly all colors, embarrassed by responsibilities they cannot or will not discharge, are devolving authority to lower levels and loosening the grip of public bureaucracies on the provision of some services.

Are the birds coming to roost? Is the center holding for the Western style democracy in Africa with over 3,000 different ethnic groups speaking more than 2,100 different languages in all of Africa? Forcing a homogenous system of governance is to encounter the difficulty and dilemma of a camel passing through the eye of the needle. The challenges are enormous with variant shades of experimental mishaps of democracy in the continent and predictable consequences.

According to Organization for Economic Co-operation and Development {OECD} (2001, p.3) First, old forms of governance in both the public and private sectors are becoming increasingly ineffective. Second, the new forms of governance that are likely to be needed over the next few decades will involve a much broader range of active players. Third, and perhaps most importantly, two of the primary attributes of today's governance systems – the usually fixed and permanent allocations of power that are engraved in the structures and constitutions of many organizations; and, the tendency to vest initiative exclusively in the hands of those in senior positions in the hierarchy – look set to undergo fundamental changes.

These predictions are apt and tend to explain the need for a system that appears organic to every clime whether it is an adaptation of democracy or something entirely different. Scholars have conceptualized the brand as postmodernism. What will be the point of departure is that as much as possible, Ghasemi

(2019, p.1) observes "postmodernism favors the diversity of human experiences, values, cultures, and identities, and thus, it critiques totality and universality... This is an effort to resist monophony and monopoly of power systems and to create pluralistic polyphony"...

There is a general paradigm shift and disquiet among old democracies. Sabel (2001, p.122) notes, where the rich democracies were once diagnosed as suffering a crisis of governability (Huntington, Crozier and Watanuki, 1975), today they are more likely to be diagnosed as suffering a deficit of democracy. More exactly, there is fear of parallel government, *imperium in imperio:* new structures of public action, outside the old ones, whose efficacy undermines the legitimacy of traditional democracy without offering an equivalent form of accountability of its own.

This was evident in the Arab Spring uprising and mass protests in post- communist regimes that capitalized on social media tools to co-ordinate and mobilize masses to challenge authoritarian regimes (Lynch 2011; Howard and Hussain 2013; Trottier and Fuchs 2014; Micó and Casero- Ripollés 2014; Tufekci 2017;). That wave of discontent swept around Nigeria in the form of #ENDSARS movement of 2020. The protests (#ENDSARS) are notable for its patronage by a demographic that is made of entirely young Nigerians. The movement used a symbolic reality instrumentalized by media platforms to demand for good and accountable governance (BBC News, Oct. 16, 2020). That media handle foreshadowed a possible lever of equalizing demands with the powers that be as well as gain opportunity for self-determination for disgruntled youth in many African society. How green is the collegial power that the new technology of ICT and its paraphernalia provide to a gapping population in a post-modernist Africa?

DIGITAL TECHNOLOGY IN AFRICA

The reality of the digital era and revolution does not segregate or leave any in doubt. The advancement and social revolution that mobile Internet has engineered because of its proliferation has transmogrified society, shaped approaches to life not without dysfunctional droppings though. One of those gaps is the obvious inequality paradox between the rich nations and the poor nations, even though the technology was granted the pass of being a great equalizer. African Digital Policy Project (ADPP, 2020) characterizes the imbalance as "the digital inequality paradox". Accordingly, it refers not only to the uneven physical access to varying forms of information and communication technologies (ICTs), but because of what people are capable of doing with digital technologies; the contexts in which they are using them, and the prices they pay for using them.

According to GSMA (2020) the prospect appears all green as "At the end of 2019, 477 million people in Sub-Saharan Africa subscribed to mobile services and half a billion mobile subscribers in 2021"... (p.3). Even then, for the "majority of people in Sub-Saharan Africa, the lack of a verifiable identity remains a major barrier to participating fully in the digital economy. Sub-Saharan Africa is home to only a sixth of the world's population – but half the global population without an ID lives in the region" (p.25).

While the advent of mobile broadband has driven Internet uptake in Africa, the representation of it as a panacea for underdevelopment masks the fact that six billion people across the world do not have access to the Internet and their lives are largely untouched by this digital revolution (World Bank 2016, v). What is the salient issue here? Increased connectivity in itself does not correlate with reduced information inequality. For those connected people, the intensity of use within Africa is highly uneven, because it is between developed economies and developing economies.

Figure 1.

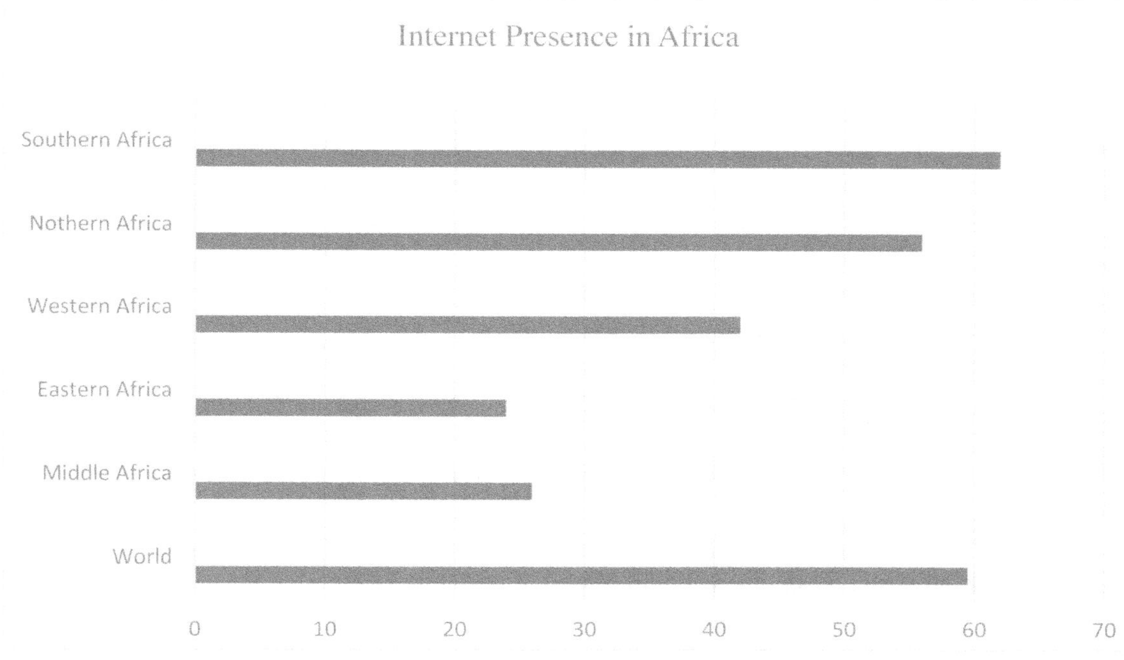

Even where networks and services appear relatively available, a swart of people majority of who are congregated in rural areas are unable to access these services affordably or use them optimally to enhance their social and economic wellbeing. This is unlike more mature economies, where levels of human development and equality are higher. Even where enabling environments have been created by legislative fiat for the extension of services, or where regulatory interventions have driven prices down, the limited demand-side data available in Africa illustrates how the socially and economically marginalized — particularly those at the intersection of class, gender, race or ethnicity, with generally lower education, employment and income — are unable to harness the benefits of the Internet (Gilwald, 2017, p.1). The 2007-2008 RIA demand-side survey across 14 African countries conducted by Gillwald, Moyo and Stork (2013) found that the bottom three-quarters of mobile phone users spent on average between 11 percent and 27 percent of their income on mobile communications, rather than the standard reference of two percent to three percent of income spent in developed economies.

Beyond the failure to policy perspectives informational asymmetries have yawning implications on social and economic wellbeing of society. In spite of divergences on the impact that the increase broadband penetration is likely to make on the economic fortune of society, there are strong indications that it has cumulative impact. Within a wider ICT ecosystem a broadband as a concept "encompasses the policies, strategies, processes, information, technologies, applications and stakeholders that together make up a technology environment for a country, government or an enterprise. Most importantly, an ICT ecosystem includes people — diverse individuals — who create, buy, sell, regulate, manage and use technology" (Kaplan 2005) cited in Gilwald (2017, p.9).

There is a cursory assumption from an empirical study that found that a broadband penetration ranging between 20-30 per cent is averagely required to propel about 0.8% increase in an average African nation

GDP. When that benchmark is hit, there might be appreciable increase in the flow of information and a concomitant reduction in transaction costs as a result of ICT diffusion outcome in holistic transformative effect on economies (Koutrompis, 2009).

Looking at the index of the development it may be easy to tell that Africa is still a long shot from that reality. There are contentions that the baggage of stereotypes is still used in telescoping Africa in the global narrative. Ya'u (2012, p.86) contends, "It would seem that the virtual public in Africa is a site of ambivalences. It is simultaneously a 'we', 'us' and 'them' space, depending on what the issues are. It is both globally and locally rooted". Africa is languidly trudging in a plane that speed is the rule of the super high way. From a policy perspective the failure to address these informational asymmetries has wider social, economic and political implications.

Quite the obvious, data network are not like voice network services. The former have effects that stretch them beyond access to intensity of use reflected in global ICT indices. Outside a monumental improvement that has a semblance of what can be reasonably described as affordable services, fertilized by improvement in human development, these hyped developments may just be some cosmetics that are abstracted for dealing with the issue of digital inequality particularly in Africa (Gilwald, 2017).

DIGITAL AFRICA AND THE E-GOVERNANCE COCKTAIL

The United Nations Educational, Scientific, and Cultural Organization (UNESCO) issued in 2009 *National Information Society Policy: A Template* (UNESCO, 2009) and in 2016 an updated version *Knowledge Societies Policy Handbook* (UNESCO & UN University, 2016). These detailed manuals for the development of national ICT institutional and policy frameworks target countries that do not possess necessary resources to develop their own, with the ultimate goal to universalize global ICT development (Budnitskiy 2018).

However, the trajectory to a webbed universe of information communication technology (ICT) is to really have all ends connected; otherwise, it is technically a turn not a web. The intention to have a bordered or borderless virtual village may be a subject of endless dialectics. What is of less controversy is the fact that its evolution seems as real as it can be. A breed with common interest, called netizens, is shaping up. Alasuutari (2015) has termed it "the global tribe of moderns." The assumption is that everyone is connected to everyone because of the commonality of the linkage being the net, the Internet.

It implies that everyone is a neighbor to everyone; hence what you do not necessarily have in geographical connection is more than made up for you in the virtual space. In all of this communication is the key player in the creation of communities. Thus, Netizens are creations of communication, not necessarily technology. The paraphernalia or apparatus of communication like the Internet is a conveyor belt. Africa is at the base of the Internet chain, more like the weakest link as we have earlier observed, with low information technology penetration ratios (Ya'u, 2012; Gilwald, 2017). As noted, it is communication that creates the virtual reality and communication is culturally contextualized by complex socio-cultural nature and orientation of the netizens. That is to say communication at the virtual frequency is still subject to cultural filters, pulls and push. How can we theorize the virtual public in Africa?

Habermas conception of the public sphere places emphasis on three key issues: participation is open to all (there is a principle of inclusivity); all participants are considered equal (social status or rank is disregarded); and any issue can be raised for rational debate. Cyberspace is potentially open to all, even though in practice there are a number of barriers - but so has it always been with other forms of communication platforms. In so far as the cyberspace is concerned, all are also potentially considered equal, though here again practical exigencies put some limit to this equality.

The bedrock of civilization has remained dialogic communication. Debate and discussion normally prefigure dialogue and that is the sine qua non of the public sphere. Like a living thing, the public sphere is ever so ambitious and longs for reach and inclusivity and often throws the gauntlet to even embrace non-interactive communication opportunities and platforms. Sometimes this inadvertent outreach creates tension between interpersonal (interactive) media like telephone and the mass media. The weakness of the later in interactivity is compensated in reach. It is the dominance of the mass media that made Habermas (1999) to think they are undermining the public sphere.

However, that gap seems being bridged by digital public sphere, or so it seems, where participants are personalized as individual netizens. The dissolution of the pyramid of communication power, held exclusively by corporations, creates a common relational ground. Visibility is almost synonymous to accessibility. Beyond just the denudation of the old communication blocs, the development is a re-constitution that demystifies their operation, constitution and contents. Now because of digitalization everyone can reach the hierarchy of media organization, respond to a content, produce and disseminate contents without the bottlenecks imposed by certification or formal orientation. Nothing encapsulates the aspirations of post-modernism than these ideals. It must be remembered particularly in Africa that these potentials of ICT are embryonic at best. In other climes ICTs have led to what MacFarlene (1993) calls the 'de-institutionalization of the process of information dissemination'.

If the media were regarded as the Fourth Estate of the Realm, now that the realm is notionally without a bar and a 'bouncer' to regulate entrants of commoners and comments about ongoing in acoustically sound-proofed executive and legislative floors, can governance remain a cult of those that qualify by criteria that is musty? It is tricky. The traditional public sphere may not be same as the cyberspace. What are the appreciable and applaud-able milestones to reckon in governance around Africa? We will chew on this question later in the work.

However, suffice to say that both, the traditional public sphere and the virtual public sphere are metaphysical and exist as construct and mental realities with veracities for socio-political concerns for netizens. One is a cocoon for the other – the traditional space provides discursive context and labyrinths for the emergence of a virtual public that has in its embryo the private and government-controlled spaces as well. Ya'u (2012, p.88) contends, "In the same vein, online communities cannot be conflated with the virtual public sphere. There are online governance structures, some of a commercial corporate nature, which are also part of the online communities".

The constitution of the public sphere by shared understanding is non-inhibitive communication styled as a Meta discursive phenomenon. A valid understanding of the virtual space ought to reflect or constitute a broad-based articulation of matters that can get expression online under a milieu of discursive normative by citizens as they engage freely. The advocacy is for the platform to make no law abridging freedom of thought and decorous talk with a clear absence of government-incubus control or profiteering threats. They ought to reflect a town-square (public sphere) that will not be puppeteer to organized platforms or those that tend towards censorship, in the spirit of post-modernist drift.

This may be the ideal but it is problematized by consistent realities. Hypothetically, the virtual spaces that are constituents of the public sphere ought to have assumptive menus like provision for blogs, text, videos, audios, chat platforms, wikis, open publications etc., but can they truly exist independently of the platform owners who are there for business profit and not public interest? Indeed very doubtful. It is reason they run the platforms, in the first place, with a propagandized make-believe that public interest is first. In a way, these public space curators are economic authorities with their sometimes-stringent brand of censorship on whatever is 'inimical' to profit or business interest. Under these ropes, can post-modernism be a realistic feature in Africa?

There are power blocs like Google, Facebook, Twitter and the others contesting the suzerainties of the virtual public spheres. This development is a truism even in Western democracies. Many countries are calling for strictures by the platform providers under the guise of national and international security concerns. The case of the Wiki leaks and Julian Assange is one out of many. Llanso, van Hoboken, Leerssen, and Harambam, (2020) stress, "automation in content moderation has increasingly been used on a voluntary basis by the most popular global online platforms. Even when not applied with intent to silence any particular voices, it in fact 'exposes all speech to a form of evaluation *ex ante* and in a way that fails to consider linguistic, social, historical, and other relevant context. Głowacka, Youngs, Pintea, and Wołosik (2021, p.27) note, "It creates substantial risks to freedom of expression, especially when coupled with a lack of due process safeguards available to users, including transparency and effective remedies. The is exacerbated by the lack of independent, external oversight of platforms' decisions and the fact that these actors, not only due to specificities of their services but also their dominant positions on the market, serve as powerful gatekeepers for public discourse and access to information".

One seeming implication of ICTs in the making of the virtual public is that they not only de-territorialized the public sphere but they also appear to create a variety of public spaces that are presumably disconnected from the national space. This gives rise to specific features of the virtual sphere, such as the fact that they cut across countries and are not necessarily organized on the basis of nationalities. When the ban on Twitter by Nigerian government happened the decentralization of the network platform made it obvious that Nigeria may have been on a different lever from other Twitter users in Europe and America who did not see the trend until desperate users had to take a bye-pass in virtual private network (VPN) to access their accounts. With de-territorialization it may be possible to weaken links through filtration of what is shared by what bloc and for what purpose.

Be that as it may, it seems the challenge is graver than imagined. The platforms that should be the emancipators are the new oligarchs with insidious tricks benched on the path of free speech to surreptitiously subvert unionize displeasures over misrule and other legit protests. The virtual space is not a no-man's land. It is owned, monopolized and manipulated by social media moguls like Facebook and Google who are more-or-less a power to themselves, operating without a scratch on their regulatory power even when they restrain, thwart competition, prevent and manipulate innovation and barricade small firms from sharing the space. Alleman (2018, p.1) reasons, "Facebook and Google – have control over what information and news we receive through 'black-box' algorithms; they select what 'we need' and maintain our attention with click-bait and other software tricks. In addition, these platforms have not taken significant measures to address false-news, bots, trolls, or other malicious software on the Internet. Indeed, they make money off the proliferation of this misinformation".

The platforms service providers bug the virtual public sphere and so a hope that a rag tag contingent of youth may, without inhibition, get a hands-free right to stake their claims is almost vacuous. Public reactions to unpopular policies of government are ringed by counter reactions either by use of subtle or covert undercut from government monitoring agents. There is a growing use of spyware across the continent to snoop on government critics. Uganda, Benin and several other states have imposed a social media tax that has excluded many users. Chad went through a 16-month social media ban while Nigeria also took a share of Twitter ban over claims of security reasons (Cheeseman, Garbe and Hassan 2020).

These giant tech corporations are polarizing society with directed click- baits, targeted ads, focused blogs, etc. In this way they appear a threat to a democratic society. How can virtual governance with participation of all and sundry be realized in such atmosphere, especially in Africa? Already Africa is now the unconquered territory of giant tech corporations where tech wars are staged. It is a test bed for AI technologies led and severally flanked by IBM, Google and Microsoft, companies believed to have invested hugely in "Africa's AI development than any African government or the African Union" (Yeboah, 2021, p. 18). Why, anyone will wonder? Meanwhile the Chinese AI firms on the other flank are also contesting for the heart of Africa and appear to have won the sympathy of many African leaders more than the Sillicon Valley trios.

One of the malaises of post modernism is a rogue fake news phinomenon that seems to run roughshod on all except those that benefit from it and studies show that the tech giants are huge benefactors "because they help retain users on the network" (Alleman, 2018 p.4). The norm for them is if it bleeds it leads, meaning the more sensational the "news" the better. False news spreads faster and wider than real news (Vosoughi, Deb and Sinan, 2018). Disinformation and Fake news seem all-good for profits! Moreover, fake accounts enhance profits; yes, even if they are fake! The more users on the platform, the more valuable the platform is to the advertiser.

In this context perhaps it is safe to surmise that there are contending elements working at cross-purpose with those that envisage a free and egalitarian society. How set then is the continent to develop an effective way to stop the flow of fake news, maximize the full benefits of digital democracy when digital exclusion driven by the high cost of data, the strategies of authoritarian governments, and in some cases the approach of major tech companies themselves are thwarting the effort and diming the hope? Postmodernism favors the diversity of human experiences, values, cultures, and identities, and thus, it critiques totality and universality. However, the idea may be a wishful thinking if it can't get through the trimester of conception to grow and resist monophony, monopoly of power systems and to create pluralistic polyphony (Ghasemi, 2019).

Nevertheless, AI technology can be a veritable window for postmodernist ambition to fruit and entrench a well-oiled leadership and governance in the continent. It holds the potential to improve governmental participation across the spectrum of a nation's demographics; it could spawn political pluralism and enhance civic participation by democratizing communication platforms and strengthening transparency. In parts of Africa like Ghana where it was utilized, it helped to defog election results and "accurately" predicted the 2016 election results before the electoral commission declared the party as the winner. All it took was the expertise of a hired Ghanaian Telecommunications Service Manager at NASA to develop an innovative system that allowed them to input data from electoral centers, via pictures of the election results sheets. The data was then transmitted simultaneously to the region and national party offices where they had set up a technology unit.

The virtue of resiliency in Africans gets them to hope and attempt to circumvent daunting challenges. Yeboah (2021, p. 19) avers that it is becoming a common sight in Africa, for citizens and marginalized groups to use AI technologies such as cloud computing systems or fact-check systems to circumvent traditional political barriers in order to have a piece of the political power to influence policy discussions, ensure respect for human rights and hold governments accountable. By using these technological tools to change the political narrative, non-elites in Africa are less dependent on political elites to define the political discourse.

A testament to that is that in October of 2020 an online campaign protest spiraled out of disgruntlement with political evasiveness of the leadership class in Nigeria to handle police excesses, extra-judicial killings some of which are at the behest of politicians. Called the #ENDSARS protest that degenerated into a brouhaha, the success in youth mobilization was like none other seen in the country. As result of that success SARS, the Special Anti-Robbery Squad (SARS) - a unit of the Nigerian Police Force that is known for arresting, intimidating and killing citizens, was dissolved.

A naughty challenge of this conflagration is the dexterity of fake information. To trim that problem and restore some sanity and trust in political statements and public debates in Africa, African Check, a South African non-partisan fact checking organization is severally employing AI driven technologies to improve its fact checking capabilities. These AI driven fact checking tools collect and monitor information from leading news sites and social media platforms, identify and label controversial claims made by a political or any public figure, claims are matched with corresponding data to confirm or declare it false Yeboah (2021, p. 19). Happily, this and other innovations are encapsulated in the objectives of e-governance, which for the moment seems the escape capsule for sanity in leadership if structured well.

E-governance is a tripartite operational element that entails e-government, e-regulation and e-democracy. Viewed together it suggests an operating system that is transparent and allows for more trust, mutual trust between government and those served. Not all e-solutions and e-services that governments provide necessarily meet fully the needs of the ordinary citizen. A well-configured one should significantly reduce corruption, although the glass is often fogged by nefarious intents. The true existence of digital governance should whittle down much of the issue of misrule and abstractive governance managed by a hand full, which is angst that postmodernism ideology decries.

As an alternative to the ideals of postmodernism ideology, e-governance could carter to issues of how well the state makes use of ICT to lubricate, regulate and provide public services like prices of things, quality of products and accessibility. E-democracy, a synonym for e-governance, deals with how the state could use ICT to improve its rule –give everyone a sense of say and belonging and the possibility of being heard by the highest authority. Where it is well coordinated a president can hold a town meeting on a social media platform, for example, and respond to concerns and questions of the common man. It is reason a UN e-government survey (2004, 2005, and 2008) described the public sector use of it as the most innovative yet (Adeyemo, 2011). The United Nations e-government global survey has adopted a five-stage e-governance model (UN e- government survey, 2004, 2005; 2008), these are:

Stage 1 - Emerging presence: In this stage a country commits to becoming an E-Government player. A formal but limited web presence is established through a few independent government websites which provide users with static organizational or political information.

Stage 2 - Enhanced presence: In this stage, a country's online presence begins to expand as the number of official websites increase, with more dynamic and specialized information content that is frequently updated. The interaction is still primarily unidirectional with information flowing essentially from government to the citizen.

Stage 3 - Interactive presence: In this stage a country's presence on the internet expands dramatically by entering the interactive mode with access to a wide range of government institutions and services.

Stage 4 - Transactional presence: In this stage two- way interactions between the citizen and the government is included.

Stage 5 - Networked (or fully integrated) presence: This stage represents the most sophisticated level in the online e-government initiatives. It is characterized by an integration of G2G, G2C and C2G (and reverse) interactions. The government encourages participatory deliberative decision-making and is willing and able to involve the society in a two-way open dialogue (UN global e-government readiness Report, 2004).

This UN model is an index that characterizes the state e-government readiness and e-government participation. The end ought to be development that is popularized by public yearning and acceptability. Adeyemo (2011, p.13) states, "The UN global e-government readiness index (UN e- government survey, 2004; 2005; 2008) is a composite index comprising the Web measure index, the telecommunication infrastructure index and the human capital index".

These ideals could be realized by nations where there is a will power and a leaning on public good by the powers that be. There is a scientific way of assessing nations on the barometer of e-governance performance and compliance. For example, Adeyemo (2011, p.16) notes that, The UN 2001 benchmarking e-government report (Benchmarking E-government, 2002) had given a detailed assessment of Nigeria's E-Readiness status, stating that Nigeria's government web sites were primarily for public affairs issues, with very little dynamic information to the citizens. It avers that the unofficial government web site is the Presidency. Quotes about combating corruption and allegiance to the presidency are common features of the page and the site is bereft of direct access to all ministries and legislative or judicial issues, including laws and regulations or court decisions. The report stresses that Nigeria had no ministries online instead the site merely provided links to an array of agencies and departments concerning export regulations, ports authority, public enterprises, corporate affairs, and investment promotions. Information (or sites) relating to education, social services, health care or women and children specifically was conspicuously absent. It also observed that this pattern of unbalanced implementation was common among developing countries.

Reflection from the report points to the fact that Africa is technologically disadvantaged in terms of infrastructure, although it is rich in human capital base. There is an absence of patriotism to develop the human capital resources because of a morbid fear of what exposing people to knowledge will do to a parochial mindset of leadership. Many leaders in Africa prefer to buy foreign services than invest in the development of indigenous service providers. This explains why many African countries may yoyo at the toddler stage of e-governance for a long time.

Some gains may have been recorded since the UN report assessment of Nigeria and by extrapolation Africa E-governance readiness in 2001. In terms of consumerism, the acquisition of telecommunication infrastructure and paraphernalia has shored up the e-government ratings of a few African countries like Nigeria, Ghana, South Africa and Cape Verde as studies show (Adeyemo, 2011). The fertile Nigerian market for ICT accessories and technologies make them the craved market for investors from Middle East, Europe, Asia and North America. A big challenge of e-government implementation in any developing country is whether the intended objective of reaching the citizens is actually achieved. E- governance, which is similar to e-democracy, should reach all the people who need government services regardless of their location, age, status, language, or access to the Internet.

The two main objectives of e-democracy are:

1. To provide citizens access to information and knowledge about the political process, about services and about choices available
2. To make possible the transition from passive information access to active citizen participation by:
    - Informing the citizen
    - Representing the citizen
    - Encouraging the citizen to vote
    - Consulting the citizen
    - Involving the citizen

The strategic objective of e-governance is to support and simplify governance for all parties - government, citizens and businesses. The use of ICTs can connect all three parties and support processes and activities (Backus, 2001, p.3).

A FINAL REMARK

Reforms and numerous theoretical expediencies prescribed from the Bretton Woods to the most recent display initial frenzies to kinetically steer a campaign, but that force is soon whittled down by razor-sharp intra-fit reactions like organic customization issues, identity question, and rules of applicability. Africa and its cultures are numerous. The collegial frames are like arteries that discreetly relate, following their route, but need not be replaced or collapsed into each other. It is reason the heterogeneity of the principle of postmodernism is worth paying attention to in looking at systems that can fit the development course of communities and the united states of Africa.

Along that field of governance shrubberies, Africa could significantly become amendable to digital governance in spite of their critical posture and suspicion of the dysfuntionality of digitalization in government operations - perhaps the suspicion can be excused because of strangeness. Beyond the synonym ology of e-governance and digital governance what ought to spring out is for communities to trace their roots in governance, and that tributary is important, before they can be forged into regional borders. Although digitalization is a technical globalization in blueprint, individual roots of evolution can strengthen regional clustering. The center need not be a system of universal replicate anymore than we will demand that individual names of nations be mortgaged for one nation. Adaptation ought not to be forced; a rainbow of uniqueness will encourage mutual respect and discourage complexes of superiority and underdogs among nations.

Digitalization does not only offer just a new technology, but also a mechanism to transform the way government operates. Moving services online involves redesigning organizational structures and processes according to the citizens' and businesses' needs. It also entails integrating services across different governmental agencies, in an effort to simplify interaction, while reducing cost structures and improving overall service delivery. E-Government initiatives need to adopt a whole-of-government approach. Many countries have implemented one-stop portals, online transactions and e-participation possibilities. However, developing public value in e-government is still at the initial stages of conceptualization and implementation particularly in developing nations of Africa.

All the same, it is not likely that any one with a sense of discernment will drop 'yes' that e-governance is a cure-all answer. Like sharks, the elements that are conditioned to incinerate exchange of ideas freely will taste blood in every innocuous intention. E-governance and its dividend will be served stepmotherly to the public to forestall a unified force that will topple the cart. They will comb restlessly the virtual halls with all tools at their disposal. The fight for democracy was never won on a bed of roses. Postmodernism has its Golgotha. The game is survival. African netizens need to own the patent to the innovations and not cede them to Silicon Valley or China. The erosion of identity has been the bane of Africa. Cultural preservation of Africa's intellectual property is one way to safeguard the heritage and existence of our virtual space. When a government is serious it will engage the people it leads and open channels for people to reach it easily and quickly. It is expected that governments in Africa will make concerted effort to boost the education and exposure level of citizens to change. Research ought to be actively encouraged to influence government significantly and understand possible loopholes in digital and data rights.

REFERENCES

Adeyemo, A.B., (2011). E-government implementation in Nigeria: An assessment of Nigeria's global e-gov ranking. *Journal of Internet and Information System, 2*(1), 11-19.

ADPP. (2020). *Technical Report.* Retrieved December 16th 2021 from https://creativecommons.org/licenses/by/4.0/legalcode

African Union. (2020). *The Digital Transformation Strategy For Africa (2020-2030).* www.au.int

Alasuutari, P. (2015). *The synchronization of national policies: Ethnography of the global tribe of moderns.* Routledge. doi:10.4324/9780203597729

Alleman, J. (2018). *Threat of Internet platforms: Facebook, Google, etc.* 29th European Regional Conference of the International Telecommunications Society (ITS): "Towards a digital future: turning Technology into markets?" Trento, Italy.

Backus, M. (2001). *E-Governance and developing countries: Introduction and examples.* Academic Press.

Budnitskiy, S. (2018). *Digital nationalisms: Identity, strategic communication, and global Internet governance* [PhD thesis]. Carleton University, Ottawa, Ontario, Canada.

Cheeseman, N., Garbe, L., & Hassan, I. (2020). Why digital democracy will take more than technology in Africa. In A collection of essays exploring the interplay between digital technologies, politics and society across Africa. Digital Civil Society Lab.

Ghasemi, M. (2019). *Paradigms of postmodern democracies.* SAGE Open. https://us.sagepub.com/en-us/nam/open-access-at-sage

Gilwald, A. (2017). *Beyond access: addressing digital inequality in Africa, Paper Series 48.* Centre for International Governance Innovation and Chatham House.

Głowacka, D. Youngs, R. Pintea, A., & Wołosik, E. (2021). *Digital technologies as a means of repression and social control.* European Parliament EP/EXPO/DROI/FWC/2019-01/LOT6/R/04.

GSMA. (2020). *The mobile economy: Sub-Saharan Africa 2020.* www.gsma.com

Habermas, J. (1996). *Between facts and norms: contributions to a Discourse Theory of Law and Democracy.* Cambridge/MIT Press. doi:10.7551/mitpress/1564.001.0001

Hamdok, A. (2015). Forward. In *Africa's youth and prospects for inclusive development: Regional situation analyses report.* United Nations Economic Commission (UNEC) for Africa.

Howard, P. N., & Muzammil, M. H. (2013). *Democracy's fourth wave? Digital media and the Arab Spring.* Oxford University Press. doi:10.1093/acprof:oso/9780199936953.001.0001

Huntington, S., Crozier, M., & Watanuki, J. (1975). Crisis of democracy: Report on the Governability of Democracies to the Trilateral Commission. New York University Press.

Kaplan, J. (2005). *Roadmap for open ICT ecosystems*. Berkman Klein Center for Internet & Society, Harvard Law School. http://cyber.law.harvard.edu/ epolicy/roadmap.pdf

Kataoka, S. (n.d.). *The plight of African states and good governance*. https://www2.jiia.or.jp/pdf/working_paper/h14_kataoka-e.pdf

Kaur, J., Miller, R., Freitas, E., Bemben, D., & Bemben, M. (2019). Racial/ethnic differences in bone mineral density, muscle function and fat mass in young women. *BJHBS*, *18*(2), 2. doi:10.12957/bjhbs.2019.53500

Koutrompis, P. (2009). The economic impact of broadband on growth: A simultaneous approach. *Telecommunications Policy*, *33*(9), 471–485. doi:10.1016/j.telpol.2009.07.004

Llanso, E., van Hoboken, J., Leerssen, P., & Harambam, J. (2020). *Artificial intelligence, content moderation, and freedom of expression*. Transatlantic Working Group.

Looker, C. A. (2002). Editorial: The skeleton, race, and Ethnicity. *The Journal of Clinical Endocrinology and Metabolism*, *87*(7), 3047–3050. doi:10.1210/jcem.87.7.8779 PMID:12107199

Lynch, M. (2011). After Egypt: The limits and promise of online challenges to the authoritarian Arab State. *Perspectives on Politics*, *9*(02), 301–310. doi:10.1017/S1537592711000910

MacFarlene, A. (1993). New news and old: revising the literature. Caejac Journal, 5, 5-20.

Micó, J.-L., & Andreu, C.-R. (2014). Political activism online: Organization and media relations in the case of 15m in Spain. *Information Communication and Society*, *17*(7), 858–871. doi:10.1080/1369118X.2013.830634

OECD. (2001). *Forward Governance in the 21st Century: Future studies*. OECD Publications Services.

Rahman, A. H. (2001). Africa In the 21st Century: prospects for political development. In A. Olugbenga & O. Arunma (Eds.), *African voices African Visions*. The Nordic African Institute.

Sabel, F. C. (2001). *A quiet revolution of democratic governance: towards democratic Experimentalism in OECD Governance in the 21st Century: future studies*. OECD Publications Services.

Sesay, A. (2014). *African governance systems in the pre and post-independence periods: enduring lessons and opportunities for youth in Africa*. For the Mandela Institute for Development Studies.

Trottier, D., & Christian, F. (Eds.). (2014). *Social media, politics and the state: protests, revolutions, riots, crime and policing in the age of Facebook, Twitter and YouTube*. Routledge. doi:10.4324/9781315764832

Tufekci, Z. (2017). *Twitter and tear gas: the power and fragility of networked protest*. Yale University Press.

UN Global E-Government Readiness Report. (2004). *Towards access for opportunity*. United Nations Department of Economic and Social Affairs/Division for Public Administration and Development Management, UNPAN/2004/11.

UN Global E-Government Readiness Report. (2005). *From e- Government to e-inclusion*. United Nations Department of Economic and Social Affairs/Division for Public Administration and Development Management, UNPAN/2005/14.

UN E-Government Survey. (2008). *From e-Government to connected governance*. United Nations Department of Economic and Social Affairs/Division for Public Administration and Development Management, ST/ESA/PAD/SER.E/112.

UNESCO. (2009). *National information society policy: A template*. UNESCO. https://unesdoc.unesco.org/images/0018/001871/187135e.pdf

UNESCO & UN University. (2016). *Knowledge societies policy handbook*. UNESCO. https://en.unesco.org/sites/default/files/knowledge_socities_policy_handbook.pdf

Vosoughi, S., Deb, R., & Sinan, A. (2018). The spread of true and false news online. *Science*, *9*(March), 1146–1151. doi:10.1126cience.aap9559 PMID:29590045

World Bank. (2016). *World Development Report 2016: digital dividends*. World Bank. http://documents.worldbank.org/curated/en/ 896971468194972881/pdf/102725-PUB-Replacement- PUBLIC.pdf

Ya'u, Z. Y. (2012). Ambivalence and activism: Netizens, social transformation and African virtual publics. *Africa Development. Afrique et Developpement*, *37*(1), 85–102.

Yeboah, K. (2021). How AI is transforming Africa's political landscape. In A collection of essays exploring the interplay between digital technologies, politics and society across Africa. Stanford Digital Civil Society Lab.

Chapter 15
Social Media Activism:
Championing and Reconstructing Causes and Values – Mapping the Social Media Ecology of "EndSARS" Protest of 2020 in Nigeria

Princewell Nwanganga Achor
Advanced Management Academy, Abuja, Nigeria

ABSTRACT

This chapter focuses on social media activism and the factors that trigger activism in developing countries. It philosophically reexamines the aftermath of the EndSARS protest via the lens of social media ecology. The epistemological and ontological underpinnings of EndSARS media ecology anchor on social media affordances. It evaluates social movements such as #EndSARS to identify their impact on addressing ills that have retarded development in Africa, particularly the Nigerian state. The chapter combines extant literature with empirical data to discuss socio-politico-environmental realities and issues contributing to social and political disorder in Nigeria. It also proposes solutions on how people can utilize lessons learned from the 'EndSARS' debacle to advance cause-oriented activities and value reorientation. Finally, the chapter suggests a paradigm shift from a violent mass movement to a peaceful one, using the public relations perspective of crisis management.The chapter focuses on social media activism and the factors that trigger activism in developing countries. The EndSARS protest and its aftermath were philosophically reexamined via the lens of social media ecology. The epistemological and ontological underpinnings of EndSARS media ecology were traced to social media affordances. The chapter also evaluates social movements such as #EndSARS for the purpose of identifying its impact in addressing ills that have retarded growth and development in Africa, particularly the Nigerian state. The chapter combines extant literature positions with empirical data to discuss socio-politico-environmental realities and issues contributing to the growing phenomenon of social and political disorder in Nigeria. The chapter also proposes solutions on how to utilize lessons learned from the 'EndSARS' debacle to advance cause-oriented activities and value reorientation. Finally, the chapter proposes a paradigm shift from a violent mass movement to a peaceful one, using public relations perspective of crisis management.

DOI: 10.4018/978-1-6684-4107-7.ch015

INTRODUCTION

Social media offers lots of benefits to like-minded individuals to champion cause-oriented activities that herald social or political change. The epistemological and the ontological interpretations of social media activism, within the frame of media ecology, need to be explored further as a way of engendering and contextualizing positive social and political change in Africa's political landscape. Ruotshalainen and Heinonen (2015) argue that "the media ecology tradition perceives media as a structure in which society and culture evolve—as an environment where people act and live their lives, and through which reality is perceived" (p.3). Media ecology has been studied through different lenses and perspectives (Strate, 2004; Polski, 2013; Polski and Gorman, 2012). Of significance in these lenses and approaches utilized in conceptualizing or contextualizing media ecology, is the emphasis on media as environment, the disruption in the environment, and advances in(media) technologies (Ruotsalainen & Heinonen, 2015; Arriagada and Ibáñez 2020). These factors have expanded the frontiers of media ecology in communication studies and perhaps opened a new vista to exploring the concept within the milieu of new media, particularly social media, which has advanced the phenomenon of ecosystemic society.

Social media have opened a new vista of understanding activism, which is a departure from the mainstream media. This new vista is embedded in the social media affordances (Bucher and Helmond, 2018) characterized by: multi-access to information, self-expressions on contentious issues, open participation in socio-political and economic discourses, users' choice of determining what is or not news, framing of issues, and users' ability to engage the political leadership and stakeholders online. The wind of social media activism which has swept across many countries in Europe, America, and Africa is still raging and portends great lessons for conflict resolution and proactive public relations practice. It is believed that some of the issues that trigger protests are akin to factors that retard development in developing countries, including Nigeria.

In October 2020, Nigeria was engulfed in intense civil protests in which Nigerians demanded the disbandment of the Special Anti-Robbery Squad (SARS) over allegations of extra-judicial killings, torture, extortion, and other crimes committed by its members. Before the protest, social media was awash with gory stories of these allegations; this eventually led to the"#EndSARS" campaign across cities. The protest got to a climax on October 20, 2020, when the Army attacked the protesters at Lekki Tollgate in Lagos State, allegedly killing and injuring some protesters. The EndSARS social media activism and its aftermath call for a philosophical reexamination using the lens of social media ecology. Hence, this chapter focuses on identifying the perceptions of social media ecologists and influencers on the incidence and marries their views with epistemological and ontological underpinnings of media ecology, within the African setting.

The chapter also aims at evaluating social movement (e.g. #EndSARS) and identifes its impact on addressing ills that have retarded growth and development in Africa, particularly the Nigerian state. The chapter also proposes solutions on how to utilize lessons learned from the 'EndSARS debacle to advance cause-oriented activities and value reorientation. Again, the chapter proposes a paradigm shift from a violent mass movement to a peaceful one and adopts a working definition of activism anchored on public relations perspective. The Chapter acknowledges the paradox of mass movement in correcting the ills of a society; and combines extant literature positions with empirical (qualitative) data in discussing socio-politico-environmental realities and issues contributing to the growing phenomenon of social and political disorder in Africa, particularly Nigeria.

The remainder of the chapter is organized in the following subtopics: historical background of social media activism, conceptualizing (social) media ecology and social media activism, methods and epistemology leanings, epistemology and ontology of media ecology and activism, EndSARS protest, and mass mobilization. Other subtopics include understanding the philosophy of activism and protest and bridging the communication gaps/strains that trigger violent mass protests in Nigeria. The chapter draws the curtain by making concluding remarks and recommendations.

HISTORICAL BACKGROUND OF SOCIAL MEDIA ACTIVISM

Historicizing activism at this juncture gives a clearer picture of mass mobilization vis-à-vis social media activism, which also makes civic engagement visible in the digital domain. Activism is as old as human existence; it predates modern democracies of the world, given the fact that, in the olden days, groups of people had always converged to protest abnormalities within their community or society. Even during the pre-colonial and colonial eras, some communities or societies had a structure that gives the youths and age-grade organizations the customary power to question perceived ills in the administration of the village or community. They used various artifacts as a symbol of resentment and chanted songs of disapproval or solidarity to convey their message and demand justice from the local and district authorities.

On the global front, modern activism can be traced to a series of non-violent demonstrations championed by Martin Luther King in the 1940s, to draw attention to racial discrimination and prejudice the Blacks or African Americans ('the Negros') were facing in the United States of America. At various times, Luther, mobilized blacks across major cities in the US to protest the injustices in the American political and social systems; he called for equal rights and justice for all peoples, irrespective of race, creed, and religion. His address at the Capitol remains one of the greatest speeches ever made by an activist to demand a change in the status quo. Also, the use of revolutionary pamphleteers of the Revolutionary War and the abolitionist press movement are part of the events that chronicle media activism in the United States. In India, Mahatma Gandhi, the father of modern India, through activism was able to advocate for social and political reforms using non-violent means. In the African continent, the struggles for independence of many colonized countries were championed by activists who mobilized various segments of the people to protest.

Across continents, activism became a tool for civic engagement and struggle for liberation—from clutches of dictatorial regimes, police brutalities, racial discriminations, social and political injustices, and inequality, including the high-handedness of repressive governments (Clayton, 2018). The media played a major role in sustaining the struggles amidst suppressive media environments. With the advent of the Internet and advancement in communication technologies, a new form of activism was birthed, variously described in the literature as digital activism, online activism, or social media activism (Cammaerts, 2015; Khazraee and

Novak, 2018; Milan and Van der Velden,2016; Cho, Byrne and Pelter, 2020). Social media activism is "a form of protest or advocacy for a cause that uses social media channels". It is a typology of activism that uses social media to call for mass action/protest (Ed Carrasco, March 26, 2012). Social media activism and all forms of digital activism, use new lexicons or grammar of protest that reflect the language of the 'digital natives/'netizens' and the vocabulary of contemporary social movements. This has introduced hybrid media ecologies within contemporary social movements and digital communication technologies (Treré, 2018).

Literature traces the emergence of active social media activism in Africa to the 2011 Arab Spring uprisings— a terminology or phenomenon used in explaining the surge in the demand for a change in the way repressive governments of Tunisia, Libya and Egypt were running their affairs (Aaron,2014; Pickard,2015; Dambo et al, 2020). The youths of these nations demonstrated how society can use social media to mobilize mass action. In Egypt, protesters used social media to advance causes and reduced the cost and difficulties associated with organizing rallies (Khan, 2012; Pfiefle, 2012). Egyptians used Twitter to create avenues for digital civic engagement to question repressive regimes and suppression of people's voices against the subjugation of the people of Egypt. Although the uprisings turned violent but helped to create a new national identity that heralded an 'elusive freedom'.

The #BlackLivesMatter is another case study where social media were/are still being used to demonstrate activism. The "#BlackLivesMatter" is a social media campaign against all forms of injustices, systemic racism, violence, and police brutality meted out to African Americans. This campaign has been sustained through social media activism that has rallied African Americans into a community of activists demanding a better life and equal rights and justice for African Americans living in the United States of America and all over the continents. In 2013, after the acquittal of George Zimmerman, for the murder of seventeen-year-old Trayvon Martin, in Florida, a group of young African Americans (Patrisse Cullors, Alicia Garza, and Opal Tometi) created the hashtag #blacklivesmatter (Erson and Paul, 2016). A Facebook post by Garza titled "A Love Note to Black People" in which she said: "Our Lives Matter, Black Lives Matter" sparked off sympathy for the way black people and indeed people of color are being treated all over the world (Rickford, 2016).

The hashtag, '#BlackLivesMatter' has been used to further blacks' causes; it has also become a rallying philosophy and sing-song in the quest for justice for blacks killed or abused by policemen, or racially abused by people of other races across the world. The story of George Floyd that was manhandled by white police personnel, leading to his sudden death is a case in point. The hashtag"#I Can't Breathe" was used on social media in the wake of his death to create awareness of the need to sustain the global campaign that 'the Black lives matter. Social media platforms such as Twitter, Facebook, Snapchat, etc were continuously used to activate and sustain the mass action.

In Nigeria, two prominent events chronicled social media activism; the Chibok girls' abduction and the EndSARS protest. Both events took activism to different levels—the former was conducted peacefully offline, while the latter turned a theater of arson and killings offline. However, within the digital domain, the two events were a success as far as digital activism is concerned. The 'bring back our girls' (#BBOG) campaign made an in-road in the use of social media in mobilizing people for mass action. Through consistent use of the #BBOG, the conveners of the campaign were able to draw the attention of the international community and mounted pressure on the Nigerian government to rescue the abducted Chibok girls (Dambo et al, 2020). The #EndSARS was a social media campaign and "mass protest against police brutality in the country calling for disbanding of the Special Anti-Robbery Squad (SARS), a notorious unit of the police force with a long record of abuses, corruption, unlawful arrest, detention, and extrajudicial killings" (Okuwob, 2022, p. 5).

The #EndSARS protest came at the heels of viral footage showing the SARS operative allegedly shooting a young man at Wetland Hotel in Ughelli, Delta State. This action sparked an "outcry on social media against SARS using the hashtag #EndSARS. By 8 October, demonstrations associated with this hashtag had begun to increase in size and number throughout Nigeria, peaking at 26 demonstration events on 13 October" (ACLED, 2021, p.1). On October 20, the Nigerian Military shot at the peaceful demonstrators who had gathered at Lekki Tollgate in Lagos, allegedly killing some of the demonstrators. The footage of the incident went viral on the social media and attracted global condemnation.

Conceptualizing Social Media, Activism, and Social Media Activism

Academic disciplines such as Communication, Public Relations, Psychology, Sociology, and Computer Science have been at the forefront of crystallizing frameworks that underpin social media research and its epistemologies. These disciplines have also produced several scholarly articles focusing on different aspects of social media, thereby deepening the call for an interdisciplinary approach to understanding a phenomenon. Social media definition is fluid, and to avoid any definitional dilemma, the author adopts a definition provided by Achor and Nnabuko (2019), which is a synthesis of different definitional approaches: "Social media are platforms and applications on the Internet that allow people, individuals, organizations and their publics, etc assemble online to converse, exchange information, opinions and share knowledge through open interactions, collaborations, and harnessing collective intelligence(p.10). This definition shows that social media is Internet-based or online, promotes social interaction, allows users to broadcast interpersonal communication to large audiences (Bayer, Triệu and Ellison, 2020), and derives value mainly from user-generated content (Carr and Hayes, 2015). Different typologies of social media exist: social networks, social blogs, weblogs, microblogging, podcast, Internet forums, picture, and video sharing platforms, etc (Kaplan and Haenein, 2010; Achor 2017; Achor, Nwachukwu, and Nkwocha, 2015). In Nigeria, the social media networks or platforms widely used include Facebook, Twitter, Instagram, WhatsApp, Google Plus, YouTube, and blogs (Achor 2017, Achor and Nnabuko, 2019; Nwodu, Ezeoke & Ezeaka, 2021).

What then is activism or social media activism? Activism is a highly discussed phenomenon in research papers and transcends disciplinary boundaries. It is a generic term that describes actions or activities used by a group or individuals geared towards changing a situation, society, or issue through advocacy, protest, and other civil means of showing collective action against something, policies, government programs, etc. The term has acquired cross-disciplinary interpretations; there are sociology, political science, and public relations perspectives. Of importance in these perspectives is their adoption of a common paradigm in advocating for change. In sociology, activism refers to collective action and a sequence of performances and contentious approaches used by ordinary people to change or advance social issues (Tilly, 2004; Chon, and Park, 2020). Sociologist, Diani (1992) defined activism as "networks of information interactions between a plurality of individuals, groups and/or organizations, engaged in political or cultural conflicts, on the basis of shared collective identities"(p.1). Information interactions facilitate information exchange and transform opinions and belief systems into collective action; by so doing, people of like-minds collectively root for change. From a political scientist's point of view, activism is seen as a kind of participation by a mass of people in cause-oriented activities, which is traditionally different from citizen-oriented participation related to elections and parties (Tarrow, 2011; Tufekci & Wilson, 2012).

In representative democracies, activism may focus on a particular policy issue, or concern whereby people voice opposition and express political grievances through collective action (Norris, 2004; Meyer, 2015). Activism, from public relations perspective, refers to a "process by which groups of people exert pressure on organizations or other institutions to change policies, practices, or conditions the activists find problematic" (Smith, 2005, p. 5). It pursues understanding by cultivating relationships using symmetrical communication with activist publics. Public relations professionals can leverage on values of activism by seeing the activists as co-creators of understanding that activates organizational-public relationships. Public relations plays a crucial role in a turbulent and polarized environment by scanning the environment for issues that can give rise to misunderstanding and promptly responding to issues and perceptions of the activist publics (Ciszek, 2015; Uysal and Yang, 2013). From the above cross-disciplinary definitions, activism has the following features:(1) contentious issues, (2) collective action, (3) solidarity or collective identity, and (4) an effort to solve problems using communication (Chon, and Park, 2020).

Social media activism is a typology of activism that uses media and communication technologies for social and political movements. The purpose is to create awareness through media of communication. Social media have been integrated into tools of activism because of their "interactive features and widespread adoption, users can quickly disseminate information and rally supporters" (Ed Carrasco, 2012, p. 12). It is seen as a tool for grassroots activists to spread information that is not in the mainstream media. Social media has evolved as a strong tool for activism, offering like-minded people the opportunity to gather online and initiate a collective action to advance causes. Specifically, social media activism is "a form of protest or advocacy for a cause that uses social media channels. Some scholars have argued that digital activism is not a substitute for offline activism (Freelon, Marwick and Kreiss(2020). Many reasons have been advanced for this line of thought. One of the reasons anchor on the difference in the structure and intents of both digital/online and offline activism; each is designed to appeal to different people and interests (Greijdanus & Postmes, 2020). People who hold such thoughts believe that majority of those who participate in online activism might not be activists; rather they are either privileged to have access to digital platforms or digital natives/netizens who follow trending hashtags to show solidarity. Another reason is that online activists may be reluctant to take their activism to the physical space (such as mass protest and other forms of civil disobedience). A counterargument is that the purpose of activism whether carried out online or offline is to champion a cause, and draw attention to or support for it.

The affordances of social media platforms help to project/promote a protest. Affordance can be explained from two perspectives. The first perspective describes how users perceive different social media sites' features that afford diverse kinds of activities (Andrew, Nicole, Cliff, and Donghee, 2011; Nicole and Vitak, 2015; Zhao, Lampe and Ellison, 2016). A Facebook user can perceive a status update as the user's ability to broadcast to many audiences (followers, friends) from their contacts. The second perspective posits that "the affordances people associate with a platform are determined by multiple sources, the design characteristics of the platform, observation of how others use the platform, and previous personal experience may all play a role in defining what affordances people perceive" (Zhao, Lampe and Ellison, 2016, p.97). The affordance perspective is expanded here to include the features, contexts, and tools, available on a single social media site or a mix of social media platforms/networks that help users meet information or communication needs and objectives. These affordance perspectives practically help social media researchers and scholars explain the epistemologies of social media and ontological underpinnings of civil movements (i.e. protests).

Affordances such as the synchronicity of message exchange (Bayer, Triệu and Ellison, 2020), persistence ((DeVito et al, 2017; Evans et al 2016), multi-access to information, information sharing, instant delivery of message/reply and reach to mass heterogeneous audiences, and mass appeal help sustain mass action (Fox and McEwan, 2017; Treem and Leonardi, 2013). The affordances offer social media users the ability to do lots of activities that were not possible in mainstream media. The EndSARS campaigners leveraged these affordances to enlist the support of activists, social media influencers, and celebrity entertainers (musicians, actors), to join the protest.

Mapping/Evaluating Social media Ecology of #EndSARS Online Activism

Several approaches to understanding media ecology exist in the literature. The common denominator of the approaches is the designation of media as environment, technology as environment, or technology as media. Marshall McLuhan provided the idea that birthed media ecology, which Neil Postman in 1968 conceptualized as media environments that are prevalent either in the past or present (Jana and, Khan,2018; McLuhan and McLuhan,2011). According to Postman, it deals with the interaction between technology and human beings, while the interaction defines the culture and the existence of humankind in a media-saturated environment (Logan, 2016). In media/communication studies, three dominant paradigms are used to explicate the term: an approach to media analysis, the study of media environments, and a research field within the broad media discipline (Lunceford, 2012; Van Den Edee, 2016; Anton, 2017; Strate, 2017). The media analysis paradigm describes media ecology as "the means and technologies of communication media rather than the messages themselves". The main emphasis here is that communication media creates a distinctive cultural milieu that provides broad paradigms of understanding. As a study of the media environment, it anchors on the idea that technology, techniques, and modes of information play a leading role in human affairs. The chapter adopts these approaches in explicating social media ecology.

Social media ecology, within the standpoint of #EndSARS online activism, reveals that the Internet and other social-mediated platforms build a community of like-minded individuals bonded by a collective intention. This is consistent with future research in communication technologies and the phenomenon of ecosystemic society. The chapter accepts that the Internet is an environment comparable to physical reality, and each social media platform is regarded as an environment where humans metaphorically live and advance social change. This assumption aligns with some scholars' argument that "the media ecology of the Internet and the ecosystemic economy point toward a future in which the whole of society organizes itself around ecosystemic principles" (Ruotsalainen and Heinonen, 2015, p.8). This assumption, according to Ruotsalainen and Heinonen (2015), sees "this kind of society as an organic whole, where different actors and spheres of life are intertwined in novel ways through the information flows of the digital media" (p.8).

In the broader sphere of social media ecology, social media networks/sites are seen as an environment, where users engage each other and the government institutions through speeches, and comments on issues that the mainstream media may not be able to grant unbridled access to. Each of the social media platforms is an environment with peculiar features that allow people to converse, share ideas/opinions and openly oppose or criticize government policies, programs, actions, and inactions(Castel,2012). The communication technologies within the social media ecological interpretations represent media. McLuhan's philosophy of the 'medium is the message' and the notion of a 'global village' is advanced through social media activism (McLuhan, 1994; Ruotsalainen and Heinonen, 2015). The epistemology of social networks explains the changes "concerning the new online social media".

The digital sphere, particularly the social media domain, has redefined how people exercise their citizenship in a contemporary networked society. Social media activism has become a tool for citizens to willingly participate in collective actions that call for change. The right to protest is becoming more visible and realizable in social media without undue interference from the government or its agents. Hence, the ecology of social media transcends the technologies that facilitate digital conversations but aligns itself to a digital/media domain (new environment) where people live and conduct daily activities. This metaphorical environment has become important in settling socio-political and economic issues for the peaceful resolution of conflicts. Despite being criticized as a harbinger of misinformation/disinformation, the social media ecology is paradoxically an environment where truth can be promoted. During the EndSARS protests, social media was used to promote truth or reasons for the protests, and also used in disseminating photo-shopped videos and pictures intended to cause more panic.

As a digital environment, the social media ecology has its language or lexicons comprising coded words and symbols such as "# hashtag" and emojis, etc. Netizens use them to communicate and draw attention to an issue. In addition, the author adopts the Social Construction of Technology (SCoT) in deepening the discourse on the social media ecology. The SCoT explores the communication that exists between or among humans and how technology and human interactions and activities affect technology (Bijker, 1995 cited in Ruotsalainen and Heinonen, 2015). The philosophical thought around social media ecology is not only premised on the metaphorical realm (environment)—where users perform lots of daily activities to advance human relationships but leverage the affordances of technologies to mediate interactions (Anton, 2016; Anton,2017). Social media is not just seen as a technology but a digital environment where people are less restricted to exercise certain freedom that was hitherto impossible in the physical space or mainstream media. The EndSARS protesters exploited these features: they lived, woke up in social media ecology, and conducted activities (like signing up petitions, sharing coded signs and information) that gave the online social movement the needed visibility and acceptance. Paradoxically, social media ecology promoted hate and misinformation that stoked the flames of violence. The social media platforms were used by unscrupulous protesters to share photo-shopped images of policemen brutalizing people even as the protests were going on across major cities. Protest artifacts such as banners, hashtags, emojis, and insignia that are associated with mass action are stored in the social media ecology. For example, the photos of the Nigerian Flag dripping with the blood of protesters shot at the Lekki toll gate during #EndSARS is an artifact of that incident.

In mapping the social media ecology of "EndSARS", there is need also to logically explore data activism that foregrounds the main facts of the protest. In the build-up to the #EndSARS campaign, data activism helped the original conveners in articulating their demands. Those activists, in the opinion of Ganesh and Hankey (2015), engaged in "information activism"—the use of data to advocate for social and political change. The activists used data generated from the Nigeria Police Commission, and Nigeria Police Force to make a case for police reforms. Data indicated the inadequate number of personnel police the nation and poor remuneration of the personnel, particularly those within the rank and file. Data activism is a facet in the domain of digital activism (Milan and van der Velden, 2016) and specifically falls within the realms of big data and datafication. As an aspect of digital activism, data activism is a "heuristic tool for the study of new forms of political participation and civic engagement in the age of datafication" (Milan and van der Velden, 2016, p.57). Within the realm of civil society, Milan and van der Velden (2016) argue that "data activism supports the emergence of novel epistemic cultures of making sense of data as a way of knowing the world and turning it into a point of intervention and generation of data countercultures" (p.57).

Methods and Epistemology Leanings

A mixed-method (of quantitative and qualitative data sourced from a semi-structured questionnaire, focus group discussions, and interviews) was adopted. Based on this method, the author adopts a three-fold classification underlying research epistemology: positivist, interpretative and critical paradigms (Rehman and Alharty, 2016) in the presentation of ideas and arguments that philosophically underpin the purpose of the chapter. These epistemology paradigms are not independently presented but are embedded into the preceding sections and those following after this. A total of 12 social media activists and influencers were interviewed on the issues that birthed EndSARS protests across major cities. Their views helped in articulating and understanding the socio-political environmental realities acting as strains and contributing to the phenomenon of social and political disorder in Africa and Nigeria. A Questionnaire containing closed-ended questions worded in a 5-point Likert scale was administered to 45 purposively selected communication practitioners: media and public relations practitioners. The questionnaire sought their opinions on how to frame contentious political issues in social media ecology for a non-violent mass movement—vis-à-vis the EndSARS debacle. Three sessions of web-based focus group discussion (FGD) comprising 4 persons per session were conducted using some active EndSARS protesters. The protesters were identified via their Facebook accounts and an invitation to participate in a web-based discussion was sent to them via messenger. The FGDs sought protesters' perceptions of the #EndSARS protests. From the transcripts, a similar pattern of meanings and expressions was identified, coded into themes as espoused by (Braun and Clark, 2014; 2019); the themes were analyzed and used to interpret or buttress the epistemological and ontological underpinning of social media activism and ecology of #EndSARS protests. The empirical results were ingrained into the discussions of various sections of the chapter.

Strains Contributory to Activism in Developing Countries: The Case of EndSARS Protest/ Mass Mobilization

Historically, the flame of activism is ignited by a desire to change situations adjudged to be inimical to the development of a nation. Every nation or region of the world has peculiar problems that hinder its development. Some of the problems are created by sheer ignorance, poor political leadership, exploitive policies, and repressive governments. Others include weak institutions, wrong policy formulation, racism and nepotism, and outright wickedness of political and non-political actors in the affairs of government. Against this backdrop, the author presents the views of social media activists and influencers interviewed on the causes of activism, including the EndSARS protest. Their views and those of the focus group discussants were combined with literature positions for a balanced discussion.

Before the advent of the Internet, activism in Africa and indeed developing countries was characterized by demonstrations and protests, merely championed by students and a few known social cum political activists, who lacked unbridled space to criticize perceived ills in the society. However, the Arab Spring became an eye-opener and ignited the flame of a new wave of media activism that has almost spread to other African countries. This was made possible by social media—which gave users unbridled access to information and other affordances (Nicole and Vitak, 2015; Donoso and Ribbens, 2020; Bucher and Helmond, 2018). From the opinions of social media activists interviewed, activism is triggered by situations that needed to be changed or challenged for the betterment of society. A synthesis of their opinions portrays Africa's political landscape as one littered with corruption, poor leadership, lack of good governance and political accountability, and lack of strong institutions to drive development. One media activist observed thus: *"These problems had given rise to other ills confronting Africa and developing countries, like Nigeria"* (Author's Personal Communication: Interview, 2021). Nigeria as well as other African countries had a chequered history of military interregnums that almost crippled their growth and national economies (Achor and Moguluwa, 2012). According to one of the social media influencers/activists, *"The dark days of the military regimes were harrowing for the civilian populace. The mainstream media were more or less a 'caged media'—whose reportage was heavily censored; media* *practitioners were always in palpable fear of being arrested by the henchmen of the juntas" (*Author's Personal communication: Focus group discussion, 2021).

Media activism during those dark days was restrained compared to this era of civilian rule.

Unfortunately, a few activists who had the guts to dare the military governments were inhumanly treated: some journalists and activists were imprisoned for months or years, and those who were not fortunate enough to gain freedom from incarceration, paid the supreme price—death. Presently in Nigeria, much has not changed in terms of the perceived anomalies that led to military incursions into politics and governance: there is still corruption, mismanagement of economic resources, poor leadership, etc. Expounding on the above observation, an activist argued thus: *"Perhaps, what seems to have changed in the fight against corruption is the establishment of EFCC and ICPC (Economic and Financial Crimes Commission; Independent Corrupt Practices Commission), and enactment of laws aimed at bringing those who have stolen public funds to justice"* (Author's Personal communication: Interview, November 2021*)*. However, these two institutions appear to be weak or selective in prosecuting some categories of allegedly corrupt individuals.

Other governmental institutions, ministries, departments, and agencies that have the mandate to implement laws, government policies, and programs also appear to be weak and pay lip service to their respective duties. The security operatives, such as the Police and Army are not left out in the web of corruption; they are accused of extortion, extrajudicial killings, torture, and harassment of innocent citizens. This situation made a social media influencer/activist comment thus: *"The eye-service or rather lip service approach to tackling these vices will always make activists demand accountability from erring institutions and individuals"* (Author's personal communication: Interview, 2021).

As rightly documented, the EndSARS protest was caused by the above-verified accusations, particularly those perpetrated by operatives of SARS (Report of Lekki Incident Investigation of 20th October 2020, 2021). In 2016, and 2018 reports were rife of how SARS operatives were manhandling innocent Nigerians at the slightest provocation. Concerned Nigerians called for the disbandment of SARS then to save Nigerians, but the Police authorities failed to take proactive steps, rather they decided to rename the squad (unit) to SWAT (Special Weapon and Tactical unit). Man, when pushed to the wall will revolt and fight back—the people fought back by demanding justice. The social structures and the entire society have not fared well either, they are held down by nauseating ills and moral decadence. Other factors that trigger activism in developing countries include brazen abuse of the constitutional provisions, disregard for rule of law, highhandedness of state actors in relating with citizens, and abuse of power. Empirical evidence from social media influencers and ecologists interviewed indicates that Africa's political leaders, abuse power and pay less attention to democratic norms and culture (Author's Personal communication: Interview, November 2021). A media activist commented thus: *"The present Buhari-led administration is renowned for flagrant abuse of the constitution and a hater of rule of law"*. Against this backdrop, activist organizations (rights groups, civil society organizations) have been at the forefront of campaigning against some of the ills mentioned above. The mainstream media have not given them the right environment to function effectively due to ownership structure, regulations, and political interference.

Epistemological and Ontological Underpinnings of Social Media Activism and Ecology

Social media sites or platforms used during the EndSARS protest can be seen as epistemic tools for advancing and curating knowledge. How can one promote knowledge beyond the traditional and linear process of sending and receiving information? The answer to this question will be provided in two broad perspectives: the literature-based perspective and the empirical-evidence perspective, which is derived from the opinions of interviewees. From the existing literature perspective, the structure of various social media platforms, their affordances, and distinct utilization in protest situations play remarkable roles in the way the epistemologies of activism are understood. First, they mark a transition from a more rigid traditional paradigm to a fluid/technologically mediated paradigm of generating and sharing knowledge. The knowledge sought and shared in social media about activism is done through what Nekmat et al (2015) refer to as connective-collective activities. Social media activism is predicated on collective action and needs communicative action. Four major ways connective-collective activities are carried out in social media include commenting, relaying information received, uploading materials, and affiliating. These activities greatly help to recruit and mobilize individuals for activism (Bennett and Segerberg, 2013).

Every form of activism is triggered by contentious issues (Bennett and Segerberg, 2013) and social media facilitates discussion of the issues, thereby making "it easier for users to express personal opinions and organize collective activities" (Chon and Park, 2020, p.76). For example, Facebook users can post their experiences of police brutality in their story status or newsfeeds; the messages posted may spread online as people share them with their friends, thereby igniting collective actions. Unfortunately, some of the messages are not verified before they are shared on social media networks—such action is susceptible to falsehood. This situation has made critics make unpleasant observations about the epistemology of social media activism and ecology. For example, some critics have wrongly described the epistemic aims of social media sites as "an 'epistemic apocalypse' narrative" (Habgood-Coote, 2021, p1). An Epistemic Apocalypse narrative argues that the traditional knowledge-generating practices and production are seriously undermined by technologies associated with social media (Habgood-Coote, 2021).

Exponents of this narrative specifically anchor their views on the technological epistemic vice of social media in selecting, filtering, and algorithmic boosting some type of content over others and circulating a large volume of false and unverified posts. This narrative does not promote civil or group ideology for social media activism, rather there should be a call for a better narrative that depicts the right epistemic purpose of social media activism. This, however, calls for evidence-based knowledge from some of the actors in a protest. A critical approach to social epistemology of (social) media activism anchors on "three distinct epistemic goals, as observed by activists interviewed in the course of writing this chapter. The first is the promotion of good epistemic outcomes for users; the second goal is on promoting knowledge and truth about contentious issues within and outside social media ecology, while the third is on achieving epistemic justice.

The epistemic outcome for users of social media activism is the huge collective action against a vice achieved through social mobilization. One of the active campaigners of the #EndSARS summarized his thoughts thus: *"Through our hashtag #EndSARS, we have been able to make a collective statement that injustice to one is an injustice to all. We did this through laying the facts on the table so that young people can see reasons to protest"* (Author's Personal communication: Interview, November 2021). The process of building and validating knowledge concerning activism is to focus attention on what triggers a protest. The majority of the interviewees believe that the epistemic goal of promoting truth and knowledge about SARS operatives was achieved through social media activism. A comment by one of the activists summarizes this notion thus: *"Nigerians and indeed the whole world needed to know the true contentious issues in the way Police and Military personnel relate with civilians, particularly young people, whom they perceive better-off than them. The language the SARS operatives understand is torture, intimidation, and killing. The facts and knowledge about the EndSARS campaign are now known".*

The structure of text or language used in expressing opinions about police brutality, torture, and extrajudicial killings on social media ontologically reveals how protesters convey knowledge and meaning underlying their desire for a change. The ontological evaluations of their expressions show a dire and urgent need to act fast to salvage an institution or country heading to the woods. Social media activism uses different forms of language, hashtags, and emojis to convey knowledge, which has implications for information management. The EndSARS protests had a common theme, which is "ending police brutality and reform of Nigerian Police Force". The ontological underpinning of "#EndSARS" online protests is expressed within the rubric of knowledge sharing and the philosophy behind the language (text, emojis) used in conveying messages that support the call for disbandment of SARS and other demands of the protesters. Expounding further on the epistemology of social networks, Bavaresco (2014), submits that "social networks act in the public sphere and the institution of democratic practices in social development, in establishing the agenda with issues more inclusive and representative of society" (p.1). This public sphere, unlike the traditional mainstream media sphere, offers the citizens a fair and democratic opportunity to participate in the decision-making process. The epistemology of social networks describes the changes concerning the new (online) media and their plural agenda setting as opposed to the conventional or unique agenda of the mainstream media.

Philosophy of Activism/ #EndSARS Movement

The social philosophy of social media activism tries to understand what motivates activists to engage in this kind of activism. It also explains the epistemic notions towards creating and sharing information concerning contentious issues. For example, people ignored other means of sharing their opinions on the contentious issues that led to the EndSARS protest but opted for the use of social media. The philosophy behind this unanimous decision hinge on the fact that social media offers them (both known and unknown individuals) a platform for identity formation, recognition, and unhindered voice to participate in a mass action/protest. The critical mass of the people distributed diverse information relating to contentious issues about SARS. By creating and sharing content about SARS, many people joined the #EndSARS campaign. People felt comfortable using social media knowing full well that government interferences would be minimal since the government has less control of the digital space.

One reason that explains the EndSARS movement could be premised on the philosophy that "when a man is consistently pushed to the wall, he is bound to react violently". The youths' elasticity of patience was overstretched leaving them with no other option than to fiercely express their anger. The government's failure to adopt proactive crisis management approaches to address the EndSARS concerns made the issue metamorphose into a full-blown crisis that had smeared the image and reputation of Nigeria. A philosophical lesson behind the #EndSARS movement hinges on a demonstration of "freedom from ethno-religious tensions that usually plague the framing of Nigeria's domestic security and political issues. Young Nigerians in the six geopolitical zones united around a common goal to end police intimidation, oppression, and brutality" (ACLED, 2021, par.8). #EndSARS protest movement demonstrated the possibility of having an accountable and transparent civil society that could be responsive to the needs of its citizens, particularly, young people. The EndSARS campaign showed the strength of the youth who represents half of the registered voters in Nigeria; it showed the need for more youths to use their civil rights and political power to speak out against wrongs and insist on change that serves the general interest of Nigerians.

Bridging the Communication Gaps that Trigger Violent Mass Protest in Nigeria

Beyond the social vices or factors that triggered the EndSARS protest, there are also communication gaps that helped to levitate the crisis. Among the gaps is Police authorities' reluctance to act sensibly and proactively communicate what has been done to investigate the allegations leveled against the operatives of SARS (Lagos State Judicial Panel of Inquiry on Restitution for Victims of SARS Related Abuses and Other Matters, 2021). The grievous allegations ought to have been promptly investigated as a way to manage trust issues between the police and the citizenry and also douse the brewing tension. Announcing a change of name from SARS to SWAT is a lopsided linear approach to passing information; this negates effective communication with the targeted audience. Such public relations stunt, however, was a wrongly conceived strategy that lacked professional and research inputs. In crisis communication, communicating with the critical stakeholders is important—the stakeholders must be carried along in any communication plan/effort designed to respond to the crisis (Achor, 2019).

Against this backdrop, public relations and communication strategies are proffered on how to manage issues and forestall violent protests. The author blends the opinions of communication experts (surveyed for the purpose of attaining the goals of this chapter) with extant literature views on crisis management. Six main items are listed (see Table1 below): inclusive communication, use of trust-building mechanisms(open-mindedness, engagement/dialogic communication, participatory communication, collaboration); situational theory of solving the problem(problem recognition, constraint recognition, and involvement recognition); recognition of offline protest coordinators; desisting from clampdown of activists, and stopping of online surveillance as strategies for bridging communication gaps during mass actions and to forestall violent protests in future. More than two-thirds (33 or 73.3%) of the communication experts advocated the use of an 'inclusive communication approach' in handling highly contentious issues (such as allegations leveled against SARS). Inclusive communication is described by the researcher as a communication effort that includes every stakeholder who is affected by an issue or crisis. The use of trust-building mechanisms (being open-minded, prompt engagement with relevant stakeholders) is recommended as a solution to bridging communication gaps. The EndSARS campaign attracted diverse stakeholders because of the gravity of the alleged crimes committed by SARS personnel. The stakeholders included known human rights organizations, individual rights activists, and social media influencers. They were among the first identifiable groups that called the attention of the Inspector General of Police to the atrocities committed by operatives of SARS.

Table 1 presents descriptive statistics of strategies for bridging communication gaps/strains that will help to reduce violent protest in developing countries, particularly Nigeria that witnessed a violent protest following the shooting of unarmed protesters at Lekki tollgate in Lagos. The strategies were carefully distilled from literature and themes derived from the analysis of interview and FGDs transcripts. Basically, the communication practitioners/scholars (respondents) were asked to indicate their level of agreement on a 5-point scale from 1= strongly disagree to 5 = strongly disagree for each of the strategies or items as shown in the table 1. Results of the analysis show that a strong agreement to each of the strategic variables (e.g. inclusive communication (M=3.78, StD = 2.307); use of trust-building mechanisms (M = 3.62, StD=2.3014); open-mindedness (M=3.51, StD=2.292); engagement/dialogic communication (M = 3.71, StD = 2.324); participatory communication (M = 3.60, StD = 2.300); collaboration (M=3.72, StD = 2.352). Other variables/strategies had the following results: situational theory of problem solving (M= 3.80, StD = 2.351), problem recognition (M= 3.81, StD = 2.364), constraint recognition (M = 3.72, StD = 2.306), involvement recognition (M = 3.80, StD = 2.351); recognition and offline protest

Table 1. Descriptive statistics of strategies for bridging communication gaps/strains to reduce violent protest

Strategies	Mean(M)	Standard Deviation(StD)
Inclusive communication	3.78	2.30731
Use of trust-building mechanisms	3.62	2.30142
*Open-mindedness	3.51	2.29211
*Engagement/dialogic communication	3.71	2.32421
*Participatory communication	3.60	2.30050
*Collaboration	3.72	2.35210
Situation theory of problem sSolving	3.80	2.35100
*Problem recognition	3.81	2.36423
*Constraint recognition	3.72	2.30632
*Involvement recognition	3.80	2.35100
Recognition and offline protest coordinators	3.71	2.32421
Desist from clampdown on activist	3.80	2.35100
Online surveillance	3.71	2.32421

Source: (Author, 2021)

coordinators (M = 3.71, StD = 2.324), desist from clampdown on activists (M = 3.80, StD = 2.351), online surveillance (M = 3.71, StD = 2.324).

Situation Theory of Problem Solving (STOPS) argues that a person's communicative action is purposive and is intended to solve a problem (Chon and Park, 2020). Expanding on this notion, Kim and Sriramesh (2009), believe that the purpose of activism is achieved if activists' efforts are channeled towards solving contentious issues through communication behaviors. For this reason, STOPS envisages that a person's communicative behavior is through situational motivation and has a background in problem-solving. Applying the variables of STOPS in solving violent protests in developing countries, government and its agencies or activist organizations should be able to identify the antecedent issues that had increased the need for situational motivation for communicative action in problem-solving (Shin and Han, 2016). Based on this, three perceptual variables underpin STOPS: problem recognition, constraint recognition, and involvement recognition. Activism is premised on an individual's discernment of a problematic situation; for example, persistent intimidation and police brutality or political crisis.

The STOPS conceptualizes problem recognition as "a perceptual discrepancy between expected and experienced states in a given situation that produces an uncomfortable feeling of badness-of-fit that one experiences in living" (Kim, Gruing and Ni,2010, p.128). Constraint recognition is the obstacles and restrictions faced by decision-makers in order to solve the problem. STOPS aligns its conceptualization of constraint recognition to the situational theory of publics, which holds that: "people perceive that there are obstacles in a situation that limit their ability to do anything about the situation" (Grunig, 1997, p. 10). The concept of involvement recognition is further expanded to connote the perceived connection between an individual and the problem. However, the situational theory of problem-solving argues that "the perceived connection of oneself to the situation triggers individuals' communicative actions" (Chon and Park, 2020, p.76); moreover, a group effort to solve a problem is achieved through communicative action or efforts.

SOLUTIONS AND RECOMMENDATIONS

The value system regulates the ethical behaviors of an individual and holds that "people should be treated with respect and dignity", and accorded equal rights and justice. The attitude and behavior of SARS personnel toward their victims are disrespectful to human dignity and infringe on their fundamental human rights. There is a need for moral reevaluation and reconstruction of values through philosophical approaches and public relations strategies. The philosophical approach will try to provide answers to "why people do what they do and in what order they choose to do them". Public relations strategies are designed to eliminate or reduce the philosophical factors underpinning people's unethical behaviors when given the responsibility of superintending over an office or establishment. Public relations approaches are meant to create and sustain mutual understanding between an organization and its stakeholders.

To prevent or reduce violent protests across Africa and indeed developing countries, the author aligns its recommendations with those of the Report of Lekki Incident Investigation of 20th October 2020. Governments across African countries should stop arresting activists or accusing them of instigating civil disobedience whenever they criticize their policies, actions, and inactions. The right to protest is a constitutional right and must be respected by the government or its agents. State agents should desist from online surveillance and monitoring of activists' social media accounts. Such behaviors do not promote healthy government-civil relations rather it widens the trust gap between leaders and the led. Government should purge itself of corruption and stop double standards in dealing with matters of corruption and other criminal acts committed by its officials.

FUTURE RESEARCH DIRECTIONS

The paradox of protest in championing causes needs further scrutiny as people continue to search for a better approach to tackle the bane of development in developing countries. The spate of violent protests across African countries has not helped in resolving most issues that trigger them; rather it has ignited the flames of destruction. One wonders why the essence of social media activism should be disrupted by uncivil and unruly behaviors of digital natives, who are at the forefront of protests. Violence never solves a problem. Scholarship on activism identifies two extreme ideologies: the leftist and rightist paradigms (Atkinson, and Berg, 2016). The leftist ideology adopts strategies or approaches that downplay some of the issues that ignite agitations and protests, while the rightists are harder and more forceful in their approach, and use strong appeals to buttress their stand on issues. None of these paradigms has resolved the causes of protest. For this reason, the chapter advocates a middle-course paradigm that consistently pursues truth and peaceful digital civic engagement with the youths. Public relations strategies with a blend of philosophical thoughts can bridge the gap between the youths and government in times of crisis or no crisis. Researchers are advised to explore the role of public relations in activism, protest, and post-protest situations. Dialogic theory can be explored to advance the citizen-government relationship, while social media affordances can be leveraged to create the right epistemic value of media ecology.

CONCLUSION

The bane of development in developing countries is legion. Oftentimes, people show their dissatisfaction over this situation by criticizing governments or engaging in protests to demand a change. The use of social media to mobilize people for mass protest is gaining ground across the world, particularly in Africa, where there are repressive governments and media environments. Like-minded individuals use social media to champion cause-oriented activities through activism. Through the epistemological and ontological interpretations of social media activism, the chapter contextualizes social media ecology and how issues are framed by activists and social media influencers. The social media ecology is "an environment where people act and live their lives, and through which reality is perceived" (Ruotshalainen and Heinonen 2015, p.3). This environment as explained in the chapter has its own culture and language, which users leverage to promote causes. The EndSARS protest or campaign reveals how the youths can begin to make their voices heard, and consistently advance cause-oriented activities that protect and respect the sanctity of human lives and dignity.

Championing causes begins when a person/group of persons identifies an issue or situation that would impact negatively on the society or mass of the people and subsequently draws attention to it by creating awareness through advocacy and use of other civil means such as protests and rallies. The issues that trigger activism are always contentious and tied to societal values or erosion of ethical values. Value can be viewed from different perspectives. One perspective that mirrors the thesis of this chapter is the ethics perspective, which indicates that value is measured by the extent to which an action or something is important and affects the sensibility of the public. It can also be seen as "broad preferences concerning appropriate courses of actions or outcomes".

REFERENCES

Achor, P. N., & Nnabuko, J. (2019). Quasi-gatekeeping and quasi-gatewatching: The dual role of public relations practitioners in the social media domain. *Canadian Journal of Communication*, *44*(1), 5–24. doi:10.22230/cjc.2019v44n1a3272

Achor, P.N. (2020). Endsars protest: Counting the gains, casualties or losses. *Emergency Digest*.

Achor, P. N., & Moguluwa, S. C. (2012). *Political marketing: Marketing, communication and politics*. Oktek Publishers.

Achor, P.N. (2019). Reputation crisis communication: Beyond what you know. *Spokespersons Digest: A Hand Journal of Public Relations & Communication*.

Ana, T. A., & Nogueira, S. (2018). Epistemology, methods and theories of communication in the big data era: A critical panorama of social media research. *Comunicacão e Sociedade*, *33*, 167–181. doi:10.17231/comsoc.33(2018).2912

Andrade, P. (2013). Sociological ontology of the digital public sphere: The case of Web 2.0/3.0. *Comunicação e Sociedade*, *23*, 202–216. doi:10.17231/comsoc.23(2013).1622

Andrew, D., Smock, N. B., Ellison, C. L., & Donghee, Y. W. (2011). Facebook as a toolkit: A uses and gratification approach to unbundling feature use. *Computers in Human Behavior*, *27*(6), 2322–2329. doi:10.1016/j.chb.2011.07.011

Anton, C. (2017). Media ecological orientations to philosophy and philosophical problems. *The Review of Communication*, *17*(4), 224–239. doi:10.1080/15358593.2017.1367830

Anton, C. (2016). On the roots of media ecology: A micro-history and philosophical clarification. *Philosophies*, *1*(2), 126–132. doi:10.3390/philosophies1020126

Arriagada, A., & Ibáñez, F. (2020). You need at least one picture daily, if not, you're dead: Content creators and platform evolution in the social media ecology. *Social Media + Society*, *6*(3). Advance online publication. doi:10.1177/2056305120944624

Armed Conflict Location & Event Data Project (ACLED). (2021). *Lessons from the #EndSARS movement in Nigeria*. Retrieved November 6, 2021 from acleddata.com/2021/02/09/lessons-from-the-endsars-movement-in-nigeria/.

Atkinson, J., & Berg, S. (2016). Right-wing activism: The next challenge for alternative media scholarship, *Activist media and biopolitics*, 117-133. https://books.openedition.org/iup/1179?lang=en

Bayer, J. B., Triệu, P., & Ellison, N. B. (2020). Social media elements, ecologies, and effects. *Annual Review of Psychology*, *71*(1), 471–497. doi:10.1146/annurev-psych-010419-050944 PMID:31518525

Bavaresco, A. (2014). Epistemology of social networks, public opinion, and theory of agenda. *Canadian Social Science*, *10*(5).

Bennett, W. L., & Segerberg, A. (2013). *The logic of connective action: Digital media and the personalization of contentious politics*. Cambridge University Press.

Bijker, W. E. (1995). *Of bicycles, bake lites, and bulbs: Toward a theory of socio-technical change*. MIT Press.

Braun, V., & Clarke, V. (2014). How to use thematic analysis with interview data. *The Counselling and Psychotherapy Research Handbook,* 183-197.

Braun, V., & Clarke, V. (2018). Using thematic analysis in counseling and psychotherapy research:A critical reflection. *Counselling & Psychotherapy Research*, *18*(2), 107–110. doi:10.1002/capr.12165

Brooker, P., Dutton, W., & Greiffenhagen, C. (2017). What would wittgenstein say about social media? *Qualitative Research Sage*, *17*(6), 610–626. Advance online publication. doi:10.1177/1468794117713058

Brown, M., Ray, R., Summers, E., & Fraistat, N. (2017). #Sayhername: A case study of intersectional social media activism. *Ethnic and Racial Studies*, *40*(11), 1831–1846. doi:10.1080/01419870.2017.1334934

Bucher, T., & Helmond, A. (2018). The affordances of social media platforms. In J. Burgess, A. Marwick, & T. Poell (Eds.), *The sage handbook of social media* (pp. 233–253). SAGE. doi:10.4135/9781473984066.n14

Cammaerts, B. (2015). Social media and activism. In *The International Encyclopedia of Digital Communication and Society* (pp. 1027–1034). Wiley-Blackwell. doi:10.1002/9781118767771.wbiedcs083

Castells, M. (2012). *Networks of outrage and hope*. Polity Press.

Chon, M., & Park, H. (2020). Social media activism in the digital age: Testing an integrative model of activism on contentious issues. *Journalism & Mass Communication Quarterly*, *97*(1), 72–97. doi:10.1177/1077699019835896

Cho, A., Byrne, J., & Pelter, Z. (2020). *Digital civic engagement by young people*. UNICEF Office of Global Insight and Policy.

Clayton, D. M. (2018). Black lives matter and the civil rights movement: A comparative analysis of two social movements in the United States. *Journal of Black Studies*, *49*(5), 1–33. doi:10.1177/0021934718764099

Dambo, T. H., Ersoy, M., Auwal, A. M., Olorunsola, V. O., Olonode, A., Arikewuyo, A. O., & Joseph, A. (2020). Nigeria's #endsars movement and its implication on online protests in Africa's most populous country. *Journal of Public Affairs*, *2583*. Advance online publication. doi:10.1002/pa.2583

DeVito, M. A., Birholtz, J., & Hancock, J. T. (2017). Platform, People, and perception using affordances to understand self-presentation on social media. In *Proceedings of the 2017 ACM Conference on Computer-supported Cooperative Work and Social Computing* (pp. 740-754). New York: ACM.

Diani, M. (1992). The concept of social movement. *The Sociological Review*, *40*(1), 1–25. doi:10.1111/j.1467-954X.1992.tb02943.x

Donoso, V., & Ribbens, W. (2010). Identity under construction. *Journal of Children and Media*, *4*(4), 435–450. doi:10.1080/17482798.2010.510011

Carrasco, Ed. (2012). *How social media has helped activism.* New Media Rockstars. Retrieved December 19, 2012 from https://www.newmedia.rockstar/how.socialmedia

Erson, M., & Paul, H. (2016, August 8). How the hashtag #Blacklivesmatter emerges: Social activism on twitter. Pew Research Center: Internet. *Sciences et Techniques (Paris).*

Freelon, D., Mcilwain, C. D., & Clark, M. D. (2016). *Beyond the hashtags: #Ferguson, #blacklivesmatter, and the online struggle for offline justice*. Center for Media & Social Impact, School of Communication, American University. Retrieved from https://cmsimpact.org/wp-content/uploads/2016/03/beyond_the_hashtags_2016.pdf

Ganesh, M. I., & Hankey, S. (2015). From information activism to the politics of data. *Fiberculture*, *26*, 275–286.

Greijdanus, P. H., & Postmes, T. (2020). The psychology of online activism and social movement: Relations between online and offline collective action. *Current Opinion in Psychology*, *35*, 49–54. doi:10.1016/j.copsyc.2020.03.003 PMID:32330859

Jana, A., & Khan, S. A. (2018). Social media's standing in McLuhan's media ecology theory: A discourse analysis. In *4th International Conference on Theory and Practice(ICTP)*. Asia Pacific Institute of Advanced Research.

Khan, A. A. (2012). The role of social media and modern technology in Arabs Spring. *Far East Journal of Psychology & Business.*, *7*(1), 56–63.

Khazraee, E., & Novak, A. N. (2018). Digitally mediated protest: Social media affordances for collective identity construction. *Social Media + Society*, *4*(1), 1–14. doi:10.1177/2056305118765740

Kim, J. N., & Sriramesh, K. (2009). A descriptive model of activism in global public relations research and practice. In K. Sriramesh,& D., Vercic (Eds.), The global public relations handbook (Rev. ed., pp. 79-97). New York, NY: Routledge.

Kitchin, R., & McArdle, G. (2016). What makes big data, big data? Exploring the ontological characteristics of 26 datasets. *Big Data & Society*, *3*(1), 1–10. doi:10.1177/2053951716631130

Lagos State Judicial Panel of Inquiry on Restitution for Victims of SARS Related Abuses and Other Matters. (2021). *Report of Lekki Incident Investigation of 20th October 2020.* Submitted to the Governor of Lagos State.

Logan, R.K. (2016). *McLuhan's philosophy of media ecology: An introduction.* Academic Press.

Lunceford, B. (2012). Posthuman visions: Creating the technologized body. *Explorations in Media Ecology, 11*(1), 7–25.

Marwick, A. E. (2013). Online identity. In J. Hartley, J. Burgess, & A. Bruns (Eds.), *A companion to new media dynamics* (pp. 355–364). doi:10.1002/9781118321607.ch23

Meyer, D. S. (2015). *The politics of protest: Social movements in America* (2nd ed.). Oxford University Press.

McLuhan, M., & McLuhan, E. (2011). *Media and Formal Cause.* NeoPoiesis Press.

Milbery, K. (2017). *Media ecology. Oxford Bibliographies Online.* https://www.oxfordbibliographies.com/view/document/obo-9780199756841/obo-9780199756841-0054.xml

Milan, S., & Van der Velden, L. (2016). The alternative epistemologies of data activism. *Digital Culture & Society*, *2*(2), 57–74. doi:10.14361/dcs-2016-0205

Nicole, B. E., & Vitak, J. (2015). Social network site affordances and their relationship to social capital processes. In S. Sundar (Ed.), *The handbook of the psychology of communication technology* (pp. 205–227). Wiley-Blackwell.

Norris, P. (2004). *Young people & political activism: From the politics of loyalties to the politics of choice?* John F. Kennedy School of Government. Retrieved from https://sites.hks.harvard.edu/fs/pnorris/Acrobat/COE%20Young%20People%20and%20Political%20Activism.pdf

Nwodu, G. B., Ezeoke, C. B., & Ezeaka, N. B. (2021). Audience perception of social media messages on security challenges in the south-east, Nigeria: Implication for audience gatekeeping. *World Journal of Innovative Research, 11*(2), 57–69.

Okuwobi, D. (2021). *Foreword to Report of Lekki Incident Investigation of 20th October, 2020.* Lagos State Judicial Panel of Inquiry on Restitution for Victims of SARS Related Abuses and Other Matters.

Pickard, V. (2015). Media activism from above and below: Lessons from the 1940s American Reform. *Journal of Information Policy.*, *5*(1), 109–128. doi:10.5325/jinfopoli.5.2015.109

Polski, M., & Gorman, L. (2012, July 10). Yuri Rozhdestvensky versus Marshall McLuhan: A triumph versus a vortex. *Explorations in Media Ecology.*, *10*(3–4), 263–278. doi:10.1386/eme.10.3-4.263_1

Polski, M. (2013). Media ecology pedagogy—Art or Techne? MEA Conference, Grand Rapids, MI.

Pfiefle, M. (2021).Social media and political activism. Huffington Post. Retrieved 14 November 2021 from https://www.huffingtonpost

Rehman, A. A., & Alharty, K. (2016). An introduction to research paradigm. *International Journal of Educational Investigation*, *3*(8), 51–59.

Rickford, R. (2016). Black Lives Matter. *New Labor Forum, 25*, 34–42. 10.1177/1095796015620171

Rotman, D., Vieweg, S., Yardi, S., Chi, E., & Preece, J. (2011). From slacktivism to activism: Participatory culture in the age of social media. CHI '11 Extended Abstracts on Human Factors in Computing Systems, 819– 822. doi:10.1145/1979742.1979543

Ruotsalainen, J., & Heinonen, S. (2015). Media ecology and the future ecosystemic society. *European Journal of Futures Research*, *3*(9), 1–10. doi:10.100740309-015-0068-7

Shin, K. S., & Han, M. (2016). The role of negative emotions on motivation and communicative action: Testing the validity of situational theory of problem-solving in the context of South Korea. *Asian Journal of Communication*, *26*(1), 76–93. doi:10.1080/01292986.2015.1083597

Smith, A. (2014). *African Americans and technology use.* Pew Research Center.

Strate, L. (2017). *Media ecology: An approach to understanding the human condition*. Peter Lang. doi:10.3726/978-1-4331-4005-1

Stefania, M., & Lonneke, V. (2016). The alternative epistemologies of data activism. *Digital Culture & Society*, *2*(2), 57–74. doi:10.14361/dcs-2016-0205

Thakora, P., & Sasib, S. (2015). Ontology-based sentiment analysis process for social media content. *Procedia Computer Science*, *53*, 199–207. doi:10.1016/j.procs.2015.07.295

Treem, J. W., & Leonard, P. M. (2013). Social media use in organizations: Exploring the affordances of visibility, editing, persistence, and association. *ACM International Communication Association*, *36*(1), 143–189. doi:10.1080/23808985.2013.11679130

Treré, E. (2018). The sublime of digital activism: Hybrid media ecologies and the new grammar of protest. *Journalism & Communication Monographs*, *20*(2), 137–148. doi:10.1177/1522637918770435

Van Den Eede, Y. (2016). Blindness and ambivalence: The meeting of media ecology and philosophy of technology. *Explorations in Media Ecology*, *15*(2), 103–112. doi:10.1386/eme.15.2.103_1

Yiran, W., Niiya, N., Mark, G., Reich, S., & Mark, W. (2015). Coming of age (digitally): An ecological view of social media use among college students. *Proceedings of CSCW'15*, 571-582.

Zhao, X., Lampe, C., & Ellison, N. B. (2016). The social media ecology: User perceptions, strategies and Challenges. Front stage on social media, 89-100.

KEY TERMS AND DEFINITIONS

Blacks Causes: Causes such as prejudices, racial abuses, discrimination, or subjugations meted out against people of African origin or actions and activities that are inimical to their advancement all over the world.

Cause-Oriented Activities: Activities or actions that promote causes or activities that people use to champion causes.

EndSARS Debacle: Tragedy associated with the EndSARS protest, which includes killings of protesters and security personnel, looting of shops, and destruction of private and public properties.

Mass Movement: A social action that requires like-minded people to stage a walk or street marches in support of or against an issue, policy, or program, etc. symbolism.

Metaphorical Environment: This symbolizes a digital environment where users of online media or social media platforms live, transact business, converse, and engage in other daily activities using digital resources.

Offline Protest: A form of protest usually carried out by people in a geographically located or physical space, compared to online protest conducted in the digital space.

Online Protest: A form of protest carried out in the online digital space in which protesters or users of online resources sign a petition, and post comments in support for or against an issue, or situation.

Social Media Affordances: Different advantages or benefits social media or the technology that facilitates their use offers to users in different contexts in the media ecosystem.

Chapter 16
Global Partnership in Technical and Vocational Education and Training:
A Pathway to Sustainable Development

James Edomwonyi Edokpolor
Benson Idahosa University, Nigeria

Innocent Otache
https://orcid.org/0000-0002-5746-5066
Federal Polytechnic, Idah, Nigeria

ABSTRACT

This chapter aims to examine the impact of global partnership in TVET (GPTVET), optimization of resources (OR), development of higher-order skills (DHOS), and equitable access to lifelong learning (EALLL) on core values of sustainable development (CVSD). A correlational design was adopted, and data were collected from a randomly selected sample of 520 TVET lecturers using a structured questionnaire. Data were analyzed using mean, standard deviation, bivariate correlational matrix, and hierarchical regression with Statistical Package for Social Sciences (SPSS) version 23.0. The results showed that GPTVET, OR, DHOS, and EALLL significantly and positively influence the accomplishment of CVSD. These findings suggest that the implementation and integration of quality TVET programme through global partnership would predict the accomplishment of CVSD.

INTRODUCTION

Since the last three decades or more, Sustainable Development (SD) has gained increased dominance in public policy discourses, with respect to sustainability issues in developing countries of the world, especially after a definition of SD was been introduced by the "Brundtland Report" in the year 1987. SD is defined as a "development that meets the needs of the present without compromising the ability

DOI: 10.4018/978-1-6684-4107-7.ch016

of future generations to meet their own needs" (World Commission on Environment and Development, 1987, p. 8). Since the "Brundtland Report" was published, which has established a landmark in activating the awareness for sustainability issues and challenges, SD has increasingly gained dominance to become one of the most salient developmental discourses today.

In September, 2015, the U.N. General Assembly launched a global SD agenda, with the theme: "The 2030 Agenda for SD", together with a set of 17 Goals, 169 sub-related targets and 230 detailed indicators, which serve as a reference point for reaching every country and community across the globe, from developed to developing countries and from rural to urban areas (UNESCO, 2020; Weiland, Hickmann, Lederer, Marquardt & Schwindenhammer, 2021). From 2015 to 2030, we are all mandated to develop our respective communities' and countries' building upon each of the 17 broad Goals, 169 sub-related targets and 230 detailed indicators, which serve as a blueprint for SD. The Sustainable Development Goals (SDGs), together with their sub-related targets and detailed indicators aimed to tackle key economic, social and environmental issues (e.g. skills gap, unemployment, dropout, insecurity, poverty, gender gap, etcetera) facing developing countries of the world. These issues and challenges are intertwined and, therefore, tackling one area can affect outcome in other areas (Nilsson, Griggs & Visbeck, 2016). Tackling each of these challenges and issues is not identified as an end to itself but as an essential catalyst for SD of developing countries.

Technical and vocational education and training (TVET), together with entrepreneurship education and training (EET), has been identified by the U.N. 2030 agenda, as represented by Goal 4 (Quality Education). Goal 4 aimed at ensuring all learners (male and female inclusive) acquire the foundational and higher-order skills (HOS); have greater and more equal chances to continually access skills training and experience core values to function effectively within the society and contribute to SD (U.N. 2017). This means that a well-implemented TVET programme would equip recipients with HOS, provide equal opportunities for all learners to continually acquire the HOS to enhance human well-being, self-esteem and freedom from social servanthood. In order to realize these obligations, there is need to adopt a different type of education programme, where all major stakeholders such as employers of labour, parents, international donor agencies and international financial institutions, among others voluntarily agree to work together to achieve a common goal.

Before and after the SDGs were launched in 2015, TVET has been facing some issues and challenges. For instance, research have shown that inadequate funding is the greatest challenge facing TVET programme in developing countries (Oviawe, 2018; Onwusa, 2021; Ramadan & Xiaohui, 2019; U.N., 2019). Governments in developing countries claim to be incapable of providing the required funds for the management of TVET (UNESCO & ILO, 2018; ILO, 2011, 2020). The argument put forward by governments concerning their inability of providing the required financial resources for the management of TVET programme is the competing demand for funds from other sectors (Akaranta, 2014; Ziderman, 2016). The financial responsibility of governments that cannot be met by mingre resources has made governments to review their involvement in funding TVET (Aryal, 2020; Center for Research and Development Services, 2018). Governments claim to be incapable of bearing full the responsibility of financing TVET programme because of its capital intensive nature (Edokpolor & Imafidon, 2017, United Nations Industrial Development Organization, 2017).

Research have shown that inadequate funding have led to inadequate provision of qualified staff and other resources such as physical facilities and instructional aids and, in turn, may affected the production of skilled and competent graduates (Ekpenyong & Edokpolor, 2015; Edokpolor, 2018). The number of qualified teachers in each specialized areas (e.g., home economics, business, agricultural science and technology, and industrial technology) are in short supply (Edokpolor, Edokpolor & Olupajimo, 2016; Kennedy, Udoetuk & Ufot, 2017). TVET graduates may not have the ability to launch a new business after graduation, due to lack of HOS, nor be able to engage in lifelong learning due to lack of self-efficacy and self-determination. This implies that TVET graduates are trained in a defective instructional environment, thus hindering them from possessing HOS to efficaciously engage in a new business and lifelong learning immediately after graduation.

Another prominent challenge facing TVET programme in developing is inadequate supply of physical facilities and instructional resources. For instance, Aworanti (2015) observed that basic physical facilities have declined in TVET programmes, both in quality and quantity. In a study by Edokpolor and Dumbiri (2019), physical facilities and instructional resources were found to be inadequate and underutilized during teaching and learning processes in TVET programmes. Edokpolor *et al.* (2016) averred that even where these physical facilities and instructional resources are inadequately provided, they are not only in bad and non-functional state but also very obsolete. The implication of these inadequacies is that graduates will not possess HOS needed to confidently engage in entrepreneurial careers and lifelong learning activities immediately after graduation.

Another conspicuous challenge faced by TVET programme in most developing countries is skills gap. For instance, Edokpolor *et al.* (2016) reported that most TVET curricula are outdated as a result require consistent renewal. Similarly, Majumdar (2011) lamented that the challenge of outdated TVET curricula appear to be a common concern, because of its salient role in contributing to skills gap or mismatch. This issue has consequently contributed to a huge dissymmetry between the skills needed by the industry and those acquired by the students at the end of the TVET programme.

Another prominent issue facing TVET programme in most developing countries is gender inequality. Generally, gender inequality has eaten deep into the fabric of most developing countries compared to developed countries (Bayeh, 2016). Specifically, gender inequality is widespread in a developing country, such as Nigeria, however the Federal Government has been putting in more effort to alleviate this situation currently ravaging the Nigerian economy (Edokpolor & Chukwuedo, 2018). Many authors have reported that there is significant differences between male and female students' access to TVET programmes in most developing nations (Ayonmike, 2014; Khan Aradi, Schwalje, Buckner & Fernandez-Carag, 2018). Studies have also shown that there is a significant difference between male and female students of TVET concerning the possession of skills required to engage in entrepreneurial career and lifelong learning (Edokpolor & Chukwuedo, 2018; Edokpolor, 2019).

These challenges and issues, as exemplified above, namely skills mismatch and gender inequalities appear to exist as a result of inadequate provision of resources. The best escape is to involve major stakeholders of TVET across the globe to invest resources that would equip students with skills to equitably engage in lifelong learning and enhance the CVSD, which in the context of this chapter involve well-being, self-esteem and freedom. The need for global partnership in TVET (GPTVET) has been documented in the U.N. SD document, where it's stipulated in the document (Partnership for the Goals, Goal 17) that there is need to strengthen the means of implementation and revitalization of the involvement of all major stakeholders across the globe to achieve SD. GPTVET has been used interchangeably with multi-stakeholder partnership in TVET (Edokpolor *et al.* 2016), cross-sector partnerships in TVET (Hazlewood, 2015), or public, private, civil society partnership in TVET (Edokpolor & Imafidon, 2019). Therefore, GPTVET must not be taken to imply public-private partnership in TVET or PPP in TVET, but a mechanism that typically operate at multiple or global scales, which have become an increasingly

Figure 1. A schematic model showing the interplay between all study variables

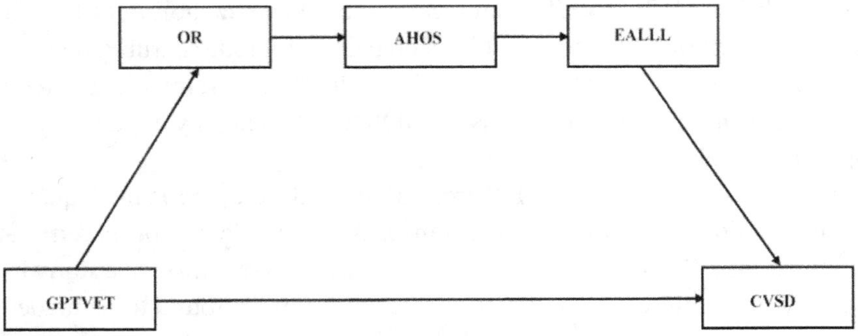

salient element of the international development feature that is strongly gaining dominance in the global (or the international) dialogue on a post-2015 SD agenda.

The adoption of GPTVET for this chapter, rather than PPP in TVET is deliberate to indicate that GPTVET is founded on shared values as well as voluntary and broader collaborative partnerships in which all stakeholders agree to work together to achieve a common purpose. Such a collaborative partnership that involves a broader partnerships among all stakeholders of TVET can be created for the purpose of advocacy, pooling core complementary resources, exchange of ideas and fostering new ways to procure infrastructural facilities or provide effective services. Therefore, GPTVET can be seen as a strategic mechanism to foster optimization of resources to equip students with HOS such as critical thinking, creative thinking, problem solving and decision-making among others to encourage EALLL and promote human well-being, self-esteem and freedom.

The purpose of this chapter is to examine the influence of GPTVET, OR, DHOS and EALLL on the CVSD. The study aimed to answer the following research question: (1) what is the impact of GPTVET, OR, DHOS and EALLL on CVSD? The results from this chapter may help inform proper management of TVET. The adequate provision of resources, DHOS and promotion of EALLL through proper implementation of GPTVET will have great impact in fostering human well-being, self-esteem and freedom in our society. In the following sections of this chapter, details were provided on conceptual framework, literature review on the impact of GPTVET, OR, DHOS and EALLL on CVSD. Details were also provided on the methods used in conducting the research, results, discussions of the results, limitations and implications of the study and conclusions based on the results.

CONCEPTUAL FRAMEWORK

The authors developed a schematic model (see Figure 1) to supports the chapter as well as to explain and describe the extent to which GPTVET, OR, DHOS and EALLL could enhance the CVSD. The authors developed a schematic model upon which the hypothetical propositions of all the variables in the chapter are to be based.

The assumptions behind the model is that when there is a strong tie among stakeholders of TVET it would provide opportunities for all students to secure huge financial resources to secure basic needs, such as food, shelter, education, self-esteem and freedom. This assumption have been supported by the stakeholder theory (Freeman, 1984), interdependence theory (Thibaut & Kelley, 1959), collaborative empowerment theory (Perkins & Zimmerman, 1995), collaborative advantage theory (Huxham, 1993), networking theory (Granovetter, 1973; Burt, 1976), and social exchange theory (Blau, 1964; Emerson, 1976). These theories proposed that if providers' of TVET partner with its stakeholders worldwide, there will be a better chance to accomplish set goals (e.g. CVSD). This underlying assumption means that TVET providers may not achieve set goals, if acting alone.

Partnerships among TVET stakeholders worldwide would further serve as a baseline that leads to OR, DHOS and EALLL which, in turn, would provide the chances for income capacities to secure human basic needs, such as food, shelter, education, self-esteem and freedom. However, previous empirical studies (e.g. Edokpolor & Imafidon, 2017; Edokpolor & Imafidon, 2018) and theoretical discussions (e.g. Ekpenyong & Edokpolor, 2015; Edokpolor *et al.* 2016) attempted to examine the role of PPP or GPTVET. None of these previous studies and discussions nor a more current article (e.g. Edokpolor & Abusomwan, 2020) examine the effect of GPTVET in enhancing CVSD through OR, DHOS and EALLL. The chapter rely on the effect of GPTVET to close this gap.

LITERATURE REVIEW

Global Partnership in TVET

Over the years, global partnership has been studied by researchers because of its important role in pooling resources, scaling up innovation and action to advance the CVSD. Hazlewood (2015) defined global partnership as *"... a wide and diverse array of institutional arrangements for expanding collaboration between government, business (and other private sector actors), civil society and/or U.N. and other multilateral agencies to address development challenges" (p. 2).* Freeman and Wisheart (2015) defined it broadly as *"... an ongoing working relationship between organizations from different sectors, combining their resources and competencies and sharing risks towards achieving agreed shared objectives whilst each also achieving their own individual objectives" (p. 3).* U.N. General Assembly (2015) defined global partnership as a *"...voluntary and collaborative relationships between various parties, both public and non-public, in which all participants agree to work together to achieve a common purpose or undertake a specific task and, as mutually agreed, to share risks and responsibilities, resources and benefits" (p. 2).*

Edokpolor *et al.* (2016) averred that GPTVET represent a strategic model to pool, combine and manage resources as well as mobilize core capabilities, competencies and commitments from government agencies, private industries, civil society groups, among others, for the purpose of enhancing the CVSD. They added that GPTVET represent a strategic model in which public sector agencies (e.g. ministries, boards, schools), private sector (e.g. corporate foundations, corporations, international financial institutions, professional bodies, business associations) and civil society sector (e.g. U.N., ILO, USAID, UNESCO) pool together resources and competencies to enhance CVSD.

OPTIMIZATION OF RESOURCES

Resources is defined as tangible and intangible assets that are adequately provided by the TVET managers to be used by teachers and students for effective teaching and learning to take place. Hitt, Ireland and

Hoskisson (2011) classified resources as tangible and intangible resources. Tangible resources are assets that can easily be observed and quantifiable. Examples of tangible resources are financial resources, entrepreneurship centres, staff quarters, workshops, laboratories, equipment, lecture halls, classrooms, ICT centres, libraries, health-care centres, hostels, educators' offices, sports grounds, structures, among others (Edokpolor & Dumbiri, 2019). Instructional resources is another example of tangible resources which include raw materials, general textbooks, course textbooks, journals and other reading materials (Kigwilu & Akala, 2017). These tangible resources can contribute directly or indirectly to the teaching and learning of TVET courses. Intangible resources, on the other hand, are assets that are less visible and quantifiable. Examples of intangible resources include knowledge, skills, creativity, competencies and core capabilities (Hitt *et al.,* 2011). Adequate provision of tangible and intangible resources would equip all students (male and female alike) with HOS necessary to secure their well-being, self-esteem and freedom.

UNESCO-UNEVOC (2018) argued that students experience high level of CVSD before and after graduation when there is optimization of resources through global partnership in TVET. UNESCO-ILO (2018) reported that students' well-being, self-esteem and freedom before and after graduation can be influenced by the optimization of resources through proper management of TVET. The optimization of resources proposed as a predictor of different dimensions of SD, which include human well-being, self-esteem and freedom can be grouped into three categories, namely: financial resources, human resources and material resources.

DEVELOPMENT OF HIGHER-ORDER SKILLS

Higher-order skills is defined *"as the abilities to perform productive tasks, think critically and solve problems"* (Edokpolor & Adeniyi, 2019, p. 3). Some empirical studies reported that HOS comprised of two aspects, namely critical and creative thinking skills (Heong *et al.* 2011; Plan, 2014; Sulaiman *et al.* 2017); logical thinking, critical thinking and reasoning skills (Marshall & Horton, 2011). Some authors focused on the three aspects of HOS such as analysis, evaluation, and creation (Ramirez & Ganaden, 2008). Meanwhile, other authors saw four aspects of HOS as critical thinking, creative thinking, problem solving and decision making (Apino & Retnawati, 2017). Creativity thinking skills involves ability to generate new and useful ideas (Certo & Certo, 2006). Problem solving skills involves a process of reaching a desired goal via the use of HOS to generate, interpret and appraise ideas, and using strategies to manage the complexity of situations (Edokpolor & Abusomwan, 2019). Critical thinking skills involve self-disciplined thinking which attempt to reason at the highest level of quality in a fair-minded way (Elder, 2007). Furthermore, decision-making skills can described as choices, and choices are not usually made directly, but after going through a process that involves multiple steps (Hitt, Tihanyi, Miller & Connelly, 2006).

Researchers maintain that HOS can be developed (Scott, Leritz & Mumford, 2004; Davis, 2006) through a real-world environment that inculcates ideas and fosters solutions to problems (Karkockiene, 2005). Various aspects of HOS cannot be acquired in formal environment alone but through a real-world environment (Edokpolor & Adeniyi, 2019). Thus, the integration of real-world learning into TVET curriculum is deemed beneficial as it would inculcate HOSs on students that advance CVSD. HOS are salient elements in TVET because of its benefits in improving problem solving. However, some authors argued that the development of HOS among students is one of salient objectives of TVET institutions because of its influence on CVSD (Edokpolor, 2020; Krstić, Ilić & Avramović, 2015).

EQUAL OPPORTUNITIES FOR LIFELONG LEARNING

Lifelong Learning is defined as *"the continuous development and improvement of the knowledge and skills needed for employment and personal fulfillment through formal and informal learning opportunities" (Chiţiba, 2012, p. 1944).* Lifelong learning also improves employability and entrepreneurship through skills development and creativity, enhances public health and well-being, and builds more cohesive and resilient communities. Learning in this context is therefore component of life which takes place in all places and at all times. In essence, lifelong learning provides people with the knowledge, skills, attitudes and creativity needed to solve problems locally and globally, and actively contributes to sustainable development of developing societies. Therefore, EALLL can lead to the advancement of human well-being, self-esteem and freedom.

Equitable opportunities for lifelong learning systems in the developing countries produce equal opportunities for skills development which tend to reinforce income equality and promote the enhancement of CVSD (Green, 2011). However, high levels of equitable access to lifelong learning fosters employment opportunities or entrepreneurial careers which enhance economic competitiveness, thus contributing to the enhancement of CVSD (Faradova, 2020). Similarly, high levels of EALLL is an important contributor to the achievement of CVSD, globally, and at national and local levels (UNESCO Institute for Lifelong Learning, 2020).

CORE VALUES OF SUSTAINABLE DEVELOPMENT

Sustainable development is defined as a *"development which meets the needs of the present without compromising the ability of future generations to meet their own needs" (WCED, 1987, p. 43).* The Brundtland Report mapped a political agenda, arguing that *"sustainable development is a process in which the exploitation of resources, the direction of investments, the orientation of technological development and institutional change are all in harmony, and enhance both current and future potential to meet human needs and aspirations" (World Commission on Environment and Development, 1987, p. 46).* SD, therefore, is about meeting basic human needs in a long term basis, which further implies that basic human needs are CVSD, but not the only core dimensions.

Sustainable development do not only fall within the confines of basic human needs, it also encompass more than life-sustaining essentials we lead and incorporate self-esteem and freedom. Therefore, SD is more concerned with advancing the lives we lead, the choices we make and the freedoms we enjoy on a continuous basis. In the context of this chapter, SD involves the continuous process of improving the quality of all human lives and capabilities by raising their levels of well-being, self-esteem, and freedom (Mensah, 2019). Life-sustaining essentials is defined as adequate stocks and flows of food and income capacity to meet well-being or livelihood. Life-sustaining essentials involves goods and services such as food, clothing, protection and healthcare that are necessary to sustain an average individual at the bare minimum level of living (Edokpolor & Egbri, 2017). Self-esteem may be seen as the ability to be a person, or the ability of not being used as a tool by others for their own ends. It is defined as a feeling of worthiness that a society enjoys when its social, political and economic systems promote human values, such as respect, honour, dignity, integrity, recognition, identity, and self-determination. Freedom may be seen as individuals' ability to choose. It involves a situation in which a society has at its disposal a variety of alternatives from which to satisfy its wants and a situation in which individuals enjoy real choices according to their preferences (Todaro & Smith, 2011). Therefore, continuously increasing high levels of livelihood, self-esteem and freedom would help in contributing to development in a sustainable manner. Based on review of the related literature, the following hypotheses were proposed as follows:

H1. Global partnership in TVET will positively predict CVSD.

H2. Optimization of resources will positively predict CVSD.

H3. Development of higher-order skills will positively predict CVSD.

H4. Equitable access to lifelong learning will positively predict CVSD.

RESEARCH METHOD

Research design. A correlational survey design where employed in this chapter. This design is appropriate for the research because it will enable authors to examine the degree to which GPTVET, OR, DHOS and EALLL predict CVSD. The degree to which these variables would predict each other will be expressed as a correlation coefficient (r).

Research Participants: A total of 520 TVET lecturers' participated in the study. These participants were from different units of TVET, namely business, industrial technical, home economics, and agriculture. Purposive sampling method were used to select participants because they were defined groups of lecturers who are directly involved in daily job performance, namely teaching, research and administration.

Research Instrument. The authors constructed an instrument for collection of data, which consists of demographic information of TVET lecturers' and questionnaire item statements. Demographic information of TVET lecturers' consist of their sex and age. Sex was represented as male (395, 76%) and female (123, 24%). Age was grouped as less than 26 years (39, 08%), 26-35 years (130, 25%), 36-45 years (170, 33%), 46-55 years (87, 17%), 56-65 years (62, 12%), above 66 years (30, 06%).

Items 1 to 3 measure GPTVET, items 4 to 7 measure OR, items 8 to 13 measure DHOS, 14 to 23 measure EALLL, and items 24 to 26 measure CVSD. The instrument was a seven-point Likert-type scale, ranging from 1 = totally disagree to 7 = totally agree. Perception of technology and vocational educators was used to measure influence of GPTVET, OR, DHOS and EALLL on CVSD. A sample of item statement for GPTVET is: "TVET providers should partner with private sector actors". A sample of item statement for OR is: "GPTVET would help in optimization of financial resources". A sample of item statement for DHOS is: "TVET students need to develop reasoning/problem solving skills". A sample of item statement for EALLL is: "it should be a passion for male and female students of TVET to learn new things throughout life". And finally, a sample of item statement for CVSD is: "TVET students' need to meet their basic needs".

A reliability test was conducted using the Cronbach's alpha method to ascertain the internal consistency of the research instrument. Coefficients alpha values provided the reliability for each variables such as GPTVET ($\alpha = .843$), OR ($\alpha = .950$), DHOS ($\alpha = .829$), EALLL ($\alpha = .727$), and CVSD ($\alpha = .953$). Thus, these coefficient values confirmed high consistency on each variables.

Data analyses. Data were analyzed through quantitative statistical tools (e.g. mean, standard deviations, bivariate correlation matrix, and hierarchical regression using Statistical Package for Social Sciences

Table 1. Mean, standard deviation, and correlation of the variables studied

S/N	Variable	*M*	*SD*	1	2	3	4	5	6	7
1.	Gender	1.26	0.52	1						
2.	Age	3.19	1.32	.108*	1					
3.	GPTVET	6.46	0.82	-.006	.144**	1				
4.	OR	6.46	1.08	-.029	.133**	.227**	1			
5.	AHOS	6.47	1.45	-.111*	.133**	.410**	.394**	1		
6.	EALLL	6.43	1.87	-.092*	.078	.323**	.478**	.229**	1	
7.	ACVSD	6.36	0.75	.005	.075	.269**	.231**	.253**	.229**	1

Note. $N = 520$, M = Mean, SD = Standard Deviation, GPTVET = Global Partnership in TVET, OR = Optimization of Resources, DHOS = Development of Higher-Order Skills, EALLL = Equitable Access to Lifelong Learning, ACVSD = Advancement of Core Values of Sustainable Development.

(SPSS) version 23.0. Hierarchical regression statistical tool were used to test the research hypotheses 1 to 4 on relationship or prediction.

RESULTS

The results of the data analyzed are presented in Tables 1 and 2.

As shown in Table 1, the mean response ranges from 6.43 to 6.47 and the standard deviation ranges from 0.75 to 1.87. Table 1 also showed that the correlation coefficient of between variables ranged from 0.75 to 0.78. The bivariate correlational analyses depicted that GPTVET (r = 0.227**, $p < .01$), OR (r = 0.394**, $p < .01$), DHOS (r = 0.229**, $p < .01$), and EALLL (r = 0.229**, $p < .01$) were significantly and positively correlated with CVSD.

H1 to *H4* were tested using hierarchical linear regression statistic to ascertain if GPTVET, OR, DHOS, and EALLL would significantly predict CVSD. In Table 2, the GPTVET in model 1 indicated

Table 2. Summary of hierarchical linear regression analysis for advancement of CVSD

	CVSD			
	Model 1	Model 2	Model 3	Model 4
Variables	*B*	*B*	*B*	*β*
GPTVET	.269***	.228***	.187***	.176***
OR		.179***	.141**	.127**
AHOS			.120*	.086 (*ns*)
EALLL				.093 (*ns*)
R^2	.072	.102	.113	.119
Adjusted R^2	.070	.099	.108	.113
F-value	F (1, 518) = 40.247	F (2, 517) = 29.510	F (3, 516) = 21.940	F (4, 515) = 17.469

* = $p < 0.05$; ** = $p < 0.001$; GPTVET = Global Partnership in TVET, OR = Optimization of Resources, DHOS = Development of Higher-Order Skills, EALLL = Equitable Access to Lifelong Learning, CVSD = Core Values of Sustainable Development.

a significant positive predictor of CVSD, F (1, 518) = 40.247, $\beta = .269$, $p < 0.001$. Adjusted R-Square (.070) indicated that 7.0% of variances in CVSD is influenced by GPTVET. Hence, the hypothesis formulated is supported, meaning that GPTVET will enhance CVSD. The inclusion of OR in model 2 indicated a significant positive predictor of CVSD, F (2, 517) = 29.510, $\beta = .179$, $p < 0.001$. Adjusted R-Square (.099) showed that 9.9% of variances in CVSD is impacted by OR. Therefore, the hypothesis formulated is supported, meaning that OR will advance CVSD.

The inclusion of DHOS in model 3 indicated a partial significant predictor of CVSD, F (3, 516) = 21.940, $\beta = .120$, $p < 0.05$. Adjusted R-Square (.108) indicated that 10.8% of variances in CVSD is partially influenced by DHOS. Therefore, the hypothesis formulated is partly supported, meaning that DHOS will partially advance CVSD. The inclusion of EALLL in model 4 indicated also a partial significant predictor of CVSD, F (4, 515) = 17.469, $\beta = .093$, $p < 0.05$. Adjusted R^2 (.113) indicated that 11.3% of variances in CVSD is partially influenced by EALLL. Therefore, the hypothesis formulated is partly supported, implying that EALLL will partially advance CVSD.

DISCUSSION

What is the impact of global partnership in TVET, optimization of resources, development of higher-order skills and promotion of equal opportunities for lifelong learning on enhancement of CVSD? To answer this question, the chapter developed a schematic model to explore the impact of OR, DHOS and EALLL on CVSD. Concerning the interplay between GPTVET and CVSD, the results showed that GPTVET was a significant predictor of CVSD *(H1)*. This result confirmed that the resources and expertise provided by stakeholders during partnership experience enhance the CVSD (UNESCO-ILO, 2018; UNESCO-UNEVOC, 2018). This result was expected given the wide range of positive reports and discourses concerning the role and impact of GPTVET in enhancing CVSD (U.N., 2017, 2019). However, the result of the impact of GPTVET in enhancing the CVSD is novel, this is because its empirical validation serves as a baseline result leading to subsequent results in the present study.

Concerning the interplay between OR and CVSD, the results showed that OR was significantly correlated with CVSD *(H2)*. This result indicated that OR play a significant role in advancing CVSD. This result authenticates assumption that adequate provision of financial resources influence adequate supply of qualified manpower, physical facilities and instructional resources that equip recipients with skills required to confidently engage in entrepreneurial careers and lifelong learning activities, thus, achieving CVSD. This finding agrees with the principles of systems theory who argued that the provision of resources (both human and materials) would transform instructional delivery effectively for the purpose of achieving set goals (Bertalanffy, 1968).

Additionally, concerning the relationship between DHOS and CVSD, the results showed that DHOS was a partial significant predictor of the CVSD *(H3)*. By implication, students with high level of HOS may have great chances to secure human basic needs such as well-being, self-esteem and freedom. This kind of skills can be developed because the process is linked to a planned and organized educational programme. This result is comparable to the study of Edokpolor (2019) and Edokpolor (2020), who found that entrepreneurial skills developed by university students is a significant positive predictor of CVSD.

Furthermore, concerning the relationship between EALLL and CVSD, the result showed that the test of the impact of EALLL on CVSD *(H4)* was not supported. This result showed that EALLL do not significantly predict the CVSD. This result means that a significant interplay do not exist between

EALLL and CVSD. This finding do not agree to the claim of authors that EALLL produce equal chances for skills development to enhance CVSD (Green, 2011; Faradova, 2020; UNESCO Institute for Lifelong Learning, 2020).

LIMITATIONS, IMPLICATIONS AND CONCLUSIONS

The study focused on the impact of OR, DHOS and EALLL on CVSD, which is relatively a less-explored area of research inquiry in development literature, especially in the context of developing countries. The study contributed to the existing literature by establishing the extent of interplay between OR, DHOS and EALLL and CVSD. The study established that OR, DHOS and EALLL are key predictors of CVSD. The findings of the research, therefore, depict some practical implications for government agencies, faith-based organizations, NGOs, international donors, international financial institutions, parents, and employers of labour. If these stakeholders collaboratively invest their resources on TVET, it will provide a real-life learning environment that would equip all recipients with HOS necessary to secure the CVSD.

In spite of the research contributions to existing literature, some limitations are identified. However, the study focused on GPTVET, as it is found in the literature as a baseline upon which the link between OR, DHOS and EALLL and CVSD is to be built. A correlational approach was adopted to achieve the objective of the research and, as such, causal inference need not to be made in the study. Therefore, longitudinal and experimental approaches are recommended to describe the rigorous process of enhancing the CVSD. If not, then what are the managerial models that can significantly predict the relationships between OR, DHOS and EALLL and CVSD?

The participants were purposively selected from the departments of technology and vocational education in the South Senatorial District of Nigeria; therefore, caution needs to be exercised in generalizing the findings of the research. However, future research should focus on using the proportional sampling procedure by covering broader Senatorial Districts (such as South-East, South-West, North-Central, North-East, and North-West Senatorial Districts of Nigeria), to provide more balanced results from all TVET programmes in the district. The participants are also homogenous, meaning that technical and vocational educators were used in the study. However, caution needs to be exercised in generalizing the results of the research, especially to technical and vocational educators in other higher institutions. Thus, the technical and vocational educators were used in the research because they are the best stakeholder to provide a useful information on global partnerships in TVET, which a factor upon which the optimization of resources, development of higher-order skills, equitable access to lifelong learning and CVSD are to be built. Hence, there is need to embark on further studies that involve educators from other higher institutions. In addition, the perception of educators was used to measure global partnerships in TVET, which does not give the true picture of educators' exposure to the TVET programme, rather it only determines what it ought to be but not what it is. Hence, future research need to incorporate the area that measure the educators' exposure to TVET programme. In addition, caution should be exercised in generalizing the results because of the social desirability of the items (Podsakoff, MacKenzie, Lee & Podsakoff, 2003), since the exposure of educators to TVET programme were not strictly measured; rather their perception of the global partnerships in TVET were measured. In addition, because the study was conducted in Nigeria, caution needs to be exercised in generalizing the findings to other developing countries. Moreover, future research should cover other developing countries to provide balanced results.

Concerning the results of the research, the authors conclude that a GPTVET is a welcome initiative, since it provides more chances for OR, DHOS and EALLL and, in turn, enhance CVSD, such as well-being, self-esteem, and freedom. Despite the results, the authors still anticipates that the research will stimulate more rigorous research that covers OR, DHOS and EALLL and CVSD in other type of institutions such as college of education, polytechnic, or innovation enterprise to determine whether the study will be consistent with the results of the present study.

REFERENCES

Akaranta, O. (2014). Building and maintaining higher education ecosystem in the 21st century. Paper Presented at *a Workshop Organized by the Centre for Higher Education Studies*, University of Port Harcourt, Port Harcourt, Nigeria.

Apino, E., & Retnawati, H. (2017). Developing instructional design to improve mathematical higher order thinking skills of students. *Journal of Physics Conference*, *812*(1), 012100. doi:10.1088/1742-6596/812/1/012100

Aryal, B. P. (2020). Financing of technical and vocational education and training in Nepal. *The Journal of Educational Research*, *10*(1), 58–80. doi:10.3126/jer.v10i1.31898

Aworanti, O. A. (2015b). *Partnership in technical and vocational education and training (TVET) for national development.* Paper Presented at the *23rd Annual International Conference of the Nigerian Vocational Association*, Yaba College of Technology, Lagos, Nigeria.

Ayonmike, C. S. (2014). Factors affecting female participation in technical education programme: A study of Delta State University, Abraka. *Journal of Education and Human Development*, *3*(3), 227–240.

Bayeh, E. (2016). The role of empowering women and achieving gender equality to the sustainable development of Ethiopia. *Pacific Science Review B. Humanities and Social Sciences*, *2*(1), 37–42.

Bertalanffy, L. (1968). *General system theory: Essays on its foundation and development.* New York: George Braziller.

Blau, P. M. (1964). *Exchange and power in social life*. John Wiley.

Burt, R. S. (1976). Positions in networks. *Social Forces*, *55*(1), 93–122. doi:10.2307/2577097

Center for Research and Development Services. (2018). *TVET financing in Nepal: Final report.* Author.

Certo, S. C., & Certo, S. T. (2006). Modern management (10th ed.). Academic Press.

Chiţiba, C. A. (2012). Lifelong learning challenges and opportunities for traditional universities. *Procedia: Social and Behavioral Sciences*, *46*, 1943–1947. doi:10.1016/j.sbspro.2012.05.408

Davis, G. A. (2006). *Gifted children and gifted education: A handbook for teachers and parents*. Great Potential Press.

Edokpolor, J. E. (2018). Systems approach in developing creative thinking and innovative capabilities for lifelong learning among TVET students in Federal Universities, South-South, Nigeria. *International Journal of Educational Development, 21*(1), 1-15.

Edokpolor, J. E. (2019). Gender differential effect of business education students' human capital on sustainable economic development. *Journal of Educational Research and Practice, 9*(1), 40-54.

Edokpolor, J. E. (2020). Entrepreneurship education and sustainable development: Mediating role of entrepreneurial skills. *Asia Pacific Journal of Innovation and Entrepreneurship, 14*(3).

Edokpolor, J. E., & Abusomwan, V. I. (2019). Students' potential abilities as correlates of self-employment start-up intentions: Evidence from private sector-led technical and vocational education institutions in Nigeria. *International Journal of Learning, Teaching and Educational Research, 18*(9), 146–169. doi:10.26803/ijlter.18.9.8

Edokpolor, J. E., & Abusomwan, V. I. (2020). Perception of TPET lecturers' on the effect of global partnerships in developing students' career human capital. *International Journal of Learning, Teaching and Educational Research, 19*(5), 125–140.

Edokpolor, J. E., & Adeniyi, I. N. (2019). Experiential and vicarious learning approaches in developing higher-order thinking skills among business education undergraduates in federal universities. *International Journal of Educational Research, 6*(1), 1–14.

Edokpolor, J. E., & Chukwuedo, S. O. (2018). Technical and vocational education and training students' lifelong-career specific human capital: Gender consideration for sustainable development. *International Journal of Gender Studies and Research, 5*(1), 51-63.

Edokpolor, J. E., & Dumbiri, D. N. (2019). Resource adequacy and utilization for teaching and learning effectiveness in vocational education programmes in south-south Nigerian universities. *Journal of Vocational Education Studies, 2*(1), 1–12. doi:10.12928/joves.v2i1.727

Edokpolor, J. E., Edokpolor, H. O., & Olupayimo, E. O. (2016). Actualizing sustainable high standard of quality in Nigerian TVET programme through multi-stakeholders partnership. *African Journal of Studies in Education, 11*(1), 47–62.

Edokpolor, J. E., & Egbri, J. N. (2017). Business education in Nigeria for value re-orientation: A strategic approach for poverty alleviation and national development. *Journal of Educational Research and Review, 5*(3), 41–48.

Edokpolor, J. E., & Imafidon, A. (2017). Effectiveness of public-private partnership in the management of technical and vocational education and training. *Education Policy, Management and Quality, 9*(1), 20–32.

Edokpolor, J. E., & Imafidon, A. (2019). Public-private-civil society partnership: A gateway to ensuring good governance practices of vocational education in South-South Nigerian Federal Universities. *Journal of Technical Education and Training, 11*(3), 121–135. doi:10.30880/jtet.2019.11.03.015

Ekpenyong, L. E., & Edokpolor, J. E. (2015). Winning the war against unemployment and poverty in Nigeria: Is there a role for TVET-private sector partnership? *Nigerian Vocational Association Journal, 20*(1), 125-132.

Elder, L. (2007). *Our concept of critical thinking (side bar), foundation for critical thinking*. Retrieved from http://www.criticalthinking.org/aboutCT/ourConceptCT.cfm

Emerson, R. M. (1976). Social exchange theory. *Annual Review of Sociology*, *2*(1), 335–362. doi:10.1146/annurev.so.02.080176.002003

Faradova, G. (2020) Adult education: Contribution to the sustainable development goals. In Quality education. Encyclopedia of the UN Sustainable Development Goals. Springer. doi:10.1007/978-3-319-95870-5_1

Freeman, C., & Wisheart, M. (2015). *Advancing the Debate: Cross-sector partnerships, business and the post-2015 development agenda*. World Vision International.

Freeman, R. E. (1984). *Strategic management: A stakeholder approach*. Pitman. doi:10.1017/CBO9781139192675

Granovetter, M. (1973). The strength of weak ties. *American Journal of Sociology*, *78*(6), 1360–1380. doi:10.1086/225469

Green, A. (2011). Lifelong learning, equality and social cohesion. *European Journal of Education*, *46*(2), 228–243. doi:10.1111/j.1465-3435.2011.01478.x

Hazlewood, P. (2015). *Global Multi-stakeholder Partnerships: Scaling up public-private collective impact for the SDGs*. Academic Press.

Hitt, M. A., Ireland, R. D., & Hoskisson, R. E. (2011). *Strategic management: Competitiveness and globalization* (9th ed.). Cengage Southwestern Publishing.

Hitt, M. A., Tihanyi, L., Miller, T., & Connelly, B. (2006). International diversification: Antecedents, outcomes, and moderators. *Journal of Management*, *32*(6), 831–867. doi:10.1177/0149206306293575

Huxham, C. (1993). Pursuing collaborative advantage. *The Journal of the Operational Research Society*, *44*(5), 599–611. doi:10.1057/jors.1993.101

ILO. (2011). *A skilled workforce for strong, sustainable and balanced growth: A G20 training strategy*. ILO.

ILO. (2020). *The digitization of TVET and skills systems*. ILO.

Karkockiene, D. (2005). Creativity: Can it be trained? A scientific educology of creativity. International *Journal of Educology,* 51-58. Retrieved from http://www.era-usa.net/images/article_5_Daiva.pdf

Kennedy, G. W., Udoetuk, U. S., & Ufot, S. I. (2017). Challenges of technical vocational teacher education and teaching in Nigeria: The need for intervention. *International Journal of Education and Evaluation*, *3*(7), 71–82.

Kigwilu, P. C., & Akala, W. J. (2017). Resource utilization and curriculum implementation in community colleges in Kenya. *International Journal for Research in Vocational Education and Training*, *4*(4), 369–381. doi:10.13152/IJRVET.4.4.4

Krstić, I. I., Ilić, A., & Avramović, D. (2015). The three dimensions of sustainable development: Environment, economy and society. *Proceedings on 50 Years of Higher Education, Science and Research in Occupational Safety Engineering*.

Majumdar, S. (2011). *Emerging challenges and trends in TVET in the Asian-Pacific Region*. Sense Publishers. doi:10.1007/978-94-6091-391-4

Mensah, J. (2019). Sustainable development: meaning, history, principles, pillars, and implications for human action: a literature review. *Cogent Social Sciences*, *5*(1), 1–21. doi:10.1080/23311886.2019.1653531

Onwusa, S. C. (2021). The issues, challenges and strategies to strengthen technical, vocational education and training in Nigeria. *International Journal of Research and Innovation in Social Science*, *5*(5), 48–59. doi:10.47772/IJRISS.2021.5502

Oviawe, J. I. (2018). Revamping technical vocational education and training through public-private partnerships for skill development. *Makerere Journal of Higher Education*, *10*(1), 73–91. doi:10.4314/majohe.v10i1.5

Podsakoff, P. M., MacKenzie, S. B., Lee, J., & Podsakoff, N. P. (2003). Common method biases in behavioral research: A critical review of the literature and recommended remedies. *The Journal of Applied Psychology*, *88*(5), 879–903. doi:10.1037/0021-9010.88.5.879 PMID:14516251

Ramadan, A., & Xiaohui, C. (2019). Challenges and opportunities of tvet in developing countries: A case of Sudan. *Developing Country Studies*, *9*(10), 77–87.

Scott, G., Leritz, L. E., & Mumford, M. D. (2004). The effectiveness of creativity training: A quantitative review. *Creativity Research Journal*, *16*(4), 361–388. doi:10.1080/10400410409534549

Thibaut, J. W., & Kelley, H. H. (1959). *The social psychology of groups*. Wiley.

Todaro, M. P., & Smith, S. C. (2011). *Economic Development*. Pearson Education.

UN General Assembly. (2015). Towards global partnerships. A principle-based approach to enhanced cooperation between the United Nations and all relevant partners (Vol. A). UNGA. RES/70/224.

UNESCO. (2020). *First meeting of the international commission on the futures of education*. UNESCO Headquarters. Retrieved from https://unesdoc.unesco.org/ark:/48223/pf0000372674?posInSet=1&queryId=4223eb90-51d6-48c5-9bd5-790d5d6df2f2

UNESCO & ILO. (2018). *Taking a whole of government approach to skills development*. Author.

UNESCO Institute for Lifelong Learning. (2020). *Embracing a culture of lifelong learning: Contribution to the futures of education initiative*. Author.

UNESCO-UNEVOC. (2018). *Open educational resources for skills development*. UN Campus.

United Nations. (2019). *Financing of education and technical and vocational education and training (TVET) in Latin America and the Caribbean*. UN.

United Nations Industrial Development Organization. (2017). *Skills policy instruments for industrial development in low and middle income countries.* Inclusive and Sustainable Industrial Development Working Paper Series WP 2 | 2017.

United Nations (UN). (2017). *The sustainable development goals report.* Retrieved from https://sdgactioncampaign.org/wp-content/uploads/2017/07/TheSustainableDevelopmentGoalsReport2017.pdf

World Commission on Environment and Development (WCED). (1987). Report of the world commission on environment and development: Our common future. Oxford University Press.

Ziderman, A. (2016). *Funding mechanisms for financing vocational training: An analytical framework* (IZA Policy Paper No. 110). Ramat Gan. Retrieved from https://ftp.iza.org/pp110.pdf

Chapter 17
Artificial Intelligence as a Catalyst for Socioeconomic Development:
Challenges and Prospects

Jude Thaddeus Chibuzo Udenkwo
Nnamdi Azikiwe University, Nigeria

ABSTRACT

The chapter explores the challenges and prospects in the role of artificial intelligence in development. Using a qualitative method of analysis, it examines evidence from crucial literature on artificial intelligence from diverse scholars and experts in the field. The research began with a conceptual review of AI and then made a foray into the ethical and epistemological basis of AI. It further highlighted the qualities of AI and the threat that AI poses to the digital divide between North and South. It also examines the importance of Ai to development, the latest advancements in AI, the importance of AI in the bid by Third World countries to catch up with development, and qualities and regulatory frameworks for harnessing and consolidating AI. Finally, it makes recommendations on the best approach to using AI to influence socioeconomic development.

INTRODUCTION

At present, Artificial Intelligence (AI) is both the current location and the next destination of global development. The various segments and dimensions of human scientific endeavors and innovative propensities—nanotechnology, machine learning, data science, military strategy, space science, corporate modeling, and so on, find a culmination in AI.

Artificial Intelligence is the engine upon which the vehicle of global change and sustainable progress is powered. Analysts have pointed at the role of artificial intelligence in achieving the Sustainable Development Goals (Vinusa, Azizpour, & Nerini, 2020). Considering the gargantuan nature of the SDGs and the ambitious nature of the tasks it arrogated to itself, there is no doubt that the founding fathers

DOI: 10.4018/978-1-6684-4107-7.ch017

envisioned a world where artificial intelligence would run concurrently with global policy implementation for development. It therefore follows that if the challenges to robust deployment of AI in industrial and domestic activities would be overcome, and if proper regulatory mechanisms are put in place to reduce the fallouts from AI, a world driven by artificial intelligence-enabled technology would be a better place for all. This paper is aimed at carrying out a brief but concise overview of the prospect of an AI-embedded economy for advancement of both the developed and the developing nations.

MEANING OF ARTIFICIAL INTELLIGENCE

What is Artificial Intelligence? According to Strusani and Houngbonon, (2019) Artificial Intelligence (AI) designates "the science and engineering of making machines intelligent, especially intelligent computer programs." Borrowing from the AI100 Panel at Stanford University, the authors defined intelligence as "that quality that enables an entity to function appropriately and with foresight in its environment."

Taking a more comprehensive and simplified look at the matter, two dominant views of AI could be seen: the *functional* view and the *process* view of AI. By their very meaning, functional definitions are those which see a thing or object from the point of view of what it does, while process definitions explain phenomena from the angle of how it does things.

Based on this, those who favor a functional approach to explaining AI see it as a computerized system that can think and act like humans. More comprehensive definitions that champion the functional approach to explaining AI define it as all computer systems that can continuously scan their environment, learn from it, and take action in response to what they sense, as well as to human-defined objectives (Strusani and Houngbonon,2019). Those who favor a process view of explaining AI sees it as the computerized process of combining large volumes of data with computing power to simulate human cognitive abilities such as reasoning, language, perception, vision, and spatial processing.

Conclusively AI can be seen as the understanding that with appropriate programming and …a computer can act as if it has a mind of its own, being able to understand complex processes, have beliefs, and experience other cognitive functions (Lawhead, 2003).

EPISTEMOLOGICAL AND ETHICAL IMPLICATIONS OF AI

The science and practice of AI has serious implications in epistemology and ethics. Epistemology is the branch of Philosophical inquiry focusing on the origin, nature and subject of knowledge. Ethics considers human actions and intentions according to how they conform to certain pre-defined values and standards. It is important to highlight the implications of these areas of human intellectual activities to Artificial Intelligence at the very beginning of this paper, so as to establish the logical and moral place of AI before delving into its various challenges and prospects.

In simple terms, epistemology judges what we learn, how we learn, and who learns. It places man at the centre of (teaching and) learning experience, and implicitly or explicitly denies the possibility of knowledge for any non-human object and entity. Arguments surrounding the epistemological basis of AI have bred two opposing camps of philosophers. One group claims that AI is equivalent of the human mind, since it can literarily understand, believe, and have other cognitive states. The other group insists that AI is not the equivalent of mind, while admitting that computers can only simulate mental activities. For this reason, they propose that AI can only help us explore various theoretical models of human mental processes (Lawhead, 2003). The question then is, is the computer a learning entity, and if yes, does it make it to have normal mental qualities? To this, philosophers have given opposing answers. The philosopher John Searle opined that "no matter how effective a computer programme might be in simulating human thought processes, it cannot simulate intelligence, though it can duplicate it." (Lawhead, 2003: 242). Those who hold this position take it further by claiming that "computers are not really intelligent, but merely doing what they have been programmed to do" (Lawhead, 246). They argued that learning, after all, is a process of following rules one has been taught in carrying out a task, receiving feedback when a mistake has been made, and learning from the mistake to improve in the task. This is also true when computers which is programmed to play chess, for instance, is performing, as it is when a human being is carrying out an activity based on previous learning s/he has undergone. Education, thus, is a sophisticated process of programming. Based on this, Lawhead concludes:

'If computers could be programmed to have cognitive states functionally equivalent to those states in human psychology that we identify as thinking, believing, wanting, remembering, willing, and so on, and if their ability to process information is comparable to ours, it would seem to follow that such computers would be intelligent and would have minds'.

Ethics measures the rightness and wrongness of human actions, and apportions either individual guilt or societal sanctions for wrongful actions (Froost, 1989). Just like in many other areas, the actions and intentions of individuals and entities in the field of Artificial Intelligence are subject to ethical consideration. Those who hold the belief that man is supreme above all creatures and creations look with acute disfavor at issues which threaten the supremacy, dignity or continuity of life. In this respect, most of the developments that prompt action in the medical field are often noted for their controversy, immediacy, and a tendency to threaten the very place of human beings in the society. For this reason, AI often violates basic values. It is therefore dangerous to perceive AI as a set of value-neutral practices and procedures which is independent of complex inter-group and intra-group behavioral dynamics. Hence, the ethical analysis of issues connected with Artificial Intelligence and development

QUALITIES OF ARTIFICIAL INTELLIGENCE

As stated above, the functional view of AI focuses on what it does. From this perspective, AI generally is thought to refer to "machines that respond to stimulation consistent with traditional responses from humans, given the human capacity for contemplation, judgment and intention." (West & Allen, 2018). They are machines which make decisions which humans alone can make, and as such, operate in an intentional, intelligent, and adaptive manner. Following West and Allen (2018), the qualities of AI would be briefly explained below:

INTENTIONALITY

Machines that embed Artificial Intelligence are designed to make decisions, often using real-time data. West and Allen (2018) contend that such machines are unlike passive machines that are capable only of mechanical or predetermined responses. The authors further explained that using sensors, digital data, or remote inputs, AI-enhanced machines combine information from a variety of different sources, analyze the material instantly, and act on the insights derived from those data. The authors then concluded that with massive improvements in storage systems, processing speeds, and analytic techniques, AI-embedded machines are capable of tremendous sophistication in analysis and decision-making.

INTELLIGENCE

Functionally defined, intelligence could said to be the ability to take on something, and observe it critically with a view to spotting underlying trends. AI machines take data and looks for underlying trends. The ability to spot something that is relevant for a practical problem, can take that knowledge and use it to analyze specific issues is a process view of intelligence. All these are possible with AI-embedded machines. The data which such machines manipulate can come in the form of digital information, satellite imagery, visual information, text, or unstructured data (West & Allen, 2018).

ADAPTABILITY

Another crucial quality of an intelligent entity is the ability to learn and adapt as it makes decisions. Explaining the mechanism of adaptation in AI, West and Allen (2018) stated:

In the transportation area, for example, semi-autonomous vehicles have tools that let drivers and vehicles know about upcoming congestion, potholes, highway construction, or other possible traffic impediments. Vehicles can take advantage of the experience of other vehicles on the road, without human involvement, and the entire corpus of their achieved "experience" is immediately and fully transferable to other similarly configured vehicles. Their advanced algorithms, sensors, and cameras incorporate experience in current operations, and use dashboards and visual displays to present information in real time so human drivers are able to make sense of ongoing traffic and vehicular conditions.

West and Allen added that in the case of fully autonomous vehicles, advanced systems can completely control the car or truck, and make all the navigational decisions based on its experience of the route, features of the road, distance involved, etc.

APPLICATION OF AI TO DIVERSE SECTORS OF THE ECONOMY

Artificial Intelligence is gradually being deployed to different industries and productive systems, fore shading its eventual takeover, if present trends continue, of the entire spheres of human activity. The key areas of advancement in the use of AI are in the following:

- **AI Advancements in the Robotics Industry**: Robotics is one of the areas that have completely adapted AI to itself. The idea of robots presupposes human-like machines deployed to routinely execute tasks which the human laborer might find risky or monotonous, or where the level of secrecy and sensitivity precludes the involvement of rank and file workforce. Robots have been effectively deployed and applied in the auto industry, the building of heavy industrial machines etc.

- **AI Advancements in Financial Services**: AI enables the performance of functions which require high level of accounting skills, which the human factor often makes vulnerable to costly errors. What is more, with rapid increase in customer base, many businesses, especially those providing financial services need to carry out calculations that match the huge day-to-day transactions with their clients. This necessitates complex financial functions which AI can conveniently enhance at little or no costs.
- **Advancements in Machine Learning for Wildlife Conservation**: The use of AI for wildlife conservation has become increasingly popular. This is mainly due to the need to respond to the high level of risk involved in the wild, coupled with the often expansive range of wildlife, which stretches available manpower. Drones and other devices have thus been developed to police the forest and identify dangers such as animal poachers, natural disasters, wildlife, cannibalism and other issues which pose danger to forest flora and fauna.
- AI Advancements in the Healthcare Industry: AI has been integrated into the healthcare industry to perform complex tasks especially in areas involving the inner parts of the body. Such areas include scanning, reading of brain waves, complex surgery and organ transplant.
- **AI Advancements in the Automobile Industry**: Artificial Intelligence has registered huge success in the auto industry. The design of automatic cars, electric cars, hybrid cars, and vehicles with different exotic features such as flying cars and driverless vehicles are all possible as a result of AI. The overall effect has been an improvement in the efficiency and effectiveness of vehicles and a reduction in the human casualty from accidents.
- **AI Advancement in security and military science:** Perhaps, no other area of industry would benefit from a future entirely dependent on AI as security and military affairs. The use of AI not only means that security has become more effective, it also reduces the human casualty from wars, terrorism and other forms of attack on human lives and properties. Increasing use is being made of drones, which are pilotless aircrafts in wars and in the protection of, at-risk populations.

AI in Commerce and the Internet: AI has become an acceptable digital assistant in a wide range of activities involving the use of mobile phones, computers and the internet. For instance, "Siri, Alexa and Google Assistant" are "A.I. -powered personal assistants are able to take in your voice commands and translate them into actions, such as adding items to your shopping list or calling a friend"

AI BENEFITS

Economic Drivers: AI is a tool for both short-term and long-term transformation of the economy. By facilitating speedy and mass performance of tasks that hitherto took a reasonable length of time to accomplish, AI has caused remarkable increase in efficiency gains, thus raising productivity and lowering costs, distance, and other natural and artificial barriers.

Human Capital Development: The increasing use of AI has led to massive uptick in human capital development. The performance of tasks which posed reasonable challenge to human effort and ingenuity has created a rich environment for those involved in AI-enabled industries to learn from. This has added to the skill set of players in cutting edge industries where AI is something of backbone. For instance, the use of AI in space aircraft and in space science extends the frontiers of human knowledge of nature and the universe, while challenging man to further explore and exploit.

Productivity Growth: AI is fundamentally a tool for productivity growth. More speed, more precision, more work, less cost, and more profit invariably lead to growth in the productivity of labor. This explains why AI has been gradually threatening to replace human workforce.

Lower Barriers to Entry for Businesses: It is generally known old barriers to the movement of goods and people are no longer in place as much as they were few decades ago. This phenomenon, known as globalization, has created a world of intense diffusion of ideas and uniformity of attitudes, outlooks and activities. Expressions like "the world is flat, and "the death of distance" increasingly mirrors the current reality. All these development would not be exponential, or even possible, without AI.

Increased Consumption: Higher output of industry and increased income growth has led to increased consumption. The world is currently witnessing the age of mass consumption, all thanks to increasing application of AI to different facets of human activities. Economists had earlier predicted the dawn of the Age of Mass Consumption, which would naturally follow from increasing economic development and modernization, but failed to envisage the relevance of AI in bringing this about. An unhealthy dimension, termed mass consumerism, has arrived.

Market Expansion: AI has spurred tremendous market expansion, through the discovery of new products and services which facilitate quick, efficient and diverse range of financial, trade, health, legal and educational services. AI-embedded solutions to climate change, space technology, wildlife conservation, agriculture, meteorology, and several other critical sectors have engineered leapfrogging solutions to complex problems of society.

HOW DEVELOPING COUNTRIES CAN USE AI TO LEVERAGE ON SOCIOECONOMIC DEVELOPMENT

Though Artificial Intelligence is a developmental silver bullet across countries, it can be particularly relevant in the drive of backward nation to deal with perennial challenges to development catch up with the rest of the world. Thus AI can be applied in the areas of other opportunities such as risk management—disease prevention, natural disaster management, humanitarian crisis management—and citizen engagement through automated and real-time analysis of online activities, including social network and telecommunications metadata (Strusani & Houngbonon, 2019)

Risk Management: AI is particularly useful as a means for developing countries to manage risks from natural disasters, epidemics, famine, wars and population displacements. Apart from poverty, and ignorance, these are typical socioeconomic issues that overwhelm the resources and efforts of people in developing countries. AI methods can help extract data on social relationships and dynamics, human mobility patterns, and appropriate methods of population response to crises (Eagle & Horvitz, 2019). The use of drones for purposes ranging from civilian life protection, detection of human and animal disease spread, oncoming drought and famine, etc, have already started to turn around the fortunes of millions of people in developing countries.

Medical Care: Developing countries face the challenge of providing cheap, available and affordable medical care to huge populations of poor and dispossessed citizens. There is a great potential for the application of AI in dealing with this challenge. According to Eagle and Horvitz, (2019), reasoning systems might one day help to extend medical care to remote regions through automated diagnosis and effective training of limited medical expertise and transportation resources.

Citizenship Engagement: AI could also be a tool for effective engagement between governments and their citizens in developing countries through automated real-time analysis of online activities, including social network and communication metadata. Eagle and Horvitz reveal that unprecedented quantities of data are being generated in the developing world on human health, financial transactions, movements, and communications. They further averred that models and systems that leverage such data are being looked upon as a means to guide public policy, monitor interventions, and provide insights about population response to crises.

REGULATORY FRAMEWORKS

Data Access Problem: As blood and oxygen are essential to human life, so is data essential to AI. Machines that embed AI make decisions solely on the basis of data imputed into them. As a result, false, incorrect or partially correct data will lead to decisions that are false, incorrect or partially true, respectively. Data integrity and open access laws are thus often put in place in order to guarantee effective functioning of AI.

AI and Ethical Considerations: Ethics is very important to AI, given the fact that though it has an intelligence that compares with humans, it is lacking in that quality called conscience, which enables humans to walk the moral and value tightrope in challenging times. To deal with this challenge, West and Allen (2018) propose that in making certain decisions and transactions, AI can be designed to spot out people in need of serious help, help people discriminate against individuals they don't like, or help screen or build rosters of individuals based on unfair criteria. They opined that the types of considerations that go into programming decisions matter a lot in terms of how the systems operate and how they affect customers.

Legal Liability: a very contentious and controversial area in AI is the issue of legal liability of AI systems. It is a thing of irony that an entity which acts like and on behalf of humans cannot be held legally answerable for infractions due to it. In most cases, the law provides that "if there are harms or infractions (or fatalities in the case of driverless cars), the operators of the algorithm likely will fall under product liability rules. A body of case law has shown that the situation's facts and circumstances determine liability and influence the kind of penalties that are imposed. Those can range from civil fines to imprisonment for major harms" (West & Allen, 2018).

RECOMMENDATIONS

Improving Data Access: Given the strategic importance of data to effective AI functioning, measures aimed at improving data access to real-time, valid and useful data should be at the heart of government policy. Data access laws and policies, data authenticity verification measures, including the use of education and software to sift relevant data from fake, unreliable ones, should be encouraged.

Investment in IT and AI: Governments should increase their budgetary allocation to AI. West and Allen (2018) noted that most AI sectors in the world, including in the United States, are still underfunded. Apart from investing in AI, governments should also invest in expansion of internet access, broadband coverage, and freedom of speech and writing should be safeguarded by the law.

Promotion of Digital Education: The integration of ICT into education has been is an inevitable policy decision for all nations in the 21st century. This is more critical in societies where the level of development of ICT is appallingly low. To rise above this challenge, and meet with the requirement for AI-powered society of the future, there is need for serous investment in digital education. As noted by OECD (2016) education can foster innovation in the society by developing the rights skills among the workforce and the citizenry. It is discouraging that, even in some of the advanced world, many students do not receive instruction in the kinds of skills that will be needed in an AI-dominated landscape. West and Allen (2018) revealed that "there currently are shortages of data scientists, computer scientists, engineers, coders, and platform developers. These are skills that are in short supply; unless our educational system generates more people with these capabilities, it will limit AI development."

Creating a Synergy between Government, Industry and Research Institutes

Research and development is a trinity involving government, industry and research institutes/universities. It is difficult to get the products of research out of the laboratory, or to deal with its problems, without creating this triangular synergy (Ekeh, 2009). The relationship between Universities, Science, Innovation (through R&D), and commercialization and the establishment of technology or innovation-based enterprises, is explained by the famous University- industry link (UIL) (Yusuf & Nabeshima, 2007).

Federal officials need to think about how they deal with artificial intelligence. As noted previously, there are many issues ranging from the need for improved data access to addressing issues of bias and discrimination. It is only when the vital concerns surrounding AI are considered in by or with all the interest of all these three actors in industry that the full benefits of this emerging technology will be gained (West & Allen, 2018).

CONCLUSION

This study has found that though AI is fraught with both ethical and epistemological challenges, there is hope that if the positive qualities of AI are harnessed, the technology has potential for closing the digital divide between North and South. It also found out that there is numerous importance of AI to development, and further highlighted the latest advancements in AI. Finally, it made recommendations on the best approach to using AI to influence socioeconomic development

REFERENCES

OECD. (2016). *Innovating Education and Educating for Innovation: The Power of Digital Technologies and Skills*. OECD Publishing. doi:10.1787/9789264265097-

Ekeh, L. (2009). *Industrialization and National Prosperity: Lessons for the Dveloping Countires*. Luzek Publishers.

Vinusa, R., Azizpour, H., & Nerini, F. F. (2020). The Role of Artificial Intelligence in Achieving the Sustainable Development Goals. *Nature Communications*, *11*(233), 233. doi:10.103841467-019-14108-y PMID:31932590

Eagle, N., & Horvitz, E. (2019). *Artificial Intelligence for Development. Papers from the AAAI Spring Symposium.*

Frost, S. E. (1989). *Basic Teachings of the Great Philosophers: A Survey of their Basic Ideas.* Anchor Books.

Lawhead, W. F. (2003). *The Philosophical Journey: An Interactive Approach* (5th ed.). McGraw-Hill Book Company.

Sharif, Y. S., & Nabeshima, K. (2007). How Universities Promote Economic Growth. The World Bank.

Strusani, D., & Houngbonon, G.V. (2019). *The Role of Artificial Intelligence in Emerging Markets.* Academic Press.

West, D. M., & Allen, J. J. (2018, April). *How Artificial Intelligence is Transforming the World.* Retrieved from, https:/www.brookings.edu>research>how-artificial-intelligence-is-transforming-the-world

Chapter 18
Adopting of Artificial Intelligence and Development in Developing Countries:
Perspective of Economic Transformation

Daniel Kwalipo Mbangula
International University of Management, Namibia

ABSTRACT

Manufactured insights has been seen by numerous governments, companies, and visionaries as another step in improvement. In spite of the fact that artificial intelligence (AI) offers numerous guarantees for the future, it too presents numerous impediments going forward, especially in African countries, and no place are those obstacles felt more distinctly than in creating nations. A few nations are as of now developing policies to upgrade capabilities for understanding issues through the utilize of AI. Any arrangement to create AI arrangements in a creating nation faces an awesome assortment of challenges, ranging from getting to power and web, the need of qualified AI pros and licensing agreements, among others. This chapter discusses the adoption of artificial intelligence and development in developing countries unloading challenges and best practices.

INTRODUCTION

The newly industrial revolution has brought about the rapid changes that every nation need to adjust to, that may allow the country to develop and catch up with the usage of artificial intelligence in the amidst of the fast growing world. AI can be defined as the combination of advances that enable what UNESCO's World Commission on the Morals of Logical Information and Innovation (COMEST) calls "machines able of mimicking certain functionalities of human insights, counting such features as recognition, learning, thinking, problem-solving, dialect interaction, and indeed creating imaginative work" (COMEST 2019).This chapter will look at the models adopted by developing countries particularly in Africa and mostly also focusing on Sub-Saharan African countries to develop and adjust themselves to

DOI: 10.4018/978-1-6684-4107-7.ch018

usage of artificial intelligence. Similarly, the chapter will address the unique cases of each country and how artificial intelligence and development are interlinked to fasten the developmental programmes in the targeted countries and how it may be deemed as a challenge to economic development for developing countries. The researcher would write on the challenges faced by the target countries in terms of Artificial Intelligence (AI) and development and how this can be addressed. The fact that the influence of big changes on the economy's functioning has been a major distress for both economists and policymakers in the period of the Fourth Industrial Revolution, Artificial Intelligence, and Digital Transformation. These changes are projected to have a significant impact on the economy's rate of growth, employment, and labour productivity, among other things (Heidi, 2020). Therefore, the researcher would like to unpack further details of why AI is assumed to be a challenge or best option to economic development and job creation in the developing countries. Conversely the goal of this chapter is to contribute to the current research on the relationship between digital transformation, development, employment, and productivity in developing countries. Policymakers must consider the ramifications of those relationships when deciding how much support to provide to encourage digital transformation and artificial intelligence promotion (Heidi, 2020).

In Africa, Counterfeit Insights (AI) is among the key empowering innovations that will drive the continent's advanced economy. AI gives endless roads for both the open and the private segments to optimize arrangements to the foremost significant issues confronting the landmass today, especially for battling industries/sectors such as healthcare and agribusiness (Travaly and Muvunyi, 2020). Imaginative shapes of benefit conveyance and back empowered by AI frameworks are paramount since of its pivotal part in expanding powerless educate and segments for the benefit of the society and economy. For illustration, supporters claim that AI venture in sub-Saharan Africa will offer assistance progress human skill, progress efficiency, and improve early disease detection and reconnaissance within the wellbeing division (Smith & Neupane, 2018). AI moreover has the control to transform the way governments provide open administrations, as this might altogether improve citizens' encounters of government whereas decreasing fetched for individuals getting to these administrations from rural and peri-urban communities. Ultimately Michael (2019) also indicated that Africa has the most youthful populace of youth within the world, so there's a requirement to build capacity with quality by training some of its exceedingly gifted youth. The youth are an opportunity for African countries to form their stamp within the AI world.

The researcher will address the aspects of economic transformation and development by discussing how different developing countries particularly in Sub-Sahara Africa implemented the usage of artificial intelligence in their different economic sectors. Artificial intelligence (AI) is a broad tool that allows people to reimagine how they integrate information, analyse data, and use the ensuing insights to make better decisions—and it is already affecting every aspect of their lives (Darrell &John, 2009). Furthermore, Darrell & John (2009) study emphasised that Artificial Intelligence (AI) is a field of science and technology that has the potential to significantly alter public policies and services in a variety of ways. In just a few years, it is projected that roughly one-third of public employees' time will be freed up, allowing them to transition from low-value job to high-value work. Governments can also utilize AI to improve policy planning and decision-making, as well as communication and interaction with citizens and communities, and the timeliness and quality of public services. Interestingly, AI is a technology that is revolutionizing every aspect of life, despite its broad lack of familiarity. It's a versatile tool that allows people to reconsider how they integrate data, evaluate it, and apply the insights gained to make better decisions. The researcher's goal with this detailed chapter review is to explain AI to policymakers, opinion leaders, and interested observers, and to show how AI is already changing the world and raising major problems for society, the economy, and governance in a developing countries (Darrell & John, 2009).

CHAPTER AIMS/OBJECTIVES

By the End of this Chapter the Following Aims and Objectives must be Achieved

- To analysis the implementation of Artificial intelligence and development in developing countries
- To discuss challenges faced to adopt AI and development in developing countries
- To elaborate best practise employed by developing countries to transform economic development by adopting Artificial Intelligence
- To describe findings of the study about embracing artificial intelligence and development in developing countries
- To draw conclusion from the study findings

IMPLEMENTING ARTIFICIAL INTELLIGENCE FOR ECONOMIC TRANSFORMATION IN DEVELOPING COUNTRIES

Malahat & Ari (2020) described intelligent / smart manufacturing as an ideas or methods of production that make use of advanced machinery and/or information. Product transactions and product optimization are the focus of these innovative technologies. Intelligent manufacturing, according to these scholars (Malahat & Ari, 2020), is a modern-day manufacturing paradigm that employs intelligent technology and scientific knowledge to dramatically improve design, production, and management. Ultimately this practice can lead to more improved services delivery in most developing countries during this area than it was a century ago. Much of these changes are due to a variety of sophisticated materials Smart sensors and sensor-based technologies, adaptive decision-making models, intelligent devices, and data analytics help products throughout their entire lifecycle. In addition the enhancement of products in terms of a) efficiency, b) quality, and c) service level in general should not come as a surprise, given the vast range of upgraded aspects of technological advancement in most developing countries now (Malahat & Ari, 2020). For that reason, related to the intelligent manufacturing, Counterfeit Insights (AI) will give producers highlights like progressed level learning, more specific thinking and quicker acting in mechanical fabricating framework. These progressions will at that point be in key role in the society automatization and digitalization steps, which builds the alter from conventional to intelligent manufacturing change in developing countries such as Namibia.

In most developing countries particularly in Sub Sahara Africa, AI is a rising innovation within the field of farming. AI-based hardware and machines, has taken today's farming framework to a distinctive level. This innovation has improved trim generation and moved forward real-time observing, gathering, preparing and promoting. To be specific, the most recent advances of computerized frameworks utilizing rural robots and rambles have made a colossal commitment within the agro-based segment. Different hi-tech computer based frameworks are outlined to decide different imperative parameters like weed discovery, abdicate discovery and edit quality and numerous other procedures (Liakos, Busato, Moshou, Pearson, & Bochtis, 2018). Because many developing countries still rely on agricultural production, hence developing economic growth starts from agricultural sector. The primary strategy was the subsurface trickle water system prepare, which minimized the sum of water misfortune due to evaporation and runoff because it is straightforwardly buried underneath the edit. Afterward analysts came with diverse sensors which were utilized to identify the require of water supply to the areas as soil dampness sensor and rain drop sensor, which were teaching through remote broadband organize and fuelled by sun based boards. The rain drop sensor and soil dampness sensor informs the agriculturist around the dampness substance within the soil through SMS in their cell phone utilizing GSM module. Appropriately the rancher can give commands utilizing SMS to ON and OFF the water supply. Thus ready to consider that this framework will identify portion or zone within the areas which required more water and seem hold off the farmer from watering when it's raining (Tanha, Dhara, Nivedita, Patelb, &Yagnik, 2020).

IMPACT OF AI ON AGRICULTURE

The innovations which are AI-based offer assistance to move forward effectiveness in all the areas conjointly oversee the challenges confronted by different businesses counting the various areas within the agrarian division just like the trim surrender, water system, soil substance detecting, edit- checking, weeding, trim foundation (Kim & Evans, 2008). In addition rural robots are built in arrange to convey tall esteemed application of AI within the said division. With the worldwide populace taking off, the agrarian division is confronting an emergency, but AI has the potential to convey much-needed arrangement. AI- based mechanical arrangements has empowered the ranchers to deliver more yield with less input and indeed moved forward the quality of yield, moreover guaranteeing speedier go-to- advertise for the yielded crops. By 2020, ranchers will be utilizing 75 million associated gadgets. By 2050, the normal cultivate is anticipated to produce a normal of 4.1 million information points every day (Kim & Evans, 2008). On the other hand, Panpatte (2018) said that manufactured insights makes it conceivable for ranchers to gather huge sum of information from government as well as open websites, analyse all of it and give agriculturists with arrangements to numerous equivocal issues as well because it gives us with a more brilliant way of water system which comes about in higher abdicate to the agriculturists. Due to fake insights, cultivating will be found to be a blend of mechanical as well as organic aptitudes within the close future which is able not as it served as distant; an improved or a distant better result within the matter of quality for all the ranchers but to minimize their misfortunes and workloads will be achieved now. UN states that, by 2050, 2/3rd of world's populace will be living in urban ranges which emerges a got to reduce the burden on the agriculturists. AI in horticulture can be connected which would mechanize a few forms, diminish dangers and give ranchers with a comparatively simple and effective cultivating (Panpatte, 2018).

CHALLENGES FACED TO ADOPT AI AND DEVELOPMENT IN DEVELOPING COUNTRIES

In the case of AI, developments may depend on get to programs outlined by other performing artists or licenses to utilize in specific advances. The cost of these licenses may be prohibitively costly for a little firm attempting to enter the advertise. Also the pre-existing asset and mental property impediments incorporate the essential components required to utilize these assets. The dialect boundary gets to be noteworthy when one consider that most programming dialects are in English and have constrained accessibility in other dialects (Johns, 2019). Too, whereas most programming does not require an especially capable computer cluster, preparing AI does require at slightest a modestly expansive preparing capacity. Moreover, get to the web and indeed steady power are required for building an environment in which AI improvement can take put. In a nutshell, components that are taken for allowed in created nations are stifling creating countries' potential to require advantage of this modern mechanical field (Johns, 2019). The capacity of a government to draw in appropriate AI specialists and hold them is key to the victory of an AI improvement program. Indeed on the off chance that a company were to procure the essential information and innovative assets, they at that point require employees able to decipher them and utilize them towards the project's objective. This is the huge gap in many developing countries to able to transform successful to artificial intelligence use and development. Agreeing to Santiago (2020) analyses, governments regularly utilize two alternatives to get these people to work in their nation, either contribute in a long term and costly instructive program or pull in specialists from other nations. In either case, companies or educate attempting to utilize them must at that point offer considerable pay rates, since of the furious around the world competition for AI experts. An instruction program that makes AI pros but offers no appropriate neighbourhood work leads to them taking off the nation for better business opportunities. As a result developing countries must take all these deterrents into thought when endeavouring to create an arrangement planned to advance the advancement of AI arrangements (Santiago, 2020).

As commandingly laid out by Kulesz (2018), AI can be anticipated to have significant impacts on the differences of broadly accessible social expressions in both the created and creating universes and, within the nonattendance of solid arrangement intercessions, the impacts have the potential to be starkly negative, especially for the world's destitute nations who are not domestic to the prevailing AI and computerized substance firms. Ndung'u & Signé (2020) concurred with Kulesz notion as they pointed out that settling the labour-skills jumble since making employments for the burgeoning youth populace could be a need in most African countries, many governments are hesitant to back innovations that undermine existing employments. A few of the current innovations tend to supplant low-skilled workers—of which Africa has an abundance —with higher-skilled labourers, compelling interest within the 4IR to economies with relevant skills. African governments must invest in instruction and reskilling programs to guarantee that technology supplements, rather than replaces, labour. Get to progressed innovation in Africa is obliged by foundation parameters such as need of power and moo tele density, web thickness, and broadband infiltration. As a result, versatile phone and web utilize remains moo. Other innovative bottlenecks incorporate a need of standardized application programming interfacing and common data dialects for the expanded integration of to a great extent self-sufficient frameworks as well as exposure to the threats of cyberattacks. Moreover, quickening the physical network of fiber-optic systems as well as the interoperability of virtual stages is basic not as it were for overhauling innovation on the landmass, but moreover for coming to and bringing down unit costs for the underserved (Ndung'u & Signé, 2020).

Michael (2019) emphasised that in Africa, major advancements in AI will be centred on tackling real-world problems influencing conventional people's lives. These will incorporate arrangements that favour the progression of AI ability, back operations in businesses like broadcast communications, energize research in wellbeing and agribusiness, direct data collection and assurance, and lastly address issues of online deception. The larger part of these will be AI pertinent arrangements taken after by roundabout AI arrangements. Where AI-relevant arrangements are those that don't specifically target

AI advancement, their presence has an effect on advance in AI such as instruction. Whereas circuitous approaches, like data protection or control, in a roundabout way influence AI advancement.

Other challenges faced includes the fact that more than 177 million individuals in Sub-Saharan Africa have a social-media account and development is expanding. This growth is due to the reasonableness of smartphone gadgets and increments in internet infiltration. The combination has driven to simple sharing of information and request for advanced substance. Social media clients share news and data like cautions of illness outbreaks and business openings. The downside of these improvements is the sharing of fake news without veracity. Researchers have proposed methods like utilizing chart investigation to detect sources of bits of gossip and dissemination of deception. In any case, it will take more than investigation to unravel such challenges. In near communities, like those in Africa, deception or disinformation that empowers the spread of divisive, xenophobic, sexist, and standard political ideals that carry noxious aim to spread fear, incite outrage, and seed retribution could be a time bomb (Michael, 2019). Malevolent people who have their claim agenda and thought processes utilize social media to spread hateful belief systems that destabilize communities.

What are the prospects for incorporating AI into education in developing nations, given this broad perspective? New opportunities have arisen as a result of technological advancements. Countries confronted with significant societal issues In Africa, access is a major issue. In the last 15 years, the number of people who have access to mobile phones has increased dramatically. Fuelling economic growth for years (Aker & Mbiti, 2010). In developing countries, there are discussions over how to employ the AI's potential for promoting social equality (BID, 2018). While AI has various benefits, as discussed in this chapter, it can also be a disruptive technology that might exacerbate existing inequities and divides by excluding marginalized and underprivileged people from AI-powered education. As a result, a new type of digital divide has emerged: a divide in how data-based information is used to inform intelligent decision making (Hilbert, 2015). The barriers to implementing AI in education in developing nations have been outlined in recent studies. 1-ICT hardware availability, 2-Electrical availability, 3-Internet reliability, 4-Data costs, 5-Students' fundamental ICT abilities, 6-Language, and 7-Lack of culturally relevant content are the key ones (Nye, 2015). More research on the usage of Big Data in poor countries reveals that a lack of basic infrastructure creates a new digital divide in the use of data-based knowledge for informed, intelligent decision-making (Hilbert, 2015). Multiple policies must be implemented to remove these roadblocks. It is critical to begin by recognizing the internet as a human right and forming several multinational alliances to create infrastructure in the developing world's poorest areas (Mutoni, 2017). The United Nations Broadband Commission's work is one vivid example work for this.

Given that data fuels AI, having complete, trustworthy, and timely data is a must before using AI-enhanced data analytics solutions. Data that is completely functional comprehensive and up-to-date data analytics system gives up new opportunities for AI-assisted prediction and machine learning. Algorithms for learning intelligent systems are made possible by data. There can be no algorithm, no matter how sophisticated, without the necessary data. Can function adequately, regardless of how complicated. As a result, AI-enabled systems require a data-rich environment. Data accessibility, on the other hand, is a necessary but insufficient need condition. As a result, any AI-enabled system can only do so much. It's only as good as the information it includes. After all, erroneous data is a problems and are more likely to lead to the creation of machine learning algorithms outputs that are wrong Predictive algorithms can only do so much. If the data they have is thorough and reliable, they can create complete and accurate forecasts. However, many countries nonetheless combat with collecting basic but necessary educational data. The UNESCO Institute for Statistics (UIS) cites the many stumbling blocks to the efficient and fantastic collection and use of instructional information (UIS, 2018). Educational data need to be open and usable at the school level. An EMIS ought to be capable to generate analyses that are granular sufficient to assist instructors and education administrators recognize the key challenges whilst also being capable to mixture statistics to disclose trends that can inform policy development. Furthermore, records have to additionally account for inequities, providing insights, for example, on studying outcomes disaggregated in accordance to demographic factors such as age, gender and socio-economic background (UNESCO, 2018). The capability to generate such analyses allows training structures to decide the educational disadvantage skilled by precise marginalised or vulnerable populations. However, data on disadvantaged groups nonetheless currently tend to be incomplete and even absent. For instance, a 2016 learn about via UNICEF showed that, out of forty nations surveyed, 19 had no facts at all on children with disabilities; for many countries that did have data, it was once solely particular that the toddler used to be on a special needs programme however failed to point out the disability (UNICEF, 2016). Data on refugees and internally displaced populations (IDPs) also continue to be limited, with most of those data coming from camps and camp-like settings (UNESCO & UNHCR, 2016). Refugees studying in country wide schools are also often no longer identified as refugees in national education statistics, thus making it more difficult to monitor and consider their studying outcomes. Furthermore, since the collection and analysis of training records usually happens on a once-a-year basis, the information are regularly unable to carry accurate records on transient populations. It is also vital to note that the training system itself is not the only supply of information applicable to learning provision. Household data, as mainly stated via the UIS, can also provide insights on exogenous factors that might account for getting to know difficulties at school. The same can be stated of records coming from different ministries, e.g. the ministry of health. Data on diet can be used to report on, for instance, the design of college meal programmes. This speaks to the significance of data integration: When government structures are integrated, more information become shared and handy throughout all sectors. This records sharing means that extra information can be used through the schooling sector to run AI algorithms and consequently, more probabilities to generate analyses, fashions or predictions.

BEST PRACTISE EMPLOYED BY DEVELOPING COUNTRIES TO TRANSFORM ECONOMIES BY USING AI

As many countries across the globe are already enjoying the transformed economies in the Fourth Industrial Revolution (4IR) many countries in Africa are not left out by this new model as it has some benefits which outsmart traditional ways of practices. Therefore, AI-powered 4IR has the capacity to move forward different perspectives of socio-economic improvement over the world. AI has the potential to make strides in business, the headway of pharmaceutical and the quality of life, make strides efficiency and proficiency of worldwide supply chains as well as raise worldwide salaries. Numerous of these opportunities are as of now developing over Africa (Sertaç & Yaman, 2020). For example, AI incorporates an expansive potential to drive economic growth, advancement, and democratization in these nations, and thus to progress open administrations, and bettering the quality of life for numerous individuals (Cisse, 2018). AI can empower labourers at all skill levels to be more competitive by upgrading human aptitudes comparable to industrial nations. More broadly, satisfactory foundation improvement will drive and maintain economic transformation in Africa. With lower transport and communication costs, nations with suitable agro-ecological conditions can deliver high-value items. Closing the web connectivity and get to crevice with progressed economies will empower more African nations to enter service export markets. Small-scale producers in Africa may moreover ended up more competitive with access to advanced stages for investigate, deals, and distribution (Ndung'u & Signé, 2020).

There's an increasing awareness of the positive impacts which AI has on African nations, in divisions such as security, agriculture, wellbeing care, and open and financial services. Consequently, a cyber security space, several countries have started utilizing AI in arrange to implement tighter supervision on their populaces. For case, at March 2018, the Zimbabwean government marked a strategic organization with the Guangzhou-based start-up Cloud Walk Innovation to start a largescale facial acknowledgment program all through the country. The assertions, supported by the Chinese government's Belt and Street activity is intended to see the innovation essentially utilized in security and law authorization and most likely be expanded to other open programs (Cisse, 2018). In this vein, AI can to help an assortment of border security and country security applications. Within the space of farming, AI technologies such as machine learning, inaccessible detecting, and data analytics move forward efficiency and productivity at all stages of the esteem chain. This process enables small-holder ranchers to extend their income through higher trim yields and more noteworthy cost control, identify and accurately treat bothers and diseases, monitor soil conditions and target fertilizer applications (Vasisht, Kapetanovic, Won, Jin, Chandra, Sinha, & Stratman, 2017). Interestingly also in African context, there's too introductory prove of utilizing AI to enhance therapeutic administrations in African countries. Specifically, portable clinical choice support systems seem broadly move forward healthcare provided in provincial ranges African nations.

According to Ndung'u & Signé (2020) study, in later a long time, the ICT segment in Africa has kept on develop, a drift that's likely to continue. For example, of late, portable advances and administrations have created 1.7 million coordinate occupations (both formal and casual), contributed to $144 billion of financial esteem (8.5 percent of the GDP of sub-Saharan Africa), and contributed $15.6 billion to the open segment through taxation. Digitization has too settled data asymmetry issues within the monetary framework and labour advertise, in this way expanding effectiveness, certainty, and security in an environment where information flow is basic for financial development and work creation. Furthermore, disappointment to recognize and capitalize on 4IR openings, alternately, will force considerable risks on African partners: Without endeavours to move past existing models of innovation, entrepreneurship, and computerized development on the landmass, African businesses hazard falling further behind, compounding the worldwide "digital divide" and bringing down their worldwide competitiveness. Going past the existing models requires teaching in administration to permit an endogenous innovative environment. At the same time, teach must secure the showcase through consumer assurance laws and controls that energize competition (Ndung'u & Signé, 2020).

Ndung'u & Signe (2020) also emphasised that the spread of computerized advances can engage the destitute with get to data, job opportunities, and administrations that move forward their standard of living. AI, the Web of Things (IoT), and block chain can upgrade openings for information gathering and examination for more targeted and viable destitution decrease techniques. As of now, one have seen the transformational power of formal monetary administrations through versatile phones, such as M-Pesa, coming to the underserved, counting ladies, who are critical drivers for economical destitution eradication. These money related administrations permit family units to spare in secure rebellious to broaden their asset base and elude cycles of poverty. This AI initiatives indeed will assist the transformation of many economies in Africa as it creates the easier opportunities for everyone who was disadvantaged in the past century. In addition, digitization has affected financial development through the comprehensive fund, empowering the unbanked to enter custom through retail electronic instalments stages and virtual reserve funds and credit supply mechanical platforms. More broadly, digitization is empowering business people and businesses to reconsider commerce models that are more impactful, maintainable, and associated with other divisions of the economy. For illustration, with fintech, digitization has gone past the financial division to influence the genuine division and family units, changing item plans and business models over showcase segments. Businesses are able to plan items and exchange online, and people are able to function budgetary administrations and instalments for shopping and investments. The government is additionally relocating to online stages to helpfully provide public administrations (Ndung'u & Signe, 2020).

Namibia is one of the newly independence country in Sub Sahara Africa which gotten its independence in 1990. After independence, the country has set a vision called Vision 2030 which stipulates that Namibia plans to be a prosperous and industrialised nation, developed by her human resources, enjoying peace, harmony and political stability by the year 2030. It furthermore sets the broad thrusts and strategies in the development agenda for the nation over the long-term. To achieve this dream the country has to align itself with other countries in the region and world at large by following the path leading to the 4IR (Fourth Industrial Revolution). Vision 2030 is a comprehensive plan to profoundly change Namibia's political and economic landscape land reform, for example, has a significant impact on the landscape. Ultimately, housing, the environment, and health are all issues that need to be addressed. Education and economic development ensures that everyone has an equal chance. It identifies the most pressing development issues human resources, for example, are important to the government. Development, creation of jobs, and provision of infrastructure, transformations. By so doing artificial intelligence and development is inevitable. Undoubtable this will lead to human resources development to capacitate them on accomplishing their tasks in the country's market.

CHAPTER FINDINGS

The following are some of the chapter's findings that were found; AI can empower labourers at all skill levels to be more competitive by upgrading human aptitudes comparable to industrial nations. Furthermore, there's also an increasing awareness of the positive impacts which AI has on African nations, in divisions such as security, agriculture, wellbeing care, and open and financial services. Consequently, a cyber security space, several countries have started utilizing AI in arrange to implement tighter supervision on their populaces. Also the spread of computerized advances can engage the destitute with get to data, job opportunities, and administrations that move forward peoples' standard of living. As supported by Cisse, (2018) in this vein, AI can to help an assortment of border security and country security applications. Within the space of farming, AI technologies such as machine learning, inaccessible detecting, and data analytics move forward efficiency and productivity at all stages of the esteem chain. AI, the Web of Things (IoT), and block chain can upgrade openings for information gathering and examination for more targeted and viable destitution decrease techniques. In addition, AI has brought the transformational power of formal monetary administrations through versatile phones, such as M-Pesa, coming to the underserved, counting ladies, who are critical drivers for economical destitution eradication in many African countries. Ndung'u & Signe (2020) also emphasised that the spread of computerized advances can engage the destitute with get to data, job opportunities, and administrations that move forward their standard of living. AI, the Web of Things (IoT), and block chain can upgrade openings for information gathering and examination for more targeted and viable destitution decrease techniques. In this vein,

AI is able to help an assortment of border security and country security applications. Within the space of farming, AI technologies such as machine learning, inaccessible detecting, and data analytics move forward efficiency and productivity at all stages of the esteem chain was found to be a necessity. This process enables small-holder ranchers to extend their income through higher trim yields and more noteworthy cost control, identify and accurately treat bothers and diseases, monitor soil conditions and target fertilizer applications. Also the study has found that AI-based hardware and machines, has taken today's farming framework to a distinctive level. This innovation has improved trim generation and moved forward real-time observing, gathering, preparing and promoting access to information in most African countries.

The study has also found some challenges brought about by the adoption of artificial intelligence in developing countries. This includes AI does requires a slightest a modestly expansive preparing capacity. By so doing the study finds that countries contribute in a long term and costly instructive program or pull in specialists from other nations. Michael (2019) emphasised that in Africa, major advancements in AI will be centred on tackling real-world problems influencing conventional people's lives. These will incorporate arrangements that favour the progression of AI ability, back operations in businesses like broadcast communications, energize research in wellbeing and agribusiness, direct data collection and assurance, and lastly address issues of online deception. Also cyber security issues are the major challenges the developing countries are facing by employing AI as they lack effective control measures to count act cyber security threat. In addition the spread of fake news and issues of exerting xenophobic attacks are all influencing by the AI developments in the continent.

DISCUSSION

With the trends unpacked in this chapter, it can be deduced that more still need to be done in developing countries to adopt artificial intelligence to bridge development in their respective countries. This can be noticed in terms of the lack of expertise and non-compliance from the central governments in developing countries to put more resources in AI skills development programs. Other issues worth noting are cost of the licenses issues which may be prohibitively costly for a little firm attempting to enter the advertise. Also the pre-existing asset and mental property impediments incorporate the essential components required to utilize these assets. The dialect boundary gets to be noteworthy when one consider that most programming dialects are in English and have constrained accessibility in other dialects. There is a need for more financially support from developing countries' central governments to avail more funds to the training institutions for better AI skills development. In addition, artificial intelligence also imbeds development in most developing nations because of the downside of these improvements is the sharing of fake news without veracity. Researchers have proposed methods like utilizing chart investigation to detect sources of bits of gossip and dissemination of deception. Furthermore, AI can be anticipated to have significant impacts on the differences of broadly accessible social expressions in both the created and creating universes and, within the nonattendance of solid arrangement intercessions, the impacts have the potential to be starkly negative, especially for the world's destitute nations who are not domestic to the prevailing AI and computerized substance firms.

Interestingly, while AI has various benefits, as discussed in this chapter, it can also be a disruptive technology that might exacerbate existing inequities and divides by excluding marginalized and under-privileged people from AI-powered education. As a result, a new type of digital divide has emerged: a divide in how data-based information is used to inform intelligent decision making. Therefore there is a need to make sure that these disparities are addressed in developing nation if bridging development via AI dream is to be comprehended. Also the major barriers in implement AI in education to upskill the developing countries workforce is another issues. This is due to unavailability of ICT hardware, electricity issues, internet reliability, data costs and students' fundamental ICT abilities as well as lack of culturally relevant content. More is still required to address the internet coverage and cost effectiveness of data usage in developing countries by either subsidising model approach. AI initiatives indeed will assist the transformation of many economies in Africa as it creates the easier opportunities for everyone who was disadvantaged in the past century to have equal opportunities to the new approaches to develop economies. Lastly, closing the web connectivity and get to crevice with progressed economies will empower more African nations to enter service export markets. Small-scale producers in Africa may moreover ended up more competitive with access to advanced stages for investigate, deals, and distribution.

CONCLUSION

The implementation of AI in African economies is indispensable as it outweigh the disadvantages of using it. For this reason, AI has the capacity to assist Africa quantum jump a few stages of development, however, it must be created in respect to information, values, and convictions of the people living there whereas paying near consideration to how these values and cultures are changing. It is obvious that advance in AI will come from the support of forward-thinking government institutions, favourable information collection, and protection and collaborations with other partners inside and exterior of Africa.

REFERENCES

Aker, J. C., & Mbiti, I. M. (2010). Mobile phones and economic development in Africa. *The Journal of Economic Perspectives*, *24*(3), 207–232. doi:10.1257/jep.24.3.207

BID. (2018). *Algoritmolandia. Intelligence artificial para una integración predictiva e inclusiva para América Latina*. Editorial Planeta.

Darrell, M. W., & John, R. A. (2009). *How artificial intelligence is transforming the world*. http://www.cemas.org.uk/index.php/17-content/publications/2009-how-artificial-intelligence-is-transforming-the-world

Cisse, M. (2018). Look to Africa to advance artificial intelligence. *Nature*, *562*(7728), 461–462.

COMEST. (2019). *Preliminary Study on the Ethics of Artificial Intelligence*. UNESCO. doi:10.1038/d41586-018-07104-7

Johns, R. (2019). *Should We Code in English Using language to reduce barriers to entry into tech*. Towards Data Science. https://towardsdatascience.com/should-we-code-in-english-d59bd7ed87c9

Heidi, A. (2020). Digital transformation, development and productivity in developing countries: is artificial intelligence a curse or a blessing? Emerald Publishing Limited. doi:10.1108/REPS-11-2019-0145

Hilbert, M. (2015). Big Data for Development: A Review of Promises and Challenges. *Development Policy Review*, *34*(1), 135–174. doi:10.1111/dpr.12142

Kim, R. G., & Evans, W. M. I. (2008). Remote sensing and control of an irrigation system using a distributed wireless sensor network. *IEEE Transactions on Instrumentation and Measurement*, *57*(7), 1379–1387. doi:10.1109/TIM.2008.917198

Kulesz, M. (2018). *Culture, platforms and machines: The impact of artificial intelligence on the diversity of cultural expressions*. UNESCO Information Document. https://en.unesco.org/creativity/sites/creativity/files/12igc inf4 en.pdf

Liakos, K., Busato, P., Moshou, D., Pearson, S., & Bochtis, D. (2018). *Machine Learning in Agriculture: A Review Sensors*. doi:10.3390/s18082674

Malahat, C. & Ari, H. (2020). *Key enablers for deploying artificial intelligence for circular economy embracing sustainable product design: Three case studies*. doi:10.1063/5.0001339

Michael, N. (2019). *Artificial Intelligence Policies in Africa over the Next Five Years*. https://www.researchgate.net/profile/Micheal-Nayebare/publication/337503231_Artificial_intelligence_policies_in_Africa_over_the_next_five_years/links/5e763a21a6fdcccd6215935e/Artificial-intelligence-policies-in-Africa-over-the-next-five-years.pdf doi:10.1145/3368075

Mutoni, D. (2017). *A revolutionary connectivity: internet access as the ultimate human right and socio-economic force*. New Degree Press.

Ndung'u, N., & Signé, L. (2020). *The Fourth Industrial Revolution and digitization will transform Africa into a global powerhouse*. Retrieved from https://fullyhuman.org/wpcontent/uploads/2020/01/NdunguSigne_The-Fourth-Industrial-Revolution-And-Digitization-Will-Transform-Africa-Into-A-Global-Powerhouse.pdf

Nye, B. D. (2015). Intelligent Tutoring Systems by and for the Developing World: A review of trends and approaches for Educational Technology in a Global Context. *International Journal of Artificial Intelligence in Education*, *25*(2), 177–203. doi:10.100740593-014-0028-6

Panpatte, D.G. (2018). *Artificial Intelligence in Agriculture: An Emerging Era of Research*. Academic Press.

Santiago, M. T. A. (2020). *Obstacles and considerations for the development and implementation of Artificial Intelligence in Developing Countries*. https://www.researchgate.net/profile/Santiago_Molina7/publication/354556278_Obstacles_and_considerations_for_the_development_and_implementation_of_Artificial_Intelligence_in_ Developing_Countries/links/613fe2cc5d9d0e131b427fab/Obstacles-and-considerations-for-the-development-and-implementation-of-Artificial-Intelligence-in-Developing-Countries.pdf

Sertaç, Y., &Yaman, Ö. E. (2020). *Artificial Intelligence in Public Sector: A Framework to Address Opportunities and Challenges*. Academic Press.

Smith, L. M., & Neupane, S. (2018). *Artificial Intelligence and Human Development: Toward Research Agenda*. Retrieved from https://www.idrc.ca/en/stories/artificial-intelligenceand-human-development

Tanha, T., Dhara, S. N., Patelb, H., & Yagnik, M. (2020). *Implementation of artificial intelligence in agriculture for optimisation of irrigation and application of pesticides and herbicides*. doi:10.1016/j.aiia.2020.04.002

Travaly, Y., & Muvunyi, K. (2020). *The future is intelligent: Harnessing the potential of artificial intelligence in Africa.* Retrieved from https://www.brookings.edu/blog/africa-in-90 focus/2020/01/13/the-future-is-intelligent-harnessing-the-potential-of-artificialintelligence-in-africa/

UIS. (2018). *A Global Framework for Reference on Digital Literacy Skills for Indicator 4.4.2*. Information Paper, no. 51.

UNESCO. (2018). *Re-orienting Education Management Information Systems towards Inclusive and Equitable Quality Education and Lifelong Learning*. UNESCO Working Papers on Education Policy, no. 5.

UNESCO & UNHCR. (2016). *No More Excuses: Provide Education to All Forcibly Displaced People*. Global Education Monitoring Report: Policy Paper no. 26.

UNICEF. (2016). *Technical Guidance: Guide for Including Disability in Education Management Information Systems*. Author.

Vasisht, D., Kapetanovic, Z., Won, J., Jin, X., Chandra, R., Sinha, S., & Stratman, S. (2017). Farm beats: An iot platform for data driven agriculture. *14th USENIX Symposium on Networked Systems Design and Implementation, 17*, 515-529.

Chapter 19
Africa in the Face of the AI Wave and the Fourth Industrial Revolution:
Leapfrog Opportunities, Developmental Backlogs, and Impediments

Cyril Chibuzo Ezeani
Nnamdi Azikiwe University, Awka, Nigeria

ABSTRACT

The major concern of the chapter is with the prospects of AI and the generality of the Fourth Industrial Revolution in the light of Africa's development and with Africa's readiness to embrace the new technology. Using the method of hermeneutics, the work discovers that efforts made in some African countries to embrace the opportunities offered by the new revolution notwithstanding, Africa seems to be at the lower rung of the new technological ladder. The chapter discusses the impeding factors and more while proffering a way out in order to catch into the opportunities created by artificial intelligence. The chapter further recognizes that AI within the context of contemporary African situation presents a dilemma given the teeming unemployed demography. Without taking light of this dilemma, the chapter tends to view AI emergence in terms of what has been described as a critical juncture, and an adequate response would ultimately lead to increased prosperity.

INTRODUCTION

The present chapter is poised to tinker with the prospects of Artificial Intelligence and the generality of the Fourth Industrial Revolution in the light of Africa's development and with Africa's readiness to embrace the new technology. Discovering that despite efforts made in some African countries to embrace the opportunities offered by the new Revolution notwithstanding, Africa seems to be at the lower rung of the new technological ladder, the chapter discusses the impeding factors and more while proffering

DOI: 10.4018/978-1-6684-4107-7.ch019

a way out in order to catch into the opportunities created by artificial intelligence. It further recognizes that AI within the context of contemporary African situation presents a dilemma given the teeming unemployed demography. Without taking light of this dilemma, the chapter tends to view AI emergence in terms of what has been described as critical juncture and an adequate response would ultimately lead to increased prosperity.

The research is informed by the understanding that Africa cannot afford to miss the transformative changes which the Fourth Industrial Revolution promises to bring. In this the Brookings Institution warns that missing such opportunities will obviously impose considerable risks on Africa stakeholders. In fact, "without attempts to move beyond existing models of innovation, entrepreneurship, and digital growth on the continent, African businesses risk falling further behind, exacerbating the global 'digital divide' and lowering their global competitiveness" (Radu, 2020). The inevitable rise of the advanced technologies of artificial intelligence and the Fourth Industrial Revolution have been marked as disruptive technologies and so while they, like other industrial revolutions will be characterized by evolution they will also disrupt economies and human society. What this means is that if nothing dramatic is done and differently, the result will be continued and more exasperating inequality. To do nothing in this regard would entail widening an already exacerbating gap and divide: There will for instance be continued skill gap, technology gap, knowledge gap and all these would inevitably translate in the long run to clear prosperity gap.

Unsettled by these concerns of the inevitability of continued prosperity gap if nothing is done, the chapter reflects on the imports of Artificial Intelligence and the Fourth Industrial Revolution on Africa; the possibility of their offering a unique launching pad for development in what has been termed leapfrogging. The second section is concerned with developmental backlogs and impeding factors on the path of leapfrogging as well as how they could be surpassed.

BACKGROUND

Artificial Intelligence (AI) is up for revolutionizing the technological sphere and as a result changing society in a profound way. It is today not just a laboratory affair, it is more than ever becoming a technological force multiplier in an ever-widening range of real world cases including drug development, healthcare, agriculture, energy, logistics and defense. From the economic perspective, the PwC analysis in its 2017 report had noted that "AI is set to be the key source of transformation, disruption and competitive advantage in today's fast changing economy." It avers that artificial intelligence can transform the productivity and GDP potential of the global economy. In this it predicted that "45% of total economic gains by 2030 will come from product enhancements, stimulating consumer demand." (PwC, 2017) This is premised on the realization that "AI will drive greater product variety, with increased personalization, attractiveness and affordability over time." (PwC, 2017) It projects the total economic impact of AI in the period to 2030 as $15.7 trillion to the global economy by 2030. While $6.6 trillion is likely to come from increased productivity, $9.1 trillion is likely to come from consumption-side effects (PwC, 2017).

Artificial Intelligence is, however, only a key element of what has been tagged the Fourth Industrial (technological) Revolution which enters into the purview of the present work. While the First Industrial Revolution used water and steam power to mechanize production, the Second used electric power to create mass production; the third used electronics and information technology to automate production. The Fourth, though, in some sense an extension of the Third but qualitatively different is "characterized by the fusion of the digital, biological and physical worlds, as well as the growing utilization of new technologies such as artificial intelligence, cloud computing, robotics, 3D printing, the Internet of things, and advanced wireless technologies, among others…" (Ndung'u & Singe, 2020) It has been described as the great tectonic shift of our time, creating new possibilities for improving people's lives and changing the way we live, the way we work and do business, and the way we govern. (Ramaphosa, 2020) Many nations are catching in and leveraging the new technology with the purpose of driving large-scale transformation and competitiveness, strategically repositioning themselves for future opportunities, all seeking to cash in on the potentials of AI and the Fourth Industrial Revolution in general. There is in fact what can be described as AI gold rush and this is evidenced by the billions of dollars in venture that have flowed into AI startups in recent times. For instance, in the third quarter of 2021 alone nearly $18 billion was invested in AI companies in USA, a record high. Such influx of capital is a sign of a belief in the potential of AI. (Bangert, 2022) Nations are striving to be at the forefront of the development and positioning to lead the revolution. China for instance is very aggressive about this. China has not hidden its ambition to be the global AI leader by 2030. China through their institution has opted for centralized direction and a massive commitment of resources. In fact "not only is China investing heavily in AI—its experts aim to set the rules of the game on global standards for the technology." (University of Pretoria, 2018)

In this race, Africa cannot be left behind as it had been in the earlier revolutions. There are, of course, signs that some African nations are taking seriously the opportunities of the Fourth Industrial Revolution. For instance, M-Pesa has recorded great success in Kenya. M-Pesa is the mobile transfer money service launched by Safaricom, Kenya's largest mobile operator and Vodafone, in 2007, has allowed millions to pay bills, buy goods, receive remittances from abroad and even access learning. This is thanks to AI-driven encryption and now AI as the new UI interfaces. In West Africa and Kenya, blockchain has enabled efficient verification of property records and transactions, and expanded access to credit in some previously informal sectors of the economy. (Foresight Africa, 2020) In Ethiopia, AI technology is helping greatly in cancer diagnostics. In Uganda, 27,000 public health workers use a mobile system to manage medicine stocks; Rwanda uses autonomous drones to air deliver blood transfusions to remote regions; Mobile banking has helped in empowering African small businesses; African farms have been seen as melding IoT, AI and data to be more precise and smarter in estimating crop yields, managing irrigation, choosing fertilizers and adjusting for weather. (Now, 2018) Some of these examples that apparently spell eagerness to embrace new technologies coupled with Africa's strong population growth as well as increased urbanization are generating optimism in many quarters concerning the near possibility of the continent jumping to a greater level of economic growth, out spacing other emerging markets while potentially becoming the world's most attractive growth region in the second half of this century. There is no gainsaying that the Fourth Industrial Revolution holds great opportunities in stall for the world and Africa in particular. In recent years for instance, ICT in Africa has had enormous economic impact. The Foresight Africa in its 2020 report (Foresight Africa, 2020) noted that of late, mobile technologies and services have contributed to $144 billion of economic value (8.5 percent of the GDP of sub-Saharan Africa) and contributed to $15.6 billion to the public sector through taxation.

Yet Africa, over all, is still both in terms of readiness to embrace the opportunities of the revolution and development in general trails far behind. For instance, the Government AI readiness Index 2020 from Oxford Insights, shows that globally, the US was the top with the rest of the top five going to UK, Finland, Germany, and Sweden, all located within Western Europe, indicating that North America and western Europe are the highest scoring regions overall. In Africa, the leading country was Mauritius in the 45th position out of 172 countries across the world, then came Egypt at 56th position, South Africa came 59th. Seychelles, Tunisia, Kenya and Rwanda took 68th, 69th, 71st and 87th positions respectively. (Oxford Insight, 2020) The report on the average shows that the lowest scoring regions were generally the global south and more particularly sub-Saharan Africa, Latin America and the Caribbean, south and Central Asia. Reacting to the generally poor performance of Africa the report notes, "these results should come as no surprise, as African countries have historically lagged the rest of the world in technological developments." (Oxford Insights, 2020) Continuing, it writes that "despite the different generations of technology that African countries have 'leapfrogged,' they still face the persistent challenge of catching up, as the pace of technological change outstrips their leaping abilities." (Oxford Insights, 2020)

AI WAVE AND FOURTH INDUSTRIAL REVOLUTION: A LEAPFROG OPPORTUNITY FOR AFRICA?

Different feedbacks from AI Africa have shown that few African nations are taking steps to promote artificial intelligence within their context and repositioning themselves to cash in on the opportunities of the Fourth Industrial Revolution. There are local and regional initiatives aimed at transforming the AI landscape in Africa especially with respect to policy dimensions to guide. For instance, in Nigeria, National Agency for Research in Robotics and Artificial Intelligence has been formed and is charged among others to collaborate with international research bodies, enhance instruction on AI topics for thousands of students, and promote Nigeria's ability to leverage these technologies for economic growth. Nigeria has also launched in November 2020 its publicly-run Centre for Artificial Intelligence and Robotics in Abuja. (FinIntell, 2020; see Gwagwa, 2020) Kenya for instance has launched an open-data portal for the purposes of accessing information on such areas as education, energy, health, population, poverty, and water and sanitation. This is with the understanding that access to public datasets is crucial for developing locally relevant AI solutions and services. Ghana has now AI research institute in Accra, thanks to Google. South Africa Department of Trade and Industry "formed a Chief Directorate for Future industrial Production and Technologies to examine the impacts of emerging digital technologies, including the internet of Things, big data AI, robotics, and new materials." The unit aims "to build government capacity to address these challenges and partner with industry to enhance South Africa's readiness." (University of Pretoria, 2018) Mauritius published an AI strategy in 2018, the first to ever have such (Gwagwa, 2020). It launched this together with the Digital Government Transformation Strategy 2018-2022 and the Digital Mauritius 2030 Strategic Plan. The AI strategy is geared towards maximizing their ocean economy as it suggests investment into a maritime internet of things. It establishes an AI council that advises the government on supporting Mauritius' AI ecosystem. Both the AI Strategy and the Mauritius 2030 Strategic Plan prioritize developing local talent such as through making programming a required university course. Egypt which leads in the North Africa launched its national AI Strategy in 2019 and this is anchored on two pillars of building human capacity and supporting scientific research and innovation. It has also created a National AI Council which is charged with supervising the implementation of the strategy. Gwagwa (2020) writes that university driven national AI capacity building programmes are present in numerous countries and these include Egypt, South Africa, Morocco, Senegal, Lesotho, and Ethiopia (See Effoduh, 2020) South Africa Centre for Artificial Intelligence Research established in 2011 links nine research groups from six universities. This is funded by the Department of Science and Innovation and coordinated by the Council for Scientific and Industrial Research. South Africa also hosts a Centre for the Fourth Industrial Revolution established at the CSIR in 2017 as part of a global network of such centre supported by the World Economic Forum. Gwagwa (2020) highlights other such initiatives at African continental and regional levels.

Interestingly, these AI springboard-enabling policies in addition to the successful applications already highlighted in the introduction to this chapter as well as the success of mobile technologies have fuelled further the optimism on the concrete realization of the metaphor of Africa's leapfrogging in the era Fourth Industrial Revolution. Many have come to be ardent believers in the metaphor of leapfrogging for Africa in the age of artificial intelligence and Fourth Industrial Revolution. The leapfrog principle is the "idea that one an innovate in environments where precedents and incumbents are poor, primitive or absent, easier than in wealthier or technologically richer environments." (Clark, 2018) In other words it refers to the concept of "bypassing intermediate stages of technology through which countries have historically passed during the development process." (UNCTAD, 2018) The idea here is that developing countries can skip stages of the path taken by industrial nations, enabling them to catch up sooner, particularly in terms of economic growth. (Clark, 2018) The catch-up here refers to "the narrowing of gaps in income and technological capabilities between a late-developing country and a front-runner country." (UNCTAD, 2018) This entails "a sequential process of learning by latecomers in skills, process technology, design and product development." (UNCTAD, 2018) These are geared towards contributing to increased productivity, new markets and filling the prosperity gap. Ton Dietz (2021) following this writes that Africa appears poised to move to a higher gear in economic activity over the coming decades. According to him, "Africa's strong population growth, increasing urbanization and eagerness to embrace new technologies are generating optimism that the continent can jump to much higher levels of growth and outspace other emerging markets..." (Dietz, 2021) Africa will potentially become, as a result, "the world's most attractive growth region in the second half of this century." The question is, can all these translate to Africa's meaningful growth and development? Can Africa actually leapfrog in a way that affects the overall growth and development? What are the stumbling blocks in achieving this? These questions are what the present paper seeks to attend to and in this way assess the trajectory of Africa's development in an increasingly AI enabled world and Fourth Industrial Revolution moment in general.

Of course not all are optimistic of the much talked of Africa's leapfrogging. Ian Moll (2020) is one of them. He does not even think that the Fourth Revolution, if at all it could be characterized as such, could be of any benefit to Africa. Moll harps on the fact that each of the preceding Industrial Revolutions had devastating consequences for Africa and so he asks, "why should we expect that a 4th Industrial Revolution would benefit this continent and its people?" Moll seems to be a proponent of dependence theory of (under)development. The main argument of this theory is that the persistent increment in industrialization in the developed countries rather subject poor countries to underdevelopment as a result of the economic surplus of the poor countries being exploited by developed countries. The basic assumption of this theory is that it is by the subjugation of poorer states which remain on the margins that wealthy nations of the world were wealthy and remain wealthy. For the proponents, the poverty of the countries in the periphery is not because they are not integrated into the world system but because of how they are integrated. They are integrated but only as to further the western agenda. This captures the whole tenure of Moll's thought as he reads history in terms of this dependence and exploitation. This skeptic and pessimist stance had already been raised by Saleem Badat in his exchange with Tshilidzi Marwala who himself is a scholar of the leapfrog optimism. In fact according to Moll, the global socio-economic order is an order skewed in favour of the global north. He points out for instance that the convergence of digitally networked information technologies have since the 1970s "created a global socioeconomic order which has systematically marginalized and exploited the countries of the global South and Africa in particular." (Moll, 2020) The same story of exploitation and dehumanization could be told of the previous revolutions. The First Industrial Revolution was founded on what historians termed the triangular trade which was about the intensification and increased brutality of enslavement, immiseration and dehumanization of African people and their labour. People were primary commodity extracted from Africa. The Second Industrial Revolution was again a skewed order in favour of the west. That both the second Industrial revolution and age of Imperialism are conventionally dated to be same, 1860s to 1914 betrays this exploitation narrative. It was a moment of scramble for Africa and Berlin's declaration of free trade, all of which are all legal backing for exploitative colonial socioeconomic system that carted African raw materials away. The free trade was for the colonial powers in Africa and the global industrial nexus comprising of the U.S., Britain, France, Belgium, Germany, Italy and some Scandinavian countries all of whom depended on raw materials found in the remote and colonial enclaves. One of the leading proponents of dependence theory, Walter Rodney in his book *How Europe Underdeveloped Africa* references this dependency with regard to Africa and the experience of colonialism. For him the greatest consequence of colonialism on Africa is the loss of power. Power according to him is the ultimate determinant in human society, being basic to the relations within any group and between groups. Power implies the ability to defend one's interests, it determines maneuverability in bargaining, the extent to which a people survive as a physical and cultural entity. When a society finds itself forced to relinquish power entirely to another, it is an unfortunate instance of dependency that entrenches underdevelopment of the society that has relinquished power. The same experience of socioeconomic exploitation and marginalization was the dominant experience of most African countries during the Third Industrial Revolution by networking of digital technologies which drove capitalism into globalized economy in which productivity and competitiveness is based on information technology. It took the form of "Western offshoring or on-shoring back to automated factories or simply discarding the people and places "no longer considered valuable, even if they are still physically there…" (Moll, 2020) According to Moll (2020) most African countries are operating as cheap labour reservoirs for the global industrial nexus or being discarded by the global economy. This long history of deep exploitation oppression creates pessimism as to how supposed massive convergence of technology can change the structural domination of Africa by the countries of the North, economically, politically and socially. Well, while one cannot gloss over this long history of deep exploitation and its telling cumulative effect on Africa, it is also true that Africa cannot just remain under the weight of this effect. It can always struggle even if at least to reduce these effects. Even if it does not succeed now in getting into the centre of global power, it can at least close the centre-periphery gap. The fact that Africa is low on the development ladder has factors that can be premised on the global politics as well as internal factors which respective countries can deal with in spite of the global politicking and long history of exploitation. The development of artificial intelligence technologies has been characterized as global race, and many countries are trying to pull ahead. Of course many of these countries leverage on the already accumulated political and economic power to others. The truth is that the more they are allowed to accumulate further data and digital power, the more their economic power and so their political power, entrenching further their global power and the latitude to bargain. Again, however one speaks about equality, collaboration, the global world order is always by power dynamics and polarization. This is a capitalist world! So to fail to take action is to expand the scope of power instead of trying to limit that power that would ensure a move towards equal grounds for bargain.

Sebastiaan Tan is among the optimists of the metaphor and practicability of leapfrogging. In his article "AI and Africa: Leapfrog to Prosperity" (2018) he shows himself an ardent believer in the ability of Africa to leapfrog from poverty to prosperity. Tan while acknowledging that African economies are still the global poorest and least developed sees this as a great opportunity which is lacking in other high-income economy, namely "the collective choice to embrace emerging technologies." With regard to why the opportunity is not as high in high-income economy, he argues that "high-income countries resist systemic change due to their size and the potential of destabilization or disruption." (Tan, 2018) What is being harped here is that there is no traditional way of doings to cling to by the general population as such. For instance it was observed that whereas other more established economic areas have been slower in adopting such technology as mobile money, it has been more received in a number of countries in Africa. Thus Africa to give an example is ahead of Western countries in adopting P2P finance. It is along this that one understands why mobile banking services such as mPesa have been so enthusiastically taken up by African consumers. (Botha, 2019) African systems are relatively in their formative period in that they have not been long established and so they stand on the cross road of defining what will be the pattern of development and this is an opportunity to take advantage of emerging economies.

One of the strength for Africa to leverage is its population boom, and this translates into what has been referred to as the biggest demographic dividend especially given that currently 60% of the African is under the age of twenty five. It is estimated that by 2035 Africa's working age population will grow by 450 million and this is an enormous potential. Adams Smith while defining human resources notes that it is a type of fixed capital next to machines, land and property. Tan (2018) following this, argues that the key to unlocking this potential and do the leapfrog magic is simply human capital investment. He underscores the economic miracles of transformation from poverty to prosperity Asian Tigres such as Korea, Hong-Kong, Taiwan and Singapore as founded on the accumulation of human capital. Human capital is the product of both talent and knowledge and skill investment. Human capital works in two ways: "on the one hand by educating people, it enhances a comparative advantage to other countries which results in economic development. On the other hand, better educated people within the market increases competition and motivates private enterprises to engage in the development of technology which in turn drives innovation." (Tan, 2018) What is lacking in Africa is not talent per se but opportunities to put the talent into use.

DEVELOPMENTAL BACKLOGS AND IMPEDIMENTS ON THE PATH OF LEAPFROGGING: LEEWAY

Unfortunately the lack of opportunities mentioned above had created a human problem in Africa, namely unemployment and underemployment. This unfortunately helps to create the pervasive narrative that AI spells doom for Africa's development especially given that in spite of the high productivity and efficiency associated with narrow artificial intelligence, it has also been associated with reducing the employment demography. This becomes more worrisome particularly in Africa where a teaming number is laboring under unemployment and underemployment. Many are also on low skilled jobs which can easily be taken over by AI agents, increasing all the more the unemployment demography. AI within the context of contemporary African situation presents therefore a dilemma, whether or not it is auspicious for Africa to engage with the AI technology. Charles Kenny (2019) in his "Automation and AI: Implications for African Development Prospects?" observes that this would not be the first time that fear of loss of job had accompanied prospects of looming automation. According to him concerns about the consequences of labour saving technology has been a longstanding tradition. What he referred to as robopocalypse has been in existence since eighty years or more, and the idea of reduction in employment rate as a result of automation has always been there. For instance New York Times of February 26, 1928 blamed unemployment on automation in one of its title "March of the Machine makes Idle Hands" This had a rider, "Prevalence of Unemplyoment with Greatly Increased Industrial Output Points to the Influence of labour-Saving Devices as an Underlying Cause." German Der Spiegel predicts Robopocalypse in 1964, 1978 and 2016. Besides there has been a wide range of literature around AI, automation and employment and it seems 1965-1970 was its peak. Another peak of concern happened in mid 1980s. Keynes predicted technological unemployment in the 1930s, Leontief in the 1950s and Heilbroner in 1965. What Kenny seems to project is that the job loss globally has not been as predicted. This is not to say that the concern about unemployment consequences of automation and AI in Africa is groundless, what Kenny argues is that the though the danger is real but it is not as bad as it might appear. In fact he makes four points in order to about the pessimism. According to him, automation has always been a vital part of development and so it is needed as a matter of necessity and urgency by Africa; second is though labour saving technology could have negative impact on jobs and incomes, it is also true that new jobs keep emerging thanks to the demand generated by greater productivity. According to him job and income losses and drop as a result of automation have been minimal; though labour saving technologies might reduce the convergence prospects of a region that has lot more labour than capital, manufacturing (export) jobs have still prospects; fourth is that the ongoing ICT revolution may present new opportunities to developing countries to speed growth. Automation has been a vital part of economic growth and this growth has engendered shifting employment patterns. Mokyr et al. argue that while, for instance, industrial revolution did away with lots of jobs in home weaving, it created new jobs for mechanics, supervisors, accountants, etc. They write further that "technological progress also took the form of product innovation, and thus created entirely new sectors for the economy, a development that was essentially missed in the discussion of economists of this time." (See Kenny, 2019) There is the observation to the effect that in OECD countries, while industry-level employment falls with rise in industry productivity, the country-level employment rises as aggregate productivity rises. The reasoning here is that "productivity increases raise incomes, consumption and employment so that the negative own-industry employment effects are more than outweighed by positive spillovers to the rest of the economy." (Kenny, 2019) What accompanies this is "significant reallocation of workers into tertiary services which employ a disproportionate share of high-skilled labor, but it has not led to overall job losses." (Kenny, 2019) It is further argued that

The reason why developing countries are poor is because they see low productivity, driven in part by limited automation. They are not intensively using technologies invented long ago to raise that productivity-technology including tractors and combine harvesters, spindles, Bessemer plants, and electricity. What is behind the slow diffusion of such technologies is complex but again, poverty and lack of well-paid formal sector jobs is associated with low use of productive technologies, not high use. (Kenny, 2019)

While the above argument is to the present writer a valid one, it is also true that the question of the burgeoning youth unemployment rate existent already in Africa cannot be swept under the carpet. It is in fact a situation that requires a state of emergency declaration. It is valid to argue that automation has always been essential part of economic growth but it is also good to recognize that in most of those countries they have been through that phenomenon through gradual and step by step technological transformation with each preceding stage placing them at a vantage point to deal with implications of subsequent and higher form of technological transformation. In Africa which is technologically backward already and where we are already talking of leapfrogging, it lacks this history of experience. Besides, the unemployment is the result of developmental backlogs and deficits. It becomes more disconcerting to talk of AI replacement of human jobs when a great number are unemployed or even unemployable and lack opportunities. In sub-Saharan Africa for instance, the ten to twelve million youth who annually join the workforce, only three million jobs are created. (Now, 2021) According to African Centre for Economic Transformation (ACET) less than a third of adults in Africa have finished primary school as opposed to nearly all adults in industrialized countries, there is a low proficiency among school children in reading and mathematics, and low enrollment in science, technology, engineering and mathematics; Africa has a low proportion of university students per population. Again it is shown that schoolchildren in developed nations get nearly 12 years of technology preparedness, while African schoolchildren receive slightly more than four years of schooling in technology. (Now, 2021) All these imply very low job prospects. The World Economic Forum submits that the overall skills base of Africa's workforce is the lowest in the world. (See Alexsandra, 2018) Moustapha Cisse decries the fact that the vast majority of experts are in North America, Europe and Asia and thus Africa seems left out or are barely represented. The danger according to him, which this limited coverage occasions is the entrenchment of "unintended algorithmic biases and built-in discrimination. This also means fewer opportunities for the improvement of the life of Africans. Noting that vast majority of AI as such expert imbalance entrench further (digital) power imbalance with some level of algorithmic biases and in-built discrimination, which are ultimately inimical to the development of the under-represented. This is within the presupposition that concentration of (digital) power increases the potential and impact of harm to others and is likely to create structural exploitation and inequality.

Here the submission of Lexi Novitske becomes apt. In her "The AI Innovation is coming to Africa (and It's a Good Thing)" (2018) she points to the need for implementing extensive education reform from primary school through university. She observes that in Ghana for instance, and this is true in Nigeria and in many parts of Africa, school curricula tends "to focus on rote memorization, rather than honing the creative and analytical ability of young minds." She underscores that Africa's education systems must adapt to the needs of the near-future job market, focusing the STEM education from an early age, providing adequate grants within the fields of STEM and information and communications for inclusive in order to help bolster domestic research and application. According to her, the faculties developed as result of engagement in these areas of studies are critical for developing the analytical and technical skills young people need to excel in job market to be dominated by AI. It is obvious that the key features of the Fourth Industrial Revolution: accelerating digitization, artificial intelligence, cloud computing, robotics, and 3D printing would be the major determinant factor in the pattern of education, employment and the future of work. We had referenced the teeming demography of African youth. According to Hanan Morsy in his "How Africa can Harness the Fourth Industrial Revolution" (2020) the share of the continent's under-20 population has expanded by more than 25% over the past decade and is projected to be the continent's largest age cohort by 2070. For Morsy (2020) this is simply the most important asset for the continent. He however noted that to reap this demographic dividend, there is the urgent need for overhauling the educational system to equip the youth to harness the opportunities that may be associated with the fourth industrial Revolution.

One witnesses in the global labour market that "demand is evolving toward adaptable social, behavioural, and non-repetitive cognitive skills, and away from routine tasks and narrow skills tied to specific jobs." (Morsy, 2020) Unfortunately Africa lags behind in ensuring that there is the type of education that provides such skills for harnessing. Besides, across Africa, education has remained concentrated in social sciences and humanities, and has lagged in the STEM fields which are crucial for repositioning for the opportunities of the fourth Industrial Revolution. The result is a growing mismatch between businesses' evolving demands and the skills furnished by African education systems. African employers often complain about inadequately prepared workers as a major constraint on their businesses' growth. If Africa could make leap then it has to deal with these skill and education mismatches. This requires a new philosophy of education which will guide national strategies for education and skills development. A key to dealing with this persistent labour-market mismatch is that education must be structured in such a way that it is demand driven. According to Morsy, one exciting option is for African countries to use new dynamic information systems to track current and future labor-market needs in the economy so as to direct the youth accordingly in terms of needed skills and education. The importance of skills development lies in the fact that it represents a major driver of innovation on the continent. In addition, Jehiel Oliver's observation in 2018 of African start-up ecosystem as being under-capitalized still persists. According to him, "in other parts of the world, you will find that the ecosystems support the growth of start-ups that eventually grow to export their technologies. In Silicon Valley the ecosystem has universities, investors, infrastructure, and the right policies that support start-ups." (African Development Bank Group, 2019) In Africa, generally the environment does not encourage start-ups and innovations. The point the present writer is making is that Africa's case need a more strategic and concerted approach. Africa has therefore to deal with lingering problems bordering on education, job preparedness and employment opportunities among others, if any genuine economic transformation can happen and in fact without them the demographic boom far from being a dividend becomes most unfortunately a doom. According to ACET, "Africa's youth are both an asset and a time bomb. At current trends, nearly half of these vibrant young people will be unemployed, discouraged or economically inactive by 2025. A well-publicized fraction is migrating, often by dangerous routes, to search for jobs. More disturbingly, some 40% of youth joining rebel and terror groups reportedly cite the lack of economic opportunity as the key motivation." (Now, 2021) It may be good to add that particularly the case of burgeoning youth unemployed population requires that government's investing, re-designing and re-engineering in educational systems and curricula as well as reskilling programs must be such that must ensure that technology supplements instead of replace labour. The watchword is education that fills the labour-market gap and impact investments.

Of course these are not the only stumbling blocks on the path of leapfrogging: infrastructural, institutional, fiscal deficits must be given adequate attention. Foresight Africa 2020 report highlights that "access to advanced technology in Africa is constrained by infrastructure parameters such as lack of electricity and low tele-density, internet density, and broadband penetration. For instance Armando Manuel, a former minister of finance in Angola and World Bank alternate executive director for Angola, Nigeria and South Africa had observed in a panel report in 2020 that "access to electricity in Africa is 45%..." He immediately added, "You can't develop in the darkness and you can't go to the Moon when you have constraints to go to the next corner." (Radu, 2020) Management consulting firm, McKinsey observes that only 1.1% of gross domestic product accounts for digital investment in African countries. And this is less than half of what developed economies spend. Internet penetration is also low, averaging less than 40% compared to 62.7% in the rest of the world. (Radu, 2020) Brookings Institute report shows this backwardness when it reports for instance that in developed countries there are nearly as many as mobile broadband subscription as there are people, where as there are only about twenty-five subscriptions per hundred people. (Now, 2021) Of course it must be noted that speaking in terms of Africa in general has a great challenge. There are some African countries that are top notch in this area and even generally in terms of readiness for the opportunities of the fourth Industrial Revolution. We had seen Mauritius, Rwanda among others. Kenya for instance has internet penetration rate of about 90%. Unfortunately such countries like Burundi, the Central African Republic, Chad and the Democratic Republic of Congo have low internet penetration rate of below 10%. Eriteria is even the worst with 1% of its population having internet access. (Now, 2021) These instances of low internet access and as a consequence expensiveness of data is unfortunately a great disadvantage to developers and AI entrepreneurs. With slower and less reliable internet access, African developers operate at a competitive disadvantage. The consequences are dire for "without reliable core infrastructure, affordable data plans, and easy access to technologies, current digital divides will only be exacerbated with the rise and continued advancement of AI." (Nwaodike, 2020) And AI risks being "an extractive industry that pulls resources out of the country to the benefit of others, designing closed source software that often cannot be used by African developers." (Nwaodike, 2020) Unfortunately, though not exclusive to African nations, UNCTAD, 2018 reports that most of the least developing countries are lacking in innovation capabilities. It observes that for example in 2014 the average intensity of research and development in most developing countries was below 0.5 per cent, much lower than the world average which is over 1.5 per cent. This ultimately tells in the differences in the productive capacities. The report observes some lack in the innovation system and strategic innovation policies. The innovation system is described thus: "The capabilities of stakeholders – firms, research and education systems, government, civil society and consumers – the connections among them and the enabling environment for innovation that they create…" On the other hand strategic innovation policies are geared towards strengthening the effectiveness of the innovation systems and in regard to leapfrogging, geared towards promoting and facilitating the deployment and adaptation of frontier technologies to the production needs of the nation and building capacity for developing them further. The report blames the thin economic impact of ICTs when compared to other regions despite their development roles in sub-Saharan Africa on the "limitations of innovation policy in Africa to co-evolve with the development of ICT and to fully exploit the opportunities to build on the mobile revolution to foster innovation and development." According to the report, "sustaining progress requires constant innovation and investment in the latest technologies to keep up with continuing swift technological change in the sector."

Other technological bottlenecks, the Foresight Africa 2020 report writes "include a lack of standardized application programming interfaces and common data languages for the increased integration of largely self-sufficient systems as well as exposure to the dangers of cyber-attacks." With regard to issue of cyber-security it notes that most African countries lack a comprehensive legal framework and institutional capacity to address cybercrime. What one finds most often is a local effort or efforts implemented by private sector actors themselves. A 2018 Atlantic Council report showed that most African countries are yet to be ready to benefit from the AI technology. This is premised on a key factor, namely the high quality data dependence nature of AI which are lacking in most part of Africa. High quality data is needed by AI for the purposes of learning and making decisions, but unfortunately while "deepening mobile phone use for instance indicate a more generation of data, the quality of the data remains poor and data-privacy regulations are mostly non-existent. It highlights that the ability of national statistic agencies to collect and analyze high-quality data about populations and economies in Africa remains the lowest in the world, in fact it has declined in the past fifteen years. The implication is that data on issues like education and household income is inaccurate or missing. Again is the challenge of connectivity which is about the fact that data is skewed in favour of Africa's urban populations as the rural areas are mainly not connected. This poses the danger of incomplete data which causes AI to learn incorrectly and also opens door to human biases. For me these are part of developmental backlogs that must be decisively dealt with before any leapfrog and sustainable transformation in Africa can happen.

THE IMPORT OF STRATEGIC PLANNING AND IMPEDING FACTORS AGAINST OPERATIONALIZATION

No doubt, all indices indicate that artificial intelligence is again a decisive moment globally and so an important opportunity for Africa. It holds key for growth, development and democratization and has the potentiality to engender and sustain productivity growth by expanding opportunities in key sectors within the context of Africa's development, namely agriculture, healthcare, financial services and government services. This is if the government of nations could painstakingly and successfully navigate the challenges. But foremost is the creation of strategic plan. In this Onaolapo writes that "before Africa can lead its AI transformation, the region needs to formulate a comprehensive continental blueprint to guide its AI strategy by involving key Pan-African institutions, academia, and the private and public sectors in its conception."(see Parker et al.) Creation of national AI and Fourth Revolution research and development strategic planning would therefore be geared towards creating a high-level framework to identify scientific and technological needs in AI over and strategic priorities; the planning would obviously speak to the national policymakers and funding agencies charged with funding research and development gives a broad perspective on priority funding in AI as well forge public discussion around AI and the Fourth Industrial Revolution in general. Strategic planning obviously is by a vision and imagination of a world in which AI is used for significant benefit to all, charting a path for future where investments and progress in AI can be harnessed, leading to increased economic prosperity, creating new efficiencies and new markets that drive further innovation, among others.

Of course these blue prints whether nationally or continentally must be located within a comprehensive development plan that strives to close the development deficits while re-strategizing to in order to the opportunities offered by AI and Fourth Industrial Revolution era. This is a matter of necessity and urgency. Like has been seen at the beginning of the chapter, there is already a good dose of effort in this regard. I do think the major challenge has always been that of operationalization of these blue prints, sometimes as a result of dearth of conscientious and responsible leadership as well as formidable institution motivated by respect for the common good.

Unfortunately, Africa has more than one hydra-headed anti-development factors to deal with: "Corruption, unstable political environments, poverty and weak regulatory environments…" (Clark, 2018) These are unfortunately preponderant in Africa and will always be impeding factors on the run way of leapfrogging. These in no way encourage investment and sustainable growth. According to Clark (2018), "to leapfrog, one must have solid ground from which to leap. Without a stable platform, these will be leaps of faith or leaps into the darkness." Continuing, he writes, that "innovation is only innovation if it is sustainable, that means stable regulations, a war on corruption and an investment environment that supports staged growth." A research carried out by Reut Institute showed what has characterized countries who have leapfrogged: "shared vision, leadership by a committed elite, 'Inclusive growth', relevant institutions, a labor market suited to cope with rapid growth and changes, growth diagnostics of the country's bottlenecks and focused reforms as well as local and regional development and national mobilization." (See Clark 2018) Also, adequate funding for AI and technological research in general. It seems that these are yet to find their footings in most of the African countries. This is among the reason that the so called digital leaps have drawbacks. The researcher thinks that it is time Africa shirks these societal anomalies! Africa cannot continue to fall further back in the ladder of prosperity.

Creating vibrant AI ecosystem would need a shared vision among all stakeholders. It requires committed stakeholder engagement that pushes the individual countries and the entire region forward by building capacity in key areas. Building this AI ecosystem "will require institution-wide changes, funding, cross-institutional and cross-sector collaboration, as well as a commitment to prioritizing AI activities." In practical terms, to fully harness the opportunities that AI and Fourth industrial Revolution offer, there will be need among others to change governance structures to support innovation, revamp education systems to cater more directly to AI related fields and other fields of the Fourth Industrial Revolution while supporting the AI these fields with adequate resources. Africa must therefore surpass existing structures, infrastructures, institutions and capacity challenges or else the digital divide will further be accentuated and this will decrease her ability to compete globally.

FUTURE RESEARCH

Future research may focus among others more on practical ways in which Africa can take advantage of the Fourth Industrial Revolution. It should also look how AI could be employed without heightening unemployed demography. More importantly, it should also be concerned on how to reduce algorithmic bias by incorporating African values and its numerous languages in the making of AI for African. For instance one of the key principles in the ethical framework for AI is autonomy. Unfortunately this does not do justice to the communitarian values common across Africa. This is a case of failing to recognize diversity of social, cultural and political contexts which make ethical technical solution ineffective or misguided. Future research must therefore focus on charting a path towards more inclusive AI systems and frameworks. It should also look at ways to reduce the gender imbalance in the participating in AI-related courses or qualifications.

CONCLUSION

There is no doubt that AI emergence and the Fourth Industrial Revolution in general are critical juncture. In fact the permissive conditions are already there. It remains productive conditions which happen by virtue of dogged determination aimed at giving an adequate response which would ultimately lead to Africa's development upward spiral. AI and the Fourth Industrial Revolution present a great opportunity for economic transformation and have seeds to leap frog development of all African countries, placing the African countries among comity of at least fast developing countries. If Africa flags in taking adequate step and addressing the historically accumulated impeding factors, then the continent would further be left behind in the rungs of development and thus be pushed further to the periphery in the dynamics of global power and economy.

REFERENCES

Africa, F. (n.d.). *Top Priorities for the continent 2020-2030.* https://www.brookings.edu/multi-chapter-report/foresight-africa-top-priorities-for-the-continent-in-2020/

African Development Bank Group. (2019). https://www.afdb.org/en/news-and-events/press-releseases/african-has-grasped-fourth-industrial-revolution-according-african-development-bank-report-its-role-globally-could-be-even-bigger-32644

Bangert, V. (2022). *AI is quietly eating up the world's workforce with Job automation.* https://venturebeat.com/2022/01/08/ai-is-quietly-eating-up-the-worlds-workforce-with-job-automation/

Botha, F. (2019). *Why Africa Has the Ability to Leapfrog the Rest of the World With Innovation.* https://www.forbes.com/sites/francoisbotha/2019/04/02/why-africa-has-the-ability-to-leapfrog-the-rest-of-the-world-with-innovation/

Cissé, F. (2019). *How Africa can Ride the Artificial Intelligence Wave.* https://www.theafricareport.com/13917/how-africa-can-ride-the-artificial-intellignence-wave

Clark, D. (2018). *9 Ways Africa can Use AI to Leapfrog into the Future.* https://donaldclarkplanb.blogspot.com/2018/01/7-ways-africa-can-use-ai-to-leapfrog.html?m=1

Dietz, T. (2021). *Will Africa Leapfrog?* https://www.ascleiden.nl/news/will-africa-leapfrog

Fabricius, P. (2021). *Playing Leapfrog: How Far Can Technology Help Africa Bypass its Developmental Backlogs.* https://www.news24.com/news24/columnists/guestcolumn/opinion-playing-leapfrog-how-far-can-technology-help-africa-bypass-its-developmental-backlogs-20210410

Gadzala, A. (2018). *Despite Rise in Mobile Technology, Most of Africa is not Ready for AI.* https://www.axios.com/despite-rise-in-mobile-technology-most-of-africa-is-not-ready-for-ai-6f4ba17a-0a7b-4c03-86f5-67a8ba28cbe8.html

Gwagwa, A. (2020). *Artificial Intelligence (AI) Deployments in Africa: Benefits, Challenges and Policy Dimensions.* https://www.scielo.org.za/sci

Kenny, C. (2019). *Automation and AI: Implications for African Development Prospects?* https://www.cgdev.org/publication/automation-and-ai-implications-african-development-prospects

Moll, I. (2020). *The First three Industrial Revolutions Stripped Africa Bare—It's hard to see why the fourth would be any Different.* https://www.dailymaverick.co.za/article/2020-08-20-the-first-three-industrial-revolutions-stripped-africa-bare-its-hard-to-see-why-the-fourth-would

Morsy, H. (2020). *How Africa can Harness the Fourth Industrial Revolution.* https://www.project-syndicate.org/commentary/how-africa-can-close-education-skills-gap-by-hanan-morsy-2020-08

Ndung'u, N., & Singe, L. (2020). *The Fourth Industrial Revolution and Digitization will Transform Africa into a Global Powerhouse.* https://www.brookings.edu/research/the-fourth-industrial-revolution-and-digitization-will-transform-africa-into-a-global-powerhouse/

Novitske, L. (2018). *The AI Invasion is Coming to Africa (and It's a Good Thing).* https://timbuktu-chronicles.blogspot.co.ke

Now. (2020). *Africa Aims to Harness the Fourth Industrial Revolution.* https://now.northropgrumman.com

Nwaodike, C. (2020). *The AI Digital Divide—An African Perspective.* https://internews.org/commentary/ai-digital-divide-african-perspective/

Parker, L. E. (n.d.). *Creation of the National Artificial Intelligence Research and Development Strategic Plan.* https://www.semanticscholar.org

PwC Global. (2017). *Sizing the Prize: PwC's Global Artificial Intelligence Study: Exploiting the AI Revolution.* https://www.pwc.com/gx/en/issues/data-and-analytics/publications/artificial-intelligence-study.html

Radu, S. (2020). *Africa Braces for the Fourth Industrial Revolution.* https://www.usnews.com/news/best-countries/articles/2020-01-23/the-stakes-for-africa-in-the-fourth-industrial-revolution

Ramaphosa, C. (2020). *A National Strategy for Harnessing the Fourth Industrial Revolution: The Case of South Africa.* https://www.brookings.edu/blog/africa-in-focus/2020/01/10/a-national-strategy-for-harnessing-the-fourth-industrial-revolution-the-case-of-south-africa/

Tan, S. (2018). *AI and Africa: Leapfrog to Prosperity.* https://newafricanmagazine.com/17686/

United Nations Conference on Trade and Development (UNCTAD). (2018). *Leapfrogging: Look Before You Leap: Policy Brief no 7.* https://unctad.org

University of Pretoria. (2018). *Artificial Intelligence for Africa: An Opportunity for Growth, Development, and Democratisation.* https://www.accesspartnership.com

ADDITIONAL READING

Amankwah-Amaoh, J. (2016). Emerging Economies, emerging Challenges: Mobilising and Capturing Value from Big Data. *Technological Forecasting and Social Change*, *110*, 167–174. doi:10.1016/j.techfore.2015.10.022

KEY TERMS AND DEFINITIONS

Algorithm: This is a procedure or formula for solving a problem, based on conducting a sequence of specified actions. It is a set of instructions for solving a problem or accomplishing a task.

Artificial Intelligence (AI): This is a wide-ranging branch of computer science concerned with building smart machines capable of performing tasks that typically require human intelligence.

Automation: This refers to the creation and application of technologies to produce and deliver goods and services with minimal human intervention.

Blockchain: This refers to a secure, decentralized, and transparent way of recording and sharing data, with no need to rely on third party intermediaries. The digital currency Bitcoin is the best known blockchain application.

Cloud Computing: This refers to on-demand availability of computer systems resources, especially data storage and computing power without direct management of the user. In simple terms cloud computing allows one rent instead of buy one's IT. Rather than investing heavily in databases, software, and hardware, companies opt to access their compute power through the internet and pay for it as they use it.

Critical Juncture: This refers to turning points that alter the course of evolution of some entity. In the analysis of institutional development, the concept of critical juncture refers to situations in which decisions of important actors are causally decisive for the selection of one path of institutional development over other possible paths.

Development: This is a process that creates growth, progress, positive change or the addition of physical, economic, environmental, social and demographic components, the purpose of which is rise in the level and quality of life, income, opportunities without damaging environmental resources.

Digitalization: This the use of digital technologies to change a business model and provide new revenue and value-producing opportunities. It is the process of moving to a digital business. Moving beyond digitization, digitalization leverages digital information technology to entirely transform a business' process—evaluating, engineering and reimagining the way you do business.

Digitization: This refers to the process of analog to digital conversion of existing data and documents for example scanning a photograph or converting a paper report into a PDF. It is about creating a digital representation of physical objects or attributes.

Fourth Industrial Revolution: This refers to a fusion of advances in artificial intelligence (AI), robotics, the internet of Things (IoT), genetic engineering, cloud computing, 3D printing etc. it is a way of describing the blurring boundaries between the physical, digital, and biological worlds. It is fourth in the series of three earlier industrial revolutions sharing with them their evolutionary and disruptive tendencies.

Internet of Things (IoT): This refers to the network of physical objects—"things"—that are embedded with sensors, software, and other technologies for the purpose of connecting and exchanging data other devices and systems over the internet.

Leapfrogging: This is a concept used in many domains of the economics and business fields whose main idea behind it is that small and incremental innovations lead a dominant firm to stay ahead. It also the notion that areas which have poorly-developed technology of economic bases can move themselves forward rapidly through the adoption of modern system without going through intermediary steps.

STEM Education: STEM is an acronym for Science, Technology, Engineering and Mathematics. STEM education refers to system/policy of education that prides these four disciplines and their subsidiaries as critical to economic success and transformation.

Chapter 20
African Multi-Wives Culture:
Human Fatality and the Media in Nigeria

Ifeanyi J. Okeke
https://orcid.org/0000-0002-7929-7649
Alex Ekwueme Federal University, Nigeria

ABSTRACT

Human life is the most prized and valued of all creation. No wonder all human activities, government policies, and the entire engagements of humanity are anchored on the betterment and sanctity of human life. Religions all over the world recognize the sacredness of human life as the highest form of creation. Sadly, the sacredness of human life has been facing a downward movement never experienced in the history of mankind in the main as a result of incidences of couples killing each other on a mere or flimsy reason of suspected marital infidelity. Nigeria media quite recently have been agog with daily reportage of such dastardly acts without a corresponding reportage of possible solution located in the multi-wives marriage or culture of the African traditional society. This work focuses on the gains of multi-wives marriage in Africa, which has been in existence since the origin of humanity in Africa. This work is a wake-up call on the media in Nigeria to rise up to the occasion and do the needful and challenge the Western culture of individualistic existentialism.

INTRODUCTION

Traditionally, Africans value human life. They have always placed the greatest premium on it. This value dates back to creation and did not just emerge in their belief system with the conquest, partitioning and subsequent inversion of their land by the colonialists assisted by the missionary religions nor with the advent of any foreign law. It was not also a product of Africa's contact with the outside world consequent upon the era of slave trade. If not for anything, the slave merchants from Europe and other parts of the world manifested the greatest dehumanization and devaluation of the human life while engaging in their nefarious trade. Onyeocha (2007) aligns himself along same reasoning as he states that "the human beings are the very center of African religious impulse and expression. The willful taking of human life was considered the worse crime and offence in African world-view and the punishment for such was

DOI: 10.4018/978-1-6684-4107-7.ch020

the killing of the culprit (Afuekwe 1992). Metuh (1987) agrees that such offence was forbidden in Igbo world-view, and its prohibition is total and absolute because its infringement threatens the natural order and the very existence of society. Metuh argues further that in the traditional African society, it was an abomination against the Earth Deity to take a human life. Both voluntary and involuntary murder were abomination and require purification rites to safeguard the society from dangers the abominations may bring on it.

In some sub-cultural areas, for voluntary murder, the murderer was allowed to hang himself honourably or he would be slain by any member of the family of his victim. Where it was known to be involuntary, the culprit was allowed to flee, and later pay an arranged compensation before his return. Such was the provisions of the traditional African Religion and culture in the value, protection and preservation of human life before the agents of social and religious change invaded Africa.

It must be noted that this work is not a comparative study of two or more froms or types of marriages and does not intend to do a bifocal study or analyses of the merits and demrits of forms of marriages nay European and African. It is a research work that seeks to profer solutions and provide alternatives in humanity's search for the panacea for the preservation of human life in Nigeria, Africa and by extension the global community against the backdrop of the incessant and contemporary abrupt termination of human lives by couples on the very flimsy reason of suspecion of infidelity which in most cases are not confirmed nor proven. If one sees the work as unifocal, he may not be far from the truth. Along this line therefore, the work argues based on the findings, that African multi-wife culture reduces and tries to eliminate petty jealousy observed in monogamous partners, creating and providing avenues for tolerance in marriages even when infidelity is suspected; further raising the human life to the value where nature/divine has so placed it from inception. By so doing, it is the well considered view of this work that development (howbeit human) in Africa will be enhanced and which will in turn stimulate other forms of developments. Accordingly, the work does not by any stoke of imagination expect a pat on the back from scholars across the divide because it seeks to adjust the the contemporary order and statue quo. Just as the 19th century theologians, church fathers and other scholars attacked the evolution theory of Charles Darwin frontally; science attacking the Jewish/Christian teachings of an earth/world with four conners and having an end, the work expects provoked scholarly reactions across board which indeed is the beauty of a venture such as this. The media (especially of Africa), wherever they may be, must continue to promote.

THE SANCTITY OF HUMAN LIFE

Both the old and new testaments as a holy book teaches that each individual is known by God from the foundations of the world, (www,cmalliance.org). Since all life exists for God's purposes and all human lives are equally sacred, it is the belief that every human is blessed of God and must be preserved and nurtured. Going by the biblical account of the creation narratives, human life is created by God and is good. Since human beings are uniquely created in the image of God (Gen 1:27) and formed by God (Gen 2:7, Job 33:4; one can safely argue and further hold to the sanctity of all human life (Gen 9:6). Further down, one understands that human life begins at conception (Psalm 139: 13-16; Jeremiah 1:4-5). It also lasts beyond death into eternity (John 5: 28-29, I Corinthians 15:51-52). God gives life and breath to every human (Acts 17:25), calling all human beings to value equally the dignity of every individual life in its entirety. This compels us to love and have compassion for all the peoples of the world

(II Corinthians 5:14-15). Gushee (2006) argues that even for Christians "the sanctity of human life" is more than a cultural wars slogan and a product of serious reflection. It is a concept that one believes in. It is a moral conviction about how human beings are to be perceived and treated. It prescribes a certain way of looking at the world, in particular its human inhabitants. The concept has a universal application being the broadest and the most inclusive understandings of our moral obligations to other human beings; demanding that we value the human life and to treat it as the most valuable gift of nature/creation.

Novak (2009), drawing from his rich knowledge as a Jewish Theologian and a trained philosopher in natural law tradition, concludes that the life of a human being refers to the sanctity of human life as a concept with an intuition that human life should not be wasted. Iwe (1986) locates this sanctity of the human life as a major component of the wider human rights establishing the facts and content of the human dignity in the equality of all men. According to him "the fact is that no one can be by nature superior to his fellows, since all men are equally noble in natural dignity and consequently there can be no differences at all between political communities from the point of view of natural dignity". This dignity is inviolable and by virtue of this dignity in natural dignity, all men are equal in the rights according to the rights allowing no one person any privilege to take away the life of any other person. He observes most importantly, that this sanctity of human life which is a component of the quantum of human rights is traceable from what he calls the Homeric Era (13th -8th century BC), down to the Era of the Athenian Polis; to the Era of the twelve tables in Rome; until it is located in the English Magna Carta of 15th June 1215; the English Bill of Rights of 1689; the American Declaration of Independence and the American Bills of Rights; The Universal Declaration of Human Rights and in the various constitutions of Nations of the world. Obiaraeri (2001) in support of the sanctity of human life observes that the Universal Declaration of Human Rights contain the minimum global prescriptions on Human right and fundamental freedoms. And when the Africa charter was adopted in 1981 at the 18th Assembly of Heads of States and Government of the then Organization of African Unity, some bodies where established to promote and protect human and people's right, and amongst such rights is "the right to life", which he sees as the sum total of human existence. Amongst the Laws or Constitution of Nigeria, the Constitution of Federal Republic of Nigeria 1999 (as amended) has section 33(1) thus "every person has a right to life, and no one shall be deprived intentionally of his life, save in the execution of the sentence of a Court in respect of a criminal offence of which he has been found guilty in Nigeria.

In Christian religion, Schmidt (1889) observes that it saw in all beings in possession of human life as worthy of its care and charity. Even humans born of adulterous union were not excluded. The Jews believe that humans are made as part of God's creation and in God's image. Therefore, human life should be valued and considered as sacred and God given (www.bbc.co.uk). The Ethics of the fathers 4:22 says "Let not your heart convince you that the grave is your escape; for against your will you are formed, against your will you are born, against your will you live, against your will you die..." Murder is forbidden in Judaism as stated in the Torah;

Anyone who destroys a human life is considered as if he had destroyed an entire world, and anyone who preserves a human life is considered to have preserved an entire world; (Talmudt Santiadrin 379).

All Jews have a belief in the sanctity of life. This is the idea that life is precious and sacred and because of this any form of murder is forbidden in Judaism. To the Hindu, all living beings are sacred because they are parts of God and should be treated with respect and compassion. In Buddhism, the first commandment is "Do not destroy life", Jainism lists as its first commandment "Do not kill or hurt any living thing". According to the Sikh Religion, human life begins at conception and is sacred from the moment of conception. Confucianism teaches a version of the "Golden Rule" "Do not do to others what you would not want them do to you". In Taoism, we observe a deep reverence for all life in its various forms. And the list goes on. If these references are in support of life and the sanctity if it, it becomes expedient that humans should seek after that which enhances the preservation of human life and supporting social tolerance. Here comes the role of multi-wife Culture in Africa. Foundational elements of every great religious tradition on the face of the earth affirm this basic ethical understanding: Being, life and human life and mysterious and tremendous gifts of transcendent value calling all to reverence, preservation and nurturing – not destruction – even in the face of great challenges, responsibilities and sacrifices. It would therefore appear that it is primarily a degenerate secular Western society that rejects this fundamental sense of reverence for human life and we shall soon know how and why (Hearly (2014).

HUMAN FATALITY AND INFIDELITY IN NIGERIA

Hardly a week or month passes in Nigeria that we are not confronted with media houses reportage and outrage of either a man killing his wife or a wife killing her husband because of mere suspicion of infidelity of one form or the other. Babajide (2021) writes about a woman who killed her husband in Ondo state over suspicions of infidelity. According to the report, the man was killed after his wife allegedly received a call from another lady. The suspect who was identified a Queen Beatrice was said to have hit her husband, Emmanuel Ikujeni with a plank during an argument over the call. According to sources, the woman had flared up after the deceased received a call from the lady whom she suspected to be her husband's girlfriend. Argument ensured thereafter and in the fight, the woman (Beatrice) picked up a plank and hit Emmanuel on the head. The man was rushed to the hospital but he died before he was admitted. Onyegbula (2021) also reports of a 46 year old man who stabbed his wife to death over suspicion of infertility. This was reported to have happened in Ogun state. The man's name was given as Sobola Olatunji and a staff of Remo North Local Government Area of the state. The suspect was said to have been arrested following a complaint by the father of the deceased who reported the matter at Owode – Egba dividional Police Head Quarters. According to the Police, the suspect, Mr. Olatunji who had a misunderstanding with his wife Momudat Sobola took a knife and stabbed his wife at the back and the victim was rushed to the hospital but while the treatment was going on Momudat died. On interrogation by the Police, Sobola alleged that he suspected his wife of over 20 years to have been having extramarital relationship because of some text messages he saw on her phone.

In a Vanguard report of September 29th 2021, Una (2021) writes about a middle-aged man whose name was simply given as Akpan who shot his wife dead on allegation of infidelity before hanging himself in Cross River state. The incident was reported to have happened in the village of Bashua in Boki Local Government Area in the Central Senatorial District of the state. The report further states that the couple had an argument following an accusation by the man that his wife was cheating on him and tempers flared leading the man to bringing out his gun to shoot the woman, killing her on the spot. The man fled into the forest immediately and a search party was organized that later found his dead body hanging on a tree in the forest.

In November 21st, 2017, Vanguard reported that one Mariam Sanda was arrested for stabbing her husband to death. The late husband was identified as Bello, 35 years old and a son of Haliu Bello, a former chairman of the People's Democratic Party (PDP) and had since been buried according to Islamic rites in Abuja. According to reports, Mariam stabbed her husband several times based on allegations of infidelity after seeing a text message on his phone. It was further reported that after stabbing Bello severally on his back and manhood, she drove him to the hospital where he was confirmed dead. The matter was later charged to court. Adebayo (2020) reports that "the Court of Appeal in Abuja has upheld the death sentence passed on Mariam Sanda for the killing of her husband, Biliyamin Bello. The Federal High Court presided by Justice Yusuf Halilu in the Federal Capital Territory had earlier convicted Ms Sanda over the killing of her husband at their Abuja residence in 2017. "She should reap what she has sown", for its been said that "thou shall not kill and whoever kills in cold blood deserves death as his own reward" Justice Halilu had said in his judgement. In a Tribune report of January 24, 2021, a wife was said to have killed her husband in Warri, Delta state by hitting him with the heel of her shoe on his head over allegation of infidelity (Adurokiya, 2021). It was gathered that the incident happened at about 11.00am, close to the community's town hall. The husband identified as Etsebanhanro Ighomi and the wife had been engaged in a misunderstanding over alleged infidelity on the part of the late husband. The woman then approached the husband and struck him with the shoe heel on the back of his head from behind. The man reportedly fainted and began to foam from his mouth and died before he could reach the hospital.

A pregnant woman allegedly hacked her husband to death over an alleged extramarital affair in Delta (www.lindaikejisblog.com). The incident happened on Monday, March 15, 2021 at Ekrejebor axis of Ughelli town in Ughelli North Local Government Area of Delta state. It was gathered that the 22 year old woman identified as Faith Okiemute allegedly killed her husband, Edafe Unuakpor (27 years) with a machete and fled to Ugholli 'A' Division Police Station to escape jungle justice. The woman was angry that her husband did not spend the night at home. After his return, she accused him of having been with another woman and macheted him in one of his hands and abdomen. The man's friends rushed him to the hospital where he was confirmed dead. Udom (2017) further reports that Mrs Folashade Bashira Idoko, an auxiliary nurse was arrested by the police in Lagos for allegedly killing her husband, identified as Lawrence Ameh Idoko (a pipeline engineer) after accusing him of having an extra-marital affair. One thing led to the other and his wife stabbed him on his leg with a knife and was left to bleed to death. It was the cry of a 3 year old son that attracted neighbours who rushed in and discovered that the man was motionless. His death was later to be confirmed by a doctor in the hospital where his body was taken to much later.

Si-Soo (2009) reports even outside of Nigeria that the police apprehended a woman on suspicion of killing her husband with sleeping pills and further choked her sleeping husband to death at midnight on January 5, 2009. The woman identified only as Cho had mixed a fatal dose of sleeping pills with soup and served it to her husband as he suspected her infidelity which was not yet confirmed. The woman initially said he'd died of unknown causes while sleeping but pled guilty following a postmortem examination.

A close observation of the incidences of these accusations and subsequent murder that followed will reveal that they were hugely premised on mere allegations and suspicion of infidelity on both sides of the victims. It is further revealing that all such incidences of murder occured in monogamous marriages and non in multi-wife marriages. One would readily want to know when the infidelity even if proved became a capital offense that should be visited with capital and maximum punishment by the spouse who feels offended or cheated. How can human life be so cheap and vulnerable to be wasted on such grounds. What is it that had informed Africans and indeed Nigerians to resort to consider human lives as so unimportant as to waste them on mere suspicion or feelings of a cheated party of a marriage union on African soil. This indeed calls for very serious attention. It is to be noted however that this paper is not in any way suggesting that infidelity justifies multiple wives marriage but that a suspicion of infidelity by a spouse against his or her partner should not be the reason to take away a human life in Africa giving that multi-wife culture or marriage encourages tolerance and patience amongst couples while reducing its incidences.

MULTI-WIVES MARRIAGE IN AFRICAN CULTURE

In the context of this research, multi-wives is to be understood as the marriage of one man and several wives. Lawrence-Hart (2013) observes correctly that in Africa, tradition and religion are synonymous and the cultural values of the people are tied to their belief system. In this vein therefore Lawrence-Hart (2019) posits further that polygamy which is another name for multi-wives as instituted in African Culture, becomes acceptable and associated with economic and social values. Perhaps in an attempt to appreciate its origin and social significance, she acknowledges that a man believes that having male children enhances his position and prominence in the community and his name in addition remains immortalized. Thus, if the first wife bears only female children, the tendency will be to contract another marriage for the expressed purpose of raising male children (Ibeabuchi, 1990). Multi-wife marriage (or polygamy) is therefore customary all over Africa, she concluded. Taking additional wives was regarded as one of the fundamental indicators of a successful established men amongst the Logoli of Kenya, as large families enhanced the prestige of Logoli men. Such men with large families were also capable of obtaining justice as they would be feared by people, who would not dare to use force to take their livestock or other goods from them (Wikipedia). In Nigeria, custom allows for the legal marriage of more than one woman by a single man and there is no limit to the number of legal wives allowed under the custom and tradition of the people (Wikipedia).

Ayodele (2021) captures the scenario vividly, positing that "African men took in women according to their capacities. They were responsible to their wives and children. Above all they commanded great respect". According to Ayodele, we should make no mistake about it that polygamy (multi-wives) is native to Africa. In polygamy (multi-wives), a man begins to have peace of mind after taking the eight wife (Ifa corpus, ensconced in African Traditional Religion (ATR). There is a big difference between adultery and polygamy. Adultery involves secrecy; polygamy is an open affair. In adultery neither of the partners want anyone to know what is going on between them. Men with multiple wives are not adulterous. The wives will always know where their husbands were at any given time. There were even incidences where wives asked other women to date their husbands; especially when the women realized they could no longer cope with the demands from their men. The word adultery is therefore a neologism, coined by this present generation. Mbiti (1969) argues that getting married to two or more wives is a custom found all over Africa. For him, the custom fits well into the social structure of the traditional African life, and into the thinking of the people, serving many useful purposes. The more wives a man has, the more children he is likely to have and the more children, the stronger the power of "immortality" in that family. In African thought and belief system, he who has many descendants has the strongest possible manifestation of "immortality', he is reborn in the multitude of his descendants, and there are many who 'remember' him after he has died physically and enters his 'personal immortality'. Such a man has the attitude that "the more WE ARE, the more I AM. Children are in African concept the glory of marriage, and the more there are of them, the greater the glory. Polygamy also raises the social status of the family concerned so much so that it earns the head great respect in the eyes of the community; in the time of need there will always be someone around to help; it helps to prevent or reduce unfaithfulness and prostitution especially on the side of the husband. Mbiti observes that this function is practically valuable in modern times when men generally go to live and work in the cities and towns, leaving their wives and children in the rural area. When a man has several wives, he can afford to take one at a time to live with him in the town while other wife(ves) remain(s) behind to care for the children and property in the country side. Later on the wives exchange their position. In such case, Mbiti observes and rightly too that the husband is unlikely to take and keep concubines or go to female prostitutes.

In African families, there are duties which cannot be adequately performed if the number of people in the family is small. Looking after the cattle in the woods or plains; babysitting; working in the fields, getting firewood from the forest and water from the river; looking for the lost sheep or cattle; going to the town to earn some money; cooking; building new houses and granaries; hunting or food gathering and the likes are demands of and needs for a larger family (Mbiti 1969). Onyeocha (2007) joins in the discussion observing that marriage institution in Africa (is based on a multi-wife system). The system is borne out of its own logic based on the perception of Africans of the world as God's gift to humanity with an injunction to populate, tame and cultivate it. The multi-wives system provides the opportunity to populate the world with a multiplicity of offspring, while on the long run granting the nursing women respite and sufficient time in-between pregnancies to concentrate on the rearing of the new children. Such multi-wives marriage in Africa is therefore functional, with its goal as offspring and the attendant assurance of continuity of the lineage. A marriage without offspring is untenable and therefore as good as dead. The logic of polygamy is therefore based on the premise that the gift of abundant offspring is a sign of divine blessing anchoring and establishing the principle that every grown-up woman or man should be able to find a spouse to enable him or her produce offspring for posterity (Onyeocha, 2007). In the views of Otite and Ogionwo (1979), polygamous marriage is the common indigenous system of marriage in most, if not in all, indigenous African societies. When a man decides to have many wives, he performs as many marriage ceremonies as he may wish. Each ceremony involves and creates a new network of relationships and new opportunities for more children, serving as a means of creating trusted and loyal relationship and of keeping a kingdom together. A few of the traditional rulers as research showed in the Cameroons were said to have had as many as 300 wives which helped the traditional rulers to keep their kingdom together.

It is manifest in all we have been able to decipher from the discussions so far that polygamy or multi-wives as a system of marriage in Africa provides for the need of the society and through such means infidelity and unnecessary hatred, suspicion and bitterness in marriages are completely checked or at worst put at abeyance while the society progresses. By the instrumentality of this form, human lives were saved, protected, preserved in line with the ultimate sanctity and sacredness which they deserve through this way Africa maintain peace and indeed saw peace. The multi-wife marriages were contracted mutually with the full consent of both parties and no party is ever forced into it. Some Scholars may be tempted to argue that multi-wife marriage can lead to genetic disorders in humans. This is not correct as researches have not proved it. Simply put, a genetic disorder is disease caused in whole or in part by a change in the DNA sequence (Kandola, 2020). Accordingly to Kandola, there are several different generic disorders with types and ways of development. Although they tend to run in families as parents pass genes on to their children, however "there is no clear pattern of inheritance". This confirms that genetic disorders develop in people of monogamous marriages as well as multi-wives marriages. From research therefore, types of marriages do not in any particular become a factor in its increase or decrease.

COMPULSORY MONOGAMY AS AN IMPORTED CULTURE IN AFRICA

The prohibition or compulsory restriction of an African man from marrying more than one wife is not part of the tradition nor culture of the Africans. In the circumstance, the African man has always exercised his natural right and privilege of the choice of how many wives to marry. The traditional African society never made it compulsory or mandatory for a man to marry only one wife. The choice of how many wives to marry had remained at the discretion of the man and his intending wives. In the consummation/ contracting of such marriage, the consent of both parties, including their families were vigorously sort and obtained. Neither the man nor his intending wife is forced into it. Expectedly, the man wooed his wife with gifts and approached his would be in-laws with offers of yam tubers, free labour in farm cultivation, cutting of palm-fruits, and the extension of other benevolent gestures. Thus, marriage in traditional African Society is a one way traffic. It is not an individual affair as it demands that intending couples must obtain the blessings and permission of their families before they could marry to prevent them from marrying from reputed bad families (Ekeopara, 2011).

Multi-wife marriage does not in any way support nor encourage inbreeding and genetical disorders. The importance of robust consultations, inquiries involving both families was amongst other things to find out if the wife or man to be are in any way related by blood or other affinities, for it is has remained a taboo in most African Traditional societies for one to marry someone that is closely related through common ancestry for this will amount to incest, which is forbidden even today in traditional African soil. To this end, Green (1964) rightly observes that "the taboo in sexual intercourse between men and women born in the same village ranks... higher than any other for importance and gravity in local feeling". Therefore any breach of this taboo was a contamination of the land, which required elaborate ritual and sacrifices to appease the earth goddess and the ancestral spirits. Such marriage perform some other socio-ethical functions such as bearing more children for the continuity of the lineage, forming bigger and broader social bonds fellowship between families and relatives and by so doing according to Mbiti (1975) "extends the web of kinship socially".

African multi-wife culture has no effect nor did it encourage human genetic disorders.... However, it was with the inversion of Africa, by the white colonialists and Christian religion that the compulsory and forceful marriage of a man and only one wife seemed to have been instituted and forced down the throat of Africa. Christianity seems to be in the forefront of this imposition. It does appear that the Christian religion clothed in the culture and tradition of the Europeans manifested a resounding opposition to the practice of multi-wives marriage in Africa while struggling for the soul of the 'untutored' Africans. Most of the Christian denominations especially the Pentecostals frown at multi-wife marriages and oppose members with more than one wife from holding any office in the church or taking holy Communion. A case in point was observed during this research of a Pentecostal church in Eleme Rivers State Nigeria where one of the ministers of the church was sacked immediately it was known that he married two wives though he claimed to have divorced the first wife. He was not only stripped of all his church duties, but was sacked vide a letter which dismissed him even as a member of the Church.

Although most of the antagonisms against multi-wives marriage by Christianity may have been lifted from some biblical passages. Jesus was quoted in Matthew 19:4-6 as having answered and said, "Have you not read that He who created them from the beginning made them male and female and said, for this reason a man shall leave his father and mother and be joined to his wife, and two shall become one flesh. So they are no longer two, but one flesh. What therefore God has joined together, let no man separate". Mark 10:6-9 records that from the beginning of creation, God made them male and female and said, for this reason a man shall leave his father and mother, and two shall become one flesh. So they are no longer two, but one flesh. Ephesians 5:31 reads that for this reason a man shall leave his father and mother and shall be joined to his wife, and two shall become one flesh. Udemba Agwuocha (2021) informed the researcher that his late father (Udeagbala Udemba) used to be an Anglican Church catechist whose first wife had only two daughters. That his father told him that he made repeated efforts to take a second wife to have male children but the church authority refused, directing him to resign from being a catechist. His late father immediately resigned and took another wife. From the second marriage, four sons were born including himself. And that his father died peacefully after attaining the age of 98 year. Further commenting, Udemba Agwuocha argues that "It is therefore in their attempt to implement these New Testament injunction that the missionaries and early church workers who came from outside their host communities attacked frontally the African institution of polygamy in an attempt to plant monogamy, as an alternative form of marriage. As a consequence, the European style of life anchored on individualism and petty jealousy accompanied by their less human value took its negative toll on the continent of Africa. This appears to be more worrisome when one considers the provision in Judaism which remains without an iota of doubt the progenitor of the Christian religion.

Several of the Old Testament patriarchs and kings had a number of wives. It is part of the lifestyle of a typical ancient middle-eastern chieftain. Genesis 4 explains that Cain's son Lamech had two wives. The patriarchs Abraham and Jacob themselves had multiple wives and concubines. Moses had two wives. The mosaic law, handed over to Moses on Mount Sanai by Yahweh Himself accommodated the practice of marrying more than one wife, including captured prisoners from foreign Conquest-(Deut. 21:1-17). It also made provision for continuing the family line by marrying a brother's wife if he died without producing heirs (Deut. 25:5-12). Gideon, one of Israel's champions had many wives; Elkanah, a presumably godly man and the father of Samuel had two wives. In summary, during the Old Testament times, polygamy was not only permitted, it was sanctioned. Other love stories in the Bible are similarly plagued with polygamous flavor. Queen Esther was undoubtedly part of a harem (Wikipedia). So also was Ruth. Boaz most likely had another wife, but was obligated to marry Ruth out of his legal obligation to his relative's family.

It gets dicer when one considers the practice of the Kings of Israel. King David, the man after God's heart had eight wives. God not only seemed to permit this activity but in one instance at least, actually took responsibility for it. In II Samuel 12, when the Prophet Nathan confronted David over his sin with Bathsheba, we read, this is what the Lord God of Israel says; "I anointed you King over Israel and I delivered you from the hand of Saul. I have given you your Master's house and your master's wives into your bosom... and I gave you the house of Israel and Judah, and as if this wasn't enough, I would have given you even more". David's son Solomon, however, went overboard flouting a stipulation in Deut. 17 that Kings should not accumulate too many wives.it is on record that Solomon had 700 wives and 300 concubines.

It is not the intention nor the design of this work to attempt a judgement on the validity of the content of the New Testament texts in its support for mandatory monogamy for Christian adherents and attack on African Multi-wives Culture, the fact which has manifested from all these overviews remain in the main that the practice of a compulsory monogamous marriage was not only alien to African soil but was the making of the Christian religious missionaries and early church workers who without the due understanding of the intricacies of the African societal demands, attempted a forceful plantation of a marriage of a man and only one wife as part of the message of God's salvation. This like the research has revealed earlier is a contradiction of the God who does not change nor pass with the passage of time like humans. They did theirs without appreciating the content and purport of the Old Testament texts that not only tolerated and allowed the practice of polygamous marriage in Israel but showed clearly and unambiguously that Yahweh authorized it. Otherwise, how would it be that a man like David remains an apple of God's eye while Abraham remains till date (in the belief of Christians) in God's bosom. Nze Okoroafor Igwe argues that it calls for questions concerning the nature and person of God. That if God loves Abraham, David, Solomon et al and at the same time turns his back to hate and indeed condemn Africans to eternal damnation and hellfire for the reason of multi-wives especially, He cannot remain the Father and creator of all human beings on earth. It is inconceivable and indeed irreconcilable to attempt a view and understanding of God in the light of such a contradiction of double speaking to mankind in matters of marriage by such a holy book or religion. It is not to be doubted that such a contradiction cannot be associated with a loving Creator who even emphasized in same Holy Book that "in Heaven, there will be no marriage nor giving to marriage".

CHRISTIANITY AND MULTI-WIVES MARRIAGE IN AFRICA

Without any fear of contradiction, it does appear that the practice of Christianity in Africa is capable of serving the dual purpose of tolerating polygamy amongst its adherents and at the same time relaying to the people the undiluted message of God. The underlying need for serving this dual purpose rests on its ability to take care and tolerate the cultural practices of the African man and further lead such African to God through the undiluted and unadulterated message of the Christian religion.

becomes more important when one considers the fact that there is no static society nor culture in the world. The incidences of globalization, modernity and cultural contacts as agents of change must give reasons for cross-culture, inculturation and acculturation. In all of these, the African society as it were will continue to place the highest value on the human life as well as freely expressing its fundamentally protected right and desire to freely practice its faith on whichever side of the religious divide the person of Africa may have found himself or herself.

Against this backdrop, some individual evangelical Christian pastors were reported to have married more than one woman (Rosenbaum 2015). Henderson (2015), also reports about a woman who lives with her husband and his 19 year old pregnant wife. Myami (2018) talks about a cleric, a Christian man who marries more than one wife. That church no doubt tolerates this and sees nothing wrong with multi-wives marriage in christiandom. Even the Presbyterian Missionary Harold Turner acknowledges the facts that the practice of polygamy is a cultural norm in some parts of the world, such as Africa, and based on it, he cautioned Western Christian Missionaries not to impose the foreign cultural norm of monogamy on the Christians of Africa because doing so would lead to the sin of divorce, leaving children without both of their parents and further leading divorced wives to remarry (Owusu, 2007). The researcher, totally agrees with this submission. The theologian was further quoted to have said:

What have we done to the Africans in the name of Christianity? Polygamy which does not forbid, we have fought against as the greatest of all evils, but divorce and remarriage which he does forbid, we have introduced. We have truly managed to Europeanized them. Mission theory should teach us to preach the gospel but not our national traditions.

According to Siron (1991), indeed in many cultures, there is the possibility that the image of Christianity can be married when a cleric in a Christian denomination which opposes polygamy "suggests that these wives may marry others while the community regards them as still married to the first man", in these cases, the Church can be seen as "a promoter of immorality and a destroyer of home and family and become a stumbling block to non-believers. The Revd. Vincent Mulwa of Christ Pilgrim Restoration Centre opines that polygamy is a biblical practice, because it was the standard for various biblical prophets, and opposition to have more than one wife sterms from Westerners imposing their views on Christians who belong to other cultures (Nyami, 2018). The practice of polygamy allows tolerance and creates more value and respect for the sanctity and dignity of the human life.

NIGERIA MEDIA TO THE RESCUE

It is not arguable that the media all over the world are known as the fourth estate of the realm whose duties among all is to inform and educate the people on the positive side of human existence and reality of life. It is part of their duties (especially of Africa) to bring to the fore the cultural practices of African origin to ensure and enhance the sanctity of life. It must be further noted that doing such job or duty is not voicing for the rights of only men to keep multi-wives, but the choice includes that of the women to support it and further tolerate their co-wives as a way of decreasing human fatality. From the discussions before now, it would appear that the media is only concentrating on one side of the story, that is, the daily reportage of the killings going on amongst couples based on mere suspicion of infidelity without a corresponding reportage of the solution provided by the practice of multi-wives marriage under which Africans forebears lived out their years in fulfilment of their days on earth. It would further appear that the media in Nigeria has been so influenced and boxed into the corner of believing what the missionary religious preachers are daily dishing out against the practice of multi-wives marriage and in support of monogamy with its non-tolerant and non-accommodating nature of Africa's communal lifestyle. We need no further emphasis that the African World-view is that cast and engraved in the WE Concept of existentialism.

The man of Africa nay Nigeria finds existence, achievement, fulfilment in the interrelatedness and Interactions of Beings devoid of and contrary to the personalised, egocentric and self-centered lifestyle of the missionary religions pervading the boundaries of Africa today. This We Concept is well captured in the multii-wives marriage which forces a man or woman of Africa to see the world as a place of sharing and communality and not a self-centered arena. The man of Africa exercises his freedom in the choice of how many wives to marry while such women also exercise their right of choice to accept such marriage, appreciating the need to be tolerant and to accommodate her co-wives. This belief system seems to be fading away and the media must rise to the occasion and dispell the errornous tag on it by the some Missionary religious bigots. Their work should not terminate at just reporting the carnage but should extend to possible solutions to the mance. Such solution no doubt lies within the corridors of multii-wives marriage and its attendant benefits. The time may ripe and due for every human being to begin to question and examine the benefits of cultural practices that encourage the development of mankind such as the one in focus.

Missionary religions are not better nor superior to African Traditional Religious beliefs and practices. Whitman's Philosophy is not better not superior to Africa's Philosophy. Agreed what has been lacking in Africa is documentation. However today the story is fast changing. Afrocentric Scholars are daily detonating the false pillars mounted by armchair Eurocentric writers about Africa's Philosophy and World-view. The media (of Africa) must not stand aloof. Europe with their common law theory defined marriage "as a voluntary union of the life of a man and a woman" in the time past and Africans simply accepted.

Today a new twist is redefining marriage to be "the voluntary union of two consenting adults" allowing same sex marriages in the name of freedom and human right of choice. The missionary religious priests are even cueing in. Africa must not take everything Europe. There is enough beauty in multi-wives marriage which can aid humans in their search for increased human life and it's attendant development. Like in other forms of marriages which find protection in the onerous right of choice, the multi-wives marriage ought to benefit from such rights. The Nigeria and the Africa's media must continue to tell all these to the whole world.

CONCLUSION

The research has left nobody in doubt that the traditional African society and its acceptance of multi-wives marriage provided a better environment for tolerance amongst the people and by extension encouraged the observation of the sanctity and sacredness of the life of the human person. The society was more organized to manage humans. The society by the instrumentality of multi-wives marriage made human beings more honourable, bold, courageous, realistic and truthful. African men took women according to their capacities. That is in sharp contrast to the present society which is full of pretentious lifestyles, hiding under the cover of imported Christian religious culture to perpetrate and perpetuate evil (murder). The traditional African man survived multi-wives without falling under the knives of their suspecting wives. They leveraged on inclusiveness of the society to live a life of truth. This traditional cultural practice was humane, practical and purely realistic. The wave of civilization especially through Pentecostalism changed African lifestyles. They told Africans that it is 'one man, one wife' directing that any man who had married two or more wives before becoming 'Born Again' must send away the second wife which they tagged "Restitution".

This idea of one man, one wife from the findings of this research is largely responsible for the present social disequilibrium, the reason why so many so-called born again, spirit filled and tongue blasting Christians fall prey to the social menace now known as side chicks leading to an increase in human fatality on both sides (if either of the partners suspects the other of infidelity).

One may be tempted to ask which one is better; a man who has three wives or more known to all and sundry; or a man who has one wife and ten mistresses in the dark streets of virtually every city? At the end giving the slightest suspicion the wife would either kill the man or he would kill the wife. Ayodele (2021) observes that the sad aspect of it is that the white people who told Africans that polygamy is bad do worse things. The Western world which exported the idea of monogamy is the same place where sexual perversions like homosexuality, lesbianism and bestiality hold sway and where it is acceptable for people to surgically alter their birth genders. Now they have redefined marriage to include same sex. What can be worse than that? Religious leaders of African descent should begin to re-examine some of the Church doctrines. The Church universal must begin to give the issue of polygamy a second thought. John Colenso, the Anglican Bishop of Natal, South Africa, championed the Zulu way of life including 'plural marriage' (Colenso, 1855).

In Liberia, the Lutheran Church began allowing plural marriage in the 1970's (Brown, 1998). The African instituted Harrist Church started to permits those who are already living in polygamous marriage to convert and join it without having to renounce their multiple marriage (Brown, 1998). Mawati III, the Christian King of Eswatimi, is reported to have 15 wives with 35 children, (www.genealogy.org). Jude Nweleke (2021) sums it up that "to check the unnecessary blood letting in Nigeria today, we must accept multi-wives marriage in our Churches as optional to those who may desire it. This is achievable". This research has further confirmed it. The Nigeria media should echoe it the more.

REFERENCES

Adebayo, A. (2020, Dec. 4). Appeal Court upholds Manyam Sanda's death sentence for killing husband. *Premium Times*.

Adurokiya, E. (2021, Jan. 24). Wife kills husband with heel over infidelity in Delta. *Tribune*.

Babajide, A. (2021, Feb. 17). *Daily Post News Paper*. www.daily post.com.

Brown, S. (1998). *WCC delay decision on membership for Church with Polygamous Clergy – Social Report from the Eight Assembly of World Council by Churches*. Ecumerical News International.

Colenso, J.W. (1855). *Remarks on the Proper Treatment of Cases of Polygamy Converts from Healthism Pieterm aritzblog*. Academic Press.

Dworkin, R. (1999). *Life's Dominion. An argument about abortion euthanasia, and individual freedom.* Knopf, Inc.

Ekeopara, C. A. (2011). *Ethical order and stability in traditional Igbo Society, Calabar*. University of Calabar Press.

Frankena, W. R. (1975). The Ethics of respect for life. In Respect for life in Medicine, Philosophy, and the Law. The John Hopkins University Press.

Green, M. M. (1964). *Igbo Village Affairs*. Frank Cass.

Gushe, P. D. (2006). *The Sanctity of Life*. The Center for Bioethics of Human Dignity, Trinity International University.

Healy, M. (2014). *The Sanctity of Life and World Religions, Commentaries*. www.ncregister.com

Henderson, E. (2015). The Woman who lives with her husband and his 19 – year – old pregnant wife. *The Independent*.

Ibeabuchi, C. (1990). *1988 Lamberth Conference and Polygamy: Its Implications for the Contemporary Nigerian Church* (B.A. Thesis). University of Calabar.

Iwe, N. S. S. (1986). *The History and Contents of Human Rights: A Study of the History and Interpretation of Human Rights*. Peter Lang Publishing, Inc.

Kandola, A. (2020). *What to know about genetic disorders*. www.medicalnewstoday.com

Lawrence-Hart, G. (2019, July). The Socio-cultural Significance of Polygamy in Africa. *International Journal of Social Science and Humanity*, *5*(1).

Lawrence-Hart, G. (2011). Sin and its Removal in African Traditional Religion. In G. Tasie & R. Olumati (Eds.), *West African Religious Heritage*. Clear Vision Publishers.

Mbiti, J. S. (1969). *African Religions and Philosophy*. Heinemann Publishers.

Mbiti, J. S. (1975). *Introduction to African Traditional Religion*. Heineman Publishers.

Metuh, E. I. (1987). *Comparative Studies of African Traditional Religions*. IMICE Publishers.

Novak, D. (2009). *The Sanctity of Human Life*. Georgetown University Press.

Nyami, F. (2018). Cleric: Christian man can marry more than one wife. *Daily Nation*.

Obiaraeri, N. O. (2001). *Human Rights in Nigeria – Millennium Perspective*. Perfect Concepts.

Onyegbula, E. (2021, Feb. 15). 46-years old man stabs wife to death over infidelity. *Vanguard Newspaper*. www.vanguardngr.com

Onyeocha, I. M. (2007). *Africa: The Country, the Concept and the Horizon*. Imo State University Press.

Onyeocha, M. I. (2001). *Africa: The country, the Concept and the Horizon*. Imo State University Press Ltd.

Otite, O., & Ogionwo, W. (1979). An Introduction to Sociological Studies. Heinemann Educational Books (Nig) Ltd.

Owusu, S. (2007). Towards a Theology of Marriage and Polygamy. *Direction, 36*(2).

Rosenbaum, S. (2015). Pastor marries pregnant teen with wife's blessing. *The New York Post*.

Schmidt, C. (1889). Social Results of Early Christianity (2nd ed.). WCM Isbister Ltd.

Si-Soo. (2009, Jan. 21). Wife kills husband for infidelity. *National*.

Siron, J.R. (1991). Polygamy: An enduring problem. *Ministry*.

Udom, E. (2017, Aug. 2). Jealous wife kills husband over alleged infidelity. *Independent*.

Una, E. (2020, Sept. 29). Man kills wife, commits suicide in Cross-River. *Vanguard Newspaper*.

Chapter 21
A Critical Evaluation of Social Media and Human Development in Nigeria

Justine John Dyikuk
https://orcid.org/0000-0003-1374-5274
University of Jos, Nigeria

Joshua Yilhikka Rotshak
University of Jos, Nigeria

ABSTRACT

Recent fraudulent online activities have drawn the attention of a sleeping nation to the alarming nature of the increasing rate of hate speech, fake news, and other sharp practices in Nigeria. The corrosion of values is blamed on the explosion of information and communications technologies (ICT). This chapter employed theories of legitimacy and dialogic communication to investigate the menacing effects of unwholesome online practices. It found overemphasis on the negative use of social media and slowness to acknowledge the significant changes in ICT as factors why people have not taken advantage of social networks. It recommended ongoing media-education through campaigns and further research on internet penetration in the country as veritable ways of measuring successes in human development. It concluded that if educationists and policy makers take advantage of social media platforms, they would remain a huge resource for human development and national integration.

INTRODUCTION

Nigeria is one of the most populous countries worldwide (Clement, 2019). "With over half of the Nigerian population under 30 years of age, they are the ones more frequent on the Internet" (Nigeria Internet Registration Association, 2019). This has brought above massive revolution in almost every sector of life. "With instant messaging and unlimited access, being a cheaper method of communication, raising awareness and generating income by promoting goods and services, social media has revolutionized

DOI: 10.4018/978-1-6684-4107-7.ch021

modern day society" (Olusola, 2018). However, many Nigerians are daily becoming circumspect of the use of social media. Perhaps it might be correct to opine that the rising number of cyber crimes across the world is alarming. The recent profiling of 80 Nigerian youths who are on the wanted list of the Federal Bureau of Investigation (FBI) in the United States of America did not help matters (BBC, 2019). This is coupled with the saturation of the virtual space in Nigeria with fake news, hate speech and calls for either secession or revolution. It is apparent that the traditional media is overwhelm with the activities of so-called "citizen journalists" who post anything online. As things stand, unsuspecting members of the public who are often gullible are left confused.

The seeming menacing effect of social media-abuse is putting journalism and media-scholarship in on trail. While the public is saturated with multiple stories, young students who are leaders of tomorrow are confused as to what constitutes truth and objectivity. The scenario is worse because apparently, experts in education and learning have not seen the need to train the masses in order to be media savvy. While mass mobilisation is far from being realized, we are left with a situation where new technology is not exploited for the advancement of the human being. Sadly, while people in other climes are cashing in on the good that Information and Communication Technologies (ICT) offers, Nigerians are busy dealing with insecurity, insurgency, hunger and other analogue malfunctioned systems which do not guarantee hatching technologically advanced global citizens who can compete with their peers in other developed parts of the world.

With this motivation and background in mind, the standalone qualitative survey aims at:

1. Drawing the attention of a sleeping nation to the alarming nature of the increasing cases of hate speech, fake news and other sharp practices in Nigeria;
2. Decrying the corrosion of values as a result of fraudulent online activities in country;
3. Investigate why Nigerians have not been able to take advantage of social media for human development;
4. Recommending veritable ways of measuring successes in human development through social networks; and,
5. Demonstrating how Nigerians, particularly students, those in business, educationists and policy makers can take advantage of social media platforms as huge resource for national integration and human development.

CONCEPTUAL ELUCIDATION

Social Media

Social media has been defined "as the facilities and tools that reduce the world to a global village; websites and applications that enables users to create, share contents and participate in social networking. The social media platform provides opportunities for users to create online communities to share ideas, information, personal messages, etc. Some of the social media applications include Facebook, Instagram, You-tube, My Space, Twitter, Skype, LinkedIn, etc" (Nigeria Internet Registration Association, 2019). However, in this study, we could conceive it as the use of modern devices such as internet enabled Smartphones for the purpose of interfacing with others who are close or far to share information, engage in social interaction, do business or make ends meet. Social media platforms such as WhatsApp,

Facebook and Twitter among many others make use of mediated-communication that is characterized by speed, interactivity and media convergence.

Human Development

In this study, we shall conceive human development as the integral or overall physical, psychological, emotional and spiritual wellbeing of the human being that is tied to improvement of tangible social amenities such as schools, roads, clean water, health care centers to mention a few. It also covers socio-economic advancements, science and technology (innovations) and aspects of culture, freedom, peaceful coexistence and living in a pluralistic society.

THEORETICAL FRAMEWORKS

This study adopts the *Theory of Legitimacy* (Deegan, 2006; Deegan & Samkin 2009) *Theory of Dialogic Communication* (Kent & Taylor, 1998) as *Theoretical Frameworks*. The former suggests that there is a social contract between the firm and society emphasizing that society constitutes a broader category than stakeholders. Drawn from the field of public administration, the central idea is that local governments often act based on what society identify as social norms that are acceptable (Dowling & Pfeffer, 1975). Frost and Semaer (2002) hold that the pressure is stronger on local governments than private sector because, while the former are politically visible, the later attracts more attention from external stakeholders. As such, they must supply a greater degree of response to make themselves genuine before society.

The latter which is *Theory of Dialogic Communication (*Kent & Taylor 1998) furnishes us with understanding on how organisations build and sustain their online social relationships. The scholars emphasized how improving the interactivity of social media aids in building social relationships, increases levels of communication, improves user-satisfaction; brings about greater transparency and participation and engenders trust between organisations and their stakeholders (Bortree & Seltzer 2009; Bonsón, et al 2013, 2014). Having been validated by experts within the last 15 years, the *Dialogic Communication Theory* is now used as a primary theoretical framework on how online social relations are established (Wright & Hinson 2009; Rybalko & Seltzer 2010; McAllister 2012). In the course of this discussion, we would demonstrate how and why the two theoretical frameworks are appropriate to the study.

SOCIAL MEDIA IN NIGERIA: PENETRATION AND EXPLOSION

Digital Report 2019 from *Hootsuite* and *We Are Social* indicates that social media use jumped nearly 9% year-over-year with upwards of 3.5 billion people now active on social media (Hootsuite, 2019). Demographics covering the number of internet users in Nigeria from 2017 to 2023 are in millions. Nigeria had 92.3 million internet users in 2018. By 2023, this number is expected to increase to 187.8 million internet users in the country. While the internet penetration was 47.1 percent of the population in 2018, it is projected to reach 84.5 percent in 2023 (Clement, 2019). Importantly too, mobile phone internet usage is popular in Nigeria as there are almost 50 million mobile internet users in the country.

Experts are of the view that in Nigeria, infrastructure and online usage development bypassed adoption of desktop PC to mobile internet usage through purchase of cheap Smartphones. About three quarters of Nigerian web traffic is generated through Smartphones. This ranks the country on the top of the list of African countries like Sudan and Ghana based on the share of traffic via mobile (Clement, 2019). On internet freedom in Nigeria, *Freedom House Index 2018* reports that: "Nigeria was ranked third in Sub-Saharan Africa and 21st out of the 65 global markets that were measured for internet freedom in 2018. Nigeria has very strong libel laws and subsequently, Nigerian internet users often do not feel free to fully express themselves online" (Clement, 2019).

By contrast, the figures had changed significant in 2019. According to a new report by *Social Media Marketing Platform Hootsuite* on the *Global State of Digital in 2019*, there are 98.39 million internet users in Nigeria. In comparison to January 2018, there is a 4 million increase in the number of internet users in the country. While the global average for internet penetration is 57%, only 50% of the population in Nigeria is connected to the internet. This demonstrates that the overall penetration of internet in the country is low. Comparatively, Kenya has (84%), South Africa 54%, and Ghana 35% levels of internet penetration (Udodiong, 2019).

On how Nigerians are using the internet in 2019, expert opinion has it that "Of the 98.39 million Nigerian internet users, 54% access the internet on a daily basis while only 12% (24 million) have active social media accounts - The report found that 3 hours 17 minutes is the average amount of time Nigerians spend using on social media. This is higher than the global average which is 3 hours 14 minutes. WhatsApp is the most active social media platform in the country with 85% of users. The second is Facebook at 78%, Instagram is third at 57%, followed by FB Messenger at 54% and Youtube at 53%" (Udodiong, 2019).

SOCIAL MEDIA-USE IN NIGERIA IN THE LIGHT OF HATE SPEECH AND FAKE NEWS

The recent blacklisting of some Nigerians in the United States of America as a result of fraudulent online activities has drawn the attention of a sleeping nation to the alarming nature of the increasing cases of hate speech, fake news and other sharp practices in Nigeria. The corrosion of values is blamed on the explosion of Information and Communications Technologies (ICT). Some of the negative effects of engaging with social media are lack of control of and over personal information, cyber bullying, mental health issues, lack of morals, spread of fake news and exposure to adult information. Others include, indirect encouragement of high rate of online- scam, poor grades in academic pursuits, long hours online, peer pressure and addiction to social media (Nigeria Internet Registration Association, 2019). We shall consider some possible causes for the negative use of social media in the country:

Possible Reasons for Negative Use of Social Media

Some scholars argue that although advances in science and technology promise a good package for humanity, the increasing use of social media handles like Facebook and WhatsApp for unwholesome acts constitute a bane of the new technology. Based on expert opinion, the following are responsible for the menace:

Lack of Being Media Savvy: The negative use of social media by many people in the country is blamed on lake of being media savvy. Because many people are still learning how to operate the Smartphone, they end up sending wrong messages to persons they did not intend to. What is more, some young people use the new technologies for sexting; that is, sharing pornographic content with their friends. This amounts to lack of being media savvy in terms of knowing what the Smartphone is supposed to be used for. In a related development, it has been argued that: "A resistance to change and a lack of social media savvy amongst senior leaders is holding organisations back from rebuilding trust and fostering cultures of openness, collaboration and innovation in their organisations" (Engage Business Media, 2019).

Slowness in Acknowledging Changes in ICT: While the world has gone far in ICT advancement, many people in Nigeria are slow in accepting these changes that ICT is offering. Technology affects the way people think and live in Nigeria but the country is yet to fully embrace e-commerce, e-banking et al. For instance, though some efforts have been made to ensure the integration of ICTs in Nigerian secondary schools, the level of ICT adoption and use is low, due to poor policy/project implementation strategies and limited/poor information infrastructure (Adomi & Kpangban, 2010).

Inability to take Advantage of New Technology: Nigeria is yet to fully take advantage of digital technologies. For example how many universities have functional websites? How many students' research works are published on university website repositories? This is what is responsible for the inability of the education sector in the country to make inroads in e-learning and research. Perhaps it is why Nigeria is unable to meet up with the Digital Terrestrial Television Benchmark, full implementation of Treasury Single Account (TSA) and E-Payment at all levels of society.

Fear and Suspicion: The nefarious activities of internet fraudsters popularly known as Yahoo-yahoo boys across the country is creating fear in the minds of prospective social media users. Unsuspecting members of the public have been robbed of their hard earned money as a result of criminal elements who pose as bank operates who are asking for details of customers to update their bank account only to defraud them. Only recently, the U.S. Justice Department reported that a four-month global operation netted a total of 281 arrests worldwide, including 167 in Nigeria and 74 in an internationally coordinated law enforcement operation aimed at disrupting a multibillion-dollar internet scam (Farivar, 2019). To this end, some scholars are of the opinion that the advent, growth and utilization of information and telecommunication technologies (ICTs) in Nigeria have been greeted with an increase in illegal activities making 419 scam a major concern for the global community (Chawki, 2009).

Cyber bullying is also on the increase. "Kids especially are vulnerable to the practice of cyber-bullying in which the perpetrators, anonymously or even posing as people to their victims terrorize individuals in front of their peers. The devastation of these online attacks can leave deep mental scars or lead to suicide" (Olusola, 2018). Since these practices have become recurrent decimals in the society, it is increasingly becoming difficult for many people to activate their mobiles for e-banking because of fear and suspicion.

DEMOGRAPHICS OF CYBER CRIME IN NIGERIA

Crime rate is on the increase across Nigeria. In particular, due to high rate of unemployment, quest for wealth, lack of strong cybercrime laws and incompetent security on personal devices, cyber crime has become a recurrent decimal. Although extant data seems obscure about these illegal activities, it is estimated that annually, financial loss in Nigeria due to cybercrime was N250 billion ($649 million) in 2017 and N288 billion ($800 million) in 2018 (Proshareng.com, 2020). As a result of cybercrimes such as fraudulent emails, identity theft, cyber harassment, spamming and ATM spoofing, businesses and individuals in Nigeria lose over $500 million annually.

In 2019, Nigeria's Economic and Financial Crimes Commission (EFCC) in collaboration with the Federal Bureau of Investigations (FBI) arrested 281 individuals for cyber-enabled financial fraud. 167 of these alleged fraudsters were Nigerians (Nnabugwu, 2020). It would be recalled that one Ramon Abbas Olorunwa popularly known as Ray Hushpuppi, was arrested in June 2020, during the COVID-19 lock-down on charges of conspiracy and laundering millions of US dollars to keep up his boisterous lifestyle. He and 11 other others were arrested in Dubai by authorities who seized about US$14 million, 13 luxury cars worth $6.8 million, 47 smart phones with computer evidence containing over 100,000 fraud files on nearly 2 million possible victims from them. He is currently in the US facing trial for cyber fraud, hacking and scamming (Igwe, 2021).

HUMAN DEVELOPMENT IN NIGERIA THROUGH SOCIAL MEDIA

It belongs to scholarship to undertake a critical review of situations and phenomena so that arguments do not end at a pedestrian level. As such, notwithstanding the position of those who are circumspect of suing social media, expert-opinion argues that advances in science and technology such as the use of social media promise a good package for humanity. It is on this note that we would like to juxtapose the seeming negative perception of social media by some Nigerians with secondary data generated from the views of scholars on why "The baby should not be thrown with the bath water."

Some of the positive opportunities various social platforms provide the youths with include: Communication tools for connecting with loved ones and old friends irrespective of locations, access to positive and free information, ways of promoting businesses to a wider audience, social capital and avenues of contributing to the emotional wellbeing of others by offering positive pieces of advice; others are, launching businesses online, marketing businesses online at little or no cost and real time sharing of information for businesses through paid and unpaid advertising (Nigeria Internet Registration Association (2019). Therefore, social media could be a rich resource for human development in Nigeria in the following ways:

Tool for National Integration: To every keen observer, Nigeria is apparently divided along ethnic, religious and political fault lines. The embers of hatred are further fueled by calls for secession or revolution from some quarters. Social media platforms are now being used as conduits for hate speech and fake news. Since we have established that internet penetration in the country is on a fast lane, users of WhatsApp, Facebook and Twitter could use these platforms to share messages which speak to the heart of patriotism and national integration. "Social media has quickly integrated into many aspects of our daily lives. Websites like Facebook, WhatsApp, Twitter, and many more make it easy to keep in touch with family and friends, to engage in online conversations and to have easy access to many goods and services. Chats and social networking are great ways to stay in touch and find new friends beyond boundaries" (Olusola, 2018).

Rich Resource for Educational Advancement: In a world of young people whom Prensky (2001) describes as "Digital Natives," social media is a huge resource for educational advancement. African students particularly those from Nigeria cannot raise their heads high if the analogue systems of the 20th century are continually being used to teach them in the 21st century. What this means is that the advent of social media is a right step in the right direction. Instead of the erstwhile negative perception of social media as a nuisance, teachers and other educators can take advantage of new technologies to share information and knowledge with their students on cloud, Yahoo, G-mail or WhatsApp and encourage them to do same with their fellow students. Scholars like Selwyn, (2018) have maintained that technologies can enhance educational outcomes and promote social inclusion in education in terms of improving educational opportunities or skills for individuals through information literacy and ICT. He contends that educational institutions such as schools, colleges, libraries and museums are used to provide access to ICTs for all.

Olusola (2018) agrees with the submission above when he opined that: "Social media is an immense contributor to the educational field. You may be shy as a student in the classroom but you can post queries to your online teachers and get your questions solved within little time. There are some sites that are dedicated specifically for education, personal development, research and developments. Certain social media platforms can also be invaluable tools for professional networking." Lectures can share materials with their colleagues from other universities; projects of students can be published online and e-libraries be established to ease learning and information-sharing. In this way, new technology would remain a huge resource for the advancement of teaching and learning between teachers and students.

Instrument for Information Sharing and Transfer of Knowledge: If we sub-divide information into hard and soft knowledge, it would be easy for us to emphasize that while people could share soft information on various social media handles, teachers and students can as well share hard information for the advancement of teaching and learning. This means that information-sharing should not be limited to sharing banters, niceties or pleasantries alone but large quantum of knowledge like latest discoveries in media studies or applied psychology. Rather than get stuck to one dimensional approach of using technology, blending the mundane with the rational could change the narrative.

In their research, Ghazali, Sulaiman, Zabidi, Omar and Alias (2016) discovered that with the invention of social media, knowledge sharing process has been more effective and easy for researchers lecturers and others in the academia as it facilitates communication, aids in idea generation and promotes group establishment. Based on the positive impact of using social media in the academia, they concluded that without doubt, social media enhances and upgrades knowledge sharing process thus assisting academics in their scholarly work.

Advancement in Science and Technology: Studies have shown that from e-commerce to e-learning, contemporary society acts out through ICTs such as the internet and other global telecommunications systems. This has resulted in technology-based reconfigurations in facets of life such as employment, education, health, welfare, politics, leisure and entertainment putting technology at the heart of almost everything (Selwyn, 2018). It is in the light of the above that other advanced nations have gone far in embracing what science and technology offers. Only recently, Rwanda launched the first set of Smartphones manufactured in that country. As such, this is a challenge for the most populous black nation on earth.

The challenge is shifting from a mono economy which survives on oil to carving a niche in a knowledge-based economy that incubates digital leaders and entrepreneurs for the next generation. Chances are that if Nigeria engages in an all-round investment in science and technology like the United States of America, United Kingdom and Asian Tigers, the phenomenon of brain drain would reduce drastically. The recent figures released recently by the National Bureau of Statistics (NBS) that ICT contributes 13.8% to GDP which includes online businesses further indicates that this may double revenues for both oil and gas in 2 years (Nigerian Communications Communication, 2019). This further points direction to potency of new technologies.

Tools for Advertising, Donations and Charity: Today, social media has become a prime news platform which exposes people to numerous business opportunities. More than ever, social networks are used as a significant marketing strategy which provides avenues for those operating a social media page to showcase their brands to wide audiences. By the same token, Social networking contributes in no small measure to making donations and or giving out in charity. Many organizations, particularly Non Governmental Organisations (NGOs) use social media handles as a marketing and fundraising strategy. They are also used for media campaigns and raising awareness about just causes which saves human lives (Olusola, 2018).

SOCIAL MEDIA AND HUMAN RESOURCE DEVELOPMENT IN NIGERIA

There is a strong relationship between social medal and human resource development in Nigeria. As such, the study would highlight indices such as training and development, social intelligence, cultural intelligence and politics and leadership which enhance integral development in the country:

Training and Development: Social media has contributed positively to human resource practices in Nigeria. For example, during and after the COVID-19 pandemic, employers employed various social media platforms for like training and recruitment of staff. As an immense human resource, social media is instrumental to improving social contacts, improving ease of doing business and helping employers reach out to their employees in the post pandemic era. Arguably, thanks to social media, human resource consultation has become a source for assessing employee well-being. The push towards integrating technology in work place environments to enhance learning is crucial. Elsewhere as in Nigeria, the next generation workforce which is tech savvy is increasingly proving to be a robust force whose learning habits, characteristics, styles, and expectations could guide innovation in corporate training. To this end, among millennials, technology and social media are driving competiveness and innovation (Hout, 2018). Besides, Ebele and Oghenetega (2014, p.21) agree that: "In an information hungry world social media is an import way to equip the undergraduates for employment of graduates."

Social Intelligence: In Nigeria, social media is employed for various educational purposes and the advancement of social intelligence. For example, studies by Oghenetega, Oyenike and Ugeh (2014) among most undergraduates concerning reasons for using social media (networking) found the following - reaching out to close or distance friends 20(41.66%), update about news 10(20.83%) and update about news 9(31.25%). Various social media platforms in vogue in Nigeria such as Facebook, WhatsApp, 2go and Twitter provide social intelligence assist in addressing national security. They achieve this through enhancing environmental surveillance, providing information on matters of security as well as creating an interactive platform for addressing security challenges and unveiling areas of individuals and entities that may sabotage national security (Samphina.com, 2022).

Cultural Intelligence: Notwithstanding that fact social media has influenced African culture in negative ways by exposing children to things that they should ordinarily not know (like pornography), new media helps in increasing connections between people and creating an environment for people from diverse cultural milieus to share a lot of stuff about their culture. In like manner, social media improves creativity and social awareness of Nigerians from the over 200 tribes in the country by interacting with other people and sharing new ideas and opinions. By the same token, a positive blend of African culture and social media is emerging as social media is helping to eradicate negative traits in African Culture like relegating women or the younger generation to the background. As a consequence, new media is now giving vulnerable groups such as children, youth and women a voice to speak out and resist all forms of oppression (Ywee, 2019).

Politics and Leadership: Social media is now impacting on politics and leadership in Nigeria. From the #EndSARS protests to the banning of Twitter, the nation seems to be witnessing a "Nigerian spring." Various #EndSARS "organisers used social media to connect with volunteers, accept donations from other parts of the world and publish accounts of disbursed funds through frequent updates" (Dark, 2020) to raise awareness about police brutality across the country. Recall that the Nigerian government suspended" Twitter's operations after the giant tech deleted a tweet by President Muhammadu Buhari that was widely perceived as offensive. The move attracted international condemnation from Amnesty International, the Embassy of Sweden in Nigeria and the British and Canadian missions in the country which described the action as an infringement of freedom of speech and the fundamental rights of Nigerians (Princewill & Busari, 2021). In a nutshell, social media gave voice to #EndSARS protesters and also led to the restoration of the activities of the micro-blogging company, Twitter.

LIMITATION OF THE STUDY AND JUSTIFICATION FOR THEORETICAL FRAMEWORKS

In this standalone qualitative survey, we tried to relay on secondary data drawn from various scholars on the subject matter. This helped us to fill in the gabs in their arguments and also propose some doable recommendations. In this way, we were able to critically juxtapose the negative and positive effects of social media-use in Nigeria. In the light of human development and national integration, we found that despite the fear and suspicion of engaging with social media handles, many Nigerians still resort to them as instruments for national integration, educational advancement, science and technology, information-sharing and human interaction.

However, given the penchant for lack of documentation in the area of study, we recommend that further quantitative research be undertaken by students and researchers on how social media is an indispensable reservoir for human development in Nigeria. This will go a long way in complimenting extant data on the subject under discussion and also provide further empirical points of view on the matter towards informed perspectives.

The choice of the *Theory of Legitimacy* (Deegan, 2006; Deegan & Samkin, 2009) as theoretical framework is justified because it encourages legislation in the area of cyber laws while stressing the role of the society. The theory recalls the social contract between the government and the people. It seemingly places society above stakeholders who are drawn from it. It also takes into cognizance what society identifies as social norms which are acceptable by all (Dowling & Pfeffer, 1975).

Dialogic Communication (Kent & Taylor, 1998) *Theory* was chosen because it reveals the importance of how organisations build and sustain online social relationships. It is appropriate to the study because the masses in Nigeria are increasingly becoming interested in improving their social media skills through improved interactivity towards building more robust social relationships, improved communication skills, user-satisfaction and trust between leaders and the led. Because the framework which has been endorsed by scholars is said to improve how online social relations are established (Wright & Hinson, 2009), it is likely to assist people in Nigeria in their use of social media.

RECOMMENDATIONS AND CONCLUSION

Recommendations

In the light of our discussion above, we make the following recommendations as veritable ways of using social media for human development in Nigeria:

1. ***Media-Education:*** We earlier made the point that people need to be media savvy in order to use social networks effectively and efficiently. To achieve this, media-education is crucial. Concretely, media-education would entail using various media platforms to de-emphasis the negative perception about the use of social media on the one hand and re-emphasize how engaging with new media can enhance learning and education. As such, "The youth should be educated on the proper use of the Internet and Social Media" (Nigeria Internet Registration Association, 2019).
2. ***Curricular Review:*** In line with international best practices, it is crucial for framers of educational curriculum in Nigeria to reconsider the inclusion of studying the rudiments of both social and traditional media in primary, secondary and tertiary syllabi. After carefully examining the influence of ICT applications in Nigerian secondary schools, Adomi and Kpangban, (2010) recommended that ICTs should be adopted in schools to improve the educational system and help the students receive a solid education, enabling them to live successfully. This will make students of all cadres across the country to catch up with their peers in terms of knowing and using new technologies. The recent disclosure by the Minister of Communications, Dr. Isa Ali Ibrahim Pantami that with 13.8% contribution to GDP, ICT (which includes social networks) may double Oil and Gas in 2 years (Nigerian Communications Communication, 2019) further proves the potency of investing in new technology for the future.
3. ***Media Campaigns:*** Today, more people are creating social media strategies to showcase their brand's authority and encourage positive actions through building savvy use of social media (Digital Marketing Skill Institute (2019) and media campaigns. It, therefore, behooves on stakeholders like the Ministers of Information and Culture and Communication as well as the government bodies such as the National Orientation Agency to drum support for media campaign which stresses unity of the nation and integral human development. This will go a long way in curbing embers of strife, hatred and the divisive tendencies that are currently being experienced in the county.
4. ***Mass Mobilisation:*** In line with the above recommendation, since the media is the fourth estate of the realm, mass mobilisation belongs to its constituency. It only takes an informed and all-round media to have an informed citizenry. The press in Nigeria ought to rise up to the occasion to not only set the agenda for discussion but engage in meaningful reportage aimed at improving poor human conditions in the country leading to robust human and infrastructural development. Since we have established that the *Theory of Legitimacy* (Deegan, 2006; Deegan & Samkin, 2009) provides a framework for the masses to act based on what society identifies as social norms that are acceptable (Dowling & Pfeffer, 1975), those who will be responsible for mass mobilisation must bear in mind their yearnings and aspirations.
5. ***Research and Documentation:*** Analysts believe that social networks will move away from advertising and try to use the data they collect to help brands better target users (Newman, 2019). Social media growth and usage is now opening new grounds for analysing various aspects of and patterns in communication as it relates to analysing data to gain insights into issues, trends, influential ac-

tors and other forms of information (Stieglitz, Mirbabaie, Ross, & Neuberger, 2018). Despite the increasing rise in the number of people using social media handles in Nigeria, there is still the challenge of documentation and data collection about users of say Facebook or WhatsApp. To this end, it is important for Service Providers, National Communications Commission, government, researchers and data analysts to document the exponential growth of social media users in the country. This would help in knowing which group of people and what type of social media handle they use as well as aid in improving or providing social networks where they are not prevalent.

6. ***Cyber Legislation:*** One serious challenge that traditional media is facing today is the increasing rate of embracing citizen journalism – a phenomenon which allows anyone who has a Smartphone which enjoys internet connection to gather and disseminate news. This new type of journalism also referred to as witness account/news makes gatekeeping difficult hence the rise in fake news. Therefore, it is crucial for scholars, journalists and experts in the media industry like the Nigerian Union of Journalists, Nigerian Press Council in collaboration with Security Agencies, Legislature, Judiciary and Executive to enforce extant cyber laws to nip the menace in the bud. In fact, we need adequate and effective Online Child Protection Laws as well as a cyber monitoring teams in schools to checkmate the effects of illegal activities of the social media (Nigeria Internet Registration Association, 2019).

As such, governments must provide (a) Effective criminalization of cyber – offences. The legislation of different countries should be as harmonized as possible; (b) Conditions facilitating direct cooperation between State institutions, as well as between State institutions and the private sector, and (c) Investigative procedures and institutional capacities which allow criminal justice agencies to cope with advance fee fraud (Chawki, 2009, p.15). These laws should be guided by the testimony of scholars that the *Dialogic Communication Theory* is a rich-resource on how online social relations should be established (Wright & Hinson, 2009; Rybalko & Seltzer, 2010). Expectedly, this should go hand in hand with ideal frameworks or well spread programmes in achieving this.

CONCLUSION

We saw how overemphasis on the negative use of social media such as lack of being media savvy and slowness to acknowledge the significant changes ICT has made in the way people think and live in Nigeria today as reasons for inability to take advantage of social networks. The study also discovered that Yahoo-Yahoo, hate speech, fake news and other sharp practices are responsible for lack of willingness by some citizens to engage with new technology. This is why the researchers argued that ongoing media-education, curricular review, media campaigns, mass mobilisation, research and documentation and cyber legislation in the country are veritable ways of encouraging people to make social media a useful resource for integral human development in the country.

It is essential for Nigerians to key into the requirements of the Sustainable Development Goals (SDGs) which stresses on the need for embracing new technologies especially social media. One participant at UNITAR's e-Learning course on social media and web 2.0 tools for development – Innovative Collaboration for Development (ICfD) during United Nations General Assembly in September 2015 rightly noted: "Indeed in the area of ICTs (that would fall under SDG 9,) their incredible potential to facilitate the achievement of the other SDGs is undeniable and should have great importance placed on it. The

Table 1. Comparative analysis of social media-use in Nigeria between 2018/2019

	Social Media-Use in 2018	*Social Media-Use in 2019*
1.	Nigeria had 92.3 million internet users in 2018	There are 98.39 million internet users in Nigeria
2.	Internet penetration was 47.1 percent of the population in 2018	While the global average for internet penetration is 57%, only 50% of the population in Nigeria is connected to the internet
3.	Nigeria ranks top in Africa based on the share of traffic via mobile	Of the 98.39 million Nigerian internet users, 54% access the internet on a daily basis while only 12% (24 million) have active social media accounts
4.	Nigeria ranks third in Sub-Saharan Africa and 21st out of the 65 global markets that were measured for internet freedom in 2018	Nigerians spend 3 hours 17 minutes on the average using social media
5.	Nigerian internet users often do not feel free to fully express themselves online" (Clement, 2019).	WhatsApp is the most active social media platform in the country with 85% of users followed by Facebook at 78%; Instagram then 57% and FB Messenger at 54%; Youtube is at 53%" (Udodiong, 2019).

Source: Authors

Table 2. Possible reasons for negative use of social media

1.	Lack of being media savvy
2.	Slowness in acknowledging changes in ICT
3.	Inability to take advantage of new technology
4.	Fear and suspicion

Source: Authors

Table 3. Veritable ways of engaging social media for human development in Nigeria

1.	Useful tool for national integration
2.	Rich resource for educational advancement
3.	Instrument for information sharing and transfer of knowledge
4.	Advancement in science and technology
5.	Tools for advertising, donations and charity

Source: Authors

ubiquitous access that ICTs allow means they as a whole can be considered as a modern utility service - like water, electricity etc. Achieve this SDG and we will then be able to leverage the incredible power of social media to change the world for the better" (United Nations Institute for Training Research, 2015).

Since the prevalent significant changes in ICT affect almost every sector of life today, it is crucial to advantage of social media for the advancement of the human race. From the foregoing, it is safe to conclude that if Nigerians particularly students, those in business, educationists and policy makers take advantage of social media platforms like WhatsApp, Facebook and Twitter, these social networks would no doubt remain a huge resource for national integration and human development in Nigeria and beyond.

REFERENCES

Adomi, E. E., & Kpangban, E. (2010). *Application of ICTs in Nigerian secondary schools*. Library Philosophy and Practice. www.researchgate.net/publication/228379384_Application_of_ICTs_in_Nigerian_Secondary_Schools. Accessed 10/09/2021.

Bonsón, E., & Ratkai, M. (2013). A set of matrixes to assess stakeholder engagement and social legitimacy on a Facebook page. *Online Review*, *37*(5), 787–803. doi:10.1108/OIR-03-2012-0054

Bonsón, E., Royo, S., & Ratkai, M. (2014). Facebook practice in Western European municipalities: An empirical analysis of activity and citizen's engagement. *Administration & Society*. Advance online publication. doi:10.1177/0095399714544945

Bortree, D. S., & Seltzer, T. (2009). Dialogic strategies and outcomes: An analysis of environmental advocacy groups' Facebook profiles. *Public Relations Review*, *35*(3), 317–319. doi:10.1016/j.pubrev.2009.05.002

British Broadcasting Corporation. (2019). *US names Nigerians in massive fraud investigation*. www.bbc.com/news/world-africa-49446845

Chawki, M. (2009). Nigeria Tackles Advance Free Fraud. *Journal of Information, Law & Technology, 1*. www.go.warwick.ac.uk/jilt/2009_1/chawki

Clement, J. (2019). *Number of internet users in Nigeria from 2017 to 2023 (in millions)*. www.statista.com/statistics/183849/internet-users-nigeria/

Dark, S. (2020). *#EndSARS: How Nigerians harness social media against police abuse*. www.aljazeera.com/news/2020/10/25/endsars-how-nigerians-use-social-media-against-police-brutality#

Deegan, C. (2006). Legitimacy theory. In Z. Hogue (Ed.), *Methodological Issues in Accounting Research: Theories and Methods* (pp. 161–182). Spiramus Press.

Deegan, C., & Samkin, G. (2009). *New Zealand Financial Accounting*. McGraw-Hill.

Digital Marketing Skill Institute. (2019). *Social media for businesses in Nigeria: How best can I market my brand on the social media?* www.digitalmarketingskill.com/social-media-for-businesses-in-nigeria-how-best-can-i-market-my-brand-on-the-social-media/

Dowling, J., & Pfeffer, J. (1975). Organizational legitimacy social values and organizational behavior. *Pacific Sociological Review*, *18*(1), 122–136. doi:10.2307/1388226

Ebele, O. C., & Oghenetega, L. U. (2014). The impact of social media on the academic performance of university students in Nigeria. *Journal of Education and Practice*, *5*(33).

Engage Business Media. (2019). *Leaders lacking social media savvy*. www.engageemployee.com/leaders-lacking-social-media-savvy/

Farivar, M. (2019). *Hundreds Arrested in Nigeria, US on Online Fraud Charges*. www.voanews.com/usa/hundreds-arrested-nigeria-us-online-fraud-charges

Frost, G., & Semaer, M. (2002). Adoption of environmental reporting and management practices: An analysis of New South Whales public sector entities. *Financial Accountability & Management, 18*(2), 103–127. doi:10.1111/1468-0408.00147

Ghazali, S., Sulaiman, N.I.S., Zabidi, N.Z., Omar, M.F & Alias, R.A. (2016). The impact of knowledge sharing through social media among academia. *AIP Conference Proceedings, 1782*. doi:10.1063/1.4966060

Hootsuite. (2019). *Survey Reveals One Million New People Online Daily; Social Media Fuels Growth Despite Industry Challenges of 2018*. www.hootsuite.com/newsroom/press-releases/survey-reveals-one-million-new-people-online-daily-social-media-fuels-growth-despite-industry-challenges-of-2018

Hout, N. (2018). *Social media in learning and development: Preparing for the next generation workforce*. www.elearningindustry.com/social-media-in-learning-and-development-next-generation-workforce

Igwe, U. (2021). *Nigeria's growing cybercrime threat needs urgent government action*. www.blogs.lse.ac.uk/africaatlse/2021/06/09/nigerias-growing-cybercrime-phishing-threat-needs-urgent-government-action-economy/

Kent, M. L., & Taylor, M. (1998). Building dialogic relationships through the World Wide Web. *Public Relations Review, 24*(3), 321–334. doi:10.1016/S0363-8111(99)80143-X

McAllister, S. M. (2012). How the world's top universities provide dialogic forum for marginalized voices. *Public Relations Review, 38*(2), 319–327. doi:10.1016/j.pubrev.2011.12.010

Newman, N. (2009). *The rise of social media and its impact on mainstream journalism: A study of how newspapers and broadcasters in the UK and US are responding to a wave of participatory social media, and a historic ship in control towards individual consumers*. Working Paper. Reuters Institute for the Study of Journalism, Oxford University.

Nigeria Internet Registration Association. (2019). *The effects of social media on the youths*. www.nira.org.ng/nira-media/news-update/288-the-effects-of-social-media-on-the-youthson%20October%2018

Nigerian Communications Communication. (2019). *Press Release: With 13.8% contribution to GDP, ICT may double Oil and Gas in 2 years, says Communications Minister*. www.ncc.gov.ng/stakeholder/media-public/news-headlines/665-press-release-with-13-8-contribution-to-gdp-ict-may-double-oil-and-gas-in-2-years-says-communications-minister

Nnabugwu, C. (2020). *Cybercrime rocks Nigeria*. www.yourcommonwealth.org/technology/cybercrime-in-nigeria/

Ogehenetega, L. U., Oyenike, O. E., & Ugeh, C. H. (2014). Comparative study of (networking) usage by undergraduates in two tertiary institutions of Nigeria. *Journal of Research on Humanities & Social Science, 4*(15).

Olusola, L. (2018). *The power of social media*. www.guardian.ng/technology/the-power-of-social-media/

Prensky, M. (2001). Digital Natives, Digital Immigrants. On the Horizon, 9(5).

Princewill, N & Busari, S. (2021). *Nigeria bans Twitter after company deletes President Buhari's tweet.* Academic Press.

Proshareng.com. (2020). *Cybercrime in Nigeria: Causes and effects.* www.proshareng.com/news/Security---Support/Cybercrime-in-Nigeria--Causes-and-Effect

Rybalko, S., & Seltzer, T. (2010). Dialogic communication in 140 characters or less: How Fortune 500 companies engage stakeholders using Twitter. *Public Relations Review*, *36*(4), 336–341. doi:10.1016/j.pubrev.2010.08.004

Samphina.com. (2022). *The impact of social media on national security: Nigeria's perspective.* www.samphina.com.ng/impact-social-media-national-securitynigerias-perspective/

Selwyn, N. (2018). The use of icts in education and the promotion of social inclusion: A critical perspective from the uk. Institution of Education, University of London. *Educ. Soc.*, *29*(104). Retrieved October 09, 2021, from Campinas.www.scielo.br/scielo.php?pid=S0101-73302008000300009&script=sci_arttext&tlng=en

Stieglitz, S., Mirbabaie, M., Ross, B., & Neuberger, C. (2018). Social media analytics – Challenges in topic discovery, data collection, and data preparation. *International Journal of Information Management*, *39*, 156–168. doi:10.1016/j.ijinfomgt.2017.12.002

Udodiong, I. (2019). *Here is how Nigerians are using the internet in 2019.* www.pulse.ng/bi/tech/how-nigerians-are-using-the-internet-in-2019/kz097rg

United Nations Institute for Training Research. (2015). *Social Media and the web 2.0 are key tools for the SDGs.* www.unitar.org/about/news-stories/news/social-media-and-web-20-are-key-tools-sdgs

Wright, D., & Hinson, M. (2009). *An analysis of the increasing impact of social and other new media on public relations practice.* Institute for Public Relations. www.instituteforpr.org

Ywee. (2019). *The effect of social media on our cultural values.* www.lagosmums.com/the-effect-of-social-media-on-our-cultural-values/

Chapter 22
The Environment and the Challenge of Technological Development:
Perspectives, Problems, and Prescription

Amaobi Nelson Osuala
https://orcid.org/0000-0001-6221-2349
University of Ibadan, Nigeria

ABSTRACT

This chapter examines the ripple effects of technological development on the environment. It exposes some of the environmental nightmares that has ensued from the exploitation of the ecosystem in the guise and pretext of attaining science and technological feat. The author argues that no doubt, humans have recorded unprecedented progress and breakthroughs in science and through the advent of technology; the boomerang environmental hazards have however remained colossal! This researcher argues that to manage the ambivalence and protect the environment from harm, technological advances must be conducted through a reasonable action undergirded with what the author has christened the law of mutual complementary exchange implied in the notion that humans can only survive through exchange and mutual positive interaction with the environment not as a being-in-the-world serving as a means to an end but a being-with-the-world; the latter of which shares a relationship of mutual dependence.

INTRODUCTION

To survive on the earth, human beings require the stable, continuing existence of a suitable environment. Yet the evidence is overwhelming that the way in which we now live on the earth is driving its thin, life-supporting skin, and ourselves with it, to destruction. To understand this calamity, we need to begin with a close look at the nature of the environment itself - Barry Commoner

DOI: 10.4018/978-1-6684-4107-7.ch022

Perhaps, the above epigraph is better captured by Ronald Engels and Gibb J. Engels in their book *Ethics of Environment and Development,* published in 1990, in which they summarized the ripple effects of our technological development on the environment as being wrong-headed. In their words:

...That our basic model is wrong is also indicated by what we have done to other species and forms of life...we increasingly destroy other animal species. Vegetation, the chemical sources of life, and the sea beds and rocky lands bounty has been the source of so much imagination, wonder, joy and creativity spring from the unending acquisitiveness of our technological way of life and concomitant decline in our sensitivity to other common organic bond with the whole of creation and thus both our own survival and that of other species (p. 31).

Before we delve into the mainstreams of the arguments captured by the above quotation, as well as those captured in the above epigraph, which is an excerpt from Commoner's classic work, *Closing the Circle,* let us first cast a bird's eye view at the nature of environmental crisis by briefly examining, some opinions and arguments by certain individuals on what according to them are the likely causes of today's global warming amongst others. It is this researcher's believe that x-raying and examining these crisis will help to better serve as a good background to the issues we hope to elucidate in this chapter.

Although, many of the arguments put forwards were made by western environmentally conscious thinkers in their attempt to salvage their environment through a declaration of what they dubbed as *A Save the Earth* campaign week of April 1970 in America (Comoner 1971, p.2). This researcher have tried to summarize the major points and also group them into sections to better capture the central theme of the discourse. They include: Those who (1) blame growth in population as the major cause of environmental pollution. (2) Blame affluence (3) Blame poverty and lack (4) gave a rebuttal from the poor. (5) Others argued from the point of appraising our industry (6) blamed man's innate aggression (7) blamed man's unchecked curiosity and his quest to know. As if to further stretch the issue (8) a minister blames profit margin and revenue generation. (9) a historian decides to complicate the matter and decides to put the blame on religion, especially the Judeo-Christian religion. (10) A politician blames Technology. This position is what this paper shall focus more on. (11) An environmentalist contends and puts the blame on politicians. (12) Others blame capitalism and capitalist economies. (13) While the capitalist, counter attacks and toes an escapist position. At last, in his attempt to avoid the ridiculous *ad hominem* arguments and those fallacious arguments against *the straw man,* a critical thinker, Pogo, who Barry Commoner described as a rather " keen observer"(7) puts the blame on the generality of the human species. Following the foregoing order, biologist Garrett Hardin avers that what we call "the pollution problem is a consequence of population. It did not much matter how a lonely American frontier man disposed of his waste...But as population became dense, the natural chemical and biological recycling processes became overloaded... freedom to breed will bring ruin to all" (commoner 1971, p.3).

Following this line of thought, Paul R. Ehrlich another biologist further informs that the causal chain of the deterioration (of the environment) is easily followed to its source. Too many cars; too many factories; too much detergent; too much pesticide; multiplying contrails; inadequate sewage treatment plan;, too little water; too much carbon dioxide- all can be traced easily to too many people. But this blame on overpopulation seems not to go down well with Walter S. Howard, who, though also a biologist like Hardin and Ehrlich yet held a contrary view thereby putting the blame of environmental crisis on our human affluent society. For him, *the affluent society has become an effluent society. The 6 percent of the world's population...produces 70 percent or more of the world's solid wastes* (p.3)

For Wayne H. Davis, impoverishment is the cause of environmental rape. According to him, we should call it *blessed be the starving blacks of Mississippi with their outdoor privies, for they are ecologically sound, and they shall inherit a nation (Closing the Circle, p.3)*. In his rebuttal of Davis' position, George Wiley, a chemist and chairman of National Welfare Rights Organization rather counsels that it will be irrational to embark on programs to curb economic growth without placing a priority on maintaining income, so that the poorest people would not simply be further depressed in their condition but will have a share, and be able to live decently.

Shifting the debate on environmental crisis to that which would require that we examine our industrial sector, Sherman R. Knapp, chairman of the board, Northeast Utility argues that

It is not industry per se, but the demands of the public. And the public's demands are increasing at a geometric rate, because of the increasing standard of living and the increasing growth of population... if we can convince the national and local leaders in the environment crusade of this basic logic, that population causes pollution, then we can help them focus their attention on the major aspect of the problem.(p.3)

However, for thinkers like William Roth and Anthony Storr, there is no need to shy away from the fact that most, if not all of environmental hazards are caused by Man. The Human inherent nature of aggressiveness should be called to question. Man's innate aggressiveness is the cause of environmental deterioration. Hence for Roth,

The first problem then, is people...The second problem most fundamental one, lies within us- our basic aggressions...As Anthony Storr has said: "the somber fact is that we are the cruelest and most ruthless species that has ever walked the earth (p.3)

For Arturo Sandoval, a foremost student and promoter of environmental action, we should put the blame on man and his acquired knowledge. Regrettably, most 'people are afraid of their humanity because systematically they have been taught to become inhuman. ...They have no understanding of what it is to love nature. And so our airs are being polluted, our rivers are being poisoned, and our land is being cut up'. For Congregationalist Minister, Channing E. Philips our overt profits and revenue is what has led to "environmental rape becoming a fact of our national life only because it is more profitable than responsible stewardship of earth's limited resources" (p.4).

However, for historian, Lynn White, there is no need to' beat about the bush'. He attacked religion, especially the *Judeo Christian* sects. According to White, "it is Christianity that should bear the huge burden of guilt...we shall continue to have a worsening ecologic crisis until we reject the Christian axiom that nature has no reason for existence save to serve man" (*Closing the circle, p.4*). Peter Singer alluded to this position of White's when he argued in his article "Animals" *that* the bibliocentric argument as well as the dominant Western tradition both of which imply that "the natural world exists for the benefit of human beings and that God gave human beings dominion over the natural world, hence does not care how we treat it...and that humans would remain the only morally important member of this world." (Singer in Jamieson, p.416) The biblical reference of Genesis 1:26-28 is for Singer grossly misguided. In his words, 'this traditional Judeo-Christian view of the world is based on a creation myth that was decisively refuted more than a century ago' (Jamieson, 2001, p.417). Strengthening his argument on the above, singer alluded to data drawn from evolutionary theories of Charles Darwin, with which he debunked this religious view and maintained that the forests and animals were not placed on earth for us to use, rather, they have evolved alongside with man (p.417).

Similarly, this author argued elsewhere that the arrogation of superiority to humans over and above the environment (biotic and abiotic) is one which is founded on a faulty humanistic philosophy (Osuala 2019, p. 28). It is this researcher's opinion that this anthropocentric arrogance which considers the human specie as capable of exhibiting exclusive dominance and superiority over the environment, the latter which comprises amongst others, non-human animals, forests,seas etc is that which is without doubt misconstrued, misconceived and serves as an outright misrepresentation of the book of Genesis chapter one. It is his position that that particular book of *Genesis 1: 26-28* is a misrepresentations and therefore is often weaponised by ignorant folks to further promote speciesism.(Osuala, 2014, p.156). This position as he would argue is what is drawn from the perspective of a "Neo-Regan" animal right scholar's mindset which for him refers to that ethical principle sustained by the foundational ethical value of *the sanctity of all life* (reverence for life) and the equality of man and animals, one which is further buttressed as well as implied in the argument that "All that which befalleth the sons of men, befalleth beasts(animals); even one thing befalleth them: as the one dieth, so dieth the other; yea, they have all one breath; so that a man had no preeminence over a beast…'' (Ecclesiastes 3:19, KJV). It is therefore evident that to ensure the future sustainability of the ecosystem man should remember that he is but a fractional part in comparison with the entire make up of the ecosystem (Osuala and Nyok 2018, p.34).

For erstwhile US Indiana senator, Vance Harke whom who puts so much blame on profits as a major threat to the ecosystem, 'A runaway technology, whose only law is profit, has for years poisoned our air, ravaged our soil, stripped our forest bare, and corrupted our water resources' (*The closing circle, p.3*). For most environmentalists like Roderick A. Cameron of the Environmental Defense Fund politicians should be blamed for the mess we are in! According to him, 'there is a peculiar paralysis in our political branches of government, which are primarily responsible for legislating and executing the policies environmentalists are urging… Industries that profit by the rape of our environment see to it that legislators friendly to their attitudes are elected, and that bureaucrats of similar attitudes are appointed (p.4).

In passing the blame over to capitalism and capitalist economies, Rennie Davis, a member of the "Chicago Seven" argues that 'politics is indeed officially- the conspiracy against pollution. And we have a simple program-arrest Agnew and smash capitalism. We say to Agnew country that Earth Day is for the Sons and Daughters of the American Revolution who are going to tear this capitalism down and set us free'(p.5). To this end, the advocates of capitalism such as Thomas R. Shepherd, Jr would contend that:

… we are solving most of our problems… that conditions are getting better not worse… that American industry is spending over three billion dollars a year to clean up the environment and additional billions to develop products that will keep it clean… and that the real danger is not from the free –enterprise establishment that has made ours the most prosperous, most powerful and most charitable nation on earth. No, the danger today resides in the Disaster Lobby- those crepe-hangers who, for personal gain or out of sheer ignorance, are undermining the American system and threatening the lives and fortunes of the American people. Some people have let the gloom-mongers scare them beyond rational response with talk about atomic annihilation… since World War II, over one billion human beings who worried about Atomic bombs (A-bombs) and Hydrogen bombs (H-bombs) died of other causes. They worried for nothing! (Closing the Circle, p.5)

While at last a keen observer in avoiding the inherent narrow-minded positions reflected above rather chose to blame everyone. For him, "we have met the enemy and it is us. (Commoner, 1971: p.1-6). All these are attempts to define the cause as well as to possibly respond to the issues of environmental crisis. This attempt by the foregoing thinkers and scholars to proffer solutions to the crisis of environment is what lies within the purview of environmental ethics (Weston, 2006, p.72) or what Singer called *practical ethics* when he attempted to argue from an animal rights perspective on the moral status of non-human animals to which he avers have equal moral status as humans. In his words:

Many people believe that all human beings are of equal value. Most of them also believe that all human beings have a moral status superior to that of non human animals. But how are these beliefs to be defended? The mere difference of species cannot in itself determine moral status. The most obvious candidate for regarding human beings or having a higher moral status than animals is the superior cognitive capacity of humans. People with profound mental retardation pose a problem for this set of beliefs, because their cognitive capacities are not superior to those of many animals. I argue that we should drop the belief in the equal value of human life, replacing it with a graduated view that applies to animals as well as to humans (Speciesism and moral status, p.564).

SOME RIPPLE EFFECTS OF TECHNOLOGY

Pollution which etymologically refers to defilement is the consequence of our use of technology on the environment. It further refers to the addition of harmful materials or energy into the environment as it makes the environment unfit and incapable to sustain life. These substances that cause harm to the environment are called pollutants and they could be biodegradable or non- biodegradable. We shall give a cursory examination of these as they affect the environment. The types of pollution are as follows: Air, water, noise and land pollution.

Air pollution are caused by many substances such as are produced when fossil fuels like coal, natural gas and oil are burnt. Others are gaseous pollutants like sulphur (IV) oxide and carbon (II) oxide produced from incomplete combustion of fuel from exhaust pipes of heavy engines. Air pollution causes global warming and greenhouse effects which results in the depletion of the ozone layer, emission of chloro-floro carbons ($CCLF_4$) acidic rain etc. leading to mankind being exposed to the ultraviolet rays of the sun. Noise pollution is the last in this list which involves the introduction of unpleasant sound to the eardrum. Its effects vary as it can be physical or psychological leading to distortion of proper coordination and balance in the brain. Noise pollution can sometimes lead to deafness in which case certain delicate parts of the ear like the semi-circular canal, auditory nerve are destroyed through high blaring sounds from heavy machines and speakers all of which are products of technology.

Other effects or consequence of technology includes the production of atomic and nuclear warheads like the machine guns, hydrogen bomb, plutonium bomb, and the atomic bomb. The ripple effects of these technologies is what led to the world war which almost wiped off the human race of Japan which they were detonated in Hiroshima and Nagasaki, that singular incident cannot be forgotten in a hurry as its ripple effects have lingered after generation as many suffer from radioactive exposition, infertility of the land as well as some unexplainable natural amputations which has defied scientific solutions.

The fact of environmental deterioration and ecological nightmare experiences such as have stared us in the face have brought us to the need to save our earth from doom, is what has created such awareness in us which implies that 'there is a need to cut back on pollution, reduce waste, save endangered species. The same way there is a need to keep air and water clean so we can breathe and drink in good health'(Weston,2006,p.75). Awareness of the need to value our environment is good but sad still is the fact that our knowledge of the environment and what Schultz calls *ecosphere* remains quite limited as we lack the understanding that the whole gamut of the ecosystem is interconnected and that just as we have value for human kind, nature itself has and should be accorded the intrinsic value such as is peculiar to it. This is what Weston observed when he argued,

Less familiar values are also often at stake with the environment. Justice often requires environmental respect, for example. Much environmental damage is also damage to other human communities. Rainforest destruction displaces whole forest communities. Whole cultures are being driven into extinction. Strip-mining, drift-netting, toxic-waste dumping—all of these immediately and profoundly affect us too. So environmental ethics may well call for radical changes to human actions. We may need to cut way back on ozone-depleters and automobiles and so many kinds of waste we now just take for granted. If it's really true in nature that "what goes around comes around," then we need to be a lot more careful about what "goes around (Weston, pp. 75-76)

Buttressing further, he maintains that, there's more, though. Ethics itself may also changing in the process. In part, of course, taking care of nature is a way of taking care of ourselves. Here the appeal is to human values: health, justice, and so on. But could it be that there are also other reasons to care about nature? Mightn't we be beginning to recognize that nature also has some claim in its own right—that the ethical world, like the actual living world, is bigger than we are? (Weston, 2006, p.76). In a more critical note, let us now examine these issues of environmental decay, more closely by putting to rest, most of the inherent anthropocentricism which obviously has bestowed so much glory to the human species for inventing technology that has enabled the former to accomplish so much. As the alleged 'most intelligent species' with "highly developed consciousness of the environment and the ability to make changes on the basis of that consciousness through invention of masterpiece equipment to conquer diseases and for the development of powerful tools to master the environment of the earth as well as to enjoy a longer, richer, and more comfortable lives.

Premised upon this, there is therefore no denying the fact that; science, technology and information technology have altogether contributed to the amazing growth of consciousness of the past 500 years or so. No doubt, pertinent questions continue to linger, one of which is if we are actually very conscious enough (Schultz, 2000, p. 160). For it is but those non-intelligent aspects of our human control of the environment that seem to have continued to pose threats not only to species survival but also to the existence of the ecosystem.

It is the attempt to curb the threat to the ecosystem as triggered by the overt growing sense of our alleged human responsibility towards the unchecked irrational plundering, exploitation and abrupt deterioration of the ecosystem that have prompted the recent upsurge of interest in that field of environmental philosophy as reflected in such books as Rachel Carson's *Silent Spring* (1962), Peter Singer's *Animal Liberation* (1975) just to mention a few. It is in line with these grave actions of man against the environment which as Audi observes:

... Led environmental philosophers have adduced a wide variety of human attitudes and practices to account for the perceived deterioration, including religious and scientific attitudes, social institutions, and

industrial technologies. Proposed remedies typically urge a reorientation or new ethic that recognizes intrinsic value in the natural world. A good example includes the land ethic of Aldo Leopold (1887-1948), which portrays humans as belonging to, rather than owning the biotic community ("the land"); deep ecology, a stance articulated by the Norwegian philosopher Arne Naess (1912) which advocates forms of identification, with the non-human world; and eco-feminism, which rejects prevailing attitudes to the natural world that are perceived as patriarchal (Audi, 1999, p.268).

In order to do justice to this discourse, it is the thrust of this chapter to examine some of the ripple effects of technological development on the environment. To achieve this task, the chapter first attempts to trace a historical trajectory of the birth of technology as catalyzed by the Protagorean maxim which posits that *Man is the measure of all things, of things that are, that they are and of things that are not, that they are not*. It is this anthropocentric drive that the author argues, raised the overt consciousness of man's intrusion on the ecosystem which can later be argued has perhaps left us in the mess we are in today! In addition, and in the attempt to delve into the mainstreams of this chapter, it becomes important to delineate the inherent conceptual distortions such as have often characterized and have thus clouded most discussions on the concept and nature of the environment and technology respectively.

This has become necessary because as Kwasi Wiredu, that celebrated Ghanian philosopher did observe "without conceptual clarification and argumentation, there is strictly no philosophy" (*Philosophy and an African Culture, p.47)*. What this means is that, conceptual delusions must be clarified if we must enjoy credible and mutual productive conversation. Furthermore, this paper examines some of the issues and problems that may arise in the attempt to explore as well as enjoy the profits and proceeds from technology in line with the adverse boomerang effects such actions may have on the environment in which case, humans only exist but as a fractional part.

From the foregoing exegesis, we could then arrive at a critical point in this essay in which a compromise must be reached as we sought out ways in which we can in the face of increased advancement in technology also ensure that our environment and the ecosystem is not left endangered at the mercy of our crave for global technological relevance and breakthroughs. By employing some ethical principles, we were able to propose and recommend a method of 'mutual service of tolerance' which allows for a complementation between the duo of environmental conservation with technological advancement, where the latter could be considered as a necessary evil.

It is perhaps a little worrisome to note that as regards the effects of human beings on the environment, most scholars seem not to concede that technology itself should be blamed for the present global problematic such as is plaguing almost if not all nation's of the world as they each seek ways to address and redress the issues of global warming such as have left our world quite unsafe. These scholars and thinkers as Schultz observed hold varied perspectives on the relationship between the environment and technology, yet have refused to crucify technology as posing a threat to the environment and human survival. As if that is not enough, some have gone further to argue that in the face of adverse threat to the environment, technology is the solution! (Schultz,2000, p.170). In a brief succession, the researcher would present the positions of some of these scholars about the role of technology in relation to the environment as posited by Schultz after which I shall attempt to critically appraise such positions in line with certain ethical principles with a view to showing their areas of strength and weaknesses from the purview of philosophy. This in line with Schultz thinking will help us decide on a more viable ethical principle concerning technology and the environment.

Suffice it therefore to say that thinkers like Al Gore and Langdon Winner both argue that technology is no threat and will not prove to be such if we (1) work within the current circumference of economic and technological systems, just as we must become more careful when doing such. It is obvious that the duo of Gore and Winner seem to be arguing that although technology has it's negative impact on the environment, it is also perhaps indispensable, hence, humans must thrive to ensure that those adverse effect it has on the environment is dutifully contained and avoided. This is what this author has criticized as an escapist philosophy, one which is tantamount to the figurative counsel that we should learn how to eat with the devil with a very long spoon. Schultz summarizes Gore and Winners' position better when he quoted them as saying that "we simply had no idea that technology could have such consequences, so we will be more careful in the future in ensuring that we comply to those ethical principle of environmental conservation" (*Intelligent life on Earth..,* p.171). Al Gore had in his 1992 publication, *Earth in the Balance,* implied misguidedly that 'Although we are not ignorant of the fact that unsustainable consumption is detrimental to the environment as it is no doubt destroying the planet, we should however be firm about not consuming so much so as to at least achieve sustainability; and we should alter our social and economic situations accordingly in order to achieve this feat!

A critical look at this suggestion by AlGore shows that he argued from the perspective of a social theorist. Although his counsel will clearly help as individuals would be not have so much choice but to reduce consumption, it still will not handle cases where the results are more indirect, such cases as global warming" - a current global nightmare involving the incessant unchecked emissions of greenhouse gases, all of which is plaguing mother earth. What Al Gore seems ignorant of, is the fact that " a society can be efficient in the sense of not consuming wastefully and still be very destructive of the environment, hence, his message to get the economy back on track in workable state in the guise to avoid wasteful consumption, does not address many aspects of the problem"(Schultz, 2000, p.172), one of which is the problem of human selfishness, a product of the his natural instinct of self preservation which is always antithetical to the other beings in the environment. Humans due to his misguided and myopic mindset supposed that *I di "to be"* means *ka so mu di* "to be alone" instead of *ka so mu adina* "to be in mutual complementary relationship" with the other beings in the world (Asouzu 2007, p.11; 2004, p.7).

For thinkers like Ehrlich, Barry Commoner and Fuller they all see the problem of environmental hazards as residing in the social and economic structure that surely needs to be changed. Erhlich for instance, in his 1968 work titled *The Population Bomb;* and in *Human Nature* (2000) published respectively; consciously blamed the cause of environmental mishap as proceeding from overpopulation, which he still thinks is an important factor of our economy that should be put to check and perhaps solved through some appropriate social and political structures being on ground. Commoner and Fuller both agreed but rather dubiously too that there would be so much to go round if social and economic production facilities are properly organized. Much of this position which seems like a rather better suggestion than those of Erhlich seems to be saying that overpopulation is not a major consideration.

But for Commoner who in his 1971 classical work, *The Closing Circle*, maintains that "there is need to understand the ecosphere which unfortunately seems rather difficult premised upon the fact that to the modern mind, it is a curiously strange place because we as humans have become so accustomed to always think of separate, singular events, each dependent upon a unique, singular cause. But the bitter truth lies in the fact that in the ecosphere, every effect is also a cause: an animal's waste becomes food for soil bacteria; what bacteria excrete nourishes plants; animals eat the plants (4). He further contends that "such ecological cycles are hard to fit into human experience in the age of technology, where machine

A yields product B, once used, is cast away, having no further meaning for the machine, the product or the user" (p.5).

Technological stages should be contrasted from one another. For instance, the older, early primitive technological stage must be contrasted with those of the pre-World -War II technologies and also with the more modern technology of today. There is therefore a great gap between the technological metamorphosis and transitions of say pasturing animals with those of factory farming; maintaining soil fertility through crop rotation as against the more easy and improved application of chemical fertilizers; the use of biodegradable soap with the present use of detergents and so on. Production technologies with adverse impact on the environment have displaced those that did not. These new technologies without gainsaying the fact are considered more profitable for the producers such as farmers, cleaning product manufacturers, and textile producers. Little wonder why Commoner's supreme salvation and solution lies in the need to reverse such kind of thinking especially at the level of social institution. But just as Schultz would contend, this action may have little or no effect on the technologist who makes this change possible, hence they will care less as they would have little or nothing to lose, or even if they do, it will not matter much as the solution may be (as the case scenario of 1965) to produce biodegradable detergent molecules with high concentration of benzene components such as would be much more toxic to the environment.

SUMMARY: TOWARDS THE THEORY OF MUTUAL COMPLEMENTARY EXCHANGE

This work have attempted an exegesis on the nature of the environment as a composite of the flora and the fauna, biotic and a biotic entities with reference to the ecosphere. Herein, it examined the ripple effects of technological development on the environment as we labored to expose some of the environmental crisis that has thus ensued from this pretext. The author maintained that despite the progress which man has made from the advent of technology, the environmental hazards of technology continue to rise as it has remained at large. This is why Lori Gruen asserts that:

The consequence of technology is surely implicated in much environmental damage, as well as the destruction of politically and psychologically sustainable ways of life. In the fast- paced world of video games, cell phones, laser guided missiles, and the like, it is indeed tempting to think that technology, in itself, is objectionable. Such an argument, however, is hard to sustain. If nature is valuable, as many have argued, then, technology can be used to inform, educate, and assist in promoting its value. Critics have done tremendous service in helping us to think more critically about the use and development of various technologies. They are right to have us examine most of our current technological trends. But ultimately, the strongest arguments for or against technology will be based on the consequences of its use for people, for animals and for the natural world (Gruen in Jamieson, p.447)

It is against this backdrop that this author has argued that man is not just to borrow Martin Heidegger's conception *a being-in-the-world* but rather *a being-with-the-world*, nor is he as J.P Sartre puts it the supposed *being-for-itself* with self-consciousness as an absolute claim to reason or reason-ability. But that he and other 'non-human' animals do share a close similarity and are in close proximity in the possession of the status of equal participatory moral right and existence. If this is to be the case, as the author supposes having argued elsewhere (see Osuala 2019) and also maintained that, "to have the sustainable future for the survival as well as the utmost security of man, nature and technology, the entire human race must realize that the environment is not just there for us and because of us, rather it is there despite the existence of humans". The bitter truth rests on the notion that "technology never creates energy; rather, it only uses up existing available energy. The larger and more complex the energy, the more available energy is used up from the environment". (Entropy: A new worldview, p.79) This energy refers to that which supports both plant and animal life.

Unfortunately, the entire human race have remained under the delusion that technology is freeing us from dependence upon our environment, when nothing could be further from the truth. It is perhaps noteworthy that what we call life is not some kind of a closed 'airtight' system (p.79) but one that requires the mutual harmonious exchange of all the biotic and abiotic factors that constitute the environment. Reality it nature is a web of interconnected opposites in mutual service with one another. It is perhaps in this sense that Innocent Asouzu(2014) would maintain from his Ibuanyidanda imperative that "everything that exists serves a missing link of reality" and that the human species like all other living things can only survive by mutual complementarity, tolerance and harmonious exchange with the environment. This theory of complementary exchange inspired from Asouzu's complementary reflection, becomes that which involves the fore knowledge that humans and the environment are ontologically connected in what seems like a web of co-existence, dependence and relationship, hence any attempt to disconnect from this link will result into a direct boomerang effect seeing that humans do not exist in isolation but in association so much so that s(he), must conduct his technological affairs in the consciousness of this truth. The theory of complementary exchange is what therefore compels humans to always will, think and act in support of those things that will promote harmony, co-benefits, conservation, exchanging, positive interaction and mutual service with the environment.

Without a constant flow of energy from the environment we would all die within days. Technology makes us more dependent upon nature, even as it physically moves us further away from it; we have become more dependent as we have required increasing doses of nature's energy to sustain our cultural patterns and personal life-styles. It is therefore worrisome that we continue to slip into deeper chaos as a result of our ill- concern attitude towards identifying the source of our problem. Rather than take measures to avert the imminent doom awaiting us as humans, we instead, wrap ourselves up even tighter in our technological garb, defending it against all criticism, unable to acknowledge what it is doing to the environment we live in, and even less able to acknowledge what it is doing to us. We continue to cling to the fiction that we are securely clothed and protected, even as we become more exposed and endangered by the disordered fragments of a world of our own making (Rifkin, 1980, p.79-80). What we must know is that if we take this to heart by taking care of the earth, then, will the earth in response take care of us! The activity of reasonable action driven by the the theory of mutual complementary exchange becomes the checker that helps to manage and as well ensure that humans in a bid to harness energy from the environment to attaining technological development do so not at the detriment or outright exploitation of the environment but with caution, tolerance and respect for the environment as an indispensable part of life itself which must not be plundered however way we please.

REFERENCES

Asouzu, I. (2004). *Innocent: Effective Leadership and the Ambivalence of Human Interest: The Nigerian Paradox in a Complementary Perspective*. University of Calabar Press.

Asouzu, I. (2007). *New Complimentary Ontology Beyond World-Immanetism, Ethnocentric Reduction and Impositions*. Lit Verlag GmbH & Co. KG Wien.

Audi, R. (1999). *The Cambridge Dictionary of Philosophy*. Cambridge University press.

Commoner, B. (1971). *The Closing Circle: Man, Nature and Technology*. Knopf Publishers.

Ehrlich, P. (1968). *The Population Bomb*. Ballantine Books.

Ehrlich, P. (2000). *Human Natures*. Penguin Group.

Gore, Al. (1992). *Earth in the Balance*. Houghton Mifflin.

Jamieson, D. (Ed.). (2001). *A Companion to Environmental Philosophy*. Blackwell Publishers. doi:10.1002/9780470751664

Osuala, A. N. (2019). How Holistic is Anthropoholism? A Critique of Samuel Bassey's environmental Philosophy. Cogito: A Multidisciplinary Research Journal, 11(4), 23-31.

Osuala, A. N. (2014). An Examination of the Question of Animal Rights. BA Project submitted to the Department of Philosophy. University of Calabar.

Osuala, A.N., & Effio-ita, E. N. (2018). A new Twist to political corruption in 4th republic Nigeria in view of non-human animals stealing millions: a case for the defense of animal rights. *Gnosis. An Inter-disciplinary Journal of Human Theory and Praxis, 1*(2), 15-37.

Rifkin, J., & Ted, H. (1980). *Entropy: A new Worldview*. Bantam Books.

Schultz, A. R. (2000). *Intelligent Life on Earth: The Pros and Cons.* Presented at the 2000 Conference of the International Association for the Management of Technology, Miami, FL.

Schultz, A. (2006). *Robert. Contemporary Issues in Ethics and Information Technology*. IRM Press. doi:10.4018/978-1-59140-779-9

Singer, P. (2009). Speciesism and Moral Status. Metaphilosophy Journal Compilation, 40(3-4).

Weston, A. (2006). *A Practical Companion to Ethics*. Oxford University Press.

Chapter 23
Environmental Degradation and Its Implication for Environmental Sustainability in the Niger Delta

Umezurike J. Ezugwu
Nigeria Maritime University Okerenkoko, Nigeria

ABSTRACT

There is a high level of abasement and decadence in the ecological and biosphere of the Niger Delta, Nigeria, due to gas flaring and oil bunkering, often carried out by illegal bunkers around the region. This has resulted to pipeline damages, caused environmental pollution, and played down on the ethical and developmental strategies of the nation. This chapter maintains that these illegal and unethical activities often carried out by both indigenes and non-indigenes, on both government and multinational companies' investments, are the reasons for environmental degradation, debasement, and underdevelopment in the Niger Delta. It further points out the causes and effects of oil bunkering in the Niger Delta and shows the need for the application of environmental ethic, to bear on the discourse on environmental degradation. This will serve as a moral code to the actors and perpetrators of the said illegal bunkery businesses and secure and sustain environment for human beings, plants, and animals within and outside the region. This chapter used conversational method to drive home its points.

INTRODUCTION

Niger Delta region (NDR) of Nigeria has not been the same since the discovery of oil in its soil in 1956. The activities of the Royal Dutch Shell (RDS), British petroleum (Shell BP), legal and illegal bunkers, in the angle of oil exploration and exploitation have increased the mineral or black gold, for the benefit of the companies and Nigeria at large, but have caused more harm than good to the people of Niger Delta region, as their environment is shattered, polluted and degraded. Ekanem et al. (2010) corroborated this when he observes that the discovery and production of oil in Niger Delta (ND) brought a tremendous

DOI: 10.4018/978-1-6684-4107-7.ch023

change to the region. "The region has ever since, not been the same, as the oil (black gold) has brought a lot of money to the Nigerian state resulting in a near total neglect and detriment of the area". Sheriff Folarin & Henry Okodua (2009) and Snapps 2011) concurred to this fact, when they aver that "the persistent anthropogenic human activities and regular emission of carbon dioxide and oil pollution, arising from the activities in the petroleum industry has contaminated the land, fishing waters and atmosphere in the Niger Delta, leading to almost total collapse of the local economy". There exist high level of environmental degradation such as soil pollution, flooding, climate change, desertification, erosion etc., which makes it difficult for the growth and development of the region's agricultural products. These agricultural products are affected due to frequent oil spillage, water pollution and soil pollution that are hazardous to the environment (Inyang 2019). These environmental decadences, which include; oil spillage, water pollution and soil pollution have resulted to severe nutrient depletion, poor crop and harvest, environmental degradation and obstruction of biodiversity in the region (Binraban, 2012). As a matter of fact, land pressure and aggravated laden tension and insensitivity of the Nigerian government to the yearning of people of the region are reasons for the decline in food production, within the geographical area. Apart from the catastrophe done on the agricultural dividends, human beings, plants and animals are adversely affected too.

Furthermore, environmental degradation is today seen as being more dangerous than war. This is because as war is a threat against human beings, environmental degradation is a threat against human beings, animals and plants. No wonder why "the United Nations has identified environmental degradation as one of six clustered threats with which the world must be concerned now and decades ahead" (UNO, 2004) Environmental degradation is the obstruction or destruction inflicted on the environment that affects and brings about depletion of resources such as ecosystem, biosphere, wildlife, water, soil, air and habitants. By Implication, any disintegration or deterioration of the environment that kicks against the ecological or bionomical order of the habitants is regarded as environmental degradation. Niger Delta communities (NDCs), where the oil and gas production primarily take place in Nigeria hardly benefit from the huge oil income, yet these communities are most degradable and affected, as their means of livelihood such as fishing, farming and conducive environment are deprived of them. A justification of this was made by Oguduvwe (2013) Oluduro & Oluduro 2012), who contend that Niger Delta indigenes have not gotten anything tangible from the multinational oil corporations (MNOCs), and have suffered terribly as a result of the persistent emission and gas flaring in the land. These adverse social, environmental deprivation and marginalisation led to the agitations and endless protests. In a bid to address the issue (s) that orchestrated the said protests, once and for all, Nigerian government established the Niger Delta Development Commission (NDDC) in 2000, as a form of government compensation scheme (Osamuyimen, 2020). The scheme under discussion has never worked, due to bribery and corruption in the commission.

This paper sets out to employ environmental ethics, for environmental sustainability and development in Nigeria (Niger Delta). This will help both illegal and legal oil bunkers in NDR to be human centric, animal centric, bio centric and ecologically holistic. It is only when they are conscious of these ethical roadmaps that they can conserve, use and secure for all Nigerians in general and Niger Delta people in particular, a quality environment adequate for their health and wellbeing, for benefit of the present and future generations. In the first section of this paper, I will bring to bear the social and economic perspectives of oil in Niger Delta. There, I shall argue that though, Niger Delta is seen as the oil-well of Nigeria, it is adversely affected by the activities of the multinational companies in the region socially and economically. And that the only way out of these menaces is through strict adherence to the principle of environmental ethics, in keeping with the laws of nature and ecosystem. Again, I will strongly recommend the need for public sensitisation to encourage individual, community and government participation, in understanding of the nexus between environment and development. Second section establishes an ethics of the environment and environmental sustainability. This will serve as moral etiquettes or codes towards oil exploration, and address the problems or effects of environmental degradation that have mitigated and deteriorated the biosphere of Niger Delta region and Nigeria at large. I shall conclude, thereafter, by pointing out 'how' and 'why' environmental ethics is the key for environmental sustainability and societal development.

OIL IN NIGER DELTA: SOCIO-POLITICAL AND ECONOMIC DIMENSIONS

From our findings, it is clear that the survival of Nigeria as a nation is dependent on the oil that exists in the Niger Delta region. In other words, Niger Delta is the oil tank of the nation. In spite of this, the activities which include legal and illegal oil bunkery, exploration and exploitation within the environment have severe economic, social and political effects in the lives of the people around the region. In fact, the emergence of oil and oil related activities by the multinational companies that operate in the Niger Delta Region have ushered in "social problems such as diseases, urbanisation, high crime rate and other social vices that characterise Nigerian society" (Ekanem etal., 2010). This ugly situation as well as deterioration in their fishing and farming occupations, due to soil pollution and gas flaring is the reason for the agitation by the Niger delta communities; that government should offer a helping hand to savage their perennial problems that have degenerated into inter and intra community war, where weapon of massive destruction have often employed to wage war of genocide and destruction or damage of pipelines. This is what Nigeria government has not been able to do for the region. The hostility and insensitivity of the government in protecting the rights and properties of the citizens of the region is evident in the manner she arrested, released and declared Government Ekpemupolo (Tompolo) and other Niger Delta warlords or militant leaders wanted. These warlords, to the best of my knowledge are only asking for nothing from the Nigeria government but integration for healthy communal environment and economy. This draconian character displayed by the Nigerian government undermines the rights to life and healthy environment, which is not negotiable, among other fundamental human rights in Nigeria.

It is no longer a hidden fact that Niger Delta is the reason for the buoyancy of the Nigerian economy. In fact, the name Nigeria is making waves or recognised as the giant of Africa because of its endowments of the natural resources found within the Niger Delta region (NDR). This, notwithstanding, "Nigeria's over dependence on oil and gas extraction has inflicted corresponding costs on the economy and the environment of the NDR" (Akhigbe, 2013). The situations of the Niger Delta communities got worsen following the State's introduction or alliance with Trans-National Corporations (TNCs). The reason for this introduction is to engage the experts who have the expertise knowledge to tap its resources. Having given the TNCs this opportunity for optimal performance, the State does not care again whether the activities of the said TNCs are detrimental to the Niger Delta communities or not (Akani, 2000). Since there is a turn up and progress in oil production, it does not matter, how the activities or processes affects. This instinct of self-preservation which is in man's nature and in controllers of the affairs of the State, contributes in no minimal way, in the war against the Niger Delta people and their environment.

More so, environmental issue being an issue that concerns all, the Niger Delta people are expected to play their own role too, in managing and curbing the environmental menaces. No doubt, it is the duty of the government to protect lives and properties of her citizenry; individual and community equally have a role to play. The depletion and environmental challenges in Niger Delta region can also be attributed to the manner in which individuals defecate and throw non-degradable elements into the river, surrounding the region. This they do persistently unknown to them that river can be contaminated through these feces and non-degradable substances. This kind of mentality can be said to have contributed to the region's environmental degradation, but the major problem that have immensely jeopardised the region is the inability of the federal government to establish a compensatory workable scheme (s) for both habitants and environment of the Niger Delta people (Osamuyimen, 2020). In other words, the less attention on the needs of the region and epileptic compensation, which serve as a government respite to the people, is the very cause of the long existed war between the Nigerian government and the Niger Delta communities. To address these problems, government must at all times, listen to the cries of the people in the Niger Delta region, hence, their lives are mystified, deeply and adversely affected by oil explorations, gas flaring, soil pollution, water pollution, and all kinds of toxic substances that are not healthy to both human beings, plants and animals. Again, schemes should also be introduced and monitored to ensuring that whatever funds mapped out for such, are utilised and not embezzled, as in the case of NDDC and the forensic propaganda, politicisation and manipulation. It is only through these financial, emotional compensations and consolations that peace can fully be restored in Nigeria and her economy boosted.

TOWARDS AN ETHICS OF THE ENVIRONMENT AND ENVIRONMENTAL SUSTAINABILITY

The survival and development of man, animal and plant is highly dependent on the conduciveness of the environment, which nature is part and parcel of. There are laws enshrined in nature, which are noticeable or discoverable with the environment. These laws must be adhered to, without which there will be internal chaos and disharmony. To avoid this internal pitfall, Omoregbe (2000) defended, "is to comply with the moral law which is the law of nature". For him:

Nobody can cheat nature and get away with it. Nature has its own way of operation and sanction. Nature does not forget easily and can be disastrous and humiliating, just to punish whoever might have offended it. In all, none is smarter than nature; hence, any attempt to outsmart nature carries with it a severe punishment or negative reward.

To avoid the untold disaster, which going against law of nature attracts, it is pertinent that we adhere to the exploration of nature in conformity with the ethical principles that will not in any manner get nature provoked. Ethics is an essential element that directs and guides human actions. As that that deals with the morality of man's act and act of man, in keeping with the normative rules and regulations of human behavior, it is capable of directing and informing our position in view of realities that exist. It is under this purview that it was prioritised in this paper as being novel and model in addressing the environmental problems confronting Niger Delta region. This claim is validated bearing in mind that the fulcrum of environmental ethics is environmental sustainability. Moreover, the question many may ask is how this research can deal with the issues pertaining to animals and plants, as aspects of nature; hence, they are not humans that should be attached with certain moral standards? Other questions may include: Can the actions taken by human beings against plants and animals be judged morally or either right or wrong? If the answer is in affirmative; are we now saying that plant and animal exhibit some traits of human behavior or conduct? Do they have anything in common with man such that whatever affects man, affects them too? These questions arose due to the fact that ethics and morality are seen by many as exclusively human things and idiosyncrasies that have nothing to do with plant and animal. Aldo Leopold (1977) explain more on this position when he observes that "early Greeks had idea of what is right and wrong but that these were limited to the free-borne while slaves were treated as property and behavior of their owners towards them involved no question of property". This notion about life is archaic and bifurcated going by the conscious effort made by Jane Goodall (1996) to prove that some other animals and plants exhibit abilities that make them eligible for ethical and moral consideration. After all, the notion of being can be understood within the context of opposites, plurality, the equal and contraries (Aristotle, 1926).

Though, we often kick against Aristotle's dichotomist and bifurcatory tendencies about realities, his above submission is useful here, hence, our intention and defense of plants and animals is not to show that both can rank at par with human beings. But to reiterate the need to protect them too, in dictate with ethics and morality of the society. The necessity of ethics has outgrown the sphere of human society or community. From the recent ecological challenges like climate change, erosion or flooding, desertification and ozone layer depletion, "it has been discovered that it is not only humans that can be affected by human conduct or morality. Non-human part of nature also suffers when the action of man towards it are devoid of moral regulations" (Leopold, 1977). This validates Goodall's assertion that some plants and animals have some innate abilities in them. With this, the ethics of the environment ought to be human oriented, animal centric, bio centric and ecologically friendly. When it is human centric or centred, it protects and conserves the environment for the wellbeing of man. It is under this ambit that the Niger Delta people and the entire Nigerians can survive and be sustained. More so, if it is animal centric, animals will be morally considered especially those of them that have human traits and resemblance. This position was expounded by Bentham (1979) who was of the opinion that these animals be considered on the ground of sentientism. For him, the facts that they feel pain and enjoy pleasurable things just like human beings do; it will be unjust to deny them that care within the environment. Ethics of the environment should hold life at high esteem. Be it plant or animal life. It is against this backdrop that it can be said to be bio centric and morally valued. It must equally be ecologically holistic. In other words, nature, like the cynics would say must be protected. It is only when all these outlined facts and ethics are obeyed and considered by government, companies and communities within the region that the environmental degradation, which has engulfed and turned Niger Delta into a war zone will be addressed, and equity and justice, which the communities in the region clamor for can be achieved.

CONCLUSION

To restore both human and environmental dignity to the region, the communities and government must join hands together. That is, government must play her own part by releasing the necessary funds that can cushion the effects of the region's environmental problems. The Niger Delta communities also have a role to play here. They must ensure that they avoid defecation and throwing of no degradable elements into the river. It is their duty to also monitor those that the said funds are being given to for accountability and transparency. This is what they hardly do; hence, a good number of them who should have asked for the statement of the account are ready to collect bribes from these embezzlers, for their own selfish reasons. This is substantiated following what happened of late between the NDDC's chairman and Nigerian House of Representatives and their forensic propaganda. For any sustainable development to exist in Niger Delta, hunger and worries salvaged and environmental degradation eradicated, the interests of all in the region must be protected and valued by both government, multinational oil companies and affected communities. Due to the instinct of self-preservation and corrupt tendencies in humans, this paper recommends that the existing environmental protection regulations be enforced. It is through this that the ethics of the environment can be obeyed for the sustainability of plants, animals and human beings, within the Niger Delta region and Nigeria in general.

REFERENCES

Akani, C. (2000). *Company / youth relationship in the Niger Delta: What Approach in the New Millennium?* Paper Presented at the Peace 2000 youth rally, Organized by the Rivers State Youth Federation, Port Harcourt, Nigeria.

Akhigbe, J. (2013). The state and development interventions in the Niger Delta region of Nigeria. *International Journal of Humanities and Social Science*, *3*(10), 255–263.

Aristotle. (1926). *Metaphysica (W. D. Ross, Trans.)*. Clarendon Press.

Bentham, J. (1979). *An Introduction to the Principle of Morals and Legislation*. Oxford University Press.

Bindraban, P. S. (2012). ISRIC Study: Assessing the Impact of Soil Degradation of Food Production. *Current Opinion in Environmental Sustainability*, *2*, 311–323.

Ekanem, S. A., & Ejue, B. J., Amimi, P. B., & Adalikwu, R. A. (2010). Living with Oil: Towards an Ethics of the Environment in Niger Delta. *Research Review: An International Multi-Disciplinary Journal, Ethiopia*, *4*(3a), 17–30.

Folarin, S., & Okodua, H. (2009). Environment and the Economics of Nationalism: Revisiting the Oil Issue and the Restless Run of Locusts in the Niger Delta. *Jadavpur J. Int'l Rel*, *141*(1), 144–152. doi:10.1177/0973598409110010

Goodall, J. (1996). *My Life with the Chimpanzees: The Fascinating Story of One of the World's most Celebrated Naturalists*. Pockets Books.

Inyang, B. (2019). Environmental Degradation and Sustainable Development in Nigeria: A Study of the South-South Region of Nigeria. *International Journal of Humanities Social Sciences and Education*, *6*(8), 33-42.

Leopold, A. (1977). *A Sand County Almanac*. Oxford University Press.

Oguduvwe, J. I. P. (2013). Poverty in oil rich Delta: A study of selected oil producing communities in Delta State, Nigeria. *Global Research Journal of Education*, (1), 1–11. http://www.globalresearchjournals.org/journal/grje3

Oluduro, O., & Oluduro, F. O. (2012). Nigeria: In search of sustainable peace in the Niger Delta through the amnesty program. *Journal of Sustainable Development*, *5*(7), 48–61. doi:10.5539/jsd.v5n7p48

Omoregbe, J. (2000). *Ethics: A Systematic Study*. Joja Educational Press.

Osamuyimen, E. (2020). *Mitigating the Effects of Environmental Degradation in the Oil Industry: An Assessment of Government Compensation Scheme in Nigeria. Law, Environment and Development Journal.*

Snapps, O. J. (2011). Africa-based oil exporting companies: The case of Nigeria. *American Review of Political Economy*, *9*, 1–56. http://www.arpejournal.com

United Nations Organisation. (2004). *A More Sure World: Our Shared Responsibility. Report of the Secretary-General's High-level Panel on Threats, Challenges and Change*. United Nations Department of Public Information.

Chapter 24
Nigerian Media's Poor Representation and Negligence of Minorities as a Breach of Ethical Journalism

Eric Ndoma Besong
Federal University of Lafia, Nigeria

ABSTRACT

The plights of Nigerian ethnic minorities, arising from marginalisation, account for various national issues, such as ethno-religious intolerance and crisis, ethnic militia, civil unrest, terrorism, banditry, among others. The study reveals that Nigerian media play crucial roles in the marginalisation, dehumanisation, and plights suffered by peoples branded 'ethnic minorities'. The poor representation and negligence of the minorities aggravate the plights of the minorities. The study argues that by breaching media ethics, the Nigerian press violates African indigenous ethical principles. Also, media's misdeeds against the minorities amount to breach of ethical journalism. The chapter concludes that besides paying little or no attention to matters concerning ethnic minorities, Nigerian media aggravate the plights of ethnic minorities by continuously exhibiting misdeeds against them.

INTRODUCTION

It is quite problematic to emphasize only three major ethnic groups along with only about ten or more others, where there are over four hundred and eighty ethnic groups (Evwierhoma, 2007; Robert, 2015; Robert, Besong & Dibie, 2016; Ugwu & Ozoemena, 2019). Also, it is quite regrettable that Nigerian media most often place undue emphasis on the three major ethnic groups (Hausa, Yoruba and Igbo) in Nigeria, to the near exclusion of the rest over four hundred ethnic groups. Hausa is the most populous ethnic group and language in Nigeria, spread across the whole of Northern Nigeria. Northern Nigeria is divided into North-East, North-West and North-Central. The Yoruba are the indigenous people of Southwestern Nigeria. Yoruba states in Southwest are Lagos, Oyo, Ogun, Osun, Ekiti and Ondo. The

DOI: 10.4018/978-1-6684-4107-7.ch024

Igbo of Southeastern Nigeria are the indigenous people of Anambra, Enugu, Imo, Ebonyi and Abia. South-South has clusters of ethnic groups and languages along with six states viz: Cross River, Rivers, Akwa-Ibom, Bayelsa, Delta and Edo. In view of problems arising from the strained emphasis on the three major ethnic groups along with the allied ten or more, this paper argues that the Nigerian mass media engages in the practice of making the image of and giving prominent attention to the three major ethnic groups and a few others, leaving out little or nothing about the other ethnic groups christened 'ethnic minorities'.

It is quite surprising that despite affirming that Nigeria has over five hundred languages (Evwierhoma, 2007; Robert, 2015; Robert, Besong & Dibie, 2016; Ugwu & Ozoemena, 2019), ethnic groups are underrepresented as being two hundred and fifty, over three hundred, or about or over four hundred ethnic groups. It is surprising because each tribe has a language and vice versa. Thus, if the languages are over five hundred, the tribes (ethnic groups) are over five hundred. The numerous other ethnic groups are perpetually silenced, disregarded, endangered and eroded (Evwierhoma, 2007; Robert, 2015; Robert & Besong, 2016). It is an indisputable fact that whatever and/or whoever pays attention to and make its (and/or his/her) image with significant media contents and jingles automatically becomes well known, relevant and prominent (Ahmed & Chiakaan, 2011; Chiakaan, 2013; Robert & Besong, 2016; Robert & Besong, 2017). The simple reality here is that once the media makes the image of the ethnic minorities with significant media contents, programs and jingles, these ethnic groups are undoubtedly bound to become prominent, relevant, formalized and (more) developed. In view of the foregoing reality, this study rises to describe the poor representation and negligence of ethnic minorities by the Nigerian mass media as a breach of professional ethics. In other words, the paper considers media misrepresentation and negligence of ethnic minorities as a breach of media and journalism ethics.

THEORETICAL FRAMEWORK

This study is grounded by the agenda setting theory of the media. This theory, developed by Maxwell McCombs and Donald Shaw, describes the ability of the media to influence the audience to give significance or importance to whatever or whoever they (the media) have made significant or important (McCombs & Shaw, 1972; Chiakaan and Ahmed, 2011; Robert and Besong, 2016; Ojie, 2020). The theorists postulate that the influence of the media on the public is so strong that the media instill in the audience what they should think and not what they think (McCombs & Shaw, 1972). This means that the frequency of media information, programs, and jingles about anything, person or group determines the attention, regard and relevance the audience gives to it/them. Again, agenda-setting revolves around creating public awareness and the concern of salient issues by news media (Ojie, 2020, p. 443). Given this expressed concern of the agenda-setting theory, there is no gainsaying that it aptly suits this study. This study advocates a reasonable level of public awareness about ethnic minorities. Also, the salient issues behind the agitations of the ethnic minorities have to be given due media coverage and reportage. Currently, the reverse is the case. Doing so would not only address the issues of marginalization and conflicts over the contestation for resources and power, but also bring the minorities to limelight and also pave way for their betterment, wide recognition, development, wellbeing and continuity/sustenance across ages.

Also, the two basic assumptions of this theory aptly theorize the central gist of this paper. The first assumption is that the media do not objectively reflect and present reality but rather filter and shape it to what they want/like. Secondly, the concentration of the media on a few selected issues and subjects makes the public perceive those issues/subjects as more important than all other not given such attention (Adebisi, 2017). By implication, one realizes and agrees with this paper that because the media exclusively concentrate on the christened major ethnic groups, the masses (public) are made to believe that the minorities are not (really) important, and their issues at stake mean little or nothing. Such perception, arising from the agenda set by the media, is largely misleading, sentimental and stereotypical. Also, this theory hints that the media, too often than not, misrepresent the realities about minorities. Apart from focusing exclusively on the majorities, they often present the ethnic majorities in good light and the minorities in bad. This practice and such others are unethical and do often generate problems that many persons do not even imagined (see Okoye, 2011).

Thus, the falsehoods generate a lot of issues that affect not just the minorities but also the society at large, as the general wellbeing and development of the society get adversely affected by issues of ethnic minorities. Given the foregoing, this study avers that the media set ethnic agenda favoring the majorities, as against the minorities, thereby negatively influencing public perception and considerations of the minorities. Thus, ethnic minorities continue to suffer various plights across ages as a result of the misdeeds of the media against them. The ethnic-based ills against the minorities are unethical (Okoye, 2011), for they involve the breach of professional media ethics and general conventionalized norms and values. The violation of these arises from internalized and shared ethnic sentiments rooted in the minds of media professionals, as with other professionals.

FACTORS BEHIND ISSUES OF ETHNIC MINORITIES VERSUS MAJORITIES

As the ethnic minorities continue to look forward to getting justice and fairness in one way or the other and get nothing, ethnic agitation becomes a consistent mechanism for fighting against perceived and/or real marginalization (Ugwu & Ozoemena, 2019, pp. 220-222). Several scholars share the viewpoint that colonialism and the amalgamation of Northern and Southern Nigeria (Northern and Southern Protectorates then) are two major factors behind the issues of majorities versus minorities in Nigeria (Ugwu & Ozoemena, 2019; Odanwu & Chukwuma, 2019). Beyond these three most populous external factors, some other inherent factors include religion, ethnicity, language multiplicity, inciting elitist orientation, negative legacies of some Nigerian elites/nationalists, leadership misdeeds of Nigerian indigenous leaders/elites, corruption and heinous crimes against the state (Achebe, 1983; Nwokora, 2000; Besong, 2019; Robert, 2020).

For many, because of ethnocentrism, ethnic hate, the national language policy, explosive population parameter and/or sheer ignorance, there are only three ethnic groups within which all others exist and operate. The three are Hausa, Yoruba and Igbo. To such persons, anyone from the North is Hausa by tribe; from the South is Igbo by tribe; from the West is Yoruba. For the traditional Yoruba and Hausa/Fulani, if one does not belong to either of the two, then the person is of Igbo ethnic group. This assumption comes with derogatory labels. For example, the Hausa and the Fulani call those from South-East and South-South 'Inyamiri', their derogatory label for the Igbo. Until the recent Fulani herders' unrest and mayhem on other tribes (Besong & Robert, 2019), the Fulani were even often misconceived by many as Hausa. These days, the spate of Fulani's attacks on other Nigerian peoples have made them known to even little children of other tribes as people who are different from Hausa. For example, Hausa-Fulani (Hausa/Fulani) is commonly used on that line of thought. Emphatically, Hausa, Fulani, Yoruba, and Igbo are the most commonly known Nigerian ethnic groups and languages. Thus, Nigerian media continue to exclusively concentrate media contents and activities on them, paying little or no attention to the others regarded as minorities.

The linguistic, social, political, and phenomenological prominence of the Fulani ethnic group and Fulfulde language rests on Hausa ethnic group and language. These are the number one ethnic groups and languages given maximum attention and relevance by the Nigerian mass media. A few other ethnic minorities considered when discussing or mentioning ethnic groups in Nigeria by the Nigerian mass media include Kanuri, Nupe, Kanuri, Gbagi, Birom, Jukun, Igala, Tiv, Idoma, etc., found in the North. Some others include Ijaw, Bini, Itsekiri, Ibibio, Efik, Annag, Urhobo and Ikwere in the South-South region of Nigeria. The rest are barely heard of. Cultural and linguistic studies are also almost the exclusive preserved of the three major ethnic groups. Given the situation espoused above, issues of marginalization have risen and have become endemic. The issues continuously degenerate on a daily basis. It should be noted that most of the other Nigerian tribes and languages gaining wide recognition and popularity are still the constituent parts of the 'ethnic minorities' in Nigeria. The peoples of these other ethnic groups, christened ethnic minorities, usually express bitterness over their marginalization. They also make a push with others on issues of ethnic marginalization and agitations.

Furthermore, although issues of ethnic minorities and majorities in Nigeria have a colonial history, this study does not subscribe to the scholarship that exclusively blames them on colonialism, exonerating or undermining the non-colonial (indigenous) factors. In the first place, the comparative advantages the trio tribes and a few others given relevance have had over the rest of the Nigerian tribes (ethnic groups) had begun from the pre-colonial era through the post-colonial era. The comparative advantages include the fortunes they had earlier over the others known today as the ethnic minorities; their earlier contact with the Westerners; their earlier acquisition of Western education; and building formidable societal structures put in place by their elites and traditional leaders. For example, the ancient peoples of the today's three major tribes as well as a few other emerging popular Nigerian tribes of these days had developed and structured their society in ways that favored the natives, which attracted foreigners and neighbors to their areas. As a result, when the colonialists came to Nigeria, they resolved for such areas, upon carrying out their feasibility studies. The then elites of the present Nigerian leading ethnic groups had taken judicious advantage of the opportunities that came their way, unlike their fellows of other ethnic groups that have come to be 'ethnic minorities.'

For example, it is not possible to compare languages, literature, knowledge, development and general societal structures and systems that developed long before and after colonialism with those that were not then or became so much later. In fact, many of today's Nigerian ethnic groups evolved much later after the majorities had become well-established and prominent for quite a long time. Most of the ethnic groups that evolved from several other earlier established groups cannot compete favorably with those they had sprawled from. That is, the latter-day emergent ethnic groups cannot compare (or be compared) with their source ethnic groups in the same magnitude. This is typically evidenced in the development experience and socio-cultural and political prominence of Idoma over Yala, Alagoe and Agatu; Jukun over Idoma, Igede, Bekwarra and Obudu; Bekwarra over Mbube and Afrike; Kanuri over Kambari, Angas, Tal and its other emergent groups across several Northern states; Bantu over the various Bantu peoples like Boki, some Ejagham and Ekoi peoples; central Bette over the Bette clusters, central Ekoi over the Ekoi clusters; and so on. Furthermore, overwhelmed or impressed by the favors they derived from groups that had already established themselves (e.g. Hausa-Fulani, Yoruba, Igbo, Efik, Bini, Kanuri, Ijaw and

Igala, among others), the colonialists became sentimental in dealing with the peoples who make-up the area later/today known as Nigeria.

In what lends credence to the preceding argument, Jimbili (2020, p. 353) claims that the British had erroneously conceived the Hausa-Fulani Islamic political institutions of the caliphate as the administrative model for all of Northern Nigeria. He adds that Lord Lugard had assumed that the future of the protectorate lies mainly with the Fulani, whose skin, color, thought system and ways of life largely appealed to the native population (Jimbili, 2020, p.353). For Jimbili (2020, pp. 352-4), issues of minorities in Northern Nigeria, which arise from their grievances and discontentment, began in 1914 when Lord Lugard forcefully amalgamated Northern and Southern Protectorates without considering the obvious pre-colonial realities and native differences among the peoples of the two protectorates. Relying almost entirely on the views of Fidelis Egbe Enang and Tochukwu Okeke, which blame the colonialists for the issues between the classified ethnic minorities and majorities (Enang & Okeke, 2015, pp. 341-3, 348-9), Jimbili (2020, p.353) considers the colonialists as those behind the ageing issues of ethnic minorities as well as their ageing plights.

He insinuates that the plights suffered by those christened 'ethnic minorities' in Nigeria would not have been in place if Lugard with its supporting British authority had not merged Northern and Southern protectorates (Jimbili, 2020, p. 354). Jimbili argues that the amalgamation presents the complexities of ethnic minorities in Nigeria. He emphasizes that even if over two hundred ethnic groups were to be merged, the Hausa-Fulani groups ought to have been separated because of their distinct population, political system, practice and level of uniformity and homogeneity in language and culture. His emphasis implies that the merging of Hausa-Fulani with the other ethnic groups by Lord Lugard brought up the sustained ethnic contestations and problems bedeviling the post-colonial Nigerian society. It is understood that for Jimbili, since a stranger does not know the house of his/her host better than the host does, Lugard merged the protectorates in error and ended up planting the problems confronting Nigeria. Consequently, ethnic contestation and marginalization issues between the minorities and the majorities have surfaced and remained endemic over the years. These issues arise from perceived and real cases of marginalization, which propel sustained agitations.

Nevertheless, Jimbili (2020, p. 356) warns that the solution to the amalgamation problems is not division (de-amalgamation), since this would lead to war and systemic instability, as in Sudan and Somalia. According to Jimbili (2020, p. 356-9), the solution rather lies in correcting the wrongs or errors of the amalgamation with the following:

i. Restructuring the extant over bloated polity, which involves returning to provincial structure and polity.
ii. Setting up new structures and portfolios for regional governance with the criteria being cultural affinity, compatible linguistic groups and shared aspirations.
iii. Evolving new revenue allocation formula, which balances shares of revenue and responsibilities between the federal government and the provinces.
iv. Moving away from the current Nigerian unitary government, tagged federalism, to true federalism, which gives regions more responsibilities than the federal body.
v. Wedging a sustained strong war against corruption, social vices and bad governance.

THE MEDIA AND ISSUES OF ETHNIC MINORITIES

Ethnic-based penchant media contents are indices or clear cases of breach of media professional ethics. Nigerian media engages in this practice (Robert & Besong, 2016; Chiakaan, 2013; Chiakaan & Ahmad, 2011). Scholars have lamented the disposition of ethnic sentiments by some media professionals in Nigeria, which are affirmed to have caused and fuelled ethnic conflicts respectively (Yusuf, 1992; Kukah, 1993; Yusuf, 1994; Galadima & Enighe, 2001, pp 62-74.; Ekeanyanwu, 2005; Nord & Stromback, 2006; Dul, 2007; Kamilindi, 2007; Oduma, 2007; Gofwen 2004; Daura, 2009; Umar, 2009; Wakili, 2009; Yoroms, 2009; Creeping Sharia, 2010; Etaghene 2010; Spero 2010; Ahmed & Chiakaan, 2011; Chiakaan, 2013; Adamu, 2013; Raphael, 2015; Robert & Besong, 2016; Pogliano, 2017; Robert & Besong, 2017; Ojie, 2020). Again, studies have lamented the negative role played by the Nigerian media in various scenes of ethnic clashes. This includes under-reportage and misrepresentation of the recurrent ethnic crises in Jos (Alozieuwa, 2010, pp. 18-31); the Ombatse ethnic upsurge in Nasarawa State (Alozieuwa, 2016; BBC, 2015; Joseph, 2013; Daniel, 2012; Eggon Association President, 2017), the attempted genocide raids on minority tribes in Taraba and Bayelsa States, aided by military invasion; elitist sponsored Fulani herders' organized genocide against other tribes to allow for Hausa-Fulani hegemony; among others (Robert & Besong, 2016; Daura, 2009; Danladi, 2008; Dul, 2007; Alubo, 2006).

The manner in which the media reports ethnic issues shows ethnic sentiments. Engaging in sensational and penchant media contents depicts ethical deviance. The Modakeke versus Hausa crisis in Ife; several ethno-religious crises in Jos; the killing of some Northerners in Onitsha following the ethno-religious attacks on some Igbo in Kano, Jos and some other parts of the North all followed the ethnic and religious sentiments expressed by the media (Alubo, 2006; Daniel, 2012; Joseph, 2013; Alozieuwa, 2016; Besong & Robert, 2019; among others). Ethical deviance (breach of professional ethics) on the part of the press either paves way for or aggravates issues of minorities versus majorities. This paper maintains that anywhere globally, where multilingualism and ethnic pluralism obtain, the media (press) ought to consider all the ethno-lingual groups equally by according them same ethical considerations and moral values. When media practitioners uphold ethics of the profession, they play commendable roles, which are capable of resolving ethnic issues between ethnic minorities and majorities. Consequent upon penchant media contents tied to ethnic sentiments, issues of disunity among the Nigerian peoples increase and remain endemic. Many studies have blamed the media for playing negative roles in crucial public matters in various societies, which often cause the societies more harm than good (Biles & Ibrahim, 2000; Danso and McDonald, 2001; Harris, 2001; McDonald and Jacobs, 2005; Ahmed & Chiakaan, 2011; Chiakaan, 2013; Robert & Besong, 2016; Pogliano, 2017; Robert & Besong, 2017; Ojie, 2020).

In other words, several studies have proven media's deviant roles in presenting and representing ethnic groups and matters concerning them. Examples of such studies include Biles and Ibrahim (2000), Danso and McDonald (2001), Harris (2001), McDonald and Jacobs (2005), Mogekwu (2017) and Pogliano (2017). For instance, Danso and McDonald (2001) are of the view that the kind of representation of a migrant by the media determines the kind of relationship between the citizens and the migrants. This implies that where the representation is negative, the relationship is also negative and finally gives rise to violence, intergroup conflicts, xenophobia and discrimination, among other issues. The above mentioned view paints a clear picture of the role played by the media in the 2019 xenophobia against Nigerian migrants in South Africa. As Onyido (2018) affirms, the 2019 xenophobic attacks on Nigerians in South Africa greatly affected Nigerian students in that country. This study adds that besides students, the 2019 xenophobic attacks on Nigerians in South Africa had devastating effects on all Nigerians there, at home and in the Diaspora. In other words, the effects still linger directly and indirectly on all Nigerians, depending on individual Nigerians. Over time, the effects undoubtedly extend to the diplomatic relations between Nigeria and South Africa.

The concept of xenophobia is mainly used interchangeably with racism, though some scholars argue that the two concepts differ considerably (Ojie, 2020; Tafira, 2011; Widfeldt, 2014). By implication, the media induce xenophobia and racism, rouse ethnocentrism and uphold ethnic brotherhood considerations and sentiments. Essentially, ethnic sentiments, prejudices and discrimination are involved in both phenomenal and practical contexts of xenophobia and racism. However, racism gives rise to or paves way for xenophobia. Xenophobia is the extreme phase of racism, bloodier and more destructive than racism. This is because racism may only end at non-violent discrimination and denial of certain rights and privileges of settlers, residents, or persons of race(s) labeled inferior by the indigenous or self-assumed *superior* persons of another race. In what lends credence to the foregoing, Harris (2002, p. 1) avers that xenophobia basically derives from the sense that non-citizens pose a threat to the recipients' identity or their individual rights, is also closely connected with the concept of nationalism. This sense in each individual is that of membership in the political nation as an essential ingredient in their sense of identity (Harris, 2002, p. 1). As Mogekwu (2017) rightly hints us, the media induces xenophobia because of individuals' socio-economic status and cultural identity. These two-set factors concern the citizens' financial security over the migrants, and ethnocentrism and ethnic brotherhood considerations/sentiments (Ojie, 2020, p. 439). Obviously, the media play a significant role in every society's daily activities. They impact on society and its members in various regards. The impactful roles played by the media are of two folds: negative and positive roles/impacts (Ojie, 2020; Robert and Besong, 2016; Chiakaan, 2013).

The implication of the foregoing is that the media play a crucial role in matters concerning ethnic majorities versus minorities. As in other public matters, the media also impact on society in ethnic matters. This study argues that the media's influence on citizens in these matters gradually culminates to or builds up ethnocentrism, ethnic hate and prejudices, racism, xenophobia, discrimination, sour intergroup relations, intolerance and violent ethnic clashes. It emphasizes that the kind of role played by the media determines the kind of impact they exert on the masses. Also, the kind of media contents, programs and/or jingles the media of a given nation disseminate to or make available to the audience about the ethnic minorities determines the awareness about, interest in and attitude towards the minorities. When the media undermine such ethnic groups, the masses do the same. It is the other way round when or if the media do otherwise. It is to this end that Herman and Chomsky (1988) have observed that besides transmitting information to the public, the media reproduce certain ideologies and discourses that support specific relations of power. Leaning on Herman and Chomsky's factual observation, it is quite clear that the Nigerian media most times reproduce certain erroneous ideologies and discourses about ethnic minorities only in ways that support specific relations of power with the majorities. They re/create what had been put in place by elites of the ethnic majorities against the ethnic minorities. By so doing, they violate ethical journalism that demands objectivity, among other principles. The media ought to be objective, and fair to all parties that make up their heterogeneous audience. Any form of sentimental journalism or journalistic practice is unethical.

Essentially, the way, manner or extent to which the press talk and/or act about, represent, depict, frame and/or present a matter, a person, a people, a group or what have you is what makes the image of the person, the group or the thing and accords relevance to it or them accordingly. Scholars have affirmed this assertion as an indisputable fact (e.g. Harris, 2001; Chiakaan and Ahmed, 2011; Chiakaan, 2013; Robert and Besong, 2016). Ethnic sentiments exhibited by the media negate media objectivity and ethical journalism. When the press allows their subjective traits and perspectives to influence their views about ethnic groups, they act against those ethnic groups that are out of their preference list. These thoughts are given credence by Mohammed (2011), who decries the negative role of the print media in covering and reporting intergroup issues like discrimination, xenophobia, racism, ethnic prejudices and hate, and so on. This paper argues that while Mohammed is right on the print media's poor and misleading coverage and reportage of such issues. He fails to be objective enough to indict the electronic (audio-visual) media. The electronic media now have a larger audience than the print media, wherever in the world that reading culture is very poor. Thus, this paper argues otherwise that the electronic media do much more harm than the print media in their coverage, reportage and depiction of the issues mentioned earlier and those concerning ethnic minorities.

For example, they commonly silence and even totally leave out important matters concerning and affecting ethnic minorities only because such groups are not the majorities and mostly have no prominent personalities to grace or sponsor the media programs. These media fail to play their role of willingly investigating, covering, reporting and developing unpopular cultures, without waiting to be paid or pushed to carry out such roles. This study goes on to argue that most often than not, both local and international mass media project and present popular ethnic groups, which are those christened ethnic majorities, in good light, and project and present the unpopular or yet-to-be popular ones in a bad light. Thus, the act of playing down the ethnic minorities by the media adversely affects the peoples along with their cultures and panorama. The foregoing views are given credence by Harris (2002), who agrees that when certain (African) media present some persons (say, foreigners) and things in good light and high esteem, and the others in a bad light or low esteem, several problems arise. Such problems include ethnic prejudices and hate, discrimination, xenophobia, stereotype, relegation, negligence, racism, interpersonal and intergroup conflicts, etc. Simply because the ethnic minorities have not gained popularity, most media either misrepresent them or merely present them in a bad light. This disposition is also evidenced in the scholarship of exonerating a few ethnic groups or races and indicting the others. For examples, expressing his Eurocentric racial perspective against other races, David Hume claimed that the Negroes and other races are naturally inferior to the European race (Popkin, 1978, p. 213). Similarly, Linnaeus (1758) claimed that all creatures were arranged by God in a great chain of hierarchy with human beings at the head; in the human hierarchy, the European is the superior race and tops others; the Black race is the closest to the lowest; the lowest being animals. Mass media are some of the major agents of the society used for spreading and sustaining such racial sentiments against other races misconceived as inferior to a popular or more developed one(s).

On his part, Immanuel Kant claimed that only Europe demonstrated regular progress, for which it has to give law to the other nations of the world. Kant unpleasantly remarked that the difference between the African and the European is the former's mental incapacity. He describes the Africans in a bad light thus: 'This fellow was quite black from head to foot, a clear proof that what he said was stupid' (Lewis W. Beck ed., *Kant on History*, p. 24, quoted in Serequeberhan, 1991, p. 6). Kant's words imply that the African has mental incapability, while the European does have mental capability. He went further to use black skin as a parameter for adjudging the African as a stupid person. He naïvely claimed that anyone who has no black skin is not stupid. Like other subjective and misleading claims of his kind, his claim is baseless and illogical. The foregoing examples of the scholarship of indicting or condemning other ethnic groups and exonerating one's own alone suffice for many others in the literature.

African and Nigerian scholars who follow such path of scholarship abound in all fields. It is for this reason that Alagoa (1993, p. 8) warns against the tendency of Nigerian scholarship to suggest that non-centralized groups of Nigeria are without history. In the same vein, Isichei (1976, p. 21) maintains the claim that larger political units are 'more advanced' than small ones could be misleading. There are such misleading thoughts and expressed ethnic prejudices here and there about ethnic minorities in specific. Although they abound among the so-called majorities against one another, theirs are insignificant and never promoted by the media. Since they have more representatives in the media and other public realms, such prejudices and ethnic framing evils are often defended and wiped out by the press and the other public-based professionals from ethnic majorities. It should be noted that like the aforementioned scholars and their likes, the media mostly exhibit and express ethnocentric prejudices against peoples of other ethnic groups. They do worse to peoples and cultures of the ethnic groups christened 'ethnic minorities'.

CONCLUSION

In all, the central position of this paper is that by continuously emphasizing and misrepresenting the ethnic majorities to the near exclusion of the ethnic minorities, the Nigerian media work against the minorities. There are various socio-cultural, economic, political, developmental and national issues confronting Nigeria that have traces to ethnic prejudices, hate, relegation and marginalization. Nigerian ethnic minorities suffer these man-tailored ills. Tribalism and ethnic crises surface among Nigerian ethnic groups result from the contestation for power and resources and the attempts by the minorities to repel continuous suppression and marginalization by the majorities. This study argues that the misrepresentation of Nigerian ethnic minorities by the media show how the media play down cultural identity and ethnic prominence of the minorities. It considers the poor re/presentation of the ethnic minorities as unethical, as doing so goes against media professional ethics. So, that amounts to breach of media professional ethics.

REFERENCES

Abdu, H., & Alabi, T. (2009). The print media and ethno-religious conflicts in Kaduna. In J.G. Yoroms & M. Abubakar (Eds.), Conflict management and the media in Nigeria. Centre for Research and Documentation (CRD).

Achebe, C. (1983). *The trouble with Nigeria*. Fourth Dimension Publishers.

Adamu, L. (2013). Media reportage of ethno-religious conflicts in Plateau State. *Journal of Communication and Media Research, 5*(1), 79-82.

Adebisi, O.O. (2017). The management of conflict in contemporary society: Prospects and challenges. *International Journal of Asian Social Sciences, 3*(12).

Alagoa, E. (1993). Oral tradition and oral history in Africa. In T. Folola (Ed.), *African Historiography: Essays in honour of Jacob Ade Ajayi.* Longman.

Alozieuwa, S.H.O. (2010). Beyond the ethno-religious theory of the Jos conflict. *African Peace and Conflict Journal, 3*(2).

Alozieuwa, S.O.H. (2016). The Ombatse crisis in Nigeria: Background, recent developments and possible solutions. *Journal of Interdisciplinary Conflict Science, 2*(2).

Alubo, O. (2006). *Ethnic conflicts and citizenship crises in the Central Region*. Eddy Asae Press.

BBC News. (2015). *Nigeria attack: Nasarawa cult ambush, kills 30 police*. Available @https://www.bbc.com/news/world-africa-22462225

Besong, E.N., & Robert, O.S. (2019). Philosophical consideration of herdsmen menace and hunger in contemporary Nigeria. *American Journal of Service Science and Management, 6*(1).

Besong, E.N. (2019). An appraisal of three Nigerian poets' perspectives on trends plaguing contemporary Nigeria. *International Journal of Arts and Literature, 3*(1).

Biles, R., & Ibrahim, D.A. (2000). *Writing xenophobia: Immigration and the print media in post- apartheid South Africa. SAMP.* Migration Policy Series, no. 17.

Chiakaan, G. J. (2013). *Broadcasting and the broadcast media in Nigeria*. Eagle Print.

Chiakaan, G. J., & Ahmed, I. J. (2011). *Mass communication for beginners*. Azaben Publishers.

Dagyang, S. D. (2008). *Jos Crisis: Another Jihad go awry? Comment*. Nigerian Tribune.

Daniel, A. (2012). We are not militias, we are a prayer group—Ombatse cult. *Vanguard*. Available at http://www.vanguardngr.com/2012/12/we-are-not-militias-we- are-aprayer-group-ombatse-cult/

Danladi, S. (2008, Dec. 12). Re the media and the genocide in Jos. Comments. *Nigerian Standard*.

Danso, R., & McDonald, D. (2001). Writing xenophobia: Immigration and the print media in post-apartheid South Africa. *Africa Today*, *48*(3), 114–137. doi:10.2979/AFT.2001.48.3.114

Daura, M. A. (2009). *Violent conflict in northern states: Bauchi, Plateau and Taraba* (Dissertation). National Institute for Policy and Strategic Studies, Kuru.

Dul, R. (2007). Roles and responsibilities of the media in conflict management and peace building. In S. Abu & C. Best (Eds.), Pen & peace. International Centre for Reconciliation, Coventry Cathedral, Centre for Conflict Management and Peace Studies, University of Jos.

Edogor, I. O., Ojo, L. I., Ezugwu, I. M., & Dike, K. (2015). Users' perception of crisis portrayals on social media: A study of Boko Haram insurgency in Nigeria. *New Media and Mass Communication, 35*. www.iiste.org

Egbon, M. (1994). Social responsibility and the Nigerian mass media: struggles and tactics for balanced media coverage of crises. *Media Review*, 16-30.

Eggon Assoc. President. (2017). *Nasarawa bloodbath: 270 people were killed, Al-Makura signed single term with us*. http://www.informationng.com/2013/05/nasarawa-bloodbath-270-people-were-killedal-makura-signed-single-term-with-us-eggon-assoc-president.html

Ekeanyanwu, N. T. (2005). The Nigerian press and political conflict reporting: A case study of the Ngige-Ubah political conflict in Anambra state. In A. M. Yakubu (Ed.), *Crisis and conflict management in Nigeria since 1980* (pp. 221–235). Nigerian Defence Academy.

Enang, F.E., & Okeke, T.I. (2015). The 1914 amalgamation and emergence of ethnic minorities problems in Northern Nigeria. *VUNS Journal of History and International Relations, 2*(2).

Evwierhoma, M. (2007). *Nigeria: A flourishing culture in diversity*. Paper Presented at the 2007 World Culture Day Celebration for the National Institute for Cultural Orientation (NICO), Abuja, Nigeria.

Harris, B. (2001). A foreign experience: Violence, crime and xenophobia during South Africa's transition. In *Violence and Transition Series 5*. Centre for the Study of Violence and Reconciliation.

Harris, B. (2002). Xenophobia: A new pathology for a new South Africa? In *Psychopathology and social prejudice*. University of Cape Town Press.

Galadima, D., & Enighe, J. (2001). The Press in Nigerian politics: An historical analysis of issues, and pattern of news coverage. *The Nigerian Journal of Communications*.

Gofwen, R. (2004). *Religious conflicts in Northern Nigeria and nation building: The throes of two decades 1980–2000*. Human Rights Monitor.

Harris, B. (2001). *A Foreign Experience: Violence*. Crime and Xenophobia During South.

Herman, E. S., & Chomsky, N. (1988). *Manufacturing consent: The political economy of the mass media*. Pantheon Books.

Isichei, E. (1976). *A history of the Igbo people*. Macmillan. doi:10.1007/978-1-349-15621-4

Jimbili, M. (2020). The origin of minority agitation in Northern Nigeria. In M. Michael, E. T. Aliegba, & A. A. Alagba (Eds.), *Human rights, religion and society: Festschrift for Rev. Fr. Prof. Jake Omang Otonko on his 60th Birthday*. Eiwa Press Nig. Ltd.

Joseph, H. (2013). Ombatse: Profile of deadly cult group. *Daily Trust*. http://dailytrust.com.ng/weekly/index.php/top-stories/12653-ombatse-profile-of-deadly-cultgroup

Kamilindi, T. (2007). Journalism in a time of hate media. In The media and the Rwandan genocide. New York: Pluto Press.

Linnaeus, C. (1758). *System of a nature*. Laurentius Salvius.

McCombs, M. E., & Shaw, D. L. (1972). The agenda-setting function of mass media. *Public Opinion Quarterly*, *36*(2), 176. doi:10.1086/267990

McDonald, D. O., & Jacobs, S. (2005). (Re)Writing xenophobia: Understanding press coverage of cross-border migration in Southern Africa. *Journal of Contemporary African Studies*, *23*(3), 295–325. doi:10.1080/02589000500274050

Mogekwu, M. (2017). *The media's role in stoking xenophobia*. Available at https://worldpolicy.org/2017/04/26/the-medias-role-in-stoking-xenophobia

Mohammed, O. A. (2011). *Xenophobia and media: An exploratory study on the public perceptions of the Nelson Mandela bay community*. Nelson Mandela Metropolitan University.

Nord, L. W., & Stromback, J. (2006). Reporting more, informing less: A comparison of the Swedish media coverage of September 11 and the wars in Afghanistan and Iraq. *Journalism: Theory, Practice and Criticism, 7*(1), 85-110.

Nwokora, L. N. (2000). *Culture, literature and nationalism.* Snaap.

Odanwu, K. O. C., & Chukwuma, J. N. (2019). Philosophical inquiry into the question of the indissolubility of Nigeria. In A. S. Ihuah, A. Idachaba, & M. I. Shenge (Eds.), *Philosophy, security and the challenge of development in Africa.* Eagle Prints Nigeria.

Oduma, A. (2007). Reporting the facts and figures of violent conflicts: Implications for conflict management and peace building. In S. Abu & C. Best (Eds.), International Centre for Reconciliation. Coventry Cathedral, and Centre for Conflict Management and Peace Studies, University of Jos.

Ojie, P. (2020). Media construct and migration in modern Africa: The 2019 South Africa's xenophobia violence in perspective. In M. Michael, E. T. Aliegba, & A. A. Alagba (Eds.), *Human rights, religion and society: Festschrift for Rev. Fr. Prof. Jake Omang Otonko on his 60th Birthday.* Eiwa Press Nig. Ltd.

Okoye, J. I. (2011). 'Ethical issues in Nigerian media management. In I. S. Ndolo (Ed.), *Contemporary issues in communication and society.* Rhyce Kerex Publishers.

Onyido, J. A. (2018). Impact of xenophobia on Nigerian students in South Africa. *Brock Journal of Education, 6*(8).

Pogliano, P. (2017). *More multicultural than thou: The news paradigm and the Sjobo affair in the Swedish press.* Paper presented at the annual meeting of the International Communication Association, San Diego, CA.

Popkin, R. (1977-1978). Hume's racism. *The Philosophical Forum, 9*(2–3).

Raphael, N. S. (2015). *Ethno-religious conflicts, mass media and national development: The northern Nigeria experience* (Unpublished thesis). School of Postgraduate Studies, Department of Religion and Philosophy, Faculty of Arts, University of Jos, Jos.

Robert, O. S. (2015). *Iwali-Ebekwaraa: A socio-cultural and political institution of a royal female dancer and performer.* Paper presented at Mabel@50 Conference, Wuse II, Abuja.

Robert, O.S. (2020). Classical and contemporary leadership misdeeds thwarting Africa's development: Nigerian case. *International Journal of Academic Multidisciplinary Research, 4*(1).

Robert, O. S., & Besong, E. N. (2017). *Unresolved degenerating nat'l issues: Nigerian govt. & media's failure.* LAP Lambert Academic Publishing.

Robert, O.S., & Besong, E.N. (2016). Nigeria media and indigenous cultures transformation: The journey so far. *Journal of Mass Communication and Journalism, 6*(7).

Robert, O.S., Besong, E.N., &Dibie, G.A. (2016). Retracing our socio-cultural norms/values for a better African society. *International Journal of Humanities and Social Sciences, 2*(4).

Serequeberhan, T. (1991). African philosophy: The point in question. In T. Serequeberhan (Ed.), African philosophy: The essential reading (pp. 3–28). Paragon House.

Tafira, K. (2011). Is xenophobia racism? *Anthropology Southern Africa, 34*(3-4), 114–121. doi:10.1080/23323256.2011.11500015

Ugwu, A. K., & Ozoemena, L. C. (2019). Structuring ethnic agitation and the survival of democracy in Nigeria. In A. S. Ihuah, A. Idachaba, & M. I. Shenge (Eds.), *Philosophy, security and the challenge of development in Africa*. Eagle Prints Nigeria.

Umar, M. (2009). The broadcast media and conflict management in Nigeria. In J. Yoroms & A. Mu'azu (Eds.), Conflict management and the media in Nigeria. Centre for Research and Documentation (CRD).

Wakili, H. (2009). The press and ethno-religious conflicts in metropolitan Kano, 1991-2001. In Conflict management and the media in Nigeria. Centre for Research and Documentation (CRD).

Widfeldt, A. (2014). *Extreme right parties in Scandinavia*. Routledge. doi:10.4324/9780203403334

Yoroms, J. (2009). The state, the media and conflict management: A conceptual approach. In Conflict management and the media in Nigeria. Centre for Research and Documentation (CRD).

Yusuf, B. (1992). The mass media: The revolt of conscience. In T.A. Imobighe (Ed.), The politics of the second republic. National Institute for Policy and Strategic Studies.

Yusuf, B. (1994, Nov.). *Sensationalism and the mass media: A case study of Soft sell Magazines* (Dissertation). National Institute for Policy and Strategic Studies, Kuru.

Chapter 25
Radio Programmes for Youth Empowerment and National Development

Emmanuel Olukunle Olumuji
Chrisland University, Nigeria

Olufemi Sunday Onabajo
Chrisland University, Nigeria

ABSTRACT

Radio as a mass medium remains the most accessible, affordable, and flexible medium of mass communication in developing countries. Radio can persuade and effectively influence large audiences, thereby contributing substantially to nation building. Over the years, radio programmes have largely focused on entertainment, religious, and political matters. There is also a paucity of programmes on youth empowerment and national development. This chapter examined the availability of youth programmes on radio through assessment of selected programme formats to ascertain the shortfalls (if any) of these programmes in mobilising youths for youth empowerment and national development. The study has as its theoretical springboard development media theory and agenda setting theory. The chapter adopted survey method to assess programme formats of radio stations in Abeokuta, Ogun State and discovered the inadequacy of programmes on youth empowerment. It recommended strategies on how to improve and use the media for youth empowerment and national development.

INTRODUCTION

The media industry has experienced a continuous technological advancement in the 20th and 21st centuries, radio as a mass medium remains the most accessible, affordable and flexible medium of mass communication in developing countries. Radio can persuade and effectively influence large audience, thereby contributing substantially to the building of a national consensus. It is an effective tool for youth mobilization and behavioural change within a society.

DOI: 10.4018/978-1-6684-4107-7.ch025

Radio is now everywhere and has recently passed its 100th anniversary in providing information (Weisenhorn, Meyer, McGoff, & Rooney, 2021). It is accessible to the taxi driver in Lagos, the itinerant fisherman in waterside and the roving nomad behind his cattle; it can be made to cater to the needs of specialised, small targeted audience of artisans, fishermen, farmers, the rural poor, the urban destitute, the elderly, lactating mothers, children and youths especially (Soola, 2003; Ojebode, 2003). It remains the cheapest to buy and these days phones have inbuilt radio in them, everyone within a community can afford one. Its cost-effective characteristic makes it more accessible and an effective tool for community mobilization. Historically, it is used for information dissemination in rural communities (Weisenhorn *et al.*, 2021).

Radio's usefulness to bring the desired changes and development to communities depends largely on the type of programme packaged. Most radio programmes however are not designed to bridge the knowledge gap between the elite and masses, thereby relegating the role of the media to inform, educate and enlighten the masses.

Furthermore, radio programmes have largely focused on entertainment, religious and political matters, there is also paucity of programmes on youth empowerment and national development. This chapter examined the availability of youth programmes on radio through assessment of radio programmes to ascertain the shortfalls of programmes in addressing (idle) youths within a society to become self-reliant for youth empowerment and national development.

RADIO IN NIGERIA

Radio in Nigeria has come a long way and gone through a lot of changes, in trying to keep pace with the intricacies of an ever-changing society. The actual beginning of broadcasting in Nigeria was in 1932, when as part of an experiment by the British Broadcasting Corporation (BBC), Lagos was chosen, as one of the centres around the world, to receive and retransmit British empire service signals from Daventry, England. Then the Lagos station began to experiment with rediffusion service, under the supervision of engineers and technicians at the Posts and Telegraphs Department, who were also mandated to design a system for distributing the signals, to major population centres across the country. This relay system of the BBC, was replicated in mainly English-speaking countries across the globe and succeeded in taking BBC news and programmes to many parts of the world (Onabajo, 2000).

Although at inception, BBC programmes dominated the Nigerian airwaves, efforts were also made to produce programmes that the local population could relate to. These were programmes and news in three main Nigerian languages (Hausa, Igbo and Yoruba), as well as dialects. However, the Nigerian Broadcasting Service (NBS) which started in 1952 became the target of criticism, based on the dominance of BBC programs in its broadcast, and for what critics described as lacking the Nigerian orientation.

In May 1960, a radio station known as Western Nigeria Broadcasting Service (WNBS), according to Chief Awolowo, the then Premier of the Western Region, was to serve as teachers, entertainers and stimuli to all and to transform Nigeria into a modern and prosperous nation. The East and North soon copied the initiative of the West, with the establishment of the Eastern Nigeria Broadcasting Service and the Broadcasting Company of Northern Nigeria in 1960 and 1962 respectively.

The Broadcasting Organisation of Nigeria (BON) started in 1973 as a child of necessity. It was then aimed at bringing together the radio and television stations in the country, to pool resources for effective coverage of national and international events.

So far, Nigeria has over 400 radio stations which ownership ranges from federal/state government, commercial/private, campus to community radio stations.

RADIO PROGRAMME

Over the years, there have been several technological advancements in the field of mass communication, presently the internet is spearheading novel advancements with a large number of users and increase in the volume of information available around the world. Despite the technological advances, radio still remains the most accessible, affordable and flexible medium of communication in developing countries. Radio can be used not only to inform and educate the people but also to mobilize them to participate effectively in a development process.

Radio programmes should be packaged to suit the larger population of people in developing countries, by so doing, the illiterate and majority living below poverty can be reached with necessary information to empower, educate and subsequently breach the development gap between Africa and the rest of the world.

Weisenhorn *et al.*, (2021) affirms that radio is an impactful medium in learning skills and it has positive impact in educating the listeners. The use of radio for development purposes is rewarding especially when programmes are packaged to communicate how the rural dwellers can be empowered in carrying out craft and trade, proper hygiene, and efficient usage of technological devices and equipment made available to them by the government. The rural dwellers also need to know government policies, how it affects them and how best to maximize them for their benefits. There is also need for them to know their rights under the law to avoid ignorance and exploitation.

The culture of packaging radio programmes for the elites has to come to end if developing nations want to experience growth and national development, Soola (2003) notes that the mass media has being one of the causes of underdevelopment in that they serve not only to reinforce but also to perpetuate existing power relations and structures of inequality. Furthermore, in many developing countries, the media are concentrated in the capital cities and heavily populated areas and so radio programmes are produced and aired in English language to suit the elite class. Instead, radio (programme) should be purveyors of progress and a means of overcoming underdevelopment, these developmental programmes can be aired in indigenous languages to reach the illiterate and rural dwellers. Successful indigenous radio programmes usually must appeal to the interest and taste of the target audience. Programmes with high listenership are more likely to have a great impact on audience loyalty which may ellicit participation and eventually a change in attitude or behaviour.

Oso (2002) adds that in order to solicit participation from the target audience and to sustain the interest of the people in the programmes, programme producers must be emphatic; enter into the socio-cultural world of the people and such programmes should be a reflection of their social world. Some radio stations are becoming popular with indigenous programmes such as OGBC Morning Flight, *Sisi Ologe*, Health Matters, *E to mi labe ofin* and Splash FM's Man and the Law. Though such programmes have a wide range of listeners, some scholars have argued that education-entertainment strategies like radio soap operas, when infused in indigenous radio programmes are more likely to promote the desired social or individual change.

Manyozo (2008) avers that the effectiveness of a radio campaign in influencing individual self-efficacy and behaviour change depends greatly on respondents' ability to recall specific messages, since this is what motivates them to change their behaviour. In other words, listening to indigenous radio programme once or more per week appears to have a stronger impact on the respondent behaviour and is capable of contributing more to the project than having heard the radio campaign once.

THEORETICAL SCAFFOLDING

This chapter is anchored on Development Media Theory and Agenda Setting Theory

Development Media Theory

The Development Media Theory was propounded by Dennis McQuail in 1987 to provide rationale and approach on how to use the media for the development of rural or underdeveloped societies. The theory seeks to explain the normative behaviour of the press in developing countries. The media have a role to play in facilitating the process of development in the developing countries (Asemah, 2011). The media are agents of development and social change in any community which can be used to complement government's efforts in carrying out programmes that will lead to positive behavioural change among the youths and the society at large.

The basic assumptions of the theory as identified by Anaeto, Onabajo and Osifeso (2008) are:

- The media should accept and carry out positive developmental tasks in line with nationally established policy.
- Freedom of the media should be open to restriction according to economic priorities and developmental needs of society.
- Media should give priority in their content to the national culture and languages.
- Media should give priority in news and information to link with other developing countries, which are close geographically, culturally or politically.
- Journalists and other media workers have responsibilities as well as freedom in their information gathering and dissemination task.
- In the interest of development ends, the state has a right to intervene in, or restrict media operation and devices and direct control can be justified.

Many media scholars have expressed concern over McQuail's point, which justifies the right of the state to intervene in the interest of development. But it is also worthy of note that at the time of formulating the theory, many of the developing countries in which the theory was designed to benefit were said to be characterised by autocratic and monarchical governments. Anaeto & Anaeto (2010) avers that McQuail did not envisage the widespread enthronement of democracies that many developing countries are now witnessing. Hence the development media theory as proposed then reflected the autocratic nature of the developing countries with little reference to the impending democratic political pluralism.

The theory may have lacked future prediction to the impending democratic political pluralism the developing countries are now facing, it is according to some scholars still anchored on communication for development which sees the mass media as ready to champion the social, economic, and political developments of the developing nations. Anaeto *et al.* (2008), clarified that the development media theory has already provided bearing for the concepts of development communication and development journalism; noting that there is no element in the origin, basis and principle of the Development Media

Theory that should be interpreted as shielding media and journalists from social responsibility or ousting the concept of press freedom.

However, this study seeks to examine radio progrmmes for national development. The use of the development media theory in this study will expose how radio programmes can be used by the media to mobilise audience to become empowered and informed, thereby complementing and assisting in the government's effort for national development.

Agenda Setting Theory

Agenda setting dates back as far back as 1922, when Walter Lippmann, a newspaper columnist was concerned that the media had the power to present images to the public. The mass media attracts the public's attention to certain issues. The media presents what the public should think about, know about, and feels about. However, it was Maxwell McCombs and Donald Shaw (1972) that put the phenomenon that other researchers referred to, to better perspective and made popular the term agenda setting. Anaeto, Onabajo & Osifeso (2008) identified the basic assumption of the theory as:

- The mass media, such as the press, do not reflect social reality because news is filtered, chosen and shaped by newsroom staff or broadcaster.
- People get their news from limited sources because people do not pay attention to all outlets; thus, they rest on the mass media.
- Few media agenda, which are chosen by professional gatekeepers, lead people to perceive given issues as important

The media should accept and carry out positive developmental tasks in line with the policies and plans of the government. The mass media have the power to increase levels of importance assigned to issues by either increasing the salience of issues or framing them in a particular way. With these subtle changes in the description of a recurrent programme, the situation may affect audience to interpret the situation in a particular way.

The media, especially radio plays a vital role in the transmission of attitudes, beliefs and perception among people in the rural areas. It has become the greatest single catalysts of our mind shift since it has the power to set agenda by telling us what to think about.

The time given to a particular programme determines audience exposure to such programme.

METHODOLOGY

This chapter is a survey of radio stations in Abeokuta, Ogun State. A self-generated list of FM radio stations in Abeokuta was used for this study, a total number of eight FM radio stations constituted the population for this study.

Two radio stations were selected based on the factors and characteristics they possess. This is in agreement with Wimmer & Dominick (2006) who observed that a purposive sampling includes subjects selected on the basis of specific characteristics or qualities and eliminates those which fail to meet these criteria.

Table 1. List of radio stations in Abeokuta

S/N	Name	Frequency	Ownership
1.	Family FM Radio	88.5	Private
2.	Ogun State Broadcasting (OGBC) FM	90.5	Government
3.	Paramount FM	94.5	Government
4.	Root FM	97.1	Private
5.	Rock City FM	101.9	Private
6.	Splash FM	106.7	Private
7.	Sweet FM	107.1	Private
8.	Fresh FM	107.9	Private

OGBC FM 90.5 was selected because it is a government owned station and its transmission covers Abeokuta and beyond. Splash FM 106.5 is a privately owned station with good coverage in Abeokuta and some other parts of Ogun State. The report of this study was based on the information gathered from the radio stations and available statistics from other reliable studies and media houses.

The programme schedule for the two selected stations were obtained, it was then categorized under nine different formats, this enabled the authors determine the frequency and percentage of each programme format.

Radio Programmes

Table 2. A week radio programmes in government owned station (OGBC FM)

Programme Format	Frequency	Percentage
Children	4	1.4%
Education	17	5.9%
Enlightenment/Empowerment	46	16.0%
Music/Entertainment	19	6.6%
News and Current Affairs	103	35.8%
Politics	7	2.4%
Sports	15	5.2%
Religious	75	26.0%
Youths	2	0.7%
Total	**288**	**100%**

The frequency of programmes in government owned radio station for a week is presented in Table 2. Findings indicate that the frequently aired programmes were: news and current affairs (35.8%), religious (26.0%) and enlightenment/empowerment (16.0%). Youths' programmes (0.7%) and children programmes (1.4%) are the least broadcasted programmes. The implication of this result in relation to enlightenment and empowerment programmes which are the focus of this study is that this programme format is the

Table 3. A week radio programmes in private owned station (Splash FM)

Programme Format	Frequency	Percentage
Children	1	0.8%
Education	2	1.6%
Enlightenment/Empowerment	3	2.4%
Music/Entertainment	39	31.8%
News and Current Affairs	51	41.5%
Politics	0	0%
Sports	17	13.8%
Religious	10	8.1%
Youths	0	0%
Total	**123**	**100%**

third position for the most frequently broadcasted radio programme in government owned radio station. Enlightenment and empowerment programmes are aired 46 times out of 288 programme formats which represent 16% of the total programmes in view.

Table 3 showed radio programmes for a week in private owned station. The result indicates that the regularly aired programmes were: news and current affairs (41.5%), music/entertainment (31.8%) and sports (13.9%). Youths' programmes and political programmes have no scheduled slot. This result in relation to enlightenment and empowerment programmes which are the focus of this study is that this programme format is neither the most frequently nor the least broadcasted radio programme. Enlightenment and empowerment programmes are aired only three times out of 123 programme formats which represent 2.4% of the private radio station. The low priority given to empowerment programmes by producers and private radio proprietors give one cause for worry because Nigeria is a developing nation and there is need to prioritize enlightenment and empowerment programmes if radio is to play its part/role in national development.

DISCUSSION OF FINDINGS

A perusal of programme formats of government-owned radio stations showed minimal impact of enlightenment/empowerment programme with frequency of dissemination being 16.0% while youth programmes stood at 2.0%. For a private radio station (Splash FM) the frequency of information dissemination of enlightenment/empowerment programmes was 2.4% while that of youth programme recorded 0%.

The understanding here is that government radio stations at 16% frequency showed more commitment to that of private radio stations. This would be understood from the point of view that government as a political party showed some commitments in catering for the interest of some of its citizens, while private radio stations recorded 0% in the frequency of transmitting youth programmers. There are possible explanations:

1. Government is no longer alive to its responsibilities of catering for the interest of its citizens because government radio stations are grossly underfunded.
2. Both government and private radio stations are now into stiff competitions for scarce adverts and programme sponsorship.
3. The axiom 'whoever pays the piper dictates the tunes' is applicable to both government and private radio and since both stations share common audience, the audience has become king and they choose the programme to listen to and those to shun.
4. Proragmme format with more audience appeal (news and current affairs 51%, music and entertainment played out at 31.8%) like news and entertainment have come into the front burner in private radio stations.
5. For government radio stations, news and current affairs appear to be the most favoured programme at 35.8% while enlightenment/empowerment programmes polled 16%.
6. Private radio stations are not into research which revealed lack of patronage of enlightenment programme (2.4%) and youth programme 0.0%.

CONCLUSION

From the figures arrived at by this study, it may be expedient to arrive at the following conclusion.

- Government of Ogun State has not been forthcoming in recognizing its priorities and deploying the appropriate media to meet these perceived needs.
- Media as the fourth estate of the realm have not been given its pride of place in disseminating radio programme that will aid youth empowerment for national development. Government should not spare expenses in information dissemination. Apart from appropriately funding its media outlets, it should also give grants to private media organisations in its domain so as to flow in the same wavelength.
- It was observed that the Agenda Setting Theory of Press has not been reactivated by both government and private radio stations as they are working at cross purpose. While it is legitimate to make money on investment, in the final analysis whatever happens to the media will reflect development indices of the citizens either positively or negatively.
- If the audience shows propensity for news dissemination and current affairs, then rural radio that will disseminate news for rural development will be the option to take.

RECOMMENDATION

As a fall-out of the research above and consequent conclusions, the following recommendations are being made.

1. The Ministry of Information should get involved in periodic research to ascertain the media needs of its citizens and sponsor production of programmes in the appropriate areas of needs. This is in accordance with the Development Media Theory which solicits the working together of both government and private radio stations for the common good of the citizens.

2. Since the audience need the media for information to gratify their needs, there should be an integral relationship among audiences, media and the larger social system. Here the government can mobilise all relevant stakeholders to participate in identifying the needs of common and shared audience in the area of need gratifying.
3. The more media an individual has for gratifying needs, the less dependent he or she will become on any single medium. Here a multi-media approach to disseminating information is advocated.
4. Whatever media approach is designed by stakeholders, the culture of the people should be significantly recognized and integrated.

REFERENCES

Anaeto, S. G., & Anaeto, M. S. (2010). Evaluating McQuail's mormative theory of developing countries. In D. Wilson (Ed.), *Perspectives on Communication and Culture*. African Council for Communication Education.

Anaeto, S. G., Onabajo, O. S. & Osifeso, J.B. (2008). *Models and theories of communication.* African renaissance Books Incorporated.

Asemah, S. E. (2011). Selected mass media themes. Jos University Press.

Dominick, J. R. (2009). *The dynamics of mass communication, media in the digital age* (10th ed.). McGraw Hill Companies.

Manyozo, L. (2008). *Communicating with radio what do we know? Findings from selected rural radio effectiveness evaluations*. Farm Radio International.

McCombs, M., & Shaw, D. (1972). The agenda setting function of mass media. Public Opinion Quarterly, 30(6), 2. doi:10.1086/267990

McQuail, D. (1979). The influence and effect of mass media. In *Mass Communication and Society*. Sage Publication.

Ojebode, O. (2003). Radio as a development communication medium: Types, format, roles and limitations. In E. O. Soola (Ed.), *Communicating for Development Purposes*. Kraft Books Limited.

Onabajo, O. S. (2000). *Fundamentals of broadcast journalism*. Gabi Concept Limited.

Soola, E. O. (2003). Development communication: The past, the present and the future. In E. O. Soola (Ed.), *Communication for Development Purposes*. Kraft Books Limited.

Weisenhorn, J., Meyer, M. H., McGoff, R., & Rooney, T. (2021). Weekly question-and-answer extension radio show helps listeners adopt environmentally sound horticulture practices. *Horticulturae*, *7*(72), 7040072. doi:10.3390/horticulturae7040072

Chapter 26
Queen Bee and Her Female Subordinate in Ifeoma Okoye's "Between Women": An Intra-Gendered Discourse

Ebele Peace Okpala
Nnamdi Azikiwe University, Awka, Nigeria

ABSTRACT

A significant number of studies have proven that women in the African cultural milieu are not only the oppressed but also are the sustainers of their own oppression. Some scholars have captured the prevalent crisis between wives and their mothers in law. Not much, however, has been written on abhorring intragender relationships between some female domestic servants and their mistresses. Using the content analysis approach of qualitative research method and the theory of Focu feminism, the chapter, therefore, studies Ifeoma Okoye's "Between Women" to highlight the daily routine activities of the domestic servant, her working hours, feeding pattern, and remuneration. These may provide insights into the type of relationships that exist between the mistress and her domestic servant. The study reveals that a desired gender justice has not been achieved. The mistress has not used her good offices to foster a fellow woman. It recommends a more harmonious intragender co-existence amongst women.

INTRODUCTION

In most patriarchal societies, the best liabilities of women incorporate giving, securing and nursing first their young siblings, their life partner, their children and grandchildren. Inconsequential female seldom participates collectively; one lady's prosperity carries little advantage to the female community. High accomplishing ladies have minimal motivator to put resources into different ladies, so most ladies benefit from rebuffing endeavoring peers (Benenson,2003). She also maintained that apart from a few selected friends, ladies are prime contenders for physical assets, mates or statuses. Do women really underestimate their fellow women? Or then again would they say they are being used? What is the relationship

DOI: 10.4018/978-1-6684-4107-7.ch026

between effective female managers and their subordinates? Do some female leaders depict queen bee disposition? What is a queen bee syndrome all about?

Some psychologists at the University of Michigan allude to ladies in an important or influential position, who treat other female subordinate more critically, as sovereign queen bees. "Sovereign queen bee", is commonly used to refer to a grown-up female honey bee that lives in a hive, generally the mother of the multitude of honey bees in the bee hive. It is uncommonly taken care of to turn out to be physically mature. A lady who acts as though she is the main individual in a specific field is likewise considered a queen bee. For example, Margaret Thatcher, the U. K's first female Prime Minister has been presumed a sovereign queen bee for not promoting the profession of ladies in her bureau. Rather than going about as coaches, some effective female supervisors pull up the stepping stool behind them on the grounds that, most likely, they see different ladies as threats. An effective lady, who doesn't utilize her great workplaces to help ladies advance or sabotages her female partners, is a sovereign queen bee. Sovereign been practices are generally set off in male dominated societies in which women are debased (BBC News, 2018).

Baykal et al (2020), in their research "Queen Bee Syndrome: A Modern Dilemma of Working Women and its Effects on Turnover Intentions", examine the Turkish white-collar women workers and the possible effect of queen bee syndrome on turnover intentions. The person-organization fit theory is adopted for the study. The research reveals that the queen bees consciously stay away from the female subordinates and make life and workplace environment difficult for them. They conclude that queen bee attitudes result to higher levels of inconveniences that may lead to turnover intentions (p.175). Despite the findings, Baykal et al (2020), however, add that not all women in leadership positions are queen bees. They maintain that "some women in higher management positions promote and motivate subordinate women and they serve as a role model for them" (p.167). In most African societies for instance, gender stereotypes suggest leadership to be a masculine and unfeminine trait (Baird, 1976). At times similar leadership style may be evaluated differently for men and women (Bartol and Butterfield, 1976). Based on some of these skewed perceptions, some high-achieving women who display "extreme competence or success in their professional sphere" may be tagged queen bees. It may be necessary to note that" a successful performance of women (as a typically male task) is not primarily attributed to their ability but to chances, extraordinary effort or even cheating, whereas men with the same achievement are simply seen as competent" (Deaux, 1976, p.318). The average female boss is afraid of being thought weak or seen as a woman rather than a boss. She detests being perceived with feminine traits who unlike the male boss is expected to be understanding and compassionate. Males seem to be rated higher for leadership (Rosen et al, 1973) even when the women's leadership qualities are more favorable. The female bosses have higher expectations for effective and successful leadership (Garland et al, 1982) and as a result, they tend to "display such stereotypically masculine behaviors" (Baril et al, 1989). This may be why, (Rosen and Jerdee, 1973) feels that the evaluation of female leaders is purely based on expectations and perceptions.

The above assumptions, nevertheless, are refuted by (Sobczak 2018) in her research "The Queen Bee Syndrome. The Paradox of Women Discrimination on the Labor Market". She argues that queen bee phenomenon is prevalent. The queen bees, according to her, exhibit similar patterns of behaviors; behaving more like men by being domineering, and emphasizing how they are different from other women (p.57). She laments that the queen bee syndrome leads to gender discrimination in the workplace. The queen bees have weak bonds with their female subordinate and like to fraternize more with the women in high-ranking positions (Shepperd and Aquino, 2013). In confirmation, Cawon et al, 1998, support that "queen bees hold a competitive attitude towards other women and see them as a threat to their success" (p.280).

Queen bee syndrome was first introduced in 1973 by G. Staines, C. Tavris and T.E. Jayaratne who describe queen bees

as professional women who have secured positions in male-dominated setting ....

These women manifest anti-feminist behaviors towards female colleagues. They are individualistic decision makers and tend to hoard information and isolate themselves with female colleagues, thereby thwarting potential competition for their positions. (p.55-56).

Unlike male managers, queen bees may not be willing to assist the female subordinates for their career advancement. (Derks et al, 2017). The female assistants, most times, seem to receive negative feedback from their female bosses (Ely, 1994). The queen bee is usually "constructed as a bitch who stings other women if her power is threatened and ... blames individual women for not supporting other women" (Marvin,2008, p. 75).

A significant number of researches prove that women employees, who are exposed to queen bee's hostilities display symptoms of depression, low productivity and intention to leave the company (Derks et al 2016). Men have been reported by (Ibarra, 1992) to promote and encourage women more than women in management. To buttress this assertion, (Kahn, 1984) reveals that young females experience more hostility toward female leaders than male leaders. The female leaders who are aggressive, selfish, insensitive, power-hungry and obstruct other women's career advancement (Zhao and Foo, 2016) are queen bees.

The role of men may not matter in the queen bee condition, the central issue is the connection between the apparent female conduct qualities and the absence of portrayal at the highest point of the board. The study is designed to deviate from the conventional discourses of inter-gender tyranny of women by men and redirect scholarly scrutiny to intra-gender subjugation. The book, *Bridging the Gap Between Philosophy, Media and Development in Developing Countries,* is a suitable platform for this study to project the ever prevalent but scarcely discussed intra-gender cruelty and also convey the ideological concepts that most of the traditional structures that induce intra- gender aggressions are Africa based. The media has unarguably made a significant impact on the various forms of discrimination and subjugation of women in most developing countries. The media has not only provided public awareness/enlightenment but also has drawn the attentions of both the government and non-governmental organizations/foundations on female marginalization. In Nigeria, for example, organizations like; FIDA (Federal International De Abogadas which is International Federation of Women Lawyers), GEM (Gender Equality Movement), NCWS (National Council of Women's Society), (Women Trafficking and Child Labor Eradication Foundation) (Lewis 2015), among others, aimed to promote equality and advancement of all persons especially women in African countries, were formed. The chapter may posit a compelling assertion that women are both the oppressed and the agents of their own oppression. The representation of this true state of affairs within the women-folk in the media, hopefully, may raise gender discussions and provide impetus for generating postulations on gender issues and identities in African consciousness.

FOCU FEMINISM

The theoretical premise of this study is hinged on the Focu Feminism which is formulated by Onyeka Iwuchukwu in 2015. The new brand of feminism proposes the requirement for every lady to zero in on herself for freedom from perceived oppression. Iwuchukwu accepts it is a panacea for self-declaration and self-completion for Nigerian women. It disproves the idea of accusing men, patriarchy and tradition as the just and significant wellspring of female abuse. She brings up that the feminists' criticism ought to be diverted to the genuine adversary which is simply the one who takes cover behind the veil of culture or show to legitimize her activities (Okpala, 2019).

Traditionally, the women's position in any case, as a peasant isn't in question. A girl child is continually reminded to comport herself well and is restricted in her longing to investigate her current circumstance. A male kid is preferred and given advantages. At the public level additionally, a lady despises the right and advantages of a resident on equivalent premise with her male partners particularly as far as arrangements to different political positions. These highlight the abuse of ladies by men, yet Iwuchukwu questions the role of ladies in the oppression of fellow women. What number of ladies supports a lady in governmental issues who chooses to compete for an elective post? When a lady prevails through difficult work in a picked vocation, do individual ladies not attribute it to "base power" and consider such a lady to be a stooge? She laments that ladies will more often than not debase and underestimate themselves. A few ladies structure associations that mirror their spouses' elevated social situations and are proud as appendages to their husbands. Instances of such affiliations are Police Officers' Wives Association, Army Officers' Wives Association, Legislators' Wives Association and so forth. Such ladies depict that their characters, self-esteem and nobility radiate from being the spouses of administrators, police or armed force officials.

A few ladies utilize their sex as modest coercion. Ladies once in a while make statements like: Is this because I am a lady? Don't you realize that you are talking with someone's wife? It is a reasonable support and induction of an inferior subordinate position just as the way that the lifted-up position of a lady comes from being a spouse and not from her capacities and abilities personally. At any smallest incitement, a few ladies shed tears and guarantee they are abused on the grounds that they are ladies. Such ladies have likewise underestimated and debased themselves and subsequently reserve no option to say they are being marginalized.

Iwuchukwu demands that the feminists' battle for privileges ought to likewise be stretched out to ladies who run down individual ladies. Although the socio-cultural oppressive structures in most cases are entrenched in society, yet ladies are typically the specialists for execution. There are different types of persecution, damage and oppression by ladies against ladies that are neither systematized nor constrained on ladies by men, culture or religion. For example, who powers the harsh and some of the time despising connections a few ladies have with their house maids, sisters, mothers, daughters, sisters-in-law, mothers-in-law? Should men, custom or male-controlled society be considered answerable for these? (Iwuchukwu, 2016) portrays that "a lady is generally answerable for most broken homes either as a mother-in-law, sister-in-law or the other lady outside, who edges herself in eventually"(p.13). A few ladies are sustainers of disgraceful and abusive variables against different ladies either as essential specialists, schemers or willing instruments. The fact that none of the various shades of feminist theories tackle the role of women in the apparent oppression resulted to the introduction of focu-feminism.

It posits that maltreatment is maltreatment, subjugation is subjugation and persecution is persecution. None is better than the other. The concept of focu-feminism will in general decrease intra-gender oppression to the barest minimum. It hypothesizes that the general public is dynamic and societies advance as they go through change. This implies that the offensive social practices will ultimately disappear.'' The woman is enjoined to ... journey into self, see what fruit it bears (because) true knowledge lies deep within the self"(Iwuchukwu,2016). This excursion into self will improve the lady's comprehension of her qualities and shortcomings, to acknowledge what her identity is, the thing that she needs, what she can do to have the option to confront her difficulties and succeed. Every lady's abuse is unconventional and ought to be tended to in an unexpected way. Every woman ought to in this way attempt to recognize her difficulties first and devise endurance methodologies. She ought to likewise study the disposition of her oppressors to enable emancipation.

Focu-feminism counters co-operation in the drive for ladies liberation, not just that it has the capability of being undermined by certain ladies to take advantage of others, but since challenges vary and hence nobody's idea can deal with every one of the issues influencing ladies in their different homes, work places and communities. It is hard to make a monolithic voice for the expression of the female experience. Rather than trusting that a women's activist development will help, every lady should attempt to distinguish her concerns and tackle it dependent on her capacities and conditions. In case every woman takes care of business, the family would be correct and the country would be better since her prosperity and that of her family lay decisively on her shoulders. The arrangement lies in the capacity of every lady to set out to work for her advancement and the well-being of individuals around her.

Focu-feminism considers positive bonding accentuated by womanism to be impractical in an exceptionally capitalist society. It contends that no sure holding can undoubtedly exist between rich ladies and their more unfortunate partners, rural and urban women, junior and senior women members of staff, the mistress and her maid, police/armed force officials' wives and the wives of ordinary ranks to make reference but a few. There might be nonetheless, at one point or the other, where a lady needs a support of different ladies.

On the issue of equality of men with women, Iwuchukwu counters that there can never be any sort of equivalence among people or between any two individuals. A man is a man and a lady, a lady. There are things a man can do and a lady can't do as well as the other way around. The attention on balance ought to be on explicit issues, for example, advancement to higher posts in associations, portrayal in government, and arrangement to higher positions dependent on merit and not on gender.

Iwuchukwu sums up that it is troubling that women experience the ill effects of different structures, shades, shapes and extents of subjugation, which don't come from men and institution alone; but also, from ladies who some of the time are the culprits of these acts as essential specialists or willing instruments. Female marginalization by females is pretty much as agonizing as some other type of oppression. Sadly, the African feminists' critics seem to neglect it. This issue has not been explicitly handled and the results of the offensive wrongdoing will more often than not hold long time adverse consequences on the unprotected victims. She suggests that women ought to set out on some cash yielding ventures to help them. The incredible requirement for self-affirmation and strengthening will upgrade her freedom. Finally, focu-feminism highlights the requirement for ladies to take care of their homes.The theory centers around self, if each woman focuses around her, attempts self-assessment and soul-search and pursues her well-being and that of other women, female subjugation may be minimized.

SYNOPSIS OF "BETWEEN WOMEN"

"Between Women" is one of the short stories contained in Ifeoma Okoye's *The Trial and Other Stories*. The book is mainly a revelation of the plights of the widows in African cultural milieu, Eastern part of Nigeria to be precise. The widows are compelled by the auspices of tradition to go through excruciating widowhood rites. The rites may require the widow to shave her hair, clad herself in white or black from head to toe throughout the mourning period, which may last for six months or one year. She may also be required to drink the water used in washing the corpse of her late husband to prove that she had in no way contributed to his death (Ibezim,2010). This is mostly common in most traditional societies which firmly uphold the belief that according to Afigbo (1986), no death, especially of a man, is accepted as a natural or biological end (p.40), hence every widow is a prime suspect. The customary law has also permitted certain male members of the family to inherit the widow of the deceased. The widow inheritance is a form of slavery and this however, bounces back on men's perception of women in patriarchal society, as property or things and accessories (Justina Okoye,2017).

In "Between Women", (Okoye,2005) presents a young widow, Ebuka, who has taken a job of domestic servant at the Edets in Enugu. Being an orphan, she leaves her five-year old daughter Amara, with her mother-in-law. She would have loved to stay with her child but Mrs. Edet insists that her job will suffer. Ebuka is twenty-two years old, she lives in Edets' domestic workers' quarters. She has been working for the Edets for two years without "annual leave or even a day off" (p.15), to enable her visit her daughter. She has severally requested Mrs. Edet for a permission to visit her family but to no avail. She has pleaded to be allowed to travel on Saturday to come back on Sunday.

Ebuka has no other choice than to stay back owing to the fact that she needs the salary for the upkeep of her family, moreover, getting another job is not easy as she has little education and no skills. She had tried plaiting women's hair in the village, but that did not fetch her enough money to take care of her child. Enugu or any other big town could have guaranteed a better pay but cost of accommodation threw the idea off.

One day, Dorcas, her Aunty, who lives in remote part of Enugu brings her news from the village that Amara is ill and has been referred from the village hospital to Abakiliki- a bigger hospital. Ebuka's attentions as well as funds are needed urgently. Her Aunty emphasized; "Your mother-in-law is now at Abakiliki hospital with her. She needs help in looking after Amara. She needs money too. And urgently … you must go to Abakiliki tomorrow" (p.23).

She meets Mrs. Edet in the evening and pleaded with her to permit her to go and see her sick child in the hospital. She vehemently refuses to grant the request. Ebuka concluded to take the bull by the horn. She packs all her belongings in a plastic shopping bag and sneaks out of the compound at about five-thirty in the morning before the Edet family wakes up.

INTRA-GENDER RELATIONSHIP BETWEEN THE MISTRESS AND HER DOMESTIC SERVANT

Okoye's significant point is to depict the difficulty of widows in South Eastern Nigeria and likely prompt insightful consideration. The majority of what widows go through are normally connected with custom, religion or male-controlled society. Okoye, very much like most female writers, projects socio-cultural and male-initiated persecution as fundamental to the propagation of female oppression. Mistreatment of the widows by the way of life, custom, religion and men isn't in question. Ibezim (2010) places that, there is not really any ethnic group in Nigeria that doesn't expose the widow to one dehumanizing condition or the other. The thing that matters is said to lie in the gravity of the technique which fluctuates from one culture to another. (Ezeifeka and Ogbazi,2014) additionally observe that the social unfairness would be a peculiarity for the widower (p.3). They reason that the opposite terms of widow and widower regarding lady and men separately appear to have a place with the arrangement of such polar terms where one of the terms serve just nomenclatural function. This is on the grounds that the widowers are not exposed to such practices and preliminaries by cultural standards and value systems. Men are totally liberated from these corrupting and brutal practices.

The study tries to investigate how ladies receive these widows, particularly the more youthful ones in their work environments and communities. What do ladies do about widow's challenges? Do they show love or sympathy understanding that they might be in a comparative position sometime in the future? How do exceptionally positioned ladies utilize their workplaces to lighten the weights of widows in Nigerian conventional society, where widowhood, according to (Ezejiofor, 2011) isn't just seen as a condition of being nevertheless more significantly as an organization. When we consider the lot of ceremonies and practices along with the guidelines and inconveniences that accompany it, we will discover that widowhood is pretty much an institution deciphered and comprehended with regards to the way of life and custom of individuals which control its activities (p.140).

Patriarchy, has unarguably been pinpointed as the repetitive decimal that subject ladies to an inferior status. (Okoye, 2005) has written to demonstrate that a few widows can work on something for themselves to tackle a portion of their problems. Ebuka, the protagonist in "Between Women" is a young widow of twenty-two years. She takes up a task of a domestic worker in Enugu at the Edets. She resides in their domestic workers' quarters while Mr and Mrs. Edet and children live in the "main house, a bungalow built for the white administrators that worked in the country before it became independent'' (p.16). The couple is introduced as truly comfortable, living in Fox road- Government Residential Area, a part of Enugu that taxi drivers were not quick to ply on the grounds that the greater part of the families living there had their own vehicles (p.21).

Ebuka would have been considered as extremely fortunate working in such a home. What is the relationship between the domestic worker and her employee? The author cautiously eliminates Mr. Edet from the picture. There is no spot in the story where he has anything to do with Ebuka. His wife is completely in control. Ebuka likewise doesn't consult him for anything. This gives adequate room for the researcher to completely analyze the intra-gender relationship between the madam and her homegrown worker.

Ebuka on account of her low level of education isn't generously compensated as her remuneration is described as "a pittance". What stressed Ebuka more than anything was cash. Her compensation was small and generally she had lain awake at night thinking about how to furnish her daughter with all she really needed (p. 22). Some domestic workers, however, are dealt with benevolent by some mistresses, but generally, domestic service has consistently been an uncertain living, as the homegrown worker could be terminated for any offense or misdemeanor (or defying house guidelines or displeases her mistress).

In spite of her pitiful compensation, Mrs. Edet's assumptions are excessively extraordinary for Ebuka to cope with. She wakes up by five a.m. and retires around eleven in the night every day. Her routine chores daily include: subsequent to clearing the rooms, she would give the kids their shower and their morning meal and afterward prepare them for school. After that she would give Mr and Mrs. Edet their breakfast. Mr. Edet generally went out first, taking the kids with him and dropping them at school while heading to work. Mrs. Edet left last as her work environment was not far away from Fox Street where they reside. Left alone in the house, she would then handle the remainder of her assignments: washing materials, going to market if need be, preparing lunch, (and later in the day, supper) and ironing the cloths she washed toward the beginning of the day. (p.17)

Ebuka is the cook, the steward, in fact the maid of all work. The responsibilities way her down. She feeds well indeed; she admits that madam doesn't investigate what and how she eats. The aunt ponders and questions: "Then what is eating you up? You're only twenty-two but you look as if you're already forty: why?" (p. 22). The question is a pointer. Ebuka works like an elephant, and procures like an insect. She is genuinely tormented. She has restless nights since her take-home can't deal with her nearby requirements. She has a lone kid who is only five years, yet her pay can't enhance her child's social, emotional and cognitive well-being. Ebuka is thus really discouraged, stressed and disappointed that nothing can make her look healthy regardless of all that she eats.

Nnaemeka's attestation, that persecution of ladies isn't just a masculine's flaw as certain women's activists guarantee, but that is additionally involves women on women violence (1998), is affirmed in the coalition between Mrs. Edet and Ebuka. Mrs. Edet sadly, is constantly battered by her husband. Usually after her fight, "Mrs. Edet would direct her unspent anger and residual aggression" (p. 16) to Ebuka. This is in accordance with the perspective on certain researchers that queen bee practices are more pervasive in male centric social orders where ladies are persecuted. The debased ladies tend to become "forceful, hazardously aggressive and uncompromisable unbiased" (Amuluche-Greg Nnamani, 2010). Mrs. Edet, at times, could be extremely unforgiving. For example, she tosses a serrated table knife at Ebuka giving her a profound cut close to her eyebrow. Dorcas' disillusionment is featured in her conversation with Ebuka:

Did I hear you right? Dorcas asked. The woman threw a knife at you? And you're still here, Ebuka? Waiting for her to kill you? What did you do? Ebuka told her about the burnt eggs. Just that? ...Threw a knife at you just because the eggs got burnt? Does she know that you're a married woman just like her?... Well, I've never liked rich people. They treat orders like dirt. Instead of being kind to you, knowing your pathetic position, she's making things worse for you. (p.21)

It may be relevant to inquire if tradition or patriarchy should be blamed for this. The eggs were not really consumed because of Ebuka's indiscretion. The fault isn't exclusively hers. "She had hardly begun frying the eggs when she was asked to be quick with the eggs" (p.17). Ebuka increased the heat under the frying pan, and her madam called her...Fetch my black shoes from my bedroom... fetch my black handbag too... it's inside the wardrobe" (p.17). By the time Ebuka could run out from the room with the shoes and bag, the eggs had burnt.

The intra-gender relationship between Mrs. Edet and Ebuka is painstakingly characterized by the author's selection of words. "Mrs. Edet ordered her to be quick with the eggs". ... come here, Ebuka, Mrs. Edet ordered". "The ones with small golden bows, Mrs. Edet shouted as if Ebuka was hard of hearing"(p.17). The assertions above and the repetitive use of the word 'ordered', depict authoritative command that exist among bosses and the subordinates. The relationship can in no way, shape or form be cheerful. The unrivaled instruction is nothing but a decree. The last order must be complied. This may most likely be the reason Ebuka couldn't request to be allowed to wind down the cooker prior to hurrying to get the shoes and bag. Dorcas' question – Does she know that you're a married woman like her? (p.21) is extremely informational in a society where "women are indeed the scape goats of tradition"(Levin,1986).

Dorcas infers that Mrs. Edet ought to have realized that each lady is a victim of persecution in African social milieu. It is necessary therefore, that a fast move ought to be made on "a disturbing phenomenon of victims victimizing victims" (Mbye and Chan, 1987). African women ought to on the other hand, improve positive bonding. Mrs. Edet ought to be a sister's keeper and keep a sensible well-disposed relationship with Ebuka. The author uncovered the limitations and sufferings of widows allotted on them by the custom as well as by individual ladies. There is no question that some domestic servants might be apathetic and at times very mischievous and should be treated with iron hands. Ebuka is introduced as delight and child friendly. Regardless of Mrs. Edet's brutal attitude, she actually relates very well with her children as can be seen when they heard Ebuka's cry of agony:

Are you going to die, Ebuka? He asked. No Effiong, I am not going to die, Ebuka said and hugged the child. Effiong brought out his lunch pack from his bag and opened it. Take some of my biscuits, Ebuka, he said, you will feel better. Thanks, Effiong ...I'm already feeling better and the biscuits are for your lunch at school. Take just one, Effiong said in a tearful voice. Ebuka loved Mrs. Edet's children and Effiong best of all. The children love her too, and feel sad if she declined their offer to share with them their biscuits, sweets and ice cream... she took one biscuit from Effiong's packs. Thanks, Effiong, she said and popped the biscuit into her mouth. Just then Eno walked into the kitchen with a ward of cotton wool and a bottle of Dettol and Affi followed, carrying a roll of plaster.... (p.19)

The children's disposition portrays care, love, appreciation and acknowledgment of Ebuka as part of their family. However, Okoye completely prohibited Mr. Edet from the image yet his unnecessary silence is presently not brilliant. One considers what will cause him to disregard the plaster on Ebuka's eyebrow, on the grounds that following the kids dressed her injury, however unprofessionally, she serves Mr. Edet his breakfast. Nothing much is said about him except that he is a wife beater. Ebuka uncovers that:"Mrs. Edet often lied about cuts and bruises that resulted from her fights with her husband. I hit my head on the door, she once heard her lie to a friend after one of the fights" (p.21). The reasons behind the fight and battery are not portrayed, however, Nnaemeka accepts that the maltreatment of the female body is worldwide and ought to be considered and deciphered within the context of oppressive condition under patriarchy (1998).

Mrs. Edet, nonetheless, is portrayed as turning out to be more brutal, both verbally and physically. Ebuka turns out to be more scared of her. The most effective method to stop the brutality is beyond her imagination. "Crying bitterly to show Mrs. Edet the amount she has hurt her, sulking all day long, and refusing to eat for a day or two had not solved the problem" (p.19). This further portrays Mrs. Edet as a pitiless detached lady without an individual inclination. She passionately would not pay for Ebuka to gain proficiency with an ability like sewing or typing since who will go about her business while she is at seamstress's workshop? (p.22). She doesn't compensate her fairly; she denies her personals upliftment through helping her to learn a skill. As indicated by Dorcas, Mrs. Edet and her husband are adequately rich to employ a second individual to assist with the house work while Ebukais learning (p.22).

Mrs. Edet utilizes her power and influence as the madam of the house to humiliate her employee. She is presented as a lady with an independent mind, who chooses unreservedly what goes on between the family and the domestic worker. No one, as depicted in the realm of the text, interferes with her issues or choices as seen what Ebuka ought to perform as her responsibilities, when she ought to retire, and the amount she ought to be paid. Her attitude to Ebuka appears to exhibit her battle to transcend her oppression, battery, badgering and disdain by her husband. To effectively accomplish this, she assumes ideal responsibility for everything, concerning Ebuka – her time, opportunity, assets. She controls her, leaves her embarrassed and disappointed without regret. This is buttressed better in the accompanying exchange:

Please, Madam, she said, almost in a whisper, I want to go home tomorrow. Mrs. Edet slowly raised her head. You want to do what? I want to go to my village.... My daughter is in hospital. She is very ill.... But you told me your mother-in-law is looking after your daughter... why can't she look after her while she's in hospital? She needs help. The hospital doesn't give food to the patients. She needs helps with going to market and with cooking. I need you during the weekend... some women are coming here for a meeting on Sunday and I want you to cook some food for them. Please, madam, let me go home tomorrow after my work. I'll come back early on Sunday morning to do the cooking. You'll be going to market tomorrow morning to buy the things you'll cook on Sunday. Please, Madam. My mother-in-law needs money... Send the money through someone... There is nobody to send... I've been here for two years and I've not visited home. I've not seen my daughter for two years. Please, Madam, let me go to see her. Just for one day. No, Ebuka. Go back to work.... (p.23-24)

The above excerpt is a vivid reflection of a potential interaction between a slave and his/her lord. The frequent use of the expression "please Madam" is unmistakably suggestive that Ebuka isn't just in a disadvantaged position but also that her whole life and sustenance rely entirely upon her madam. Mrs. Edet attempts to affirm her power yet neglects to understand that everyone is extremely essential in all aspects of life. The interdependent nature of human beings is symbolized by the palm tree, which from top to bottom, has and produces all (Ojukwu,2014). Wozabia affirms:

...From leaves, to thatch, to shade, to broom. From fruit, to wine, to oil to kernel.... That is the palm. Each part has its own value and yet interdependent on all other parts. We all, men, women, child must be schooled to actualize these potentials for full benefit for all with none posing an obstacle to another, with the left hand washing the right, and the right hand, the left.... (Onwueme,1992, p.33)

Mrs. Edet is depicted asself-centered and lacks the capacity to deal with others. She has no compassion toward a debilitated kid whose mother works in her home. She isn't liberal, doesn't manage the affairs of her family well and won't aid in any house chores. Who can say for sure why she isn't cherished by her husband?

CONCLUSION

In line with focu feminism, women on women violence is evident in the relationship between Mrs. Edet and her domestic worker. Women are still subjected to humiliation by both men and fellow women. The action of Mrs. Edet may have been exaggerated, but the truth remains that she is ruthless in her dealings with Ebuka. Based on her state, as a young widow and orphan, Ebuka relies so much on her madam, hence vulnerable to exploitation. Her working hours and daily activities are not commensurate with her remuneration. She is denied both the freedom to visit and be visited. There is no law or any form of protection against abuse of domestic workers in their places of work. Mrs. Edet's children love Ebuka, but unfortunately, they are too tender to protect her interest. There is hardship, unemployment coupled with Ebuka's lack of skill acquisition or certificate; she is left with little or no choice. Tracing the roles of women in the text, Mrs. Edet, to a large extent, lends a support towards enhancing most of the factors that debase Ebuka. The unfair treatment given to her is, however, not glorified by the author, but she has not used her poetic license to address the predominant intra-gender brutality. The author has not also offered adequate poetic justice to put a check on further oppression of female domestic servants. Mrs. Edet is a representative of a queen bee who has not used her position to assist a poor widow, who is her subordinate.

The study is a clarion call for female solidarity. The "discovery of the deepening cracks in the walls of women alliances has exposed the need for a re-assessment of women's inter-personal interactions" (Utoh-Ezeajugh, 2015, p.151). The presentation of cold war, witch-hunting, gender jealousy, intimidation and coercion within the cult of womanhood, which undermine female assertiveness and justify the patriarchal dictatorship of women, deserve a wider pulicity. Awua (2010) sums that "it is only when women learn to understand, appreciate and love one another that they can redress the very many prejudices which have reduced them to second-class status" (p. 145).

REFERENCES

Afigbo, A. E. (1986). *An Outline of Igbo History. RAA*. Publishing Company.

Awua, B. (2010). Women on Women Violence: A Survey of Women Characters in Mairama Ba's So Long A Letter and Flora Nwapa's Efuru. In Gender Studies: A Reader (pp. 139–145). Great Publishers.

Baird, J. E. Jr. (1976). Differences in group communication: A review of relevant research. *The Quarterly Journal of Speech*, *62*(2), 180–192. doi:10.1080/00335637609383331

Baril, G.L. (1989). Are androgynous managers really more effective? *Group and Organizational Studies, 14*, 234-249.

Bartol, L. M., & Butterfield, D. A. (1976). Sex effects in evaluating leaders. *The Journal of Applied Psychology*, *61*(4), 446–454. doi:10.1037/0021-9010.61.4.446 PMID:947881

Baykal. (2020). *Queen Bee Syndrome: A Modern Dilemma of Working Women and its Effects on Turnover Intentions.* www.semanticscholar.org>papers

Benenson, J.F. (2013). The Development of Human Female Competition: Allies and Adversaries. *Philosophical Transactions of the Royal Society B Biological Sciences*, 1-11.

Bonjean, C. M. (1982). Sex and power in the federal bureaucracy: A comparative analysis of male and female supervisors. *Work and Occupations*, *9*(2), 233–254. doi:10.1177/0730888482009002005

Cowan, Neighbors, C., DeLaMoreaux, J., & Behnke, C. (1998). Women's hostility toward women. *Psychology of Women Quarterly*, *22*(2), 267–284. doi:10.1111/j.1471-6402.1998.tb00154.x

Deaux, K. (1976). *The behavior of women and men*. Brooks/Cole.

Derks, B. (2017). Queen bee syndrome, In The SAGE Encyclopedia of Industrial and Organizational Psychology (2nd ed.). Sage Publications.

Derks, B., Ellemers, N., van Laar, C., & de Groot, K. (2011). Do sexist organizational cultures create the Queen Bee? *British Journal of Social Psychology*, *50*(3), 519–535. doi:10.1348/014466610X525280 PMID:21884548

Derks, B., Van Laar, C., & Ellemers, N. (2016). The queen bee phenomenon: Why women leaders distance themselves from junior women. *The Leadership Quarterly*, *27*(3), 456–469. doi:10.1016/j.leaqua.2015.12.007

Ely, R. J. (1994). The effects of organizational demographics and social identity on relationships among professional women. *Administrative Science Quarterly*, *39*(2), 203–238. doi:10.2307/2393234

Ezeifeka, C., & Ogbazi, I. (2011, September). You're responsible for His Death: Widowhood in Igbo Gender Construction and Struggle for Agency in Selected Literary Texts. *International Journal of Languages and Literatures.*, *2*(3), 1–10.

Ezejiofor, A. O. (2011). Patriarchy, Marriage and the Rights of Widows in Nigeria. *Unizik Journal of Arts and Humanities*, *12*(1), 139–157. doi:10.4314/ujah.v12i1.9

Garland, H., Hale, K. F., & Burnson, M. (1982). Attributions for the success and failure of female managers: A replication and extension. *Psychology of Women Quarterly*, *7*(2), 155–162. doi:10.1111/j.1471-6402.1983.tb00827.x

Ibarra, H. (1992). Homophily and differential returns: Sex differences in network structure and access in an advertising firm. *Administrative Science Quarterly*, *37*(3), 422–447. doi:10.2307/2393451

Ibezim, E. (2010). Gender Discrimination Against Women. A focus on Widowhood Practices in Nigeria. In *Gender Studies: A Reader* (pp. 164–181). Great AP Express Publishers.

Iwuchukwu, O. (2016, Apr. 24). Women Empowerment is Key to Self-actualization Through Focu. *The Guardian*, p. 15.

Kahn, L. S. (1984). Group process and sex differences. *Psychology of Women Quarterly*, *8*(3), 261–281. doi:10.1111/j.1471-6402.1984.tb00636.x

Levin, T. (1986). Women as Scapegoats of Culture and Cult: An Activist's View of Female Circumcision in Ngugi's The *River Between*. In C. B. Caries & A. A. Graves (Eds.), *Ngambika Studies of Women in African Literature* (pp. 205–221). African World Press.

Mavin, S. (2008). Queen Bees, Wannabees and Afraid to Bees: No More "Best Enemies" for Women in Management? *British Journal of Management*, *19*(s1), 75–84. doi:10.1111/j.1467-8551.2008.00573.x

Mbye, B. C. (1987). Contemporary Society and the Female Imagination: A Study of the Novels of Mariama Ba. In *Women in African Literature Today* (pp. 89–101). African World Press.

Nnaemeka, O. (1998). *Sisterhood, Feminism and Power*. African World Press.

Ojukwu, C. (2014). The Politics of Power and the Struggle for Self-Assertion: Tess Onwueme's*The Reign of Wazobia,* AkachiAdimora-Ezeigbo's *Hands that Crush Stone* and Julie Okoh's *Edewede*. In E. A. Adedun & O. B. Nweke (Eds.), *New Perspectives on Literary Enigma* (pp. 315–335). University Press.

Okoye, I. (2005). *Between Women. In The Trial and Other Stories.* African Heritage Press.

Okoye, J. (2017). *The Woman Today: Viewing Her in African Literature in French.* Noben Press Ltd.

Okpala, E. P. (2019) *Intra-Gender Subjugation in Selected African Female Writers' Novels* [Unpublished doctoral dissertation]. Nnamdi Azikiwe University, Awka, Nigeria.

Onwueme, T. (1992). *The Reign of Wazobia.* Heinemann Plc.

Queen bees: Do Women Hinder the Progress of other Women? (2018). www.bbc.com-new

Rosen, B., & Jerdee, T. H. (1973). The influence of sex-role stereotypes on evaluations of male and female supervisory behavior. *The Journal of Applied Psychology*, *57*(1), 44–48. doi:10.1037/h0034198 PMID:4784751

Sheppard, L. D., & Aquino, K. (2013). Much ado about nothing: Observers' problematization of women's same-sex conflict at work. *The Academy of Management Perspectives*, *27*(1), 52–62. doi:10.5465/amp.2012.0005

Sobczak, A. (2018). The Queen Bee Syndrome. The Paradox of Women Discrimination on the Labour Market. *Journal of Gender and Power*, *9*(1). www.semanticscholae.org>papers

Staines, G. (1974). The queen bee syndrome. *Psychology Today*, *7*, 55–66.

Utoh-Ezeajugh, T. C. (2015). Nigerian Female Playwrights and the Evolution of a Literary Style: Gendered Discourse in the Plays of Tess Onwueme, Irene Salami-Agunlonye and Tracie Utoh-Ezeajugh. In Gender Discourse in African Theatre, Literature and Visual Arts. Kraft Books Ltd.

Zhao, S., & Foo, M. D. (2016). *Queen Bee Syndrome. The real women do not promote women.* Center for Creative Leadership. Available from: https://www.ccl.org/wp-content/uploads/2016/09/Queen-Bee-Syndrome.pdf

ADDITIONAL READING

Okpala, E. P., & Utoh-Ezeajugh, T. C. (2018). Inter and Intra-Gender Discourse in African Prose: An Interrogation of the Female Image in Selected Literary Texts. *Journal of Arts And Humanities*, *19*, 1–14.

Chapter 27
The Fate of Nigerian Women in Armed Conflict Situations:
An Appraisal of Adichie and Agbasimalo's Novels

Adaobi Olivia Ihueze
https://orcid.org/0000-0002-3956-1134
Nnamdi Azikiwe University, Awka, Nigeria

ABSTRACT

Armed conflicts in many parts of the globe have a major detrimental influence on many aspects of life, particularly in the affected areas. The destiny of women in armed conflict scenarios, as well as their survival techniques, was investigated in this research. The chapter employed feminist and psychoanalytical theories to examine the unpleasant experiences of women in conflict zones by analyzing two female novels, Half of a Yellow Sun by Chimamanda Adichie and Forest Dames by Adaokere Agbasimalo. It revealed that the armed conflict had far-reaching and terrible consequences for women and children. The study, therefore, recommends that women are better positioned to write about their life experiences that leave an everlasting mark.

INTRODUCTION

Literature has evolved into a critical instrument for comprehending and interpreting elements of our evolving society and experiences. These experiences are communicated through media and this can be printed or online. Therefore, literature and media are two sides of the same coin. Hence, literary writing is the writer's soul expressed for the consumption of his audience. The writer, as a speaker, must exhibit an attitude while speaking to other men. He designates, protests, resists, persuades, insinuates, and appeals to the masses. The thoughts he expresses reflect his message to his audience. As a result, there is no better place to seek and comprehend people's reactions to their situations than in the works of their writers. These writers' works especially the novel have three phases of development in African history.

DOI: 10.4018/978-1-6684-4107-7.ch027

Palmer (1979) stated that the last of the three phases was the period of post-independence, largely one of re-adjustment in an attempt to rediscover lost values. This phase showed the development of the new political class that was incapable of facing the challenges of nation building and providing moral and civic leadership. This political setup broke down as a result of instability orchestrated by coups and counter-coups with major violence (Obiechina, 1993). The crises later led to the roots of the greatest armed conflict in Nigerian history – The Nigerian Civil War.

The Nigerian Civil War/armed conflict of 1967-1970 formally began on July 6, 1967, when the Eastern Provinces (Biafra) declared their independence and Nigeria launched a relentless military effort to re-establish their independence. Millions of Biafrans were uprooted, malnourished, raped, slain, and pushed to the brink of human agony during this time. Even though the combat officially ended on January 12th, 1970, little attention has been devoted to resolving the war's deep social, political, and psychological wounds (Ademoyega, 1981; Forsyth, 1977; Effiong 2000). The hardship unleashed by the armed conflict brought new inspiration to the writing on war themes. As a result, some committed writers have taken it as their responsibility to confront the 'traumatic conflict' (Jones, 1996). It was revealed that the majority of works on armed conflict are dominated by male voices but now as Ogbazi (2012) averred that women's voices must be heard on crucial historical and national issues; that their voices must complement those of men for any story to be holistic. They have also chosen to convey their ideas from a female perspective, being visible rather than invisible by presenting their narratives. Through their literary output, female authors embrace and participate in the battle for the restoration of an ideal society with social and economic equality. This they achieved by writing about the immense damage and suffering endured by the people throughout the conflict and painting a bleak image of Biafra elites and businessmen/women who abandoned their jobs, families, possessions, and future endeavors to carry out the Civil War. This paper explores the fate of Nigerian women in armed conflict situations using Adichie and Agbasimalo's novels *Half of a Yellow Sun* and *Forest Dames* respectively. They have expressed their feelings from the female stance and their works were assessed to see how effectively they have recreated women's experiences in an armed conflict situation.

THEORETICAL FRAMEWORK

The study is based on the theoretical frameworks of Feminism and Psychoanalysis to provide a more accurate assessment of the impacts of the conflict from a female perspective. The feminist theory seeks to analyze gender inequality and is primarily concerned with gender politics, power relations, and sexuality. It criticizes these societal and political reactions and focuses on the advancement of women's rights and interests (Beauvoir, 1949/2009; Hooks, 1994; Friedan, 1963; Walker, 1983). In 1792, Mary Wollstonecraft, a philosophical feminist, published *A Vindication of the Rights of Woman*, which advocated for female equality, particularly in education. Wollstonecraft rejected the cultivation of conventional feminine characteristics like submission and service, arguing that women could not be competent mothers, spouses, and household administrators unless they were well educated. The book is broken into thirteen chapters in which Wollstonecraft addressed issues such as the significance of educating women equally, treating women with respect, and giving women the necessary training to be decent wives, mothers, and intellectual companions to their husbands.

In general, feminists' critiques investigate how literature promotes or destroys women's economic, political, social, and psychological oppression (Beauvoir, 1949/2009; Showalter, 1977/1999). Their ultimate purpose is to transform the world by supporting gender equality, increasing our awareness of women's experiences in the past and today, and increasing our respect for women's importance in the world. They regard sexism as dysfunctional because it deprives society of one-half of its creative workforce. They also believe that no gender is more significant than the other and that everyone, regardless of gender, should be treated equally. Walker (1983) goes further to portray women as powerful and capable, in contrast to the stereotype of a woman as subservient and inferior. Feminists are fighting to communicate their sentiments and sorrows during violent battles from their side and with their voices, rather than via males (Ogbazi, 2012). Their literature is a protest dedicated to challenging traditional and accepted male ideals about the nature of women and how they feel, act, and think concerning war narratives and the way women's participation is portrayed as active instead of passive, in an attempt to deconstruct these stereotyped single stories and give voice to the female personality. Umeh adds that without the female voice, there will be no entire image of the Nigerian Civil War preserved in Nigerian literary history (as cited in Ogbazi, 2012, p.17). In other words, the writers employed in this work were inspired to create their works to portray their own and their people's experiences and in portraying their experiences many feminist writers appear to rely on components of psychoanalytic theory, inadvertently because they find them beneficial in addressing themes pertinent to women's lives (Tyson, 1999).

Dobbie (2009) described the psychoanalytic theory as a personality theory which holds that an individual is driven more by unseen forces that are controlled by conscious and logical reasoning. This literary critique stems especially from a therapeutic approach created at the end of the nineteenth century by the Viennese neurologist Sigmund Freud for the treatment of hysteria and neuroticism. According to him, human behavior is generated by the interaction of three components of the mind: the id, Ego, and Super ego. All of Freud's work is based on the concept of the unconscious - the portion of the mind that exists outside of consciousness yet has a profound impact on our behavior. This is linked to the concept of repression,' which is the 'forgetting' or ignoring of unresolved conflicts, unaccepted desires, or painful past events to drive them out of conscious consciousness and into the domain of the unconscious.

Thus, a work of art, according to the psychoanalytical viewpoint, is a veiled manifestation of the author's unconscious desire. The nature of creative work may be comprehended if the author's mind is known. Wilson's (1941) book of literary criticism "The Wound and the Bow: Seven Studies in Literature" expanded on the part of psychoanalytic criticism in which an author's personality is tied to his works (1941). Wilson establishes a connection between a writer's life and his creative works. He begins with Freud's idea that an artist is not far removed from neurosis, and he makes art to relieve his neurotic feelings. According to Wilson, every author goes through terrible events, which he explains to himself and the rest of the world through his works. As a result, the character of his art is influenced by his terrible experiences. Wilson employs the wound and bow paradigm in his analysis, where the wound alludes to psychic trauma and the bow to the healing force of insight. He puts this notion into action, and it was revealed that the writer utilizes art to transcend pain. The researcher employs feminist and psychoanalytic theory based on these observations. The writers attempt to describe the female experience, expose patriarchy, and liberate women from the role of the other.

Brief Synopses of Adichie and Agbasimalo's Novels

Chimamanda Adichie's *Half of a Yellow Sun* and Adaokere Agbasimalo's *Forest Dames* published in 2006 and 2014 respectively offer a heart-wrenching account of the Biafran war of 1967 – 1970. It is a story of loyalty, betrayal, resilience, and hope and it revolves around the normal life of people who are shaken and overturned by war. They offered a glimpse into the lives of people of several different and multifaceted characters who were traumatized by the war. In *Half of a Yellow Sun*, the story is told from the perspective of five characters – Odeingbo, Olanna, Kainene, Richard, and Ugwu. Odenigbo, one of the major characters, is a lecturer at the University of Nigeria Nsukka, a revolutionary thinker and an enthusiastic Biafran who struggles with the psychological impact of the violence. Olanna, Odenigbo's wife is an elite who was trying to keep her family intact. Kainene, Olanna's twin sister who is strong and hardworking, tries everything possible to survive the war while Richard is a British expatriate who is in love with Kainene. Ugwu is Odenigbo's house boy who transforms from a village boy to an intelligent boy who is forced to grapple with the unpredictable situation that surrounds him. In *Forest Dames*, the war came with ugly incidence, one of which was the hunt for and abduction of girls and women to be forcibly converted to bedmates. Families sought places to hide their daughters but two women decided that their daughters will not be victims and therefore found them a safe place in the evil forest. The forest dames Deze, Sofuru, Lele, and Gonma survived the war and one of them decides to tell the unfortunate story of human suffering.

APPRAISING ADICHIE AND AGBASIMALO'S WAR NOVELS

Every full-fledged battle must result in the loss of life and property. The civil conflict that erupted between Nigeria and Biafra ripped many people's lives apart. The novels *Half of a Yellow Sun* (2006) and *Forest Dames* (2014), vividly depict the mayhems of 1966, with breathtaking descriptions and painful recollections. It demonstrates that hundreds of innocent individuals were slain or vanished without a trace. Some are raped and subjected to various horrors before being maimed. The novels thoroughly and powerfully illustrated the psychological and physical repercussions of war. The stories transport the reader to the battlefields to observe the horrors of war and then return him or her to various homes and lifestyles to emphasize the effects.

The author explores the pogrom that led to the Igbo people's migration to the east in *Half of a Yellow Sun*. The heroine, Olanna, begs Mohammed to assist her in rescuing her relatives so that they might move to the east together during the Northern uprising. She was so traumatized that she could not describe her experiences when she saw the dead bodies of Uncle Mbaezi and Auntie Ifeka. Richard, Kainene's lover in *Half of a Yellow Sun* also recounted his experiences of the massacre. Many able-bodied young men and women were slain or murdered, as Adichie and Agbasimalo related in *Half of a Yellow Sun* and *Forest Dames,* with young boys, men, and even unborn infants were butchered mercilessly. As a result, many were widowed, and children were left orphaned. Adimora-Ezeigbo (1991) in *Facts and Fiction in the Literature of Nigeria Civil War* summarizes this by asserting that it is supremely ironic that the war said to be waged against rebels was just cold-blooded murder of innocent people none of whom contributed to the decision that triggered the war. During the conflict, the women were subjected to psychological trauma that permeated their beings and left a permanent impact. In *Half of a Yellow Sun*, the lady holding her daughter's skull and Olanna both experience inward trauma that will leave lifelong scars on their lives. Kainene's emotional turmoil following Ikejide's death was extremely moving though the writer showed 'Kainene, Olanna's sister, who is an emotionally strong lady, showing the weakness that usually characterizes women. Harrison and Richard were able to manage their shock well unlike Olanna who was completely beaten.

Again, the execution of Madam Rosa in *Forest Dames* demonstrates the extent to which the people were devastated by the war circumstances. They were looking for a method to vent their frustrations when Madam Rosa gave them a fantastic chance. She was buried alive for they felt betrayed because she was sleeping with the enemy soldiers. This is consistent with Freud's concept of the unconscious, which is the portion of our mind that is not aware yet has a tremendous impact on our behavior (Dobbie, 2009).

Another terrible repercussion of war is malnutrition, and these female writers wrote extensively on the effects of starvation on people, particularly women and children. Hunger reigned supreme, wreaking havoc on the people. It increased the number of deaths in the community, particularly among youngsters, the old, and those who relied on others for their livelihood and daily affairs. In *Forest Dames,* Lillian complained, "Yesterday we ate the last grain of food in this house. Nothing has been cooked today" (Agbasimalo, 2014, p.77). Soldiers' deaths in battle are reasonable, but what about the deaths of millions of children due to malnutrition and sudden death owing to a lack of medication? The economic embargo proved to be the true battle on the civilian population, many of whom watched helplessly as their newborns died gradually. We also saw young schoolgirls and women who have become willing victims as a result of hunger. In *Half of a Yellow Sun,* Father Marcel is accused of impregnating a girl (Urenwa) while helping Kainene distribute crayfish and other food items in a refugee camp. When Kainene discovered it, she dismissed him. Ogbazi (2012) affirms that "... some of the women... who experience sexual exploitation in form of rape or sexual manipulation owe their experiences to their lack of security, food and /or protection. The men who abused them knew this and took undue advantage" (p.26). The hunger at that time compelled people to violate their faith and integrity and this can be seen in *Half of a Yellow Sun,* where Eberechi was forced by her parents to sleep with an army commander.

Aside from the deaths reported during conflicts, numerous more demeaning and chaotic circumstances, such as sexual harassment, have emerged. Troops' behavior in conflict varies greatly, both individually and as groups or armies. In some cases, forces may commit genocide, war rape, or ethnic cleansing. The United Nations condemns violations of human rights, particularly those of women in crisis circumstances. In other words, gender equality and the abolition of all forms of discrimination against women are essential human rights and United Nations ideals. This is clearly stated in Article 1 of the United Nations General Assembly's Declaration on the Elimination of Violence against Women. It states that for this Declaration, violence against women is defined as any act of gender-based violence that causes or is likely to cause physical, sexual, or psychological harm or suffering to women, including threats of such acts, coercion, or arbitrary deprivation of liberty, whether committed in public or private life. This resolution declared that women must be free from violence, yet women all over the globe continue to face violations of their human rights throughout their lives, and valuing women's rights is not always a priority.

The violence against women takes serious forms in violent conflict settings. Much worldwide attention has been devoted to the relationship between gender-based violence and war during the last decade. Conflicts, whether civil and political or economic and social, have far-reaching consequences for women's enjoyment of their fundamental rights. Manjoo and Calleigh McRaith (2011) are of the view that, despite efforts to combat gender violence in conflict and post-conflict settings, women continued to be subjected to these abuses such as rape, sexual slavery, kidnapping or trafficking, forced impregnation or miscarriages, and sexual abuse. This shows that nothing has been achieved in stopping the sexual violation of women during armed conflict situations. They are frequently victims of sexual assault, which appears throughout society, particularly during times of armed war. The literary authors employed in this discourse discussed the role of sex in combat conditions, how women in crisis scenarios are raped by marauding or bored troops, and how women barter sex for protection, favors, and food.

They appear to suggest that army officers use drugs and alcohol to help them cope with the stress and sight of what they experience, and as a result, they may behave inappropriately. To this, Ogbazi writes that "oftentimes, it is the women who bear the brunt of different levels and forms of wickedness and depravities in conflict situations" (p.27).

With rape, a woman's life changes because she has been violated, and in *Body Sexuality and Gender: Versions and Subversions in African Literatures* they refer to rape victims as tainted or violated bodies. The writer addressed the issue of rape in *Half of a Yellow Sun* because, as a woman, she understands the psychological repercussions of that societal crisis on women. She describes Ugwu and his buddies going to a bar to drink after a successful attack on the vandals. They raped a bar girl while they were drinking and smoking. Even Anulika Ugwu's sister was manhandled beaten and raped. So many other women in the novels were abducted and violated. These violated women were emotionally traumatized and they find it extremely difficult to adjust to society.

In any armed combat situation, men perceived women as the booty of war. It demonstrates how women, particularly minors, maybe sex objects in a combat environment and be sexually exploited without understanding the men's actual intentions or even being coerced. Lynn Hancock affirms that the revelation of sexual assault is perilous and can result in estrangement from family, mistreatment of children, and social marginalization. Several young women and girls had returned, some with children and others with pregnancies. Some of them never returned and were never found. It was too embarrassing for these girls to return with pregnancies or newborns. For their plight, they are cajoled, mocked, and caricatured. Some of them, like Ojiugo in *Forest Dames*, couldn't bear the shame and committed suicide. The rape victims often need support and time to heal from the traumatic experiences and also regain emotional and mental stability.

The agonies felt by the women in the books could only be vividly represented by female authors whose membership in the same gender inspires them with the required insight needed to depict the inner sentiments of women in the light of their experiences from their point of view. The representation of the violence against women in the books might be interpreted as an attempt by the writers to counter the gendered bias of war discourse, which is exhibited mostly in the novels written by male writers. One cannot help but admire these female writers for reviewing and judging, from a feminist standpoint, the devaluation, violence, and deep psychological damage faced by women throughout the Nigerian Civil War. During the tragic struggle that decimated the people and their future, the writers employed in this discourse, represent their female characters as being abused and denied their human rights.

The Civil War was also marked by the willful disruption of social order and, in many cases, utter dissolution of social and family relationships. This signifies that the family's purpose as a social unit has been lost, and its values have been destroyed. In investigating the issues, the writers unwittingly illustrated how the flow of communal life is interrupted and familial bonds are shattered. Many individuals moved from one location to another in search of protection, and many solid relationships were shattered as a result. One of the novels' assertions is that the Nigerian Civil War destroyed many wonderful, great, and beautiful things, particularly human connections and lives. It also wreaked havoc on property and infrastructure, shattering aspirations and hopes.

The Resilience and Capabilities of Women

In their distinct literary styles, Adichie and Agbasimalo have also conveyed to us the problem of women in a male-dominated world, particularly during times of armed war, and how they may be of immense assistance to their children and society. They portrayed women as capable members of society, particularly in times of conflict. The writers employed in this discourse critique stereotypes of women as "mothers" and "mistresses," as well as the weaker sex. In doing so, they emphasize the significance of women in country formation and national growth. Women's resilience is influenced by their capacity to adjust to new events and circumstances more quickly and easily than males. They have demonstrated that women can have the courage required to persevere amidst adversity. In the words of Nnolim when he was referring to Adichie's *Half of a Yellow Sun,* he writes that 'The women she creates were no longer there to carry fufu and soup to men discussing important matters. They have been empowered by education ..., (as cited in Fubara, 2011, p. 245).

Despite the devastation of the war, women are perceived to have transcended the reality of trauma to fully utilize their creative and resourceful potentials, as well as their survival instincts, in sourcing materials and providing basic needs for the sustenance of their families and society. The authors illustrate a shift in values, shifting views about life, and the presence of women in the conflict zone. According to Nnaemeka, (1997) women battled "on all fronts" to bring normality (or a semblance of it) to an abnormal environment - a job they considered a moral imperative and civic duty. Women fought their everyday fights by performing many roles as the lines between public and private, personal and political, individual and collective were blurred. Men were rarely seen on the roadways during the period, while women worked hard to support their families. "Most of the women took up the duty of providing food for the family so that their children would not starve" (Agbasimalo, 2014, p. 83). Literary characters like Dora in *Forest Dames,* Olanna, Kainene, and Mrs. Muokelu in *Half of a Yellow Sun* were strong, compassionate, diligent, and quick thinking. They were not passive but active participants who stood firm in helping to soften the effects of the war. Most often they take the roles of men in the home.

Based on patriarchy's prevailing worldview, they think that women are oppressed because of their gender. The origins, nature, and scope of female subjugation and oppression have long been a topic of contention in African literary disputes. These female authors have been acknowledged for their writings, which they utilize to demonstrate what African women experience in modern Nigerian culture, including violent circumstances, and to argue why they should be treated equally. In her book, *A Vindication of the Rights of Woman*, Mary Wollstonecraft (1792) urged equality and greater education for women, and she provided the first continuous critique of a social order that degraded women to other creatures.

The authors, used in this discourse, undermine patriarchy's belief in female weaknesses through its portrayal of women's strength by giving them a voice, an identity, and an emotional entity, especially in a conflict situation. Women must tell their and other people's experiences for their education and enlightenment as well as the society and it is important to hear it from the 'horse's mouth' (Adimora-Ezeigbo, 2005). To support this, Smith (2001) wrote that it will be told without embellishment so that those who suffered to die did not die in vain. This is a better way of relieving this painful past, which is to confront it and not live perpetually in the past. Some individuals to deal with the painful events try to record their recollection of the events apparently for posterity to read and learn from the records to avoid those things that triggered off the armed conflict.

CONCLUSION

Adichie and Agbasimalo in their works highlighted the killings that preceded and later defined the Nigerian Civil War. They chronicled the thirty-month war's air attacks, bombardment, famine, rape, and heartbreak in compelling detail. The writers have detailed how the war took away Biafrans' normalcy and how they continued to live and love during the conflict. They highlighted the physical and literal truths of war before moving on to the psychological and emotional aspects. The physical wounds of war and violence may heal in the tales, but the psychological scars inflicted on the characters may never heal. They discussed warfare as a watershed event that serves as a stepping stone into the psychological and emotional impacts of war on individuals, relationships, ethnic groups, and the nation as a whole.

As a result, this article includes female war novels that address topics of women's suffering during battle situations. Despite this, they maintain a strong and assertive connection with the opposite sex. They dive into the social issues that women face during times of armed war. They present their female characters as clever, ambitious, and forward-thinking. They demonstrate the bravery of women in a world that strives to stifle their ambitions. The authors explore the position of women from various perspectives and philosophies. They accomplish this by utilizing their heroes as a cover to advocate for women's equality in society.

REFERENCES

Ademoyega, A. (1981). *Why we struck*. Evans Brothers.

Adichie, C. (2006). *Half of a Yellow Sun*. Farafina.

Adimora-Ezeigbo, A. (1991). *Facts and fiction in the literature of Nigeria civil war*. Unity Publishing and Research.

Adimora-Ezeigbo, A. (2005). From the horse's mouth: The politics of remembrance in women's writing on the Nigerian civil war. In F. Veit-Wild & D. Naguschewki (Eds.), *Body sexuality, and gender: Versions and subversions in African literatures* (pp. 221–230). Rodopi B.V. doi:10.1163/18757421-029030015

Agbasimalo, A. (2014). *Forest dames*. Parrèsia Publishers.

Beauvoir, S. (2009). *The second sex* (C. Borde & S. Malovany-Chevallier, Trans.). Vintage Books, A Division Random House Inc. (Original work published 1949)

Dobbie, A. (2009). Theory into practice: An introduction to literary criticism (2nd ed.). Academic Press.

Effiong, P. (2000). *Nigeria and Biafra: My story*. Business Forum Publications.

Fosyth, F. (1977). *The making of an African legend: The Biafra story*. Penguin Books.

Frieden, B. (1963). *Feminine Mystique*. W.W. Norton.

Fubara, A. (1997). Rhetoric of pain: unearthing the ugly as a tool for the good in Chimamanda Adichie's half of a yellow sun. In C. Nwahunanya (Ed.), A harvest from tragedy: Critical perspectives on Nigerian civil war literature. Academic Press.

Hancock, L. (2012). *Drowning out the silence: Nigerian civil war literature and the politics of gender-based violence*. escholarship.org.

Jones, E. D. (1996). New trends and generations in African literature. African Literature Today, 20, 1-2.

Manjoo, R., & McRaith, C. (2011). Gender –based violence and justice in conflict and post-conflict areas. *Cornell International Law Journal*, *44*(11), 11–12.

Nnaemeka, O. (1997). Fighting on all fronts: gendered spaces, ethnic boundaries, and the Nigerian civil war. *Dialectical Anthropology, 22*(3–4), 253.

Obiechina, E. (1993). *Language and theme. Essays on African literature*. Heinemann Educational Books.

Ogbazi, I. (2012). The female voice and the experiences of women in conflict situations: The truce in Chimamanda Ngozi Adichie's half of a yellow sun. *Journal of English Literature and Literary Studies*, *3*(1), 17–33.

Palmer, E. (1979). Ngugi in petals of blood. *African Literature Today*, *10*, 153–166.

Showalter, E. (1999). *A literature on their own: British women novelist from Bronte to Lessing*. Princeton University Press. (Original work published 1977)

Smith, C. (2001). *Proud of me: Speaking out against sexual violence and HIV*. Penguin.

Tyson, L. (1999). *Critical theory today*. Garland Publishing Inc.

United nations general assembly. 'A/res/48/104- declaration on the elimination of violence against women – united nation documents: gathering a body of global agreements'. un- documents.net.

Veit-Wild, F., & Naguschewki, D. (Eds.). (2005). Body sexuality, and gender: versions and subversions in African literatures. Rodopi B.V.

Walker, A. (1983). *In search of our mother's garden: Womanist prose*. Harcourt Brace Javanoich.

Wilson, E. (1941). *The wound and the bow: seven studies in literature*. Riverside Press.

Wollstonecraft, M. (1792). *A vindication of the rights of women*. J. Johnson.

Chapter 28
Rethinking the Idea of Sustainable Development in Africa

Vitalis Chukwuemeka Ugwu
Alex Ekwueme Federal University, Nigeria

ABSTRACT

Africa has a long history of exogenous development initiatives usually directed at addressing various developmental challenges in the continent. For instance, at the dawn of the 21st century, there was the Millennium Development Goals (MDGs) meant to address the indignity of poverty especially in Africa. After that, came the New Partnership for Africa's Development (NEPAD). Like the MDGs before it, the objective of NEPAD was to eradicate poverty and place Africa on a sustainable process of development. The latest in the list of these development initiatives was the 2030 Sustainable Development Goals (SDGs) meant again to address the issues of poverty, hunger, health, gender equality, among others. However, in spite of this long history of exogenous development initiatives, Africa remains largely underdeveloped – a pointer to something intrinsically and specially wrong with Africa. This chapter therefore calls for a more endogenous approach to tackling African development challenges as the continent has peculiar problems requiring endogenous solutions.

INTRODUCTION: CONTENDING PERSPECTIVES ON DEVELOPMENT AND SUSTAINABILITY

This author hopes that his topic which is 'Rethinking the Idea of Sustainable Development in Africa' will be better appreciated if we first understand, though not in their entirety the ideas of development and sustainability. Therefore we ask: What is Development?

This author in 2018 had observed elsewhere that the term 'development' is a multidimensional concept judging from the fact that it enjoys a mass of contextual definitions emanating from different disciplines. It is a term that is defined and understood along so many lines of human experience. Thus

DOI: 10.4018/978-1-6684-4107-7.ch028

we talk about economic development, cultural development, educational development, moral development, infrastructural development etc.

Therefore, development has economic, cultural, practical, social, human or personal dimensions. However, most people understand development only from the angle of economics and infrastructural provisions. They view development as advancement and growth only on economic and environmental conditions of peoples and nations. That explains the reason why it seems the only yardsticks employed in determining a nation's level of development at any given period are the Per Capital Income (PCI), National Income (NI), Gross National Product(GNP) and the Gross Domestic Product (GDP). With these economic tools, economists measure only incomes accruing to nations and peoples within nations, while using indices such as economic growth rate, income of the population, level of school enrolment and level of industrial production measured against primary production among others. Noteworthy, is the fact that the above economic tools employed in measuring levels of development represent only quantitative indices of development. They provide information only on the total wealth of a country, material living conditions of the people, values of goods produced etc., and they neglect entirely issues bothering on the quality of life of the people, such as decent accommodation, level of calorie intake, clothing, education, healthcare, social amenities and others. Consequently, the only nations considered as developed are those that have outstanding growth levels in most of the quantitative indices over a given period, whereas all those that trail behind others in the quantitative measurement are called 'underdeveloped' and sometimes 'developing' as a sign of courtesy. Perhaps, it is the above lacuna in our conception of the meaning of development, that prompted S.O Opafola (1998;160) to remind that:

Parameters for measuring or determining improvement in the quality of life of a country's citizens include food availability and affordability, water supply, clothing, shelter, health-care, wholesome environment, human dignity, literacy, employment, security, education, transportation, availability and affordability of energy and communication.

It is very regrettable and disappointing that in many countries of Africa, most of these human parameters are visible absent due largely to endemic corruption in the continent. Again sense of duty and responsibility is also lacking among a good percentage of African population and the consequences are very glaring. For instance, Nigeria is in a very terrible security situation at the moment. Human lives are wasted daily because of separatist agitations and unholy activities of militant groups and organized criminal gangs. Available online statistics have shown that in 2019 alone, one thousand, two hundred and forty five (1,245) persons died in agitations and terror related attacks. This very ugly situation is direct consequence of corruption, abandonment of duties and responsibilities, lack of proper education, especially moral and values education. There cannot be security which is one of the important indices of development where large percentage of a people's population lacks a sense of moral and ethical values. It may not be out of place to say that Nigeria and indeed the whole Africa's development crises are caused primarily by moral and ethical underdevelopment of her citizens. Moral decadence, not only destroys human capacity for good citizenship but also peace, security and real development of the people. As a matter of fact, no economic advances are made where the citizens have no sense of duty, and lack the right attitude to work as well as sense of patriotism which engenders a feeling of moral responsibility towards society.

Therefore for any development drive to be meaningful, it must be people-oriented. Every development initiative or drive which neglects the quality of life of the people cannot be said to be meaningful.

Development is primarily about the people and therefore should be human centered and people-inspired. In fact, the advancement, expansion, growth and change which development is supposed to represent, must depend on human resources as well as on human socio-political conditions among other human factors. Onwuliri (2008) stresses that:

Development....goes beyond the narrow lines of economic and material advancement. It is all encompassing. Development is a multidimensional process involving the totality of man in his political, economic, psychological social relations among others. It is erroneous to see underdevelopment as an original state which must be characterized by indices of traditionalism and therefore development consists in abandoning these characteristics and adopting those of the Western world.

The above submission justifies the necessity of the human index in determining levels of development. The humanistic view of development sees development not as a project as believed by economists, but as a process which is driven by the people. Thus according to Claude Ake (2001:140):

Development is not a project but a process by which people create and recreate themselves and their life circumstances to realize higher levels of civilization in accordance with their own choice and values.

Writing still on the necessity of the human index, Okolo (2015:202) emphasizes that:

Development... is used ... to incorporate a wide range of assumptions implied by words such as advancement, expansion, growth, progress and change... that takes place in a society as a result of the effort, support and participation of the people. It defines a situation in which there is freedom for people to interact on an equal basis. It specifies a condition in which no set of people are hindered from realizing their full potential due to any imposed disadvantage.

Interestingly, the above remarks which underscore the importance of the human index also points to the necessity of 'freedom' in defining development. Freedom as a determinant factor in development is so crucial that Oladipo (2008:83) had rightly observed that:

In measuring national development...our primary focus should be on two keys variables. The first one is freedom. In the context of national development, the meaning of this concept should be fixed at two levels. At the first level, it involves not only the absence of constraints on individual self realization through the provision of means for the fulfillment of the human bio-social needs..., but also the provision of absolute security. Crucial to the meaning of freedom at this level, then is the achievement of a level of social efficiency that guarantees that things work- for instance, that the services which make modern social life tolerable and fulfilling, including education, health services, water, electricity, telephones, transportation and so on, work.

In effect, this write-up stands to prove that balanced development requires attention to both quantitative and qualitative aspects of development and that paying greater attention to the qualitative aspect (especially personal/individual development) has positive implications. Perhaps, it is in support of this view that Wily Brandit et al (1980:18) had noted that:

Development must mean improvement in living conditions for which economic growth and industrialization are essential. But if there is no attention to the quality of growth to social change, one cannot speak of development.

Understanding Sustainable Development in Africa

Sustainability is the underlying aim in every development drive. When developments are initiated and implemented, they are meant to be sustained in order to have lasting impact on the population. Sustainability is a challenge to many development plans, hence the continuous emphasis on sustainable development by serious world leaders. The Oxford dictionary meaning of the word 'sustain' from which the adjective 'sustainable derives is to make something continue for some time without becoming less. Usually, the idea behind the contemporary politics of sustainable development in our world today, is according to this author in the work already cited "the ensuring of a better life for everyone now and generations to come". However, the World Commission on Environment and Development (WCED), also known as the Brundtland Commission (1987) is reputed to have coined what in the recent times, has become the most often quoted definitions of sustainable development. This commission, views sustainable development as "development that meets the needs of the present without compromising the ability of future generations to meet their own needs" (WCED, 1987:43)

Meanwhile, Omoyeni (2015:30) in Ugwu (2018), sees development as a 'pattern of resource use that aims to meet human needs while preserving the environment so that these needs can be met not only in the present but in the indefinite future'. To further explain the concept, Onyeshola (2008) in Ugwu (2018) argues forcefully that sustainable development implies three primary factors of economic, environmental and social. According to Onyeshola(2008:162) as highlighted in Ugwu (2018):

An economically sustainable system must be able to produce goods and services on a continuing basis and maintain manageable economy without jeopardizing sectoral balances of economic activities of the country. Environmentally, sustainable system must maintain a stable resource base, avoiding over exploitation of renewable resource systems... and depleting non-renewable resources only to the extent that investment is made in adequate substitutes...The last factor (social) must achieve distributional equity, adequate provision of social services, including health and education, gender equity and political accountability, transparency and participation. This must be with dynamic understanding of human rights.

The above is an excellent submission on the real meaning of sustainable development as well as the conditions that can make it achievable. It is also exposition of the challenges of sustainable development, especially in African, where leadership failure has become a serious recurring decimal for decades of her political independence, and has equally become the major reason for the high level of underdevelopment often associated with the continent over the years.

The United Nation World Summit Outcome document (2005), rightly observes that "the three factors of economic sustainability, environmental sustainability and social sustainability, are interdependent as well as mutually reinforcing pillars of sustainable development". However, a crucial point to note here, is the indispensability of good leadership in achieving sustainable development be it in economic, environmental or social dimensions. This is because the sustainability or otherwise of developments in any nation depends on the manner leadership in that nation is driven along these sustainable development components of economic, environmental and social "(Ugwu).

Leadership failure has become the greatest challenge of African development. Leaders in Africa have become fantastically corrupt and corruption brings retardation in all spheres of human existence. The common people of Africa are not also helping matters in this regard. In fact, according to Oguejiofor (2001:36):

Many among the so-called common people in many African countries today would readily taunt a highly placed official who did his duty creditably, and left office a poor man on account of his honesty.

The above, shows the extent African citizens are helping to underdevelop themselves. And the continent. Again, recognizing the indispensability of good leadership in driving sustainable development in African, Onyeshola (163) avers:

Any development that will be sustaining, especially in the developing countries will include the following: increases in the real income especially for the 'wretched of the earth'. This implies poverty eradication on the long run; improvement in the health and nutritional status of especially children and young mothers who are vulnerable to most preventable diseases; education achievement; access to resources; a fairer equitable distribution of income...,increases in basic freedom and guaranteed security of all citizens; respect and responsible relationship with ecosystem.

A critical examination of the above submission shows how most Africa leaders and peoples are wasting efforts in the wrong direction in their quest for sustainable development by not addressing the real parameters that can actually guarantee sustainable development in the continent. It is a common knowledge that almost the whole of the sub-saharan African countries are bedevilled by man-made poverty, malnutrition, insecurity, diseases, social inequality, lack of education, environmental degradation and pollution etc. Therefore, one wonders how sustainable development can be achieved in the sub-region if the above issues are largely unattended to in the name of construction of roads and bridges alone.

Furthermore, Africa must also recognize the challenge of building national unity in her quest for sustainable development. Unity is very important for peace and for unity to be achieved, justice must be seen to be done to all at all times. Economic differences created by the leaders can weaken national cohesion and cause strife and wars and the urge to secede as is currently evident in Nigeria. The national unity being canvassed here, is one that must recognize the uniqueness of each region and encourage them to develop along the lines of their peculiar circumstances and interests. Lack of national unity can lead to civil wars and ethnic tensions, resulting to a halt in every economic and social activity that may aid development.

Again, for Africa to achieve sustainable development, Africans must work to establish stable governments. Iftichar Ahmad et al (2004:112) inform us that:

After independence countries that had stable government made the most economic progress. The economy of Cote d voire... grew under a single, strong ruler. With stable government, Gabon and Kenya also made economic gains.

Therefore, there must be sincere efforts towards true democratization in the whole of Africa to ensure not only peace and unity in the continent but also continuity and sustainability of all programmes of development.

Another important challenge to sustainable development in African is the issue of population explosion. Even though African traditions encourage large families as children are seen as valuable resource to the family. One African saying notes that "each extra mouth comes attached to two extra hands". However, there is need to tred with caution in this regard. Iftickhar Ahmad et al (115) observe that:

Since independence, birth rates have risen in Africa.....The result was soaring population in some countries. Africa's Population continues to grow today...in 2000, Africa's population was about 800 million. At the current growth rate, it will be more than double by 2050.

Continuing, they noted that:

Africa's population increase has created many problems for government leaders and economic planners. Almost half of the people of Africa are less than 15 years old. Government have to find money for schools, housing and jobs for these young people. They must improve conditions in cities, which are becoming more crowded every year.

We can see that large population explosion can be a very big stress to especially poor countries of Africa, who are economically dependent on foreign aids. It is true that government are established to provide social amenities and provide information on family planning among other things. Africans themselves must recognize the need for them to embrace the present realities of our time where population explosion can only increase the level of poverty, increase the rate of diseases and infections, and make management of diseases and crises very difficult. It adds strain to the wealth of nations and make allocation of scarce resources difficult among others.

Furthermore, there is the challenge of decreased agricultural activities in African countries. All over the world, agriculture is seen as the bedrock of development. But that awareness is lacking almost in the whole of Africa recently. In Nigeria, the decrease in agricultural practices is largely blamed on the incessant farmers-herders clashes which have caused many people to abandon farming. But very disturbing is the fact that Nigerian government has no concrete agenda aimed at addressing the problem. The result is high cost of food in the market, malnutrition, ethnic tension, hunger and in most cases death. Also worrisome is the fact that:

Although most Africans are subsistence farmers government programmes often neglect their needs. Instead, most focus on cash crops for export. As a result, farmers have stopped planting food crops... Government also have kept prices for food crops low. This policy helps poorly paid city workers to buy food. Farmers, however suffer from low prices. Many have left the land to join swelling city populations (Iftickhar,114)

The picture painted above may not be true for all African countries. Example is Nigeria where government is not only helping to increase food prices but also discouraging many people from investing in agriculture due to her policies that are akin to 'divide and rule' especially in the case of herders-farmers clashes and tackling insecurity. One often wonders how development of any sort can be sustained under the circumstance.

Finally, to sustain positive developments in the African continent, Africans must learn to cherish the values of industry and build a sense of duty and responsibility. Africans must work hard to achieve the much desired sustainable economic, environmental and social developments. The only way to do this is to accept duties and responsibilities while working hard to deliver positive results wherever one may find him/herself. This is because contemporary Africans have learnt to transfer duties and responsibilities while blaming unseen forces for their failures. Most Africans have a warped sense of religion. They erroneously believe that God does everything for men. Lao Russell has told us in her 'A Living Philosophy' published in America in 1955, that "God will work with you but not for you" but most Africans think otherwise. For example, according to Ugwu (2018):

We shift everything we should do to bring development to God, hoping that God would do everything for us. we spend hours in churches and mosques, neglecting long time African cherished values of hard work and perseverance.

Continuing, he however hinted that:

Religion no doubt is necessary for harmonious existence of society. It also makes for tolerance and inner peace, but unreasoned adherence to, and reliance on unfounded religious beliefs at the expense of active involvement in the realities of existence can hinder development, be it human, environmental, social or economic development.

Therefore, this write-up also calls on Africans in all strata of social existence to avoid religious extremism and work hard towards solving the many developmental challenges of Africa. It is said that Africans are deeply religious, but we must be guided by reason and logic in our collective existence. It may not be out of place to say that our lack of development is partly attributable to our inactions caused by our obsession with religion. We must do our part for God to do His part. God knew this when he blessed us with our individual talents and wisdom and commissioned us to go and conquer the world.

To buttress this point, Oladipo (2008:88) avers that:

It should be clear…that there is a lot in our mentality that is responsibility for our situation of underdevelopment and decadence, and that, unless we as individuals begin to cultivate the attitude of critical and reflective thinking about ourselves and the things we do or do not do, not much in our society will improve.

Another serious challenge to development in Africa generally is the issue of African belief in superstitions, especially her belief in witchcraft. This is a belief that pervades almost the whole of the continent and results in witch-hunting and ritual killings. This very belief which is known to lack foundation in truth and reality is a serious bane to African development as it can hamper safety. The belief could directly or indirectly impede scientific and technological innovations in Africa. M.O Maduagwu (2010) had sought to explore the perception of selected Nigerian Senior Executives (NSE) and Students of University of Nigeria, Nsukka; University of Ibadan; and Ahmadu Bello University, Zaria in a research he carried out to discover the extent of belief in witchcraft in contemporary Africa. Reporting his findings, Maduagwu (42) informs us that 58% of the selected NSE believe in the existence of witches, 27% believe in the possibility of their existence, while only 13% do not believe that witches exist. And for the selected Nigerian Students, he noted that there was no much difference. The perceptions are aptly demonstrated in the table below:

Table 1.

Response	Yes	No	It's possible	It's unlikely	N. R
NSE	30 (58%)	7 (13%)	14 (27%)	1 (2%)	-
100 LEVEL STUDENTS	73 (51%)	11 (8%)	50 (35%)	4 (3%)	6
400 LEVEL STUDENTS	106 (67%)	3 (2%)	43 (27%)	4 (3%)	2

Source: Maduagwu (2010:41)

The table above proves the pervasiveness of the belief in Africa. The greatest consequence of this belief in witchcraft, however, could be lack of critical or philosophical thinking as well as scientific reasoning among large percentage of African population. A defective thinking system, no doubts, cannot guarantee the much needed national development.

RECOMMENDATIONS/CONCLUSION

As already noted in this write-up, Africa has had a long history of especially exogenous development programmes which have all failed to achieve the much desired sustainable development in Africa. To solve this problem, there must be an African redefinition of sustainable development as Africans have needs that are especially peculiar to them. Replication of development strategies of the west may not always work for African nations. Therefore Africa must seek African solution to her varied development problems. African leaders must acknowledge the ultimate purpose of development which is the development of man himself, as it concerns the unfolding of his creative potentials through a planned improvement in his general conditions of living. The whole of his physiological, psychological, spiritual and emotional needs must not be neglected in development plans. Therefore, African governments and peoples should pay greater attention to the issues of poverty, health, education, security, unemployment, gender equality, ecology etc., as sustainable development in Africa cannot be possible if the above indices are neglected.

Furthermore, African peoples should work collectively to stem the rising tide of superstitions and taboos in the continent as such beliefs and practices are dealing deadly blows to Africa's development efforts, especially at the local levels.

Finally, to achieve lasting security which is a much needed factor for development in the continent, African governments must unite and take seriously the issues of economy and military strength. This is because the economy not only provides the resources for food, shelter, industrial production, and trade, but is also the foundation of military strength. It is only when the above issues and more like them, are sincerely addressed, that sustainable development in all fronts can be achievable in Africa.

REFERENCES

Ahmad/ (2004). *World Cultures: A Global Mosaic*. Academic Press.

Ake, C. (2001). *Democracy and Development*. Spectrum Book Ltd.

Oguejiofor, J. O. (2001). *Philosophy and the African Predicament*. Hope Publications Ltd.

Okolo, M. S. C. (2015). *Philosophy: Contemporary Concerns in African*. Book- Konzult.

Oladipo, O. (2008). *Thinking About Philosophy*. Hope Publications Ltd.

Omoyeni, B. A. (2015). *Principles and Applications of Environmental Impact. Assesment (EIA)*. McOr-nels Ventures.

Onwuliri, C. E. C. (2008). The Church as Agent of Progress and Development. In I Onyeocha (Ed.), The Church as Agent of Progress and Development, CIP Jubilee Essays (pp. 70-83). Imo State University Press.

Opafola, S. O. (1998). Developmental Philosophy and the Concept of People Oriented Development. In Philosophy: An Anthology. ARK Publishers.

Oyeshola Dokun, O. P. (2008). *Sustainable Development: Issues and Challenge for Nigeria*. Daily Graphics Nig. Ltd.

Pearson Prentice Hall Maduagwu, M. O. (2010). *The Belief in Witchcraft in Contemporary Africa: A Philosophical Discourse*. Stirling – Horden Publishers Ltd.

Ugwu, V. C. (2018). *Sustainable Development Goals (SDGS) and Africa's Development Challenges. Nigerian Journal of Educational Leadership and Management.*

UN. (2015). *Transporting our World: The 2030 Agenda for sustainable Development General Assembly Seventieth Session Agenda, 15 and 16, A/70/L*. Retrieved on 18 May, 2018, from http:/www.un.org

Compilation of References

Aas, K. F. (2007). Beyond "the desert of the real": Crime control in a virtualised reality. In Y. Jewkes (Ed.), *Crime Online*. Willan.

Abakare, C. O., & Okeke, V. C. (2016, July). Philosophy in contemporary time: Relevance vs. public perception. *Mgbakoigba. Journal of African Studies*, *6*(1).

Abdu, H., & Alabi, T. (2009). The print media and ethno-religious conflicts in Kaduna. In J.G. Yoroms & M. Abubakar (Eds.), Conflict management and the media in Nigeria. Centre for Research and Documentation (CRD).

Achebe, C. (1958). *Things Fall Apart*. Heinemann Educational Books.

Achebe, C. (1983). *The trouble with Nigeria*. Fourth Dimension Publishers.

Achor, P.N. (2019). Reputation crisis communication: Beyond what you know. *Spokespersons Digest: A Hand Journal of Public Relations & Communication*.

Achor, P.N. (2020). Endsars protest: Counting the gains, casualties or losses. *Emergency Digest*.

Achor, P. N., & Moguluwa, S. C. (2012). *Political marketing: Marketing, communication and politics*. Oktek Publishers.

Achor, P. N., & Nnabuko, J. (2019). Quasi-gatekeeping and quasi-gatewatching: The dual role of public relations practitioners in the social media domain. *Canadian Journal of Communication*, *44*(1), 5–24. doi:10.22230/cjc.2019v44n1a3272

Adamu, L. (2013). Media reportage of ethno-religious conflicts in Plateau State. *Journal of Communication and Media Research, 5*(1), 79-82.

Addis, A. (2004). The Thin State in Thick Globalisation Sovereignty in the Information Age. *Vanderbilt Journal of Transnational Law*, (January), 3–107.

Adebayo, A. (2020, Dec. 4). Appeal Court upholds Manyam Sanda's death sentence for killing husband. *Premium Times*.

Adebisi, O.O. (2017). The management of conflict in contemporary society: Prospects and challenges. *International Journal of Asian Social Sciences*, *3*(12).

Ademoyega, A. (1981). *Why we struck*. Evans Brothers.

Adeyemo, A.B., (2011). E-government implementation in Nigeria: An assessment of Nigeria's global e-gov ranking. *Journal of Internet and Information System, 2*(1), 11-19.

Adichie, C. N. (2021). *Speech at the Humboldt Forum*. YouTube.

Adichie, C. (2006). *Half of a Yellow Sun*. Farafina.

Adimora-Ezeigbo, A. (1991). *Facts and fiction in the literature of Nigeria civil war*. Unity Publishing and Research.

Adimora-Ezeigbo, A. (2005). From the horse's mouth: The politics of remembrance in women's writing on the Nigerian civil war. In F. Veit-Wild & D. Naguschewki (Eds.), *Body sexuality, and gender: Versions and subversions in African literatures* (pp. 221–230). Rodopi B.V. doi:10.1163/18757421-029030015

Adomed, I. O. C. (2008). Sociology theories of education. In R. O. A. Aluede & E. O. Omoregie (Eds.), *Sociology of education*. Alltime Publishing Company.

Adomi, E. E., & Kpangban, E. (2010). *Application of ICTs in Nigerian secondary schools*. Library Philosophy and Practice. www.researchgate.net/publication/228379384_Application_of_ICTs_in_Nigerian_Secondary_Schools. Accessed 10/09/2021.

ADPP. (2020). *Technical Report*. Retrieved December 16th 2021 from https://creativecommons.org/licenses/by/4.0/legalcode

Adurokiya, E. (2021, Jan. 24). Wife kills husband with heel over infidelity in Delta. *Tribune*.

Afigbo, A. E. (1986). *An Outline of Igbo History. RAA*. Publishing Company.

Africa, F. (n.d.). *Top Priorities for the continent 2020-2030*. https://www.brookings.edu/multi-chapter-report/foresight-africa-top-priorities-for-the-continent-in-2020/

African Development Bank Group. (2019). https://www.afdb.org/en/news-and-events/press-releseases/african-has-grasped-fourth-industrial-revolution-according-african-development-bank-report-its-role-globally-could-be-even-bigger-32644

African Union. (2020). *The Digital Transformation Strategy For Africa (2020-2030)*. www.au.int

Agbasimalo, A. (2014). *Forest dames*. Parrèsia Publishers.

Agbedo, C. U. (2000). *General linguistics: An introductory reader*. ACE Resources Konsult.

Ahmad/ (2004). *World Cultures: A Global Mosaic*. Academic Press.

Ahmed, Y. (2017). *Language, rhetoric, and politics in a global context: A decolonial critical discourse perspective on Nigeria's 2015 presidential campaign* (Dissertation). Michigan Technological University. doi:10.37099/mtu.dc.etdr/400

Ai, W., Lu, X., Liu, X., Wang, N., Huang, G., & Mei, Q. (2017). Untangling Emoji popularity through semantic embeddings. *Proceedings of the International AAAI Conference on Web and Social Media*, 11.

Ajala, J. (1991). *Public relations: In search of professional excellence*. African Link Book Ltd.

Akani, C. (2000). *Company / youth relationship in the Niger Delta: What Approach in the New Millennium?* Paper Presented at the Peace 2000 youth rally, Organized by the Rivers State Youth Federation, Port Harcourt, Nigeria.

Akaranta, O. (2014). Building and maintaining higher education ecosystem in the 21st century. Paper Presented at *a Workshop Organized by the Centre for Higher Education Studies*, University of Port Harcourt, Port Harcourt, Nigeria.

Ake, C. (1996). *Democracy and development in Africa*. The Brookings Institution.

Ake, C. (2001). *Democracy and Development*. Spectrum Book Ltd.

Aker, J. C., & Mbiti, I. M. (2010). Mobile phones and economic development in Africa. *The Journal of Economic Perspectives*, *24*(3), 207–232. doi:10.1257/jep.24.3.207

Akhigbe, J. (2013). The state and development interventions in the Niger Delta region of Nigeria. *International Journal of Humanities and Social Science*, *3*(10), 255–263.

Alagoa, E. (1993). Oral tradition and oral history in Africa. In T. Folola (Ed.), *African Historiography: Essays in honour of Jacob Ade Ajayi*. Longman.

Alasuutari, P. (2015). *The synchronization of national policies: Ethnography of the global tribe of moderns*. Routledge. doi:10.4324/9780203597729

Alesina, A., & Dollar, D. (2000). Who Gives Foreign Aid to Whom and Why? *Journal of Economic Growth*, *5*(1), 33–63. doi:10.1023/A:1009874203400

Alexander, M. (2010). *The new Jim Crow: Mass incarceration in the age of colorblindness*. The New Press.

Ali, W. (2013). *Introduction: Watershed, Principles of Watershed Management*. National Centre of Excellence in Geology University of Peshawar. Retrieved 2021, from http://nceg.uop.edu.pk/workshops/workshop-geoscience/WorkshopMaterial/Lectures/Day4/lecture-1-wajidali.pdf

Alić, S. (2010). Philosophy of media – Is the message. *Synthesis Philosophica*, *50*(2), 201–210.

Alleman, J. (2018). *Threat of Internet platforms: Facebook, Google, etc.* 29th European Regional Conference of the International Telecommunications Society (ITS): "Towards a digital future: turning Technology into markets?" Trento, Italy.

Alozieuwa, S.H.O. (2010). Beyond the ethno-religious theory of the Jos conflict. *African Peace and Conflict Journal*, *3*(2).

Alozieuwa, S.O.H. (2016). The Ombatse crisis in Nigeria: Background, recent developments and possible solutions. *Journal of Interdisciplinary Conflict Science*, *2*(2).

Alubo, O. (2006). *Ethnic conflicts and citizenship crises in the Central Region*. Eddy Asae Press.

Alvares, C., Cardoso, G., Crespo, M., & Pinto-Martinho, A. (2021). Seeking the Legitimation of Mainstream Journalism: A Portuguese Case-Study. *Journalism Practice*, 1–16. doi:10.1080/17512786.2021.2008808

Anaeto, S. G., Onabajo, O. S. & Osifeso, J.B. (2008). *Models and theories of communication*. African renaissance Books Incorporated.

Anaeto, S. G., & Anaeto, M. S. (2010). Evaluating McQuail's mormative theory of developing countries. In D. Wilson (Ed.), *Perspectives on Communication and Culture*. African Council for Communication Education.

Anagbogu, P. N. (2001). *Introduction to linguistics*. J.F.C. Ltd.

Anastaplo, G. (2021). *Censorship. Encyclopædia Britannica*. Ultimate Reference Suite. Encyclopædia Britannica Inc.

Ana, T. A., & Nogueira, S. (2018). Epistemology, methods and theories of communication in the big data era: A critical panorama of social media research. *Comunicacão e Sociedade*, *33*, 167–181. doi:10.17231/comsoc.33(2018).2912

Andrade, P. (2013). Sociological ontology of the digital public sphere: The case of Web 2.0/3.0. *Comunicação e Sociedade*, *23*, 202–216. doi:10.17231/comsoc.23(2013).1622

Andress & Winterfeld. (2014). What is Cyber Warfare. In *Cyber Warfare: Techniques, Tactics and Tools for Security Practitioners*. Elsevier.

Andrew, D., Smock, N. B., Ellison, C. L., & Donghee, Y. W. (2011). Facebook as a toolkit: A uses and gratification approach to unbundling feature use. *Computers in Human Behavior*, *27*(6), 2322–2329. doi:10.1016/j.chb.2011.07.011

Anton, C. (2016). On the roots of media ecology: A micro-history and philosophical clarification. *Philosophies*, *1*(2), 126–132. doi:10.3390/philosophies1020126

Anton, C. (2017). Media ecological orientations to philosophy and philosophical problems. *The Review of Communication, 17*(4), 224–239. doi:10.1080/15358593.2017.1367830

Aper, I.C., & Iorhemen, I.P. (2015). Dissecting academic and church corruption in Nigeria: The way forward. *Fidei Journal of Management and Business Studies, 1*(1).

Apino, E., & Retnawati, H. (2017). Developing instructional design to improve mathematical higher order thinking skills of students. *Journal of Physics Conference, 812*(1), 012100. doi:10.1088/1742-6596/812/1/012100

Appadurai, A. (1996). *Modernity at large: Cultural dimensions of globalization.* University of Minneapolis Press.

Arendt, H. (1973). *Origin of Totalitarianism.* A Harvest Books.

Arendt, H. (1958). *The human condition* (2nd ed.). The University of Chicago Press.

Aristotle. (1926). *Metaphysica (W. D. Ross, Trans.).* Clarendon Press.

Aristotle. (1947). Metaphysics. In R. McKeon (Ed.), The basic works of Aristotle. Clarendon.

Armed Conflict Location & Event Data Project (ACLED). (2021). *Lessons from the #EndSARS movement in Nigeria.* Retrieved November 6, 2021 from acleddata.com/2021/02/09/lessons-from-the-endsars-movement-in-nigeria/.

Armingeon, K., Engler, S., & Leemann, L. (2021). *Supplement to the Comparative Political Data Set – Government Composition 1960-2019.* Institute of Political Science, University of Zurich.

Arriagada, A., & Ibáñez, F. (2020). You need at least one picture daily, if not, you're dead: Content creators and platform evolution in the social media ecology. *Social Media + Society, 6*(3). Advance online publication. doi:10.1177/2056305120944624

Aryal, B. P. (2020). Financing of technical and vocational education and training in Nepal. *The Journal of Educational Research, 10*(1), 58–80. doi:10.3126/jer.v10i1.31898

Asemah, S. E. (2011). Selected mass media themes. Jos University Press.

Asouzu, I. I. (2012). Ibuanyidanda and the philosophy of essence (philosophy, the science of missing links of reality). 50th Inaugural Lecture, University Calabar, Calabar, Nigeria.

Asouzu, I. I. (2017). *Changes, adaptation and complementary noetic transformation.* A Keynote Address delivered at the 2nd African Philosophy World Conference (UNICAL 2017): Jointly Hosted by the University of Calabar, Nnamdi Azikiwe University, Awka, and the University of the Witwatersrand in Collaboration with the Conversational School of Philosophy (CPS), University of Calabar.

Asouzu, I.I. (2007). *Ibuanyidanda: New complementary ontology beyond world-immanetism, ethnocentric reduction and impositions.* LitverlagGmBh & Co. KGWien.

Asouzu, I. (2004). *Innocent: Effective Leadership and the Ambivalence of Human Interest: The Nigerian Paradox in a Complementary Perspective.* University of Calabar Press.

Asouzu, I. (2007). *New Complimentary Ontology Beyond World-Immanetism, Ethnocentric Reduction and Impositions.* Lit Verlag GmbH & Co. KG Wien.

Asouzu, I. I. (2004). *The method and principles of complementary.* Calabar University Press.

Asouzu, I. I. (2007). Ibuanyidanda: New complementary ontology, beyond world-immanentism, ethnocentric reduction and imposition. *Trans-Action.*

Asouzu, I. I. (2011). Ibuanyidanda and the philosophy of essence. *Filosofia Theoretica: African Journal of Invention and Ideas*, *1*(1), 79–118.

Atkinson, J., & Berg, S. (2016). Right-wing activism: The next challenge for alternative media scholarship, *Activist media and biopolitics*, 117-133. https://books.openedition.org/iup/1179?lang=en

Attfield, R. (1984). Value in the wilderness. *Metaphilosophy*, 15.

Audi, R. (1999). *The Cambridge Dictionary of Philosophy*. Cambridge University press.

Aworanti, O. A. (2015b). *Partnership in technical and vocational education and training (TVET) for national development.* Paper Presented at the *23rd Annual International Conference of the Nigerian Vocational Association*, Yaba College of Technology, Lagos, Nigeria.

Awua, B. (2010). Women on Women Violence: A Survey of Women Characters in Mairama Ba's So Long A Letter and Flora Nwapa's Efuru. In Gender Studies: A Reader (pp. 139–145). Great Publishers.

Ayonmike, C. S. (2014). Factors affecting female participation in technical education programme: A study of Delta State University, Abraka. *Journal of Education and Human Development*, *3*(3), 227–240.

Babajide, A. (2021, Feb. 17). *Daily Post News Paper*. www.daily post.com.

Backus, M. (2001). *E-Governance and developing countries: Introduction and examples*. Academic Press.

Baird, J. E. Jr. (1976). Differences in group communication: A review of relevant research. *The Quarterly Journal of Speech*, *62*(2), 180–192. doi:10.1080/00335637609383331

Banerjee, I., & Seneviratne, K. (2005). *Public Service Broadcasting: A Best Practices Source Book*. UNESCO.

Bangert, V. (2022). *AI is quietly eating up the world's workforce with Job automation*. https://venturebeat.com/2022/01/08/ai-is-quietly-eating-up-the-worlds-workforce-with-job-automation/

Bankler, Y. (2006). *The wealth of networks*. Yale University Press.

Baran, S. J., & Davis, D. K. (2010). *Mass Communication Theory: Foundations, Ferment and Future*. Wadsworth Cengage Learning.

Baril, G.L. (1989). Are androgynous managers really more effective? *Group and Organizational Studies, 14*, 234-249.

Bartol, L. M., & Butterfield, D. A. (1976). Sex effects in evaluating leaders. *The Journal of Applied Psychology*, *61*(4), 446–454. doi:10.1037/0021-9010.61.4.446 PMID:947881

Barzilai-Nahon, K. (2008). Toward a theory of Networking Gatekeeping: A Framework for Exploring Information Control. *Journal of the American Society for Information Science and Technology, 59*(9), 1493–1512.

Baudrillard, J. (1998). The Consumer Society: Myths and Structures. *Sage (Atlanta, Ga.)*.

Bauman, Z. (2000). *Liquid modernity*. Polity Press.

Bavaresco, A. (2014). Epistemology of social networks, public opinion, and theory of agenda. *Canadian Social Science*, *10*(5).

Bayeh, E. (2016). The role of empowering women and achieving gender equality to the sustainable development of Ethiopia. *Pacific Science Review B. Humanities and Social Sciences*, *2*(1), 37–42.

Bayer, J. B., Triệu, P., & Ellison, N. B. (2020). Social media elements, ecologies, and effects. *Annual Review of Psychology, 71*(1), 471–497. doi:10.1146/annurev-psych-010419-050944 PMID:31518525

Baykal. (2020). *Queen Bee Syndrome: A Modern Dilemma of Working Women and its Effects on Turnover Intentions.* www.semanticscholar.org>papers

BBC News. (2015). *Nigeria attack: Nasarawa cult ambush, kills 30 police.* Available @https://www.bbc.com/news/world-africa-22462225

Bearce, D. H., & Tirone, D. C. (2010). Foreign aid effectiveness and the strategic goals of donor governments. *The Journal of Politics, 72*(3), 837–851. doi:10.1017/S0022381610000204

Beauvoir, S. (2009). *The second sex* (C. Borde & S. Malovany-Chevallier, Trans.). Vintage Books, A Division Random House Inc. (Original work published 1949)

Bedriñana, K. G. A., Martín, J. A. R., & Añaños, F. T. (2021). Human Rights in the Least Developed Countries of Asia: An Index for Quantifying Sustainable Development Goal 3 (Good Health and Wellbeing). *International Journal of Environmental Research and Public Health, 18*(9), 4747. doi:10.3390/ijerph18094747 PMID:33946837

Belch, G. E., & Belch, M. A. (2001). *Advertising and promotion: An integrated marketing communication approach.* McGraw Hill.

Bendall, M. J., & Robertson, C. (2018). Crisis of democratic culture. *International Journal of Media and Cultural Politics, 14*(3), 383–391. doi:10.1386/macp.14.3.383_7

Benenson, J.F. (2013). The Development of Human Female Competition: Allies and Adversaries. *Philosophical Transactions of the Royal Society B Biological Sciences*, 1-11.

Bennett, W. L., & Segerberg, A. (2013). *The logic of connective action: Digital media and the personalization of contentious politics.* Cambridge University Press.

Bentham, J. (1979). *An Introduction to the Principle of Morals and Legislation.* Oxford University Press.

Berengueres, J., & Castro, D. (2017). *Differences in emoji sentiment perception between readers and writers.* A Paper presented at the 2017 IEEE International Conference on Big Data. https://arxiv.org/pdf/1710.0888

Berger, L. P., & Luckmann, T. (1971). *The social construction of reality: a treatise in the Sociology of knowledge.* Hamondswoth Penguin.

Berry, W. D., Ringquist, E. J., Fording, R. C., & Hanson, R. L. (1998). Measuring citizen and government ideology in the American states, 1960-93. *American Journal of Political Science, 42*(1), 327–348. doi:10.2307/2991759

Bertalanffy, L. (1968). *General system theory: Essays on its foundation and development.* New York: George Braziller.

Besong, E. N. (2016). *Lingering aspects of human bondage in Nigeria: A reflection on Nyerere's true freedom.* Paper presented at the Nigeria Philosopher Association Annual Conference, University of Uyo.

Besong, E. N., & Robert, O. S. (2018). *Rousing parents' and students' interest to Arts/Humanities through early career guidance and counselling.* Paper presented at the International Conference on 'The arts/humanities: Past, present and future', University of Calabar.

Besong, E.N. (2019). An appraisal of three Nigerian poets' perspectives on trends plaguing contemporary Nigeria. *International Journal of Arts and Literature, 3*(1).

Besong, E.N., & Robert, O.S. (2019). Philosophical consideration of herdsmen menace and hunger in contemporary Nigeria. *American Journal of Service Science and Management, 6*(1).

Besong, E. N. (2017). The imperative of indiscriminate and rural-centred educational broadcasting in Nigeria. In O. S. Robert & E. N. Besong (Eds.), *Unresolved degenerating nat'l issues: Nigerian govt & media's failure* (pp. 49–64). LAP Lambert Academic Publishing.

Best Media Info. (2016). *TV Channels create awareness about AIDS*. Retrieved from https://bestmediainfo.com/2016/12/tv-channels-create-awareness-about-aids/

BID. (2018). *Algoritmolandia. Intelligence artificial para una integración predictiva e inclusiva para América Latina*. Editorial Planeta.

Bijker, W. E. (1995). *Of bicycles, bake lites, and bulbs: Toward a theory of socio-technical change*. MIT Press.

Biles, R., & Ibrahim, D.A. (2000). *Writing xenophobia: Immigration and the print media in post- apartheid South Africa. SAMP.* Migration Policy Series, no. 17.

Bindraban, P. S. (2012). ISRIC Study: Assessing the Impact of Soil Degradation of Food Production. *Current Opinion in Environmental Sustainability, 2*, 311–323.

Blackburn, S. (2005), The Oxford Dictionary of Philosophy (2nd ed.). Oxford University Press.

Blakley, J. (2001). *Entertainment goes global: mass culture in a transforming world*. The Norman Lear Center Publications.

Blau, P. M. (1964). *Exchange and power in social life*. John Wiley.

Bliss-Carroll, L. N. (2016). *The nature, function, and value of Emojis as contemporary tools of digital interpersonal communication*. https://digitalcommons.gardner-webb.edu/english_etd

Block, D. (2019). *Post-Truth and Political Discourse*. Springer Nature Publishers. doi:10.1007/978-3-030-00497-2

Bonjean, C. M. (1982). Sex and power in the federal bureaucracy: A comparative analysis of male and female supervisors. *Work and Occupations, 9*(2), 233–254. doi:10.1177/0730888482009002005

Bonsón, E., & Ratkai, M. (2013). A set of matrixes to assess stakeholder engagement and social legitimacy on a Facebook page. *Online Review, 37*(5), 787–803. doi:10.1108/OIR-03-2012-0054

Bonsón, E., Royo, S., & Ratkai, M. (2014). Facebook practice in Western European municipalities: An empirical analysis of activity and citizen's engagement. *Administration & Society*. Advance online publication. doi:10.1177/0095399714544945

Bork, P. (2011). *Misunderstanding Africa: The West's misrepresentation of Africa, an insufficient notion of evil seen through the lens of the Rwanda genocide and child slavery in Ghana*. https://keep.lib.asu.edu/items/150395

Bortree, D. S., & Seltzer, T. (2009). Dialogic strategies and outcomes: An analysis of environmental advocacy groups' Facebook profiles. *Public Relations Review, 35*(3), 317–319. doi:10.1016/j.pubrev.2009.05.002

Botha, F. (2019). *Why Africa Has the Ability to Leapfrog the Rest of the World With Innovation*. https://www.forbes.com/sites/francoisbotha/2019/04/02/why-africa-has-the-ability-to-leapfrog-the-rest-of-the-world-with-innovation/

Boulianne, S. (2015). Social media use and participation: a meta-analysis of current research. *Information, Communication & Society, 18*. doi:.1008542 doi:10.1080/1369118X.2015

Braun, V., & Clarke, V. (2014). How to use thematic analysis with interview data. *The Counselling and Psychotherapy Research Handbook,* 183-197.

Braun, V., & Clarke, V. (2018). Using thematic analysis in counseling and psychotherapy research:A critical reflection. *Counselling & Psychotherapy Research*, *18*(2), 107–110. doi:10.1002/capr.12165

Brenner, S. W. (2007). Cybercrime: Rethinking crime control strategies. In Y. Jewkes (Ed.), *Crime Online*. Willan.

British Broadcasting Corporation. (2019). *US names Nigerians in massive fraud investigation*. www.bbc.com/news/world-africa-49446845

Brooker, P., Dutton, W., & Greiffenhagen, C. (2017). What would wittgenstein say about social media? *Qualitative Research Sage*, *17*(6), 610–626. Advance online publication. doi:10.1177/1468794117713058

Brownlee, B. J. (2017). Media development in Syria: The Janus-faced nature of foreign aid assistance. *Third World Quarterly*, *38*(10), 2276–2294. doi:10.1080/01436597.2017.1333420

Brown, M., Ray, R., Summers, E., & Fraistat, N. (2017). #Sayhername: A case study of intersectional social media activism. *Ethnic and Racial Studies*, *40*(11), 1831–1846. doi:10.1080/01419870.2017.1334934

Brown, S. (1998). *WCC delay decision on membership for Church with Polygamous Clergy – Social Report from the Eight Assembly of World Council by Churches*. Ecumerical News International.

Bruner, J. (1991). The narrative construction of reality. *Critical Inquiry*, *18*(1), 1–21. doi:10.1086/448619

Bucher, T., & Helmond, A. (2018). The affordances of social media platforms. In J. Burgess, A. Marwick, & T. Poell (Eds.), *The sage handbook of social media* (pp. 233–253). SAGE. doi:10.4135/9781473984066.n14

Budnitskiy, S. (2018). *Digital nationalisms: Identity, strategic communication, and global Internet governance* [PhD thesis]. Carleton University, Ottawa, Ontario, Canada.

Bukht & Heeks. (2019, February 17). *Defining, Conceptualising and Measuring the Digital Economy*. Retrieved from Centre for Development Informatics, University of Manchester, UK: https://www.gdi.manchester.ac.uk/research/publications/working-papers/di/

Burnside, C., & Dollar, D. (2000). Aid, policies, and growth. *The American Economic Review*, *90*(4), 847–868. doi:10.1257/aer.90.4.847

Burt, R. S. (1976). Positions in networks. *Social Forces*, *55*(1), 93–122. doi:10.2307/2577097

Calhoun, C. (1996). Social theory and the public sphere. In B. S. Turner (Ed.), *The Blackwell companion to social theory*. Blackwell Publishing.

Callicott, B. J. (1989). *In defense of the land ethic*. State University of New York Press.

Callicott, B. J. (1999). *Beyond the land ethic: More essays in environmental philosophy*. State University of New York Press.

Cammaerts, B. (2015). Social media and activism. In *The International Encyclopedia of Digital Communication and Society* (pp. 1027–1034). Wiley-Blackwell. doi:10.1002/9781118767771.wbiedcs083

Carrasco, Ed. (2012). *How social media has helped activism*. New Media Rockstars. Retrieved December 19, 2012 from https://www.newmedia.rockstar/how.socialmedia

Carta, C., & Higgott, R. (2020). Conclusion: On the Strategic Deployment of Culture in Europe and Beyond. In Cultural Diplomacy in Europe. The European Union in International Affairs.

Cassirer, E. (1985). *Filozofija simboličkih oblika* [Philosophy of symbolic forms]. Dnevnik-Književna zajednica Novog Sada.

Castells, M. (2001). *The internet galaxy*. Oxford University Press. doi:10.1007/978-3-322-89613-1

Castells, M. (2012). *Networks of outrage and hope*. Polity Press.

Cater, D. (1965). *Power in Washington: A critical look at today's struggle to govern in the U.S.A.* Collins.

Center for International Media Assistance. (n.d.). *What is media development?* Center for International Media Assistance. Retrieved December 02, 2021, from https://www.cima.ned.org/what-is-media-development/

Center for Research and Development Services. (2018). *TVET financing in Nepal: Final report*. Author.

Cerovac, I. (2016). 'The Role of Experts in a Democratic Society'. *Journal of Education Culture and Society*, *2*(2), 75–88. doi:10.15503/jecs20162.75.88

Certo, S. C., & Certo, S. T. (2006). Modern management (10th ed.). Academic Press.

Chandler, D., & Munday, R. (2011). *A Dictionary of Media and Communication*. Oxford University Press. doi:10.1093/acref/9780199568758.001.0001

Charles, M. (2013). News, Documentary and Advocacy Journalism. In K. Fowler-Watt & S. Allan (Eds.), *Journalism: New Challenges* (pp. 384–392). Centre for Journalism and Communication Research: Bournemouth University.

Charles, M. (2019). Advocacy Journalism. In T. P. Vos & F. Hanusch (Eds.), *the International Encyclopedia of Journalism Studies* (pp. 1–5). John Wiley & Sons.

Chawki, M. (2009). Nigeria Tackles Advance Free Fraud. *Journal of Information, Law & Technology, 1*. www.go.warwick.ac.uk/jilt/2009_1/chawki

Cheeseman, N., Garbe, L., & Hassan, I. (2020). Why digital democracy will take more than technology in Africa. In A collection of essays exploring the interplay between digital technologies, politics and society across Africa. Digital Civil Society Lab.

Cheng, B. (2018). *21st Century Motif: relevance and (r)evolution*. Paper presented at the LABAN 2018 International Conference Celebrating the 40th Anniversary of the Laban/Bartenieff Institute of Movement Studies. https://labaninstitute.org/wp-content/uploads/2018/07/21st-Century-Motif-Relevance-and-REvolution-Brenton-Cheng.pdf

Chen, M. (2019). Modelling Public Mood and Emotion: Blog and News Sentiment and Politico-economic Phenomena. In A. Visvizi & M. D. Lytras Effat (Eds.), *Politics And Technology In The Post-Truth Era* (pp. 57–72). Emerald Publishing Limited. doi:10.1108/978-1-78756-983-620191005

Chiakaan, G. J. (2013). *Broadcasting and the broadcast media in Nigeria*. Eagle Prints.

Chiakaan, G. J., & Ahmad, J. I. (2011). *Mass communication for beginners*. Azaben Publishers.

Chimakonam, J. O. (2017). African Philosophy and Global Epistemic Injustice. *Journal of Global Ethics*, *13*(2), 120–137.

Chiţiba, C. A. (2012). Lifelong learning challenges and opportunities for traditional universities. *Procedia: Social and Behavioral Sciences*, *46*, 1943–1947. doi:10.1016/j.sbspro.2012.05.408

Cho, A., Byrne, J., & Pelter, Z. (2020). *Digital civic engagement by young people*. UNICEF Office of Global Insight and Policy.

Chon, M., & Park, H. (2020). Social media activism in the digital age: Testing an integrative model of activism on contentious issues. *Journalism & Mass Communication Quarterly*, *97*(1), 72–97. doi:10.1177/1077699019835896

Choucri, N. (2012). *Cyber-politics in international relations*. The MIT Press. doi:10.7551/mitpress/7736.001.0001

Cissé, F. (2019). *How Africa can Ride the Artificial Intelligence Wave*. https://www.theafricareport.com/13917/how-africa-can-ride-the-artificial-intellignence-wave

Cisse, M. (2018). Look to Africa to advance artificial intelligence. *Nature*, *562*(7728), 461–462.

Clark, D. (2018). *9 Ways Africa can Use AI to Leapfrog into the Future*. https://donaldclarkplanb.blogspot.com/2018/01/7-ways-africa-can-use-ai-to-leapfrog.html?m=1

Clayton, D. M. (2018). Black lives matter and the civil rights movement: A comparative analysis of two social movements in the United States. *Journal of Black Studies*, *49*(5), 1–33. doi:10.1177/0021934718764099

Clement, J. (2019). *Number of internet users in Nigeria from 2017 to 2023 (in millions)*. www.statista.com/statistics/183849/internet-users-nigeria/

Cohen, J. (1989). Deliberation and democratic legitimacy. In A. Hamlin & P. Pettit (Eds.), *The good polity* (pp. 12–24).

Cohen, S. (2002). *Folk devils and moral panics: The creation of the mods and rockers* (3rd ed.). Routledge.

Cohn, N., Engelen, J., & Schileroord, J. (2019). The grammar of emoji? Constraints on communicative pictorial sequencing. In *cognitive research: Principles and implications*. doi:10.1186/s41235-019-0177-0

Colenso, J.W. (1855). *Remarks on the Proper Treatment of Cases of Polygamy Converts from Healthism Pieterm aritzblog*. Academic Press.

Collaboratarium for Social Media and Online Behavioural Studies (COSMOS). (2020). https://www.cosmos.ualr.edu/misinformation

COMEST. (2019). *Preliminary Study on the Ethics of Artificial Intelligence*. UNESCO. doi:10.1038/d41586-018-07104-7

Commoner, B. (1971). *The Closing Circle: Man, Nature and Technology*. Knopf Publishers.

Copeland, B. J. (2020). The Modern History of Computing. *The Stanford Encyclopedia of Philosophy*. Retrieved from Stanford Encyclopedia of Philosophy: https://plato.stanford.edu/archives/win2020/entries/computing-history/

Cowan, Neighbors, C., DeLaMoreaux, J., & Behnke, C. (1998). Women's hostility toward women. *Psychology of Women Quarterly*, *22*(2), 267–284. doi:10.1111/j.1471-6402.1998.tb00154.x

Cowen, M., & Shenton, R. (1998). *Doctrines of Development*. Routledge.

Craig, E. (n.d.). *Routledge Encyclopedia of Philosophy*. Routledge.

Crosbie, V. (2002). *What is new media? Digital deliverance*. www.digitaldeliverance.com

Daghrir, W. (2013). Globalization as Americanization? Beyond the Conspiracy Theory. *IOSR Journal of Applied Physics, 5*(2), 19-24.

Dagyang, S. D. (2008). *Jos Crisis: Another Jihad go awry? Comment*. Nigerian Tribune.

Dahlman, C. M. (2016). *Harnessing the Digital Economy for Developing Countries*. Retrieved from OECD, Paris: https://www.oecd-ilibrary.org/docserver/download/4adffb24-en.pdf

Daldal, A. (2014). Power and Ideology in Michel Foucault and Antonio Gramsci: A Comparative Analysis. *Review of History and Political Science*, *2*(2), 149–167.

Dambo, T. H., Ersoy, M., Auwal, A. M., Olorunsola, V. O., Olonode, A., Arikewuyo, A. O., & Joseph, A. (2020). Nigeria's #endsars movement and its implication on online protests in Africa's most populous country. *Journal of Public Affairs*, *2583*. Advance online publication. doi:10.1002/pa.2583

Danesi, M. (2016). *The semiotics of Emoji: the rise of visual language in the age of the Internet*. Bloomsbury.

Daniel, A. (2012). We are not militias, we are a prayer group—Ombatse cult. *Vanguard*. Available at http://www.vanguardngr.com/2012/12/we-are-not-militias-we- are-aprayer-group-ombatse-cult/

Danladi, S. (2008, Dec. 12). Re the media and the genocide in Jos. Comments. *Nigerian Standard*.

Danso, R., & McDonald, D. (2001). Writing xenophobia: Immigration and the print media in post-apartheid South Africa. *Africa Today*, *48*(3), 114–137. doi:10.2979/AFT.2001.48.3.114

Dark, S. (2020). *#EndSARS: How Nigerians harness social media against police abuse*. www.aljazeera.com/news/2020/10/25/endsars-how-nigerians-use-social-media-against-police-brutality#

Darrell, M. W., & John, R. A. (2009). *How artificial intelligence is transforming the world*. http://www.cemas.org.uk/index.php/17-content/publications/2009-how-artificial-intelligence-is-transforming-the-world

Das, S. (2018). Maternal health, human rights, and the politics of state accountability: Lessons from the Millennium Development Goals and implications for the Sustainable Development Goals. *Journal of Human Rights*, *17*(5), 550–567. doi:10.1080/14754835.2018.1496012

Daura, M. A. (2009). *Violent conflict in northern states: Bauchi, Plateau and Taraba* (Dissertation). National Institute for Policy and Strategic Studies, Kuru.

David, R. (2020). *India Confirm its first corona virus case*. CNBC. https://www.cnbc.com/2020/01/30/india-confirms-first-case-of-the-coronavirus.html

Davis, G. A. (2006). *Gifted children and gifted education: A handbook for teachers and parents*. Great Potential Press.

Davis, Y. A. (1998). Race and criminalization: Black Americans and the punishment industry. In J. Jones (Ed.), *The Angela Y Davis Reader* (pp. 61–73). Blackwell Publishing.

DD News. (n.d.). *About us*. Retrieved from http://ddnews.gov.in/about/about-us

De Mesquita, B. B., & Smith, A. (2007). Foreign Aid and Policy Concessions. *Journal of Conflict Resolution, 51*(2), 251–284. . doi:10.1177/0022002706297696

De Mesquita, B., & Smith, A. (2009). A Political Economy of Aid. *International Organization*, *63*(2), 309–340. doi:10.1017/S0020818309090109

Deaux, K. (1976). *The behavior of women and men*. Brooks/Cole.

Debebe, A. D. (2017). Socio-Economic Contributions of Community Based Participatory Watershed Development on Rural Farm Households at Gammo Gofa Zone of Demba Gofa Woreda, Ethiopia. *Journal of Economics and Sustainable Development*, *8*(13), 15–27. Retrieved 2021, from https://core.ac.uk/download/pdf/234647914.pdf

Deegan, C. (2006). Legitimacy theory. In Z. Hogue (Ed.), *Methodological Issues in Accounting Research: Theories and Methods* (pp. 161–182). Spiramus Press.

Deegan, C., & Samkin, G. (2009). *New Zealand Financial Accounting*. McGraw-Hill.

Denning, D. (2000). Cyber-terrorism: The Logic Bomb versus the Truck Bomb. *Global Dialogue*.

Derks, B. (2017). Queen bee syndrome, In The SAGE Encyclopedia of Industrial and Organizational Psychology (2nd ed.). Sage Publications.

Derks, B., Ellemers, N., van Laar, C., & de Groot, K. (2011). Do sexist organizational cultures create the Queen Bee? *British Journal of Social Psychology*, *50*(3), 519–535. doi:10.1348/014466610X525280 PMID:21884548

Derks, B., Van Laar, C., & Ellemers, N. (2016). The queen bee phenomenon: Why women leaders distance themselves from junior women. *The Leadership Quarterly*, *27*(3), 456–469. doi:10.1016/j.leaqua.2015.12.007

DeVito, M. A., Birholtz, J., & Hancock, J. T. (2017). Platform, People, and perception using affordances to understand self-presentation on social media. In *Proceedings of the 2017 ACM Conference on Computer-supported Cooperative Work and Social Computing* (pp. 740-754). New York: ACM.

Diani, M. (1992). The concept of social movement. *The Sociological Review*, *40*(1), 1–25. doi:10.1111/j.1467-954X.1992.tb02943.x

Dibie, G.A., & Robert, O.S. (2016). Significance of arts and languages in polytechnic education. *International Journal of Education Research.*

Dibie, G. A., & Robert, O. S. (2014). Appraising the significance of arts and languages in polytechnic education. *5th National Conference of the Nasarawa state: Polytechnic ASUP chapter.*

Dibie, G. A., & Robert, O. S. (2015). *A thankless task for Nasarawa parents, schools and mass media in marketing library resources. International Journal and Publications.*

Dibie, G. A., & Robert, O. S. (2017). Highlevel of corruption in Nigerian tertiary institutions. *National Annual Conference of ASUP.*

Dibie, G. A., & Robert, O. S. (2018, January). Towards transforming sub-Sahara Africa through collective rural development. *International Journal of Engineering and Information Systems*, *2*(1), 159–167.

Dietz, T. (2021). *Will Africa Leapfrog?* https://www.ascleiden.nl/news/will-africa-leapfrog

Digital Marketing Skill Institute. (2019). *Social media for businesses in Nigeria: How best can I market my brand on the social media?* www.digitalmarketingskill.com/social-media-for-businesses-in-nigeria-how-best-can-i-market-my-brand-on-the-social-media/

Dobbie, A. (2009). Theory into practice: An introduction to literary criticism (2nd ed.). Academic Press.

Dokotum, O.O. (2020). *Hollywood and Africa recycling the 'Dark Continent' myth, 1908–2020.* NISC African Humanities Program.

Dominick, J. R. (2009). *The dynamics of mass communication, media in the digital age* (10th ed.). McGraw Hill Companies.

Donoso, V., & Ribbens, W. (2010). Identity under construction. *Journal of Children and Media*, *4*(4), 435–450. doi:10.1080/17482798.2010.510011

Dowling, J., & Pfeffer, J. (1975). Organizational legitimacy social values and organizational behavior. *Pacific Sociological Review*, *18*(1), 122–136. doi:10.2307/1388226

Downing, D. H. J. (2001). *Radical Media Rebellious Communication and Social Movements.* Sage Publications, Inc.

Dul, R. (2007). Roles and responsibilities of the media in conflict management and peace building. In S. Abu & C. Best (Eds.), Pen & peace. International Centre for Reconciliation, Coventry Cathedral, Centre for Conflict Management and Peace Studies, University of Jos.

Dusek, V. (2006). *Philosophy of technology: An introduction.* Blackwell.

Dutta, N., & Williamson, C. (2016). Can foreign aid free the press? *Journal of Institutional Economics*, *12*(3), 603–621. doi:10.1017/S1744137415000557

Dworkin, R. (1999). *Life's Dominion. An argument about abortion euthanasia, and individual freedom.* Knopf, Inc.

Dyer & Petersen. (2021). Design culture of thinking: the theory, history and critics. *Cumulus Conference Proceedings.*

Eagle, N., & Horvitz, E. (2019). *Artificial Intelligence for Development. Papers from the AAAI Spring Symposium.*

Easterly, W. (2003). Can foreign aid buy growth? *The Journal of Economic Perspectives*, *17*(3), 23–48. doi:10.1257/089533003769204344

Ebele, O. C., & Oghenetega, L. U. (2014). The impact of social media on the academic performance of university students in Nigeria. *Journal of Education and Practice*, *5*(33).

Eckstein, D., Künzel, V., Schäfer, L., & Winges, M. (2019). Global climate risk index 2020. *Germanwatch.* Available at https://germanwatch.org/en/17307

Edogor, I. O., Ojo, L. I., Ezugwu, I. M., & Dike, K. (2015). Users' perception of crisis portrayals on social media: A study of Boko Haram insurgency in Nigeria. *New Media and Mass Communication, 35.* www.iiste.org

Edokpolor, J. E. (2018). Systems approach in developing creative thinking and innovative capabilities for lifelong learning among TVET students in Federal Universities, South-South, Nigeria. *International Journal of Educational Development, 21*(1), 1-15.

Edokpolor, J. E. (2019). Gender differential effect of business education students' human capital on sustainable economic development. *Journal of Educational Research and Practice, 9*(1), 40-54.

Edokpolor, J. E. (2020). Entrepreneurship education and sustainable development: Mediating role of entrepreneurial skills. *Asia Pacific Journal of Innovation and Entrepreneurship, 14*(3).

Edokpolor, J. E., & Chukwuedo, S. O. (2018). Technical and vocational education and training students' lifelong-career specific human capital: Gender consideration for sustainable development. *International Journal of Gender Studies and Research, 5*(1), 51-63.

Edokpolor, J. E., & Abusomwan, V. I. (2019). Students' potential abilities as correlates of self-employment start-up intentions: Evidence from private sector-led technical and vocational education institutions in Nigeria. *International Journal of Learning, Teaching and Educational Research*, *18*(9), 146–169. doi:10.26803/ijlter.18.9.8

Edokpolor, J. E., & Abusomwan, V. I. (2020). Perception of TPET lecturers' on the effect of global partnerships in developing students' career human capital. *International Journal of Learning, Teaching and Educational Research*, *19*(5), 125–140.

Edokpolor, J. E., & Adeniyi, I. N. (2019). Experiential and vicarious learning approaches in developing higher-order thinking skills among business education undergraduates in federal universities. *International Journal of Educational Research*, *6*(1), 1–14.

Edokpolor, J. E., & Dumbiri, D. N. (2019). Resource adequacy and utilization for teaching and learning effectiveness in vocational education programmes in south-south Nigerian universities. *Journal of Vocational Education Studies*, *2*(1), 1–12. doi:10.12928/joves.v2i1.727

Edokpolor, J. E., Edokpolor, H. O., & Olupayimo, E. O. (2016). Actualizing sustainable high standard of quality in Nigerian TVET programme through multi-stakeholders partnership. *African Journal of Studies in Education*, *11*(1), 47–62.

Edokpolor, J. E., & Egbri, J. N. (2017). Business education in Nigeria for value re-orientation: A strategic approach for poverty alleviation and national development. *Journal of Educational Research and Review*, *5*(3), 41–48.

Edokpolor, J. E., & Imafidon, A. (2017). Effectiveness of public-private partnership in the management of technical and vocational education and training. *Education Policy, Management and Quality*, *9*(1), 20–32.

Edokpolor, J. E., & Imafidon, A. (2019). Public-private-civil society partnership: A gateway to ensuring good governance practices of vocational education in South-South Nigerian Federal Universities. *Journal of Technical Education and Training*, *11*(3), 121–135. doi:10.30880/jtet.2019.11.03.015

Effiong, P. (2000). *Nigeria and Biafra: My story.* Business Forum Publications.

Egbon, M. (1994). Social responsibility and the Nigerian mass media: struggles and tactics for balanced media coverage of crises. *Media Review*, 16-30.

Eggon Assoc. President. (2017). *Nasarawa bloodbath: 270 people were killed, Al-Makura signed single term with us.* http://www.informationng.com/2013/05/nasarawa-bloodbath-270-people-were-killedal-makura-signed-single-term-with-us-eggon-assoc-president.html

Ehrlich, P. (1968). *The Population Bomb*. Ballantine Books.

Ehrlich, P. (2000). *Human Natures*. Penguin Group.

Ejaz, W., Ittefaq, M., & Arif, M. (2021). Understanding Influences, Misinformation, and Fact-Checking Concerning Climate-Change Journalism in Pakistan. *Journalism Practice*, 1–21. doi:10.1080/17512786.2021.1972029

Ekanem, S. A., & Ejue, B. J., Amimi, P. B., & Adalikwu, R. A. (2010). Living with Oil: Towards an Ethics of the Environment in Niger Delta. *Research Review: An International Multi-Disciplinary Journal, Ethiopia*, *4*(3a), 17–30.

Ekeanyanwu, N. T. (2005). The Nigerian press and political conflict reporting: A case study of the Ngige-Ubah political conflict in Anambra state. In A. M. Yakubu (Ed.), *Crisis and conflict management in Nigeria since 1980* (pp. 221–235). Nigerian Defence Academy.

Ekeh, L. (2009). *Industrialization and National Prosperity: Lessons for the Dveloping Countires*. Luzek Publishers.

Ekei, J. (2017). *Philosophy, human development and national question* (Special edition). UJAH. http://dx.doi./org/10.4314/ujah.v18i2.1

Ekeopara, C. A. (2011). *Ethical order and stability in traditional Igbo Society, Calabar*. University of Calabar Press.

Ekpenyong, B., & Ikegbu, E. A. (2018). The language of philosophy and the philosophy of language: A symbiotic paradigm. Budapest International Research and Critics Institute- Journal, 1(3), 296-305.

Ekpenyong, L. E., & Edokpolor, J. E. (2015). Winning the war against unemployment and poverty in Nigeria: Is there a role for TVET-private sector partnership? *Nigerian Vocational Association Journal, 20*(1), 125-132.

ElAlfy, A., Darwish, K. M., & Weber, O. (2020). Corporations and sustainable development goals communication on social media: Corporate social responsibility or just another buzzword? *Sustainable Development, 28*(5), 1418-1430. doi:10.1002/sd.2095

Elder, L. (2007). *Our concept of critical thinking (side bar), foundation for critical thinking.* Retrieved from http://www.criticalthinking.org/aboutCT/ourConceptCT.cfm

Elkins, J. (2012). Concerning Practices of Truth. In J. Elkins & A. Norris (Eds.), *Truth and Democracy*. University of Pennsylvania Press. doi:10.9783/9780812206227.19

Ellington, J. W. (Ed.). (1994). *Immanuel Kant Ethical Philosophy*. Hackett Publishing Company.

Ely, R. J. (1994). The effects of organizational demographics and social identity on relationships among professional women. *Administrative Science Quarterly*, *39*(2), 203–238. doi:10.2307/2393234

Emeka-Nwobia, N. U. (2015). The place of indigenous Nigerian languages in national development. *Research on Humanities and Social Sciences*, *5*(12). www.iiste.org

Emeka-Nwobia, N. (2007). *Sociolinguistics: An introductory reader*. Larry Caleb- Copy Craft International Ltd.

Emerson, R. G. (2016). Limits to a cyber-threat. *Contemporary Politics*, *22*(2), 178–196. doi:10.1080/13569775.2016.1153284

Emerson, R. M. (1976). Social exchange theory. *Annual Review of Sociology*, *2*(1), 335–362. doi:10.1146/annurev.so.02.080176.002003

Enang, F.E., & Okeke, T.I. (2015). The 1914 amalgamation and emergence of ethnic minorities problems in Northern Nigeria. *VUNS Journal of History and International Relations, 2*(2).

Engage Business Media. (2019). *Leaders lacking social media savvy*. www.engageemployee.com/leaders-lacking-social-media-savvy/

Engelhardt, H. T. Jr. (1996). *The foundations of bioethics* (2nd ed.). Oxford University Press.

Ericson, R., & Stehr, N. (2000). The ungovernability of modern societies: states, democracies, markets, participation, and citizens. In R. Ericson & N. Stehr (Eds.), *Governing Modern Societies*. University of Toronto Press. doi:10.3138/9781442675452

Erson, M., & Paul, H. (2016, August 8). How the hashtag #Blacklivesmatter emerges: Social activism on twitter. Pew Research Center: Internet. *Sciences et Techniques (Paris)*.

Eskilson, J. S. (2019). *Graphic Design: a New History* (3rd ed.). Yale University Press.

Etieyibo, E. E., & Chimakonam, J. O. (2018). The state of African philosophy in Africa. In E. E. Etieyibo (Ed.), *Method, substance, and the future of African philosophy*. doi:10.1007/978-3-319-70226-1_5

Evans, W. D. (2006). How social marketing works in health care. *BMJ, 332*(7551), 1207-1210. Retrieved 10 8, 2021, from https://bmj.com/content/332/7551/1207.2

Evwierhoma, M. (2007). *Nigeria: A flourishing culture in diversity*. Paper Presented at the 2007 World Culture Day Celebration for the National Institute for Cultural Orientation (NICO), Abuja, Nigeria.

Eze, E. (1997). *Race and the Enlightenment: A Reader*. Wiley-Blackwell.

Ezeifeka, C., & Ogbazi, I. (2011, September). You're responsible for His Death: Widowhood in Igbo Gender Construction and Struggle for Agency in Selected Literary Texts. *International Journal of Languages and Literatures.*, *2*(3), 1–10.

Ezejiofor, A. O. (2011). Patriarchy, Marriage and the Rights of Widows in Nigeria. *Unizik Journal of Arts and Humanities*, *12*(1), 139–157. doi:10.4314/ujah.v12i1.9

Ezeogu, U. A., & Ezugwu, U. J. (2021). African Philosophy beyond Eurocentric Concepts and Categories. *Nnamdi Azikiwe Journal of Philosophy*, *12*(2), 1–10.

Fabricius, P. (2021). *Playing Leapfrog: How Far Can Technology Help Africa Bypass its Developmental Backlogs.* https://www.news24.com/news24/columnists/guestcolumn/opinion-playing-leapfrog-how-far-can-technology-help-africa-bypass-its-developmental-backlogs-20210410

Faradova, G. (2020) Adult education: Contribution to the sustainable development goals. In Quality education. Encyclopedia of the UN Sustainable Development Goals. Springer. doi:10.1007/978-3-319-95870-5_1

Farivar, M. (2019). *Hundreds Arrested in Nigeria, US on Online Fraud Charges.* www.voanews.com/usa/hundreds-arrested-nigeria-us-online-fraud-charges

Fayissa, B., & El-Kaissy, M. I. (1999). Foreign aid and the economic growth of developing countries (LDCs): Further evidence. *Studies in Comparative International Development, 34*(3), 37–50. doi:10.1007/BF02687626

Fields, B. J. (1990). Slavery, race and ideology in the United States of America. *New Left Review, 181*, 95–118.

Firmstone, J. (2019). Editorial journalism and newspapers' editorial opinions. In J. Nussbaum (Ed.), *Oxford Research Encyclopedia of Communication.* Oxford University Press. doi:10.1093/acrefore/9780190228613.013.803

Fisher, C. (2016). The advocacy continuum: Towards a theory of advocacy in journalism. *Journalism, 17*(6), 711–726. doi:10.1177/1464884915582311

Fisher, C. (2018). News Sources and Journalist/Source Interaction. In J. F. Nussbaum (Ed.), *Oxford Research Encyclopedia of Communication* (pp. 1–18). Oxford Oxford University Press. doi:10.1093/acrefore/9780190228613.013.849

Fluck, W. (2011). The Americanization of modern culture: A cultural history of the popular media. In *Romance with America? Essays on culture, literature, andAmerican Studies.* https://www.jfki.fu-berlin.de/en/v/publications_fluck/2000/Romance_with_America/Fluck__Winfried_-_The_Americanization_of_Modern_Culture.pdf

Folarin, S., & Okodua, H. (2009). Environment and the Economics of Nationalism: Revisiting the Oil Issue and the Restless Run of Locusts in the Niger Delta. *Jadavpur J. Int'l Rel, 141*(1), 144–152. doi:10.1177/0973598409110010

Forough, H., Gabriel, Y., & Fotaki, M. (2019). Leadership in a Post-Truth Era: A new Narrative Disorder? Sage. doi:10.1177/1742715019835369

Fortner. (2021, March 31). *The Origins of Media Theory: An Alternative View.* Retrieved from Researchgate: https://www.researchgate.net/publication/278316913

Foster, C. (2010). *Researching ICT micro-enterprise in developing countries.* Retrieved from The Electronic Journal of Information Systems in Developing Countries: https://www.ejisdc.org/ojs2/index.php/ejisdc/article/view/695

Fosyth, F. (1977). *The making of an African legend: The Biafra story.* Penguin Books.

Frankena, W. R. (1975). The Ethics of respect for life. In Respect for life in Medicine, Philosophy, and the Law. The John Hopkins University Press.

Frankfurt, H. (2005). *On Bullshit.* Princeton University Press. doi:10.1515/9781400826537

Fraser, N. (1990). Rethinking the public sphere: A contribution to the critique of actually existing democracy. *Social Text*, (25/26), 56–80. doi:10.2307/466240

Freeden, M. (2003). *Ideology: A Very Short Introduction.* Oxford University Press. doi:10.1093/actrade/9780192802811.001.0001

Freedman, D. (2014, June 16). *Paradigms of Media Power.* Goldsmiths.

Freelon, D., Mcilwain, C. D., & Clark, M. D. (2016). *Beyond the hashtags: #Ferguson, #blacklivesmatter, and the online struggle for offline justice.* Center for Media & Social Impact, School of Communication, American University. Retrieved from https://cmsimpact.org/wp-content/uploads/2016/03/beyond_the_hashtags_2016.pdf

Freeman, C., & Wisheart, M. (2015). *Advancing the Debate: Cross-sector partnerships, business and the post-2015 development agenda*. World Vision International.

Freeman, R. E. (1984). *Strategic management: A stakeholder approach*. Pitman. doi:10.1017/CBO9781139192675

Frieden, B. (1963). *Feminine Mystique*. W.W. Norton.

Frost, G., & Semaer, M. (2002). Adoption of environmental reporting and management practices: An analysis of New South Whales public sector entities. *Financial Accountability & Management, 18*(2), 103–127. doi:10.1111/1468-0408.00147

Frost, S. E. (1989). *Basic Teachings of the Great Philosophers: A Survey of their Basic Ideas*. Anchor Books.

Fubara, A. (1997). Rhetoric of pain: unearthing the ugly as a tool for the good in Chimamanda Adichie's half of a yellow sun. In C. Nwahunanya (Ed.), A harvest from tragedy: Critical perspectives on Nigerian civil war literature. Academic Press.

Fuchs, C. (2014). Social media and the public sphere. *TripleC, 12*(1), 57–101. doi:10.31269/triplec.v12i1.552

Gadzala, A. (2018). *Despite Rise in Mobile Technology, Most of Africa is not Ready for AI*. https://www.axios.com/despite-rise-in-mobile-technology-most-of-africa-is-not-ready-for-ai-6f4ba17a-0a7b-4c03-86f5-67a8ba28cbe8.html

Gaita, R. (2016). *When Politicians Lie: Reflections On Truth, Politics And Patriotism*. https://griffithreview.com/contributors/raimond-gaita/

Galadima, D., & Enighe, J. (2001). The Press in Nigerian politics: An historical analysis of issues, and pattern of news coverage. *The Nigerian Journal of Communications*.

Galus, A. (2020). What is Media Assistance and (Why) Does It Matter? The Case of Polish Foreign Aid to the Media in Belarus and Ukraine. *Central European Journal of Communication, 13*(27), 390–408.

Ganahl, J. P. (2013). *Corruption, good governance, and the African state: A critical analysis of the political-economic foundations of corruption in sub-Saharan Africa*. Postdam University Press.

Ganesh, M. I., & Hankey, S. (2015). From information activism to the politics of data. *Fiberculture, 26*, 275–286.

Garland, D. (2001). *The Culture of Control*. Oxford University Press.

Garland, H., Hale, K. F., & Burnson, M. (1982). Attributions for the success and failure of female managers: A replication and extension. *Psychology of Women Quarterly, 7*(2), 155–162. doi:10.1111/j.1471-6402.1983.tb00827.x

Garnham, N. The media and the public sphere. In C. Calhoun (Ed.), *Habermas and the public sphere* (pp. 359–376). The MIT Press.

Gartner. (2011). *Gartner Says 4.9 Billion Connected*. Retrieved January 12, 2022, from https://www.gartner.com/newsroom/id/2905717

Ge, J., & Gretzel, U. (2018). Emoji rhetoric: A social media influencer perspective. *Journal of Marketing Management, 34*(15-16), 1272–1295. doi:10.1080/0267257X.2018.1483960

Gerritsen, D., Gagnon, K., Stefanucci, J., & Drews, F. (2012). I'd Like to Introduce you to my desktop: toward a theory of social, human-computer interaction. In *Proceedings of the Human Factors and Ergonomics Society Annual Meeting* (Vol. 56, No. 1, pp. 2098-2102). SAGE Publications. 10.1177/1071181312561445

Ghasemi, M. (2019). *Paradigms of postmodern democracies*. SAGE Open. https://us.sagepub.com/en-us/nam/open-access-at-sage

Ghazali, S., Sulaiman, N.I.S., Zabidi, N.Z., Omar, M.F & Alias, R.A. (2016). The impact of knowledge sharing through social media among academia. *AIP Conference Proceedings, 1782.* doi:10.1063/1.4966060

Ghernaouti, S. (2013). Cyber Conflicts, Cyberwars and Cyber Power. In *Cyber Power: Crime, Conflict and Security in Cyberspace*. EPFL Press.

Ghosh. (2012). *Dead son face of anti – cancer fight, family lives in penury*. Retrieved from http://archive.indianexpress.com/news/dead-son-face-of-anticancer-fight-family-lives-in-penury/1049922/1

Giddens, A. (1990). *The consequences of modernity*. Polity Press.

Gilley, B. (2009). Is democracy possible? *Journal of Democracy*, *20*(1), 113–127. doi:10.1353/jod.0.0052

Gilwald, A. (2017). *Beyond access: addressing digital inequality in Africa, Paper Series 48*. Centre for International Governance Innovation and Chatham House.

Głowacka, D. Youngs, R. Pintea, A., & Wołosik, E. (2021). *Digital technologies as a means of repression and social control.* European Parliament EP/EXPO/DROI/FWC/2019-01/LOT6/R/04.

Goff, P. M. (2013). Cultural Diplomacy. In The Oxford Handbook of Modern Diplomacy. Oxford University Press. doi:10.1093/oxfordhb/9780199588862.013.0024

Gofwen, R. (2004). *Religious conflicts in Northern Nigeria and nation building: The throes of two decades 1980–2000.* Human Rights Monitor.

Goldman, E. (2018). Emojis and the law. *Washington Law Review (Seattle, Wash.)*, *93*, 1227.

Goodall, J. (1996). *My Life with the Chimpanzees: The Fascinating Story of One of the World's most Celebrated Naturalists*. Pockets Books.

Goode, L. (2005). *Jurgen Habermas: Democracy and the public sphere*. Pluto Press.

Gore, Al. (1992). *Earth in the Balance*. Houghton Mifflin.

Gore, C. (2000). The rise and fall of the Washington consensus as a paradigm for developing countries. *World Development*, *28*(5), 789–804. doi:10.1016/S0305-750X(99)00160-6

Grabosky, P. N. (2001). Virtual criminality: Old wine in new bottles?'. *Social & Legal Studies*, *10*(2), 243–249. doi:10.1177/a017405

Gramsci, A. (1975). History, Philosophy and Culture. In The Young Gramsci ed. (pp. 352-353). New York: Telos Press.

Granovetter, M. (1973). The strength of weak ties. *American Journal of Sociology*, *78*(6), 1360–1380. doi:10.1086/225469

Green, A. (2011). Lifelong learning, equality and social cohesion. *European Journal of Education*, *46*(2), 228–243. doi:10.1111/j.1465-3435.2011.01478.x

Greenberg, D. (2015). *Truth in Politics Now*. https://prospect.org/article/truthpolitics-now

Green, M. M. (1964). *Igbo Village Affairs*. Frank Cass.

Greijdanus, P. H., & Postmes, T. (2020). The psychology of online activism and social movement: Relations between online and offline collective action. *Current Opinion in Psychology*, *35*, 49–54. doi:10.1016/j.copsyc.2020.03.003 PMID:32330859

Gruzd, S. (2018). *Multi-Stakeholder Initiatives: Lessons Learned.* SAIIA Research Paper.

GSMA. (2020). *The mobile economy: Sub-Saharan Africa 2020.* www.gsma.com

Gushe, P. D. (2006). *The Sanctity of Life.* The Center for Bioethics of Human Dignity, Trinity International University.

Gwagwa, A. (2020). *Artificial Intelligence (AI) Deployments in Africa: Benefits, Challenges and Policy Dimensions.* https://www.scielo.org.za/sci

Habermas, J. (1962). *The structural transformation of the public sphere: An inquiry into a category of bourgeois society.* The MIT Press.

Habermas, J. (1984). *The theory of communicative action.* Beacon Press.

Habermas, J. (1992). Further reflections on the public sphere. In C. Calhoun (Ed.), *Habermas and the public sphere* (pp. 421–461). The MIT Press.

Habermas, J. (1996). *Between facts and norms: contributions to a Discourse Theory of Law and Democracy.* Cambridge/ MIT Press. doi:10.7551/mitpress/1564.001.0001

Habermas, J. (1997). The public sphere. In R. E. Goodin & P. Pettit (Eds.), *Contemporary political philosophy: An Anthology* (pp. 143–146). Blackwell Publishers.

Habermas, J. (1998). Modernity – An incomplete project. In H. Foster (Ed.), *The anti-aesthetic: Essays on postmodern culture* (pp. 3–15). The New Press.

Haider, H., Mcloughlin, C., & Scott, Z. (2011). *Topic Guide on Communication and Governance.* Academic Press.

Hall, M. (2021, July 21). *Barter System vs. Currency System.* Retrieved from Economics and Macroeconomics: https://www.investopedia.com/ask/answers/061615/what-difference-between-barter-and-currency-systems.asp

Halliday, M. A. K. (1985). *An introduction to functional grammar.* Edward Arnold.

Halliday, M. A. K., & Webster, J. (2006). *On Language and Linguistics.* Continuum International Publishing Group.

Hall, S. (1996). *Critical Dialogues In Cultural Studies.* Routledge.

Hamdok, A. (2015). Forward. In *Africa's youth and prospects for inclusive development: Regional situation analyses report.* United Nations Economic Commission (UNEC) for Africa.

Hancock, L. (2012). *Drowning out the silence: Nigerian civil war literature and the politics of gender-based violence.* escholarship.org.

Hariman, R., & Luciates, L. J. (2007). *No Caption Needed: Iconic Photographs, Public Culture, and Liberal Democracy.* University of Chicago Press.

Harris, B. (2001). A foreign experience: Violence, crime and xenophobia during South Africa's transition. In *Violence and Transition Series 5.* Centre for the Study of Violence and Reconciliation.

Harris, B. (2001). *A Foreign Experience: Violence.* Crime and Xenophobia During South.

Harris, B. (2002). Xenophobia: A new pathology for a new South Africa? In *Psychopathology and social prejudice.* University of Cape Town Press.

Harris, S. T. G. (2018). Questioning the Role of Foreign Aid in Media System Research. In B. Mutsvairo (Ed.), *The Palgrave Handbook of Media and Communication Research in Africa.* Palgrave Macmillan., doi:10.1007/978-3-319-70443-2_22

Hartley, J. (1992). *The politics of pictures: The creation of the public in the age of popular media.* Routledge.

Hartmut, W., & Freudenthaler, R. (2018). Public sphere. In P. Moy (Ed.), *Oxford bibliographies in communication.* Oxford University Press., doi:10.1093/obo/9780199756841-0030

Hasa. (2018). *Difference between Philosophy and Literature.* Retrieved from www.differencebetween.com/difference-between-philosophy-and-literature/

Hazlewood, P. (2015). *Global Multi-stakeholder Partnerships: Scaling up public-private collective impact for the SDGs.* Academic Press.

Healy, M. (2014). *The Sanctity of Life and World Religions, Commentaries.* www.ncregister.com

Hebbar, N. (2020). P.M. Modi announces 21- day lockdown as COVID-19 toll touches 12. *The Hindu.* https://www.thehindu.com/news/national/pm-announces-21-day-lockdown-as-covid-19-toll-touches-10/article31156691.ece

Hegel, G.W.F. (1955). *Fenomenologija duha* [The phenomenology of spirit]. Grafički zavod Hrvatske.

Heidi, A. (2020). Digital transformation, development and productivity in developing countries: is artificial intelligence a curse or a blessing? Emerald Publishing Limited. doi:10.1108/REPS-11-2019-0145

Henderson, E. (2015). The Woman who lives with her husband and his 19 – year – old pregnant wife. *The Independent.*

Herman, E. S., & Chomsky, N. (1988). *Manufacturing consent: The political economy of the mass media.* Pantheon Books.

Hettne, B. (2002). Current trends and future options in development studies. In V. Desai & R. B. Potter (Eds.), *The companion to development studies.* Arnold.

Hilbert, M. (2015). Big Data for Development: A Review of Promises and Challenges. *Development Policy Review, 34*(1), 135–174. doi:10.1111/dpr.12142

Hitt, M. A., Ireland, R. D., & Hoskisson, R. E. (2011). *Strategic management: Competitiveness and globalization* (9th ed.). Cengage Southwestern Publishing.

Hitt, M. A., Tihanyi, L., Miller, T., & Connelly, B. (2006). International diversification: Antecedents, outcomes, and moderators. *Journal of Management, 32*(6), 831–867. doi:10.1177/0149206306293575

Hlabangane, N. (2021). The underside of modern knowledge: an epistemic break from Western science. In M. Steyn & W. Mpofu (Eds.), *Decolonizing the human: reflections from Africa on difference and oppressions.* Wits University Press. doi:10.18772/22021036512.12

Hockett, C. F. (1958). *A course in modern linguistics.* Macmillan. doi:10.1111/j.1467-1770.1958.tb00870.x

Hootsuite. (2019). *Survey Reveals One Million New People Online Daily; Social Media Fuels Growth Despite Industry Challenges of 2018.* www.hootsuite.com/newsroom/press-releases/survey-reveals-one-million-new-people-online-daily-social-media-fuels-growth-despite-industry-challenges-of-2018

Hopkin, J., & Rosamond, B. (2017). Post-truth Politics, Bullshit and Bad Ideas: 'Deficit Fetishism' in the UK. *New Political Economy.* Advance online publication. doi:10.1080/13563467.2017.1373757

Hountondji, P. (1990). Scientific Dependence in Africa Today. *Research in African Literatures, 21*(3), 5–15.

Hout, N. (2018). *Social media in learning and development: Preparing for the next generation workforce.* www.elearningindustry.com/social-media-in-learning-and-development-next-generation-workforce

Howard, P. N., & Muzammil, M. H. (2013). *Democracy's fourth wave? Digital media and the Arab Spring.* Oxford University Press. doi:10.1093/acprof:oso/9780199936953.001.0001

Huddlin, W. E. (1979). Film Language. *The Journal of Aesthetics Education*, *13*(2). doi:10.2307/3331928

Human Development Index 2019: Pakistan ranks lower than all South Asian countries. (2019, December 13). *The News*. Retrieved from https://www.thenews.com.pk/print/582826

Human Rights Watch. (2019). *Nigeria: Widespread Violence Ushers in President's New Term*. Human Rights Watch. https://www.hrw.org/news/2019/06/10/nigeria-widespread-violence-ushers-presidents-new-term

Hume, D. (1994). *Political essays* (K. Haakonssen, Ed.). Cambridge University Press. doi:10.1017/CBO9781139170765

Huntington, S., Crozier, M., & Watanuki, J. (1975). Crisis of democracy: Report on the Governability of Democracies to the Trilateral Commission. New York University Press.

Huxham, C. (1993). Pursuing collaborative advantage. *The Journal of the Operational Research Society*, *44*(5), 599–611. doi:10.1057/jors.1993.101

Ibarra, H. (1992). Homophily and differential returns: Sex differences in network structure and access in an advertising firm. *Administrative Science Quarterly*, *37*(3), 422–447. doi:10.2307/2393451

Ibeabuchi, C. (1990). *1988 Lamberth Conference and Polygamy: Its Implications for the Contemporary Nigerian Church* (B.A. Thesis). University of Calabar.

Ibezim, E. (2010). Gender Discrimination Against Women. A focus on Widowhood Practices in Nigeria. In *Gender Studies: A Reader* (pp. 164–181). Great AP Express Publishers.

Iftikhar, M., & Yousaf, M. (2021). The Impact of Climate Change Coverage on Public Adherence towards Health Threat: An Empirical Validation of the Health Belief Model. *Sir Syed Journal of Education & Social Research*, *4*(2), 402–413. doi:10.36902jesr-vol4-iss2-2021(402-413)

Igwe, U. (2021). *Nigeria's growing cybercrime threat needs urgent government action*. www.blogs.lse.ac.uk/africaatlse/2021/06/09/nigerias-growing-cybercrime-phishing-threat-needs-urgent-government-action-economy/

Ijiomah, C. (2014). *'Harmonious monism' a philosophical logic of explanation for ontological issues in supematuralism in African thought*. Jochrisam Publishers.

ILO. (2011). *A skilled workforce for strong, sustainable and balanced growth: A G20 training strategy*. ILO.

ILO. (2020). *The digitization of TVET and skills systems*. ILO.

IMDB. (n.d.). *All Shows of Star Plus*. Retrieved from https://m.imdb.com/list/ls021951507

IndiaNetzone. (2013). *History of Private Television in India*. Retrieved from https://www.indianetzone.com/42/history_private_television_india.htm

Innes, M. (2004). Reinventing Tradition? Reassurance, Neighbourhood Security and Policing. *Criminal Justice*, *4*(2), 151–171. doi:10.1177/1466802504044914

Innes, M. (2005). Why Disorder Matters? Antisocial Behaviour and Incivility as Signals of Risk. Paper given to the *Social Contexts and Responses to Risk (SCARR) Conference*, Kent, UK.

Innis, H. A. (1964). *The bias of communications, with a new introduction by Marshall McLuhan*. University of Toronto Press.

Inya-Egwu, A. (2018). Philosophy in diverse modes: An appraisal of the musicsophical contents in the music of Fela Anikulapokuti and Prince Nico Mbarga. In P.B. Bisong & O.J. Alexander (Eds.), Essays on feminism in honour of Prince Nico Mbarga (pp. 498-515). e20Media Limited.

Inyang, B. (2019). Environmental Degradation and Sustainable Development in Nigeria: A Study of the South-South Region of Nigeria. *International Journal of Humanities Social Sciences and Education*, *6*(8), 33-42.

IPA. (2011). *The Impact of Savings Groups on the.* Innovations For Poverty Action. Retrieved 2021, from https://www.poverty-action.org/study/evaluating-village-savings-and-loan-associations-ghana

Isichei, E. (1976). *A history of the Igbo people*. Macmillan. doi:10.1007/978-1-349-15621-4

Ittefaq, M., Ejaz, W., Fahmy, S. S., & Sheikh, A. M. (2021). Converged journalism: Practices and influences in Pakistan. *Media International Australia*, *181*(1), 167–182. doi:10.1177/1329878X211017329

Iwe, N. S. S. (1986). *The History and Contents of Human Rights: A Study of the History and Interpretation of Human Rights*. Peter Lang Publishing, Inc.

Iwuchukwu, O. (2016, Apr. 24). Women Empowerment is Key to Self-actualization Through Focu. *The Guardian*, p. 15.

James, G. (1988). *The stolen legacy*. Julian Richard.

James, J. (1999). Black revolutionary icons and 'neoslave' narratives. *Social Identities*, *5*(2), 135–159. doi:10.1080/13504639951536

James, W. (1907). *A New Nature for Some Old Ways of Thinking*. Longman Green & Co.

Jamieson, D. (Ed.). (2001). *A Companion to Environmental Philosophy*. Blackwell Publishers. doi:10.1002/9780470751664

Jamil, S., & Appiah-Adjei, G. (2020). Battling with infodemic and disinfodemic: The quandary of journalists to report on COVID-19 pandemic in Pakistan. *Media Asia*, *47*(3-4), 88–109. doi:10.1080/01296612.2020.1853393

Jana, A., & Khan, S. A. (2018). Social media's standing in McLuhan's media ecology theory: A discourse analysis. In *4th International Conference on Theory and Practice(ICTP)*. Asia Pacific Institute of Advanced Research.

Janowitz, M. (1975). Professional models in journalism: The gatekeeper and the advocate. *The Journalism Quarterly*, *52*(4), 618–626. doi:10.1177/107769907505200402

Jay, M. (2010). *The Virtues of Mendacity*. University of Virginia Press.

Jefferson, T. (1787). Notes on the state of Virginia. In Race and the enlightenment: A reader. Wiley-Blackwell.

Jensen, R. (2008). *Advocacy journalism*. The International Encyclopaedia of Communication., doi:10.1002/9781405186407.wbieca029

Jewkes, Y. (Ed.). (2003). Dot. In Cons: Crime, deviance, and identity on the internet. Cullompton.

Jewkes, Y., & Andrews, C. (2007). Internet child pornography: international responses. In Y. Jewkes (Ed.), *Crime Online*. Willan.

Jewkes, Y., & Sharp, K. (2003). Crime, deviance and the disembodied self: Transcending the dangers of corporeality. In Y. Jewkes (Ed.), *Dot. Cons: Crime, Deviance, and Identity on the Internet*. Willan.

Jibril, A. T., & Abdullah, H. M. (2012). Relevance of emoticons in computer-mediated communication context: A review. *Asian Social Science*, *9*(4), 201–207. doi:10.5539/ass.v9n4p201

Ji, D., Hu, Z., & Muhammad, Y. (2016). Neighboring competitor? Indian image in Chinese media. *Global Media and China*, *1*(3), 234–250. doi:10.1177/2059436416668186

Jimbili, M. (2020). The origin of minority agitation in Northern Nigeria. In M. Michael, E. T. Aliegba, & A. A. Alagba (Eds.), *Human rights, religion and society: Festschrift for Rev. Fr. Prof. Jake Omang Otonko on his 60th Birthday*. Eiwa Press Nig. Ltd.

Johns, R. (2019). *Should We Code in English Using language to reduce barriers to entry into tech.* Towards Data Science. https://towardsdatascience.com/should-we-code-in-english-d59bd7ed87c9

Jones, E. D. (1996). New trends and generations in African literature. African Literature Today, 20, 1-2.

Joseph, H. (2013). Ombatse: Profile of deadly cult group. *Daily Trust.* http://dailytrust.com.ng/weekly/index.php/top-stories/12653-ombatse-profile-of-deadly-cultgroup

Kahn, L. S. (1984). Group process and sex differences. *Psychology of Women Quarterly*, *8*(3), 261–281. doi:10.1111/j.1471-6402.1984.tb00636.x

Kalpokas, I. (2019). *A Political Theory of Post-Truth.* Springer Nature Publishers. doi:10.1007/978-3-319-97713-3

Kamboh, S. A. (2019). Missing links in practical journalism in developing Pakistan. In B. Dernbach & B. Illg (Eds.), *Journalism and journalism education in developing countries* (pp. 157–168). Manipal University Press.

Kamboh, S. A., Ittefaq, M., & Sahi, A. A. (2021). Journalistic routines as factors promoting COVID-19 vaccine hesitancy in Pakistan. *Third World Quarterly*. Advance online publication. doi:10.1080/01436597.2021.1995713

Kamboh, S. A., Ittefaq, M., & Yousaf, M. (in press). COVID-19: A window of opportunity to influence environmental policies through media advocacy in global south. *International Journal of Communication.*

Kamboh, S. A., & Yousaf, M. (2020). Human development and advocacy journalism: Analysis of low editorial coverage in Pakistan. *Development Policy Review*, *38*(5), 646–663. doi:10.1111/dpr.12443

Kamilindi, T. (2007). Journalism in a time of hate media. In The media and the Rwandan genocide. New York: Pluto Press.

Kanbur, R. (2006). *What's Social Policy got to do with Economic Growth?* Retrieved from https://www.arts.cornell.edu/poverty/kanbur/

Kandola, A. (2020). *What to know about genetic disorders.* www.medicalnewstoday.com

Kant, I. (1983). To perpetual peace. In *Immanuel Kant: Perpetual peace and other essays on politics, history, and morals* (pp. 107–144). Hackett. (Original work published 1795)

Kaplan, J. (2005). *Roadmap for open ICT ecosystems.* Berkman Klein Center for Internet & Society, Harvard Law School. http://cyber.law.harvard.edu/ epolicy/roadmap.pdf

Karkockiene, D. (2005). Creativity: Can it be trained? A scientific educology of creativity. International *Journal of Educology,* 51-58. Retrieved from http://www.era-usa.net/images/article_5_Daiva.pdf

Karras, G. (2006). Foreign aid and long-run economic growth: Empirical evidence for a panel of developing countries. *Journal of International Development: The Journal of the Development Studies Association*, *18*(1), 15–28. doi:10.1002/jid.1187

Kataoka, S. (n.d.). *The plight of African states and good governance.* https://www2.jiia.or.jp/pdf/working_paper/h14_kataoka-e.pdf

Kaur, J., Miller, R., Freitas, E., Bemben, D., & Bemben, M. (2019). Racial/ethnic differences in bone mineral density, muscle function and fat mass in young women. *BJHBS*, *18*(2), 2. doi:10.12957/bjhbs.2019.53500

Keane, J. (2018). *Post-Truth Politics and why the Antidote isn't simply 'Fact-Checking' and Truth.* https://theconversation.com/post-truth-politics-and-why-the-antidoteisnt-simply-fact-checking-and-truth-87364

Kelley, J. R. (2010). The New Diplomacy: Evolution of a Revolution. *Diplomacy and Statecraft, 21*(2), 286–305. doi:10.1080/09592296.2010.482474

Kelly, R., and Watts, L (2015). Characterizing the inventive appropriation of Emoji as relationally meaningful in mediated close personal relationships. In *Experiences of technology appropriation: Unanticipated users, usage, circumstances, and design.* Academic Press.

Kendall, L. (2002). *Hanging out in the virtual pub: Masculinities and relationships Online.* University of California Press. doi:10.1525/california/9780520230361.001.0001

Kennedy, X. J. & Gioia, D. (1995), *Literature: An Introduction to Fiction, Poetry, & Drama.* Harper Collins College Publishers.

Kennedy, G. W., Udoetuk, U. S., & Ufot, S. I. (2017). Challenges of technical vocational teacher education and teaching in Nigeria: The need for intervention. *International Journal of Education and Evaluation, 3*(7), 71–82.

Kenny, C. (2019). *Automation and AI: Implications for African Development Prospects?* https://www.cgdev.org/publication/automation-and-ai-implications-african-development-prospects

Kent, M. L., & Taylor, M. (1998). Building dialogic relationships through the World Wide Web. *Public Relations Review, 24*(3), 321–334. doi:10.1016/S0363-8111(99)80143-X

Keyes, R. (2004). *The Post-Truth Era.* St Martin's Press.

Khan, A. A. (2012). The role of social media and modern technology in Arabs Spring. *Far East Journal of Psychology & Business., 7*(1), 56–63.

Khan, M. A., Khan, M. M., Hassan, M., Ahmed, F., & Haque, S. M. (2017). *Role of Community Radio for Community Development in Bangladesh. The International Technology Management Review.* doi:10.2991/itmr.2017.6.3.3

Khazraee, E., & Novak, A. N. (2018). Digitally mediated protest: Social media affordances for collective identity construction. *Social Media + Society, 4*(1), 1–14. doi:10.1177/2056305118765740

Kigwilu, P. C., & Akala, W. J. (2017). Resource utilization and curriculum implementation in community colleges in Kenya. *International Journal for Research in Vocational Education and Training, 4*(4), 369–381. doi:10.13152/IJRVET.4.4.4

Kim, J. N., & Sriramesh, K. (2009). A descriptive model of activism in global public relations research and practice. In K. Sriramesh,& D., Vercic (Eds.), The global public relations handbook (Rev. ed., pp. 79-97). New York, NY: Routledge.

Kim, J. (2011). Foreign aid and economic development: The success story of South Korea. *Pacific Focus, 26*(2), 260–286. doi:10.1111/j.1976-5118.2011.01065.x

Kim, R. G., & Evans, W. M. I. (2008). Remote sensing and control of an irrigation system using a distributed wireless sensor network. *IEEE Transactions on Instrumentation and Measurement, 57*(7), 1379–1387. doi:10.1109/TIM.2008.917198

Kitchin, R., & McArdle, G. (2016). What makes big data, big data? Exploring the ontological characteristics of 26 datasets. *Big Data & Society, 3*(1), 1–10. doi:10.1177/2053951716631130

Klapper, J. T. (1960). *The Effects of Mass Communication.* Free Press.

Kling, R., & Lamb, R. (2000). IT and organizational change in digital economies. In Understanding the Digital Economy. Cambridge, MA: MIT Press.

Konvitz, M. R. (2006). Censorship. *Microsoft Encarta 2007* [DVD]. Microsoft Corporation.

Koutrompis, P. (2009). The economic impact of broadband on growth: A simultaneous approach. *Telecommunications Policy*, *33*(9), 471–485. doi:10.1016/j.telpol.2009.07.004

Kovach & Rosenstiel. (2001). *The Elements of Journalism: What Newspeople Should Know and the Public Should Expect*. Three Rivers Press.

Krstić, I. I., Ilić, A., & Avramović, D. (2015). The three dimensions of sustainable development: Environment, economy and society. *Proceedings on 50 Years of Higher Education, Science and Research in Occupational Safety Engineering*.

Kulesz, M. (2018). *Culture, platforms and machines: The impact of artificial intelligence on the diversity of cultural expressions*. UNESCO Information Document. https://en.unesco.org/creativity/sites/creativity/files/12igc inf4 en.pdf

Kumar, K. J. (2007). *Mass Communication in India*. Jaico Publication House.

Kurbalija, J. (2019). An Introduction to Internet Governance (6th ed.). Princeton University Press.

Lagos State Judicial Panel of Inquiry on Restitution for Victims of SARS Related Abuses and Other Matters. (2021). *Report of Lekki Incident Investigation of 20th October 2020*. Submitted to the Governor of Lagos State.

Lamola, J. M. (2021). *Africa in the Fourth Industrial Revolution: A Status Questionis, from the Cultural to the Phenomenological. In African Values, Ethics and Technology*. Palgrave Macmillan.

Lane, N. (1999). Advancing the digital economy into the 21st century. *Information Systems Frontiers*, *1*(13), 317–320. doi:10.1023/A:1010010630396

Lasswell, H. D. (1951). The Political Writings of Harold D. Lasswell. The Free Press.

Laursen, B., & Trapp, N. L. (2021). Experts or advocates: Shifting roles of central sources used by journalists in news stories? *Journalism Practice*, *15*(1), 1–18. doi:10.1080/17512786.2019.1695537

Lawhead, W. F. (2002). The voyage of discovery: A historical introduction to philosophy (2nd ed.). Wadsworth/Thomson Learning.

Lawhead, W. F. (2003). *The Philosophical Journey: An Interactive Approach* (5th ed.). McGraw-Hill Book Company.

Lawrence-Hart, G. (2011). Sin and its Removal in African Traditional Religion. In G. Tasie & R. Olumati (Eds.), *West African Religious Heritage*. Clear Vision Publishers.

Lawrence-Hart, G. (2019, July). The Socio-cultural Significance of Polygamy in Africa. *International Journal of Social Science and Humanity*, *5*(1).

Laws, N., & Chojnicka, J. (2020). "A Future to Believe in": Introducing Varieties of Advocacy Journalism. The Examples Sustainability and the Sanders Campaign. *Journalism Studies*, *21*(9), 1261–1283. doi:10.1080/1461670X.2020.1742773

Lee, M. Y. H. (2015). Donald Trump's False Comments connecting Mexican immigrant and Crime. *The Washington Post*. https://www.washingtonpost.com/news/fact-checker/wp/2015/07/08/donald-trumps-false-comments-connecting-mexican-immigrants-and-crime/

Lemarchand, R. (2009). The dynamics of violence in Central Africa. University of Pennsylvania Press. doi:10.9783/9780812202595

Leopold, A. (1977). *A Sand County Almanac*. Oxford University Press.

Lerner, D. (1958). *The passing of traditional society: Modernizing the Middle East*. Free Press.

Lerner, D., & Schramm, W. L. (1967). *Communication and change in the developing countries*. East-West Center P. doi:10.1515/9780824885663

Levin, T. (1986). Women as Scapegoats of Culture and Cult: An Activist's View of Female Circumcision in Ngugi's The *River Between.* In C. B. Caries & A. A. Graves (Eds.), *Ngambika Studies of Women in African Literature* (pp. 205–221). African World Press.

Lewis, D. (1978, January). Truth in Fiction. *American Philosophical Quarterly*, *15*(1).

Lhamon, W. T. Jr. (2000). *Raising Cain: Blackface performance from Jim Crow To hip hop*. Harvard University Press.

Liakos, K., Busato, P., Moshou, D., Pearson, S., & Bochtis, D. (2018). *Machine Learning in Agriculture: A Review Sensors*. doi:10.3390/s18082674

Linnaeus, C. (1758). *System of a nature*. Laurentius Salvius.

Lippmann, W. (2004). *Public Opinion*. Dover Publications.

Llanso, E., van Hoboken, J., Leerssen, P., & Harambam, J. (2020). *Artificial intelligence, content moderation, and freedom of expression*. Transatlantic Working Group.

Lockie, S. (2017). Post-truth Politics and the Social Sciences. *Environmental Sociology*, *3*(1), 1–5. doi:10.1080/23251042.2016.1273444

Logan, R. (2021, December 24). *Understanding Man: The Extensions of Digital Media.* Retrieved from https://www.researchgate.net/publication/313601251 doi:10.13140/RG.2.2.32821.47847

Logan, R.K. (2016). *McLuhan's philosophy of media ecology: An introduction*. Academic Press.

Looker, C. A. (2002). Editorial: The skeleton, race, and Ethnicity. *The Journal of Clinical Endocrinology and Metabolism*, *87*(7), 3047–3050. doi:10.1210/jcem.87.7.8779 PMID:12107199

Lu, X., Ai, W., Liu, X., Li, Q., Wang, N., Huang, G., & Mei, Q. (2016). Learning from the ubiquitous language: an empirical analysis of emoji usage of smartphone users. *Proceedings of the 2016 ACM International Joint Conference on Pervasive and Ubiquitous Computing*.

Lugo-Ocando, J. (2018). A Mouthpiece for Truth: Foreign Aid for Media Development and the Making for Journalism in the Global South. *Brazilian Journalism Research*, *14*(2), 412–431. doi:10.25200/BJR.v14n2.2018.1101

Lunceford, B. (2012). Posthuman visions: Creating the technologized body. *Explorations in Media Ecology*, *11*(1), 7–25.

Luuk, E. (2018). *Symbol and its evolution*. doi:10.12775/3991-1.064

Luuk, E. (2013). The structure and evolution of symbol. *New Ideas in Psychology*, *31*(2), 87–97. doi:10.1016/j.newideapsych.2012.06.001

Lynch, M. (2011). After Egypt: The limits and promise of online challenges to the authoritarian Arab State. *Perspectives on Politics*, *9*(02), 301–310. doi:10.1017/S1537592711000910

Lyon, D. (2001). *Surveillance society: Monitoring everyday life*. Open University Press.

Lyon, D. (2003a). *Surveillance after September 11*. Polity Press.

Lyon, D. (2003b). Surveillance as social sorting: Computer codes and mobile bodies. In D. Lyon (Ed.), *Surveillance as Social Sorting: Privacy, Risk, and Digital Discrimination*. Routledge.

MacCormack, C. (1983). Community Participation in Primary Health Care. *Tropical Doctor, 13*(2), 51-54. Retrieved 9 18, 2021, from https://ncbi.nlm.nih.gov/pubmed/6679395

MacFarlene, A. (1993). New news and old: revising the literature. Caejac Journal, 5, 5-20.

Machiavelli, N. (1992). Of Auxiliary, Mixed, and One's Own Soldiers. In *The Prince*. University of Chicago Press. (Originally published 1532)

Mair, P. (2013). *Ruling the Void. The Hollowing of Western Democracy*. Verso.

Maitland, D. (1994). Forging New Links for Telecom Development. *Transnational Data and Communications Report*, (March/April), 17–20.

Majumdar, S. (2011). *Emerging challenges and trends in TVET in the Asian-Pacific Region*. Sense Publishers. doi:10.1007/978-94-6091-391-4

Malahat, C. & Ari, H. (2020). *Key enablers for deploying artificial intelligence for circular economy embracing sustainable product design: Three case studies*. doi:10.1063/5.0001339

Malek, J. (2018). Bridging the gap between theory and practice: Philosophy through a wide- angle lens. *The Journal of Medicine and Philosophy*, *43*(1), 1–7. doi:10.1093/jmp/jhx031

Manin, B. (1987). On legitimacy and political deliberation. *Political Theory, 15*(3). Doi:10.2307/191208

Manjoo, R., & McRaith, C. (2011). Gender –based violence and justice in conflict and post-conflict areas. *Cornell International Law Journal*, *44*(11), 11–12.

Mantovani, G. (1996). Social context in HCI: A new framework for mental models, cooperation and communication. *Cognitive Science*, *20*(2), 237–296. doi:10.120715516709cog2002_3

Manyika, J. e. (2013). *Lions Go Digital: The Internet's Transformative Potential in Africa*. Retrieved from McKinsey Global Institute. https://www.mckinsey.com/industries/high-tech/our-insights/lions-go-digital-the-internets-transformative-potential-in-af

Manyika, J. e. (2016). *Digital Globalization: The New Era of Global Flows*. https://www.mckinsey.de/sites/mck_files/files/mgi_digital_globalization.pdf

Manyozo, L. (2008). *Communicating with radio what do we know? Findings from selected rural radio effectiveness evaluations*. Farm Radio International.

Marchant, R. E. (2018). Anyone anywhere: narrating African innovation in a global community of practice. *Publicly Accessible Penn Dissertations*. 2746. https://repository.upenn.edu/edissertations/2746

Markman, K., & Oshima, S. (2017). *Pragmatic play? Some possible functions of English emoticons and Japanese Kaomoji In computer-mediated discourse*. Paper presented at the Association of Internet Researchers Annual Conference 8.0: Let's play! Vancouver. 10.31235/osf.io/qa764

Martin, D. (2016, June 20-21). *Socio-digital practices of collective action in online labour platforms*. Paper presented at Connected Life Conference.

Marty, E. M., & Moore, J. (2000). *Politics Religion and the Common Good*. Jesse-Bass Publisher.

Marwick, A. E. (2013). Online identity. In J. Hartley, J. Burgess, & A. Bruns (Eds.), *A companion to new media dynamics* (pp. 355–364). doi:10.1002/9781118321607.ch23

Maryniarczyk, A. (2016). *Rationality and Finality of the World of Persons and Things*. Polskie Towarzyztwo Tomasza z Akwinu.

Mathiesen, T. (1997). The viewer society: Michel Foucualt's "Panopticon" revisited. *Theoretical Criminology*, *1*(2), 215–234. doi:10.1177/1362480697001002003

Mavin, S. (2008). Queen Bees, Wannabees and Afraid to Bees: No More "Best Enemies" for Women in Management? *British Journal of Management*, *19*(s1), 75–84. doi:10.1111/j.1467-8551.2008.00573.x

Mayoux, L. (2018). *Participatory Methods*. Retrieved 2021, from Watsan Mission Assistant: https://www.google.com/url?sa=t&rct=j&q=&esrc=s&source=web&cd=&cad=rja&uact=8&ved=2ahUKEwiV-bXWjsnzAhUGlhQKHanlBJAQFnoECCAQAQ&url=https%3A%2F%2Fwatsanmissionassistant.org%2Fwp-content%2Fuploads%2F2018%2F08%2Fparticipatory-methods-_linda-mayoux.pdf&usg=AOv

Mbiti, J. S. (1969). *African Religions and Philosophy*. Heinemann Publishers.

Mbiti, J. S. (1975). *Introduction to African Traditional Religion*. Heineman Publishers.

Mbye, B. C. (1987). Contemporary Society and the Female Imagination: A Study of the Novels of Mariama Ba. In *Women in African Literature Today* (pp. 89–101). African World Press.

McAdams, P. D., Josselson, R., & Lieblich, A. (2006). *Identity and story: creating self in narrative*. American Psychological Association. Retrieved from http://psycnet.apa.org/psycinfo/2006-01746-000/

McAllister, M., Dunn, G., Payne, K., Davies, L., & Todd, C. (2012). Patient empowerment: The need to consider it as a measurable patient-reported outcome for chronic conditions. *BMC Health Services Research, 12*(1), 157-157. Retrieved 10 8, 2021, from https://bmchealthservres.biomedcentral.com/articles/10.1186/1472-6963-12-157

McAllister, S. M. (2012). How the world's top universities provide dialogic forum for marginalized voices. *Public Relations Review*, *38*(2), 319–327. doi:10.1016/j.pubrev.2011.12.010

McAnany, E. G. (1978). Does Information Really Work? *Journal of Communication*, *28*(1), 84–90. doi:10.1111/j.1460-2466.1978.tb01568.x

McCombs, M. E., & Shaw, D. L. (1972). The agenda-setting function of mass media. *Public Opinion Quarterly*, *36*(2), 176. doi:10.1086/267990

McCormick, P. (2006). Our hearts of darkness. *U.S. Catholic*, (May), 42–43.

McDonald, D. O., & Jacobs, S. (2005). (Re)Writing xenophobia: Understanding press coverage of cross-border migration in Southern Africa. *Journal of Contemporary African Studies*, *23*(3), 295–325. doi:10.1080/02589000500274050

McInery, R. (Ed.). (1998). *Aquinas, T. Selected Writings*. Penguin Books.

McIntyre, A. (2006). *Ethics and Politics: Selected Essays* (Vol. 2). Cambridge University Press. doi:10.1017/CBO9780511606670

McIntyre, A. (2007). *After Virtue* (3rd ed.). University of Notre Dame Press.

McIntyre, L. (2019). *Post-Truth*. The MIT Press.

McKee, A. (2005). *The public sphere: An introduction*. Cambridge University Press.

McLuhan, M. (1964). *Understanding media*. Routledge & Kegan Paul.

McLuhan, M. (1967). *The Medium is the Massage. New York*. Bantam Books.

McLuhan, M., & McLuhan, E. (2011). *Media and Formal Cause*. NeoPoiesis Press.

McNair, B. (2018). *An Introduction to Political Communication*. Routledge.

McQuail, D. (1979). The influence and effect of mass media. In *Mass Communication and Society*. Sage Publication.

McQuail, D. (1983). *Mass Communication Theory: An Introduction*. Sage.

Mearsheimer, J. J. (2011). *Why Leaders Lie: The Truth About Lying in International Politics*. Oxford Press.

Media. (2021, December 23). Hypodermic Needle Theory. *Media - The study of what we hear, watch and read*. http://www.mediaknite.org/hypodermic-needle-theory/

Mefalopulos, P. (2007). Theory and Practice of Participatory Communication - The Case of the FAO Project "Communication for Development in Southern Africa. *Communication Initiative Network*. Retrieved 2021, from https://www.comminit.com/africa/content/theory-and-practice-participatory-communication

Mehta, N. (2008). *India on Television: How Satellite News Channel have Changed the Way We Think and Act?* Harper Collins.

Memmi, A. (1999). *Racism*. University of Minnesota Press.

Mensah, J. (2019). Sustainable development: meaning, history, principles, pillars, and implications for human action: a literature review. *Cogent Social Sciences*, *5*(1), 1–21. doi:10.1080/23311886.2019.1653531

Mesenbourg, T. (2001). *Measuring the Digital Economy*. Retrieved from US Bureau of the Census, Suitland, MD.: https://www.census.gov/content/dam/Census/library/working-papers/2001/econ/umdigital.pdf

Metuh, E. I. (1987). *Comparative Studies of African Traditional Religions*. IMICE Publishers.

Meyer, D. S. (2015). *The politics of protest: Social movements in America* (2nd ed.). Oxford University Press.

Michael, N. (2019). *Artificial Intelligence Policies in Africa over the Next Five Years*. https://www.researchgate.net/profile/Micheal-Nayebare/publication/337503231_Artificial_intelligence_policies_in_Africa_over_the_next_five_years/links/5e763a21a6fdcccd6215935e/Artificial-intelligence-policies-in-Africa-over-the-next-five-years.pdf doi:10.1145/3368075

Micó, J.-L., & Andreu, C.-R. (2014). Political activism online: Organization and media relations in the case of 15m in Spain. *Information Communication and Society*, *17*(7), 858–871. doi:10.1080/1369118X.2013.830634

Milan, S., & Van der Velden, L. (2016). The alternative epistemologies of data activism. *Digital Culture & Society*, *2*(2), 57–74. doi:10.14361/dcs-2016-0205

Milbery, K. (2017). *Media ecology. Oxford Bibliographies Online*. https://www.oxfordbibliographies.com/view/document/obo-9780199756841/obo-9780199756841-0054.xml

Millington, R. (2012). *Types Of Community And Activity Within The Community*. Retrieved July 2021, from https://www.feverbee.com/types-of-community-and-activity-within-the-community/

Moemeka, A. (1994). *Communicating for development: A new pan-disciplinary perspective*. State University of New York Press.

Moemeka, A. A. (1994). Development communication: A historical and conceptual overview. In A. A. Moemeka (Ed.), *Communicating for development: A new pan-disciplinary perspective* (pp. 3–22). State University of New York Press.

Mogekwu, M. (2017). *The media's role in stoking xenophobia.* Available at https://worldpolicy.org/2017/04/26/the-medias-role-in-stoking-xenophobia

Mohammed, O. A. (2011). *Xenophobia and media: An exploratory study on the public perceptions of the Nelson Mandela bay community.* Nelson Mandela Metropolitan University.

Moll, I. (2020). *The First three Industrial Revolutions Stripped Africa Bare—It's hard to see why the fourth would be any Different.* https://www.dailymaverick.co.za/article/2020-08-20-the-first-three-industrial-revolutions-stripped-africa-bare-its-hard-to-see-why-the-fourth-would

Monday, H. G., & Eze, C. C. (2012). *Basic studies in English and communication skill for tertiary institutions.* Shola Publishers.

Morley, D. (2000). *Home territories: Media, mobility, and identity.* Routledge.

Morris, M. (2010). The idea of words as signs. In *Philosophy of language and linguistics* (Vol. II). The Philosophical Turn. Ontos Verlag.

Morsy, H. (2020). *How Africa can Harness the Fourth Industrial Revolution.* https://www.project-syndicate.org/commentary/how-africa-can-close-education-skills-gap-by-hanan-morsy-2020-08

Moschini, I. (2016). The 'face with tears of joy' emoji. A Socio-Semiotic and multimodal insight into a Japan-America Mash-Up. *HERMES-Journal of Language and Communication in Business, 55*, 11–25.

Msibi, F., & Penzhorn, C. (2010). Participatory communication for local government in South Africa: A study of the Kungwini Local Municipality. Information Development. *Information Development, 26*(3), 225–236. doi:10.1177/0266666910376216

Muhammad, K. (2010). *The condemnation of blackness: race, crime, and the making of modern urban America.* Harvard University Press. doi:10.2307/j.ctvjsf4fx

Murphy, J. A. (2015). *Africa's Information Revolution.* John Wiley.

Mutoni, D. (2017). *A revolutionary connectivity: internet access as the ultimate human right and socioeconomic force.* New Degree Press.

Myers, M., Juma, L. A., & O'Maley, D. (2018). *Defending independent media: A Comprehensive analysis of aid flows.* Center for International Media Assistance. https://stats.oecd.org/Index.aspx?DataSetCode=crs1

Myers, M., Harford, N., & Bartholomew, K. (2017). *Media Assistance: Review of the Recent Literature and Other Donors' Approaches.* Imedia Associates.

Nabi, R. L., & Riddle, K. (2008). Personality Traits, Television Viewing, and the Cultivation Effect. *Journal of Broadcasting & Electronic Media, 52*(3), 327–348. doi:10.1080/08838150802205181

Ndlovu-Gatshen, S. J., & Ndlovu, P. P. (2021). The invention of blackness on a world scale. In Decolonizing the human: reflections from Africa on difference and oppressions. Wits University Press. doi:10.18772/22021036512

Ndung'u, N., & Signé, L. (2020). *The Fourth Industrial Revolution and digitization will transform Africa into a global powerhouse.* Retrieved from https://fullyhuman.org/wpcontent/uploads/2020/01/NdunguSigne_The-Fourth-Industrial-Revolution-And-Digitization-Will-Transform-Africa-Into-A-Global-Powerhouse.pdf

Ndung'u, N., & Singe, L. (2020). *The Fourth Industrial Revolution and Digitization will Transform Africa into a Global Powerhouse.* https://www.brookings.edu/research/the-fourth-industrial-revolution-and-digitization-will-transform-africa-into-a-global-powerhouse/

Neff, D. (1998, Nov. 16). The Water Station. The Capital Times.

Negroponte, N. (1996). *Being Digital*. Vintage Books.

Nelson, M. P. (1993). A defense of environmental ethics: A reply to Janna Thompson. *Environmental Ethics, 15*(3), 147–160. doi:10.5840/enviroethics199315318

Nelson, M. P. (1998). Aldo Leopold, environmental ethics, and the land ethic. *Wildlife Society Bulletin, 26*(4), 741–744. www.jstor.org/stable/3783545

Neumann, I. B. (2018). Diplomacy, the Arts, and Popular Culture. In G. Martel (Ed.), *The Encyclopedia of Diplomacy*. John Wiley & Sons, Ltd. doi:10.1002/9781118885154.dipl0080

Newman, N. (2009). *The rise of social media and its impact on mainstream journalism: A study of how newspapers and broadcasters in the UK and US are responding to a wave of participatory social media, and a historic ship in control towards individual consumers*. Working Paper. Reuters Institute for the Study of Journalism, Oxford University.

News, D. D. (2020). *Actor Amitabh Bachchan shares precautionary measures on Coronavirus*. Retrieved from http://ddnews.gov.in/videos/health/actor-amitabh-bachchan-shares-precautionary-measures-coronavirus

Nicole, B. E., & Vitak, J. (2015). Social network site affordances and their relationship to social capital processes. In S. Sundar (Ed.), *The handbook of the psychology of communication technology* (pp. 205–227). Wiley-Blackwell.

Nigeria Internet Registration Association. (2019). *The effects of social media on the youths*. www.nira.org.ng/nira-media/news-update/288-the-effects-of-social-media-on-the-youthson%20October%2018

Nigeria. (1999). *Constitution of the Federal Republic of Nigeria 1999*. Federal Government of Nigeria. Retrieved 2021, from https://www.icnl.org/wp-content/uploads/Nigeria_constitution2.pdf

Nigerian Communications Communication. (2019). *Press Release: With 13.8% contribution to GDP, ICT may double Oil and Gas in 2 years, says Communications Minister*. www.ncc.gov.ng/stakeholder/media-public/news-headlines/665-press-release-with-13-8-contribution-to-gdp-ict-may-double-oil-and-gas-in-2-years-says-communications-minister

Nnabugwu, C. (2020). *Cybercrime rocks Nigeria*. www.yourcommonwealth.org/technology/cybercrime-in-nigeria/

Nnaemeka, O. (1997). Fighting on all fronts: gendered spaces, ethnic boundaries, and the Nigerian civil war. *Dialectical Anthropology, 22*(3–4), 253.

Nnaemeka, O. (1998). *Sisterhood, Feminism and Power*. African World Press.

Nord, L. W., & Stromback, J. (2006). Reporting more, informing less: A comparison of the Swedish media coverage of September 11 and the wars in Afghanistan and Iraq. *Journalism: Theory, Practice and Criticism, 7*(1), 85-110.

Norris, P. (2004). *Young people & political activism: From the politics of loyalties to the politics of choice?* John F. Kennedy School of Government. Retrieved from https://sites.hks.harvard.edu/fs/pnorris/Acrobat/COE%20Young%20People%20and%20Political%20Activism.pdf

NOUN. (2008). *MAC 111 Introduction to mass communication: Course guide*. National Open University of Nigeria.

Novak, D. (2009). *The Sanctity of Human Life*. Georgetown University Press.

Novitske, L. (2018). *The AI Invasion is Coming to Africa (and It's a Good Thing)*. https://timbuktuchronicles.blogspot.co.ke

Now. (2020). *Africa Aims to Harness the Fourth Industrial Revolution*. https://now.northropgrumman.com

Nwala, M. A. (2008). *Introduction to linguistics: A first course* (rev. ed.). Osi and Alozie Ltd.

Nwaodike, C. (2020). *The AI Digital Divide—An African Perspective.* https://internews.org/commentary/ai-digital-divide-african-perspective/

Nwodu, G. B., Ezeoke, C. B., & Ezeaka, N. B. (2021). Audience perception of social media messages on security challenges in the south-east, Nigeria: Implication for audience gatekeeping. *World Journal of Innovative Research, 11*(2), 57–69.

Nwokora, L. N. (2000). *Culture, literature and nationalism.* Snaap.

Nyami, F. (2018). Cleric: Christian man can marry more than one wife. *Daily Nation.*

Nye, B. D. (2015). Intelligent Tutoring Systems by and for the Developing World: A review of trends and approaches for Educational Technology in a Global Context. *International Journal of Artificial Intelligence in Education, 25*(2), 177–203. doi:10.100740593-014-0028-6

Nye, J. S. Jr. (2008, March). Public Diplomacy and Soft Power. *The Annals of the American Academy of Political and Social Science, 616*(1), 94–109. doi:10.1177/0002716207311699

O'Connell, J., & O'Connell, K. (2008). Rabrindranath Tagore as cultural icon. *University of Toronto Quarterly, 77*(4), 961-970.

O'Reilly, M. D. (2017). *An investigation into metaphoric competence in the L2: A linguistic approach.* https://etheses.whiterose.ac.uk/19853/2/An%20investigation%20into%20metaphoric%20competence%20in%20the%20L2%2C%20a%20linguistic%20approach_O%27Reilly%2C%20D_PhD%20thesis%202017.pdf

Obiaraeri, N. O. (2001). *Human Rights in Nigeria – Millennium Perspective.* Perfect Concepts.

Obiechina, E. (1993). *Language and theme. Essays on African literature.* Heinemann Educational Books.

Ocheje, D. O. (2020). *Philosophy of education* (2nd ed.). Yinkus and Sons Ent.

Ochsner Health. (2020). *How TV can Help Kids Eat Healthy Foods.* Retrieved from https://blog.ochsner.org/articles/how-tv-can-help-kids-eat-healthy-foods

Odanwu, K. O. C., & Chukwuma, J. N. (2019). Philosophical inquiry into the question of the indissolubility of Nigeria. In A. S. Ihuah, A. Idachaba, & M. I. Shenge (Eds.), *Philosophy, security and the challenge of development in Africa.* Eagle Prints Nigeria.

Odugbemi, A. (2008). Public opinion, the public sphere, and quality of governance: An exploration. In A. Odugbemi & T. Jacobson (Eds.), *Governance reform under real-world conditions: Citizens, stakeholders, and voice* (pp. 15–37). The World Bank. doi:10.1596/978-0-8213-7456-6

Oduma, A. (2007). Reporting the facts and figures of violent conflicts: Implications for conflict management and peace building. In S. Abu & C. Best (Eds.), International Centre for Reconciliation. Coventry Cathedral, and Centre for Conflict Management and Peace Studies, University of Jos.

OECD. (2001). *Forward Governance in the 21st Century: Future studies.* OECD Publications Services.

OECD. (2015). *OECD Digital Economy Outlook.* Retrieved from OECD: https://www.oecd.org/sti/oecddigital-economy-outlook-2015-9789264232440-en.htm

OECD. (2016). *Innovating Education and Educating for Innovation: The Power of Digital Technologies and Skills.* OECD Publishing. doi:10.1787/9789264265097-

OECD. (2021, April 13). *COVID-19 spending helped to lift foreign aid to an all-time high in 2020*. OECD Detailed Note. Retrieved December 02, 2021, from https://www.oecd.org/dac/financing-sustainable-development/development-finance-data/ODA-2020-detailed-summary.pdf

Ogbazi, I. (2012). The female voice and the experiences of women in conflict situations: The truce in Chimamanda Ngozi Adichie's half of a yellow sun. *Journal of English Literature and Literary Studies*, *3*(1), 17–33.

Ogehenetega, L. U., Oyenike, O. E., & Ugeh, C. H. (2014). Comparative study of (networking) usage by undergraduates in two tertiary institutions of Nigeria. *Journal of Research on Humanities & Social Science*, *4*(15).

Oguduvwe, J. I. P. (2013). Poverty in oil rich Delta: A study of selected oil producing communities in Delta State, Nigeria. *Global Research Journal of Education*, (1), 1–11. http://www.globalresearchjournals.org/journal/grje3

Oguejiofor, J. O. (2001). *Philosophy and the African Predicament*. Hope Publications Ltd.

Ojebode, O. (2003). Radio as a development communication medium: Types, format, roles and limitations. In E. O. Soola (Ed.), *Communicating for Development Purposes*. Kraft Books Limited.

Ojie, P. (2020). Media construct and migration in modern Africa: The 2019 South Africa's xenophobia violence in perspective. In M. Michael, E. T. Aliegba, & A. A. Alagba (Eds.), *Human rights, religion and society: Festschrift for Rev. Fr. Prof. Jake Omang Otonko on his 60th Birthday*. Eiwa Press Nig. Ltd.

Ojukwu, C. (2014). The Politics of Power and the Struggle for Self-Assertion: Tess Onwueme's*The Reign of Wazobia,* AkachiAdimora-Ezeigbo's *Hands that Crush Stone* and Julie Okoh's *Edewede*. In E. A. Adedun & O. B. Nweke (Eds.), *New Perspectives on Literary Enigma* (pp. 315–335). University Press.

Okolo, M. S. C. (2015). *Philosophy: Contemporary Concerns in African*. Book- Konzult.

Okoye, I. (2005). *Between Women. In The Trial and Other Stories*. African Heritage Press.

Okoye, J. (2017). *The Woman Today: Viewing Her in African Literature in French*. Noben Press Ltd.

Okoye, J. I. (2011). 'Ethical issues in Nigerian media management. In I. S. Ndolo (Ed.), *Contemporary issues in communication and society*. Rhyce Kerex Publishers.

Okpala, E. P. (2019*) Intra-Gender Subjugation in Selected African Female Writers' Novels* [Unpublished doctoral dissertation]. Nnamdi Azikiwe University, Awka, Nigeria.

Okuwobi, D. (2021). *Foreword to Report of Lekki Incident Investigation of 20th October, 2020*. Lagos State Judicial Panel of Inquiry on Restitution for Victims of SARS Related Abuses and Other Matters.

Oladipo, O. (2008). *Thinking About Philosophy*. Hope Publications Ltd.

Olela, H. (1984). The African foundations of Greek philosophy. In R. Wright (Ed.), *African philosophy: An introduction*. University Press of America.

Oluduro, O., & Oluduro, F. O. (2012). Nigeria: In search of sustainable peace in the Niger Delta through the amnesty program. *Journal of Sustainable Development*, *5*(7), 48–61. doi:10.5539/jsd.v5n7p48

Olusola, L. (2018). *The power of social media*. www.guardian.ng/technology/the-power-of-social-media/

Oluwasemilore, I. (2018). A critical analysis of Nigeria's freedom of information act. *The Gravitas Review of Business and Property Law, 9*(2).

Omoregbe, J. (1985). African philosophy, yesterday and today. In P. Bodurin (Ed.), *Philosophy in Africa: trends and perspectives*. University of Ife Press.

Omoregbe, J. (2000). *Ethics: A Systematic Study*. Joja Educational Press.

Omoregbe, J. I. (1991). *A Simplified History of Western Philosophy: Ancient and Medieval Philosophy* (Vol. 1). Joja Educational Research and Publishers Limited.

Omoyeni, B. A. (2015). *Principles and Applications of Environmental Impact. Assesment (EIA)*. McOrnels Ventures.

Onabajo, O. S. (2000). *Fundamentals of broadcast journalism*. Gabi Concept Limited.

Onobe, J. M., & Beida, O. J. (2016). Commoditization of cultural communication: buying back Nollywood from the trans-Atlantic and neo-classic market of alien values. *Journal of Communication and Media Research, 8*(1).

Onwueme, T. (1992). *The Reign of Wazobia*. Heinemann Plc.

Onwuliri, C. E. C. (2008). The Church as Agent of Progress and Development. In I Onyeocha (Ed.), The Church as Agent of Progress and Development, CIP Jubilee Essays (pp. 70-83). Imo State University Press.

Onwusa, S. C. (2021). The issues, challenges and strategies to strengthen technical, vocational education and training in Nigeria. *International Journal of Research and Innovation in Social Science, 5*(5), 48–59. doi:10.47772/IJRISS.2021.5502

Onyegbula, E. (2021, Feb. 15). 46-years old man stabs wife to death over infidelity. *Vanguard Newspaper*. www.vanguardngr.com

Onyeocha, I. M. (2007). *Africa: The Country, the Concept and the Horizon*. Imo State University Press.

Onyeocha, M. I. (2001). *Africa: The country, the Concept and the Horizon*. Imo State University Press Ltd.

Onyido, J. A. (2018). Impact of xenophobia on Nigerian students in South Africa. *Brock Journal of Education, 6*(8).

Opafola, S. O. (1998). Developmental Philosophy and the Concept of People Oriented Development. In Philosophy: An Anthology. ARK Publishers.

Orwell, G. (1990). *1984 Nineteen Eighty-Four*. Penguin Books.

Osamuyimen, E. (2020). *Mitigating the Effects of Environmental Degradation in the Oil Industry: An Assessment of Government Compensation Scheme in Nigeria. Law, Environment and Development Journal.*

Osuagwu, N., & Chimakonam, J.O. (2018). African Studies through language-based techniques. *Filosofia Theoretica: Journal of African Philosophy, Culture and Religions, 7*(1), 101-124. . doi:10.4314/ft.v7i1.5

Osuala, A. N. (2014). An Examination of the Question of Animal Rights. BA Project submitted to the Department of Philosophy. University of Calabar.

Osuala, A. N. (2019). How Holistic is Anthropoholism? A Critique of Samuel Bassey's environmental Philosophy. Cogito: A Multidisciplinary Research Journal, 11(4), 23-31.

Osuala, A.N., & Effio-ita, E. N. (2018). A new Twist to political corruption in 4th republic Nigeria in view of non-human animals stealing millions: a case for the defense of animal rights. *Gnosis. An Interdisciplinary Journal of Human Theory and Praxis, 1*(2), 15-37.

Otite, O., & Ogionwo, W. (1979). An Introduction to Sociological Studies. Heinemann Educational Books (Nig) Ltd.

Outhwaite, W. (1996). General introduction. In W. Outhwaite (Ed.), *The Habermas Reader* (pp. 1–22). Polity Press.

Oviawe, J. I. (2018). Revamping technical vocational education and training through public-private partnerships for skill development. *Makerere Journal of Higher Education, 10*(1), 73–91. doi:10.4314/majohe.v10i1.5

Owusu, S. (2007). Towards a Theology of Marriage and Polygamy. *Direction, 36*(2).

Oyedeji, V. A. (2018). *Indigenous Language Education and the Challenges of Insecurity in Nigeria. Zaria Journal of Educational Studies* (special edition, Vol. 19). ZAJES.

Oyeshola Dokun, O. P. (2008). *Sustainable Development: Issues and Challenge for Nigeria.* Daily Graphics Nig. Ltd.

Pałka-Suchojad, K. (2021). *Who Keeps the Gate? Digital Gatekeeping in New Media.* Retrieved from Zeszyty PRASOZNAWCZE: https://www.ejournals.eu/Zeszyty-Prasoznawcze/ doi:10.4467/22996362PZ.21.012.13477

Palmer, E. (1979). Ngugi in petals of blood. *African Literature Today, 10*, 153–166.

Panpatte, D.G. (2018). *Artificial Intelligence in Agriculture: An Emerging Era of Research.* Academic Press.

Parfit, D. (1984). *Reasons and persons.* Oxford University Press.

Parker, L. E. (n.d.). *Creation of the National Artificial Intelligence Research and Development Strategic Plan.* https://www.semanticscholar.org

Parker, E. B. (1978). An Information-Based Hypothesis. *Journal of Communication, 28*(1), 81–83. doi:10.1111/j.1460-2466.1978.tb01567.x

Pashkova, V. (2016). *Arendt's political thought: the relationship between truth and politics.* http://hdl.handle.net/1959.7/uws:37675

Pavalanathan, U., & Eisenstein, J. (2016). More emojis, less: The competition for paralinguistic function in micro blog writing. *First Monday, 21*(11). Advance online publication. doi:10.5210/fm.v21i11.6879

Pearson Prentice Hall Maduagwu, M. O. (2010). *The Belief in Witchcraft in Contemporary Africa: A Philosophical Discourse.* Stirling – Horden Publishers Ltd.

Pearson, M. (2021). Global Justice, Factual Reporting and Advocacy Journalism. In S. J. A. Ward (Ed.), *Handbook of Global Media Ethics.* Springer. doi:10.1007/978-3-319-32103-5_30

Pensky, M. (2014). Historical and intellectual contexts. In B. Fultner (Ed.), *Jurgen Habermas: Key concepts* (pp. 13–32). Routledge.

Perritt, H. H. (1998). The internet as a threat to sovereignty? Thoughts on the internet's role in strengthening national and global governance. *Global Legal Stud., 2*, 475–491.

Peuchaud, S. R. (2021). Objectivity, advocacy, and critical pedagogy in the race, gender, and media classroom: Individual, interpersonal, and structural tensions and recommendations. *Journalism, 22*(2), 519–536. doi:10.1177/1464884918779943

Pfiefle, M. (2021).Social media and political activism. Huffington Post. Retrieved 14 November 2021 from https://www.huffingtonpost

Philosophy and Literature. (n.d.). Retrieved from https://en.wikipedia.org/wiki/Philosophy_and_literature

Philosophy of Language. (2019, March 25). *New World Encyclopedia.* Retrieved 19:35, January 15, 2022 from https://www.newworldencyclopedia.org/p/index.php?title=Philosophy_of_language&oldid=1019212

Pickard, V. (2015). Media activism from above and below: Lessons from the 1940s American Reform. *Journal of Information Policy., 5*(1), 109–128. doi:10.5325/jinfopoli.5.2015.109

Pinter, H. (2012). Art, Truth and Politics. In J. Elkins & A. Norris (Eds.), *Truth and Democracy.* University of Pennsylvania Press. doi:10.9783/9780812206227.9

Pitts, L. (2001, December 17). Objectivity might be impossible, so we strive for fairness. *Austin American Statesman*, p. A13.

Podsakoff, P. M., MacKenzie, S. B., Lee, J., & Podsakoff, N. P. (2003). Common method biases in behavioral research: A critical review of the literature and recommended remedies. *The Journal of Applied Psychology, 88*(5), 879–903. doi:10.1037/0021-9010.88.5.879 PMID:14516251

Pogliano, P. (2017). *More multicultural than thou: The news paradigm and the Sjobo affair in the Swedish press.* Paper presented at the annual meeting of the International Communication Association, San Diego, CA.

Polletta, F. (2009). *It was like a fever: Storytelling in protest and politics.* University of Chicago Press. https://proxy.library.upenn.edu:2265/books/about/It_Was_Like_a_Fever.html?id=hBY2OUKingUC

Polski, M. (2013). Media ecology pedagogy—Art or Techne? MEA Conference, Grand Rapids, MI.

Polski, M., & Gorman, L. (2012, July 10). Yuri Rozhdestvensky versus Marshall McLuhan: A triumph versus a vortex. *Explorations in Media Ecology., 10*(3–4), 263–278. doi:10.1386/eme.10.3-4.263_1

Pool, I. d. (1979). The Influence of International Communication on Development. *Media Asia 6*(3), 149-156.

Poole, R. (1989). Public spheres. In H. Wilson (Ed.), *Australian Communications and the Public Sphere: essays in memory of Bill Bonney* (pp. 6–26). The Macmillan Company of Australia. doi:10.1007/978-1-349-11077-3_2

Popkin, R. (1977-1978). Hume's racism. *The Philosophical Forum, 9*(2–3).

Popkin, R. H., & Stroll, A. (1993). *Philosophy made simple.* W.H. Allen.

Porat, M. U. (1978). Global Implications of the Information Society. *Journal of Communication, 28*(1), 70–80. doi:10.1111/j.1460-2466.1978.tb01565.x

Prensky, M. (2001). Digital Natives, Digital Immigrants. On the Horizon, 9(5).

Princewill, N & Busari, S. (2021). *Nigeria bans Twitter after company deletes President Buhari's tweet.* Academic Press.

Proshareng.com. (2020). *Cybercrime in Nigeria: Causes and effects.* www.proshareng.com/news/Security---Support/Cybercrime-in-Nigeria--Causes-and-Effect

Pudovkin, V. I. (n.d.). *Film Technique and Film Acting.* New York: Dutton.

Puiu, Y. V., Puiu, D. A., Sablin, I. V., Georgieva, E. S., Vladimirovich, I., & Bykov, A. Y. (2015). Conceptual framework of mass media manipulative models forming. *International Review of Management and Marketing, 5*(special issue). http: www.econjournals.com

PwC Global. (2017). *Sizing the Prize: PwC's Global Artificial Intelligence Study: Exploiting the AI Revolution.* https://www.pwc.com/gx/en/issues/data-and-analytics/publications/artificial-intelligence-study.html

Quartiroli, I. (2011). *The Digitally Divided Self: Relinquishing Our Awareness to the Internet.* Silens Publishers.

Queen bees: Do Women Hinder the Progress of other Women? (2018). www.bbc.com-new

Radu, S. (2020). *Africa Braces for the Fourth Industrial Revolution.* https://www.usnews.com/news/best-countries/articles/2020-01-23/the-stakes-for-africa-in-the-fourth-industrial-revolution

Rahman, A. H. (2001). Africa In the 21st Century: prospects for political development. In A. Olugbenga & O. Arunma (Eds.), *African voices African Visions.* The Nordic African Institute.

Raja, F. (2021). *Amplifying rural needs and voices: A conversation with Helene Papper*. Retrieved 2021, from IFAD: https://www.ifad.org/en/web/latest/-/amplifying-rural-needs-and-voices-helene-papper

Rajan, R. G., & Subramanian, A. (2008). Aid and growth: What does the cross-country evidence really show? *The Review of Economics and Statistics*, *90*(4), 643–665. doi:10.1162/rest.90.4.643

Ramadan, A., & Xiaohui, C. (2019). Challenges and opportunities of tvet in developing countries: A case of Sudan. *Developing Country Studies*, *9*(10), 77–87.

Ramaphosa, C. (2020). *A National Strategy for Harnessing the Fourth Industrial Revolution: The Case of South Africa*. https://www.brookings.edu/blog/africa-in-focus/2020/01/10/a-national-strategy-for-harnessing-the-fourth-industrial-revolution-the-case-of-south-africa/

Raphael, N. S. (2015). *Ethno-religious conflicts, mass media and national development: The northern Nigeria experience* (Unpublished thesis). School of Postgraduate Studies, Department of Religion and Philosophy, Faculty of Arts, University of Jos, Jos.

Rasmussen, T. (2000). *Social theory and communication technology*. Ashgate.

Raza, S. H., Zaman, U., & Iftikhar, M. (2021). Examining the Effects of Media-Generated Stereotypes on Receivers' Trust and Attitude in Pakistan. Moderating Influence of Ethnicity and Gender. *Information (Basel)*, *12*(1), 35. doi:10.3390/info12010035

Reeves, B., & Nass, C. (1996). *How people treat computers, television, and new media like real people and places*. CSLI Publications and Cambridge University Press.

Rehman, A. A., & Alharty, K. (2016). An introduction to research paradigm. *International Journal of Educational Investigation*, *3*(8), 51–59.

Reporters Without Borders. (n.d.a). *2021 World Press Freedom Index: Journalism, the vaccine against disinformation, blocked more than 130 countries*. Reporters Without Borders. Retrieved November 2, 2021, from https://rsf.org/en/2021-world-press-freedom-index-journalism-vaccine-against-disinformation-blocked-more-130-countries

Reporters Without Borders. (n.d.b). *World Press Freedom Index 2021*. Retrieved October 10, 2021, from https://rsf.org/en/ranking_table

Report, S. I. S. T. (2016). *Trends for January–June 07* (Vol. XII). Symantec.https://www.symantec.com/content/dam/symantec/docs/reports/cyber-security-trends-report-africa-interactive-en.pdf

Repucci, S. (2019). *Freedom and Media 2019: Media Freedom: A Downward Spiral*. Freedom House. https://freedomhouse.org/report/freedom-and-media/2019/media-freedom-downward-spiral

Rickford, R. (2016). Black Lives Matter. *New Labor Forum, 25*, 34–42. 10.1177/1095796015620171

Rifkin, J., & Ted, H. (1980). *Entropy: A new Worldview*. Bantam Books.

Rist, G. (2001). *Le developement: une histoire de croyance ocidentale*. Presses de Science Po.

Robert, O. S. (2015). *Iwali-Ebekwaraa: A socio-cultural and political institution of a royal female dancer and performer*. Paper presented at Mabel@50 Conference, Wuse II, Abuja.

Robert, O.S. (2020). Classical and contemporary leadership misdeeds thwarting Africa's development: Nigerian case. *International Journal of Academic Multidisciplinary Research, 4*(1).

Robert, O.S., & Besong, E.N. (2016). Nigeria media and indigenous cultures transformation: The journey so far. *Journal of Mass Communication and Journalism, 6*(7).

Robert, O.S., Besong, E.N., &Dibie, G.A. (2016). Retracing our socio-cultural norms/values for a better African society. *International Journal of Humanities and Social Sciences, 2*(4).

Robert, B. P. (2019). *Filmed Thought: Cinema as Reflective Form.* University of Chicago Press.

Robert, O. S. (2017). *Contemporary trends plaguing Public schools in Nigeria.* Kindle Direct Publishing.

Robert, O. S. (2018). Formation, types and processes of questions in Bekwarra language of Northern Cross River. *International Journal of Language, Literature and Culture, 5*(3), 27–34.

Robert, O. S., & Besong, E. N. (2016). *Nigerian media and indigenous cultures transformation: The journey so far* (Vol. 6). J Mass Communicat Journalism.

Robert, O. S., & Besong, E. N. (2016). Nigerian media and indigenous cultures transformation: The journey so far. *J Mass Communicat Journalism, 6*, 317.

Robert, O. S., & Besong, E. N. (2017). *Unresolved degenerating nat'l issues: Nigerian govt. & media's failure.* LAP Lambert Academic Publishing.

Robertson, R. (n.d.). *Glocalization: Time-Space and Homogeneity-Hetrogeneity.* https://warwick.ac.uk/fac/arts/history/students/modules/hi31v/syllabus/week18/robertson-1995.pdf

Rogers, E. M. (1978). The Rise and Fall of the Dominant Paradigm. *Journal of Communication, 28*(1), 64–69. doi:10.1111/j.1460-2466.1978.tb01564.x

Rolston, H. I. II. (1988). *Environmental ethics: Duties to and values in the natural world.* Temple University Press.

Rolston, H. I. II. (1994). *Conserving natural value.* Columbia University Press.

Rose, J. (2017). Brexit, Trump, and Post-Truth Politics. *Public Integrity, 19*(6), 555–558. doi:10.1080/10999922.2017.1285540

Rosen, B., & Jerdee, T. H. (1973). The influence of sex-role stereotypes on evaluations of male and female supervisory behavior. *The Journal of Applied Psychology, 57*(1), 44–48. doi:10.1037/h0034198 PMID:4784751

Rosenbaum, S. (2015). Pastor marries pregnant teen with wife's blessing. *The New York Post.*

Rosenberg, S. (2002, May 10). *Much Ado About Blogging.* Retrieved from Salon.com: https://www.salon.com/tech/col/rose/2002/05/10/blogs/

Rostow, W. (1971). *Etapas do desenvolvimento econômico.* Zahar Editores.

Rotman, D., Vieweg, S., Yardi, S., Chi, E., & Preece, J. (2011). From slacktivism to activism: Participatory culture in the age of social media. CHI '11 Extended Abstracts on Human Factors in Computing Systems, 819– 822. doi:10.1145/1979742.1979543

Rouse, M. P. (2016). *Digital Economy.* Retrieved from Techtarget, Newton, MA.: https://searchcio.techtarget.com/definition/digital-economy

Ruggiero, T. (2000). Uses and Gratifications Theory in the 21st Century. *Mass Communication & Society, 3*(1), 3–37. doi:10.1207/S15327825MCS0301_02

Ruotsalainen, J., & Heinonen, S. (2015). Media ecology and the future ecosystemic society. *European Journal of Futures Research*, *3*(9), 1–10. doi:10.100740309-015-0068-7

Rutherford, P. (2000). *Endless propaganda: The advertising of public goals*. University of Toronto Press. doi:10.3138/9781442674455

Rybalko, S., & Seltzer, T. (2010). Dialogic communication in 140 characters or less: How Fortune 500 companies engage stakeholders using Twitter. *Public Relations Review*, *36*(4), 336–341. doi:10.1016/j.pubrev.2010.08.004

Ryniejska-Kieldanowics, M. (2009). *Cultural Diplomacy as a Form of International Communication*. Institute for Public Relation BledCom Special Prize for the best New Research on the Cultural Variables in Public Relations Practice.

Sabel, F. C. (2001). *A quiet revolution of democratic governance: towards democratic Experimentalism in OECD Governance in the 21st Century: future studies*. OECD Publications Services.

Samphina.com. (2022). *The impact of social media on national security: Nigeria's perspective*. www.samphina.com.ng/impact-social-media-national-securitynigerias-perspective/

Santiago, M. T. A. (2020). *Obstacles and considerations for the development and implementation of Artificial Intelligence in Developing Countries*. https://www.researchgate.net/profile/Santiago_Molina7/publication/354556278_Obstacles_and_considerations_for_the_development_and_implementation_of_Artificial_Intelligence_in_ Developing_Countries/links/613fe2cc5d9d0e131b427fab/Obstacles-and-considerations-for-the-development-and-implementation-of-Artificial-Intelligence-in-Developing-Countries.pdf

Sapir. (1991). *Linguistic Theory: The Discourse of Fundamental Works*. Longman.

Sarup, M. (1996). *Identity, culture and the postmodern world* (T. Raja, Ed.). Edinburgh University Press.

Savun, B., & Tirone, D. C. (2011). Foreign Aid, Democratization, and Civil Conflict: How Does Democracy Aid Affect Civil Conflict? *American Journal of Political Science*, *55*(2), 233–246. doi:10.1111/j.1540-5907.2010.00501.x

Schiff, J. L. (2015). Repressive democracy: Pathological and ontological distortion in Habermas' theory of communicative action. In B. Fischer & M. Mergenthaler (Eds.), *Cultural transformations of the public sphere: Contemporary and historical perspectives* (pp. 65–92). Peter Lang.

Schmidt, C. (1889). Social Results of Early Christianity (2nd ed.). WCM Isbister Ltd.

Schramm, W. L. (1964). *Mass media and national development: The role of information in the developing countries*. University Press Stanford.

Schudson, M. (1992). Was there ever a public sphere? If so, when? Reflections on the American case. In C. Calhoun (Ed.), *Habermas and the public sphere* (pp. 143–164). The MIT Press.

Schultz, A. R. (2000). *Intelligent Life on Earth: The Pros and Cons*. Presented at the 2000 Conference of the International Association for the Management of Technology, Miami, FL.

Schultz, A. (2006). *Robert. Contemporary Issues in Ethics and Information Technology*. IRM Press. doi:10.4018/978-1-59140-779-9

Scott Brennen and Daniel Kreiss. (2014, September 8). *Digitalization and digitization*. Retrieved from Culture Digitally: https://culturedigitally.org/2014/09/digitalization-and-digitization/

Scott, Z., Haider, H., & Mcloughlin, C. (2011). *Topic guide on communication and governance*. Retrieved 10 8, 2021, from http://gsdrc.org/docs/open/commgap1.pdf

Scott, G., Leritz, L. E., & Mumford, M. D. (2004). The effectiveness of creativity training: A quantitative review. *Creativity Research Journal*, *16*(4), 361–388. doi:10.1080/10400410409534549

Selwyn, N. (2018). The use of icts in education and the promotion of social inclusion: A critical perspective from the uk. Institution of Education, University of London. *Educ. Soc.*, *29*(104). Retrieved October 09, 2021, from Campinas. www.scielo.br/scielo.php?pid=S0101-73302008000300009&script=sci_arttext&tlng=en

Serequeberhan, T. (1991). African philosophy: The point in question. In T. Serequeberhan (Ed.), African philosophy: The essential reading (pp. 3–28). Paragon House.

Sertaç, Y., &Yaman, Ö. E. (2020). *Artificial Intelligence in Public Sector: A Framework to Address Opportunities and Challenges*. Academic Press.

Sesay, A. (2014). *African governance systems in the pre and post-independence periods: enduring lessons and opportunities for youth in Africa*. For the Mandela Institute for Development Studies.

Shapin, S. (2019). Is there a Crisis of Truth. *Los Angeles Review of Books*. https://lareviewofbooks.org/article/is-there-a-crisis-of-truth/

Sharif, Y. S., & Nabeshima, K. (2007). How Universities Promote Economic Growth. The World Bank.

Shayne Bowman and Chris Willis. (2003). *We Media: How audiences are shaping the future of news and information*. Retrieved from Academia: www.hypergene.net/wemedia/

Sheppard, L. D., & Aquino, K. (2013). Much ado about nothing: Observers' problematization of women's same-sex conflict at work. *The Academy of Management Perspectives*, *27*(1), 52–62. doi:10.5465/amp.2012.0005

Sheptycki, J. (2002a). Accountability across the policing field: Towards a general cartography of accountability for post-modern policing. *Policing and Society*, *12*(4), 323–338. doi:10.1080/10439460220000055

Sherin, A. (2013). *Design elements, using images to create graphic impact*. Rockport Publishers.

Shields, R. (2003). *The virtual*. Routledge.

Shin, K. S., & Han, M. (2016). The role of negative emotions on motivation and communicative action: Testing the validity of situational theory of problem-solving in the context of South Korea. *Asian Journal of Communication*, *26*(1), 76–93. doi:10.1080/01292986.2015.1083597

Shoemaker, P. J., & Reese, S. D. (1996). *Mediating the message: Theories of influences on mass media content* (2nd ed.). Longman.

Showalter, E. (1999). *A literature on their own: British women novelist from Bronte to Lessing*. Princeton University Press. (Original work published 1977)

Sibanda, B. (2021). 'Language as Being' in the politics of Ngugi wa Thiongo. In M. Steyn & W. Mpofu (Eds.), *Decolonizing the human: reflections from Africa on difference and oppressions*. Wits University Press. doi:10.18772/22021036512.11

Sidaway, D. J. (2002). Post-development. In V. Desai & R. B. Potter (Eds.), *The companion to development studies*. Arnold.

Signitzer, B. (2008). Public Relations and Public Diplomacy: Some Conceptual Explorations. In A. Zerfab, A. A. Van Ruler, B. Van Ruler, & K. Sriramesh (Eds.), *Public Relations Research: European and International Perspectives and Innovations*. VS Verlag fur Sozialwissenschaften. doi:10.1007/978-3-531-90918-9_13

Sikarwar, R. (2016, december 29). *Definition of Digital Media*. Retrieved 2021, from Linkedin: https://www.linkedin.com/pulse/definition-digital-media-rahul-sikarwar-digital-marketing-expert

Simon, J. (2007). *Governing through Crime: How the War on Crime Transformed American Democracy and Created a Culture of Fear*. Oxford University Press.

Singer, P. (2009). Speciesism and Moral Status. Metaphilosophy Journal Compilation, 40(3-4).

Singer, P. W., & Friedman, A. (2014). *Cybersecurity and Cyberwar: What Everyone Needs to Know*. Oxford University Press. doi:10.1093/wentk/9780199918096.001.0001

Sirbu, A. (2015). The significance of language as a tool of communication. 'Mircea cel Batran'. *Naval Academy Scientific Bulletin*, *18*(2), 405–406.

Siron, J.R. (1991). Polygamy: An enduring problem. *Ministry*.

Si-Soo. (2009, Jan. 21). Wife kills husband for infidelity. *National*.

Smejkalovd-Strickland, J. (1994). Censoring canons: Transitions and prospects of literary institutions in Czechoslovakia. In R. Burtn (Ed.), *The Administration of aesthetics: Censorship, political criticism, and the public sphere* (pp. 195–215). University of Minnesota Press.

Smiley, C., & Fakunke, D. (2017). From "brute" to "thug:" The demonization and criminalization of unarmed black male victims in America. *Human Behavior Society Environ.*, *26*(3-4), 350–366. doi:10.1080/10911359.2015.1129256 PMID:27594778

Smith, G. (n.d.). An Electronic Pearl Harbor? Not likely. *Issues on Science and Technology*.

Smith, L. M., & Neupane, S. (2018). *Artificial Intelligence and Human Development: Toward Research Agenda*. Retrieved from https://www.idrc.ca/en/stories/artificial-intelligenceand-human-development

Smith, A. (2014). *African Americans and technology use*. Pew Research Center.

Smith, C. (2001). *Proud of me: Speaking out against sexual violence and HIV*. Penguin.

Snapps, O. J. (2011). Africa-based oil exporting companies: The case of Nigeria. *American Review of Political Economy*, *9*, 1–56. http://www.arpejournal.com

Soares & Quintella. (2008, April 28). *Development: An Analysis of Concepts, Measurement and Indicators*. Retrieved from Brazilian Administrative Review: http://www.anpad.org.br/bar

Sobczak, A. (2018). The Queen Bee Syndrome. The Paradox of Women Discrimination on the Labour Market. *Journal of Gender and Power*, *9*(1). www.semanticscholae.org>papers

Soola, E. O. (2003). Development communication: The past, the present and the future. In E. O. Soola (Ed.), *Communication for Development Purposes*. Kraft Books Limited.

Sotunde, A. (2021, October 2). *#ENDSARS movement: From Twitter to Nigerian streets - The "soro soke" generation won't give up*. Retrieved from Amnesty International: https://www.amnesty.org/en/latest/campaigns/2021/02/nigeria-end-impunity-for-police-violence-by-sars-endsars/

Splichal, S. (1999). *Public opinion, developments and controversies in the twentieth century*. Rowman & Littlefield.

Staines, G. (1974). The queen bee syndrome. *Psychology Today*, *7*, 55–66.

Statista. (2015). *Internet users' number 2005-2015*. Author.

Steen, G. (2008). The paradox of metaphor: Why we need a three-dimensional model of metaphor. *Metaphor and Symbol*, *23*(4), 213–241. doi:10.1080/10926480802426753

Stephens, J., & McCallum, R. (2013). *Retelling stories, framing culture: traditional story and metanarratives in children's literature*. Routledge. doi:10.4324/9780203357750

Stieglitz, S., Mirbabaie, M., Ross, B., & Neuberger, C. (2018). Social media analytics – Challenges in topic discovery, data collection, and data preparation. *International Journal of Information Management*, *39*, 156–168. doi:10.1016/j.ijinfomgt.2017.12.002

Stillman, F. A., Cronin, K. A., Evans, W. D., & Ulasevich, A. (2001). Can media advocacy influence newspaper coverage of tobacco: Measuring the effectiveness of the American stop smoking intervention study's (ASSIST) media advocacy strategies. *Tobacco Control*, *10*(2), 137–144. doi:10.1136/tc.10.2.137 PMID:11387534

Stoklossa, U. (2007). *Advertising: New techniques for visual seduction*. Thames and Hudson.

Strate, L. (2017). *Media ecology: An approach to understanding the human condition*. Peter Lang. doi:10.3726/978-1-4331-4005-1

Strausbaugh, J. (2006). *Black like you: Blackface, whiteface, insult and imitation in American popular culture*. Tarcher.

Strusani, D., & Houngbonon, G.V. (2019). *The Role of Artificial Intelligence in Emerging Markets*. Academic Press.

Suiter, J. (2016). Post-Truth Politics. Political Insight, 7(3), 25-27. doi:10.1177/2041905816680417

Symantec. (2015). *Internet Security Threat Report* (April ed., Vol. 20). Symantec.

Tafira, K. (2011). Is xenophobia racism? *Anthropology Southern Africa*, *34*(3-4), 114–121. doi:10.1080/23323256.2011.11500015

Tan, S. (2018). *AI and Africa: Leapfrog to Prosperity*. https://newafricanmagazine.com/17686/

Tandoc, E. C. Jr, & Duffy, A. (2019). *Routines in Journalism*. Oxford Research Encyclopedia of Communication., doi:10.1093/acrefore/9780190228613.013.870

Tandon, Y. (2015). Development is resistance. *Africa Development. Afrique et Developpement*, *XL*(3), 139–159.

Tanha, T., Dhara, S. N., Patelb, H., & Yagnik, M. (2020). *Implementation of artificial intelligence in agriculture for optimisation of irrigation and application of pesticides and herbicides*. doi:10.1016/j.aiia.2020.04.002

Tapscott, D. (1996). *The Digital Economy: Promise and Peril in the Age of Networked Intelligence*. McGraw-Hill.

Taylor, P. M. (2007). *Global Communications, International Affairs and the Media since 1945*. Routledge.

Tellis, J. G. (2007). *The sage handbook of Advertising* (1st ed.). SAGE Publications Ltd. doi:10.4135/9781848607897Tran, T., Nguyen, D., Nguyen, A., & Golenz, E. (2018). Sentiment analysis of emoji-based reactions on marijuana-related topical posts on Facebook. *IEEE International Conference on Communications (ICC)*.

Terzis, G. (2015). *INFOCORE Definitions: "Media Assistance"*. Brussels: Global Governance Institute. Retrieved November 30, 2021, from https://www.infocore.eu/results/definitions/

Thakora, P., & Sasib, S. (2015). Ontology-based sentiment analysis process for social media content. *Procedia Computer Science*, *53*, 199–207. doi:10.1016/j.procs.2015.07.295

The Communication Initiative Network. (2015, June 9). Retrieved 9 23, 2021, from https://www.comminit.com/governance-africa/content/participatory-budgeting-project

The World Bank, World Development Indicators. (2021). *GNI*. Retrieved November 10,2021, from https://data.worldbank.org/indicator/NY.GNP.PCAP.CD

Thibaut, J. W., & Kelley, H. H. (1959). *The social psychology of groups*. Wiley.

Thomas, A. (2004). *The Study of Development*. Paper prepared for DSA Annual Conference.

Thomas, A. (2000). Development as practice in a liberal capitalist world. *Journal of International Development*, *12*(6), 773–787. doi:10.1002/1099-1328(200008)12:6<773::AID-JID716>3.0.CO;2-7

Thompson, A. (1988). The news media and international relations: Experience and the media reality. *Canadian Journal of Communication*, *13*(1). doi:10.22230/cjc.1987v13n1a440

Thornton, S. H., & Thornton, W. H. (2008). *Development without freedom: The politics of Asian globalization*. Ashgate Publishing Limited.

Thorson, K. (2014). Sampling from the civic buffet: Youth, new media, and do-it-yourself citizenship. In New technologies & civic engagement: New agendas in communication series (pp. 3 - 22). New York, NY: Routledge.

Tierney, M. J., Nielson, D. L., Hawkins, D. G., Roberts, J. T., Findley, M. G., Powers, R. M., Parks, B., Wilson, S. E., & Hicks, R. L. (2011). More dollars than sense: Refining our knowledge of development finance using AidData. *World Development*, *39*(11), 1891–1906. doi:10.1016/j.worlddev.2011.07.029

Todaro, M. P., & Smith, S. C. (2011). *Economic Development*. Pearson Education.

Toffler. (1970). *Future Shock*. Bantam Books.

Tomasello, M. (2010). On the different origins of symbols and grammar. In Language evolution. doi:10.1093/acprof:oso/9780199244843.001.0001

Topic, M., & Sciortino, C. (2012). Cultural Diplomacy and Cultural Hegemony: A Framework for the Analysis. In Cultural Diplomacy and Cultural Imperialism: European Perspective(s). Peterlang.

Torres, C. D. (2014). *Literature and Film in Postmodern Metanarratives*. Palgrave Macmillan. doi:10.1057/9781137439734_3

Travaly, Y., & Muvunyi, K. (2020). *The future is intelligent: Harnessing the potential of artificial intelligence in Africa*. Retrieved from https://www.brookings.edu/blog/africa-in-90 focus/2020/01/13/the-future-is-intelligent-harnessing-the-potential-of-artificialintelligence-in-africa/

Treem, J. W., & Leonard, P. M. (2013). Social media use in organizations: Exploring the affordances of visibility, editing, persistence, and association. *ACM International Communication Association*, *36*(1), 143–189. doi:10.1080/23808985.2013.11679130

Treré, E. (2018). The sublime of digital activism: Hybrid media ecologies and the new grammar of protest. *Journalism & Communication Monographs*, *20*(2), 137–148. doi:10.1177/1522637918770435

Trottier, D., & Christian, F. (Eds.). (2014). *Social media, politics and the state: protests, revolutions, riots, crime and policing in the age of Facebook, Twitter and YouTube*. Routledge. doi:10.4324/9781315764832

Tufekci, Z. (2017). *Twitter and tear gas: the power and fragility of networked protest*. Yale University Press.

Turianskyi, Y. (2020). *Policy Insights 77, Africa And Europe: Cyber Governance Lessons African perspectives Global insights. The South African Institute of International Affairs*. SAIIA.

Tyson, L. (1999). *Critical theory today*. Garland Publishing Inc.

Uche, B. G. (1994). The interaction between science and language. *The Nigeria Teacher Today: A Journal of Teacher Education*, *3*(1), 101.

Udigwomen, A. F. (2014). The Greek cultural context: The transition from poetry to philosophy. In A. F. Udigwomen & C. A. Udofia (Eds.), *A critical history of philosophy: Ancient and medieval* (pp. 1–13). Ultimate Index Book Publishers.

Udodiong, I. (2019). *Here is how Nigerians are using the internet in 2019.* www.pulse.ng/bi/tech/how-nigerians-are-using-the-internet-in-2019/kz097rg

Udofia, C. A. (2014). Early pioneers: The myth and reality about their authorship and origination of Western philosophy. In A. F. Udigwomen & C. A. Udofia (Eds.), *A critical history of philosophy: Ancient and medieval* (pp. 14–20). Ultimate Index Book Publishers.

Udom, E. (2017, Aug. 2). Jealous wife kills husband over alleged infidelity. *Independent.*

Uduma, O. U. (2000). *The fundamentals of philosophy.* WAP Coy.

Ugwu, A. K., & Ozoemena, L. C. (2019). Structuring ethnic agitation and the survival of democracy in Nigeria. In A. S. Ihuah, A. Idachaba, & M. I. Shenge (Eds.), *Philosophy, security and the challenge of development in Africa.* Eagle Prints Nigeria.

Ugwuanyi, L. (2006). Disabusing the mind of the prejudices against the world of philosophy. In Philosophy and Africa. UNIZIK UNESCO World Philosophy Day Celebrations, Lumos Nig Ltd.

Ugwu, V. C. (2018). *Sustainable Development Goals (SDGS) and Africa's Development Challenges. Nigerian Journal of Educational Leadership and Management.*

UIS. (2018). *A Global Framework for Reference on Digital Literacy Skills for Indicator 4.4.2.* Information Paper, no. 51.

Umar, M. (2009). The broadcast media and conflict management in Nigeria. In J. Yoroms & A. Mu'azu (Eds.), Conflict management and the media in Nigeria. Centre for Research and Documentation (CRD).

UN E-Government Survey. (2008). *From e-Government to connected governance.* United Nations Department of Economic and Social Affairs/Division for Public Administration and Development Management, ST/ESA/PAD/SER.E/112.

UN General Assembly. (2015). Towards global partnerships. A principle-based approach to enhanced cooperation between the United Nations and all relevant partners (Vol. A). UNGA. RES/70/224.

UN Global E-Government Readiness Report. (2004). *Towards access for opportunity.* United Nations Department of Economic and Social Affairs/Division for Public Administration and Development Management, UNPAN/2004/11.

UN Global E-Government Readiness Report. (2005). *From e- Government to e-inclusion.* United Nations Department of Economic and Social Affairs/Division for Public Administration and Development Management, UNPAN/2005/14.

UN. (2015). *Transporting our World: The 2030 Agenda for sustainable Development General Assembly Seventieth Session Agenda, 15 and 16, A/70/L.* Retrieved on 18 May, 2018, from http:/www.un.org

Una, E. (2020, Sept. 29). Man kills wife, commits suicide in Cross-River. *Vanguard Newspaper.*

UNDP. (2021). *United Nations Development Programme strategic plan 2022 - 2025.* UNDP.

UNESCO & ILO. (2018). *Taking a whole of government approach to skills development.* Author.

UNESCO & UN University. (2016). *Knowledge societies policy handbook.* UNESCO. https://en.unesco.org/sites/default/files/knowledge_socities_policy_handbook.pdf

UNESCO & UNHCR. (2016). *No More Excuses: Provide Education to All Forcibly Displaced People.* Global Education Monitoring Report: Policy Paper no. 26.

UNESCO Institute for Lifelong Learning. (2020). *Embracing a culture of lifelong learning: Contribution to the futures of education initiative.* Author.

UNESCO. (2008, March 26-28). *Media Development Indicators: A Framework for assessing media development.* Intergovernmental Council of the International Programme for the Development of Communication (IPDC). Retrieved December 02, 2021, from https://unesdoc.unesco.org/ark:/48223/pf0000163102

UNESCO. (2009). *National information society policy: A template.* UNESCO. https://unesdoc.unesco.org/images/0018/001871/187135e.pdf

UNESCO. (2018). *Re-orienting Education Management Information Systems towards Inclusive and Equitable Quality Education and Lifelong Learning.* UNESCO Working Papers on Education Policy, no. 5.

UNESCO. (2020). *First meeting of the international commission on the futures of education.* UNESCO Headquarters. Retrieved from https://unesdoc.unesco.org/ark:/48223/pf0000372674?posInSet=1&queryId=4223eb90-51d6-48c5-9bd5-790d5d6df2f2

UNESCO-UNEVOC. (2018). *Open educational resources for skills development.* UN Campus.

UNICEF. (2016). *Technical Guidance: Guide for Including Disability in Education Management Information Systems.* Author.

United Nations (UN). (2017). *The sustainable development goals report.* Retrieved from https://sdgactioncampaign.org/wp-content/uploads/2017/07/TheSustainableDevelopmentGoalsReport2017.pdf

United Nations Conference on Trade and Development (UNCTAD). (2018). *Leapfrogging: Look Before You Leap: Policy Brief no 7.* https://unctad.org

United nations general assembly. 'A/res/48/104- declaration on the elimination of violence against women – united nation documents: gathering a body of global agreements'. un- documents.net.

United Nations Industrial Development Organization. (2017). *Skills policy instruments for industrial development in low and middle income countries.* Inclusive and Sustainable Industrial Development Working Paper Series WP 2 | 2017.

United Nations Institute for Training Research. (2015). *Social Media and the web 2.0 are key tools for the SDGs.* www.unitar.org/about/news-stories/news/social-media-and-web-20-are-key-tools-sdgs

United Nations Organisation. (2004). *A More Sure World: Our Shared Responsibility. Report of the Secretary-General's High-level Panel on Threats, Challenges and Change.* United Nations Department of Public Information.

United Nations. (2019). *Financing of education and technical and vocational education and training (TVET) in Latin America and the Caribbean.* UN.

University of Pretoria. (2018). *Artificial Intelligence for Africa: An Opportunity for Growth, Development, and Democratisation.* https://www.accesspartnership.com

Utoh-Ezeajugh, T. C. (2015). Nigerian Female Playwrights and the Evolution of a Literary Style: Gendered Discourse in the Plays of Tess Onwueme, Irene Salami-Agunlonye and Tracie Utoh-Ezeajugh. In Gender Discourse in African Theatre, Literature and Visual Arts. Kraft Books Ltd.

Uvin, P. (1998). *Aiding Violence: The Development Enterprise in Rwanda.* Kumarian Press.

Vaccari, C., Valeriani, A., Barberá, P., Bonneau, R., Jost, J. T., Nagler, J., & Tucker, J. A. (2015). Political expression and action on social media: Exploring the relationship between lower- and higher-threshold political activities among Twitter users in Italy. *Journal of Computer-Mediated Communication, 20*(2), 221–239. doi:10.1111/jcc4.12108

Valier, C. (2004). *Crime and punishment in contemporary culture*. Routledge.

Van Den Eede, Y. (2016). Blindness and ambivalence: The meeting of media ecology and philosophy of technology. *Explorations in Media Ecology*, *15*(2), 103–112. doi:10.1386/eme.15.2.103_1

van Leeuwen, T. (2005). Three models of interdisciplinarity. In R. Wodak & P. Chilton (Eds.), A new agenda in (Critical) discourse analysis: Theory, methodology and interdisciplinarity (pp. 3-18). John Benjamins. doi:10.1075/dapsac.13.04lee

Vasisht, D., Kapetanovic, Z., Won, J., Jin, X., Chandra, R., Sinha, S., & Stratman, S. (2017). Farm beats: An iot platform for data driven agriculture. *14th USENIX Symposium on Networked Systems Design and Implementation, 17*, 515-529.

Veit-Wild, F., & Naguschewki, D. (Eds.). (2005). Body sexuality, and gender: versions and subversions in African literatures. Rodopi B.V.

Velarde, O. (2017). *Commonly used Advertising techniques in visual marketing*. https://visme.co/blog/visual-advertising-techniques/#XAcjK-wo0ApoBc8Gf.99

Vidal, L., Ares, G., & Jaeger, R. S. (2016). Use of emoticon and emoji In Tweets for food-related emotional expression. *Food Quality and Preference*, *49*, 119–128. doi:10.1016/j.foodqual.2015.12.002

Vinusa, R., Azizpour, H., & Nerini, F. F. (2020). The Role of Artificial Intelligence in Achieving the Sustainable Development Goals. *Nature Communications*, *11*(233), 233. doi:10.103841467-019-14108-y PMID:31932590

Vogler, C. (2016). Anscombe on Two Jesuits and Lying. In L. Gormally, D. A. Jones, & R. Teichmann (Eds.), *The Moral Philosophy of Elizabeth Anscombe*. Imprint Academic.

Vosoughi, S., Deb, R., & Sinan, A. (2018). The spread of true and false news online. *Science*, *9*(March), 1146–1151. doi:10.1126cience.aap9559 PMID:29590045

Wacker, W. (2002). *The Deviant's Advantage*. Crown Publishing.

Waisbord, S. (2009). Advocacy journalism in a global context. In K. Wahl-Jorgensen & T. Hanitzsch (Eds.), *The handbook of journalism studies* (pp. 371–385). Routledge.

Wakili, H. (2009). The press and ethno-religious conflicts in metropolitan Kano, 1991-2001. In Conflict management and the media in Nigeria. Centre for Research and Documentation (CRD).

Walker, A. (1983). *In search of our mother's garden: Womanist prose*. Harcourt Brace Javanoich.

Wallack, L. (1994). Media Advocacy: A Strategy for Empowering People and Communities. *Journal of Public Health Policy, 15*(4), 420-436. Retrieved 9 14, 2021, from https://ncbi.nlm.nih.gov/pubmed/7883943

Walt, S. (1985). 'Alliance Formation and the Balance of Power' 9. *International Security*, *9*(4), 3. doi:10.2307/2538540

Webster, F. (1975). *Theories of the information society*. Routledge.

Weisenhorn, J., Meyer, M. H., McGoff, R., & Rooney, T. (2021). Weekly question-and-answer extension radio show helps listeners adopt environmentally sound horticulture practices. *Horticulturae*, *7*(72), 7040072. doi:10.3390/horticulturae7040072

West, D. M., & Allen, J. J. (2018, April). *How Artificial Intelligence is Transforming the World.* Retrieved from, https:/www.brookings.edu>research>how-artificial-intelligence-is-transforming-the-world

West, R., & Turner, L. (2010). *Introducing Communication Theory. Analysis and Application. Fourth Edition* (4th ed.). McGraw-Hill. Retrieved 2021, from https://silo.pub/introducing-communication-theory-analysis-and-application-fourth-edition.html

Weston, A. (2006). *A Practical Companion to Ethics*. Oxford University Press.

Widfeldt, A. (2014). *Extreme right parties in Scandinavia*. Routledge. doi:10.4324/9780203403334

Wikipedia. (2021a). *DD News*. Retrieved from https://en.m.wikipedia.org/wiki/DD_ News

Wikipedia. (2021b). *Pulse Polio*. Retrieved from https://en.wikipedia.org/wiki/Pulse_Polio

Williams Fayne, M. (2021). Advocacy journalism in the 21st century: Rethinking entertainment in digital Black press outlets. *Journalism*. doi:10.1177/14648849211023166

Williams, B. (2002). *Truth and Truthfulness: An Essay in Genealogy*. Princeton University Press.

Willoughby, F. J., & Liu, S. (2018). Do pictures help tell the story? An experimental test of narrative and emojis in a health text message intervention. *Computers in Human Behavior*, *79*, 75–82. doi:10.1016/j.chb.2017.10.031

Wilson, E. (1941). *The wound and the bow: seven studies in literature*. Riverside Press.

Wiredu, K. (1999). Society and democracy in Africa. *New Political Science*, *21*(1), 33–44. doi:10.1080/07393149908429850

Wollstonecraft, M. (1792). *A vindication of the rights of women*. J. Johnson.

World Bank. (2016). *World Development Report 2016: digital dividends*. World Bank. http://documents.worldbank.org/curated/en/ 896971468194972881/pdf/102725-PUB-Replacement- PUBLIC.pdf

World Commission on Environment and Development (WCED). (1987). Report of the world commission on environment and development: Our common future. Oxford University Press.

Wright, D., & Hinson, M. (2009). *An analysis of the increasing impact of social and other new media on public relations practice*. Institute for Public Relations. www.instituteforpr.org

Wright, H. K. (2002). Editorial: Notes on the (Im) Possibility of articulating continental African identity. *Critical Arts: a Journal of Media Studies.*, *16*(2), 1–18. doi:10.1080/02560240285310111

Ya'u, Z. Y. (2012). Ambivalence and activism: Netizens, social transformation and African virtual publics. *Africa Development. Afrique et Developpement*, *37*(1), 85–102.

Yar, M. (2006). *Cybercrime and society*. Sage. doi:10.4135/9781446212196

Yarow, J. (2013). *Here's an awesome story about Steve Jobs telling an employee he's going to become the world's best story teller in 1994*. https://www.businessinsider.com/steve-jobs-story-teller-2013-7

Yassin, A. K. (2021). Emojis as a new visual language in Advertising creativity. *Journal of Design Sciences and Applied Arts*. doi:10.21608/jdsaa.2021.29904.1037

Yeboah, K. (2021). How AI is transforming Africa's political landscape. In A collection of essays exploring the interplay between digital technologies, politics and society across Africa. Stanford Digital Civil Society Lab.

Yiew, T. H., & Lau, E. (2018). Does foreign aid contribute to or impeded economic growth? *Journal of International Students*, *11*(3), 21–30. doi:10.14254/2071-8330.2018/11-3/2

Yilmaz, G. (2019). Post-truth politics in the 2017 Euro-Turkish crisis. *Journal of Contemporary European Studies*, *27*(2), 237–246. doi:10.1080/14782804.2019.1587390

Yiran, W., Niiya, N., Mark, G., Reich, S., & Mark, W. (2015). Coming of age (digitally): An ecological view of social media use among college students. *Proceedings of CSCW'15*, 571-582.

Yoroms, J. (2009). The state, the media and conflict management: A conceptual approach. In Conflict management and the media in Nigeria. Centre for Research and Documentation (CRD).

Young, I. M. (2000). *Inclusion and democracy*. Oxford University Press.

Yousaf, M., Rahman, B. H., & Yousaf, Z. (2020). Constructing reality: Framing of the Kashmir conflict in dictatorial and democratic regimes in the Pakistani English Press. *Media Watch*, *11*(3), 401–415. doi:10.15655/mw/2020/v11i3/203045

Yusuf, B. (1992). The mass media: The revolt of conscience. In T.A. Imobighe (Ed.), The politics of the second republic. National Institute for Policy and Strategic Studies.

Yusuf, B. (1994, Nov.). *Sensationalism and the mass media: A case study of Soft sell Magazines* (Dissertation). National Institute for Policy and Strategic Studies, Kuru.

Ywee. (2019). *The effect of social media on our cultural values*. www.lagosmums.com/the-effect-of-social-media-on-our-cultural-values/

Zarrilli, B. P. (2009). *Psychological Acting: An Intercultural Approach after Stanislavski*. Routledge Taylor & Francis Group.

Zerilli, L. M. G. (2020). Fact-Checking and Truth-Telling in an Age of Alternative Facts. *Le foucaldien, 6*(1), 1–22. doi:10.16995/lefou.68

Zhao, S., & Foo, M. D. (2016). *Queen Bee Syndrome. The real women do not promote women*. Center for Creative Leadership. Available from: https://www.ccl.org/wp-content/uploads/2016/09/Queen-Bee-Syndrome.pdf

Zhao, X., Lampe, C., & Ellison, N. B. (2016). The social media ecology: User perceptions, strategies and Challenges. Front stage on social media, 89-100.

Ziderman, A. (2016). *Funding mechanisms for financing vocational training: An analytical framework* (IZA Policy Paper No. 110). Ramat Gan. Retrieved from https://ftp.iza.org/pp110.pdf

About the Contributors

Desmond Onyemechi Okocha, PhD, is a Social Scientist with specialisation in management, development, media, journalism and communication with over 15 years experience in consulting, research and lecturing. Aside his numerous professional certifications, he obtained a Bachelor of Arts (BA) degree in Management from the United Kingdom, a Master of Arts (MA) degree in Journalism and Mass Communication from Sikkim Manipal University, India and a Doctor of Philosophy (PhD) in Journalism and Mass Communication from Nims University, Rajasthan, India. Additionally, he has Postgraduate Diplomas in Education Management and Leadership, and Logistics and Supply Chain Management. Aside working and consulting for World Bank, Global Fund for Women and Open Society Initiative for West Africa (OSIWA) funded projects, he was the pioneer National Knowledge Management and Communication Coordinator for the International Fund for Agricultural Development project in the Niger Delta, Nigeria. He also served as Special Adviser on Digital Media and Strategic Communication to the Executive Governor of Abia State, His Excellency Dr. Okezie Victor Ikpeazu from 2020 to 2022. His working career spans over several countries including The Gambia, Ghana, India and Nigeria. Presently, Dr Okocha is a Senior Lecturer and Postgraduate Programme Coordinator at the Department of Mass Communication, Bingham University, Nigeria. He is also the Founder of Institute for Leadership and Development Communication, Nigeria. As a prolific writer, he has published widely and has more than 40 scholarly publications in reputable local and international journals to his credit, in addition to being on the editorial board. He is a reviewer for some Scopus journals including Journal of Information Technology Research (JITR), International Journal of Virtual and Augmented Reality (IJVAR), International Journal of Digital Literacy and Digital Competence (IJDLDC), International Journal of Social Media and Online Communities (IJSMOC) and Jurnal Studi Komunikasi (Indonesian Journal of Communications Studies). As an international voice, Dr. Okocha is a frequent speaker in conferences across continents. In 2018, he was invited to speak at Harvard University, USA, Vienna University, Austria, and at the MIRDEC-8th, International Academic Conference on Social Sciences, Portugal.

Melchizedec J. Onobe, PhD, is a Communication Scholar with socio-scientific interest in media and society development issues, cultural communication, digital media and brand communication. He has about 18 years combined work exposure and experiences as a researcher, journalist and editor. He holds a B.A degree, M.A and a PhD in Mass Communication from universities in Nigeria. He has taught in some prestigious universities in Africa and published widely. He is a co-editor of a book of Reading, Nigeria: Journeying in Socio-Economic and Political Development and also Social Spiral of Silence and the Narratives of African Culture in Contemporary Media. He is a Reader in the Department of Mass

Communication, Bingham University Karu. Nasarawa state, Nigeria and was a sabbatical Professor in the Department of Mass Communication, Nasarawa State University Keffi, Nasarawa State, Nigeria.

Mirian Ngozi Alike, PhD, is a Philosopher and Researcher who specializes in Metaphysics and African Philosophy. She had her B.A, M.A and PhD degrees in Philosophy from Nnamdi Azikiwe University Awka, Nigeria. Mirian has great passion for youth leadership development and community services. She has attended several International conferences and has published in reputable peer reviewed journals. Additionally, she is a co-editor of the festschrift in honour of The African Philosopher, Professor Paulin Hountondji. Presently, Mirian is a Lecturer in the Department of Philosophy, Nnamdi Azikiwe University, Awka, Anambra State, Nigeria.

* * *

Princewell Nwanganga Achor, PhD, is a trained Political Communicator, Scholar, Researcher, Public Relations Professional, and an emerging star writer. He possesses both academic and professional qualifications in Communications, Public and Business Administration, Marketing, and Public Relations. Dr. Achor obtained his M.Sc Public Relations, MBA in Marketing, and PhD in Public relations from the prestigious University of Nigeria Nsukka, Enugu State, Nigeria. He is the lead author of the flagship book, Political Marketing: Marketing, Communication, and Politics. The book can be described as an intellectual and practical meeting point for three great disciplines or professions: Marketing, Communications, and Politics. He has published in reputable peer-reviewed journals. His research interest ranges from social media, political public relations, political marketing, media studies, advertising, and marketing communications to political communication. He is a guest reviewer for some International Journals and was recently appointed also a member of the Editorial Board of Journal of Digital Marketing and Communications (JDMC), and Journal of New Age Marketing and Management Sciences (NAMMS). Dr. Achor is a consummate Media, Management, and Marketing Communications Consultant with over twenty-two years of industry experience. He is also a project supervisor and course facilitator at the National Open University of Nigeria; he has also taught courses in Public Relations, Advertising, Marketing Communication, and Business Management in academic institutions and training organizations in Nigeria. He is presently the Head, Research, Media and Public Relations, South East Region, Advanced Management Academy, Abuja, Nigeria.

Ejike Akpa is a lecturer in the Department of Philosophy, Madonna University, Nigeria, Okija Campus, Anambra State. He is currently the Acting Head of the Department. He holds an M.A. and B.A. in Philosophy from University of Nigeria, Nsukka and University of Uyo, respectively, with specialization in Social and Political Philosophy. He is completing his Ph.D dissertation at the University of Nigeria, Nsukka. He has garnered reasonable teaching and administrative experiences having taught in Madonna University for more than a decade and having occupied several administrative positions and having served in several University committees. He has contributed articles to several academic journals and has authored some books. He is married with children.

Eric Besong is a lecturer in the Department of Philosophy, Federal University of Lafia, Nasarawa State, Nigeria. An erudite scholar and career academia, from Nsadop in Boki L.G.A, Cross River State, Nigeria.

Christiana Danjuma, a consultant, researcher and writer, is a promising multidisciplinary scholar. She is a philosopher, who had her B.A. in Philosophy from Federal University of Lafia, Nasarawa, Lafia, Nigeria. She is of Jaba tribe in Southern Kaduna, Northern Nigeria. She has many well-researched articles published by several foreign and Nigerian publishing outlets and institutional bodies. She is also a biographer, with several books, finished and ongoing, on some female dignitaries. Her research interests include Aesthetics, Ethics, Feminist Philosophy and Gender Studies, Environmental and Sociopolitical Philosophies, Metaphysics, Media, Education, Entrepreneurship, and International Relations.

Justine John Dyikuk is a Lecturer in the Department of Mass Communication, Faculty of Arts, University of Jos, Nigeria. In 2015, he graduated with a Master of Arts Degree in Pastoral/Communication Studies from the University of Calabar, Nigeria. He holds two Bachelors' Degree in Philosophy and Theology from the Pontifical Urbaniana University, Rome and the University of Jos. He bagged a Diploma in Pastoral/Communication Studies from the Catholic Institute of West Africa, Port Harcourt, Nigeria. He has contributed over 50 articles in both local and international peer reviewed journals with 3 books to his credit. He is the convener of Media Team Network Initiative, a Non Governmental Organisation through which he compliments teaching and research with community service. Dyikuk's areas of interests include media and society, investigative reporting and strategic communication in conflict resolution. He occasionally writes for Premium Times, Nigeria's premier investigative online newspaper and is a regular contributor to Union of Catholic Asian News and other diocesan newspapers. He is engaged with The Kukah Centre, Abuja as a trainer and facilitator. The Catholic priest who was ordained on 13 June, 2009 by Bishop John Moore, SMA of Blessed Memory at Saint John the Evangelist's Cathedral, Bauchi is the Dean of Wuntin Dada Deanery and a Consultor in Bauchi Diocese.

James Edomwonyi Edokpolor is a lecturer in Benson Idahosa University with 6 years teaching experience, where he has served as a member and representative in different committees. He holds a BSc and MSc in Business Education from Ambrose Alli University and University of Benin, respectively. Because of the relevance of business education, his research interest is focused on career and workforce education with specific emphasis on entrepreneurial skills development; experiential and vicarious learning; stakeholders-driven TVET education; work/organizational psychology and human resource management in business education. He has published several articles in top-tier journals indexed by Scopus, Web of Science and ProQuest and published by Sage, Elsevier, and Emerald within his research interest.

Cyril Ezeani holds a Bachelor of Arts (Philosophy) from the University of Ibadan as well as Bachelor of Theology from Urban University Rome. He obtained Post Graduate Diploma in Education from Federal College of Education (Technical) Umunze. He bagged Masters in Arts (Philosophy) from Nnamdi Azikiwe University, Awka. He is currently on his Doctoral programme at the same University where he also lectures in the Department Philosophy.

Uchenna A. Ezeogu is a Lecturer in General Studies Unit (Philosophy), Nigeria Maritime University Okerenkoko Warri South West Local Government Area Delta State Nigeria. Studied philosophy at Nnamdi Azikiwe University Awka, B.A. 2008, M.A. 2012 and PhD 2016. His area of research interest are African Philosophy, Ethics, Conflict resolutions, Problems of Western Epistemic Hegemony and epistemic marginalisation.

Umezurike J. Ezugwu is a research fellow, Conversational Society of Philosophy. He did his first degree in the Department of Philosophy, Nnamdi Azikiwe University Awka, Anambra State, Nigeria. He obtained his Masters and Doctorate degrees in the Department of Philosophy, University of Calabar, Calabar. Currently, he is a lecturer in General Studies Unit (Philosophy) at Nigeria Maritime University Okerenkoko, Delta State, Nigeria. There, he teaches Philosophy and Logic, History and Philosophy of Science, Use of Library Skill and ICT and Nigeria Peoples and Culture. He is an appointed member of Research and Development Committee, and an associate editor of International Journal of Maritime and Interdisciplinary Research (IJMIR). He is also a Co-editor of a book entitled: Conversations on African Philosophy of Mind, Consciousness and Artificial Intelligence, to be published by Springer Nature. He has contributed different chapters in books, attended national and international conferences, and has published in both local and international journals. His research interests include but are not limited to African Philosophy, Environmental Philosophy, Political Philosophy, Philosophy of Education, Ethics and History and Philosophy of Science.

Adaobi Olivia Ihueze is a lecturer with the Department of English Language and Literature of Nnamdi Azikiwe University Awka, Anambra State of Nigeria. She holds her Ph.D. in English Language and Literature (Literary Studies) in 2017, MA in English (Literature) in 2011 both from Nnamdi Azikiwe University, Awka, and BA (ED) in English Language and Literature (2003) from Imo State University, Owerri. She bagged the Award of Excellence by the Faculty of Arts of Nnamdi Azikiwe University, Awka on their “Grand Alumni / Friends Homecoming” on April 26th 2018. She has a special interest in Gender Studies and African Literature. She has participated in many conferences, seminars, and workshops and has published many critical essays/articles. She is married to Prof. C. C. Ihueze and the marriage is blessed with children.

Michael Agbo John is a Political Scientist with specialization in Development Studies, Political Economy, Conflicts, Wars, Displacement and International Terrorism. He holds a BSc. Degree in Political Science from the University of Maiduguri, Nigeria, an MSc. In Political Economy and Development Studies from the Nasarawa State University, Keffi, Nigeria. He is currently undertaking his Ph.D. in Defence and Strategic Studies in the Nigerian Defence Academy, Kaduna, Nigeria. He is a lecturer, Department of Political Science, Bingham University, Nigeria and a member, Nigerian Political Science Association.

Shafiq Ahmad Kamboh is Senior Lecturer at the School of Communication Studies, University of the Punjab, Lahore, Pakistan. Currently, he is a doctoral candidate in the Centre for Media, Communication, and Information Research (ZeMKI) at the University of Bremen, Germany. His research focuses on development communication, climate and environmental justice, health communication and the Global South. His recent work has been published in the Journal of Media Ethics, Development Policy Review, Third World Quarterly, International Journal of Communication and Psychology & Health. He has worked on several research projects funded by local chapters of international development organisations in Pakistan including UNESCO, WHO and Micronutrient Initiative (MI).

Johnson Okeke holds a Ph.D in African Traditional Religion & Intercultural hermeneutics. He teaches Indigenous African Religion, African Philosophy and Cultural hermeneutics in the University. He is also a researcher in Culture and Religion. He is a trained Lawyer and called to the Nigerian Bar.

Bassey Ibiang Okon is the Acting Deputy Commandant of Nigerian Air Force Institute of Administrative Management and Dean, School of Public Relations and Information, Kaduna, Nigeria. He was the Deputy Director of Public Relations of the Nigerian Air Force prior to his current appointment. He has edited several magazines and newspapers. He has also reported for the Nigerian Chronicle, Vanguard and Daily Times newspapers. He was the Command Public Relations Officer for Tactical Air Command, Mobility Command and Air Training Command at different times. He attended the university of Nigeria, Nsukka; University of Lagos; University of Uyo and Cranfield University, Shrivenham, United Kingdom. He was the University of Nigeria best graduating Mass Communication Student in 1997, winner of the Professor Donald Ekong's Book Prize for academic excellence and NAOS Award. He is a Chevening scholar and member of the International Communication Association as well as the Nigerian Institute of Public Relations.

Ebele Peace Okpala is a committed literary scholar. She obtained her B.A. (Educ English) from University of Calabar, Cross River State, Nigeria. She is a lecturer in the Department of English Language and Literature, Nnamdi Azikiwe University, Awka, Anambra State, Nigeria, where she obtained her M.A. and PhD in Literature. Her area of interest is Gender Studies. She has published scholarly articles in both national and international journals solely and with well- known humanity scholars. She is a native of Mbaukwu in Awka South Local Government Area of Anambra State, Nigeria. She is married to Hon. Kennedy Chukwudi Okpala and the union is blessed with children.

Roxie Ojoma Ola-Akuma is a PhD candidate in the Department of Mass Communication, Bingham University, Nigeria. She holds a B.Sc. in Mass Communication from NTA Television College Jos, Plateau State, and an M.Sc. in Media & Communications from Pan-Atlantic University, Lagos State. She has built a professional career in broadcast media, spanning over ten years, of blended experience in multimedia practices with media, humanitarian and development agencies, including Mennonite Economic Development Associates (MEDA), Action Against Hunger International Damaturu, CNBC Africa/ABN Productions Lagos and Confluence Cable Network Lokoja. Her research interest includes digital technologies, Artificial Intelligence, cyber journalism, gender & culture including risk, strategic and development communication.

Emmanuel Olumuji is a Lecturer in the Department of Mass Communication, Chrisland University Abeokuta, Nigeria. He attended the University of Jos, Usmanu Danfodiyo University and Federal University of Agriculture, Abeokuta, Nigeria. He has taught for close to two decades and he is involved in training and humanitarian services. His research interests include New Media Studies, Participatory Journalism, Print/Online Journalism, Media and Education.

Olufemi Onabajo is a Professor of Mass Communication and the former Vice-Chancellor of Lead City University, Ibadan. He is currently the head of department of Mass Communication in Chrisland University, Abeokuta.

Thaddeus Akagbulem Oparah is a lecturer in philosophy at the Madonna University Nigeria, Okija, Anambra State, Nigeria. He holds a doctorate degree in philosophy of the University of Nigeria, Nsukka. He has interest in philosophy of science, philosophy of development, socio-political philosophy and Epistemology. He worked as ad-hoc staff with the Nigeria's Independent National Electoral Commission (INEC) in two consecutive elections (2011 and 2015). He has written a number of scholarly articles including “Postcolonial Dreams, Neocolonial Realities and National Consciousness: Assessing Nigeria 50 Years After”.

Taiwo Wesley Osemwegie (PhD) is a Senior Lecturer with over twelve years of research and teaching experience at the department of Philosophy Faculty of Arts, University of Benin, Benin City. He holds a Doctor of Philosophy (PhD) in Metaphysics and Philosophy of Mind from the Nnamdi Azikiwe University, Akwa, a Master of Arts (MA) degree in Philosophy from the University of Lagos, Akoka Lagos, a Bachelor of Arts (BA) Philosophy degree (First Class Honours) from the University of Benin and a certificate of Applied Ethics (Summer School) from the Central European University, Budapest, Hungary. He has received several awards including the University of Benin Best Scholar Prize Award from 100 level to 400 level & best graduating student of the department. He also received the University of Lagos Teaching Assistantship Award during his MA degree in 2010. He was the pioneer Head Master (HM) of the staff school (Nursery & Primary) of Government Secondary School (GSS), Isa, Sokoto state in 2008 during his compulsory NYSC service year. Dr Osemwegie has been appointed to serve in many capacities including his appointment as Lecturer-in-Charge of the department of Philosophy in 2019 & elected into several committees of the University of Benin. He has contributed several articles to national & international peer-reviewed journals. His main areas of research interest are Metaphysics, Philosophy of Mind, Applied Ethics, Symbolic Logic, Philosophy of Language, Philosophy of Education & African Philosophy.

Amaobi Nelson Osuala is a Doctoral student in the university of Ibadan Ibadan-Nigeria. He had his Bachelor's degree in Environmental philosophy from the university of Calabar, Calabar-Nigeria and his Master's in African philosophy of Logic from the university of Ibadan Ibadan-Nigeria. His research interests covers African philosophy of Environment, Logic, Science, and decolonial Epistemologies. He has published in local and international journals of repute while employing contemporary original African inspired methods of complementary reflection, Conversationalism, Integrativism etc towards addressing global issues of philosophical concerns spanning from global warming to animal ethics, decoloniality and many more. His current research is on employing an African alternative methods towards addressing the question/problems of rationality, diffused identity and decoloniality in African philosophy.

Innocent Otache is currently a Senior Lecturer at the Department of Business Administration and Management, Federal Polytechnic, Idah, Kogi State, Nigeria. He holds a PhD in Entrepreneurship from Universiti Utara Malaysia (UUM). His research interests include entrepreneurship, entrepreneurship education, small business management, graduate employability and general management. He has published articles in top-tier journals published by Emerald, Elsevier and SAGE and presented papers at both national and international conferences. His publications can be viewed at https://orcid.org/ 0000-0002-5746-5066.

Sevinc Ozturk is a lecturer at Bitlis Eren University, Turkey. She finished her Ph.D. in the Political Science department at Rutgers University. Ozturk's research interests include regime types, Turkish foreign policy, and foreign aid policies.

Syed Hassan Raza is an Associate Professor, Department of Communication Studies, Bahauddin Zakariya University, Multan, Pakistan. He does research in area of Advertising, Marketing communication, Social Marketing, Health Communication, and Environmental communication. He has published in many reputed Web of Science (Impact Factor) and Scopus indexed journals including, sustainable production and consumption (Elesvier), Journal of Islamic Marketing (Emerald), Journal of Creative communication (Sage), Journal of Public Affairs (Wiley) International Journal of Environmental and Public Health (Mdpi), Journal of Asian Pacific Communication (John Brinjamins) etc. He also served as Reviwer for several Web of Science journals published by world leading Publishers such as Sage, Emerald etc.

Odey Robert is a Bekwarra-born multidisciplinary scholar, with over forty publications to his credit. This erudite linguist of Ebonyi State University, Abakaliki, Nigeria is a PG student, consultant, researcher, writer and an editor, currently working with Ropah Ventures' Educational Services, Research and Consultancy, and Bridge Gate Consult Ltd, Abuja/Lafia respectively. He has taught English Language, Literature and related courses/subjects in both secondary and tertiary institutions for several years. His research interests include Languages and Linguistics, English, Literature, Philosophy, Religion, Feminism and Gender Studies, Politics, Leadership and Development, Media Studies, Sociology, Psychology, History, Education, Entrepreneurship and International Relations.

Joshua Yilhikka Rotshak is a Lecturer in the Department of Educational Foundations, Faculty of Education, University of Jos, Nigeria. The scholar was awarded a PhD in Psychology with specialization in "Psychology, Conflict, Education and Early Childhood Education" having completed his postgraduate studies in the University of Jos between 1997 and 2018. He is also a seasoned Psychologist and Therapist. The accomplished scholar has 21 publications in different learned journals apart from books he has published. Dr. Rotshak is a graduate of Saint Thomas Aquinas Major Seminary, Makurdi (1987-1990) and Saint Augustine's Major Seminary, Jos (1990-1994) where be bagged two Degrees in Philosophy and Theology respectively. He was ordained a Catholic Priest in 1994 by Archbishop Gabriel Gonsum Ganaka at Our Lady of Fatima Cathedral, Jos. He has worked in different parishes both in the Archdiocese of Jos and his home Diocese of Pankshin, Plateau State.

Kingsley Mbamara Sabastine received his Master's degree in Philosophy from the Catholic University of Eastern Africa, Nairobi-Kenya in 2012. In the same year (2012) he was hired as a lecturer at the Good Shepherd Major Seminary Kaduna, Nigeria and is currently a doctoral student at the Catholic University of Lublin, Poland. His work focuses on ethics, theories of truth and epistemology.

Subir Sinha is an Indian scholar and a Lecture (State Aided College Teacher) in the Department of Journalism and Mass communication of Dum Dum Motijheel College (Affiliated under West Bengal State University). He was formerly attached with the Department of Journalism of Surendranath College (Affiliated under University of Calcutta) and Vijaygarh Jyotish Ray College (Affiliated under University of Calcutta) as a Guest Faculty. He was also remained attached with Indra Gandhi National Open University (IGNOU) under convergence scheme with Dum Dum Motijheel College as an Academic Counsellor of PGJMC for a short period. He presented papers in various National and International conference and published various articles in several books and journals.

Vitalis Ugwu (Ph.D) is a graduate of the Nnamdi Azikiwe University, Awka, Nigeria. He holds a doctorate in Philosophy and at present teaches in the department of Philosophy & Religion, Alex Ekwueme Federal University, Ndufu-Alike, Ebonyi State, Nigeria.

Muhammad Yousaf is an assistant professor, Centre for Media & Communication Studies, University of Gujrat, Pakistan. Dr. Yousaf earned his doctorate in Communication Studies at the Communication University of China in 2018. He is the recipient of three Gold Medals in M.Sc. Communication from University of the Punjab. Dr. Yousaf does research in media effects, public opinion & health communication, environmental communication & advocacy journalism. He is an HEC approved Ph.D. supervisor. Dr. Yousaf has published in Scopus & SSCI journals such as International Journal of Communication, Vaccine Journal, Vaccines Journal, Information Discovery and Delivery, Global Media and China, Psychological Research and Behavior Management, Media Watch, Journal of Media Studies, etc.

Index

E

F

G

H

I

K

L

M

N

O

P

R

S

www.ingramcontent.com/pod-product-compliance
Lightning Source LLC
Chambersburg PA
CBHW080501051126
54379CB00005B/144